P9-EJZ-528

The Shadow of Blooming Grove

Books by Francis Russell

THREE STUDIES IN 20TH-CENTURY OBSCURITY

THE AMERICAN HERITAGE BOOK
OF THE PIONEER SPIRIT [co-author]

TRAGEDY IN DEDHAM

THE FRENCH AND INDIAN WARS

THE GREAT INTERLUDE

LEXINGTON, CONCORD AND BUNKER HILL

THE WORLD OF DÜRER

THE MAKING OF THE NATION, 1783–1860

THE SHADOW OF BLOOMING GROVE

The Shadow of Blooming Grove

Warren G. Harding in His Times

BY FRANCIS RUSSELL

McGraw-Hill Book Company · New York · Toronto

Copyright © 1968 by Francis Russell. All Rights Reserved.
Printed in the United States of America. No part of this publication may be reproduced, stored in a retrieval system, or
transmitted, in any form or by any means, electronic, mechanical, photocopying, recording, or otherwise, without the
prior written permission of the publisher.

Library of Congress Catalog Card Number: 68-29916
FIRST EDITION   54338

For
Lynn Staley Beals
1910–1968

Preface

This book, as it now appears, has a scattering of blank spaces in the text of several chapters where I had originally quoted from Harding's love letters to Carrie Phillips. I have been forced to these deletions because of a restraining order issued by Judge Henry L. Holden of the Court of Common Pleas in Columbus, Ohio, on a motion by Harding's nephew, George T. Harding. This order, which has been "temporarily" in effect now for four years, forbids the publication, production, copying, exhibition, or making any use whatsoever of the letters of Warren G. Harding to Carrie Phillips; and it has served its intended purpose of delaying *The Shadow of Blooming Grove.*

But rather than postpone my book further, I have decided to publish it, bearing in mind the court order by leaving blanks where quotations from the letters would have appeared. In itself it is a smallish omission, a matter of a dozen or so spaces and some 800 words from a text of 300,000. Yet, to my regret, something of the full flavor of Harding is thereby inevitably deleted. Compared to what is available today at any drugstore book rack, Harding's eroticism as expressed in his letters is naïve, and even pathetic as the quality of his mind peeps through the boudoir phrases. In his sexuality he was Adolphe rather than Don Juan. The letters, if they can be considered shocking — as some of them can — are more so because they were written by a President of the United States than through the tumescence of their content. When I first read them I felt a sense of pity for the lonely Harding; for Carrie Phillips was clearly the love of his life, and he was more loving than loved. Eventually, of course, the letters will be published as a part of history. Meanwhile each reader must make his own interpretation of them.

Francis Russell

Contents

Foreword

With better luck Warren Gamaliel Harding might have gone down in history as another McKinley or Garfield, or at the least the equivalent of a Pierce. After his death his reputation plummeted so quickly that only with the greatest reluctance could a Republican successor be persuaded to dedicate his tomb. As President he has come to be rated last in the hearts of his countrymen, along with Grant, who at least had the merit of being a great general and—as he demonstrated in his memoirs —an impressive writer of English.

Yet, whatever the tone of the Harding administration, one cannot say that it was shot through with scandal when it contained such men as Herbert Hoover, Charles Evans Hughes, and the elder Henry Wallace in the Cabinet and the Harding-appointed Chief Justice William Howard Taft. Other Presidents since have suffered or tolerated scandals in their family and administration without being branded by them. Franklin Roosevelt's reputation never suffered from the marital vagaries of his children or from the financial exploitation of his name by his sons Jimmy and Elliott. That Lucy Rutherford, the woman he had long loved and once wanted to marry, was with him when he died did not discredit him when knowledge of it leaked out two decades later, even though it may have chipped the Eleanor idyll a little.

The "five-percenters," mink coats, and deep freezes current in the Truman administration have receded to a limbo that requires explanation by footnotes, along with such egregious characters as the bumbling General Harry Vaughan, the weeping Assistant Attorney General and the convict-to-be T. Lamar Caudle, and former convict and White House intimate John Maragon. Truman's close association with Kansas City's Boss Tom Pendergast does not seem to be held against him by history, any more than Sherman Adams's débâcle has left its mark on Eisenhower. Nor, more recently, do Billie Sol Estes's nimble peculations reflect on Kennedy's presidential years. No incident so gross as that of Johnson's chief aide, Walter Jenkins, being caught in an indecent act in a public lavatory was recorded in Harding's administration. The roguery of Harding's Jess Smith was from all evidence exceeded by that of Johnson's Bobby Baker, and Harding at least repudiated Smith.

Whatever his shortcomings, Harding was personally honest. As President he gambled privately on the stock market (and lost), but he never used his official position to get inside knowledge of a sure thing. His Marion *Star* was a flourishing paper by the time he came to Washington as a senator, nor did he use his privileges to make it more so. By comparison Senator Lyndon Johnson operated on a lower ethical level when he applied the subtle pressures of his senatorial position to create his Texas radio-television fief, as did General Eisenhower in contriving to have the royalties of his ghost-written *Crusade in Europe* considered capital gains.

Of course the *ad hominem* argument that Harding was not the only President touched with scandal does not answer the underlying question: Why have the lapses of other administrations been shrugged away, shelved and forgotten, while his remain a living reproach to his memory? One can say that there were more scandals under Harding—although their number can be exaggerated—and that they were not compensated for by other accomplishments. But I think the real answer is that they lasted so long. The various oil-lease conspiracy trials went on for years, trial after trial. At each election Teapot Dome was ready to be revived as a slogan by the Democrats. Not until six years after Harding's death did his Secretary of the Interior Albert Fall go on trial for receiving a bribe, and not until 1931 did Fall finally go to jail. A generation later the preparations for Harding's hundredth birthday celebration were jolted by the discovery of a number of love letters he had written to another man's wife.

Then, too, the mysteries of Harding's life, because of their very enigmatic quality, have proved more durable and persistent than politics. Was Harding a mulatto? Did he have a child by his mistress? Was he murdered? What were the papers his wife so hastily burned after his death? The questions have continued to be asked and the answers debated long after his budget, his support of the World Court, and his Disarmament Conference—by which he himself felt he would be remembered longest—have been forgotten.

Harding, with his tarnished reputation, has never claimed the serious attention of historians. In this he has been the most neglected of Presidents. His centennial passed without an adequate general biography of him ever having appeared. For the most part his prevailing image has been formed from the journalistic impressions of William Allen White, Mark Sullivan, and Samuel Hopkins Adams, and so thoroughly accepted by scholars that it has scarcely seemed worth while to pursue the image further. Here was a puppet, a handsome straw man with a rhetorical voice and empty head, taken from a small Ohio town by a set of curious chances to the United States Senate, and finally propelled into the presidency by a cabal of reactionary senators and the oil interests. "If ever there was a he-harlot, it was this same Warren G. Harding," White wrote in 1926. Then the image was unforgettably fouled by three meretricious books: the naïve chatterings of Harding's girl-mistress, Nan Britton; the psychotic swindler 'Gaston Mean's *The Strange Death of President Harding*, in which he hints that Harding's wife poisoned her husband to avoid scandal; and former Attorney General Harry Daugherty's apologia in which he deifies himself by claiming to have formed Harding from the Ohio mud.

In spite of the legend, Harding was neither a fool nor a tool, but an astute and able Ohio politician (not the highest breed of that animal) who knew how to get what he wanted—a place in the state senate, the United States Senate, the White House—while all the time disclaiming that he wanted any such thing. Even his weedy rhetoric had a purpose in its attempt by unanchored verbosity and a pleasant manner to reconcile the irreconcilable. Harding was not a creation of Daugherty's. In essence he was nominated for the presidency because he had done the necessary political spadework in the grass roots and because, in one politician's words, he was "everybody's second choice." Harding was the available man, as Andrew Sinclair pointed out in his recent political biography, even though that may not be the most adequate reason for choosing a candidate.

By a twist or two of fate Harding has come to be regarded right, left, and center as the worst President this country ever had; while the President who most resembled him, Dwight Eisenhower, for all his ineptitudes as general and chief executive, has remained the Little Father. One former President is honored, one disgraced in his tomb, yet both are very similar. A political commentator wrote of Harding not long after his death that "he came to office at a time of extraordinary public irritation. Everybody was cross, there had been a deadlock in government for months, and the main occupation of the articulate was in fixing the blame for it on the man or group they did not like." The same words could have been written to describe the "I Like Ike" phenomenon of 1952.

I suspect that Harding and Eisenhower had about the same IQ. Certainly they had the same easy, engaging manner. Both held to the idea —as long as they could—that Congress proposes and the President disposes. Both shared roughly the same cultural values, in life, in books, in music, in art. Both got themselves entangled in the syntax jungles of their mother tongue. Harding longed for a return to "normalcy." Eisenhower felt that the real problem of the world was "malnuition." One was essentially a lieutenant governor manqué, the other essentially a lieutenant colonel. Both played compulsive golf. Both had mothers who were religious fanatics; Harding's a Seventh-day Adventist, Eisenhower's a Jehovah's Witness. Both had faith in faith. Neither one made a decision if he could avoid it—and usually he could. I think it is indisputable that this country would have had a better history if General Wood had been elected President in 1920 and Senator Taft in 1952.

With his centenary year past, Harding deserves a biography, not so much for himself—though in many ways his life was more interesting than those of more notable Presidents—but because he came at a dividing point in history, when men moved forward and looked back. The first President after World War I, he was also the first President to be born after the Civil War. His election was in one sense a nostalgic yearning to recapture the years before the war, seen through the imperfect haze of memory, at a moment when twentieth-century America was inevitably if belatedly taking form.

The Shadow of
Blooming Grove

CHAPTER I

March 4, 1921

When President James Monroe, on March 4, 1817, delivered his inaugural address from "an elevated portico" in front of the Capitol—still in ruins after the burning of Washington by the British in 1814—he set the open-air tradition that American Presidents have since followed. The tradition has not always squared with the weather. Spring comes early to Washington, but the first week in March can still be as capricious as it was on Inauguration Day, 1841, when the northeast wind blew so cruelly on the President-elect General William Henry Harrison that the elderly hero of Tippecanoe died of the aftereffects a month later. Rain fell in gusty torrents on the bare heads of Benjamin Harrison and William McKinley as they took their oaths before the Chief Justice. And the tradition itself temporarily yielded to ice and snow in 1909 when William Howard Taft had to take his oath in the shelter of the Senate Chamber.

In contrast to those turbid occasions the morning of Inauguration Day, 1921, although chill, promised fair, with a cloudless sky that had already begun to lose the steel-blue of winter. As a day it would ring down the curtain on the World War era for the United States, when at one o'clock Senator Warren Harding of Marion, Ohio—who had coined the phrase "return to normalcy"—would replace the broken war leader, Woodrow Wilson.

Four years before, Wilson in his pride had ridden to his second inaugural between solid ranks of soldiers, with machine guns set up at every corner. In the afternoon he had reviewed a vast military parade, and the relentless tramping feet had seemed a prelude to his declaration of war a month later. By contrast, this postwar inauguration day lacked the earlier sense of drama and urgency. In spite of the great Republican electoral victory of the previous November, the public mood was apathetic. Those whose partisan spirits rejoiced that the man from Ohio would now replace the remote invalid in the White House did not on the whole feel it worth a trip to the capital to see the change. By train or by car, people simply stayed away from Washington. Crowds were thinner than on ordinary days, as the taxi drivers were the first to notice. The big hotels—the Willard, the Shoreham, the Washington and Raleigh—were filled, though not overfilled. The tourist hotels stood half empty. Conspicuous in the bare streets about the Capitol were several hundred Harding rooters from Marion who had arrived at sunrise in Washington on a special bunting-decked train to cheer their home-town boy. They wore large red, white, and blue booster badges to which were attached buckeyes, the symbol of their state.

In the long morning light, the fresh bunting and the little clusters of flags on each lamppost along Pennsylvania Avenue looked bleak and somewhat garish. Over the Capitol building the flags were at half-mast in memory of the former Democratic Speaker of the House of Representatives Champ Clark, who had died two days before. At the site of the inauguration, held on the East Terrace of the Capitol ever since Chief Justice Roger Taney had administered the oath to Abraham Lincoln there, the customary balcony and wooden stands were in place. A rectangular baldachin of classic design, supported by four simulated marble columns, had been set up over the spot where the President-elect would stand to take his oath. Reporters referred to it as a kiosk. H. L. Mencken, with somewhat more precision, called it an Ionic temple—although the columns themselves were Corinthian. A flag, spread over the vaulting of the baldachin, concealed an amplifier—for speakers, though admitting the need, were still a little shamefaced about artificially extending the range of their voices. Directly under the flag was a desk—made especially by employees of the Bell Telephone Company—and just below the desk, on the laurel-entwined balcony, the Great Seal of the United States.

As chairman of the Inaugural Committee the dapper Ned McLean, old friend of the Hardings and court jester-designate of the new administration, had originally been in charge of all arrangements. He himself had planned to make the inaugural day ten times as lively as the Fourth of July, with parades, bands by the score, fireworks, and a mammoth inaugural ball. Never had he worked so hard at anything in his casual life. But Senator Borah and a few more killjoy senators complained to the President-elect about the extravagance, and Harding—to Ned's chagrin—decided to cancel everything, even the parade. This, the simplest of inaugurals, would consist of the swearing-in ceremony, a brief White House reception, and nothing more.

Harding and his large official party, that included his campaign manager Harry Daugherty, were staying at the Willard, as was Vice President-elect Calvin Coolidge. At half-past ten a congressional committee was to call for the President and Vice President-elect and take them to meet Wilson at the White House. Just before the committee arrived, a delegation from Oklahoma appeared at the hotel with a huge broom for the new President. The leader said that it was made of broom corn to demonstrate how the Republicans had swept Oklahoma clean out of the solid South. Harding remarked in taking it that as a boy he had often wound such brooms.

Wilson's final day as President was one to tax his strength to its limits. Stubbornly he insisted that he had recovered sufficiently from his stroke of a year and a half before to follow the official routine of the inaugural, even though a Secret Service man who had traced the distance reported dubiously that he would have to walk 190 steps from an elevator in the Capitol to the President's Room in the Senate wing, 270 steps from there through the Rotunda to the steps leading to the wooden stands, down 16 steep stone steps, and then 50 steps to his seat, "all in full view of probably 50,000 people and hundreds of motion-picture cameras." He rose early from the massive Lincoln double bed that he had had brought to the southwest bedroom after his second marriage and where he now slept alone. After eating the breakfast already set out for him on the side table, he dressed slowly. His Negro valet, Major Arthur Brooks[1] helped him into his gray trousers and morning coat, then handed him the rubber-tipped blackthorn stick that he called his third leg. With its help the President shuffled across to his study and the flotsam of last-minute papers on the desk waiting his signature.

Not until his personal physician, Rear Admiral Cary Grayson, arrived to tell him that he could not possibly negotiate the Capitol steps did he at last agree to forego the inaugural. Grayson was followed by the wispy, sharp-faced Joseph Tumulty, Wilson's private secretary since 1911 when the President was governor-elect of New Jersey. After Grayson had left, the two old friends sat alone. Tumulty asked Wilson if he remembered four years ago, that second inaugural, and how the President had said it would be "great to be free" once March 4, 1921, arrived. Wilson remembered well. Then the words between them seemed to freeze. "Well, Joe!" Wilson said finally. "Well, Governor!" "Well, Joe, you've served me faithfully through it all." "Well, Governor, I'm glad to hear you say so." And Tumulty said he was glad as a Catholic to have shown he could work with a Presbyterian, and maybe it would open a few people's eyes to things.

Tumulty now brought out a pardon paper he had made up for an old man in Nebraska serving time in a Federal penitentiary. The man reminded Tumulty of his own father. He had a son and a crippled daughter who thought the world of him. "Governor," said Tumulty, handing Wilson the paper, "let the curtain go down on an act of mercy—the last act an act of mercy. And I know, some way, when you need mercy, the last will be

---

[1] Brooks held a major's commission in a Negro militia unit. He had first been employed as a confidential servant in the White House by President Taft.

remembered for you." Wilson glanced at the paper and shook his head. "No, Tumulty, no. The case has been reviewed." "But it's an act of mercy and your last act, Governor," Tumulty persisted, "and there is something in the balance of things." "No, Joe," Wilson said, "the country needs to see the law vindicated. The country needs the spectacle of a stable, just, and righteous government more than an old man needs a pardon or I need an act of mercy." He took his pen and in the strongest hand he had written in months wrote *Disapproved* across the paper.

Five years before the fifty-eight-year-old Wilson, on his second honeymoon, had danced a jig in the railroad car and whistled, "Oh, You Beautiful Doll." Four years before he strode down Pennsylvania Avenue in a Preparedness Parade, jaunty in white flannels and a straw hat. Now he had become an old man, with the querulous twitching look of age, his gray hair wisping unkemptly about his ears, the inherited strength of his eroded features only dimly apparent.

Generations of dominies and Calvinist preachers had formed that long-jawed, long-toothed professorial face that had been God's gift to cartoonists. But after the stroke that cut short Wilson's tour of the country in the autumn of 1919 defending his League of Nations, his face contracted overnight to a mask, with drawn lips, desiccated cheeks, and the long jaw sunk into itself. Only the eyes remained alive, as if imprisoned.

While the rejected leader sat at his desk, facing Tumulty, the downstairs rooms of the White House filled with aides, senators, and congressmen, Cabinet officers, reporters and photographers, all waiting the arrival of the new. A few minutes after half-past ten the cavalcade of open-topped touring cars carrying the President and Vice President-elect and their wives, with Senate Majority Leader Philander Knox and Speaker of the House of Representatives Joseph G. Cannon, swung under the White House porte-cochère.

Edith Bolling Wilson had left her husband to go downstairs and distribute her parting gifts and say her goodbyes to the White House staff. As soon as she heard the crush of the car tires in the driveway she returned upstairs to notify him that the official party had arrived. She was wearing a corsage of orchids, not for the day but for the time of their courtship when Wilson had complimented her as "the only woman I know who can wear an orchid." At forty-eight Edith Wilson still preserved much of the rounded kittenish charm of her girlhood. "Well fleshed," the knowing Ned McLean called her. But the last months had dimmed her complexion and given a sag to her chin and sent streaks of gray through her dark hair.

Wilson stood up shakily as his wife entered the room. Brooks, with silk hat and gloves in one hand, came forward to offer him the blackthorn. Then husband and wife walked slowly to the elevator. Ike Hoover, the head usher, waited with door open. Downstairs they went at once to the Blue Room where the Hardings and the members of the Congressional Inauguration Committee were waiting.

The concept that Edith Wilson felt for the Hardings in the abstract had achieved concrete immediacy the day before when the new President and his wife had come to tea in the Red Room. For Edith Wilson, the plantation-bred Virginian with the soft voice that was almost English, the Hardings were parvenus of parvenus. Harding's Duchess, as he called her—a caricature of a nickname that somehow fitted this haggard, rouged old woman—had clamped her pince-nez over her veil and talked on and on in a rasping voice that with its nasal a's and guttural inverted r's seemed to echo the parched Midwestern earth in a summer drouth. "Wurr-'n," she kept saying as she looked at her husband, "Wurr-'n." Harding, ill at ease, slouched silently in an armchair, one leg thrown over the arm.

Tumulty had gone in ahead of the Wilsons to greet the Hardings. The President-elect, as he stepped into the oval formality of the Blue Room to shake Tumulty's hand, was an impressive sight. His lusty black eyebrows contrasted with his steel-gray hair to give the effect of force, his massive shoulders and bronzed complexion gave the effect of health. Although fifty-five years old, he looked older, but with an unimpaired statesman-like virility. If he had been wearing a toga instead of a double-breasted chesterfield he could have stepped on stage in a production of *Julius Caesar*. Of all the members of the United States Senate in the years that he had served there, he most resembled the classical model.

"Why, the son of a bitch *looks* like a senator!" an enthusiastic rural supporter had exclaimed overloudly at a banquet some years back, carried away by his first close view of the Roman from Ohio.

On this morning Harding, silk hat in hand, sleek and pomaded, bore himself with the assurance of a politician fresh from the barbershop. If he did not actually smell of bay rum, he gave that effect. Behind him stood his Duchess, possessively determined, as if she held him on an invisible check rein.

Florence Kling Harding was five years older than her husband, but in contrast to his assertive masculinity she appeared sexless, with the brittle quality of an autumn leaf after the chlorophyll has receded. For the inauguration she wore a sealskin coat with a vast chinchilla collar. Her thin mouse-colored hair, marcelled to a machine precision and resembling a wig, was topped by a wide-brimmed blue hat with spiky darting feathers. The fretful lines of her face still flickered under a heavy layer of paint, but her look as she had entered the Blue Room was challenging and triumphant.

Wilson and his wife met them a minute later. Edith Wilson, whatever she wore, had a flair for clothes. This morning she was wearing a mink stole and a veiled, close-fitting hat like a toque trimmed with a gull's wing. In spite of the care written into her face she still looked young enough to be the Duchess's daughter—as both women were undoubtedly aware. Wilson and Harding, with Grayson hovering in the background, chatted together with somewhat strained amiability. Grayson stepped forward solicitously and gave Wilson a jigger of whisky. As the President and President-elect moved toward the door they were joined by Senator Knox and that ancient of days, Uncle Joe Cannon. Harding offered Wilson his arm, who took it haltingly. Camera and moving-picture men were clustered at the White House entrance. Wilson, as he shuffled along, essayed a frail witticism, saying that the Senate had thrown him down once and he did not want to fall again. The Pierce-Arrow touring car with the presidential seal on the tonneau door-panel waited directly under the porte-cochère. Wilson shook off Harding's arm and walked unaided from the portico to the car, but then Brooks and the Secret Service men had to help him onto the running board and almost lift him into the rear seat while the police shielded him from the photographers. Harding sat beside him, on his left. Senator Knox and Uncle Joe Cannon took the two collapsible seats directly in front. The two Presidents and the Senator wore the customary velvet-collared chesterfields and silk hats, Harding wearing his hat cocked jauntily to one side.

Knox, the ailing senator from Pennsylvania—McKinley's old friend and attorney general and Taft's secretary of state—looked solemn and withdrawn. With his silk hat on, he bore a surprising resemblance to the Mad Hatter. Uncle Joe Cannon, who feared neither God, man, nor Presidents, was wearing his old brown fedora and an overcoat with a turned-up astrakhan collar. His one concession to the day was to discard the stogie that had become almost his trade-mark. Inaugurals meant nothing to him. His narrow, calculating eyes had watched them all since he had helped nominate Lincoln. The old czar of the House of Representatives, with his white beard and rapacious nose, looked more a strangely surviving Civil War general than a party elder. In spite of his age—he was born in 1836— he was to outlive the other three in the tonneau with him.

Four troops of cavalry sent from Fort Myer accompanied the presidential cortège. As soon as Wilson and Harding and the others were settled in their places, the head of the White House Secret Service detail, Colonel Edmund Starling, gave the signal to the cavalry captain. The captain raised his arm, dropped it forward sharply as he spurred his horse and barked out an order, and the lead troop moved off down the curving drive at a quick trot, lance swords drawn, red-and-white guidons fluttering. Two more troops trotted in hollow-square formation on either side of the presidential car as it moved out, with a fourth troop closing the square at the rear of the procession. Five other official cars and five more containing Secret Service and newspapermen followed within the square. The two wives rode in the second car. As it moved down the drive past the circular fountain, the Duchess kept leaning from one side to the other calling out in her hoarse voice to the reporters along the way. "My boys," she remarked to Edith Wilson, primly silent, muffled in her stole.

With a clatter of hoofs the procession passed the gate and turned right past Lafayette Park to the cheers and handclaps of those gathered there. Wilson, as if to insist that the cheers were for the new President, stared straight ahead without bowing acknowledgment. Harding, with a quick, deprecating gesture, silenced the applause. At Fifteenth Street the troopers turned right again, past the Treasury Building, then swung left into the eight-carriage width of Pennsylvania Avenue that sloped uphill in a gentle, unbroken rise to the Capitol on the horizon. In the muted sunshine the great classical dome seemed—as was intended—the focal point of the imperial city, drawing all vistas like filaments to it. As the procession neared, the flags, still at half-mast, were now raised.

Uneasy at the aloof, ravaged figure and embarrassed by the silence, Harding began to talk about the various dogs he had owned and how much he had cared for them. Someday, he said, he hoped to own a pet elephant. Wilson twisted his lips to essay another witticism, saying that he hoped it would not prove to be a white elephant. Glad at last to find something harmless to talk about, Harding went on to tell of an old elephant named Tuskie that his sister Carolyn had written him about from Burma where she was a missionary. One morning the animal's keeper found him down and dying. As long as the elephant could watch the keeper he seemed content, but when his sight dimmed he began feeling in all directions with his trunk. The keeper came nearer to speak to him, and Tuskie reached out and wrapped his trunk about his friend and held him close until he died. As Harding finished his little story he noticed with dismay that the tears were running down Wilson's withered cheeks.

So Wilson left the White House, the old leader cast out by the herd yet forced by the cruel ritual of succession to take part in the ceremony of his rejection. Only two years before, when he had arrived in Europe with the gospel of his Fourteen Points, he, the star-crossed schoolmaster, had seemed a demigod. Wilson, Veel-son—to the millions who had massed to see him—his was the magic name that would banish war forever, the name people had shouted in the streets in a dozen different accents, the name at which kings and prime ministers bowed. Peasants had lighted votive candles before his picture, clipped from newspapers. As he had ridden down the Champs-Élysées with the President of the French Republic, spectators burst into tears. At London's Charing Cross Station, spread with a crimson carpet, the King and Queen of England waited to receive him. In his tumultuous welcome in Rome, as he sat in an open victoria beside the King, violets and mimosa showered down on him endlessly from roofs and windows and balconies.

Since those golden weeks, that still seemed only yesterday, his name had lost its magic, had become a tattered garment to be trampled on by gutter politicians. Today, finally, instead of kings there was this Ohio senator beside him, the symbol of America's repudiation of the League of Nations, of the peaceable kingdom that had seemed so near two years before. There were no flowers on this ride. The spectators gathered along Pennsylvania Avenue had come to cheer the new and not the old. There was not even the consolation of high tragedy, for the star-crossed schoolmaster in his defeat had become the dogmatic college professor.

Echoed by the insistent clatter and jingle of the cavalry escort, the procession passed the Patent Office, the tower of the fortress-like Post Office Building, the Raleigh Hotel with its irrelevant cupola. Ahead, as the cars wound up the tree-lined rise in second gear, the Capitol loomed larger, more overwhelming. Crawford's Freedom statue above the dome had grown from a speck to a looming feather-crested giant. The verdigrised lower roofs were visible now, as was the flag over the West Front.

It is customary for the incoming and outgoing Presidents to drive to the East Front of the Capitol before the inaugural and walk up the steps together. Wilson now excused himself to Harding, explaining that this would be beyond his strength and that he had made arrangements to use the Senate elevator. Edith Wilson and Florence Harding in the car behind spoke little, but the Duchess's face was stiff with disregarding pride.

Crossing Constitution Avenue, the procession passed through the seedy district of rooming houses and junk dealers and nondescript shops known as Chinatown before it turned into the steep, curving drive running through the still-muffled greenery of the Capitol grounds. At the Peace Monument, just before the sharp turn uphill, there was a burst of music from the waiting Harding-Coolidge Band of Washington.

The presidential car moved slowly up the drive, made a complete arc, and came to a stop before the triple flight of stairs leading to the Capitol's Senate wing. To the left the crowd formed a solid, expectant block in front of the temporary balcony of the East Portico. Harding sprang out of the car with professional amiability, waving his hat and nodding as he walked briskly up the steps. Wilson, his face an ashen mask, was driven to the freight entrance where a wheel chair was waiting to take him to the elevator and the President's Room on the floor above. Florence Harding hopped from the second car and dashed after her husband, "fairly raced up the steps," according to Edith Wilson.

The small, ornate President's Room, splashed with gilt and bowed under the weight of the allegorical ceiling paintings by Constantine

Brumidi (the American Tiepolo), was crowded by the time Wilson arrived. Harding, still smiling and nodding as he edged his way jovially along the corridor, had preceded him. Vice President Coolidge, incapable of either a smile or a nod, stood with his wife near the quarter-size bronze statue of McKinley in the corner.

Wilson had insisted on walking into the room by himself. Courtly even in his disability, he bowed slightly to the senators, Cabinet members, and friends who stood waiting for him. They gathered round to take off his coat. As he slipped his right arm out of the sleeve, he hooked the black-thorn to the upper coat pocket. Without its support he wavered, and the former mayor of Boston, "Honey Fitz" Fitzgerald,[2] reached out to steady him. Coatless, leaning heavily on his blackthorn, he limped across the Minton-tiled floor to the oval walnut table under the massive chandelier. He sat down and began to sign the left-over documents—several dozen minor bills relating to fortifications, water power, agricultural needs—that would take up the minutes before the committee from both Houses arrived to notify him formally that the Sixty-sixth Congress was ready to adjourn. There was no sound but the scratch of his pen and a subdued wave-murmur of conversation. The first measure he signed had to do with funds for the care of wounded soldiers. Every now and again he would interrupt his work to shake hands with some newcomer. To General Pershing, in impeccably cut tunic and boned crossbelt, he excused himself for not rising. At that same green-covered table where he sat writing, outgoing Presidents had sat since Lincoln's day and signed similar bills. The gilded hands of the mahogany grandfather clock opposite McKinley's statue showed eleven-eighteen. That clock slowly ticking away the last forty-two minutes of the Wilson administration was known as the Gold Clock be-cause once—until they were stolen—it had had hands of pure gold.

Wilson's old Cabinet members—Colby, Burleson, Baker, Daniels, and the others—stood by to wish him luck. He thanked them, calling each man by name. "Well," he said, glancing at the clock, "I think I had better scoot now." He beckoned to Senator Knox standing gravely near him, saying that he doubted he could negotiate the few steps to the Senate Chamber for Vice President Coolidge's inaugural shortly to take place there. The notification committee had still not arrived. As the hands of the Gold Clock neared twelve they were set back to give a few fictitious minutes to the old administration.

Just after noon Senator Henry Cabot Lodge strode across the threshold. The room hushed. Someone touched Wilson on the arm. He had kept his composure all the morning. Only at the entrance of the gentleman from Massachusetts, his old enemy, did his lopsided face stiffen. A small gray

[2] John F. "Honey Fitz" Fitzgerald, former mayor, Democratic former congressman, and grandfather of the four-year-old John Fitzgerald Kennedy.

man, waspish and arrogant, with tight curly hair and narrow spade beard, Lodge boasted—with truth—that he had destroyed Wilson's League of Nations in America. In his clipped Boston voice the Senator now notified Wilson that Congress had completed its business and stood ready to adjourn, unless the President had any further message to communicate.

"I have no communication to make," Wilson answered him in a voice of icy contempt. "I appreciate your courtesy; good morning, sir!"

Unruffled, Lodge glanced at his watch and remarked, "It's time we're moving." Wilson gave him a last cold stare as he left the room.

The others shifted toward the door, following the outgoing Vice President, Thomas Marshall, as he led Coolidge to the Senate Chamber. Harding stepped over to Wilson, bent down, and said in his kindly way—for he was, above all, a kindly man—that he would not consider it discourteous if Wilson did not appear at the inaugural. "I guess I had better not try it," Wilson told him. "I'm afraid I shall have to beg off." Harding said he understood. "All the luck in the world," Wilson wished him as he left.

Sonorously the Gold Clock struck twelve. Tumulty counted the strokes under his breath. Wilson reached spastically toward his throat and took off his scarf pin engraved with the President's Seal. It had been made from a nugget of gold that the state of California had given him and his bride as a wedding present in 1915. Their wedding rings had come from the same nugget. He struggled to his feet, crawled into his coat, and stumbled away with his wife, Tumulty, Admiral Grayson, and two Secret Service men, shuffling down the corridor with pathetic slowness, his blackthorn tapping on the flags. At the corridor's opposite end, in the larger area of the Marble Room, the diplomats and military chiefs of the various nations had assembled; many of the ambassadors in the peacock splendor of their formal uniforms of blue or red trimmed with gold, assorted attachés in hussar uniforms. Now they were joined by Pershing, the brown eagle, in olive-drab. They, too, began to head upstairs toward the gallery of the Senate Chamber.

The chamber itself was in an uproar of unfinished business, the chatter of the visitors in the galleries so shrill that Senator Lodge finally appealed to the president pro-tempore. Not until the new Vice President's appearance did the galleries finally quiet down. Throughout Coolidge's swearing-in, Harding—breaking precedent by being there at all—sat in a leather armchair just to the right of the rostrum. He sprawled there at ease, his knees crossed. Above him Florence Harding's spiky blue hat was the most conspicuous feature of the left gallery. Next to her were Harding's two sisters Carolyn and Abigail, and his father, Doctor George Harding, in the brass-buttoned GAR uniform that he wore for dress-up occasions. Close by them, with her two boys, Grace Coolidge in a red picture hat provided a graceful contrast to the Duchess.

The new Vice President was sworn in at twelve twenty-one; retiring Vice President Marshall announced that the Senate of the Sixty-sixth Congress was adjourned *sine die* and handed the gavel to his successor. Coolidge's inaugural address, in his atavistic Vermont twang that at times made even his wife giggle, was the shortest ever made, scarcely more than a formal compliment to the senatorial body. As he concluded, there was a polite ripple of self-contained applause. The galleries and the Senate Chamber emptied quickly.

Capitol Park before the East Portico was solid with waiting people. They stretched back under the leafless trees—where small boys were perched like starlings in the branches—as far as the Library of Congress. Just before one o'clock the crowd grew restive, began to stir in anticipation. Fifty wounded soldiers who had been brought from the Walter Reed Hospital were carried in wheel chairs to a special wooden platform near the baldachin. The scarlet-coated Marine bandsmen in the foreground readied their instruments. Marines in felt campaign hats were guarding the whole length of the East Front. A naval color guard stood at each side of the temporary platform. Directly below the desk where the President was to take his oath, under the Great Seal, a second color guard of four soldiers displayed the United States and presidential flags. Behind the baldachin the central doors of the Capitol had opened and congressmen, diplomats, Cabinet members, generals, admirals, and their wives were beginning to make their way to the reserved sections of the stands. Senator Lodge appeared, hatless, brisk and cocky as a sparrow, as he stopped to exchange a few words with the outgoing Secretary of the Navy Josephus Daniels and A. Mitchell Palmer, Wilson's Red-harrying attorney general.

The band struck up a dance tune. There were no longer any empty spaces to be seen. The members of the old administration grouped in the stand to the left, the new Cabinet sat on the right. The air itself seemed to contract. Then the Duchess appeared, sweeping along like a real duchess, accompanied by a military aide and followed by Harding's spinster sister Abigail and his married sister Carolyn. There were a few cheers from the crowd as the Duchess took her seat by the railing to the right of the desk used to hold the Bible. Her leathery features cracked into a smile of acknowledgment, she nodded, swaying slightly in time to the music. The solemn and bearded Charles Evans Hughes, Harding's designated secretary of state, made his way forward to greet her. Coolidge and former Vice President Marshall arrived unobtrusively and faded into their places.

Abruptly the band stopped playing. The almost ominous hush that followed dissolved in a murmur like the rustle of leaves as the justices of the Supreme Court—led by the enormous bulk of the former Confederate soldier, Chief Justice Edward Douglass White [3]—filed in gravely, two by two, wearing their black gowns and close black skullcaps. They were preceded by the Marshal of the Court bearing the Bible belonging to St. John's Masonic Lodge of New York on which Washington had taken his oath.

Then the President-elect appeared, walking forward quickly with springing step as he was escorted to the lectern by Senator Knox. At his appearance the band broke into "Hail to the Chief!" Harding carried his silk hat in his hand. The top button of his chesterfield, unbuttoned, showed the white piping of his waistcoat. In the bright sunshine his handsome solid figure loomed up almost stylized, like a ship's figurehead. The marshal laid the Bible open on the desk. Harding turned to face Justice White, resting the tops of his left fingers on the book as he slowly raised his right hand. His voice was clear and resonant, a silver voice:

> I, Warren Gamaliel Harding, do solemnly swear that I will faithfully execute the office of the President of the United States and will, to the best of my ability, preserve, protect, and defend the Constitution of the United States, so help me God.

At "so help me God," he nodded his head in affirmation, then bent over to kiss the Bible. The passage his fingers had rested on was one he had chosen from the Book of Micah.

> What doth the Lord require of thee, but to do justly, and to love mercy, and to walk humbly with thy God.

Applause filtered through the stands, was taken up in the plaza, and echoed like a wave among the trees. Harding turned to Knox and whispered, "Was it done all right?" The band struck up "The Star-Spangled Banner."

As the last notes crashed, quavered, and faded, the new President stood at the desk between bouquets of roses, facing the crowd below him. Slowly he adjusted his corded black-rimmed pince-nez, then took a small packet of notes from his pocket. To his right rows of silk toppers bobbled like enameled corks on a placid bay; to his left were the sooty skullcaps of the justices, and behind him the plumed hats of diplomats and the stiff visored caps of the military.

"If I say so myself," Harding had once remarked to a friend, "I do think I turn out a good speech." By "turning out" a speech he meant more the manner than the content. His conception of speechmaking derived from the full-blown style current in his youth, when oratory was like a set fireworks piece and Fourth-of-July orators filled the air with showers of

---

[3] A Roman Catholic, White, in the Reconstruction period, had been a local leader of the Ku Klux Klan. President Taft had appointed him chief justice.

rhetorical sparks and Roman-candle phrases. Brought up in this frock-coated school, Harding had early assimilated the alliterative generalities, the mellifluous polysyllables applied without too much regard for exactitude of meaning, favored by the imitators of Henry Clay, Harry of the West. Harding's speeches were meant to glow and expire. At the moment of their utterance, spoken so unhesitatingly by this virile neo-Roman in his silver voice, they overwhelmed most of his hearers.

Thrusting his left hand into his coat pocket, the stance of Harry of the West, he began:

> My countrymen—
> When one surveys the world about him after the great storm, noting the marks of destruction and yet rejoicing in the ruggedness of things which withstood it, if he is an American he breathes the clarified atmosphere with a strange mingling of regret and new hope. We have seen the world passion spend its fury, but we contemplate our Republic unshaken and hold our civilization secure. Liberty—liberty within the law and civilization are inseparable, and though both were threatened, we find them now secure and there comes to Americans the profound assurance that our representative government is the highest expression and surest guarantee of both.
> Standing in this presence, mindful of the solemnity of the occasion, feeling the emotions which no one may know until he senses the great weight of responsibility for himself, I must utter my belief in the Divine Inspiration of the founding fathers. Surely there must have been God's intent in the making of this New World Republic. . . .

On other inaugurals the presidential voice scarcely carried beyond the first few rows of spectators, but today with the concealed amplifiers it could be heard as far as the House and Senate office buildings:

> Our supreme task is the resumption of our onward normal way. Reconstruction, readjustment, restoration—all these must follow. I would like to hasten them. If it will lighten the spirit and add to the resolution with which we take up the task, let me repeat for our Nation, we shall give no people just cause to make war upon us; we hold no national prejudices; we entertain no spirit of revenge; we do not hate; we do not covet; we dream of no conquest nor boast of armed prowess. If, despite this attitude, war is again forced upon us, I earnestly hope a way may be found which will unify our individual and collective strength and consecrate all America, materially and spiritually, body and soul, to national defense. . . .
> Out of such universal service will come a new unity of spirit and purpose, a new confidence and consecration, which would make our defense impregnable, our triumph assured.

After demanding a reduction from wartime spending, he turned a phrase that would echo again in the same place forty years later:

"Our most dangerous tendency [he said solemnly] is to expect too much of government, and at the same time do for it too little."

The crowd listened in deferential unemotional silence. The first applause came among the silk hats, when, in oblique reference to the League of Nations, he spoke of "the wisdom of the inherited policy of non-involvement in old world controversies." The League was the key point of Harding's address, the unavoidable tightrope that he had to walk. Mention it he must, yet in such general terms that he could at the same time satisfy its implacable enemies led by Lodge and soothe those who like Taft basically believed in it. Harding did his best to spread the oil of rhetoric on those troubled waters:

> America builded on the foundations laid by the inspired fathers can be party to no permanent military alliance.
>
> Since freedom impelled and independence inspired and nationality exalted, a world super-government is contrary to everything we cherish and can have no sanction by our Republic. This is not selfishness, it is sanctity.
>
> We are ready to associate ourselves with the nations of the world, great and small, for conference, for counsel, to seek the expressed views of world opinion to recommend a way to approximate disarmament and relieve the crushing burden of military and naval establishments.
>
> We must strive for normalcy to reach stability.
>
> The supreme inspiration is the commonweal. Humanity hungers for international peace, and we crave it with all mankind. My most reverent prayer for America is for industrial peace, with its rewards, widely and generally distributed, amid the inspirations of equal opportunity.
>
> We would not have an America living within and for herself alone, but we would have her self-reliant, independent, and ever nobler, stronger, and richer. Believing in our higher standards, reared through constitutional liberty and maintained opportunity, we invite the world to the same heights. But pride in things wrought is no reflex of a completed task. Common welfare is the goal of our national endeavor. . . .

The generalities flashed and glittered as they soared over the throng and the bare trees of Capitol Park. Harding accompanied his speech with stiff, set gestures recalling the illustrations of books of declamation. The mellow voice concluded:

> We ought to find a way to guard against the perils and penalties of unemployment. We want an America of homes, illumined with hope and happiness, where mothers, freed from the necessity of long hours of toil beyond their own doors, may preside as befits the hearthstone of American citizenship. We want the cradle of American childhood rocked under conditions so wholesome and so hopeful that no blight may touch it in its development.
>
> Service is the supreme commitment of life. I would rejoice to acclaim

the era of the Golden Rule and crown it with the autocracy of service. I pledge an Administration wherein all the agencies of Government are called to serve, and ever promote an understanding of Government purely as an expression of the popular will. One cannot stand in this presence and be unmindful of the tremendous responsibility. The world upheaval has added heavily to our tasks. But with the realization comes the surge of high resolve, and there is reassurance in the belief in the God-given destiny of our Republic. If I felt that there is to be sole responsibility in the Executive for the America of tomorrow I should shrink from the burden. But there are a hundred millions, with common concern and shared responsibility, answerable to God and country. The Republic summons them to their duty, and I invite cooperation.

He stood there silent at last, gracious, immobile, as the applause welled around him. Then as he tucked his notes in his pocket and made ready to leave, a Secret Service man presented the Duchess with a bouquet of American Beauty roses. The Marine Band burst forth with "America," and the crowd mumbled the words in indistinguishable syllables. A cold wind blew along the plaza. The stands were clearing quickly, but most of those below waited for the start of the procession and a close glimpse of the new President.

To the surprise of the senators, met in closed session immediately after the inaugural, Harding appeared again in the Senate Chamber to submit in person the names of the members of his Cabinet. Although the custom had been initiated by Washington, it had fallen out of use and even memory since Jefferson's day.

Harding ascended the rostrum and took his seat beside Vice President Coolidge, then almost immediately rose to speak. "I have chosen my Cabinet," he told the senators, "in accordance with my best judgment and my personal wishes. I trust it will meet with your approval." He then read the names.

Among the senators ranged behind their desks like pliant schoolboys sat the gaunt, weather-scored Albert Fall, senator from New Mexico and designated secretary of the interior. At Harding's mention of his name, his colleagues whooped and cheered. He rose from his seat, snake-eyed and impassive, and tendered his resignation as United States senator. It was immediately accepted, and for a few moments Fall found himself on the Senate floor a private citizen. At once his cheering colleagues flocked around him, slapping him on the back, and then in ham-handed humor feigning anger with shouts of "Get out!" "Throw him out!"

Senator Lodge finally moved that Fall be confirmed as secretary without reference to committee. The motion was carried with jovial unanimity. Names of the other Cabinet officers had to await the brief formality of a committee report.

At half-past two Harding emerged from the Senate wing with the fur-swathed Duchess. The waiting cars were still surrounded by the cavalry escort. Restlessly the horses pawed the ground, their hoofs chinking, while the troopers yanked at the bridles. As Harding and his wife entered the presidential car the officers' swords flashed in salute.

Police whistles shrilled, motorcycles backfired, rattling commands rang out. The auto exhausts filled the air with puffs of blue smoke. And all in a moment the new President had gone. The Pierce-Arrow, top still down, moved slowly to the north drive of Capitol Park, then spurted along the slope to Pennsylvania Avenue and the waiting White House.

CHAPTER II

The Shadow of Blooming Grove

Exactly a century before Harding's inauguration as America's twenty-ninth and Ohio's seventh President,[1] his great-great-grandfather, Amos Harding, had left Pennsylvania for the Ohio country. Amos was of the sixth generation of American Hardings, descended from the English Puritan Richard Harding, "a mariner engaged in fishing," who had crossed the Atlantic in 1623 to settle in Braintree, Massachusetts. From the beginning the Hardings were a restless tribe, stiff-faced swarthy men, apt at establishing themselves on new soil but then, instead of garnering their harvests, moving on to some fringe of settlement. Richard's son Stephen, a blacksmith by trade, became a Baptist convert and followed this suspected sect to the non-sectarian air of Providence, Rhode Island. Future generations of Hardings would retain the hard substance of their Baptist shell.

Stephen's son, the second Stephen, started out in Providence as a tanner and currier, but before he was thirty he had become a successful shipbuilder and sea captain. In his middle years he bought a farm of 400 acres in New London County, Connecticut, and moved there with his brother Israel. His second son, Abraham, married a neighbor's daughter, Anna Dolson. Twenty years later, in 1761, Abraham and Anna with six accumulated sons moved on to Orange County, New York, to a fertile area nine miles east of the present Fort Jarvis. In that rapidly expanding rural community Abraham soon made his mark as a prosperous farmer and leading citizen. He was elected highway master, fence viewer, and in 1775 his tax assessment reached the respectable sum of fourteen shillings. During the Revolution he served as a second lieutenant in the Continental Army, and after the war was raised to a second major in the State Militia. He liked to be addressed by his title of major.

The Major's eldest son, Abraham, Jr., born in 1744, went back to Con-

---

[1] Ohio's other Presidents were: Ulysses S. Grant, Rutherford B. Hayes, James A. Garfield, Benjamin Harrison, William McKinley, and William H. Taft.

necticut in 1762—the year after his arrival in Orange County—to marry Huldah Tryon of the New London Tryons. Returning with his bride to Orange County, he settled on a farm near his father and worked the land for ten years. It was rich land, repaying labor with abundance. Nevertheless, in June, 1772, young Abraham, accompanied by his wife, three sons, and a daughter, left with his brother Lemuel for the Wyoming Valley in northeastern Pennsylvania.

The valley had long been in dispute between Pennsylvania and Connecticut, the Connecticut Assembly claiming that the whole Wyoming country had been granted to Connecticut by Charles II nineteen years before he had deeded the same region to William Penn. In 1755 the assemblymen chartered the Connecticut-Susquehanna Company to survey and settle their valley. This river region of rich bottom earth and wide meadows, abounding in fish and game, its hillsides thick with massive walnut trees, towering buttonwoods, pine, ash, hickory, and elm, drew the Connecticut farmers irresistibly from their thinner acres. During the summer of 1762 the first large party of Yankee settlers arrived in the valley, planted grain, and returned to Connecticut late in the autumn both to avoid the unsheltered winter and because of difficulties with the local Delaware chief, the alcoholic "King" Teedyuscung. The following year the settlers returned and circumspectly set fire to Teedyuscung's log castle, roasting him while he slept. Some months later the avenging Delawares ambushed a number of settlers, killing about twenty. Then both whites and Indians fled the valley, and it remained deserted for the next six years.

In February, 1769, a new band of 40 Connecticut farmers arrived in the valley only to find that a smaller group of Pennsylvanians—Pennamites, the Yankees called them—had preceded them. Their armed encounter was the beginning of a series of incidents known as the Pennamite War. Three times that year the Pennamites drove the Yankees from the valley. Three times the following year reinforcements from Connecticut drove out the Pennamites. But when Captain Zebulon Butler with 150 Connecticut militia arrived in 1771, the Pennamites reluctantly conceded that the Yankees were there to stay. The newcomers now felt free to bring their wives and children from Connecticut to the spreading fields beside the Susquehanna.

It was in that interlude of peace that Abraham Harding, in 1772, staked out his future farmstead east of the river within range of Fort Pittston's protective stockade. Like his father before him, when placed in a new environment he quickly emerged as a man of standing. At the first Wyoming town meeting he was elected fence viewer, and that same year appointed to a committee to investigate land titles. Three years later his tax valuation was twenty-eight pounds and he was paying thirty-eight shillings in taxes.

The peace interlude was shattered in the spring of 1788 when Colonel John Butler with his loyalist Rangers in their green-and-buff uniforms slipped down from the Mohawk Valley to raid the Wyoming country. The Rangers were supported by a detachment of Sir John Johnson's Royal Greens and 700 Iroquois auxiliaries led by a Seneca chief and the relentless Queen Esther.

When the news of the Tory advance reached the Wyoming Valley late in May, the settlers left their farms for the protection of the forts. Abraham and his family took refuge in Fort Pittston. On the other side of the river, a few miles to the south, stood Fort Jenkins. Captain Stephen Harding, the son of the Connecticut mariner, commanded this fort which was soon crowded behind its palisades with his relatives and neighbors.

During the day armed working parties often went out from the fort to cultivate the fields. On June 30 such a party left Fort Jenkins to work in a cornfield belonging to Captain Stephen. In the party were Stephen's sons Benjamin, Stukely, and young Stephen, and a grandson David. A Tory scout spotted them at their hoeing and carried the news to Butler's Indians. As the Hardings and their companions filed back along the bank of the Susquehanna at the end of the afternoon, the Indians lay in ambush waiting for them. In the sudden attack that followed, Benjamin and Stukely fought back as long as they could raise a hand, but with a third settler were finally overpowered, tomahawked, and scalped. Two others, who were taken prisoner, were later tortured and killed. David Harding saved himself by plunging into the river and hiding among the rushes. At one point the Indians were so close they could have touched him.

For three days and nights the Indians invested Fort Jenkins. In spite of his grief Captain Stephen repulsed each assault. On July 3, in a sudden woodland engagement known afterward as the Wyoming Massacre, the Tory Colonel Butler surrounded and overwhelmed Capt. Zebulon Butler and his 300 hastily assembled defenders. Most of the beaten Yankees who attempted to surrender were struck down by the swooping Indians. A hundred and sixty settlers died during the battle. Of some twenty prisoners seized by the Indians, Queen Esther personally tomahawked eight that evening.

Colonel Butler with his Rangers now appeared before Fort Jenkins and demanded its capitulation, expressing regret for the death of Captain Harding's sons whose mutilated bodies he now returned, at the same time offering a safe-conduct to the Yankees if they would leave the valley at once. Captain Harding was forced to accept the terms. In spite of Butler's promise, it proved impossible to control the Indians who ranged up and down the valley plundering, burning, and murdering at will. In a rush of panic the surviving Wyoming families abandoned their possessions and fled across the mountains to their old homes in New York and Connecticut in what was known afterward as the Big Runaway. Many died on the terrible journey through the Shades of Death Swamp, among them the eleven-year-old Joseph Harding. Abraham's second son, John, had died two years earlier.

In spite of this catastrophe, Abraham returned three months later to the charred remains of his cabin in the desolate valley. With the help of his only remaining son, the fourteen-year-old Amos, he cleared and planted his acres, and although he seems from the surviving records to have gone into debt he managed at last to build himself a comfortable home. When Amos at the age of twenty married a neighbor's daughter, Phoebe Tripp, his father gave him half the cleared part of his farm. There Amos lived for sixteen years, and there Phoebe bore nine of the seventeen children she was to bear him.

After the Revolution the Pennamites renewed their attempts to eject their Yankee cousins, and men died in haphazard skirmishes until their differences finally drifted into the calmer if more extended waters of litigation. Discouraged by the uncertainty of his land titles, and stirred by the old family restlessness, Amos got rid of his Pittston land and in March, 1800, moved forty miles north to an empty corner of the recently created Luzerne County known as the Beech Woods, a valley wilderness with scarcely a cabin or clearing between it and the Susquehanna River. There were not even trails to follow, and he and his family dragged their household goods through the snow on sledges.

A solitary settler had preceded them, an Adam Miller, who had arrived the year before to claim the land in the southern end of the valley and build himself a log cabin on the west side of the creek. Amos bought enough land from Miller for a farm on the creek's east side, and there he built his own cabin. Between them, the two men founded the village of Clifford. More settlers followed, but for years Amos Harding and Adam Miller were the heaviest taxpayers of the new community. They laid out the first road, built the first schoolhouse, and Amos organized the Baptist Church. In 1802 old Major Harding came from Orange County to live with his grandson, and somehow a place was found for him in the small cabin that already held two adults and ten children within its two rooms and a loft.

From time to time Amos bought more land from Miller, finally in 1812 acquiring Miller's cabin as well. To this more commodious building Amos now added an extra room, making it the largest cabin for miles around. There the first school was held—for several years the Harding and Miller children were the only pupils—until the schoolhouse was built, and on Sundays the new room was used for religious services. Amos, the founding father, was long remembered in Clifford. Tall, wiry, with long black hair, he looked almost like an Indian. He is described as "a high-spirited man of adventurous nature, stern, unbending in matters affecting his convictions of right and justice, with strong religious beliefs, a 'Hard-shell Baptist' of the old school, a shrewd and prosperous businessman but generous and kindly in his dealings with his family and neighbors." He often preached at meetings of the County Baptist Association, and when his four-year-old daughter Huldah was drowned, he conducted the funeral services and preached the sermon then customary. He might have remained in Clifford honored and prosperous, to have become a patriarch in his old age, but in his middle years news of the Ohio country stirred him to move on again.

Since Washington's young manhood the Ohio region, in spite of the French and Indian threat, had remained a beckoning if perilous dream of wealth. Brig. John Forbes's capture of Fort Duquesne in 1758 had eliminated the French. The Indian threat lasted until, after the Revolution, Gen. "Mad Anthony" Wayne avenged the humiliation of Arthur St. Claire's earlier rout by defeating and shattering the forces of Chief Little Turtle at the Battle of the Fallen Timbers in 1795. Wayne opened up the Northwest Territory. By the Treaty of Greenville he forced the Indians to give up eastern and southern Ohio and confine themselves to the northern section bounded by the treaty line. In the wake of the treaty, settlers poured across the flat Ohio landscape; old soldiers eager for their promised land grants, New Englanders, Germans, Scotch-Irish, Quakers from Pennsylvania, dissenting farmers turning their backs on the slave states of Virginia and Kentucky. The rapid increase in population led to Ohio's admission to the Union in 1803 as the seventeenth state.

North of the treaty line the Indians remained restive, and danger still lurked in the forests for unwary or unlucky whites. Not until the War of 1812, when Gen. William Henry Harrison commanding the Army of the Northwest defeated and killed the Shawnee chief Tecumseh, who as a last resort against the white advance had allied himself with the British, would the Indians realize the helplessness of their destiny and agree to cede away northern Ohio. Then, on foot, on horseback, in two-wheeled carts and covered wagons, over turnpikes and along the Cumberland Road—the new national highway—the land-hungry Easterners swarmed into the newly opened wilderness.

The Ohio fever, the lure of the fertile Northwest, of that Beulah land where a man could buy 160 acres for $200, reached even into the beechwood settlement of Clifford. Colonization agents circulated through rural Pennsylvania, glib and persuasive, with accounts of virgin farmland in the Western Reserve.

Again the restless Harding blood quickened. Several settlers from Clifford had already left for the West. In October, 1815, Amos Harding paid to John Maxwell, recently of Clifford, the first instalment on a quarter section of 160 acres in Richland County, Ohio, at the government price of two dollars an acre. Two years later Salmon Harding made a down payment to another emigrant Clifford neighbor, Charles Pond, for a second quarter section.

In 1818 Amos's third son, the twenty-three-year-old Mordecai, packed his belongings on an ox-drawn wagon and set out with his bride on the overland journey of some four hundred miles to "spy out" the Harding lands in what had just become the township of Blooming Grove, Ohio.[2] It was a forest terrain of gently rolling hills that tapered off into the central alluvial plain. The abundance of black walnut, blue ash, and red elm—as any pioneer farmer could tell at a glance—was the sign of a rich soil, and the spruce undergrowth indicated depth.

Mordecai approved. He ran up a squatter's cabin on a quarter section of land that he later bought from the government. Shortly after his arrival, while exploring the wilderness, he wandered off a marked trail and became lost in the dense woods. As it grew dark he made out the light of a campfire through the trees and followed its glow until he found himself at the camp of Chief Pipe, one of the rulers of the local Indians. The chief gave him food, a place to sleep, and skins to protect him—and at daybreak escorted him back to the trail. Afterward they remained friends, and the chief often visited him in Blooming Grove.

The other tribes were growing so restive at the sight of the white intruders in the north that another Indian uprising seemed imminent. Most of the settlers left. Mordecai decided to go back for the time to Pennsylvania. But by the following year the Federal government had persuaded the Indians to a final withdrawal. The Public Land Act of 1820, by which a man with $100 could buy himself 80 acres and take four years to pay for it, brought a rush of poorer settlers. Late in 1820 Amos sold off his holdings in Clifford and, together with his twelve surviving children, prepared for the long journey—that was to be his last—to Ohio.

There is no record of that springtime trek of the Hardings over the Alleghenies along Braddock's old military road, of the fording of the rivers, the days of rain and sleet, the frosty mornings by the campfire, the lowering evenings. They carted their belongings in oxcarts and covered wagons, and led what livestock they could on foot. It was a miniature tribal migration: Amos the patriarch; two married sons, Salmon (or Solomon) and Mordecai, with their families; two married daughters, Abigail Stearnes and Welthy Baker, and their husbands; William, a widower whose wife Minerva had either been killed by wild beasts or carried off by the Indians several years before; Ebenezer and Benjamin

[2] Blooming Grove Township in Richland County was erected in 1816 when it was split off from Madison Township. Three years later the township was cut in half by the separation of Sharon Township. Blooming Grove remained part of Richland County until Morrow County was organized in 1848.

Franklin, bachelors; sixteen-year-old Hilah and her sister Mahala, aged seven; the two boys, thirteen-year-old John and twelve-year-old Chauncey; and several grandchildren. George Tryon Harding, the eldest son, who was to be Warren Gamaliel's great-grandfather, stayed behind in Clifford with his second wife, Elizabeth Madison, to settle the last of the family affairs. He did not leave for Ohio until late summer.

The small caravan finally reached Blooming Grove in August. Although other settlers had had their cabins burned and their crops destroyed, Mordecai—thanks to his friendship with Chief Pipe—found his cabin still intact and the staked-out Harding lands undisturbed.

Now, in this tangle of forest, the work of settlement had to be undertaken all over again. Cabins had to be raised quickly with the early frost in mind, sheds set up for the stock, the land cleared and prepared for next season's planting. Amos built his cabin on a slight eminence not far from a spring. George on his belated arrival ran up his cabin near his father's.

On his land about a quarter of a mile away Salmon, now beginning to assume the leadership of the clan, commenced to survey and lay out the village of Blooming Grove. Amos donated land and saw to it that a log school was erected, one that could be used temporarily on Sundays for Baptist worship. In turn Salmon gave the land for the Blooming Grove cemetery. Other settlers arrived, transplanted Yankees and Virginians and Dutch from Pennsylvania with names such as Chambers, Appleman, Baggs, Marshman, Johnson, Kreps, and Foglesong. On March 5, 1835, the plat of Blooming Grove was recorded in Richland County and acknowledged by David Kilgore, justice of the peace.

Johnny Appleseed passed through Blooming Grove with his seeds and his seedlings, and was befriended by Mordecai. Scattered bands of Indians still wandered by on their way from Sandusky to Mount Vernon, but they gave no trouble to the settlers, merely stopping off to trade venison for tobacco and whisky. More troublesome for some years were the wolves.

Salmon organized the Bloomfield Baptist Church and built the first church building, a small frame structure some two miles beyond the village crossroads. The Hardings were passing devout. Of Amos's eight adult sons, Ebenezer became an "old school" Baptist preacher, Benjamin Franklin often officiated as pastor, and Mordecai remained for fifty years a deacon of the Blooming Grove Church. Salmon, outliving two wives, later moved to the county seat of Mount Gilead where he organized the Bethel Baptist Church and served for many years as its minister. Hardest of Hard-shells, he would wither any modernist dissenter with: "My Bible don't say so!" Amos always kept a young steer to fatten up for the meetings of the Baptist Association.

For many of the Hardings, Blooming Grove itself was not the last stopping place. Ebenezer, the first to leave, went farther west, as did

Benjamin. John became a wagon maker and continued his trade in LaPorte County, Indiana. Chauncey, after the customary early frontier marriage, settled in Marion County. Salmon, although he preferred the relative urbanity of Mount Gilead, requested in his will to be buried in his own Blooming Grove cemetery.

Within a few years of their arrival the Hardings banded together and bought a sawmill. After sawing their own lumber and using what they needed, they sold to or bartered the surplus boards with their neighbors. Soon clapboard houses began to replace the cabins as the settlement gave way to the village. The population of Blooming Grove crept toward the hundred mark. Clark Johnston set up a blacksmith shop at the north-south, east-west crossroads. Next to it was whiskery old Jake Day's general store, and there was even a wayside halting place that served as a tavern and called itself Adams's Hotel.

Amos Harding still kept thin and erect, but his black hair had turned completely white and he was beginning to feel his years. In 1826 he divided his original land purchase, deeding it equally to his sons Ebenezer and George Tryon. Since Ebenezer did not intend to stay in Blooming Grove, he sold his land to George. In 1831 George took over another 80 acres that his ailing father had contracted to buy from the government. The following year Amos died.

Not long after his father's death, George built himself a more substantial house to the west of the family log cabin. The new house, two stories high, was built of oak and walnut. It measured twenty-eight feet by twenty-eight feet with a one-story wing on the northwest corner. Hand-cut shingles covered the roof. The twin front doors, flanked by windows, were shielded by an overhead porch that extended seven feet and was enclosed at the base with lattice. Although the house was not large, it was the most substantial one in Blooming Grove. Inside, the ceilings were eight feet high. The fireplace in the dining room was six and a half feet wide.

Life in that crude burgeoning community was self-contained, remote, measured more by the progress of the seasons than by days or years. The outside world, news of which was read aloud from the Columbus weekly journal to those gathered at the post office, seemed scarcely real to husbandmen struggling, within the limits set by Hesiod 2,500 years before, to "plough and plant and set one's house in order." Social gatherings were for the most part practical extensions of daily activities—cabin raisings, log rollings, quilting parties, paring bees, cornhuskings, shooting matches. The men wore coarsely woven hunting shirts and deerskin breeches or trousers, the women at their finest wore American cotton check. The customary drink at these gatherings was whisky toddy which one old pioneer reminiscently thought "fit for a king." Brawls were not uncommon in such settlements. John May, the first lawyer in Mansfield, recalled that "every neighborhood had its bully or chief fighter, and these were pitted against each other like gamecocks. These fights often ended in a general melee in which whole neighborhoods were sometimes engaged against each other."

Three miles south of Blooming Grove a post office was set up in the house of William Wallace and called Barcelona. Then, in 1841, the office was moved to Whitaker's general store in the village. One of the early postmasters was Doctor James McCune, Blooming Grove's first physician. Since Ohio already had a Blooming Grove post office elsewhere, it was decided to call the new one Corsica out of respect for Napoleon.[2]

Salmon's rural backwater that he had laid out so carefully flourished with the rest of Ohio. In 1800 the territory numbered 42,000 inhabitants. By 1820 the population of Ohio had grown to 580,000 and the new state had become seventh in size in the Union. Yet of these numbers all but 35,000 inhabitants lived on farms and villages of less than a hundred persons. Cincinnati, with a population of 9,642, was the only real city. But Cincinnati was the glittering exception whereas Blooming Grove, hacked from the forest, was the type.

George Tryon Harding, although twice married, had only five children —three girls, Huldah, Phoebe Ann, and Mary Miranda, and two boys, William Oliver Perry and Charles Alexander. In 1856, when he was sixty-five, he prepared to turn over his farm to Charles who had been living with his wife Mary Anne Crawford and their five children in the family log cabin ever since his father had moved into the new homestead.

George pulled down the old cabin and built a small house for himself on the site. Two months after George's death, in 1860, his widow Elizabeth deeded the farm to her son William and four days later he conveyed the land, except for one small strip, to his brother Charles "for a consideration of $2,200."[3] Elizabeth now moved into the homestead with her son Charles. Charles's two eldest daughters slept in the small house.

George was buried in Salmon's cemetery on a ridge near his father's grave. By this time a fair scattering of Hardings had been buried in Blooming Grove. Their gravestones, as well as their holdings, gave evidence of a family that had made its mark. The first Harding headstones were of austere slate incised with inverted torches and weeping willows. A small marble obelisk testified to George Tryon's substance.

In church and meeting, in ownership of land and in the quality of their gravestones, the Hardings appeared the oldest and most prominent family in the village. Blooming Grove was even referred to as Harding Corners.

[2] Corsica it remained on the post-office records until long after Harding's childhood. In official documents he always described his birthplace as Corsica, Ohio.
[3] Land values had, of course, increased, but this figure represents more the inflation of the currency caused by the circulation of paper money.

Yet there was a flaw in this successful family, a shadow that the Hardings could not escape, a rumor that would never quite die down, that they and every family in Blooming Grove were aware of. For it was said, usually in whispers, and had been said almost from the arrival of the Hardings in Ohio, that the Harding veins had Negro blood in them. The stories varied. Some had it that Amos, the patriarch, was a West Indian Negro; others that Anna Roberts, George Tryon's first wife, was a Negress; still others that Elizabeth Madison was a mulatto.

The Hardings were all aware of the legend of their mixed blood. Amos in his old age, with his sons William, Salmon, and Chauncey present, explained it solemnly to his great-granddaughter Helen Harding Meredith who had run to him in tears after being taunted by her playmates. Just after he had arrived in Blooming Grove, he told her, he had come to an unexpected clearing with a log cabin on it. When he went up to the cabin, he found a man living there whom he had known in Pennsylvania. This man (he did not name him) had quarreled with one of his Pennsylvania neighbors—not a Harding—and afterward for spite had girdled all the man's apple trees, then cleared out when he was discovered. Now, discovered again, he threatened to kill Amos if he said anything about what had happened in Pennsylvania. Amos merely told him that he wanted no trouble and left him alone.

Later, after the first corn harvest, Amos found that someone had been robbing his corncribs. He and his sons lay in wait for several nights until at last they spotted a man filling his sack with their corn. The man they caught in their struggle in the darkness turned out to be the Pennsylvania fugitive. Exposed to everyone as a thief, and furious at being exposed, the man started the story that the Hardings were part Negro. Then, alarmed at the thought of Harding vengeance, he sold his land quickly and left for the West. But the story, once started, never did die out.

Whatever the truth of Amos's explanation, the rumor of their blood would haunt the Hardings down the years. Later generations would not be able to say for certain whether the rumor was true or false, but its shadow would darken their lives and follow them to their graves.[4]

[4] The collateral descendants of President Harding are to this day extremely sensitive on the subject.

[CHAPTER III]

The Father

The second George Tryon Harding, father of the future President, was the third child and only surviving boy among the five surviving daughters of Mary Anne and Charles Alexander Harding. Tryon they called him. He was born on June 12, 1844, in the log cabin built by his great-grandfather Amos. Three sisters and a brother died in infancy. The remaining girls, Phoebe, Sophia, Lydia, Margaret, and Sarah were to live on into the twentieth century.

During Tryon's boyhood, Ohio, although still facing the frontier, had become the country's leading agricultural area. The population had grown to over a million and a half, making it the third largest state in the Union. Panics, like that of 1837, might strike at the financial centers of Cincinnati and Columbus, money might grow scarce, but the rural self-sufficiency of most of the inhabitants remained unshaken. The canal network of the thirties and the expanding railroads of the forties and fifties did not touch Blooming Grove. Where other settlements grew to towns and cities with thriving new industries, Salmon's village remained a village, outwardly enlivened only by the annual flurry of elections and by the occasional revival or camp meeting.

Tryon was twelve years old by the time his father abandoned Amos's log cabin for the new house. Although no description of the Harding homestead exists beyond the catalogue of its dimensions, it resembled the general run of prosperous farmers' dwellings of the place and period. Francis Weisenburger, in his history of the Ohio frontier, describes such a homestead in which

> the eastern section was used for every-day purposes—kitchen, dining room, dormitory, and work shop; the lower part of the western section was an old-fashioned parlor, set aside for Sundays and special occasions. On the second floor were the sleeping quarters, notably lacking in light and air. In the much-used eastern section of the house, there was a large fireplace, with an iron crane and brass andirons. Above hung a long rifle, and on the

27

opposite wall, powder-horns and shot-pouches arranged in decorative fashion. In the corner of the room there was a loom operated by hand. Candles were the only means of illumination. The parlor was fitted out in more formal style. On the walls were two colored wood cuts or engravings, protected by frames and glass. One was an heroic likeness of Daniel O'Connell, the Irish patriot. The other represented "Isabel," a cherry-lipped damsel with spangled bodice and a smart hat bedecked with waving ostrich feathers. A porch used for informal relaxation was attached to the south side of the house, where a long bench and a number of stools invited the weary adult to an interval of smoking and chatting. A tin wash-basin, a pitcher and towels provided adequate toilet facilities, while the scythe, sickle, hoe, rake, axes, fishing poles, and husking pegs were on hooks near-bye ready for work or recreation. The well-curb a short distance away was equipped with an iron-bound bucket attached to a grape-vine rope. The cool milk house in the yard had a flat earth floor on which rested crocks of butter, pots of cream, and a variety of pans. In the barnyard, a log building served as a horse-stable, corn-crib, and cow-shed. . . . A chicken-coop, a hog-pen, and a sheepfold were near-bye. Not far away was the more decorative, enclosed vegetable and flower garden, where food for the table, and flowering shrubs—the lilac, snow-ball, and burning bush—were growing. An orchard produced its yearly crops of cherries, apples and peaches.

Such was the farm, but Tryon was neither by nature nor inclination a farmer. For boys like himself, eager to leave the family acres, three traditional paths lay open—law, medicine, and schoolteaching. A keen, aggressive boy with a neat hand would make his way to the nearest county seat and prevail on some provincial attorney to allow him the corner of an office. In exchange he would take on the routine clerical tasks, reading law in his spare time, until in a few years he would stand between the American flag and the brass cuspidors facing the judge in the courthouse and find himself admitted to the bar. The path of the law led to politics, a broadening highway that ran to the state capital and even beyond to Washington.

A quieter, more scientifically minded boy might prefer to apprentice himself to the local doctor. "Reading medicine," this was called, though it consisted more of accompanying the doctor on his rounds, learning to dress wounds and compound drugs, and recognize the common diseases. After three years of this itinerant teaching it was the custom for doctor and pupil to dissect a cadaver taken from some not too closely guarded country cemetery.

Teaching was a temporary calling, engaged in by young men "getting under way" and by young ladies unable to get under way.

The schoolmaster's way was the easiest but also the narrowest. At thirteen or fourteen a boy or girl need spend only two years at one of the new training schools that had begun to dot the landscape. Founded in imitation of New England academies, grandiloquently named colleges, such institutions awarded *baccalaureatus in artibus* degrees to raw farm adolescents whom they sent out to the one-room district schools across the state.

Most of the boys who finished their course at Blooming Grove's new brick schoolhouse—the school had been built by Charles Harding who numbered bricklaying among his other skills—had received all the education, in their opinion and that of their parents, that any farmer needed. But Tryon as a prosperous farmer's son went on to a subscription school run by his aunt Clara. He was small for his age—his height at maturity would be below average—dark-complexioned, with dark curly hair and over-large ears. Some would have called him ferret-faced.

It was at an entertainment in the new school that Tryon first noticed a prim-faced little girl in brown pigtails as she gave a recitation. He knew that she was Phoebe [1] Elizabeth Dickerson, the daughter of Isaac Haines Dickerson whose farm adjoined the Harding land, but this was the first time he had ever really noticed her. After that he noticed her more. Phoebe, in the gawky, wall-scribbled school term, became his "girl" and he her "fellow."

In 1858, at the age of fourteen, Tryon entered Iberia College in the village of the same name seven miles east of Blooming Grove. The college had been chartered four years before by the synod of the Free Presbyterian Church with the aim of making it "positively Christian in management and influence." It consisted of a two-story brick dormitory with separate entrances and floors for the boys and girls, perched on a hill and capped by a small belfry. Attached limpet-like to the side was a somewhat bleaker, bulkier structure, built later, that held the classrooms. Between thirty and forty boys and girls aged from thirteen to sixteen, and drawn from the surrounding farmlands, made up the student body. The three clergymen-teachers, calling themselves professors, taught grammar, history, arithmetic, a little elementary science. Three terms made up the academic course: the first, from the first Wednesday in September to the third Wednesday in December; the winter term, from the first Wednesday in January to the fourth in March; and the spring term, from the first Wednesday in April to the third in June. Commencement came on the first day of summer.

Tryon, the smallest boy in his class, received his bachelor's degree in June, 1860. Commencing in the autumn, he taught for two terms at a rural school four miles north of Mount Gilead. Most of his minute salary he saved and then a few months after the outbreak of the Civil War—and in spite of his bachelorhood in arts—he enrolled for another term at

[1] Her name was also spelled Phebe.

Ontario Academy six miles north of Blooming Grove, where Phoebe was already a student. She had never been wholly out of his mind. One night that winter they found themselves sitting side by side on a sleighing party to which each had been invited unknown to the other. "When I climbed into my place under the buffalo robes," Tryon recalled in his old age, "whom should I find, elbow to elbow with me, but Phoebe. . . . There in the night shadows we squeezed hands. In a month we were engaged."

At the graduation exercises that year he gave an address on "Brough and Vallandigham." Ostensibly a defense of John Brough, the candidate for governor of the Unionists—the Republicans and those Democrats supporting the war—it was much more an attack on Clement Vallandigham, congressman and candidate of the anti-war Democrats, now directing his campaign from exile in Canada. The Hardings, earlier abolitionists and Free Soilers, were now true-blue Republicans—all except the stubbornly Democratic Uncle Salmon who persisted in his loyalty to the memory of Andrew Jackson.

Tryon, though not tall enough at first to be a soldier, was as restless as most young men at school in wartime and as filled with romantic notions about war. He left Ontario Academy, returned to Blooming Grove, and the following Sunday took the train from Galion to Delaware where in spite of his lack of height he managed to enlist as a fifer in Company C of the 96th Ohio Volunteer Infantry. Almost at once the 96th was sent to Camp Dennison, north of Cincinnati. But before the young recruit had even begun to harden into a soldier, he was laid low with pleurisy after a long march in the rain. When the rest of the regiment left Ohio he had to stay behind. A few weeks later he was mustered out.

He returned to Blooming Grove and his father's house. It took him a year to get his health back, the climactic year of Chancellorsville and Gettysburg, of Vicksburg's surrender, and the emergence of Grant and Sherman. Belatedly, in the fine print of the Columbus weekly, the heroic news of Union activities reached Blooming Grove. Regiments from the old Northwest Territory fought in every engagement. As Tryon's health improved, he grew restless again at the thought of a blue tunic and brass buttons. The 136th Regiment of the Ohio National Guard—one of the ephemeral hundred-day regiments—was to be mustered in at Camp Chase on May 3, 1864. Tryon once more tried his luck at the recruiting booth, and again he was allowed to enlist, this time as a "drummer boy," in Company D. He was given a few days to go back to Blooming Grove to arrange his affairs and say his goodbyes. That evening he went to the Dickersons', told Phoebe he was going to war, and asked her to marry him before he left. She said yes. The next day he drove to Mount Gilead for a license, his father's written permission in his pocket—since he was under twenty-one.

Both of them knew what Isaac Dickerson would have said to the marriage of his twenty-year-old daughter to a boy who might never come back. Charles Harding had given his consent with silent reluctance, vexed enough that his son wanted to take up soldiering again after his first unlucky attempt, especially as he needed the boy to help out on the farm.

On the afternoon of May 7 Tryon hitched up the family buggy and drove over to the Dickerson farm to "take Phoebe and her sister Deb for a ride." It was a wild ride, for they drove eight miles to Galion so fast and over a road so bumpy that a buggy spring broke. Once in Galion, they went to the "Methodist preacher's house" [2] where, with Deb as a witness, they were married.

They wanted to be back in Blooming Grove before anyone might become suspicious, but with the broken spring the return journey was not very fast. Tryon had to lead the horse most of the way. While he walked ahead Phoebe asked him for his watch, and as the buggy lurched lamely along she scratched four lines on the back case:

> Phoebe Dickerson is no more
> May 7th 1864
> Phoebe Harding now it is
> Didn't we fool Mal and Liz?

Mal and Liz were Phoebe's older sisters, Malvina and Elizabeth Ann. Tryon left Phoebe at the farm. He was not to see her again until he returned from his soldiering.

By 1864 the lustiest of the Ohio boys had long since marched away. The 136th was a skeleton regiment, a cadre made up of only a hundred men and designated for guard and garrison duty. Tryon's military career was fated to be unheroic. On May 11 the 136th left Camp Chase in a belated flurry of snow for Fairfax, Virginia. A week later the regiment arrived in Washington and was split up to reinforce the garrisons of Forts Ellsworth, Williams, and North, part of the defenses of the capital just south of the Potomac. Company I was stationed in Fort Williams.

A bunk mate of Tryon's from Blooming Grove who had enlisted with him had ideas of his own about courting Phoebe. He often wrote her and received friendly if impersonal replies which he shared with his comrade. Tryon did not share his own love letters. Not until after the bunk mate had been mustered out did he discover that the girl he had been writing to was Tryon's wife. Phoebe and Deb kept their secret so well that not even Bets Johnston found out about it although Bets was the Blooming Grove gossip who knew about everybody's business almost before it happened.

Company I's garrison duty turned out to be uneventful and routine, remote from the actuality of war, its calm broken only by a flutter of alarm at the Confederate Gen. Jubal Early's feints at Washington. While

[2] The Reverend F. Marriott.

on a pass to the capital Tryon and two comrades, with the extraordinary informality that was then possible, dropped in at the White House to shake hands with the President. A colored attendant told them that the President was busy but if they waited awhile they would have a chance to see him. In about an hour they were taken to Lincoln's study. With proud embarrassment they announced themselves as Buckeye boys come to defend the Union. The gaunt, towering man thanked them, saying that the Buckeye State had been loyal to him, and he grasped each extended hand in both his great hairy paws. "And now"—he smiled at them—"you can tell your people at home that you have seen the handsomest man in the United States!" It was a moment that the three young soldiers would talk about for the rest of their lives.

The short-term 136th was scheduled to return to Camp Chase for mustering out on August 31. Two weeks before then Tryon came down with typhoid fever. Word reached Blooming Grove that he was in the army hospital at Fort Williams. When the regiment finally moved back to Ohio he had recovered sufficiently to travel with it, if not to march. On his arrival in Columbus on August 24 he was admitted to the Seminary U. S. General Hospital as a fever convalescent.

When Phoebe heard the news she was all for leaving at once for Columbus to help take care of her Tryon. Since any of Tryon's sisters could equally well have nursed him, Isaac Dickerson was outraged at his daughter's "unseemly" forwardness. He demanded an explanation and he received it. Whatever his amazement on learning about the marriage, he accepted it as irrevocable.

After four days in the hospital Tryon was granted a certificate of disability "arising from an attack of typhoid contracted while in service" and ordered to report to his regiment the following day to be honorably discharged. On August 29, with his discharge in his pocket, he left Columbus several days before the rest of the 136th was mustered out at Camp Chase, and started for Blooming Grove. A week later Phoebe's brother Thomas wrote to his married sister Clara:

> Well, Clarie, I suppose you will hear before you get this that Phoebe has been playing sharp and getting married. Tryon and her and Deb went to Galion on the *7th of May** and she and Tryon were married at the Methodist preacher's house and his sisters nor no one else but Deb knew of it till near the time he was to come home from war. Then she told mother and she told father, and that was all the family that knew it until *after** he came home. They fooled Bets Johnston completely. They have been married almost four months. He had the fever and by that means got home first. He was going back to be mustered out and then they were going to let it be known.

* Italic expressions underlined in original.

Back in Blooming Grove Tryon took his bride to live in the crowded Harding homestead. Phoebe's in-laws made her welcome, but Tryon after a few months was filled with his old restlessness and began to hanker again after the war which he had managed to experience only second-hand. In March, 1865, Phoebe anxiously wrote Clara:

> I almost wish Tryon had a bad leg so he would not be liable [to go to war]. Oh no, I'll take that back, for I am glad that he is sound in body as well as in mind. For if his body was one bit weaker than it is, then his mind would be entirely too strong for his body and would go soaring around like a raging lion seeking whom it might devour.

On April 9 her sister Abbie (Abigail Dickerson) wrote from Blooming Grove to Clara that Tryon was going to war again soon. Since news traveled slowly, Abbie did not know that on the very day she wrote General Lee had surrendered to General Grant at Appomattox Court House.

In Blooming Grove it was as if the war had never been. The echoes of outside events, Lincoln's assassination, the accession of President Johnson, the turbulent beginnings of Reconstruction were as muted and distant as the thin murmurings from a seashell. Tryon went back to teaching at the brick school north of Mount Gilead. In his spare time he began building a house on the site of his great-grandfather Amos's log cabin. By this time Phoebe was well along in pregnancy. On November 1 she gave birth to a son, Warren Gamaliel. She had wanted to name him Winfield, but Tryon insisted he be named after his aunt Malvina Dickerson's husband, Warren Gamaliel Bancroft, a Methodist clergyman of Wisconsin.

In January, 1866, her sister Elizabeth Ann wrote to Clara:

> I'll bet you'd like to see Phoebe's baby. It grows so fast that she can't keep its clothes large enough or alter them fast enough as he grows out of them. She calls him Warren Gamaliel, and for a pet name she calls him "Winnie."

When Winnie was only ten days old his mother had taken him to the Methodist preacher to have him blessed. She felt her baby was dedicated to some large purpose. It was her belief, part of the American myth and common to many a farmer's wife, that he might grow up to become President of the United States. She said so, often. As soon as she thought he was old enough she brought him to meeting rigged out in the costume she had made him, a braided "delaine" dress and a "mareno" cape trimmed with ribbons. "His big fat white face looked very pretty under a blue-and-white hat," Aunt Elizabeth Ann observed.

Toward the end of 1866 Phoebe wrote Clara:

> I have plenty of housework, sewing, knitting to do, besides taking care of the sweetest, dearest little brother you ever saw, and you would say so if you could be with him awhile. But I tell you, Clara, they are a troublesome

comfort. When I think of the great charge that is upon my shoulders, the responsibility of training him as he should be, and the care and anxiety I feel about his future. But I still would not part with him for anything in the world. I think if every child just knew the love a parent has for a child, they would never wound their feelings or do anything contrary to their wishes; but that, they will never know until they see their own offspring figuring on the stage of this life. Winnie is always walking. He will walk all along the walls, but does not go alone. He has a head as large as Joe Flack [her sister Priscilla's husband] and a beautifully shaped one too. It attracts a great deal of attention. Oh, we think he is all right, but it is an impossibility to get his picture taken. We have tried several times, but to no effect—he won't sit still. So you will have to come to see him . . . , I have a large house and everything in it that any farmer's wife around here has to do with. Tryon has bought property, and we will move in there in the Spring so as to be by ourselves. His father gave him the deed by [Tryon's] paying six hundred dollars.

In her letter Phoebe also described the new minister and his family, the affairs of the neighboring farms, her own "preserves of 14 cans of tomatoes, 9 of blackberries, 3 of peaches, 4 of molasses, 6 of elderberries," as well as apple butter and cider. "Oh," she concluded, "we really live up our way; and I have made a piece of carpet in my loom for my sitting room this Winter. I made 23 yards last Fall for our parlor."

On New Year's Day, 1867, Priscilla Flack wrote to Clara:

I have written four letters since yesterday noon and now my arm is so tired carrying Winnie around that I can scarcely write at all. Phoebe and Try were here today. Tryon is cutting wood and Pa is hauling it while there is snow, and then Pa is going to get the woodsaw and have it sawed on shares. . . . And New Year's Eve we had an oyster supper here at our house. Those three boys, Abner, Hat and Chat, Lizzie Chandler, Mrs. Tipton, Gust and Liddy Harding, Josie Harbison, Sarah McFarland, Isaac Dickerson, Ellie Wheeler, Wiley, Phoebe and Try were here. We had a good old time indeed. There were 12 of them staying all night and then we had lots of fun the next day, riding down hill on the hand sled and caveing around in the snowdrifts. For the supper I baked 8 mince pies, 5 cherry pies, 2 jelly cakes, 1 white and 1 golden cake, 24 light cakes and some bread. . . . We have a fresh cow and are making lots of butter, but it has come down to 22 cents and other things in proportion.

Late in February Tryon and Phoebe moved into their own rough-clapboarded house. On March 1 a daughter was born to them. A week later Elizabeth Ann wrote to Clara:

Phoebe's time was up two weeks ago last Friday. She brought forth a daughter which weighs 7 pounds. She calls her Charity. Winne was 16 months old the next day after she was born. There was no one there but

Sillie until about five minutes before. She ran to the Hardings and gave Mrs. Harding a pluck by the sleeve and she followed her out and they had the young one on hands before anyone knew it. Tryon was at a raisings at Dr. Mac's, and they didn't send for him or the Doc either. Sillie says she only called Mrs. Harding in for the looks of the thing, and not because she really needed her. She is getting along very well; has had two or three baths and sits up a little each day. Both Mother and I went up there Saturday, and while we was up there Winnie upset a tinful of hot water on his bosom and scalded himself so badly that when we took his clothes off his skin came too, as big as your hand on his left shoulder and breast. His hands and face were scalded too but they didn't blister.

Though the new house was small there was "an awful sight of company" there. In spite of the children Phoebe never seemed to mind. Relatives might "drive over" for the day or Tryon arrive for supper with a strange face but—to the wonder of her sisters—she found it no trouble "to get up a meal" on short notice. The household went through the usual childhood diseases. In June, 1867, both Warren and Charity—Chat they called her—came down with whooping cough. On April 26, 1868, another daughter was born. Phoebe named her Mary Clarissa. Even before she could walk, it was clear that something was wrong with her eyes.

In 1869, after eight terms in the brick schoolhouse, Tryon decided that he had had enough of teaching. In him the inherited restlessness that had driven his ancestors West came out less directly. Other Hardings had gone on to Indiana and beyond. He would shift jobs rather than states. The solid quality that had made his ancestors leaders in their communities was lacking in him. He was unstable, with a slackness that was both inward and outward. Although he was to shift from place to place, from house to house, his moves would be limited to Morrow County and adjacent Marion. He would play out his life on the fringes of small towns, usually in debt, never accepted by the "better people" anywhere. Whatever fire was in his nature came out in his passion for "swapping." Always he was ready to exchange anything he had for something he did not have —jobs, horses, cattle, farm implements, teams, wagons, machinery. Wherever he happened to live he mortgaged his uncertain future in real-estate speculations. In treating farm animals he developed a certain amount of skill, and for a while thought of becoming a veterinary. But on abandoning his schoolroom he decided to become a doctor.

He bought a set of secondhand medical books and began "reading medicine," going the rounds with Blooming Grove's Doctor Joseph McFarland. Doctor McFarland, an intense evangelical man with a square-cut white beard, had come to Blooming Grove in 1852, buying a farm and house from Salmon. Besides practicing medicine the doctor preached occasionally in the Baptist Church and superintended the Sunday school.

He had a fine singing voice and in his younger days had given music lessons, and had even composed a popular religious tune, "I'll Wait for You All at the Gate." A generation before, he himself had read medicine on rural rounds, climaxing his practical training with a year at the Western College of Homeopathy in Cleveland.

Tryon, having once more swapped jobs, now jogged about the countryside in Doctor McFarland's buggy between intervals of farming. Phoebe tried to add to their meager budget by going out to the neighbors as a practical nurse and midwife. Toward the end of 1870 Tryon felt he had served his apprenticeship and went on to Cleveland where he spent a term at Doctor McFarland's old medical college. The school had changed its name six times in a twenty-year period, to become known finally as the Homeopathic Hospital College. After his one session, during which he registered with Doctor Hamilton Biggar,[5] Tryon was admitted to practice on a certificate issued by the Northwest Medical Society. He returned in 1872 to Blooming Grove and his rounds with Doctor Mc-Farland. His third daughter, Eleanor Persilla, arrived on November 11, 1872.

Two sessions at the Homeopathic Hospital were required before a student was allowed to put an M.D. after his name. Tryon was not able to go back for his final session until the spring of 1873. Before leaving for Cleveland he moved his family from the Blooming Grove farm to the small town of Caledonia, fourteen miles to the west in Marion County.

[5] Doctor Biggar was to become personal physician to John D. Rockefeller.

[CHAPTER IV]

The Son

"Winnie is bright beyond his years, and Chattie is everywhere present," Phoebe wrote to Clara at about the time the baby girl was beginning to walk. Winnie did not have to be very old before he learned to find his way to his grandfather's farm. There was much visiting between the small house and the homestead where Winnie's younger aunts were only a few years older than he. Tryon, between intervals of schoolteaching and later of accompanying Doctor McFarland, did farming on his own. Children were expected to help in the fields from the time they were of school age, and the long summer gap between school terms was arranged for just that purpose. The life of the Harding children in its rural self-sufficiency was typical of Ohio of the period. James Cox, who was to be three times governor of Ohio and Harding's unsuccessful Democratic opponent in the 1920 presidential election, lived through a similar boyhood at about the same time on a farm in Butler County. Years after Harding's death, Cox in his autobiography recalled that farm life, only one generation removed from the pioneers:

> It was hard work in season and out. In summertime we were in the fields at sunrise; we came in for dinner at eleven o'clock, had supper at four o'clock and then followed the plough or the sickle until sundown. On some occasions in the cornhusking season we went to the fields by morning moonlight. When the moon went down, there was not enough light to work by and we ran up and down the fence corners to keep warm till the labor of the field could start.
>
> Grain was cut by the scythe and the cradle. The cradle had wooden hands three or four feet long parallel to the blade. When the implement was properly handled the grain was caught by these "hands" and laid in even swathes to be bound into sheaves. . . .
>
> In the winter evenings corn was popped and apples were brought from the cellar. The diversion was usually history and geography tests. There was not a playing card in the house and definitely no liquor. . . .

37

With the first thaw of spring when the sap was running in the maple trees came a joyful season. The gathering of buckets filled with sugar water, the boiling processes running through the night as well as day, and then the taffy pulls—those were the times!

And who can forget the butchering season? The wood fires were set under the kettles before daylight to heat water for scalding the hair off the animals—the same vessels to be used later for the making of lard. . . .

April Election Day was the beginning of the barefoot season and "stone bruises." On the Sabbath, for Sunday school and church, shoes that pinched painfully were worn. We went barefooted until frost time and sometimes later than that. . . .

Then there were other customs—the ice-cream social at the church in the summer, the county fair, in the autumn, the oyster supper in the winter, and the Christmas celebration.

The budget on the farm was rather simply conducted. The sale of lambs and wool usually took care of the June taxes. The December assessments were met by the sale of hogs. These taxes were the major expenses. Groceries, in the main, were purchased by the marketing of butter, eggs, and chickens. The early part of the winter was the clothing era. It was usually the sale of surplus wheat or corn that met this requirement.

As Winnie grew from a toddler to a walker Phoebe taught him his letters, using the printed cards from the Methodist Sunday school. Unlike the staid Baptist convictions of the Hardings, Phoebe's Methodism held something of the fanatic glow of the Wesleyans of the previous century. Except for her religious zeal she was a quiet, dark woman, always ready to help with self-acquired efficiency when any Blooming Grove woman was in labor. She loved flowers, and cared for her small garden of pinks, petunias, fuchsias, and ribbon grass. Coached by her, the four-year-old Winnie made his first declamation at a country-school entertainment in the Buckhorn Tavern School.

Oratory, with its Victorian pomposities, had in mid-nineteenth century America developed into a national vice; declamation had become its handmaiden. Children, whose descendants at a similar age might learn tap dancing, were taught to lisp in numbers. It was considered "cute" for a preschool child to be able to stand up and parrot a few lines of verse. The great favorite was still David Everett's set piece that he had written for a New Hampshire school declamation. It may have been the one that Winnie, in Kentucky trousers and a gingham shirt, and watched with expansive pride by his mother and aunts, then recited:

> You'd scarce expect one of my age
> To speak in public on the stage;
> And if I chance to fall below
> Demosthenes or Cicero,
> Don't view me with a critic's eye,

But pass my imperfections by.
Large streams from little fountains flow,
Tall oaks from little acorns grow. . . .

Before Winnie left Blooming Grove he spent several terms in the village
school his grandfather had built. Those rectangular one-room schools had
become perhaps the most familiar objects in the rural landscape. There
were two front-door entrances—one for the boys and one for the girls—a
belfry with its warning bell, and in the rear the woodshed and the out-
house. Inside were rows of double desks where boys sat with boys, girls
with girls. A potbellied cast-iron stove had replaced the square sheet-
metal burner of an earlier period, but the familiar wooden water bucket
and drinking cup had survived, as had the dunce cap. The children came
to school barefoot in the spring and in the autumn almost to the frost. In
the winter the air was rancid—heavy with the stench of wet woolens and
rawhide.

Under the stern eye and ready ferrule of the schoolmaster, James
Boggs, the pupils learned the elementals of reading, writing, spelling,
arithmetic, history, and geography. The Eclectic Readers of Ohio's
William H. McGuffey, those firmly didactic little books that formed the
moralistic attitudes of generations of Americans, were the most familiar
general textbooks.

Winnie and his schoolmates learned in McGuffey's *First Reader,* mouth-
ing the syllables in phonic repetition as they followed the illustrated
story of the boy George and his horse Jack: "George is kind to Jack and
Jack loves him, because he is kind." Even then Boggs noticed that Winnie
liked to declaim.

Too remote from canals and railroads to attract industries, Blooming
Grove remained a village. Jake Day's general store at the crossroads
had become weather-pitted and the roof was sagging. Across the road the
tavern that had hoped to grow with the stagecoach trade was mouldering
away, the porch pump for watering horses rusty with disuse. Before the
store the single street lamp on a much-scarred post looked almost medieval·
A towering red oak, survivor of the ancient forest, stood nearby, shading a
bench much notched and nicked by decades of whittlers who sat there on
long summer afternoons carving abstractedly and spitting tobacco juice
into the dust.

Beyond the school that rural backwater was world enough for a small
boy. It was a world still fixed in tradition. Summer brought swimming and
fishing. In the autumn there were wild grapes, hickory nuts, walnuts,
butternuts to gather. The older boys followed after the men as they
hunted wild turkeys, geese, ducks, squirrels, quail, partridge, and sometimes raccoons and foxes. Winter brought its own joys. Yet in that crudely
pastoral setting the shadow over the Harding family persisted.

As soon as the Hardings were old enough to go to school they became aware of the shadow. Whenever there was a schoolyard quarrel the jeering cry would go up: "You Hardings are part nigger!" The older Harding children might respond with violence, but the taunt persisted. Outside the shelter of his home, Winnie, like his cousins and junior aunts and uncles, learned that there were things for which neither father nor mother nor even grandparents offered protection. To be "part nigger" in Blooming Grove meant to be flawed, meant never to be wholly admitted or admissible to the herd. Winnie's awareness at the age of five of this barrier, of the fact that he was not to be considered like the others who sat at the double benches in the schoolroom, left an ineradicable mark on him, first began to shape him toward the man he was to become. Some, faced with such a challenge, would have rebelled against the conventions of the community, turning bohemian or radical or revolutionary. Young Warren's response was to try to placate, expressing his inner doubt in an almost mindless conformity. The doubt, the insecurity never left him. His first words after he had become President were the whispered: "Was it done all right?"

Always in his growing up he would be haunted by this sense of alienation from the world to which he wanted with all his heart to belong—a quite different feeling from being born a Negro among Negroes and identifying himself with the group as such. Since he never felt secure in his group identification, he would demonstrate his right to belong by the strictness of his conformity. The roots of Harding's conservatism lay in the shadow of his inheritance. As a man he did not lose his temper often, but any challenge to his hardly won self-image would set him off in high anger. The shadow of Blooming Grove was something that in later years he could scarcely bring himself to talk about. Once he managed to discuss the matter briefly with his old friend James Miller Faulkner, a political reporter on the Cincinnati *Enquirer.* "How do I know, Jim?" he remarked finally. "One of my ancestors may have jumped the fence."

The Harding house in Caledonia, a few doors from the town square, was a small yellow-brown frame structure with gingerbread-work trimmings. Compared to Blooming Grove, Caledonia seemed a metropolis, with several large churches, a two-story school opposite the Methodist Church, and over seven hundred inhabitants. During the summer the fifteen-piece Caledonia Aeolian Band gave Saturday-evening concerts on the wide barren square near the town pump.

The Hardings arrived from Blooming Grove early in 1873 in a hayrack filled with their household goods. For Warren, Caledonia was a large and glittering new world. In a suit of perpendicular striped trousers and black jacket, bought for the occasion, he attended the new school with Chat. Phoebe, while her husband was in Cleveland, now set herself up as a professional midwife. In Caledonia the nearness of the Methodist Church gave her religious zeal daily outlet. She became one of the most conspicuously devoted church members. Sunday after Sunday Warren sat on the wooden benches in the Sunday-school room across from his sisters "whittling and whispering." The Hardings attended all church services, suppers, entertainments. Phoebe's ingrained piety hardened. She hummed hymns as she went about her housework and pointed up all her conversation with apt scriptural quotations.

Late in the spring Tryon returned from Cleveland with his M.D. and put up his shingle. The letters were no magic sign to conjure up prosperity. The new doctor lacked and always would lack the grave professional presence of a Doctor McFarland. Tryon's practice was marginal, lived-out on the fringes of several communities, where he would become a character, known to everyone but never wholly accepted. He made his rural rounds, often as not taking payment in kind—eggs, butter, and such farm produce—while Phoebe, between intervals of bearing her own babies, practiced her midwifery. For a time he ran a drugstore. His itch to exchange whatever came his way developed into a gambler's passion, his "one vice" according to his son. More exciting to Tryon than medicine was the glitter of the sure but as yet unobserved opportunity waiting only to be grasped, the dream of wealth lying just beyond the next street extension. He bought odd lots of land, mortgaged them, and used the mortgage money to buy more lots. On the thinner outskirts of Caledonia he acquired a section of land that he subdivided, convinced that it would soon be worth much when the town expanded. Horses appeared and disappeared in his barn like casual boarders. Carts, wagons, carriages, and farm implements cluttered his yard in transit. From the day he arrived in Caledonia he was never out of debt.

A few months before the Hardings left Blooming Grove, Phoebe's third daughter, Eleanor Persilla, was born. Seventeen months later, when they were settled in Caledonia, Phoebe gave birth to a son, Charles Alexander. Three more children followed in the next five years; Abigail Victoria in 1876, another George Tryon in 1878, and finally, in 1879, Phoebe Caroline.[4]

By the summer of 1873 Warren and Chat had finished their first term in the school across from the Methodist Church, a term in which they were introduced with awe to Parson Weems's account of George Washington and the cherry tree in McGuffey's *Second Reader*. When in the *Third Reader* Warren encountered Southey's "Bonaparte Crossing the Alps," Napoleon became his hero. He continued to take resounding part in Friday-afternoon declamation contests, with Patrick Henry's "Give Me

[4] Caroline, she was called. Later she took to spelling it Carolyn. Abigail was always called Daisy.

Liberty or Give Me Death," "The Boy Stood on the Burning Deck," and "Horatius"—all selected from McGuffey.

The McGuffey readers in their didactic annual sequences were standard school fare. By the time the pupils, at the age of eleven or twelve, had finished the *Sixth Reader* they had read nine selections from Shakespeare that included "Hamlet's Soliloquy" and the "Fall of Cardinal Wolsey"; Scott's "Marmion and Douglas" and "Lochinvar"; Longfellow's "A Psalm of Life" and "Evangeline"; "Elegy Written in a Country Churchyard"; Felicia Dorothea Hemans's "The Landing of the Pilgrims"; Emerson's "Value of the Present"; Bulwer-Lytton's "The Surrender of Granada." In addition they had practiced declaiming such sonorous showpieces as Poe's "The Raven"; "Dawn," by Edward Everett; Disraeli's "Description of a Storm"; "The Death of Little Nell"; Macaulay's "Impeachment of Warren Hastings"; Webster's "Reply to Hayne"; and "Mark Antony's Funeral Oration."

When Warren was almost ten his father brought home a cornet. It became the boy's most precious possession, to be guarded from the inquisitive fingers of the younger children. An elderly harness maker, who was also an expert on the valve trombone and whose interest was more in the Aeolian Band than in his leather business, gave him his first music lessons. Later a house painter, the new leader of the band, instructed the boy on the cornet. It was not too many months before Warren was able to join the band itself and tootle as loudly on his B-flat cornet as any member of it.[5]

In the summer of 1875, some time after school had closed, Tryon in one of his bouts of trading acquired the local newspaper, the *Caledonia Argus*. The paper, sustained by a small trade in job printing, appeared spasmodically. Whenever its founder-owner, editor, and printer, an eccentric by the name of Will Warner, was able to pay for the newsprint he would get out another edition. Besides being the local publisher, Warner was also the local dude, courtly in manner, the wearer of Caledonia's only top hat. After Tryon became the owner of the *Argus*, Warner continued to stay on as editor.[6] Warren and another small boy were taken on in the office as printer's devils. They swept the floor, ran errands, fed the press, washed rollers, and learned to "throw in pi"—to distribute back into the proper boxes the jumbled letters from the mass of type that had been used. No doubt they experienced the hoary joke of being sent out to get type lice.

---

[5] Sherwood Anderson's father Irwin moved with his family to Caledonia in 1878 to take over the harness maker's shop. Like his predecessor he was a brass musician, always ready to close his shop for the day to play in the band. For at least a year he and Harding playing in the band together.

[6] After two months Tryon turned back his interest in the paper to Warner who continued to edit and publish it until the autumn of 1876.

There was little money in being a printer's devil, but the messy little plant with its ink-smeared press was considerably more attractive than household or farm chores. When Hi Henry's Circus came to town and the usual two complimentary tickets for the *Argus* got no farther than Warner's desk, the two outraged printer's devils demanded from the editor and finally received what they considered their perquisites. In time Warren, perched on a stool, began tentatively to set type. One afternoon a Caledonia lawyer brought in a brief that had to be printed and ready for delivery next morning. Warren and Warner worked late into the night over it, and when it was finished the old man gave the boy a 13-em make-up rule—a thin bit of sheet steel about two and half inches long—the craft sign of a full-fledged printer. Harding kept the rule with him for the rest of his life as a lucky piece.

Although robust and large, Warren was not notably energetic. Like the other boys in that semi-rural community he curried horses, milked cows, worked at times in the fields during the summer vacation, moulded bricks, made brooms, or helped with barn painting. When he was twelve, it is said, a farmer gave him a job shucking corn at fifty cents a day, but after five minutes he gave it up, saying it was too hard. On warm summer afternoons—until Tryon exchanged the *Argus* for something else—the boy preferred hanging about the print shop to more arduous tasks. He took considerable pains to teach his sister how to milk a cow so that she could take over this particular chore from him. When the band went on a free trip to Chicago for the opening of the Erie Railroad, he went along, too, for his first journey outside the boundaries of Ohio.

He ran with the gang of boys his own age, swimming in Whetstone Creek, playing scrub baseball in the Rice Bottom, galloping his father's bay, Prince, on the pike road just outside the town whenever he got the chance. Yet the shadow of Blooming Grove followed him to Caledonia, as it would follow him wherever else he went. According to William E. Chancellor, the avid pursuer of derogatory Harding gossip, Warren because of his olive skin was called Nig by the other boys.[7]

In the autumn of 1878 tragedy came to the Harding family, and to Warren the first intimate experience of death. Tryon was away when Charles and Persilla took sick with what seemed at first only a mild form of jaundice. Then, on November 9, both children suddenly became much worse. In spite of all Phoebe's efforts to nurse them they died that day within a few hours of each other.

Warren was nearly fourteen when Caroline was born. He had almost

---

[7] Because of Chancellor's violent obsession with racial issues one cannot be certain of his unsubstantiated statements, yet he spent much time in Blooming Grove and Caledonia and in his book on Harding he set down a number of facts that have never been mentioned elsewhere and that are corroborated by later evidence.

reached his full growth; a gawky, swarthy six-footer with a head that was still too large for his adolescent body. The painter–band leader who had taught him the cornet now took him on as a helper in painting barns and also showed him how to grain wood. Before long the boy was priding himself on his ability to turn honest white pine into imitation oak, cherry, and mahogany. When the Toledo & Central Railroad began to extend a line beyond Caledonia the company recruited all the strong farm boys it could get hold of for grading and track laying. Young Harding arrived with one of his father's transitory mule teams and drove a scraper during the construction—an easier and much better paying job than track laying.

For all his hot hopes, Tryon's speculations had a way of ending in cold disappointment. By 1880, shorter than ever of cash, he not only had lost most of his mortgaged land but was forced to give up the Caledonia house. He moved to a 40-acre farm two miles to the east, just over the county line. Phoebe with her midwifery became the steady family bread-winner. Warren still played in the band, still stuck to his friends in Caledonia, sometimes arriving in town in a wagon incongruously drawn by a horse and a mule. In later years Tryon liked to tell how he had given his son a half acre to grow in wheat. The crop came to eighteen bushels and when the boy took it over to a warehouse at the village of Climax he received a dollar a bushel for it. "He was happy as a sunflower," Tryon recalled long afterward, and added with some parental exaggeration that "Warren was never afraid of hard work."

In spite of his family's shaky financial status, Harding managed to enter Iberia College—now known more grandiloquently as Ohio Central College—for the autumn term of 1880. Some of these backwater Ohio schools had gone on to become actual rather than nominal colleges, but the Iberia institution (although prior to the war a way station in the underground railroad smuggling Negroes to Canada) had scarcely changed in curriculum or in its annexed building since Tryon had graduated twenty years before. There were fewer students now.[8] Tuition came to seven dollars a term. The faculty of three was composed of the president and professor of philosophy, the Reverend John P. Robb, A.M.; Albert C. Jones, A.B., dean of the faculty and professor of ancient languages; and the Reverend A. C. Crist, A.M., professor of mathematics and natural sciences.

The fourteen-year-old Harding arrived in the "thriving village containing three flourishing churches and no groggeries" in the midst of the Garfield-Hancock presidential campaign to find the cabalistic anti-Republican slogan 329 chalked on sidewalks and fences. James A. Garfield, while a congressman, had been accused of receiving a bribe of $329 from the

[8] Soon after Harding graduated, the college was sold to the state for use as a school for the blind. In 1885 the building burned down and was not rebuilt.

Crédit Mobilier funds, and now that he was the Republican candidate for President the accusing numbers sprang up everywhere. Politics was one of the chief diversions of rural Ohio, and the students talked glibly about candidates and issues, airing the opinions they had picked up from their elders. Most of the students considered themselves Democrats, for outside the larger towns the Jacksonian tradition still survived in that part of Ohio.[9] Harding was, of course, the effusive young Republican. He boarded with a number of other students at Professor Crist's where he talked easily and readily, if vaguely, on all offered occasions. One of his roommates said later that his main interests were in debating, writing, and making friends. As a boarding student he was expected to attend one of Iberia's churches. He picked the Methodist. Later he managed to earn some extra money by helping paint the church and by his skill in graining the pews.

Harding the student had never been to a theater or seen an actual play on the stage. Nevertheless, on October 25, 1880, he took the affirmative in a school debate on the subject: "Has the Stage a Moral Tendency?" Doubtless he cribbed his opinions and many phrases as well from some ephemeral encyclopedia, but he managed to mouth them resonantly to an audience that for the most part knew no more of the theater than he did:

> Mr. President, Honorable Judges, respected audience. The question of morality and immorality of the stage is one of the most important that can engage us. When we reflect upon the universal passion that has been exhibited to us through this species of amusement, when we further remember that some of the noblest productions of human intellect have been offered to the world through the medium of the stage, and lastly when we bear in mind that the theater is one of the chief pleasures of the youthful members of society in all times and countries we should see at once that we have a subject worthy of debate.

He went on to describe the theater of his time as presenting "tragedies of milk and water, dramas of blood, blue fire and slang, and operas of the most irredeemable silliness." The theater had obviously no attraction for Warren Harding at fourteen.

In his last year he became president of the Philomathic Literary Society which met every Monday evening. His interest in newspapers persisted, and he was able to earn a little money working in the printing shop of William Beebe, the editor and proprietor of the *Union Register*. Here he and a classmate, Frank Miller, conceived the idea of getting out a college paper on the same press. They called it the *Iberia Spectator,* and the first issue appeared in February, 1882. It was published fortnightly, a sub-

[9] Anti-Negro feeling was an equally important source of support of the Ohio Democratic party.

scription costing thirty cents. For the two young editors the little four-page journal was a creditable production, as lively as many a county paper, full of local items and jokes and advertisements, its editorials ranging over such varied topics as the anti-polygamy bill and the aurora borealis. It was a popular venture. "The *Spectator*," Harding noted editorially, "is taken by every family in our city excepting a few stingy old grumblers who take no more interest in home enterprise than a mule takes in a hive of bees." Six issues were published, but with the graduation of the editors the paper died.

Harding was one of three to graduate from the college that spring, and gave the commencement address, "It Can Never Be Rubbed Out." But before the Reverend Professor Robb conferred the degree of bachelor of science on him, his parents had already made another move, this time from the farm to the county seat of Marion nine miles to the west. Some time before their move Tryon had taken Phoebe to a camp meeting of the Seventh-day Adventists then recently arrived in Ohio. On her return home she insisted that their Methodist preacher rebaptize her by immersion. Soon she began a Bible-study group, and in spite of her position as a pillar of the Methodist Church she found herself drawing closer and closer to the Adventists. Their apocalyptic vision of the return of Christ almost any day, their belief in prophecy, their vegetarian conviction of being the elect, their blinkered dogmatism filled her days with a more burning certainty than she had ever been able to find in the evangelism of John Wesley. Shortly after she arrived in Marion she gained her redemption in the new church. Then with all the ardor of a convert she harried her children and relations into the new faith.[10] Only Tryon remained an impervious Baptist. Warren, in spite of compulsory church attendance at Iberia, had begun to doubt. After his first college encounter with the doctrine of evolution he imagined himself a freethinker, even an atheist, although he would soon relapse into a mild Baptist conformity untouched by his mother's zeal.

In Marion, Tryon hoped to build up a respectable town practice where his patients would pay their bills in cash instead of eggs and butter and other farm products. He bought a shabby house—possibly with the remnants of the money that came to him after his father died in 1878—on North East Street [11] opposite the old interurban station. There, on the wrong side of town, he set up his office.

After graduation Warren went back for a few days to the as-yet-unsold Caledonia farm. On July 1 he saddled his father's mule, an animal too

[10] The Harding descendants in an expanding line have remained Seventh-day Adventists ever since. Doctor George Harding, a nephew of the President and a practicing psychiatrist in Columbus, is a present-day member of the church.

[11] Now North Prospect Street.

valuable to be left behind and too well known in the vicinity to find a buyer, and set out at last for the county seat. "I started early in the afternoon," he reminisced at the Marion Centenary Celebration in 1922, "but this mule had only one gait. The evening shades were falling when I reached the vicinity of Roberts' farm, three or four miles out of Marion. The situation was looking dark to me and I stopped to ask an old fellow, who was smoking his pipe, how far it was to Marion. Without cracking a smile, he replied: 'Well, if you are going to ride that mule, it is a farther distance than you will ever get.'

"As I neared the town the evening bells were ringing for the mid-week prayer. I do not know that I have ever heard a concert of bells that sounded so sweet."

[CHAPTER V]

Marion and the Star

The dust-streaked young man who rode his balky mule into the county seat on that long-shadowed July evening of 1882 was too inconspicuous for anyone to pay much attention to his picaresque appearance. Yet as he rode through the unfamiliar streets, he was riding forward into his own unsuspected future. Inwardly he would never leave Marion again. Unlikely as it might seem to a casual passer-by, this gangling adolescent perched on a mule was to become in the next four decades the town's leading editor, its leading politician, its leading citizen, its success symbol. In the end he would move beyond Marion, but the flat, lush countryside stretching away on all sides would always bound his horizon. For the rest of his life he would remain inwardly rooted in an obscure courthouse town in Ohio. And after his death, his massively columned mausoleum would set its seal on the expanding city of Marion.

When the Harding tribe settled in Blooming Grove, Marion was still part of the wilderness of north central Ohio. Jacob Foos, a chainman in a survey team running a center line for a military road through Indian country, stumbled on the site in 1808. The team, after a waterless meal of salt pork, had camped for the night on a small rise twenty miles south of the Wyandot village of Upper Sandusky. Jake finally got up in the darkness and in his thirst swore he would find water if he had to dig to hell. With his ax he cut a crude shovel and dug down several feet in a moist spot until clear water oozed out of the ground.

Later travelers enlarged Foos's spring and lined the sides with stone, and good, sweet water continued to bubble up there. Jacob's Well they called it. The woods surrounding the spring became a favorite stopping place. Gen. William Harrison bivouacked there during the War of 1812 on his march toward Upper Sandusky.

In 1821 Alexander Holmes of Newark, Ohio, bought the oak forest near Jacob's Well from the Delaware Indians, surveyed it, and sent his agent, Eber Baker [1]—a man of more initiative than money—to plot and sell lots.

[1] Eber Baker is remembered today in Marion's Eber Baker Junior High School.

Baker, called the founder of Marion, was born at Litchfield Corners, Maine, but as a young man had wandered south to Cape Cod, then to Virginia where he served for a while in the Army during the War of 1812. Finding Army life not to his taste, he hired a substitute and moved off to Newark before going West. On arriving at Jacob's Well he first occupied a squatter's cabin that he set up as a tavern. For laying out the oak grove in lots and managing their sale he received the land east of Main Street. On April 18, 1822, Baker and Holmes filed for the record their plat of the new town which they called Marion after the county, named in turn after Gen. Francis Marion, the "swamp fox" of the Revolution. Fortunately for the town-to-be, Holmes had enough influence with the legislative commissioners to persuade them to pick Marion as the county seat. Baker as director of the settlement set aside land for schools, churches, the courthouse, a cemetery, a jail. The log jail he built himself, donated it to the town and, after being caught selling a short measure of whisky, nearly served as its first tenant. He outlived two wives, to become the local patriarch, and died the year before Warren Harding was born.

By 1830 the village had only 285 settlers. The countryside was still a wilderness, its few highways infested with robbers and its taverns more often than not thieves' dens. One settlement near Marion was known locally as Sodom. But by mid-century Marion had grown to a respectable county center of 1,311 inhabitants. Baker lived to see schools and churches flourishing on the lots he had set aside. A Greek-revival courthouse—characteristic of Ohio—lifted its rounded gilt dome above the surviving oaks.

Such a quiet county seat Marion might have remained. The coming of the railroads in the fifties was to make the difference between town and city, and give Marion the impetus to growth that would never have come to Caledonia or Blooming Grove. In 1852 the Bellefontaine & Indiana Railroad extended its tracks west to connect Marion to the expanding world of industry. The Chicago & Atlantic soon ran east through the village; while from the south came the Columbus & Sandusky Short Line—ephemeral names, to be absorbed by the Pennsylvania, the Erie, the Chesapeake & Ohio lines. German immigrants began to arrive after 1830, followed from 1850 by survivors of the Irish famine.

Marion's growth from a county seat to a small manufacturing city needed the nodal potential of the railroads, yet without the energy and ingenuity of Edward Huber, who arrived in Marion in 1865 and began manufacturing hayrakes, that growth might have been stunted. Huber, whose father came from Germany, started out in life as a cabinetmaker and blacksmith. Of a practical and original turn of mind, he had invented in his smithy a number of useful gadgets, the most important of which was his revolving hayrake. After setting up a small factory in Marion he constructed road scrapers, reapers, separators, and other farm implements of his own design, always filling a want that up until then nothing else had filled. By 1874 his business had so expanded that he was able to form the Huber Manufacturing Company. Six years later he patented a threshing machine and engine that sold all over the country. When another local young man, H. M. Barnart, invented a steam shovel, Huber supplied the capital to build the first machine and took a large block of stock in the new concern. In 1884 he became the first president of the Marion Steam Shovel Company.[2]

If Huber was Marion's leading industrialist, Amos Kling was its entrepreneur. Kling's Pennsylvania Dutch parents had brought him to Ohio as a child. As a young man he had learned tailoring, but in 1854, at the age of twenty-one, he left his stitching to take a commercial course in Mansfield. With double-entry bookkeeping behind him, he settled in Marion as clerk to the local hardware merchant. Before long he had taken over the business. He ran it for nine years. During the Civil War two of his brothers joined the Union Army and were killed in battle, but he remained behind his counter, making so much money during the war boom that, after the South's surrender, he abandoned hardware for mortgages and real estate. As the town's first financier he organized banks and loan companies, backed the construction of the $30,000 Hotel Marion, took the lead in inducing the railroads to extend their lines to Marion. As a by-product of all this activity he became the richest man in town.

Of the men of wealth and property who now formed the dominant group in Marion, Kling and Huber represented the new dispensation. There were a few older and more urbane families with fortunes derived from earlier acquisitions of land who were aware of horizons beyond the Ohio plain, who sent their children East to school and even traveled to Europe. To them Kling and Huber were parvenus, but new and old combined instinctively in a power oligarchy that controlled both Marion and Marion County. In a town still small enough for everyone to know everyone else they were the "best people," and they and everybody else knew it. The town hall might be Republican, the courthouse Democratic, but the clique at the top knew how to manage both. Huber was a Democrat, Kling a Republican. A man was born one or the other, just as he was born a Baptist or a Presbyterian, and gave an emotional allegiance to his church and party without, however, letting either interfere with his practical life.

The Marion that Warren Harding on muleback observed so casually that summer evening had about 4,500 inhabitants. Soon—one sensed it in the air—it would have more. From the market town of an agricultural community it had first become a grain-selling center, and now industries

[2] The company was soon Marion's leading industry, its giant steam shovels known all over the world. It has been said that the Panama Canal was dug in Marion, Ohio.

were beginning to take hold. The new First Baptist Church, of yellow and red mottled brick, was the largest building in town, and the violent colors of its rose window were something to marvel at on a Sunday morning. There was a new jail, with a sheriff's residence and a brick Gothic tower on which perched a weathervane in the shape of a key. A Music Hall—more hall than music—soon followed the jail. Plans were already drawn up to replace the austere Doric courthouse with a mock-renaissance building four times its size. New residential streets extended in a north-south, east-west grid, the houses wedged together on small lots, all within walking distance of the courthouse square. The houses fronted the streets nakedly, their angularity relieved only by the occasional irrelevant wooden tower or castellation. Yards coalesced with a neighborly good will that would have considered intervening hedges or fences undemocratic. A few large brick mansions survived from before the Civil War, aftermaths of the Federalist style, but most of the elite of the town lived in ornate wooden castles with wide surrounding porches, stained-glass windows on the stair landings, and cast-iron stags on the front grass. Yet these, too, though on larger lots, were not set apart from their neighbors by fence or shrubbery. A mile or so beyond Marion the countryside reasserted itself—patches of cornfields, pasture land, orchards, swales where cattails bent before the hot wind of "good weather for corn," large barns, gaunt if trim farmhouses, and long yellow ribbons of county-numbered roads.

Once settled in Marion, Tryon again hopefully hung up his shingle and put advertisements in the local papers announcing the opening of his homeopathic practice. His son did not settle so easily. For a while he served customers in a hardware shop—another one of Tryon's ephemeral ventures—at Crestline, half-a-dozen miles north of Galion. Returning after a few weeks, he took the examination required by the county school board for a district teacher's job. One of the examiners happened to be a man from Caledonia who had earlier taken a great liking to him. Not only did young Harding pass, but he was given one of the best jobs the county had to offer, one that paid $20 a month, and double that in winter when the teacher had to light the fires and sweep the floors. Even better than the pay was the fact that the school was only two miles from Marion, in the one-room school on the north highway known as the White Schoolhouse. Instead of being boarded and bundled from farm to farm like most rural teachers, he would be able to live handily at home.

Almost on his arrival in Marion, Harding had joined the Huber Silver Band. This turned out to be a disappointment. At one time the band had had 25 players, but as a company organization it had never been very popular and was now falling apart. When Harding's old cornet instructor, the house painter from Caledonia, moved to town, the two of them reorganized the players into the Marion People's Band with Harding as man-

ager and first B-cornetist. The new band made an immediate hit, giving
street concerts every Saturday night, playing at political rallies, and
occasionally supplying the background waltzes at the Merry-Roll-Round,
the local roller-skating rink.

With the autumn term Harding began his teaching career in the White
Schoolhouse. The tall, gray-eyed young man with the heavy eyebrows
and close-clipped black hair had wisely done his best to look mature,
since several of his scholars were older than himself. He wore a stiff collar,
a black stock tie, and the large double-looped watch chain that was the
insigne of a teacher in those days. His lunch he brought with him, just as
did his pupils. He taught them reading, writing, arithmetic, and some
algebra. But teaching, he soon realized, was not for him. "It was the
hardest job I ever had," he admitted later. And the shadow followed him
even into the schoolroom. The whisper of children behind his back, the
suppressed but not-too-suppressed titter.[3]

His evenings were happily free, and as manager of the band he had a
pass to the Merry-Roll-Round. The roller-skating fad was just then sweeping the country, and any town of even moderate size had at least one rink.
In a day of limited amusements, skating became the principal one and a
rink the chief meeting place for young people, especially during the winter
months. The Merry-Roll-Round was open every evening except Sunday.
Harding spent much of his time there. Outside the school he *bloviated*.[4]
He met with the "boys" who hung around the courthouse or Tregor's
livery stable, pitched silver dollars with them in the rear of Prussia
Hoberman's drugstore, watched Mike O'Shane, the town drunkard,
stagger down the street. Saturday nights he was introduced to poker—a
somewhat expensive introduction, he confessed afterward. While never a
drunkard, he never crossed the road to avoid a brass rail. From a late
poker session or band rehearsal he and a few of his cronies would often
slip away with surreptitious eagerness to that raw street of shaded houses
near the railroad junction—Dan Fritz's White Pigeon, Annie Marie's,
Lizzie Lazalere's Red House. As a true-blue Republican he attended all
local political meetings. But for his job, as the days grew shorter and the
new year approached, he found only increasing distaste. One term of
keeping his unruly pupils in order was, he decided, enough. On February
12, 1883, he wrote from his school desk to his aunt, Sarah Harding Dickerson:

[3] An elderly woman in Marion who as a little girl was one of Harding's pupils in the
White Schoolhouse told me in 1963 how infuriated she used to be when pupils from
another school taunted her with having a "nigger teacher."
[4] A word then current in Ohio, but long since obsolete, meaning to loaf about and
talk and enjoy oneself. It became a favorite expression of Harding's, so much so that
outsiders later credited him with having coined it.

Your good letter should have been answered ere this, but my excuse is good enough to secure my pardon from the terrible punishment of not having another trial. As I always am, was glad to hear from you and the other friends, although Pa got the first peep at your letter's contents. However, he doesn't always open epistles addressed to me, but seems to know when, and where they are from.

I am still fighting ignorance with fair success. Of course there are some chronic kickers, but I deem THAT the best evidence of MY SUCCESS. Next Friday, one week, i.e., the 23rd inst., forever my career as a pedagogue will close, and—oh, the joy! I believe my calling to be in some other sphere and will follow out the belief. I sincerely hope that my winter's labors are not lost, but that those with whom I labored are somewhat benefited. How often it is that one's most arduous toils are without appreciation! I will never teach again without better (a good deal, too) wages, and an advanced school.

The winter is passing off very pleasantly and we are all glad to near spring. There are plenty of amusements but the principal attraction is the skating rink. I attend quite frequently and always enjoy myself superbly. Chat has attended but cannot as yet manage the rollers. Her brother CAN, and he represents the family. Quite frequently young ladies show more of themselves than is meant for general observation, but the boys, all the boys, look the other (?) way.

Hasn't it been wet and slippery? The ice facilitated falling and all seemed to embrace—the opportunity of an easy fall. One morning I saw several new constellations when on my way to educational headquarters but, they soon disappeared only to be seen by a similar fall. The floods, however, did not effect the Marionites to any extent. How is Uncle Dan, Mother, Grandma'am, and the rest of the relatives? I am coming up when school closes then I will visit all, Gert included PERHAPS. How does Cass sail forth? Stingy as ever, I suppose. Does he "mash"?

Uncle D.K. and Aunt Clara are visiting at our house at this writing. Will return home this even, I suppose. Uncle Trav. dropped in upon us and we all had to laugh many a time. Pa is very busy, making over $500 per month.[5] Ma is on the healthy list again, having had three monstrous old teeth pulled yesterday by the dentist. The children are well, myself included, for I am gaining in flesh every day.

Must now call my herd together and give them their brain fodder.

> Bye Bye
> With love to all
> Your affectionate neph.

The second school term found Warren idle and at home. Phoebe had gone for a few weeks to Cleveland to take a course in obstetrics under Doctor Biggar. Tryon somewhere in his trading had picked up a set of

---

[5] Harding is of course being facetious. It is doubtful if Doctor Harding ever made $500 in any month of his long life.

old lawbooks. If his son would not be a teacher, he now decided, let him be a lawyer. Superficially acquiescent, Harding agreed and settled down for a while with his calf-bound volumes in the corner of a Marion law office near the courthouse. "I entered the office with misgiving," he told his friend Joe Chapple years later. "Lashing my feet to the top of a desk and tilting back in a chair, I glued my eyes on Blackstone four or five hours a day. It was slow work and money ran out."

To the tort-weary young man with the restless feet it seemed there must be an easier way than the law of earning a living. For the next desultory year he thought he had found that way as local agent for three insurance companies. Although the money that he made was scanty and came in driblets, his expenses were low and his time free. With the spring he became substitute first baseman and manager of the Marion baseball team. The People's Band flourished, although not yet to the point of having uniforms. When Harding learned that a State Band Tournament was to be held at Findlay, fifty miles away in Hancock County, he sent in an entry for his band, undaunted by the precondition that all entrants must be uniformed. By persuading a local merchant to endorse his note he borrowed enough money to buy the uniforms, optimistically hoping to pay the sum back out of the tournament prize money. The uniforms—blue trousers with stripes down the legs, braided coats and caps—were on display in the merchant's window for several days before the band strutted off to Findlay. Thirty bands entered the tournament, ten of them in the class with the Marion band. Each band in the competition played an overture and a march. Harding on that occasion was substituting on the helicon bass, a huge horn that encircled his head like a life preserver as he played the notes of "Doc Munger's Quickstep." "We blew our heads off," he recalled afterward, "but there were so many bands from the big cities that for the first time I felt discouraged and thought we had failed." So disheartened were the Marion bandsmen that by the time the prizes were given out they had all left except for Harding, the bass drum, and the clarinet. To Harding's relieved surprise the judges announced that the Citizens' Band had won the first prize in its class, $150—more than enough to pay for the uniforms. When Manager Harding and his bandsmen arrived back at the Union Depot, most of Marion was waiting to welcome them. Years afterward he recalled the noisy triumph of that reception as his "great day of glory."

Harding's career as an insurance agent came to an end late that spring. The Hotel Marion was just being completed and all the brokers in town were out to write a policy for it. Harding, the beginner, won out over the others and deducted several hundred dollars' commission from the premiums. Only after he had sent in his policy did the company discover that the reason he had won out was that he offered a rate a quarter of a per cent lower than that established by the insurance combine. Harding had to return his premium, and the policy was then written by a broker who knew his business.

Marion, at the time of Harding's arrival, had three newspapers of sorts, the weekly *Mirror,* the biweekly *Independent,* and the daily *Star.* Most substantial by far was the *Mirror,* whose editor, Col. James H. Vaughan, ran the paper together with Miller Eugene Sweney, brother of the superintendent of the Marion Steam Shovel Company. The Colonel, a square-faced man in his late forties with a challenging oval mustache, was not a Civil War veteran but held his military title as a postwar Saturday-night militia soldier. Sweney had come to the paper as a printer in 1876. The *Mirror,* the voice of the county's Democratic majority, dated from 1842. From 1877 to 1882 its owner and editor had been Col. George B. Christian, a leading county Democrat and, like Vaughan, a militia colonel. In 1880 Vaughan had moved to Marion to take over the job of publishing the paper under Christian. Two years later he, L. A. Brunner, and a former editor, R. D. Dumm, bought out the Colonel. In 1884 Brunner and Dumm retired, and Vaughan became editor as well as publisher. Sweney handled the paper's printing and advertising.

George Crawford, the cantankerous editor-publisher of the *Independent,* was spokesman for the minority Republicans, and his paper received its minority share of the county advertising—election notices, tax delinquencies, calls for contract bids. Such official advertising was the main source of income for most rural dailies, and according to the law of Ohio it was split between the newspapers officially representing each party. Crawford, after a short-term enlistment in the Army, had bought his paper in 1862, when it was known as the *Marion County Unionist,* and renamed it the *Independent.* In the autumn of 1864 another former soldier, Samuel Dumble, came to the *Independent* as its sole reporter. After two years he managed to buy a half-interest in the paper, but Crawford remained its editor and the dominating personality in the new partnership.

The irregularly twinkling *Star,* although one of two county dailies in the state, was too insignificant to claim any political emoluments. Two Marion boys scarcely out of school, Willis and Harry Hume, had started it in 1877 in their father's ramshackle printing office on the second floor of the Miller Block. Sam Hume, the father, a garrulous pitchman with an untidy white beard, did odd-job printing in the intervals he was not selling peanuts, brass rings, and pinchbeck jewelry at county fairs. On a third-hand Fairhaven press the boys cranked out their first edition of the *Pebble* on March 24, 1877, proclaiming bravely:

> If Marion can support a daily paper, let it be ever so small, it will be a commendable feature of the place. While we do not know of any town with so small a population sustaining one of any size, we are positive that *NO TOWN* can boast of one at the extremely low price of 7 cents per week.

That hopeful issue of four 11- by 8-inch five-column pages was scarcely more than a flier, with a few small notices, charity inserts by the *New York Sun* and *Church's Musical Visitor,* and several columns of village gossip arranged under the head of "Local Pebbles." Most important for the young editors were the paid timetable announcements of the railroads: the Baltimore & Ohio; the Columbus & Toledo; the Cleveland, Columbus, Cincinnati; the Atlantic & Great Western. Railroads—the first industry to become sensitive to public relations—were always happy to support the press, even the minute rural press, and with their patronage went free passes on their lines.

Within a few issues the Hume boys had changed the name of their paper to the *Star,* and Sam grew interested enough in the project to take over as editor. By the end of the year the *Star's* four pages had doubled to five-column folio size. Now ten cents a week by carrier—although often given away—it was still more an advertising sheet than a newspaper, with its inconsequential local items, windy stories cribbed from Eastern journals, and dovetailed advertisements for corn and cancer cures, trusses, beard elixirs, Dr. Dye's Voltaic Belt, Samaritan Nervine, Lydia E. Pinkham's Vegetable Compound, and other hopeful curatives. The itinerant Sam picked up most of the county items while vending peanuts. Now and again the Main Street coal and wood yard or the Chinese laundry, or the inventor of the Right Speedy Corn Sheller would dole him an advertisement. In those easier days doctors proclaimed their presence, and Tryon not long after his arrival in Marion called attention through the *Star* to: "G. T. Harding, M.D., Homeopathist. Office and Residence on East St., second door south of county jail."

Hume and his boys ran the *Star* for seven years, but it proved no gold mine. Although the paper had a padded circulation list of over five hundred, neither the *Mirror* nor the *Independent* regarded it as a competitor. In fact they disregarded it. Subscribers failed to pay their subscriptions for years; the cut-rate advertisements for elastic corsets and sarsaparilla scarcely paid for themselves. Faced with a rising tide of debts, Hume's editorial zest finally evaporated after he had printed an incautious domestic item for which he was "visited" by an outraged Marionite with the traditional horsewhip in hand. On May 18, 1884, he let the *Star* go to Ben Demster, a carpenter friend of Harding's, just before it was to be auctioned off at a sheriff's sale. Tryon, his trading instinct stirred, gave Demster a house lot he had picked up in another trade for a half-interest in the paper. The last week in May Demster and Warren Harding ran off a new edition with Harding assuming the august title of editor.

A hand-operated Fairhaven press, several hundred mostly non-paying subscribers, enough body type to set out all the news that the town could produce from day to day, a few fonts of job and advertising type, and four railroad passes—those were the current assets of the *Star*. The staff consisted of a bearded eccentric journeyman, Luther Miller, and a beardless printer's devil. Fortified by free transportation, the new editor left on June 2 for the Republican national convention in Chicago. Harding had never seen more than a country caucus until he watched the nomination of James G. Blaine. Although he would not be able to vote for another two years, he had the freedom of the press section where, awestruck by his own standing as a newspaperman, he mingled with editors and reporters from all parts of the country. The tumult of that convention reached its climax when Judge West, speaking for Blaine, implored the assembly to "nominate him and the campfires and beacon lights will illuminate the continent from the Golden Gate to Cleopatra's Needle. Nominate him and the millions who are now waiting will rally to swell the column of victory that is sweeping men on!" As he shouted Blaine's name, men jumped onto their chairs, tossed hats and umbrellas in the air, danced and paraded in the aisles, cheered with a roar "fully as deafening as the voice of Niagara."

Harding's Republican spirit soared on the somewhat tarnished pinions of the Plumed Knight. He rode back to Marion "a real nut on Blaine," determined to put the whole weight of the *Star* behind the magic name. On his eager return he found himself the editor of a non-existent paper, for while he was away a judgment had been entered against the house lot his father had put up to satisfy the creditors. "The sheriff," Harding remarked wryly, "found an extra *Star* on his hands."

Time hung loosely around the young ex-editor's shoulders for the next few weeks. In his enthusiasm for Blaine he took to wearing the gray plug hat that had become the symbol of the Plumed Knight. At Democratic Mantel, near Caledonia, where his father had set up an overnight office, he made his first political speech. There were less than a dozen to listen to him, in the district schoolhouse, but even at his awkward beginning he had the blarney manner. His only income now was the small percentage he drew as manager of the band, plus the fugitive minor insurance commission. In a real pinch, he knew he could always borrow five dollars from his mother. Despite lack of funds, life in Marion with its band concerts and baseball games and bars and political gabble and frowsy poker sessions with their midnight aftermath in the houses down by the railroad junction was agreeable enough to this affable, friendly, and not overly ambitious young man in the plug hat. But if Warren was content to live in the immediacy of the summer present, the sight of his casual son "riled" the doctor. Tryon spoke with Colonel Vaughan and suggested that since the boy was hanging around doing nothing, the Colonel might give him a job on the *Mirror*.

Vaughan was willing. He liked young Harding, and for a few dollars a week could use an extra hand with some newspaper experience.[6]

So Harding went back to his chosen calling, this time as an odd-job reporter who scribbled local notes, set type, wrote editorials, solicited advertisements, and even delivered some of the papers. He soon lost the job —according to legend, because he insisted on wearing his Blaine plug hat to work, and at the office keeping it conspicuously on his desk. Years later Vaughan told a visitor that he had really fired Harding for "loafing about town and putting time on the Blaine-Logan Club instead of his job." Harding had disarmingly admitted to Vaughan that this was true, and the two parted with no hard feelings on either side.

During the summer months the *Star* appeared so fitfully that it became known as the *Comet*. In the last week of July, Kelly Mount—a fanatic Blaine supporter and imitator of the humorist Bill Nye—managed to keep it flickering a whole month. Early in the autumn Demster as mortgagee resumed control of the now almost extinct luminary. A few weeks before the November 4 presidential election he and Harding started the press up again, but in the heat of the Blaine-Cleveland campaign the press stopped within the week.

With the reform Republicans—the Mugwumps—breaking angrily from their Blaine-dominated party to support Cleveland, the Democrats secured a national victory for the first time since 1856. In Marion the county Democrats hired both the Marion and Caledonia bands for the evening of what they felt would be their triumph. And so it was, for although Blaine managed to carry Ohio by a 32,000 majority, he lost the key state of New York—and hence the election—by 1,149 votes.[7]

When the news came through just before midnight and the kerosene torches flared, Harding, his neck encircled by the helicon bass, tootled grimly before the courthouse in involuntary celebration of his party's defeat. After the sooty torchlight procession had come to an end and the marchers were crowding through the swinging doors of Blofogle's and the other saloons on Center Street, he ran into two old friends from the Aeolian Band, Jack Warwick and Johnnie Sickle, who had hitched up a pair of borrowed yellow ponies and driven over from Caledonia. The three of them dropped in at Meily's Restaurant on North Main Street— noted for its bean sandwiches—for a round of oysters. Warwick asked Harding what he had been doing that fall. "I've been working on the *Star*

[6] Harding's weekly earnings at the *Mirror* have been set by various biographers at anywhere from one to seven dollars. Since skilled reporters, according to William Allen White, then got eight dollars a week, the seven-dollar figure is too high, but whatever Harding's pay it did not continue long.

[7] The final voting tabulation in New York was Cleveland 563,154, Blaine 562,005. The state's 36 electoral votes going to Cleveland gave him 219 electoral votes to Blaine's 182.

for a week," Harding told him, "but the ghost didn't walk and I don't know what I'll do next."

They talked over the inambulant ghost, and Harding remarked that Demster would probably sell what was left of the *Star* for $300. Sickle, a railroad brakeman, had just inherited $1,600 and the money was burning a hole in his pocket. He suggested that the three of them buy the *Star*. Harding with his newspaper experience could act as editor. He himself was willing to put up $100 plus a working fund of $400. Neither Warwick nor Harding had $100, but Sickle offered to lend Warwick the money for his share, and Harding thought he might be able to borrow $100 from his father.

Vaughan had already suggested to Crawford that they buy up the *Star* and junk it. But when his rival editor refused, Vaughan, to spite Crawford, encouraged Harding to take over the paper. It was Vaughan, rather than the doctor, who in the end lent Harding the necessary minimum.

While Harding was still trying to rustle up his $100, Demster made one last effort to put the *Star* in orbit. On Monday, the twenty-fourth, the paper appeared again under his signature with an announcement "to the good people of Marion:"

> The *Star* again makes its appearance among you hoping under new management to stay and shine for the benefit of all who may assist me with their patronage. Hereafter this paper shall be conducted as a local and advertising medium, all other matters of communication must be in bounds with respectible [sic] journalism and without an opinion from the editor on either side.

Two days later, just three weeks and four days after Harding's nineteenth birthday, the *Star* recorded under its masthead:

> I have sold out the *Star*.
> BEN DEMSTER

Under this announcement appeared the bold if anonymous challenge of Harding, Warwick, and Sickle:

> We have purchased the *Star* and will stay.
> STAR PUBLISHING CO.

Near it Harding inserted a quatrain that he had composed for the occasion: [8]

> Who says that the *Star* of our village is dead,
> That its glory has faded away?
>   Look! and behold, how bright as pure gold
> It is smiling and dancing today.

[8] Harding often felt moved to write occasional verses although he never printed them under his name.

Only a loving editor could have found much brightness in that next day's issue. Most of the reading matter consisted of fillers, "boiler plate" in newspaper parlance; items and stories lifted from the larger papers on the *Star's* exchange list. The front page, at least, was cleared of Hume's corn and cancer advertisements. More than half the page was taken by a boiler-plate reprint, "STAGE-STRUCK. Spoopendyke's Cruel Criticism of His Wife's Histrionic Attempt." Accompanying Spoopendyke [9] was an explanation of "How Flies Walk on Glass," taken from *Popular Science News,* and a poem from the *Merchant Traveler,* "The Poet's Difficulty." A shorter column contained advice about dead letters and how to diminish them. Bob Burdette of the Brooklyn *Eagle* gave "a Little Good-Natured Advice to Railroad Directors," and *Leisure Hours* commented on "A Cat That Committed Suicide." There were briefer borrowings from the Providence *News* and the *Arhansas Traveler* (sic). The remaining three pages were a litter of small announcements and items: advertisements for the Lowell Clamp Roller Skate, Colt's Repeating Rifle, and the Mason & Hamlin piano; and come-on cures for catarrh, piles, consumption, and drunkenness.

Three days later Editor Harding formally addressed what he claimed were his 700 readers in an editorial, "Pardon Us":

> Thus far we have, contrary to the usual custom, said nothing in the *Star* about the intentions of the new publishers. Since Sam Hume disposed of the paper its changes have been varied and numerous. It seems that each succeeding proprietor, by unpopular management, has lost public favor rather than gained it. Under the management of Kell Mount success was expected but Kelly's ardent administration for a political party carried him too far and his Democratic patrons left him. By the mistakes of others we should learn the way for improvement. Many times we have been interrogated as to our intentions: "Are you going to sell soon? When will the next change occur?" and like questions reach us daily. To answer these questions emphatically, we say, "Look for no more changes." Our egotism tells us that if we can't make the *Star* a success no one can. . . . The unfavorable circumstances under which the present firm issued a paper were discouraging, but up to the time we write our subscription list has been increased one-tenth. There is room for more. We believe we will gain your confidence. . . .
>
> Try the *Star* and if it don't suit you, stop it. We are pleasantly located on the second floor of the Miller Block, where we invite you to call and see us. Pardon us for these remarks concerning ourselves, and hereafter we will not parade the columns of the *Star* with the publishers' intentions.

The "unfavorable circumstances" referred to the unhappy discovery by the new owners that Demster, along with his title to the paper, had trans-

---

[9] Spoopendyke was the creation of one Stanley Huntley who wrote a series for the Brooklyn *Eagle* that he called "The Spoopendyke Papers."

ferred to them some nine hundred dollars in past debts. The following week the *Star* observed tartly that "Ben Demster, after making divers misrepresentations concerning various matters, has changed his loafing place and now roams in Indiana."

Nevertheless the energy of the young proprietors did bring a noticeable if not startling change to the little paper. There were more, and more elaborate Marion items: The Reverend Bonebrake was complimented for his preaching at the United Brethren Church; "Where are the Merry Hayrakers?" the inquiring reporter asked: Would there be another charity ball during the winter? Would the Bag of Tricks insist on making a trip to the Cleveland workhouse a punishment for them?

Order took over in the news columns as Spoopendyke and his heirs gradually retreated. Advertising matter receded from the front page until only a double-column square in the upper left-hand corner continued to announce that Sam Oppenheimer still had special prices on hats and caps, gloves and mitts, undershirts and drawers. Tentatively, news from Washington and overseas began to make its appearance.

Harding gathered up and wrote most of the local news, solicited and wrote the advertisements, and helped set the type, using plugs of burned matches to fasten the loose forms. He and Warwick worked at feeding the wobbly press, running the paper through twice to print each side, then after it was printed rounding up the carrier boys. Since there was only enough type for a single issue, the partners had to unlock the forms and distribute the type for the next day as soon as one edition was off the press. The *Star* sold over the counter for three cents, or ten cents a week delivered.

On December 6 the *Star* recorded that "W. G. Harding of the Star Pub. Co. is in Chicago today, having gone thither on a business trip." He returned with a Favorite job press, "bought on faith and sold on a bet," as Warwick explained it. The new press and the expense of the journey brought a certain amount of hard feelings between Harding and Sickle. Sickle's pocketbook had been deeper in the venture than his heart, and he now observed the *Star's* orbit from a distance, a silent though critical partner.

For all the hustle of the two active proprietors, the paper's survival chances seemed modest. Defiantly they announced on December 13:

> Some man is a wilful liar. We refer to the man who is telling around that there will be another change in the *Star*. The only change anticipated is that of making the paper better. People expecting to damage the *Star* by their silly lies are wasting their breath.

Yet in spite of their brave words there seemed little call for a town daily in the rural-minded agricultural county. Partisan Democrats could find their news once a week in the *Mirror*, Republicans in the *Independent*.

The *Star* claimed to be independent in a day when in partisan Ohio the independent voter was considered a freak of nature.

For months it took a neat juggling of credits and debits just to get the *Star* a sufficient supply of newsprint that invariably arrived C.O.D. A lien or writ was always in the offing, with Harding at times dodging out the back door as the sheriff entered the front. The townspeople felt that the odds were against the young editor. Yet the day of the daily paper was closer than Marion residents realized. The town was growing—over a thousand newcomers in the short time since the Hardings had arrived. Early in December the *Seneca Advertiser* noted with approval that:

> Marion is a wide-awake, enterprising place. Old fogeyism kicked the bucket about ten years ago and his remains were interred amid the loud hallelujahs of the young stirring live businessmen of the place. . . . It enjoys an unprecedented tide of prosperity. Within the last five years it has almost doubled its population. It has four railroads and the fair prospect of securing another, a line that will connect it with Pittsburgh at the head of the Ohio River navigation. Its business houses are large and roomy. The papers published in this city are not filled with medical advertisements and other announcements of a foreign character. . . . Marion has a large number of manufacturing establishments chief of which is the Huber Manufacturing Co. It employs over seventy hands and the sale of its machinery amounts annually to the sum of a million dollars. Marion has two first-class hotels. . . .

The changes in Marion were part of the common pattern. America's postwar industrial expansion was shifting from capital to consumer goods. Local merchants were beginning to enlarge their stock with unheard-of novelties. Hardware men offered all sorts of new labor-saving gadgets. Dry goods merchants and clothiers, used to ordering their consignments twice a year, now took smaller and more varied monthly selections. Advertising, storekeepers were beginning to realize, could clear their loaded shelves. No longer were advertisements merely a nuisance bribe to avert the malice of an impoverished local paper, but, properly inserted, they could be the magic key to a quick turnover. The newspaper business was changing its character from that of a beggar and blackmailer to become one of the major industries of every little town.

It was at this turn of the tide that Harding, conscious of neither the turn nor the tide, had taken command of the *Star*. Yet on his ambles through Marion selling space he sensed the pragmatic if still not obvious truth that it paid to advertise, and made this his pitch. "W. G.," as he now preferred to be called, grew a cigarillo-shaped mustache to emphasize his maturity.[10] A glib good fellow, persuasive and anxious to please, with

[10] The mustache lasted only a few months.

the latest traveling man's joke on his lips, he sauntered affably from store to store soliciting advertising, offering to write the advertisements himself and even to forget about the bill if they did not bring results. "As an advertising solicitor or persuader," Warwick wrote, "W. G. always got on the right side of the cow. He convinced her that she ought to 'give down.'"

While Colonel Vaughan looked on in Democratic detachment, the *Star* commenced to cut into the circulation and the advertising of the *Independent*. Crawford reacted with a snarl to the competition and to the occasional flip reference to his sheet. A little more than two months after Harding had become editor the *Star* commented:

> Ever since the *Star* has been in existence there has been a perpetual kick against it being a legal advertising medium, the objection coming mainly from our home contemporaries. Why they should be jealous is not known as the morsel of legal work given the *Star* is a small affair.

During those struggling months Harding often slept at the office. Sometimes in the rush of going to press he would find himself composing news items directly into the case. Always he printed names. He aimed to print the names of every man, woman, and child in Marion at least once a year. The more prudent Warwick became alarmed when he insisted on having a telephone installed. Since Warwick objected, Harding bought him out —or, to be more accurate, won his share of the *Star* in a cold hand of poker. Warwick nevertheless stayed on as a salaried assistant and later city editor, and remained all his life Harding's trusty and admiring friend.

In those early weeks Vaughan continued agreeable and obliging, lending equipment and even his press when the old Fairhaven broke down. "Our accommodating neighbor, Bro. Vaughan," the *Star* called him. But the testy Crawford repulsed any conciliatory overtures. Already the new proprietors had broken Kelly Mount's summer endurance record, and each evening there were a few less copies left over on the counter. The day before Christmas Harding printed several hundred copies and distributed them broadside.

> This evening [he explained] the *Star* is sent to a great many persons whose names do not appear on our subscription list. We send these extra copies out as a reminder that the *Star* still exists despite the many predictions that the last change would end its existence. There are many who have said "prove your stability and we will patronize you."
>
> For one month the present firm has sent out the *Star* better than ever before and the prospects for its future could not be more encouraging. In fact the *Star* has become a necessity and we believe that sobriety and enterprise will make a good paying paper. At the price it is offered there is no one but that would not prefer it to our behindhand weekly contemporaries. Read this issue and if you like it send us your name by the beginning of the new year and try it for three months at least.

Although the *Star's* front page continued to be padded out with stories from *Hearthstones,* jokes taken from *Texas Siftings,* Spoopendykes and fugitive verse such as the poem about falling leaves from *Chambers' Journal,* there were more and pithier local items, court news, a more professional layout. Already by February, 1885, the Delaware *Chronicle* could remark:

> The little twinkling *Star* at Marion has at last fallen into good hands, and shows its effect by getting out a daily that contains much more news and with each succeeding issue is improving. Marionites could do no better thing than by giving it a most liberal support.

The *Star* still drew most of its substance from the metropolitan papers, but with increasing discrimination. Much more space was now given to national and foreign news, yet in a curious alternation. In one issue [11] the front page contained a column on events in Congress, a list of President-elect Cleveland's probable Cabinet, an obituary of Sen. Robert Logan of Illinois who had dropped dead in the Capitol, the resolutions of the Prohibitionists, and an account of a murderer executed in Kentucky. News from abroad was abridged into sentences. The following day, as if the editors had exhausted themselves, the front page relapsed to boiler plate. Half the page was occupied with "Chinese Folk Lore," from the Washington *National Republican.* There were "Pungent Paragraphs" (all reprints), a humorous column on "Train Fever" from the London *Globe,* "The Dress of Great Men," and a poem from *Harper's Bazaar* by Thomas B. Conant. The same alternation of facts and boiler plate continued week after week. On March 16 the *Star* appeared on somewhat larger pages, and four days later Harding produced his triumph of "giving down" a half-page advertisement from a new drygoods store, Warner & Edwards, announcing that it was selling "desirable Dry Goods at prices that Demand Attention." That same day the *Star* warned that "J. O. Sickel has disposed of his entire interest and is authorized to make no contracts and collect no accounts for this firm." On March 28 the Local Gossip column recorded that "J. O. Sickel left Caledonia for the far West. John has tired of Ohio and the social unpleasantries that some of its towns afford."

By the month's end Harding's persuasiveness had managed to secure two lots of political advertising for his rising *Star:* the Mayor's proclamation for the Marion election of April 6, and a public accounting of the school funds of Marion Township. By now he felt confident enough to move from the Miller Block to larger quarters on the second floor of the Fite Block at the corner of East and Center streets opposite the Methodist Church, although he still did not feel up to replacing the Fairhaven press. Tryon several months earlier had shifted his office to a small front room

[11] March 2, 1885.

in the Fite Block and was selling insurance and dealing in real estate on the side.

At the end of May, 1885, against all predictions, the *Star* completed an unbroken half year under its new editor. Harding wrote:

> On the 24th instant the present management of the *Star* will have completed six months. During those six months the "Twinkler" has always been on time and won favor among its readers. When we began we thought to do away with the continuous clamor for money and make our collections on subscriptions quarterly and adopting the plan no call was for money for three months and then not one-fourth of our readers obliged us by calling and settling. Now that we have reached six months we must demand the payment of back subscriptions. We can't run a daily paper on wind. We must pay our bills and to do so those owing us must settle. . . . We are not running a daily paper at the mark required for glory, and we want no dead-beat subscribers for they are no good to us or our advertisers. There is no one but who can understand just what we mean, and their knowledge of their standing with us will indicate whether this applies to them or not. Come and see us or be prepared for us when we come.

In June Harding took another bold step forward by issuing a Republican weekly, made up for the most part from features selected from the week's daily *Stars,* for county distribution. The daily *Star* by its professed independence could have no regular claim on political advertising since this, according to Ohio law, had to be divided between recognized party organs. As both the *Independent* and the *Mirror* circulated for the most part among farms and rural areas of Marion County, a small town daily had represented no real threat to them. But an announced Republican weekly distributed through the county became not only a challenge to the *Independent's* circulation but a direct bid as well for the Republican share of the county printing, Crawford's most reliable source of income.

The *Weekly Star* first appeared on June 14, twice the length of the four-page daily and with rocket announcements: "The Telegraph News! Miscellaneous! General and Local!" Harding celebrated its advent with doggerel glee:

> All sing the praises of the Marion *Weekly Star:*
> The old gent will hustle for it,
> The old lady'll rustle for it,
> The small boys will tussle for it,
> The old maids will bustle for it,
> And all unite in saying 'tis THE BEST by far.

Two weeks after its appearance Harding secured a franchise from the Associated Press and the *Star* began to receive AP news direct by wire. From then on the latest domestic and foreign events, as well as stock-market reports, produce and cattle market quotations, and baseball scores replaced boiler plate on the front page. Harding himself began to write Ohio political notes, brief paragraphs of political comment. In July he could boast that the *Star* had double the circulation of any other Marion paper.

Colonel Vaughan, his Democratic advertising pie slice unthreatened, and not unwilling to encourage intra-mural Republican ink battles, complimented the appearance of the new *Weekly Star* in the pages of the *Mirror* and wished the venture well. Crawford, alarmed, reacted with fury. He taunted Harding with being a Republican "for revenue only," and added that "the Republican paper needs a certificate of good character from a Democratic paper these days it seems." . . .

Harding replied in a relatively restrained editorial:

> Should the *Independent* be taken as authority our people must have learned strange ideas on political policy. . . .
>
> The old gentleman's [Crawford's] ideas of political differences is enmity and hate. To be a good Republican one must hate the Democrats and vice versa. The *Mirror* saw fit to give our new paper a fraternal notice, a thing that no newspaperman could expect from Mr. Crawford and this leads the old gentleman to infer that we are not "offensively" partisan and, in a later notice, "Republican for revenue only." We admit the first charge and glory in it. . . . We are common people with common interests and the idea that political differences, so essential to our perpetuity, must make us bitter enemies is one that comes from minds warped by prejudice and schooled in hatred. Mr. Crawford has edited a paper for many years and ought to know decidedly more than we could claim to about the business, but if he insists upon us being offensively partisan we must be permitted to run the *Star* without his fatherly advice.

Crawford answered in turn with waspish malice, but Harding refused to be stung. On July 8 he wrote, "Mr. Crawford, we can't notice you again so we must bid you adieu. We can't occupy our space answering or noticing the vents of sarcasm, spleen, and dislike you invariably give a contemporary whether with or without cause."

September brought a purge of the *Star's* "dead-beat" subscribers who "owe us over $600 back accounts." The carrier boys would now collect bills weekly and thus do away with the dead beats, "a class of readers we wish to avoid." Marion remained for some time insulated from the spreading business depression commented on in an August *Star* editorial, and trade still flourished. That novel conception, "It pays to advertise," began to take on with the Center Street merchants. Jno. Frash, observing Warner & Edwards with a calculating eye from his New Dry Goods house, took a flaring half-page to announce unheard-of bargains in Dress Goods. Sam Oppenheimer called attention to his new fall line of Gents' Furnishing

Goods. S. E. DeWolfe, the coal dealer, warned that winter was on the way. Hoberman & Co. had on display 1,500 rolls of new wallpaper. "There was a time," Harding wrote, "when the *Star* got only what advertising the weeklies didn't want, but now our readers will observe it is different. . . . Being engaged in publishing a daily newspaper we haven't time to consult our contemporary protozones [12] concerning our course."

With prosperity peering around the corner, Harding acquired a kerosene engine for the Fairhaven press. The more cautious Warwick predicted that the engine would blow the place up and one day as the editor was tinkering with it, it did just that, filling the shop with steam and broken parts. Luckily for Harding, no one was hurt.

Money still remained as transient as ever in the *Star* office. At one point the paper almost failed to go to press on time while Harding's only pair of trousers was being repaired. Yet the young editor somehow always managed to meet his Saturday-night payroll, paying off with new money and with the quip, "Here's your insult." In a pinch he might win some of the insult back afterward in a poker game. Life at the *Star* was breezy. If Harding felt the need for a chaw of tobacco he would drop into the composing room and ask who had a plug. Once, when Lew Miller produced a small remnant, Harding left and returned a few minutes later with a long plug which he nailed to the wall for community use after cutting off a slice for himself. He chewed tobacco constantly, even keeping a brass cuspidor on his desk.

If not aroused by the *Independent*, Harding basked in his natural good nature. The *Star* had not been long in the Fite Block when a worker at the Huber factory was ridden through town on a rail by his fellow workers and ducked in the public horse trough. Henry Sheets, the *Star*'s first regular reporter, was delighted. He could see an exciting story, to be trimmed with grandiloquent phrases. But Harding was pained. It was against his easygoing ways to hurt anyone, except when sharply challenged. He would even walk carefully on the sidewalk to avoid treading on ants. If he could do so without detriment to the *Star* he was always willing to cover up the prints of some local misstep.

Sam Hume, when he was back from the popcorn business he had started in Chicago, dropped in at the *Star* office with an occasional gossip item. Kelly Mount contributed humorous articles in his Bill Nye manner. A succession of tramp printers came and went, seldom staying for more than a month and often sleeping in the back room. There were itinerants such as "Colonel" Hargot who always wore a Prince Albert and a battered

[12] Besides misspelling the word, Harding confused the adjective with the noun. If piqued, he often thumbed the dictionary for ammunition, as on December 23 when—this time confusing the noun with the adjective—he labeled Crawford "the nystagmus editor."

silk hat, Shorty Johnson with his invariably "How ya fixed?", and a Civil War veteran who slept behind the press on a pile of old newspapers and always cautioned the others before he crawled into his cubbyhole, "Wake me up when Kirby dies!" But the most permanent of the transients was a vastly disheveled dog, mostly Newfoundland, that wandered in from nowhere and stayed until he died. Harding called him Senator.

In the early months Harding was too concerned with the day-to-day operations of getting out the paper to bother much with editorials. His first extended editorial on a controversial subject—this time prohibition— did not appear until August, 1885:

> Every good citizen desires that this evil which is certainly not becoming less widespread from year to year shall be repressed and so on. *The difficulty that confronts the policy of prohibition is the fact that it does not prohibit.* The stubborn fact is that where prohibition has never been found competent to prohibit, other marks of controlling the liquor traffic have been effective, with advantage more or less marked because of temperance. The three months of experience of Wisconsin with the high license is notable proof of this. Restraint people will submit to. They do in every relation, and there are very few who will not make every reasonable concession for the general good. But absolute interdiction, that is felt to be destructive of personal liberty when the object sought is believed to be obtainable without it, and when the interdiction is proved to be, except in a very limited degree, inoperative, always has and always will be resisted.
>
> Theories that contravene all facts will not solve the question. It must be dealt with in the practical way which experience unmistakably points out.

The following month found him lecturing the suffragettes:

> Now a woman has a perfect right to talk temperance, and the good her sex has done is undisputed, but her right to wear pants and make the night hideous on the street is questioned.

From his first days at the editorial desk, Harding was an ardent supporter of Ohio's governor-elect, the magnetic Joseph Benson Foraker. Foraker, known as "Fire Alarm Joe" and "Boomtara" for his rampageous spread-eagle oratory, represented the new generation of Republicans. Only eight years old when Ohio's senior Republican senator, the staid but colorless John Sherman, had first been elected in 1854 (as a Whig) to Congress, Foraker ten years later had marched as a young soldier with Sherman's general brother to the sea. Though later he would become the none-too-scrupulous ally of predatory corporations and city bosses, in the immediate postwar years this still-boyish figure with the eyes that shot sparks above a drooping mustache seemed a fighter against corporate greed and corruption, full of idealistic courage. Eloquent on the rights of the people, passionate in defense of the Union soldier, he sent his audiences into frenzies with his stars-and-stripes invective. When President Cleveland requested Northern governors to return captured Confederate battle flags, Fire Engine Joe announced: "No rebel flags will be returned while I am governor!"

Harding wrote in his defense:

> Governor Foraker has been charged with being particularly bitter with Confederate soldiers, but it will be observed that the Governor pursues a worthy plan . . . he loathes one that has sought to destroy the Republic and still glories in it.

Fire Alarm Joe had first appeared in Marion as a second-time candidate for governor in September, 1885, and some months later Harding wrote a glowing account of this visit. Foraker became his state hero, a leader to set beside his national hero, Blaine. Harding early showed an instinct for practical politics, and as an editor he developed an instinct for the political labyrinths of Ohio. Nor did he hesitate to say what he thought of the labyrinths. When the Ohio legislature adjourned he noted that "respectable people may now pass through Columbus in the cars without being compelled to wear clothespins on their noses." In his early days Harding often seemed the young Turk, although his inner need of acceptance was too great for him ever to stray very far. The Republican party, whatever its leaders, always remained for him the party of union and prosperity. As a Republican he would take the high tariff road and let the Democrats take the low. That was within the decent bounds of two-party rivalry. But for the off-limit roads beyond the two-party highway, for the Mugwumps, Prohibitionists, Populists, he had only scornful anger.

Although he had just reached voting age himself he could not contain his indignation when the Negroes of New Albany failed to support the Grand Old Party:

> Now the colored voters have the privilege . . . of voting just for whom and what they please, but just how they can display so much ingratitude as to vote against the true representatives of the party that proved itself their liberator is difficult to understand; and the colored voter who will vote against the party that proved its savior, if he isn't, ought to be damned.

An attack on the dying General Grant sent Harding's pen stabbing at the paper:

> A cowardly, sneaking copperhead in Van Wert County in a newspaper correspondence says: "I expected to see General Grant recover as soon as he received his pension." If that low-down pup knew the contempt he brought for himself by that utterance he would feel so small that a thimble could contain him and then show no evidence of being filled.

Editorially the *Star* was anti-outsider. Of the Mormons Harding wrote in 1885:

"What a pity that the cyclones that played such frightful havoc on Washington Court House were not transformed to Mormon settlements in the West."

After Chicago's Haymarket Massacre of 1886, presumably carried out by bomb-throwing anarchists, Harding suggested that the New York anarchist writer and propagandist Johann Most "be cured by allopathic doses of cold lead." For the *Star*, Gov. John Peter Altgeld of Illinois, who sympathized with the Pullman strikers, was "the anarchist governor." Foreign immigration, that had once made America, was "now promising to ruin it."

Marion was too familiarly small town to experience class warfare in the urban sense. Harding had no objection to his men joining a union, and in fact later joined the printers' union himself, but he opposed the Knights of Labor because of their "radicalism" and their heretical tendency to form a third party. The opposition did him no harm in Marion. In spite of his earlier schoolboy views on the moral tendencies of the stage, he preferred to spend his evenings elsewhere than on the hard benches of the Music Hall watching touring-company productions of *The Octoroon, Ticket-of-Leave Man, Kit the Arkansas Traveler,* or even *The Lights o' London* "with all the magnificent scenery, properties, and mechanical effects used at the Union Square Theatre, N.Y." Maggie Mitchell appeared at the hall in her great success *Little Barefoot,* as did Minnie Maddern (later Fiske) in *In Spite of It All,* the latter—according to the *Star*—attracting a very small attendance. Just before Christmas of 1885 Rice's Opera Company arrived to present a week of *The Mikado,* the first opera to be seen in Marion. "A real live opera company," Editor Harding commented. "Well, I'll be darned!" The *Star* now had a Boys and Girls column, Fashions, Science and Progress; and it appealed to its readers for more items of local interest.

Eber Baker—his widow was still alive—would have marveled at the Music Hall, although he might scarcely have appreciated Professor Fisher's Dancing Academy, with Thursday-afternoon classes for ladies and children and evening classes for ladies and gentlemen. The Harmonic Society's rehearsal of Haydn's Imperial Mass (at the Music Hall) he would not have appreciated at all. For Harding, even as a bystander, these were all heartening signs of progress, of his slogan "Marion for Everything." The roller-skating fad had passed its peak, and the rink—under new management—tried vainly to attract customers, lowering its price from a quarter to a dime. But the gayer blades of the town now scorched about on the new high-wheeled bicycles until the snow fell.

In January, 1886, Harding was at last able to replace the old Fairhaven with a new Babcock press. It took two days to get it installed during which "our always accommodating friend Jim Vaughan" gave Harding the use of his printing plant. But as the February snow deepened, the word-volleys between the *Star* and the *Independent* quickened. "We regret to speak disrespectfully of an old gentleman," the *Star* announced on February 26, "but when George Crawford, while worrying over a printer's plum, says the *Weekly Star* has a circulation of but 150, HE LIES AND HE KNOWS IT." A month later Harding observed editorially that the "old drunk boat who wrote that piece for the *Independent* of last week was so drunk at Essex last week that they had to thaw the medicine out as soon as he was gone." Crawford attacked the "almost Republican" again after Harding announced that he was supporting Marion's Democratic Mayor Gailey in opposition to the Republican candidate, the former Democrat, former Mayor Mohr, whom the *Star* called a "flopper." As for Doctor Harding, he, according to the *Independent,* was no more than a quack and a fake Republican. Harding, in spite of having bid Crawford adieu nine months earlier, replied with a volley that rattled the editorial page:

We beg the indulgence of our readers to devote a few lines to George Crawford and the sheet he edits. This lying old gentleman has made Doctor Harding the subject of his venomous remarks, and we must correct him.

To begin with, the *Independent* is bitterly jealous of the *Star* and everybody knows it. When it was of doubtful stability he cared little for it, but when it began to receive the merited support and a weekly was established, he began to regard it as formidable, and used every opportunity to throw stones in our way. Crawford seeks to divest us of Republican support, he representing that our father is responsible for the utterances of this paper, and then portrays him as a traitor to the Republican party—calls him a bogus and a fraud Republican and resorts to other disreputable means to have the party taboo him and the *Star;* refers to him as the "quack who engineered the attempt to defeat Hane for School Board." In every such assertion George Crawford lies outright. In the first place, the Doctor is not responsible for any utterances in the *Star,* and he is by far a more loyal and respectable Republican than Crawford or his sneaking partner. He always diligently worked for the party from principle, and does so still, and Crawford knows this.

This Crawford, who works the temperance and pious racket for church support, while his inebriate associate caters to the saloon patronage, has no business questioning anyone's loyalty. His co-workers know him. Instead of being a political writer for the sake of principle, he is a Republican for patronage, as his support of kicked-out Democrats indicates. It was Crawford who picked out Doctor Hahn from the Democratic ashpile and supported him for auditor, after abusing him in the *Independent* three years continuously, simply to get financial support of the auditor's office. There are plenty of instances. He plays the lickspittle to a class of men who like such parasites. Then he swells up, and believing no good can be done without his sanction and advice, he foams at the mouth whenever his sordid mind grasps anything done politically without his counsel; and he rolls his eyes and straightway evolves from his inner consciousness a double-twisted, unadulterated, canvas-back lie, that would make the devil blush. His sordid soul is gangrened with jealousy. This sour, disgruntled and disappointed old ass gets frenzied at the prospects of a successful rival, and must vent the feelings of his miserable soul by lying about those he cannot browbeat or cajole. He belittles men whose shoes he is unfit to lace, and his mind has become a heterogeneous mass of jealous ideas and dissatisfaction. But his colossal self-adulation is tumbled mightily, for no one trembles when he barks. His acquaintance is tottering him; he only remains an imbecile whose fits will make him a paralytic, then his way of spitting venom will end.

The depression spread further. By spring the mortgage on the Merry-Roll-Round had been foreclosed and the rink with all its appurtenances sold at a sheriff's auction. Marion merchants began pulling in their advertising horns. No longer did Warner & Edwards challenge Jno. Frash across the half-pages. On May 24 Harding had to cancel his Associated Press franchise. "It has been a popular feature with a few," he wrote, "and we prefer it ourselves, but the heavy expense does not justify its continuance." On the following day the *Star's* front page was taken up chiefly with "Mabel Lightfoot or The Fortunes of a Ferryman's Daughter." All the summer the page continued to be graced with such fillers as "Love Among the Daisies," poems from the Chicago *Sun*, Mrs. Julia Ward Howe's opinions on Goethe's Sweethearts, and free pieces from the Detroit *Free Press*.

In spite of the depression-clouded future, Charity Harding was married to Elton E. Remsberg on June 23, four months after her nineteenth birthday. Chat's wedding caused little interest and no comment in Marion. Remsberg might be from the wrong side of the tracks, but that seemed right enough for Doc Harding's daughter. Not long after their marriage the young couple moved West.

By autumn the business tide had turned, carrying the *Star* along in the current. It was in September that Sheets arrived from the Pittsburgh *Daily Post*. A week later Harding announced that he was resuming the Associated Press service, and foreign and domestic news now reclaimed the front page. In October the *Weekly Star* was able to elbow the *Independent* out of its contract for the sheriff's proclamation of the next month's election, Harding's first taste of county printing. Crawford complained with loud vindictiveness that the *Star*, weekly or daily, was not a

Republican paper. He did his best—with some success—to undercut Harding in job printing. Harding returned to the fight:

> The same sneaking whelp who argues about that politics has nothing to do with commercial printing is the same lying dog that for more than a year has gone among Republican merchants and begged for the commercial work given us on the pleas that it was all done in the *Mirror* office. He hopes in this way to prejudice Republicans against us and get their work. Very fortunately Republicans of Marion know better.

Crawford did succeed in getting hold of the annual report of the county commissioners in December, but Harding was able to show that if the *Independent* had published the report in the compact form specified by law, it would have saved the county $168. The exchange of fire continued. On December 8 Harding wrote:

> If Crawford will secure a copy of our "Family Physician" he can find good advice possibly that will help to alleviate the nauseated stomach the weekly *Star* has given him. If the malady is not treated in its first stages it may become serious. We fancy we see symptoms of drivelling idiocy already.

By the spring of 1887 Marion's newspaper battle was reaching a crescendo. "Almost Republican," Crawford jeered at the *Star*, calling attention to his *Independent* as "an out-and-out Republican paper that does not sail under false colors." He discovered that the name of the "pretended Republican paper" was Rats spelled backward. He also discovered that Vaughan had endorsed a note of Harding's. "The time has never been in Marion County," he wrote, "since the party existed when help could not be got for a Republican paper when it needed it, from Republicans."

Harding felt the hit. On the following day, May 17, he replied:

> We will spare our readers from a long tirade against the venerable old idiot of the *Independent*. It is simple justice to ourselves and the gentlemen he names to say that the *Star* doesn't owe J. H. Vaughan or S. A. Court one cent, but we do owe the Farmers' Bank part of a $250 note on which these two men are security and which is being paid as fast as it becomes due. If this servile old man says we are debtors to them in any other manner, or that there is any mortgage on our office besides the one voluntarily given to protect them in securing our note, he wilfully lied. We are not ashamed of our debts, we are proud to say we are reducing them, and are looking forward to a date when they shall be wiped away. The *Weekly Star,* a splendid Republican paper with over a thousand readers, is a terrible thorn in the old man's flesh and it tortures him more than he can bear. His list is dwindling and it pains him so that he growls at us and abuses our friend. We cannot answer the old growler as we would like, for we respect gray

hairs, even if on a dog, and we can never consent to devote any space to the slimy snake that is associated with him.

He discovered in turn that "sneaking Sam" had a "$1,200 plaster on his home for money borrowed of a very estimable East Center Street lady last December, and which he is supposed to have borrowed to aid his associate in his great scheme of closing up his side show."

> The reference to debts has not trampled our toes to hurt them, but we are moved to refer to this mortgage on lot 323 for the simple purpose of proving to Mister Crawford that debts are quite common nowadays, and very few can loan money without security and he himself isn't included in that few. We didn't take time to inquire whether the lady that loaned him the money is Republican or not, but we presume she is. This latter point is important.

Crawford in fury finally struck back where Harding was most vulnerable. In the *Independent* of May 20 he announced that "we have no desire to draw the COLOR line on the kink-haired youth that sees fit to use his smut machine only as a receptacle for a low order of adjectives—as nature did it for him."

From boyhood Harding had been one to avoid fisticuffs, but he was ready to "mop up the street" with anyone who challenged his blood. Tryon, always shorter in temper and quicker in a fight, tucked a shotgun under his arm as father and son set out for the *Independent* office. There they cornered and temporarily cowed the elderly Crawford and Dumble. Crawford agreed to print a retraction. Next day the still-spluttering *Star* was able to report:

> Malicious persons, who are attempting to make capital out of an ambiguous paragraph in Friday's *Independent,* that through lying reports of some sneaking scoundrels seemed to have application to the editor of this paper, are hereby informed of the positive disavowal of such an application of the article by Messrs. Crawford and Dumble, who have given us their personal assurance that they had no such intention, and will furthermore make a statement of similar nature in Tuesday's *Independent.* And while the subject is up we notify the retailer of Harding's genealogy, whoever he is, that he is a contemptibly, sneaking, lying dog, who hasn't the sand or nerve to make the statement in a manner that can be traced to him. If he doesn't desire to stand branded as a miserable coward, let him make himself known.

Three days later the *Independent* concluded its somewhat equivocable disavowal:

> For ourselves, we think, even were the objectionable stories referred to by the young man mentioned, in his paper of Saturday last, true, they would not be a proper foundation for newspaper controversy, unless for some

good reason. If such stories as he mentions are in circulation we are in no way responsible for their circulation, as they are none of our make.

However lame the apology, Crawford—as everyone in Marion realized —had been forced to back down. Not for many months would he again refer to Harding and the *Star* on his editorial page. The *Independent*, as if nothing had happened, resumed its long-term political feud with the *Mirror*. Crawford might remark offhandedly that Vaughan hired the brains to edit his paper and they were "of poor quality and detrimental to society"; Vaughan, before a county election, might refer to the "vile and unprincipled position assumed by Crawford and his gang of greedy spoils seekers." But both men understood that nothing personal was implied so long as each paper received its share of official printing. Harding now disturbed this profitable equilibrium by demanding that Marion's printing be awarded through competitive bids. A large saving of money would result he pointed out with accurate, uncomfortable insistence.

As times improved, the circulation of the *Star* continued to rise. That of the *Mirror* and the *Independent* did not. Before the county fair in September, Harding printed 4,000 copies of the *Weekly Star*, heavy with advertising, for distribution at the fairgrounds. The year also brought an end to his amiable relations with Colonel Vaughan. Some time early in the summer he had enticed the Colonel to Lizzie Lazalere's down by the tracks, and then with barnyard humor staged a fake raid in which Vaughan was seized and to which the *Star* jocosely alluded the next day. The Colonel never forgave Harding. He retaliated by printing a whole page of the *Mirror* devoted to the Hardings' supposedly negroid ancestry, with sneers at Doctor Harding's "woolly" head and elaborations of the rumor that the family had always been considered and treated as Negroes in and around Blooming Grove. Before the edition could be distributed, Vaughan had second thoughts and suppressed it.[13] His revenge now took the more conventional form of starting a daily rival to the *Star*.

From the beginning the *Daily Mirror* was not a success. A few months of getting it out showed the editor that he lacked the temperament, the staff, and the means to undercut his rival daily. Just after Christmas he announced that Doctor J. W. Thatcher, "a well-known citizen and prominent physician of Marits, Morrow Co.," had bought a half-interest in the *Mirror*. Vaughan stayed on for the time as senior editor, but the doctor's son, Ned Thatcher, a young man given to fierce bouts of drinking, who had left his reporter's job in Columbus to take over as local editor, did

[13] "Before Harding's death Vaughan told Doctor Alderfer that the last copy extant was in his safe, that he had refused $5,000 for it, and that his will provided for its destruction unread. He is dead, and the newspaper has been destroyed." *The Incredible Era*, S. H. Adams.

most of the work of getting out the paper. Sweney and Doctor Thatcher managed the business side.

So 1887 passed, with a sudden cold wave from Canada that froze the ponds overnight. Although there had been a run of casual entertainments at the Music Hall, from *East Lynne* to the Bennett English Opera Company's production of *Fra Diavolo*, what Harding remembered longest from that year was the appearance at the town hall of Ohio's homespun poet, Will Carleton.[14] With Harding in the audience, Carleton recited his narrative poem, "The First Settler," about a farmer who had used such harsh words to his wife for letting the cattle stray that she had gone out into the night to look for them. After finally bringing them back, she sank exhausted on the cabin floor where he later found her dead. The farmer had rhymed his remorse:

> Boys flying kites haul in their white-winged birds;
>   You can't do that way when you're flying words.
> "Careful with fire" is good advice, we know:
> "Careful with words" is ten times doubly so.
> Thoughts unexpressed may sometimes fall back dead:
>   But God himself can't kill them when they're said.

These lines so impressed the young editor that he memorized them. They became his favorite verses, to be quoted—and sometimes misquoted—ever afterward, even when he had become President.

With the spring of 1888 Harding was able to enlarge the size of the *Star* by a column. Always ahead of his competitors in publicity sense, in May he printed an edition of 2,000, his carrier boys distributing the extra copies free as samples. Marion dry-goods merchants were again taking up their rivalry in the *Star's* pages, and Harding with an expanded *Weekly Star* was validating claims for city and county printing. In November he was able to boast that "from a despised, knocked-about, and generally uncertain sheet, the *Star* has grown, in the passing years, to be the real newspaper of Marion. It has marched in the line of progress with Marion and will continue to do so."

To Vaughan it was all too clear that Harding's boasting had substance. He had not forgiven his former protégé the insult of the previous year, and the success of the *Star* fanned his anger. As the *Daily Mirror* continued to falter, he sought out his old adversary of the *Independent* and suggested that the two of them band together to hamper Harding and shut him out of any share of county advertising. Harding soon got wind of this politically contradictory combination, and on September 29 he twitted them:

[14] Carleton's best-known poem, "Over the Hill to the Poor-House," was a popular declamation piece in its day. "The First Settler" appeared in his book, *Farm Legends*.

Not so long ago but what it is within memory of all who have watched the newspaper clashings in this city did the *Independent,* the "only official organ of the Republican party in this county," set up a great howl because this office was financially aided though at a high rate of interest, by . . . the very able and brilliant editor of the *Mirror,* Col. Jas. H. Vaughan. He was accused of aiding, abetting, and sustaining a Democratic aid society and the old gentleman of the "official organ" raised his hands in holy horror, snarled, and danced at the outrage. Indeed his antics were so frightful that we paid the debt as quickly as possible, and the hysteria ended. Now the circumstances are changed and what do we behold? Gaze and see the distinguished pair composed of Colonel Vaughan, the aforesaid brilliant editor and George Gordon Bennett Crawford, marching together like brothers with a single thought, visiting various county offices and trying to down the *Star* in the matter of a little legal advertising that seems likely to be placed with us. What a spectacle, fellow citizens! These able men marching and pleading together against the *Star,* Jimmy telling Georgie in a loving way what an "old Nancy" he is, and Georgie affectionately illustrating to Jimmy what a "brainless mullet head" he is—we quote these expressions from back numbers of their respective papers. Why, it is a sight to amuse everyone.

On November 11 the *Daily Mirror* ceased publication. "The baby is dead," Harding jeered. "Born to elevate Marion journalism, to show our benighted people what a real, flourishing daily was, it has filled its mission and more, too. It taught its proprietors that the publication of a daily was not boys' play, that it required work unknown even in a GREAT weekly office. . . ."

The following week Vaughan retired from the still-surviving weekly *Mirror,* and Ned Thatcher became sole editor. Eugene Sweney remained to keep the feud with Harding green. On January 17, 1889, the *Star* was able to display its personal and financial trophy of victory with a front page given over wholly to the printing of the Financial Statement of the Commissioners of Marion County.

By the end of the decade Marion's population had grown to 8,200 and the *Star* had become accepted as a permanent part of the scene. Newcomers, unaware of old quarrels, read it because it had the most news and it printed their names. Up until 1889 the paper had appeared as the impersonal responsibility of the Star Publishing Company. Now in February Harding announced that the *Star* was "Published Every Evening Except Sunday by W. G. Harding." This, he explained, was no change of proprietorship:

When we took the *Star* after the innumerable changes of 1884, it was deemed wise to adopt a plan under which the owners could change as rapidly as they went broke, without the fact appearing in the paper. Then it was not sure how long the paper could hold out in variable financial trade winds and no one would have particularly cared to appear as foster father of the concern. The indications are such now that the paper is likely (to be) permanent—yes, surely so unless some fatal blunder occurs to blast its foundations—and we conclude to drop the burdensome name of the Star Publishing Company, and put what responsibility there is where it belongs.

The fatal blunder almost occurred the following summer when Harding found himself arrested for criminal libel on the complaint of Mary Lynn, the wife of a prosperous county farmer. On July 13 the *Star* reported that she had eloped with a Marion clergyman.[15] Her husband indignantly asserted that she was visiting an aunt in Indiana and spoke of "horsewhipping, tar and feathers, and railroading through the streets of the . . . mean dastardly coward who gave credence to the rumor before investigation." Next day the *Star* printed what was meant as a full retraction, and when the Lynns rejected this and in addition demanded $10,000 damages, the matter went to the grand jury. "It comes high to be Alexy," the *Mirror*, remarked, "but some people must have it." At last, on October 24, the *Star* was able to report:

> Those who have neglected to subscribe to the *Star* for fear that it would be branded with criminal libel send in their names at once. The criminal suit of Mrs. Lynn has been laid in an early grave by an intelligent grand jury, fourteen out of fifteen of whom voted that the attempted prosecution was too silly to be countenanced in court.

It was during this year that the rising *Star* made another and this time final move from the Fite Block to the lower half of a much more substantial building on the south side of East Center Street next to the brick Gothic Episcopal Church and almost opposite the county jail. Compared to the old, the new quarters were vast, set off by a counter so long that for the first few weeks after the move jokers kept dropping in to ask for "two beers." Harding installed new presses, new engines, new equipment, all bought on credit. The interest of the *Star's* debts was now larger than the debts themselves had been five years before.

For all Harding's progress upward, the "best circles" of Marion remained pointedly unaware of him. In 1885 he had become a Knight of Pythias in Marion's Canby Lodge No. 51, but the more aristocratic circles of Masonry remained barred to him. One of his humiliations he recalled in the mellow glow of success before a convention of the Society of Newspaper Editors after he had become President of the United States:

[15] This July 13, 1889, edition of the *Star* is missing from the files of the Ohio Historical Society and is unrecorded on the microfilm of the paper both at the Marion Public Library and at the office of the *Star*.

In the early days of the newspaper business, we felt an obligation, and it was quite the custom in the small towns to have the editor specially invited for the all-important event, social or otherwise, and there was a very prominent wedding in my town and I was not invited. I took it very much to heart, and, like a culprit, on that occasion, after the wedding, I published the news of the marriage as an obligation but limited it to a three-line item without a headline.

And the little notice of the wedding was so remarked about that there came to me the inevitable remorse of conscience that I concluded never after that, in the newspaper with which I was associated, should the news in any manner be appraised by the prejudices of the editor and the paper.

With the move to the new building, Jack Warwick became the *Star's* city editor. Aylmer Rhoads, a brilliant reporter when he was sober, replaced Henry Sheets. The staff grew with the size of the plant. A cartoonist, Arthur Porter, came to sketch and caricature the town and the people. Kelly Mount returned to contribute his dialect humorous bits. Among the more casual reporters was Fred O'Brien, later to become famous as the author of *White Shadows in the South Seas*. "Fred came to us a straggling remnant of Coxey's Army in which he was a 'general,'" Warwick recalled. "He stopped off in Marion between meals—how long between I am unable to say. W. G. found work for him to do at the *Star* office. Where there was an opportunity for decorations Fred could elaborate a story and write it beautifully, but prosaic facts annoyed him; he was never at home with them."

Harding now gave up most of his news gathering, spending the better part of his time soliciting advertising, hailing his fellows, well meeting newcomers as he felt his way into Marion's political scene. In the spring of 1890 he took his first and second degrees as a charter member of the Marion Lodge of Elks. He joined the Young Men's Republican Club, formed as an aggressive challenge to the entrenched party elders of the Republican County Executive Committee. The committee—made up of Crawford, J. F. McNeal, and others hostile to the *Star*—was always willing to work with the Democrats, and in that predominantly Democratic county even to endorse their candidates. To these elderly encrusted men Harding threw down his challenge. In 1888 he supported W. Z. Davis in his contest with McNeal at the congressional district convention. When McNeal captured the local delegates, Harding agreed to support him for Congress, but at the convention switched to a candidate who succeeded in defeating McNeal. That same presidential year Harding became a delegate to the Republican state convention and continued a delegate for many years afterward. Gradually W. G. was building up a following. The County Committee members might be his enemies, but they as the elite of the town had their opponents who sided with the impatient younger

Republicans. "We know the bosses, henchmen and all," he wrote, "and care little for the regard of any of them."

Although Benjamin Harrison was nominated by the Republican National Convention in Chicago, Harding remained true to his old hero Blaine.

> Mr. Blaine [he wrote in the *Star*] is unquestionably the idol of his party. Even in this state, where every Buckeye is proud of our own great Sherman, Blaine is as greatly estimated as any man should be, and he is pre-eminently the first choice. Even if he should persist in refusing, he has a place in the hearts of his political friends that is more lasting than any honor that office can confer.

His satisfaction in Harrison's victory was tempered by Governor Foraker's defeat for a third term the following year. An increase in the tax to be paid by saloonkeepers turned the Cincinnati Germans against Foraker— the Saloonkeepers' Rebellion, Fire Engine Joe called it—and he lost to a Civil War veteran, James E. Campbell—by 368,551 to 379,423 votes. Following the election Harding wrote:

> There is too much doubt about the Ohio results to admit of an expiation upon the causes. There is defeat, however, even in the doubtful result. . . . There is no use repeating the old "I told you so." The Republicans did not expect it so nor did the Democrats. The latter are surprised at the victory they have achieved. . . . In all probability they are not responsible for it. The "Saloon attics" in Hamilton County, who have always proven the anarchists of the political world, have done the greater part of the work, while jealous Republicans who turned green with envy at Foraker's shining star have completed the work by stabbing him in the back amid protestations of friendship and fidelity.

Just after the election Harding suffered what he later called a nervous breakdown. On October 16 the *Star* had reported that its editor was "indisposed to such an extent that he is unable to attend to any newspaper duties, being scarcely able to reach the office for half an hour each day." Urged by his father, he left on November 7 for the Battle Creek Sanitarium in Michigan. Battle Creek, sponsored by the Seventh-day Adventists, was a vegetarian establishment run by the autocratic Doctor J. P. Kellogg, the inventor of peanut butter and corn flakes. After some weeks of Battle Creek's Spartan regimen Harding returned early in 1890 to Marion renewed in spirit and twenty pounds lighter. This was the first of five visits he would make to Battle Creek during the next twelve years.

In June, 1891, he was again a delegate to the Republican state convention. With a sort of prescience he had even then begun to dress the part of the statesman—the inevitable Prince Albert and the slouch hat that was its Ohio political complement. A fellow delegate, the editor of another small-town newspaper, described him at the time as "a big, rosy-complexioned young man, handsome, enthusiastic, eager for McKinley's nomination, and evidently on the best of terms with life. No hint fell from him, in our talks, that he was making the fight of his young life to keep the Marion *Daily Star* off the rocks."

The following month, on July 9, 1891, the *Star* reported:

> It isn't often that the *Star* records marriages of its own force, and there might be pardon for unusual notice to the nuptials of the editor, but it is quite sufficient to say that Warren G. Harding and Florence M. Kling were happily married at their own home on Mount Vernon Avenue, Wednesday evening (July 8, 1891), at 8:30. Reverend R. Wallace officiated. Quite a pleasant company of friends were present to witness the ceremony and extend congratulations.
>
> Mr. and Mrs. Harding were most handsomely remembered by their friends, using this term in the fullest meaning.
>
> They leave tonight for Chicago, St. Paul, and the Northwest, expecting to return by way of the lakes. They will be at home to their friends on and after August third.

It was the turning point in Harding's life.

[CHAPTER VI]

Marriage

Florence Mabel Kling was the one girl of the three children of Amos Kling, and many times her father wished she had been a boy. His square Teutonic face had grown puckered with the determination to get what he wanted out of life, and this quality he had passed on to his daughter. With the narrow arrogance of the self-made man, he insisted that he was the head of his house, the arbiter, the ruler. His wife Louisa so accepted him, but to his daughter he insisted in vain. She had inherited his stubbornness as well as his intelligence. What she had not inherited was her mother's womanliness. There was nothing feminine about her. Even the most awkward girls often have a moment of charm as they bloom into womanhood. Flossie Kling never had that moment. Her gawky face was not so much masculine as assertively neuter. Even her walk was ungainly. No man would ever turn to stare at her plain figure as she passed. Yet within herself she was a female, too, responsive to men.

She was born the year before the outbreak of the Civil War. From her emergent childhood days her father found her as headstrong as he was. They quarreled at the sight of each other. Nevertheless, he gave her what he thought was her due: piano and riding lessons, several years at a good if not fashionable boarding school. At the school she continued her piano lessons, and afterward even took a course at the Cincinnati Conservatory of Music. Then she returned to the sullen atmosphere of her father's brick and plate-glass house. Her relations with her two brothers, Clifford and Vetallis, were never close.

There were few outlets in Marion for this restless, sharp-witted, if unintellectual girl. She went to the church socials, she rode her horse Billy like a man, and sometimes she slipped away to the Merry-Roll-Round. The few boys who took her roller skating were usually from the wrong side of town. Amos locked and chained the double front door at 11 P.M. If Flossie did not return by then, as sometimes happened, she had to spend the night at some girl friend's and face her father's temper next day.

The Klings' nearest neighbors were the DeWolfes, an older family by Marion's brief measuring stick, if not quite so rich. Simon DeWolfe was the local coal dealer. The son Henry, known as Pete—an amiably idle young man with no purpose in life beyond amusing himself—would from time to time go with Flossie to the skating rink. He was two years older than she, but once that self-willed young woman decided to marry him he had no chance. Their closest friends were not surprised when, in March, 1880, she and Pete eloped. In the euphemistic language of the day, he married her "because he had to." Six months afterward their son Eugene Marshall was born.[1]

Far from settling Pete, marriage to the dominating Flossie broke whatever small spirit he had and turned him to drink, a turning to which he had already shown himself inclined. Incapable even of making the effort to earn a living, resentful of his wife and indifferent to his child, he idled away his days and roistered his nights. Sometimes he would be gone from his home for weeks at a time. The jobs his father found for him he soon lost or gave up. Kling in obdurate anger at the marriage refused to help his daughter, who in turn refused to go to him for help, although behind his back his wife supplied her with clothing and money. The less obdurate Simon DeWolfe guaranteed his daughter-in-law's grocery bills. As if in defiance of her father, Flossie borrowed a piano and began giving music lessons. Her friends took pity on her, if her father did not. Even the most reluctant of the neighborhood children were sent to her to learn their scales. Whether Amos was impressed by her independence or whether he found the hound tongues of local gossip too sharp, in any case after a time he asked her to return to her old room in the brick mansion. She and the child could both take the name of Kling. She refused.

In September, 1884, Florence M. obtained a legal separation from Henry A. DeWolfe. Their child—Marshall she called him—was now four years old. But once he was past his babyhood she felt no overpowering affection for him, and after the separation let him go to his Kling grandparents in the proud house with its cupola and oval-topped plate-glass windows. Her petition for divorce was granted in May, 1886, on the grounds of gross neglect of duty, and she was permitted to resume her maiden name. She continued giving piano lessons at fifty cents an hour, renting several rooms in a house on East Center Street a few doors from the stark little Victorian-utility house with its jutting bay window that Tryon had recently built for himself and his family. Although her father ignored her, she often took short trips with her mother and sometimes with her brother Vetallis. When Louisa Kling went to Cincinnati in the winter of 1887 for an eye operation, Flossie went with her. The previous summer Louisa had supplied the money for her to join a Raymond excur-

[1] September 22, 1880, in Prospect, eight miles south of Marion.

sion party to Yellowstone Park. Florence's former husband moved on to Columbus. From time to time he came back to Marion, to the humiliation of his parents. She never saw him again.

In March, 1885, Simon DeWolfe felt forced to insert a notice in the *Star* that H. A. DeWolfe had no authority to collect money in his name. Two months later Pete DeWolfe and two companions, "all somewhat drunk," were arrested for attempting to rob a passenger on the Marion–Columbus train. In July Pete left for Nebraska where he wandered from odd job to odd job and from saloon to saloon. Another year found him returning from Chicago, "to make Marion his home for a while," according to the *Star*. Not long afterward John Lazalere of the Red Bird was arrested for selling liquor "to a person in the habit of getting drunk— Henry DeWolfe." Simon made a final effort the following year to provide for his son's incompetency by setting him up in the tobacco and fruit business in the old post office. Six weeks later found Simon advertising that he was disposing of the stock. Pete again drifted West. He became a railroad brakeman, and on one less-than-sober run fell between the wheels of a freight car and lost an arm. His father agreed to send him money on condition that he stay away from Ohio. In 1894 he was once more in Columbus. That spring, a wasted alcoholic, he returned to Marion to die, his death being charitably certified as due to laryngitis. He was buried in his family's lot in the Marion cemetery, but in an unmarked grave. He was thirty-five years old.

One of Florence's piano pupils was Harding's sister Chat. It was in Tryon's parlor at the old upright piano that she first met the editor of the *Star*, perhaps not wholly by accident. Beneath her unlikely exterior she still kept a susceptible heart, and from her upstairs window she had noticed this handsome young man and marked him down for hers.

When, at the age of twenty-five, Harding met his match in Flossie Kling, he had developed a swatch of gray hair above his forehead and a dusting of white at his temples. The effect was to refine his good looks, even to accentuate his virility. Strolling down Center Street on a morning, he seemed the bull of the herd. Girls were drawn to his blatant maleness. He responded casually and directly. Crudely experienced in the flesh, he had never been in love in any deeply involved emotional sense. Flossie wooed him with all the tenacity she had inherited from her father. His lack of response increased her infatuation. She determined never to let him escape. At first he was affably evasive, but his easygoing personality was no match for her will. Soon it was being gossiped about that Flossie DeWolfe and Warren Harding were keeping company. If he attempted to stray, she was there to check him. When—as he sometimes did—he sneaked off on the afternoon train to visit an old flame in Caledonia, he would find her waiting at the station on his return. Once he glimpsed her from the train window and got off on the other side of the tracks. "You needn't try to run away, Warren Harding," she called out to him through the couplings. "I see your big feet!"

Harding was flattered, if not overpowered, by the attentions of Amos Kling's daughter. For him she represented the pinnacle of that small-town world: wealth, position, assurance. Through her he could foresee the acceptance that had been denied him. He never loved her, but he did not say no to her. In time he would achieve a qualified affection for her, the feeling of reluctant but essential dependence that a bachelor feels in living with his mother.

If Harding had thought that Kling would, however reluctantly, accept him as a son-in-law, he soon learned otherwise. Amos, when he heard the gossip, flew into a fury. Pete DeWolfe had been bad enough, but this newspaper upstart with empty pockets and tainted blood was a thousand times worse. Flossie continued to see Warren and paid no attention to her father's tirades. But when Kling happened to meet Harding in the courthouse, he cursed him out at the top of his voice, called him a nigger, and threatened to blow his head off. Since Kling could not manage his daughter, he took what means of revenge lay at hand. After buying up all of Tryon's debts he could find—notes of seventy-five or a hundred dollars that the doctor had given for his picayune land speculations—he began a series of suits against him. He forbade his wife and sons to have anything to do with Flossie. For the next seven years he would not even nod to his daughter on the street. One of his friends, Bartholomeo Tristram, had been a wedding guest. When the two met shortly afterward, Kling cursed him and denounced their friendship. Any chance he found to thwart Harding, financially or otherwise, he took. In his old age Amos would become sentimentally reconciled to his daughter and son-in-law, but not for another fifteen years would he cross their threshold.

Harding and Flossie sent out their own wedding invitations and were married in the front hall of the house on Mount Vernon Avenue that they themselves had planned and had built by their friend, Captain Jacob Apt.[2] Young George Christian, in his best knickerbocker suit, proudly opened the door for the hundred or so guests. A harpist from Dayton played the "Weddng March." Just before the ceremony, Louisa Kling slipped in the side door unobserved, leaving immediately afterward before even her daughter knew she had been present.

How much Flossie contributed to the house, she always kept secret. Her mother had privately given her money for the furniture. The house was like most of the others on that flat, friendly maple-shaded street—a large, style-less, two-story frame structure trimmed with wooden curlicues, scalloped shingles, and inserts of garish stained glass. A short concrete walk led from the street to a front porch that was just wide enough for

[2] A carpenter and old soldier who in the housing boom after the Civil War became Marion's best-known builder.

a hammock. The door was set off by a long plate-glass window. Inside, oak woodwork sparkled under yellow varnish. Everywhere there was oak: oak balustrades, oak arches, oak fireplaces with mottled green or brown tile trim, oak floors, oak mouldings, oak bookcases, oak furniture, even an oak toilet seat in the single bathroom. From the downstairs hall an archway on the left led to the long combination parlor and sitting room. To the right beyond the staircase the brown-papered dining room absorbed the opalescent glow from a stained-glass central window of intricately worked leaf-and-cherry pattern. Upstairs were four square bedrooms, the edges of their wide-paned windows trimmed with alternating squares of red and yellow glass. Uncompromisingly ugly as its Victorian pattern would seem to the eyes of the next generation, the house was solidly built—the solid middle-class house of the solid middle-class citizen that Harding aspired to be and that he was on his way to becoming.

By the time of Harding's marriage the *Star*, in spite of perennial financial crises, could hold up its head to any county paper. "There is not a daily paper in Ohio published in a town of like population that is half as enterprising or does as much for its town as the Marion *Daily Star* does for Marion," was the comment of the LaRue *News*. The Toledo *Blade*, Ohio's best-known metropolitan evening journal, remarked that "the Marion *Star* publishers continue to get out a splendid paper." On Saturdays the *Star* expanded to eight pages. The *Mirror*—declining in circulation—took over Crawford's vituperative role and in a sensational election edition in November, 1890, denounced the *Star's* politics, comparing the paper to the dogs of Lazarus, "ever ready to lick the sores on the festering carcass of the grand old party." Harding sneered back at the "lickspittle of municipal affairs." He could afford to sneer, for a few months later the hard-pressed *Mirror* was reduced to a semi-weekly, leaving the *Star* as the only weekly paper in the county seat. Harding's old enemy Sweney now abandoned the *Mirror* to the two Thatchers.

In July, 1890, Marion, until then still technically a village, became officially a city. The board of trade, organized as a progressive aftermath, grouped incongruously Harding, Crawford, Vaughan, Amos Kling, Simon DeWolfe, and the Sweney brothers among the other members. There were enough German immigrants in the burgeoning city now to start a weekly paper, *Die Deutsche Presse*.[3] Progress seemed written in the heavens as Marion expanded. By the first of the year the new Huber plant was in operation. "We are getting quite citified," the *Weekly Star* noted. "We have the dime museum necessary to every city; we are to be in a racing

---

[3] The *Presse* was a passionate advocate of minority German-language schools. When Harding opposed such schools in the interest of "a common language," the *Presse* editor denounced him as a Know Nothing.

circuit and see the flyers go in the summer meets; the waterworks are about completed and sewerage—well, it is coming."

For New Year's, 1891, the *Star* requested "various prominent inhabitants" to send in their prophecies for Marion for the coming year. Paved streets and sidewalks, streetcars, a union depot, sewerage, an opera house, a dyke to prevent flooding from Goose Creek, churches, and much else that seemed to Harding landmarks on the path of progress were suggested. Newly-built smokestacks poured out soot, and the smudge was a welcome sign. Stock was being raised for a carpet-sweeper factory and for the Implement Manufacturing Company to make hayrakes. A franchise had been granted for a street railway. Harding announced the facts with pride. He always took a few shares in any new Marion enterprise, paying for them with advertisements in the *Star*. To anyone who, like Harding, had watched a dusty courthouse seat transform itself into a humming little city, progress became a fact of nature. It surrounded him, obvious, as tangible in new paving blocks and asphalt sidewalks as in the increasing pages of the *Star*. His belief in progress was as literal a fundamentalism as his mother's belief in the Old Testament.

With Rhoads taking care of the news and Warwick managing the editorial side, the circulation of the daily *Star* by the spring of 1892 had reached 2,000 copies. Harding still wrote the longer political editorials and attended personally to any attacks on Crawford or the *Mirror*. He still liked to saunter into the composing room, his green eyeshade slanted across his forehead, to lean over the "stone" and take a turn at making up the front page, then wash his hands with a cake of tar soap and dry them on the smeared rag that was the print-shop towel. But the now-established paper took up less of his time, and his interest shifted more and more to politics. Increasingly county printers and politicians coming to Marion found their way up the stairs to the *Star's* editor. He, leaning back in his squeaky swivel chair behind a littered desk, always had time for them. His office walls were emblazoned with lithographs of Lincoln, Grant, Garfield, and Blaine, as well as specimens of *Star* job printing—public sale bills, horse posters, dodgers, and fair notices. On the wall opposite his desk hung a carbon print of Napoleon at the tomb of Frederick the Great. "The greatest man that ever lived," he would tell callers who happened to glance at the print.

His earlier restlessness showed itself in the frequency with which he now used his railroad passes, traveling up and down the state, sometimes with a political goal in mind but as often as not with none. Traveling was to become a vertiginous necessity for him. He crisscrossed Ohio, meeting additional editors and minor party leaders, leaving his amiable impression behind. Harding would always have a capacity for easy, casual friendship. Any Republican meeting or caucus in the county found him present.

Always willing to speak, he began to achieve a small reputation as an orator. People were impressed by the coaxing friendliness of his manner, his young-statesman face, and by the resonant voice and the verbiage it commanded. At a rally at Bellefontaine before the Republican state convention of 1892 he was asked to introduce the "brilliant Foraker." His speeches were full of local pride, patriotic, Republican, jovial. They appealed to audiences conditioned from their own school elocution lessons to appreciate not so much what was said as how it was said. And W. G. could be relied on to make the eagle flutter.

Marion County was so discouragingly Democratic that the Republicans had difficulty in finding candidates willing to let their names be sacrificed on the county ballot. Seven times the Republican County Executive Committee had browbeaten one Jerry Ellmaker into accepting the Republican nomination for county auditor, and seven times Jerry had been, as he called it, "skunked." The eighth time he balked. At the Marion County Republican convention in September, 1892, Crawford, on behalf of the Executive Committee, suggested that the Republicans endorse the Democratic candidate for auditor, Upton R. Guthrie.

Harding, as the young Republican spokesman, challenged Crawford, demanding that the party name a candidate of its own for every office on the ballot. Crawford ironically agreed and offered Ellmaker's old place to Harding. Harding could do no less than accept. He explained afterward in the *Star:*

> To avoid any erroneous impressions it may be well to say that the editor of the *Star* is not seeking to be auditor of Marion County, and is not insanely dreaming of being Auditor Clarke's successor. It was necessary to round out the Republican ticket, and in a vein of humor, the editor of the *Star* was named.

Most of the Democratic leaders had come to dislike Crawford, and increasingly they were shifting the Republican share of the county printing from the *Independent* to the *Star*. Crawford, fearing for his perquisites, felt that this time he had put his rival in a dilemma. Harding would be buried at the election. The *Independent,* by supporting Guthrie, would have first claim on the printing from the auditor's office.

Guthrie was of course overwhelmingly elected, running far ahead of the other Democrats. Harding reserved his venom for Crawford, taking pains to say nothing but kind things of Guthrie—a conciliatory policy he would always follow in dealing with his Democratic adversaries. "It is easy to explain Guthrie's majority," he wrote after the election, "——— he had an easy mark for an opponent."

Harding's defeat was, nevertheless, not a failure for it left him the spokesman of the Marion young Republicans and the *Star* their instrument. Though the Crawfords and the Klings remained implacable, they in turn had their enemies who were glad to side with the young editor. In his late twenties the affable Harding was beginning to appear a potential political figure. His world was expanding. Following the election he made his first trip to Washington, saw the Capitol, and talked with Ohio congressmen and senators. Nationally it was a sad year for the Republicans, with Cleveland emerging from his involuntary retirement of four years before to defeat Harrison for the Presidency. Even in Ohio Harrison carried the state by only 1,072 votes, although in his defeat he was perhaps luckier than he realized in being able to shift the onus of the coming Panic of 1893 onto the massive shoulders of his opponent.

That financial panic and the great unrest that followed—the strikes, riots, and lynchings that swept the large Ohio cities—were muted in the smaller dimensions of Marion. Hard times were there, but no one starved or froze as they did in Chicago and other metropolitan centers. The rural-based city had not the need for the "soup houses" set up in Cleveland and Cincinnati. "Marion has reason to be thankful today," Harding wrote at Thanksgiving, "that the misfortunes of 1893 have touched us so slightly." Though men from the closed-down machine shops tramped the pavements or idled around the courthouse, they were less apparent than the members of the Marion Bicycle Club who scorched the streets as the bicycle fad conquered the country and dust settled on the roller-skating rinks.

During 1893 the *Star* printed regular advertising for the Chicago World's Columbian Exposition—to celebrate the four hundredth anniversary of Columbus's discovery of America—and received a number of complimentary tickets. In the autumn Harding visited the fair, recording his impressions of the White City with its buildings and exhibits and gleaming lagoons. He saw the network of incandescent lights, the great Yerkes telescope, a ten-ton cheese from Canada (the world's largest), and listened over the telephone hookup to a concert from New York. He gaped at the magical Court of Honor and the McMonnies Fountain—like Venice, or at least like photographs of Venice. In the Fine Arts Palace Thomas Hovenden's painting, "Breaking Home Ties," of the country boy leaving his family for the city moved him almost to tears. On Chicago Day, October 9, with nearly a million others, he wandered through the White City, past the great Ferris wheel, down the Midway, and along the lagoons. The progress that he so firmly believed in he found comfortably tangible in the exhibits, a cheering antidote to the depression outside. "The World's Fair is fascinating to me," he told an editorial association group at the Hotel Mecca, "and I derived more profit browsing about the exposition grounds and in the buildings, visualizing concrete things marking the progress of the world, than in the many hours of my school days." He made little mention of the Midway with its Irish Village, Old Vienna, the South Sea Islanders, and the Moorish palace with its "chamber of horrors"; and none at all of the Streets of Cairo. But Harding would not have been Harding if he had missed seeing the sinuous Little Egypt in her hootchy-kootchy dance.

For all his appearance of jovial good health, Harding kept a hazardous balance between his outer and inner being. He complained of heartburn and sudden attacks of indigestion. On so many nights did he send for his father in the weeks following his marriage that Tryon finally persuaded the young couple to come and stay temporarily at the Center Street house. For almost six months Harding and his wife lived under his parents' roof before returning to Mount Vernon Avenue. His home life remained tense. In that barren household Florence either nagged at him or retreated to her bedroom in neurasthenic collapse. By the end of the following year he found himself at the edge of another breakdown. On January 7, 1894, he again entered the Battle Creek Sanitarium, staying until late in February, and then after two months in Marion returning to Battle Creek where he remained until autumn.

Florence Harding loved her husband, but her opinion of his business ability was not high. For a long time she had been dinning it into him that he was not getting the money out of the *Star's* circulation that he should. While he was away at Battle Creek, the circulation manager quit. The next morning Flossie rode down to the *Star* office on her bicycle and announced that she was taking over. "I went down there intending to help out for a few days," she wrote, "and I stayed fourteen years." She was her father's daughter, autocratic and efficient. With her shrewd, directing mind she soon brought system to that casually conducted office. Her health improved with her busyness. She reorganized the delivery service. Her boys were drilled and supervised—she was even known to spank an occasional recalcitrant. Under her command there was no delivery of the *Star* after the second week if the ten-cent weekly subscription had not been paid. She kept a sharp eye on the small change that her husband had not bothered to watch. "No pennies escaped her," Warwick wrote. "They may have disappeared before her advent, but none got away and none was unaccounted for after she took over the management of the newsboys. She took them home from day to day, and after the accumulation reached bankable size it was carried downtown and banked. I have seen W. G. marching down to the bank with a gallon of pennies in either hand. I was always curious to know how many pennies made a gallon, but never found out." [4]

[4] Samuel Hopkins Adams, William Allen White, Norman Thomas—a former *Star* delivery boy—and others have managed to create the impression that Florence Harding made the *Star,* that she walked into the office when it was moribund and by

"Duchess," Harding began to call his wife not long after his return from Battle Creek, and the odd nickname somehow suited this domineering female with the burred voice. Yet, wherever he had picked it up, he applied it not wholly with affection. Something in the term suggested an unspoken protest—and the name stuck. If the Duchess had inherited her father's business ability, she had also inherited his bluntness. Perhaps her lack of tact was inherent in her deficiency as a female. When she and Harding attended a banquet in Columbus to celebrate his election as lieutenant governor, the staff of the *Star* gathered to welcome and congratulate them on their return. She eyed them coldly, thinking less of their good fellowship than of the pay raise of fifty cents or a dollar a week that they had come to expect at the end of each year. "You needn't look for a raise this time," she rasped at them. "That little show cost us $1,300."

In the spring interval before his return to Battle Creek Harding was able to deal the *Independent* so telling a blow that it never really recovered when he caught Crawford brassily swindling the city on official printing. Until 1893 Marion's public printing had been a perquisite of the *Mirror* for so long that the editors had come to regard it as a right. Crawford had always received a large enough minority share to keep him quiet. The printing was handed out privately by the city clerk without bids or discussion at the rate of a dollar a square of print. Ordinary commercial advertising then sold in Marion for ten cents a square. Month after month for several years the *Star's* editorial pages had been denouncing the printing sinecure. Finally in May, 1893, the city council voted to let the city printing through contract bids. Harding's bid for this advertising was thirty-three cents a square. The *Independent* offered twenty-three cents a square for the first insertion and eleven-and-a-half cents for each additional one. Its bid was accepted, and Crawford was able to announce himself the Official City Printer.

When the new legal notices began to appear in the *Independent*, Harding took to measuring them with his make-up rule. After some months of comparing them with the bills submitted to the clerk's office,

---

her energy and business shrewdness transformed it into a successful daily. Actually the *Star* was already a going concern before she arrived. Although she did bring a needed system to its distribution, the paper would have continued its successful growth without her. Undoubtedly one of her reasons for staying was to keep an eye on her husband. But in those days a woman in an office was a novelty. "It was this conspicuousness, perhaps," Mark Sullivan wrote, "that gave rise to the legend that the active and aggressive and talkative woman who bustled about the *Star* office was the source of much of its growth, and of Harding's. Passers-by on the street had seen, on a thousand hot summer afternoons, Harding's outstretched feet reposing on the window sill of the editorial sanctum on the second floor, and an equal number of times had seen Mrs. Harding chattering at the newsboys whom she managed in the first-floor office. From the contrast, some had deduced incorrect conclusions."

he determined that Crawford had been regularly overcharging the city by seven to ten cents a square—a matter of several hundred dollars in the course of a year. After Crawford got wind of what Harding was up to, he denounced his rival with the old vituperation. "Kick a skunk and be perfumed with its villainous odor," he wrote of Harding; and of the *Star:*

> That odorous sheet is filled with accounts of every family quarrel its editor can get hold of. Every scandal is aired with particularity. Gossip of the meanest kind finds place in its columns. The sanctity of the Sabbath is sneered at and the religious sentiment of the country is defied and scorned in its nasty columns. And yet people will read the dirty bantling and allow their children to read it and when their children go to bad they whine and cry over the natural result of allowing their children to read moral filth.
>
> While pretending to be a Republican, it will meanly twist figures and call statements false which are true, to defend the party which gave *Mephetis Americana* (sic) its life blood, and which yet maintains it.

Harding retorted by accusing Crawford flatly of "robbing and stealing" in regard to city advertising and gave figures to prove it. Crawford tried to disregard the proofs:

> We do not care to bandy filthy lying epithets with the moral leper who edits the *Star.* His heart, mind, blood, and flesh form a mass of corruption. No one who differs from him in any respect escapes his slanderous attacks. Some of the best men in the city have been assailed by him in the coarsest and most brutal manner.
>
> When called to account personally, he whines about his illness, as if that was the fault of others. In politics he shows the real "yaller dog" that he is unless he can have his own way. The matter the Slop Bucket editor refers to was but a mistake of ours in figuring. . . .

The *Mirror,* smugly detached, attempted irony:

> The *Star* a day or so ago read the *Mirror* a lecture on its lack of "newspaper courtesy," and the very next day called the *Independent* a "lickspittle organ" and its editor a "lying thief." Brother Harding is a nice young man —and we like him—and he is smart too— most too smart. He talks so much about "newspaper ethics" and makes such nice distinctions between "journalists" and "newspapermen" that we are bewildered at times—but as we said before we like him—we do for a fact. All he needs to do is to tone down the estimate he puts on himself. Not too much of course because he is a smart young man and his abilities should not be underestimated, even by himself.

From Battle Creek Harding replied, unruffled, with the assurance of a poker player who knows he holds the winning hand, twitting the "esteemed organs" at their unhappiness because the one had been caught with its fingers in the municipal till and the other was losing its "city pull."

As a result of his exposure, the *Independent*—"that obscure journal" as he now called it—lost its city printing contract, and on June 3 the *Star* was at last able to display on its masthead: Official City Paper.

Harding had scarcely returned to the *Star* in the autumn before he was caught up in another town dispute that nearly sent him back to the sanitarium. After years of bickering, the city council had finally voted to lay the dust of Marion's chief thoroughfares. The Marion firm of Coleman & Hallwood, Harding's friendly advertiser, received the contract for paving Center and Main streets. But before the first block had been laid, the Canton Shale Brick Company protested the contract award, claiming that the Marion firm was not the lowest bidder and that its Wassal-Hallwood paving block was inferior to the Canton brick product. Concealed by the legal camouflage of J. J. Hane, a Marion lawyer, two of the larger shareholders of the Canton Brick, Amos Kling and Edward Huber, were manipulating the suit.

Hane found a straw man, Lewis Gunn, to bring the injunction in his name. Gunn, a former soldier living on a pension, had a small house strategically located on the corner of Center and Main streets. Householders living on the streets were to be assessed 2 per cent of the paving costs semi-annually for five years. Gunn claimed in his petition that it would work him irreparable damage to pay his share of these costs. The *Star* ridiculed a dependent pensioner, a man who had taken an oath that he was unable to support himself, bringing suit as a suffering taxpayer. Harding pointed out editorially that Gunn's total tax assessment for paving would be $16.30, and wondered why it was necessary to retain two prominent law firms to fight an improvement costing so little. "Mr. Lewis Gunn," Harding appealed to him: "Let us all live in peace and hurry the paving. We need it so very badly. The *Star* feared it might be wrong in suggesting your motive of injunction, thought perhaps the cost of an injunction might work an irreparable injury to you. A public official . . . fixes your paving tax at $1.63 for semi-annual payment for five years. That is outrageously high, of course. But we are for peace and for paving, so we propose to you that if you will withdraw your unpopular injunction suit the *Star* will pay in cash, now, your paving tax. . . . Come, now, we are in earnest. . . . This proposition is not made in the spirit of charity, but for peace and paving. We jingle the coin while we wait for your answer. We don't believe the Canton brick kickers can get another man to sign the petition if you will pull off. Are you with us, Mr. Gunn?"

Gunn's reply was to announce that he was going down to the *Star* to "clean out the office." The tall but short-tempered ex-soldier arrived in the afternoon bustle just as the last proofs were being rushed to the press. Followed by his older brother, he stormed into the upstairs office and—according to his later and expurgated version of the conversation—told the editor: "You must stop this abuse of me or take the consequences." Harding, with the desk between them, called him a tool of Huber and Kling. He called Harding a damned liar and picked up a chair. Harding grabbed a poker. Tryon, who several months earlier had rented a cubby-hole office across the hall, was paring his nails with his jackknife when he heard the shouting. Always more pugnacious than his son, he dashed into the editor's office, knife in hand. Gunn swung, while he stabbed. In spite of three slashed fingers, the much larger Gunn pummeled Tryon into a corner while his brother threatened Harding. Members of the *Star* staff dashed upstairs, and soon fists and chairs were flying. The fight ended when Charlie Kramer, the head job printer, knocked Gunn out with a shower of blows. By the time a constable arrived the office was strewn with broken glass and furniture, Gunn had one black eye and Tryon two. The Gunn brothers were arrested, bound over, and released when Hane furnished $500 bond.

The next day the *Mirror* noted primly:

> The little unpleasantness in the *Star* sanctum yesterday, with its incidental thumps, broken chairs, cuts, bruises, and bloody noses, ought to have been avoided. It was the result of offensive personalities indulged in by the *Star* that might well have been omitted. That kind of newspaper work don't pay. It lowers the standard of journalism and besides its unsafe. You never can tell how soon some fellow with blood in his eye will drop in, and insist on cracking your skull to even things up. A soft answer not only turneth away wrath but saves us a peck of trouble very often besides.

"*Kitchen Oracle*"; "The *Slander Monger* or *Star*," Crawford jeered. "As a journalist we have always felt it our duty to shut up this foul slanderer's mouth that our citizens might be freed from being befouled by his villainously low billingsgate and fish-woman tirades. To do this will require the use of very filthy gloves to handle the *Slop Bucket*. . . . Frequently we have kept the jackal from being severely cowhided by advising parties, who had been outraged through his dirty columns, to desist as he would only plead the baby act to gain sympathy, as was the case in which Mr. Gunn was interested."

When Harding, mellowed with success as the editor of the only surviving Republican paper in a prosperous and growing town, was beginning to rise in the political world, he wrote a creed for the *Star* that he distributed to each of his employees:

> Remember there are two sides to every question. Get them both.
>   Be truthful. Get the facts.
>   Mistakes are inevitable, but strive for accuracy. I would rather have one story exactly right than a hundred half wrong.
>   Be decent, be fair, be generous.
>   Boost, don't knock.

There's good in everybody. Bring out the good and never needlessly hurt the feelings of anybody.

In reporting a political gathering, give the facts. Tell the story as it is, not as you would like to have it. Treat all parties alike. If there is any politics to be played, we will play it in our editorial columns.

Treat all religious matters reverently.

If it can possibly be avoided, never bring ignominy to an innocent man, woman, or child in telling of the misdeeds or misfortunes of a relative.

Don't wait to be asked, but do it without asking, and above all be clean and never let a dirty word or suggestive story get into type.

I want this paper so conducted that it can go into any home without destroying the innocence of any child.[4]

Such pieties, suitable for framing, were often found on office walls with scarcely more relevance to daily living than the Ten Commandments. Certainly the *Star* was not hampered by rules in its last engagements with the *Independent*. "As was expected," Harding jeered at Crawford in return, "the lickspittle organ gives a report of the disturbance at the *Star* office that is a collection of fabrications and misrepresentations from beginning to end. We expected little else from the lying thief who was detected in robbing the city, and admitted the robbery but claimed it was an inadvertence. We do not care, anyhow. The senile organ has so manifestly lost prestige and circulation that a lie in its columns might as well be buried."

Harding had never been free or handy with his fists, and the set-to unnerved him. Senator, his Newfoundland, had grown so old and lame and mangy that Harding regretfully had him shot.[5] Not long after the "little unpleasantness" he acquired the more aggressive Jumbo, a cross between a sledge dog and a mastiff. No Gunn would ever cross the threshold with Jumbo watching at the door! Harding loved the dog, as he loved all animals. He even wrote an editorial about him. It was the sort of subject that stimulated his pen. When Jumbo had been there eight years, someone poisoned him. Harding knew that whoever had poisoned the dog would have preferred to poison the man, and for a long time he could not get over the thought that Jumbo had suffered for his master.

[4] Mark Sullivan, who spent some time in Marion as a correspondent in 1920, maintained that the *Star's* "Creed" was a piece of propaganda concocted by the then editor, George Van Fleet, for the presidential campaign of that year.

[5] Harding was always tender with animals. One of the haunting memories of his childhood was of the death of his black-and-tan mongrel. His great-uncle Perry had come over to complain that the dog had been mangling his sheep, and Tryon in the barn had told him to do as he pleased with the animal. "I saw Uncle Perry reach down and take my dog by the hind legs, one in each hand," Harding wrote almost half a century later. "Then he whirled the terrified animal about his head and dashed its head against the side of the corn crib. I can feel the horror of it yet."

Jumbo was succeeded by Hub, a Boston terrier, who followed Harding to work each day and stayed a number of years in the office until he, too, fell to a dog poisoner. Harding composed a eulogistic editorial on Hub's death that, though it owed its unacknowledged inspiration to Sen. George Vest's *Eulogy on the Dog*, was an apt fusion of his own emotions and literary style:

> Edgewood Hub in the register as a mark of his breeding, [he wrote] but to us just Hub, a little Boston terrier, whose sentient eye mirrored the fidelity and devotion of his loyal heart. The veterinary said he was poisoned; perhaps he was—his mute sufferings suggested it. One is reluctant to believe that a human being that claims man's estate could be so hateful a coward as to ruthlessly torture and kill a trusting victim, made defenseless through his confidence in a human master, but there are such. One honest look from Hub's trusting eyes was worth a hundred lying greetings from such inhuman beings, though they wore the habiliment of men.

In the aftermath of the Gunn encounter Harding grew more conscious than ever of his ailments. Rather than return to Battle Creek, in January, 1895, he took a trip with the Duchess to Florida. It was the first of many such trips to various parts of the United States. Now that he was able to leave the *Star* in competent hands for longer periods, he traveled endlessly and indiscriminately over the next two decades—to Florida, Texas, Wyoming, the Great Lakes, to New England and Nova Scotia, to the Caribbean, Hawaii, and finally Europe. These flights from himself were made possible in his earlier years by the free railroad and steamship passes that he acquired in exchange for advertisements. Harding's *Star* correspondence is dotted with requests for additional travel passes.

In Florida the Hardings first stayed at the Indianola House on Merritt Island, fifty miles south of Daytona Beach. Some years before a small colony of Marionites had established a refuge there against the Ohio winter. Harding's friend and next-door neighbor, Colonel Christian, at whose house he often dropped in evenings to play parcheesi, used to leave his crushed-stone business in Marion for the island at the beginning of each new year, and it was he who had persuaded Harding to make the trip. The Colonel with his family also stayed at the Indianola House. Not far away, at the Wallace Villa—belonging to a Marion banker—were Florence's brother Clifford, his wife, and the bachelor Vetallis. The Kling boys were fond of their sister and, removed from their implacable father, were willing to be friendly with Harding. Often the two families joined up for trips and beach parties.

Even in Florida 1895 was a chill winter. Harding wrote to the *Star* that a cold snap of six degrees below freezing had destroyed much of the fruit and vegetable crops. Not until April did he return for the county Republican convention. During his absence the old Music Hall had been demolished and the *Mirror* had again changed hands. The new *Mirror* proprietor was a newspaperman from Zanesville, George L. Padgett, and with his editorship the personal feud with Harding ended. Ned Thatcher soon afterward started up a rival weekly, the *Dollar Democrat,* in which he continued to attack the *Star* editor with alcoholic virulence, in one issue printing a silhouette of Harding and explaining in a caption that because of the color of the subject he could not reproduce the features. On seeing this black caricature Harding threatened to kill Thatcher, although his innate dread of physical combat kept him from doing more than threaten. Tryon, in spite of his size, was never so hesitant about using his fists. Shortly after the silhouette appeared, as he was passing the Kling house, Amos coming down the walk mouthed "nigger" at him and Tryon knocked the larger man to the ground.

For a period of several months after the Democrats had taken over City Hall, Thatcher managed to get hold of Marion's legal printing for his *Dollar Democrat.* Not so fortunate was Sam Hume, who returned from his popcorn exploits in Chicago to launch the Marion *Astonisher,* "devoted to society" and bearing the motto TRUTH on its masthead. The new paper, a tabloid before its time, astonished for half-a-dozen issues before it disappeared in the wake of a criminal libel suit.

On April 1 George H. Van Fleet came to the *Star* with the compliments of the *Mirror* to take charge of the advertising department. Harding now began working on something he had long had in mind, an industrial edition of the *Star,* illustrated with halftone cuts of all the Marion enterprises and industries, to show the growth of the county seat from a village to a city and the promise of future growth. In the middle of this project he had another crisis of "nerves" and on May 12 returned to Battle Creek. The attack was brief and he was able to be back in his office before the industrial edition appeared on June 15. That thirty-two-page supplement with a glowing front-page lithograph in color of the idealized city was the most ambitious publishing effort yet to appear in Marion County. Every achievement was chronicled, from the newest machine works to an illustration of the proposed new Opera House austerely conceived behind a pilastered classical façade. Whatever might be whispered about Harding, everyone had to admit that he had made a remarkable achievement with his *Star* in a little over ten years. Editorial compliments poured in from all over Ohio. "A great paper," the Cardington *Independent* agreed. "At the head of Marion County papers," seconded the Prospect *Monitor,* while the Wadsworth *Banner* praised the *Star* as "one of the spiciest local dailies in the state, if not the very best." "Cannot be too highly appreciated by Marion's people," thought the editor of the Upper Sandusky *Chief.* And from beyond the state boundaries the Chester, Pennsylvania, *Times* wished "long life and prosperity to the *Star,*" even as the Battle

Creek *Daily Journal* found "Brother Harding the publisher, an adept at newspaper work, and this magnificent edition adds another to the laurels won by him."

On his return from the Chicago Exposition, Harding had bought his first linotype machines. Novelties in the way of machinery always appealed to him enough to keep his paper's debt constant. With the *Star's* position consolidated as Marion's leading newspaper, Harding's editorial tone grew more benign even as his physical appearance began to shape itself into the pattern of the frock-coated McKinley image. The *Star* plant was a loyal, friendly, and happy one. Harding always paid above, if not excessively above, the going wage. Almost never did he discharge anyone.

While the *Star* expanded, Tryon continued to vegetate in the office across the hall from his son. On first moving in, he had partitioned off a cubbyhole as a consulting room and had the single window facing Center Street lettered in gilt, GEORGE T. HARDING M.D. "A hoorah's nest," a young reporter of the early staff described the frowzy interior. A congoleum rug, chipped at the edges and its pattern almost worn away, covered the floor. On the wall, flanking a roll-top desk littered with medical-supply catalogues, hung lithographs of Lincoln and Betsy Ross. Next to the window stood a rocking chair with a broken cane seat. Dust lay over everything, including a couple of old coats on the window sill. "I remember," the young reporter wrote years afterward to Samuel Hopkins Adams, "there was a shabby, sagging sofa in the inside office where he held his consultations. The old boy would often bed down on that for the night with his long overcoat thrown over him. I don't think he ever had much of a practice: mostly old people, and farmers and their families who stopped in from their Saturday marketing. He was slow and kind and patient. He could look wise. With his experience I expect he was plenty competent to handle most of the cases that came his way. But he didn't strike my youthful eyes as very antiseptic."

On the side Tryon sold insurance and still plotted his jigsaw real-estate deals. Occasionally his son ran a hopeful notice that Doctor George T. Harding was giving "exclusive attention to the general practice of medicine." The bulk of the family income derived from Phoebe who, according to a periodic *Star* announcement, gave "especial attention to treatment of women at their homes. Hygienic and Electric Baths with marked curative and restorative effects, with the pronounced advantages of Sanitarium practice, at home and at moderate cost."

Phoebe, after decades of delivering babies, had taken to calling herself a doctor. Until 1896, when the legislature passed a Medical Practice Act, anyone in Ohio who wished to take the title of doctor and practice medicine needed only to register with the nearest probate court. There were no educational requirements. Following the passage of the act, those engaged in the practice of medicine were required to set down their qualifications for the newly established State Medical Board. Tryon received a license from the board on the strength of his Homeopathic Hospital diploma. In July, 1896, Phoebe applied for a license as a "legal practitioner," on the basis of "having spent twenty-five years in the practice of medicine, studying under G. T. Harding, M.D." She asked to be classed as "homeopathic," [6] and gave Doctor A. Rhee and Doctor John Martin of Marion as references. On being granted her license she began to refer to herself as a specialist in obstetrics and children's diseases.

While Tryon napped in his back office, and Phoebe delivered babies and treated infants for the croup, their younger children were growing up. Daisy was among the ten graduates of Marion High School in 1894. A year later George Tryon, Jr., received his diploma, demonstrating—with a certain confusion of number—in his graduation address that "one of the greatest existing injuries to the working man is labor organizations." The Deacon, his classmates had nicknamed him for his solemn adherence to the Seventh-day Adventist tenets. Of all the Harding children he was the most pious, the most influenced by his mother. By the time he finished high school, everyone, even his brother, called him Deac. Mary Harding, through her older brother's nascent political influence, was in 1896 appointed a kindergarten teacher with a salary of $400 a year at the Ohio Institution for the Education of the Blind in Columbus, where she herself had been educated. Her faulty sight had deteriorated as she grew older, so that by the time she reached adolescence she was purblind and had had to leave Marion for the Columbus school. A gentle, sad-faced girl, she had the darkest complexion of all that brunette family.

Eighteen ninety-six saw the end of both the *Dollar Democrat* and the *Independent*. Crawford, old and tired, had watched his paper's advertising melt away, his circulation shrink. With another winter at hand, he felt he had had enough. On December 8, after thirty-four years as editor, he published his last issue. Kling took the *Independent's* demise as his opportunity. Although careful to cover his traces, he became one of the chief financial backers of the Marion Publishing Company that took over the *Independent,* and with a capital stock of $20,000 launched the daily *Republican Transcript.* A trained newspaperman, George E. Kelley, came on from Washington as editor. Harding angrily charged in the *Star* that Kling and his county committee associates had begun the new paper in an effort to destroy him. Kelley replied:

> The *Star* has been saying to its advertisers that the *Transcript* was started to ruin its proprietor, because Amos Kling desired it, that he was support-

[6] Chat Harding wrote in 1930 that her mother spent a term studying at the Cleveland Homeopathic College about 1882, but Phoebe in her application to the Medical Board stated that she "did not attend any courses of instruction at a medical institute."

ing the *Transcript* for the purpose of beating a son-in-law objectionable to him for reasons expressed to him on the street and elsewhere. The advertising man of the *Transcript* meets this talk everywhere and it has been a sweet morsel under the tongue of the *Star* staff ever since the starting of the *Daily Transcript*. It is the desire of the *Transcript* to correct this error and to prove that the lie of the *Star* is a known and wilful one. Amos Kling never owned a share of stock in the Marion Publishing Company, the owner of the weekly and daily *Transcript*, never loaned the company a dollar and has no interest therein, direct or indirect, so far as the Marion Publishing Company knows.

The *Transcript* was started because the Republican field was not occupied by the *Star*. The *Star* pretended to publish an independent daily, without a partisan predilection and fear, and a Republican weekly. . . . The *Star* would not do it, and now when its Republicanism was to be tried, it flunked and joined the Democracy, being one out of two dailies in this state, owned by Republicans, which proved a traitor to its party.

For all its funds, and the talents of its city-trained reporters, its flourishes and metropolitan airs, the *Transcript* was not a success. No outside editor could have Harding's personal concern and his intimate knowledge of Marion byways. Above all, the new paper represented the defensive older group of entrenched Republicans. Harding with the *Star* had come to speak for the young Republicans, the challengers, restive against the reins held by stubborn, liver-spotted hands. As Harding's political sun rose, the *Transcript* slipped below the horizon.

In February, 1897, Harding and his Duchess were again in Florida, courtesy of the Florida East Coast Railway. Back at the Indianola House with his old friends, he came down with the grippe in spite of the sunshine and was in bed for several days. When he had recovered he moved on to Daytona Beach where, he wrote Colonel Christian, he was staying with their friends the MacMurrays and "enjoying the facilities" of the Daytona Yacht Club. After his return from Florida he paid another, if briefer, visit to Battle Creek. The end of May found him again at his desk.

More embarrassing and potentially damaging to Harding than the comet's trail of the *Transcript* was the disaster that overtook his mother in the summer. On Friday morning, July 18, Phoebe was called in by Thomas Jefferson Osborne—in spite of the eloquence of his name, merely the local fish and meat dealer—to treat his ten-month-old son Dudley who had come down with diarrhea and vomiting. Phoebe diagnosed the illness as "cholera infantum" and gave him a powder of "lacti-pepsin and carbo vegetables." After being given the pepsin the child fell into a deep sleep. When by afternoon his baby could still not be awakened, the frightened Osborne sent again for Phoebe. After examining the child, she thought it seemed under the influence of an opiate and called Tryon. Since the baby would not wake, Tryon brought in Doctor Charles E. Sawyer, his diminutive younger homeopathic colleague and recent founder of the Sawyer Sanitorium "for the treatment of Nervous and Mental Diseases" at White Oaks Farm two miles south of Marion. By evening the child seemed out of danger.

Next day, however, little Dudley went into spasms. Sunday morning he died. When Osborne realized that his son was dying, he took one of the pepsin powders to a druggist who tested it and said that it contained morphine, though not in sufficient quantity to cause death. Osborne next day accused Phoebe of having killed the baby through her negligence. She denied that there was morphine in the pepsin, pointing out that she had given doses from the same bottle to other children without any harm coming to them.

With the Osborne baby's death, the Hardings were in a panic. The *Star's* reaction was hysterical, denouncing the morphine story as "rank idiocy or dangerous lunacy." Harding even went so far as to suggest that Osborne's mother might have drugged the child. The day after the funeral Osborne wrote to the *Transcript:*

> I desire to say through the columns of the *Transcript* that my heart is too sad at present to answer the statements in Monday's *Star,* yet I feel it my duty to defend my mother from any false accusation. I never did nor do I now entertain the insane idea that my mother would conspire with anyone to kill my beloved child. I feel that the statement was made merely to lower me in the eyes of the people. I will leave the truth of it to be judged by the people themselves. The other statements will be answered later on.

Feeling was sharp against Phoebe, and for a few days it seemed that the Hardings' medical practice was in ruins and Warren's career indirectly marred. But Doctor Sawyer, from the respectable background of his sanitorium, pronounced the death as owing to a brain fever "that often develops from cholera infantum." He did not say that there was no morphine in the pepsin powder, but he assured the public that the baby had not died from the effects of the drug. "This statement," even the *Transcript* admitted, "from a man of Doctor Sawyer's ability and standing in the community relieves Mrs. Harding from all responsibility in the affair."

The Osborne misadventure passed over more easily than the Hardings had expected. Phoebe quietly resumed her practice. Harding a few weeks later joined a group of editors on a chartered boat trip up the Detroit and St. Clair rivers to Georgian Bay. When at one point the boat stopped near a Canadian Indian reservation, it was Harding who got up a scrub team of editors to play the Indians in baseball. That same year a half-page sketch of the *Star* editor appeared in the *Portrait and Biographical Record of Marion County*. True, Harding had had to pay for the insertion, but at least it was there as one more sign of his growing reputation. Outside papers continued to hail him as "a clever gentleman and able editor, . . . a faithful and untiring Republican worker." His silver voice with its cheer-fully polysyllabic phraseology became more and more in demand at local functions.[7] His silver hair gave him the air of an incipient statesman; and the Duchess had tidied him up, doing her relentlessly nagging best to make him look the part.

His world, the world now of editors and politicians, was expanding. He had come to know the state political leaders, reported local speeches by party orators, received Republican campaign advertising. And he was becoming known. Foraker, the magic-tongued, had not forgotten the young editor's bright-worded introduction on the platform at Bellefon-taine. "I trust you will be able to come to the convention with the right kind of delegation," Fire Engine Joe wrote him in April, 1895. Two years later, after Mark Hanna had outmaneuvered Bryan and his free-silver crusaders to put the gold-plated McKinley in the White House and had claimed his reward of a United States Senate seat, his secretary was writing to say that the Senator would see Harding at any time.

At the close of 1897 the *Star* had grown to eight daily pages with four more added on Saturday. International and national news from the Asso-ciated Press filled the front page. An increase of young reporters took care of the local news on the inside pages, covering all Marion happenings and accidents, lodge meetings, church and school events, and the rest. Van Fleet, a more aggressive type than Warwick, had been taking over more and more of the editorial supervision of the paper. Whenever Harding was away he now, to Warwick's silent chagrin, left Van Fleet in charge.

The year's end saw the rise of war sentiment in the country, roused by William Randolph Hearst's assiduously circulated reports of Spanish brutality in Cuba. Traditional anti-monarchical feeling combined with outrage at a Spanish colonialism functioning so callously close to the borders of the United States. Men who had forgotten what war was, now began to demand it again. Yet Harding did not join the jingo press in the agitation against Spain. Even after the battleship *Maine* was blown up in Havana Harbor, on February 15, 1898, the *Star* continued to suggest that keeping cool was a good idea and quoted Senator Hanna's observation that the destruction of the *Maine* might have been an accident. As the

---

[7] Typical of these growing requests was that of the mayor of Milford Center asking Harding to be the orator at their 1895 Fourth-of-July celebration. "We want an up-to-date young man," he wrote, "who can make a rattling good 30-minute speech. From what our people saw of you at Bellefontaine two years ago we believe you are the man."

war clouds gathered over Cuba while the belligerent Hearst kept goading the non-belligerent McKinley, the *Star* still maintained that this was "not a time for nervous excitement."

Nevertheless, with war apparently inevitable and the President's War Message only four days away, Harding capped his newspaper successes by gearing in with the Scripps-McRae Press Association. "Over our own wire," the *Star* boasted, "we now get the telegraphic news of the world smoking hot, in fact fairly sizzling from the griddle of the world's affairs. . . . Marion is served with the highest-grade news service that goes to any afternoon paper in the land."

The cost was six times that of the Associated Press service—which Harding still kept—but the outbreak of hostilities proved it was worth it. A few weeks before, the *Star's* daily circulation was about 2,300. By May, with the population of Marion inching above 10,000, the war increased the paper to over 3,350 copies, with almost 5,000 for the Saturday edition. In towns of Marion's size a daily paper rarely circulated as many as 1,000 copies, but the *Star* had more than doubled that number and was now being read in a score of neighboring towns. With banner headlines, photographs replacing sketches, and direct-wire news "at points of vantage from London to Hong Kong," the *Star* had become a small metropolitan paper.

William Jennings Bryan, erstwhile champion of populism and free silver, was now in a blue uniform astride a black horse commanding a regiment of Nebraska volunteers. Harding's patriotic enthusiasm was not so martial. He had inherited none of his father's zest for soldiering—Tryon was trying to volunteer again as a doctor—but he did his best to encourage the others. Marion's Company G of the Fourteenth Regiment of the Ohio National Guard was being recruited to full strength for service in Cuba, and the *Star* greeted each new day with: "Good morning, have you enlisted?"

On Sunday, April 24, Company G—still the boys in blue, since new-issue khaki uniforms had not yet arrived—paraded from the armory to attend service at the Baptist Church wearing red badges that read To Hell with Spain. Two days later, at eight thirty in the morning, Company G, led by its mascot Sport, an Irish setter, marched from the armory down Center Street to the railroad station behind the People's—now called the Citizens'—Band to the tune of "The Girl I Left Behind Me." The bell in the Corinthian courthouse rang out above the young men as they marched, just as the old Ionic courthouse's bell had rung for their fathers in 1861. In the foot-tapping music, in the crowds lining the sidewalks, in the women dabbing their eyes with their handkerchiefs, there were the same obvious sentiments, the same sentimentality, and beneath everything else the same ultimate poignancy that are always there when men march away.

Brief as the war was, it had consolidated the *Star's* position. Circulation never again sank below 3,500. Harding might remain in debt for web presses, linotype machines, and other equipment he could not resist buying, but the *Star* was established among the Ohio dailies. With Van Fleet occupying the editor's desk in Harding's absence, Warwick, hurt and disappointed, made up his mind to leave. He wrote Harding that he felt he was getting stale at his work even though there had been "many delightful days that cannot be forgotten." He admitted that he had hoped to become editorial head of the *Star* "with authority subordinate only to your own," and he spoke of his need of earning more money. The following spring he left Marion to become a reporter and paragrapher for the Toledo *Blade*. Yet, in spite of his disappointments and the buried bitter thought that he had given up his initial partnership in the *Star* for a few hundred promissory dollars, he never lost his feelings of friendship and affection for Harding.

After Crawford's retirement, time had begun to erode Harding's other enemies of the Sherman vintage on the Republican County Committee. As in the rest of Ohio, most Marion Republicans were divided between Cincinnati's Foraker and Mark Hanna, "the Red Boss of Cleveland." Foraker, twice governor and at the height of his power, had in the spring of 1895 so thoroughly packed the Republican state convention at Zanesville in order to force the nomination for governor of Asa S. Bushnell that the convention became known as the "Zanesville Rout." Bushnell, a wealthy farm-implement manufacturer, had financed and managed Foraker's campaign for governor in 1885. Awed by the dynamic Foraker, he aped his mannerisms and appearance, grooming his white hair in the same theatrical manner and wearing a drooping white Foraker mustache. He continued to express his admiration more practically by large contributions to Foraker's political ventures. After his election he gratefully cracked the whip over the Republican legislature that elected Foraker to the United States Senate. Inwardly Harding sided with Foraker, but he aimed to make no enemies in the Hanna camp. "The *Star* has neither assailed nor opposed Senator Hanna," Harding wrote in 1898. "It has simply declined to abuse the opposition to him." Harding's thought, his invariable political reaction was always to get two warring party factions to combine for an immediate goal. "Harmonizing," he called it, and over the years it became his favorite expression—as verb, adjective, or noun. Lacking the ruthless self-confidence necessary for a boss or a leader, he saw himself as the affable middle man, the third party who brings two bargainers together, breaks the tension by the latest traveling salesman joke, suggests a compromise, and then takes the two off to have a drink.

Harding's ear was always close to the political grass roots, so close, in fact, that he could hear the grass grow. With middle age approaching he sensed that if he was to move forward politically, it must be soon or never. Marion County was hopelessly Democratic. He had learned that lesson in his defeat for auditor. Marion City Hall remained in control of his Republican enemies, still determined and still able to shut the doors to him.

There remained only the alternative of the state senate. Although Marion County stayed mulishly Democratic, the 13th Senatorial District— composed of Marion, Hardin, Logan, and Union counties—was Republican. Ohio senators were elected every other year, and by 13th-District custom each county in rotation was given the chance of nominating its choice. Marion's turn, after the usual eight-year interval, came in 1899, and Harding determined to become the Republican candidate of that year. He consulted first with one of the Young Republican leaders, Grant E. Mouser, a Marion lawyer. Mouser agreed to defy the City Hall clique and support him.

On July 5, 1899, a week before the meeting of the Republican County convention, Harding announced his decision in the *Star:*

> I am a candidate for the Republican nomination for state senator in the 13th District. There has been no formal announcement of this previously, but the current rumor seems to have been well founded and my chances have been thought of importance enough to set to work a system of organized misrepresentation that would make me wonder that I have not been drummed out of the Republican camp, did I not know that the good, hard sense of the people will reveal the true inwardness of the matter.
>
> As a candidate I would like to be considered on merit—on availability, capacity, and deserts as a Republican who has cared to be only a private in the ranks and has stayed there through thick and thin. Some of this may seem unseemly through the lack of modesty, but the drift of the campaign has been to promote a factionalism rather than contemplate candidates on their merits, and I prefer the latter. . . .
>
> I have not thought the senatorial contest serious enough to involve a bitter fight. My own candidacy shall not be promoted by any plan that involves a conscienceless attack on other aspirations. . . . I am a candidate until the Republicans of Marion County express their preferences at next week's caucuses.

The Kenton *News-Republican* greeted "the polished and pushing editor of the Marion *Star,* . . . candidate for the nomination for state senator in this district . . . an enthusiastic Republican, a most agreeable gentleman. If the nomination is to go to Marion County it can fall on none worthier than Warren G. Harding." There were kind words from the Mt. Gilead *Register,* the Bellefontaine *Index,* the Cardington *Independent,* the Mansfield *News,* the Fostoria *Times.* Even the reconstituted *Mirror* recognized

Harding as "a congenial fellow. . . . The Republicans could not select a better man." Only the *Transcript*—in a special anti-Harding edition—dissented, accusing Harding of being a traitor to his party in the 1897 election by having supported his "highly valued friend and fellow townsman," the Democratic Colonel Christian, for senator in the 13th District instead of the Republican candidate, Henry J. May.[8] Harding replied that although he had supported May he had refused to make any personal attacks on Christian. Then Harding's enemies, still guided and financed by Kling, managed to persuade Grant Mouser to become a candidate against Harding.

The Republican caucuses [9] of Friday, July 15, held in each of the city's nine precincts to pick delegates for the county senatorial convention on the following day, were among the "hottest" ever seen in Marion. Every rig in Tregor's livery stable had been hired, and in spite of a driving rain each caucus room was "full of ginger" by the 7 P.M. opening hour. Harding carried every part of the city except Mouser's home precinct. Only in Precinct B of the Third Ward was there any doubt as to the result. There two caucus groups, both claiming to represent the precinct, met separately—the Harding supporters at the People's Barn, Mouser's people in the City Hall—and each nominated six delegates.

On Saturday morning 128 delegates—plus the rival sextets from the Third Ward's Precinct B—gathered in the courtroom of the Marion Courthouse. Though Harding had carried the city, Mouser was the stronger in the county. So close were the two candidates that the votes of Precinct B would be more than enough to carry the nomination. The convention chairman, Henry Hane, having with a lawyer's ease put aside old animosities, was now a Harding supporter. However, J. P. Patten, the chairman of the Rules and Credentials Committee, was a Mouser man and made it clear that in the Third Ward dispute his majority report would favor Mouser. When Harding learned this, he passed the word along to his floor leader, Charles C. Fisher, to vote down the report. Unexpectedly, it was the committee's minority report favoring Harding that reached the convention first. In the confusion four pro-Harding delegates

---

[8] Harding in a *Star* editorial, "Christian for Senator," admitted that the Colonel had no real chance in the 13th District but added that the Democrats had nominated the best man they could have selected. "We trust the fact that Colonel Christian has been reported to own the *Star*, in part or solely," he wrote, "and the further fact that he has been ofttimes made to bear the suspicion of furnishing the little gray matter that *Star* columns have contained, and the still further fact that the figurehead publisher of the *Star* and the Colonel are sufficiently intimate friends to break a bottle of sarsparilla water or nervine together occasionally—we trust all these will not forbid a word of comment on his nomination."

[9] This curiously loose term is generally applied to an informal meeting of leaders of a party to decide on policy. Here it is used to describe a voice-vote choice of candidates.

from Grand Township voted against it, and the report was rejected 67 to 61.

For a moment it seemed that the Harding forces had accidentally defeated themselves. Again Harding gave out his orders: "Vote down the majority report." The Grand Township delegates reversed themselves, and the majority report was in turn defeated 65 to 63. Chairman Hane "in a pandemonium of yells" now ruled that both delegations from the Third Ward's Precinct B were ineligible.

The balloting did not take place until afternoon. On the first ballot Harding received 64 votes, Mouser 63, and a George E. Lawrence, 1. On the second ballot the lone Lawrence delegate switched his vote to give Harding a one-vote majority. Mouser protested that there ought to be 134 votes in the convention, but Hane ruled him out of order. He manfully accepted the ruling and made an "eloquent" speech praising Harding who thanked him and then proceeded to pick his 27 delegates for the 13th District senatorial convention to be held in the courthouse on Monday.

The district convention was merely a ratification by the Hardin, Logan, and Union delegations of Marion's choice. There was no contest. To a later generation there is something extraordinary in the frequency of such caucuses and conventions, in the zeal with which men flocked to sweaty halls to listen to windy speeches by minor candidates. But such events were then welcome interludes from overlong workdays; half-holidays of talk and male conviviality, arousing a recreative excitement later supplied more passively by the moving pictures, radio, and television. More than that, to those identifying themselves with a tribal party they provided a catharsis, an Aristotelian purging of the emotions, whether the results of the voting were comedy or tragedy.

Harding's nomination, almost the equivalent of his election, was approved by his colleagues across Ohio. The Republican Columbus *Journal* predicted that he would be "an honor to the district in the next assembly." Nor were Democratic papers less reticent. The Upper Sandusky *Union*, after bestowing on Harding the honorific of colonel, called him "one of the most brilliant young men in Marion"; and the Marysville *Journal* felt he was the best man to be nominated by the Republicans of the 13th District in more than a decade. With his Democratic opponent, John P. Bower of Logan County, he maintained the friendliest of relations, making Bower's law office in Rushsylvania his headquarters whenever he spoke in Logan. "And he always carried my town!" Bower used to remark ruefully in after years.

In the November election the Democrats, as usual, swept Marion County, Bower carrying the county by 3,677 votes to 3,413 for Harding and carrying Hardin County as well. Harding, however, picked up enough votes in Republican Logan and Union counties to win the district by a 1,667 plurality. With his election to the Ohio senate, his discomfited enemies had to face the fact that he had become the leader of the Republican party in Marion County. The next convention would be his convention, and he would control it.

Election evening was open house at Mount Vernon Avenue. The large lamp—a wedding present—with the spherical glass shade on which was painted a small boy in colonial costume bowing and presenting a nosegay to a little colonial girl, glowed like a beacon in the front hall. By the time enough returns had come in to make the election certain, several hundred supporters had gathered under the buckeye trees in front of the green-shingled house. The Citizens' Band arrived in uniform to serenade its old cornetist and new senator with "There'll Be a Hot Time in the Old Town Tonight." So many well-wishers crowded up the concrete walk onto the narrow front porch to congratulate Harding that the structure finally collapsed.

The new porch, built some months later to replace the old, ran the whole length of the house. Topped by an ornate railing, supported by pairs of Ionic wooden columns, it terminated on the far side in a rounded protuberance that resembled a medium-sized bandstand. Twenty-two years later its curves and columns would become familiar from coast to coast as the background to presidential candidate Harding's "Front Porch" campaign.

Harding's political career might have ended with a few terms in Columbus and a comfortably obscure six years in the U. S. Senate but for his chance meeting with Harry Daugherty a week before the 1899 election. That casual morning encounter was to alter their lives, even though it left no great impression on Harding at the time.

Both men had stopped off at the crossroads village of Richwood, fifteen miles from Marion, to attend a Union County Republican rally. They spent the night before at the Globe Hotel, a ramshackle two-story frame structure on the main street. Daugherty was to be the principal speaker at the evening's rally, to be held at the overoptimistically named Opera House, a single-story brick building that could crowd in at most 600 spectators. Harding knew who Daugherty was—the former chairman of the Republican State Committee, the man who had nominated McKinley for governor six years before, a power behind conventions, who only this last summer had failed in his own bid for the Republican gubernatorial nomination by a mere 77 votes in a convention of 1,200. Daugherty was scarcely aware of the editor of the *Star*. There are variant versions of their meeting, but Daugherty's own seems the most authentic.

As there was no running water in the hotel, he had come down from his room with a morning-after thirst to get a drink and had made his way to the cast-iron pump in the unkempt back yard. There in the fly-blown debris he had found a tall, gray-haired man brushing his shoes. In spite of, perhaps in contrast to, the littered yard, the man looked impressive. With a warm-voiced easiness he introduced himself as Warren Harding of Marion, and offered the other a plug of tobacco. Daugherty ceremonially bit off a chaw and handed the plug back. Harding took his chaw and tucked the plug in his pocket. They chatted a few minutes. Daugherty was struck. "Gee," he mused as he watched Harding's graceful, retreating figure until it disappeared around the corner, "what a great-looking President he'd make!"

It was a remark no one would ever have made of Daugherty. One glance at his combative middle-aged figure slipping along the corridors of the State House in Columbus told what he was—the professional behind the scenes, the astute manipulator.

Physically he was stocky and thickset, the type of a district boss or Tammany chief. One of his eyes was brown, the other blue, and a cast in his brown eye compounded by a twitch of muscle made him seem to look around rather than at anyone. His ears lay flat against his square head; his short neck supported a pugnacious jaw and an ominously narrow mouth that turned down at the corners; his legs were slightly bowed. At forty he was growing pudgy, and the thin hair that he wore parted in the middle was obviously not going to last many years longer.

From 1890 to 1893 he had served two terms in the Ohio legislature as representative from Fayette County and had never held office since, but there were few more skilled guides through that uncharted morass where politics and business overlap. Corporations with legislative problems in Ohio had long since found it expedient to consult him. He became counsel for the American Tobacco Company, Armour & Company, the American Gas & Electric Company, and the Ohio State Telephone Company. The clerk of the House of Representatives—an old friend—made a habit of reporting to him on all bills about to be introduced to the assembly. Those inimical to Daugherty's clients were somehow buried.

Harry—not Henry—Micajah Daugherty was five years older than Harding, and his three names combined in apt incongruity to describe him, for he was at the same time a back-slapper, as relentless as his Old Testament namesake, and a subtle wily Celt.[10] He was born in Washington Court House, a small town with its domed central courthouse not unlike Marion in size and flavor, and the seat of Fayette County. While he was a boy, his father died and left his mother almost destitute. Young Harry worked after school and Saturdays in a grocery store when he was still so little he had to stand on a box to reach the cash drawer. By clerk-

[10] Daugherty was of Scotch-Irish descent, by which is meant Protestant stock from the north of Ireland. He pronounced his name "Dokerty."

ing and other odd jobs he managed to put himself through high school, then worked his way through the University of Michigan. He returned with his degree to Washington Court House where he read law in Judge H. B. Maynard's office and waited for his twenty-first birthday. Shortly after his birthday he was admitted to the bar. Within four years he had worked up the best law practice in Fayette County. At the beginning much of his practice was criminal, and he boasted later that there was never a murder in the county in those early days that he was not involved in the trial. In the twenty or so murder cases he defended, no accused was ever convicted in the first degree. One of his first corporation clients was a local railroad construction company. Other corporations came to him as his political influence grew. He established a law firm, later to become Daugherty, Todd and Raney, then opened a second office in Columbus. As a personality he was to be reckoned with. "Handsome Harry," they called him, in spite of his defective eye. In 1884 the young and charming Lucie Walker came to Washington Court House to teach music in the public schools. Handsome Harry heard her sing at a concert, and that was his undoing. He courted her impetuously, the most vociferous and determined of many suitors, and married her in December. They had two children, a son Draper and a daughter Emily Belle. Lucie in later life became an invalid, crippled with arthritis, but Daugherty's devotion to her never wavered. Although scandals beat about him all his days, there was never any hint of a woman scandal. Lucie, even as an ailing old woman, always remained for him the girl he had fallen in love with at the concert when he heard her sing "Love's Old Sweet Song."

Daugherty's interests were law and politics, and indeed the two became for him a single Janus-faced image. Before he was twenty-five he ran successfully for clerk of the township. Following this he was twice elected town councilman from the Fourth Ward. Republican leaders in the state soon became aware of his intrusive personality. John Sherman, the elder statesman and senior United States senator from Ohio, offered to appoint him district attorney for the southern district of Ohio. "I refused the job," Daugherty wrote, "because I did not think I had sufficient experience and because I preferred to build up a private practice."

In his early political years he was close to Foraker. The year after his final legislative term he tried unsuccessfully for the Republican nomination for state attorney general. Acclimated to the smoke of back rooms, from then on whenever he came out into the light as a candidate he failed. Although he twice ran for Congress, and for years nursed the ambition of being governor or even United States senator, he lacked the indefinable but necessary magnetic quality that attracts voters. "Harry Daugherty was what we used to call a fringe politician," an old Columbus acquaintance told Samuel Hopkins Adams. "He was the fly on the rim of the wheel. You'd always find him outside, looking in. When a good office was to be filled, Harry would always be among those mentioned—he'd see to that—and that let him out. He kept himself surrounded by we-men but they couldn't deliver the vote."

Like most men who have fought their way up in the political world, Daugherty was pitted and toughened by the battle. The struggle made him morally ambiguous. A shrewd judge of men and their weaknesses, he knew when to flatter, when to threaten, when to bluff. Wealth and political power, if not public office, came easily to him. He was feared and he was liked, but even in his own party he was not wholly trusted. Though he would never in his long life be convicted of any wrong doing, the outlines of his solid figure would always be blurred by a cloud of rumors and suspicions.

Although it was not too obvious a defect in the backwaters of Ohio politics, Daugherty lacked an ethical sense. Before he was of age, he and his younger brother Mally had been caught tapping telegraph wires under a culvert a few miles from Washington Court House to pick up advance news of sporting events in order to make sure-thing bets. Not long after his admission to the bar he was charged with unethical conduct by the bar association's grievance committee. The committee found the charges true, but Daugherty was rescued from the consequences by the friendly intervention of Fayette County's Judge John Mayberry. In the decade to come, when Daugherty was one of the engineers in the control room of the Ohio legislative machine, Judge Mayberry's son as clerk of the House of Representatives became the gravedigger for the bills Daugherty opposed.

It was Foraker who financed Daugherty's two successful campaigns for the Ohio Assembly. Daugherty was considered his Fayette County outpost. In 1892 Fire Engine Joe caused a national sensation by opposing Sen. John Sherman in his re-election to the United States Senate. Senators were still elected by vote of their state legislatures, and Daugherty was taken for granted as Foraker's man. When, however, the Fayette County Republican Convention endorsed Sherman, Daugherty appeared on the platform and pledged his support. Then the evening of that same day he met Foraker's manager, Charles Kurtz, in Columbus and assured him of his unqualified allegiance to Foraker.

Fire Engine Joe, contrary to his mathematical calculations and much to his surprise, found himself defeated. Shortly before the legislature's vote Sherman's manager, William H. Hahn, had drawn a number of $500 bills from the Deshler Bank. Before these were passed over the counter, a suspicious young teller secretly inked a small W on each bill. After Sherman's election the marked bills began to surface in the state capital. The Columbus *Press-Post* accused Daugherty of switching his vote to Sherman for "seven crisp $500 bills." A grand-jury investigation was ordered. Daugherty, in defending himself on the floor, told the assembly:

"I do not claim to be so honest that I cannot sleep at night—but I didn't get any of those crisp $500 bills." The investigation dragged on for almost a week. Finally the jurors were discharged without having returned an indictment. But people remembered the inked bills for years.

After he had given up his seat in the assembly, Daugherty continued in Columbus as a lobbyist. An old-time member described him as "paymaster for the boys." He became noted as a deft instigator of "milker bills" that ostensibly aimed at regulating or hampering various large corporations. The fearful corporation executives would then engage Daugherty to smother the bills he had secretly spawned. Among the more familiar "milkers" were the perennial anti-cigarette bills. Mark Sullivan, who knew Daugherty most of his adult life, considered him a man of high talent and low tastes, a competent lawyer who might have been an outstanding one. But Daugherty's restless temperament preferred the marketplace excitement of lobbying and manipulation to the staid respectability of a law office.

> It was a time [Sullivan wrote] when small, local telephone, gas, and electric plants were being merged into larger systems; the operation in many cases called for new charters from legislatures, consents from regulatory bodies, negotiations with minority groups of stockholders, suits in the courts, suits in which the main consideration was compromise, or other quick and definite conclusion, to be attained either by appeasement or by resoluteness. In all this Daugherty became adept; he almost never appeared himself in court nor before a legislative committee or public utility commission; but always he knew who could make the appearance with the best advantage; always he knew what wire to pull; always he kept a web of wires running from his office out to all sorts of men who occupied places of leverage; always he knew how to get results.[11]

[11] Characteristic of Daugherty's deviousness was the pardon that he managed to secure a number of years later for Charles W. Morse, a New York banker and Wall Street operator who had been sentenced to a long term in the Federal penitentiary for fraud and larceny. Morse engaged Daugherty and another lawyer, Thomas B. Felder, later disbarred, to act for him in getting a pardon.

On August 4, 1911, Morse sent Daugherty a retainer of $5,000, promising to pay another $25,000 when he was released. Only President Taft could commute Morse's sentence, and the upright Taft was from Ohio and knew Daugherty too well to be approached directly. Daugherty appealed to his Democratic friend, the newspaper publisher John McLean. McLean sent a reporter to Atlanta and then claimed that Morse was in a dying state. An Army physician was found to certify that Morse was suffering from cardiac dyspnœa and that even if released he could not live another six months. Morse asked to be allowed to die outside prison, and Taft agreed to pardon, as he thought, a dying man. Once free, Morse took a curative trip abroad and managed to survive the next fifteen years. Gossip had it that he owed most of his symptoms to having eaten a bar of soap before his medical examination. Whether Daugherty knew of this or the actual state of his client's health has never been determined.

All that is known of Harding's fateful day in Richwood is that after his morning meeting with Daugherty it rained. Restricted by the weather to the hotel lobby or the local bar, the political figures gathered together and told their smoking-room tales while waiting for the evening rally. Daugherty warmed to Harding as he talked with him, finally to the surprise of the other politicians suggesting that the *Star* editor make the first speech of the evening.

The Richwood *Gazette* recorded his unscheduled appearance on the platform, editorial pride exaggerating the rally's attendance:

> Attorney J. F. Miller of this place called the meeting to order and introduced Honorable F. T. Arthur of Marysville as the temporary chairman. Mr. Arthur made a few remarks and then introduced Honorable W. G. Harding of Marion, editor of the Marion *Star*. Mr. Harding is the Republican candidate for state senator. He made an able speech and pleased the immense audience by his humorous illustrations and bursts of eloquence. Most of our people had been led to believe that Mr. Harding was not much of a speaker, and had been placed on the program as a sort of "filler." He surprised everybody present, even his most intimate friends. While he appeared a little awkward on the stage, his language was well chosen and his argument convincing. In a short time we predict he will be one of the leading political orators of the state. His visit to Richwood made him many warm friends both in the Republican and Democratic parties.

It was at the Richwood meeting that Harding emerged from his chrysalis of private self-doubt into public life. Up until then his efforts had been tentative; set speeches and Fourth-of-July orations. But facing his most formal audience to date in an impromptu speech, he discovered within himself the gift of political glossolaly. Never again would he appear awkward on any stage. He knew now that, regardless of meaning, his voice could hypnotize. The printer had at last become the politician.

[CHAPTER VII]

Ohio Politics

The state political scene onto which the neophyte Harding now emerged was for any outsider a confusing and contradictory spectacle. "I think there is only one thing in the world I cannot understand," Theodore Roosevelt wrote at about this time, "and that is Ohio politics." Although the Republicans had carried the state in every presidential election since 1856, they would never take Ohio's large electoral vote comfortably for granted. The Grand Old Party, in spite of occasional gubernatorial defeats in off-year elections, managed to control the legislature and elect most of the state officials, but Republican leaders meanwhile fought one another more vindictively than they did the Democrats. Factions split or incongruously combined. Bosses who were friends today were tomorrow's enemies, and allies the next day. Regional Republican leaders there were, but no undisputed state leader. If there had been such a leader, unchallengeable in his state-wide authority, Ohio politics even in corruption might have been more comprehensible. Instead, authority and influence seesawed between Ohio's United States senators, Fire Engine Joe Foraker and Mark Hanna, and their subordinates, with a few independents such as the scholarly Theodore Burton standing aside and bosses such as George Cox concealed in the background shadows.

In their separate ways both senators were post-Civil War phenomena, representing the forces unloosed by the nascent machine age under the iron determinism of war, forces that crudely and corruptly but inevitably —and with great human cost—were resolving the rural America of Jefferson's dream. Rising entrepreneurs, leaders in transportation, industry, and finance were conquering the continent for the new industrialism. To obtain what they wanted of the country's natural resources they bribed legislatures and congressmen as a matter of course. With *laissez-faire* self-righteousness they sweated their workers. The novel concept of progress seemed to them eternal. Any attempt of the government to control or regulate their activities was "revolutionary." The gaudy brutality of this unfolding industrialism would mask the thesis of its inevitability, although its uncontrolled dynamism in turn would breed its own antithesis in the sub-cerebral indignation of the Populist revolt and later the more considered, more respectable, more effective evangelicalism of the Progressives.

Although political exigencies might link Foraker and Hanna arm in arm as they walked down the aisles of some applauding convention, their rivalry remained not only political but personal. Each knew how to smile with the knife under the frock coat. Both were maneuvering for their party's presidential nomination in 1904 when the re-elected McKinley would have finished his second term. Until Hanna turned from his business interests to politics, the magnetic Foraker was the dominant if not dominating Republican leader in Ohio. Like his older rival, Senator Sherman, Foraker was a lawyer, but there any resemblance ended. Sherman had his roots in the prewar era when ambitious young men in back offices read Robertson, Vattel, and the three volumes of Blackstone by the light of a tallow candle, to model themselves on Webster and Henry Clay.

Sherman's personality was formed by the image of such statesmen as Harry of the West, austere in their black stocks and stylized gestures. Beyond all his ambition—and he was an ambitious man—there was always a detached sense of obligation to public service and a relative indifference to wealth. During the Civil War and until 1877 he had served as United States senator from Ohio. From 1877 to 1881, as secretary of the treasury in President Hayes's Cabinet he had brought an end to the wartime greenback inflation, resuming the payment of gold dollars with a skill that placed him among the great treasury names of Hamilton, Gallatin, and Chase. Once more in the Senate, in 1880 and again in 1888 he was considered as a candidate for President, and might have been nominated if he had been less scrupulous in the use of patronage and more skillful in manipulating politicians. Hanna, after successfully managing McKinley's 1896 presidential campaign, elbowed the elderly senator aside to make way for his own appointment by Governor Bushnell to Sherman's vacant Senate seat. In order to remove the failing and fading Sherman from the Senate, McKinley made him his nominal secretary of state, a position the old man held inactively until overwhelmed by the Spanish-American War.

If Sherman was the older type of lawyer-statesman, Foraker was the new type of lawyer-politician that would eventually become the stereotype. While active in politics, he was equally active as counsel for railroads, public utilities, a tobacco trust, and a dozen other corporations. Conflicts of interest never troubled him. The corporations that he represented made him wealthy, and he felt such money was his due. He looked after their political interests with a clear if elastic conscience, never doubting that what was good for business was good for him, for the state, and the country.

His first inauguration as governor on a bitter January day in 1886 marked for Ohio the change that the Republican party was experiencing nationally. For the party of embattled freedom was transforming itself into the party of big business. Foraker approved the evolution, holding it to be in the nature of things that corporations, trusts, and monopolies should lead politics along that GOP highway of prosperity where the guideposts were dollar signs.

As a governor who knew how to manage the legislative strings, he was also an able administrator. In emergencies such as the Johnstown Flood of 1888 he showed how decisively and efficiently he could act. Yet, impatient with the details of political manipulation, he was more the boom-ta-ra leader than the entrenched boss, sustaining his position through his deft personal touch and almost limitless quantities of personal and friendly letters. Among Republican precinct and ward workers he could fire an enthusiasm that Sherman could not even spark. His manager, Charles L. Kurtz—a wispy man with a black mustache, receding hair, and pince-nez-veiled eyes who looked more like a Sunday-school superintendent than a politician—took care of the practical management of his campaigns.

In 1883 Foraker in his first bid for the governorship was defeated by a fellow Cincinnatian, and former Republican, George Hoadly. Since Hoadly won by a mere 12,529 votes out of the 706,957 cast, Foraker maintained that he was not damaged in his defeat. Two years later he managed to turn the tables on Hoadly by 17,451 votes without, however, carrying Cincinnati. Foraker realized that he needed his home city as a solid base of support. His politically minded medical friend, Doctor Thomas Graydon, the "Conqueror of Consumption"—a patent-medicine manufacturer who had also invented a cure for deafness, marketed as Brahmo Yan—suggested that he make approaches to Cincinnati's rising Republican boss George Barnstable Cox.

Cox could have given Tammany lessons in ward management, but his city's deep and bipartisan corruption long antedated him. Until the climactic riots of March 8, 1884, Cincinnati under a series of Democratic mayors was controlled by two bosses: a Republican criminal lawyer, Tom Campbell, and his close friend, the Democratic dandy, John Roll McLean. McLean, a newspaperman, had inherited the Cincinnati *Enquirer*—Ohio's leading Democratic daily—from the paper's founder, his father Washington "Wash" McLean. He and Campbell formed their own Tweed ring to rule the city, buying votes, fixing juries, taking their shakedowns from graft, vice, and crime. Campbell controlled the law courts. When in 1884 a local livery-stable owner was hacked to pieces by two of his stablemen, Campbell defended the murderers. Although the men—a young German, William Berner, and Joe Palmer, a mulatto—had confessed, Campbell persuaded the jury to bring in a verdict of manslaughter. Even for Cincinnati this was too raw. A mob stoned the jurymen as they left the courthouse. Hundreds more held an indignation meeting at the Music Hall, then marched on the jail. Pitched street battles with the police followed. By the time the governor called out the militia several men had been killed and the courthouse burned to the ground. Before the rioting ended, 45 rioters and militiamen had died and over a hundred and fifty were wounded. In the smoky aftermath Campbell abandoned Cincinnati for New York, and McLean—although keeping his legal residence in Ohio— moved on to Washington. The shambles were left to Boss Cox.

Before his alliance with Foraker, the thirty-year-old Cox merely controlled Cincinnati's 18th Ward. With Foraker's help, although Cox was never in that time to hold municipal office, he became the absolute ruler of the city from the late eighties until his death in 1916. He had started out in life as a ragged street urchin, his first job that of a butcher boy. Being tall and strong for his age, he was made a bouncer at the polls before he was old enough to vote. That was his introduction to politics. In the early seventies he drove a grocer's delivery wagon, graduating from that to selling tobacco. For a while he tended the Keno game at the Empire, an elaborate gambling joint on West Fifth Street. Then he turned bartender. Finally he bought into a grubby but strategically located saloon and small-time gambling den in Ward 18 at a juncture of Longworth Street and Central Avenue known as Dead Man's Corner. When— as he soon did—he found his business obstructed by the police, he was told to get elected to the city council "and his troubles would cease." He ran successfully for the council in 1879. With his election, his power in the ward grew. By 1884 he could deliver the 12 ward delegates at any Republican convention. One thing distinguished him in his bossism— would always distinguish him from other bosses. His dishonor was rooted in honor. In splitting the boodle he always divided it "on the square." When he gave his word, he never broke it.

Foraker, as soon as he had settled comfortably into the governor's chair, brought enough pressure on the legislature to abolish the Cincinnati Board of Public Works, just then engaged in a $4 million job of relaying the city's streets. He saw to it that a board of public affairs, appointed by the governor, replaced this elective body. The patronage of the new board he threw to "Old Boy" Cox. Among the board members was "Medicine Man" Graydon. Cox used the 2,000 or so jobs of dispossesed Democrats at his disposal like counters to make himself absolute boss of the city and of surrounding Hamilton County.

He sold the saloon at Dead Man's Corner, and set up his headquarters in a mean front-hall room over the Mecca Saloon near Fourth and Vine streets where he received supplicants, gave out his judgments, and planned with his lieutenants. Seldom did he leave the city. State and city politicians, bankers, businessmen, police captains, and ward heelers trudged up the dank stairs to state their case before the bulky, impassive man chomping on a cigar behind his roll-top desk. He spoke little, and then in a sepulchral voice "unmodulated by sympathy."

Much of Cox's boodle came from public utility franchises and from bribes given by banks in exchange for illegal deposits of county funds. He controlled about 5,000 jobs and through them a core of 25,000 votes. In Cincinnati a judge could not select his own bailiff or stenographer, a mayor could not choose his assistant or clerks. Cox did the selecting. Job holders paid him 10 per cent of their first year's salary and after that 2½ per cent a year. In return he demanded reasonably good service. Through his organization the Loyal Republican League—known more informally as the Stranglers—he made his private nominations in advance of the conventions. No hopeful candidate in the city dared announce his intentions without paying off first at the Mecca. Before his death Cox was reputed to be worth over $2 million. "This is the age of the boss," he announced in 1911, "and I am the boss of Cincinnati . . . I am hardened to attacks . . . I am living my life as I believe I should live it. My enemies cannot affect me."

In his middle years he weighed 225 pounds and looked like a boss cartoon by Davenport, with his solid bartender's body, thick neck encased in its stiff collar, square, solid head, black mustache drooping about the rattrap jaw, and fleshy nose with eyebrows that almost met above it. Only his luminous and penetrating dark eyes seemed unfitted to the rest of his face. His three lieutenants, Augustus (Garry) Hermann, Mike Mullen, and Rudolph (Rud) Hynicka, represented the three racial strains of his mass support—German, Irish, and Hunky. Garry Hermann took care of City Hall and its patronage. Mike Mullen—a former policeman and one-time Democrat whom Cox had enticed over the party fence—called the tunes to which the city council pranced. He was also in charge of handouts, picnics, and parties. Rud Hynicka, a smooth if heavy-faced young man with relentless blue eyes, was Cox's second-in-command. He had started out as a political reporter for the *Enquirer* and through his contacts got himself elected police court clerk. Soon he found that by closing the office early he could collect three to five dollars for each late entry in his register. After joining Cox he was put in charge of building up a campaign "war chest." Between elections he kept a card catalogue of the adult males of Hamilton County, their jobs and voting habits. At the county courthouse he looked after the "boys."

In 1887 Foraker with Boss Cox's help carried Hamilton County for the first time. As recompense he appointed Cox state oil inspector, the only office the Boss would ever again hold. As inspector Cox was brought into palm-greasing contact with Standard Oil and other large oil corporations. It was a lucrative position for anyone who knew how to work it—and Cox did know. Foraker and Cox together controlled the southern part of Ohio. In any election Cox could deliver twenty to thirty thousand votes, and this solid, undeviating majority, added to Foraker's own more mercurial support, was usually enough to carry a state election. "He [Cox] is not a Sunday-school superintendent," Foraker said of his colleague, "neither is he a man of as much culture as some others, but he is a man of ability, always reliable, not a bummer or a politician for revenue."

One of Cox's most troublesome opponents in his home city was Charles P. Taft, the white-bearded older half-brother of Judge William Howard Taft of the Ohio Superior Court. Charlie Taft was a lawyer, a scholar, a graduate of Yale with a doctor of laws degree from Heidelberg. He owned the Cincinnati *Times-Star* and used his paper to attack Cox and in 1889 to expose the Stranglers. When the Citizens' Municipal League ran a candidate for mayor to oppose Cox's puppet, Taft vociferously supported the reform candidate. But Cox knew how to deal with the high as well as the low. He saw to it that the *Times-Star* received large blocks of city advertising, and the attacks ceased. And when in 1894 the politically ambitious Taft accepted the nomination for Congress from Cox's stubby hands, the *Times-Star* became the Mecca boss's fanatical supporter.

In 1895, with Cox's backing, Foraker routed the Sherman forces at Zanesville and was given the convention's endorsement for United States senator. He was elected at the first meeting of the new legislature in January, 1896. A few months later, backed by Foraker, Cox steered the Rogers Law through the Ohio Assembly, giving the Cincinnati Street Railroad a fifty-year franchise. But so great had public opposition become to such franchises that it took several hundred thousand dollars distributed judiciously among the legislators to get the law passed.[1]

From his Cincinnati bastion Foraker might control the southern part of his state and at times dominate the Assembly, but his influence at the state capitol fluctuated and in the North it was diminished by the looming shadow of Mark Hanna. "The difference between Foraker and me," Mark Hanna once remarked, "is that I buy and he sells." Hanna's was a more novel appearance than Foraker's in the post-Civil War political world. Businessmen in politics were to become common enough before the century ended, but he was the prototype. Big business never hesitated to seek

---

[1] Foraker's fee for his services was over a hundred thousand dollars. But even Cox's influence was not sufficient to still the opposition to the Rogers Law, and two years later public opinion forced its repeal.

out complacent politicians as its instrument; yet politics, especially at the ward and county level, seemed too dirty a stream for any businessman to swim in. Hanna was the first businessman to take the plunge. And in so doing he remade the Republican party.

They called him the Red Boss of Cleveland, but Hanna was never a boss in the sense of organization, patronage, tribute, and vote control. When a campaign was over, an objective gained, he tended to lose interest in the details of politics, most of which in any case he left to his more assiduously political lieutenant, Charles Dick. He tolerated or at least was indifferent to his enemies within the party, tending to underestimate them. Even when he had made McKinley President and himself a United States senator, he could not control his own Northern lake city.   .

The afterimage of Hanna has endured in the distortions of Homer Davenport's New York *Journal* syndicated cartoons where Dollar Mark appeared like some modern apocalyptic beast trampling women and children underfoot until their eyes bulged from their sockets. In Davenport's sketches—and they were cruel enough at times to bring the tears to Hanna's eyes—Hanna wore a suit covered with dollar signs. Dollar signs were branded into his distended ear lobes and on the end of his thumb. He always carried a huge cigar and wore a glittering lump of coal in his shirt front. His sharp pig eyes glittered coldly in a blob of a face that was like a carved lump of suet. Davenport himself eventually came to regret the grossness of his caricature. Hanna felt most bitterly the implication of his injuring women and children. Within the paternalism of his business empire he prided himself on being a good employer and a generous citizen. He paid higher wages than his competitors. He was not as a rule anti-union. Nor was he mealy-mouthed like his boyhood schoolmate John D. Rockefeller. He faced his men, talked with them, mixed with them. Any worker of his who felt he had a grievance was free to come to Hanna, and Mark would listen. He was not cold and he was not aloof. Even arch-reformers such as Frederick Howe and Harold Ickes were moved by his personality. "He was bullet-headed, cruel-lipped," Howe wrote, "dynamic in all his relations. Many of his associates loved him. I came to have affection for him." Ickes found him personally "a likable man—short and squat with a round, friendly face. The most distinguishing of his features were his eyes. They were full of life and vitality and power."

Hanna's were not the hard beginnings to shape a flinty character. He was born in 1837 in New Lisbon, then one of the busiest towns in eastern Ohio. His father was a doctor, his grandfather and six uncles the town's leading wholesale and commission merchants until they lost their fortune in the collapse of the canal boom. Hanna's father and his uncle Robert left New Lisbon for Cleveland in 1852 to make a new start in the grocery and commission business.

After finishing high school, young Mark entered the family firm just as it was beginning to expand into the shipping trade of Lake Superior region. He started at the bottom as an overalled warehouse clerk and worked his way down. For a time he was a roustabout on the docks, then a purser on one of his family's lake steamers, and not long afterward one of the first traveling salesmen in the United States. Like most offshoots of a pioneer society, he was not introspective and cared little about books. Yet his eye was not fixed undeviatingly on the main chance. As a young man he was gay and sociable and spent as much time in entertaining and being entertained as he did at the family business. He danced and he went on excursions with the other young people of Cleveland's upper segment, he played cards (but not poker), and rowed well enough to become captain of the Ydrad Boat Club. When the Civil War came he would have liked to join the Army but since his elder brother Howard had gone he was practical enough to hire a substitute and stay home himself to tend the family business. Finally, in the spring of 1864, he joined the Perry Light Infantry—a company made up of young Cleveland businessmen—as a hundred-day soldier. Commissioned a lieutenant, he spent his hundred days in garrison duty in the forts near Washington.

When the sprightly lieutenant with the brown chin whiskers and the unspotted uniform returned, he married the daughter of Daniel P. Rhodes, one of Cleveland's most successful coal-and-iron merchants. Rhodes, an anti-war Democrat, at first objected to his daughter marrying "a damned screecher for freedom." The screecher kept to his own affairs until after losing two lake steamers and a small oil refinery in which he had invested all his money, he reluctantly entered the Rhodes firm as Daniel was preparing to retire. Mark had shrewdness to spare, but he also had the advantage of starting just at the right time. Soon the firm became M. A. Hanna & Company, one of the largest concerns in the coal-and-iron trade in the entire Ohio lake district.

At the beginning of the Midwest's industrial development, Cleveland on its lake was a most favorably located import-export center where coal, iron ore, and pig copper were routed from mines to furnaces and factories. Hanna saw to it that his firm did most of the routing. To create system and order out of this originally haphazard distribution, M. A. Hanna & Company began to mine its own coal and ore which it shipped in its own lake steamers to its own docks. Often the ore was melted in Hanna furnaces. Through prosperity and depression Hanna's firm expanded. Hanna's nature was to expand. In his acquisitiveness he seemed to act by instinct rather than by conscious thought, gathering his empire twig by twig like a bird building a nest. Almost by accident he bought the bankrupt Opera House, Cleveland's largest and handsomest theater, reorganized it, and made it pay. With the same casualness he founded the Rockland National Bank.

His chance take-over of a broken-down horsecar line became the means of bringing him into politics. On his father-in-law's death he inherited a directorship in the West Side Street Railway Company, a horse-drawn service for Cleveland's West Side. The service was as cheap as it was poor, the stock consisting of fifteen miles of rusty track and a few dozen worm-eaten cars and decrepit nags. Such commercial decay was intolerable to Hanna's temperament. He bought out the other directors and took over the company himself, purchasing new horses and cars, and soon combining with another line. In 1889 he began to electrify. Then, after consolidating still further with the Cleveland City Cable Company, he became president of the new Cleveland City Railway Company, popularly known as the Little Consolidated. With the postwar expansion of the cities and the new demands for public transportation, transit lines became sudden money-makers. "My bank account," Hanna used to call his Little Consolidated.

Cleveland was then as corrupt as most American cities of the period. The politicians on the city council controlled transit-line franchises. Hanna soon discovered that for the franchises he needed most in his expanding company he either had to bribe the councilors or go out of business. He bribed. At the beginning he had tried to fight civic corruption, but he was too practical a man to continue to fight against his own interests. He found himself dealing with politicians and controlling councils in spite of himself. His transit lines made money, but this was not the prime object of his restless entrepreneurial mind. For him it was the joy of making things run, *his* things, and he was ruthless in seeing that they kept running.

In 1880 he had bought the Cleveland *Herald,* another impulsion toward political life. By degrees he became a power in local and state politics. Yet he did not have a machine behind him so much as the cash registers of businessmen. Professional politicians disliked and continued to dislike him even as they came to him with outstretched palms. In 1884, with Foraker and Congressman William McKinley, he was delegate-at-large to the Republican national convention that nominated Blaine. He himself favored Senator Sherman. Foraker made the nominating speech for Sherman, and then, typically, switched to Blaine. Nevertheless, Hanna was impressed by the flamboyant boom-ta-ra. "Among the few pleasures I found at the convention," he wrote to Foraker afterwards, "was meeting and working with you. . . . It will not be my fault if our acquaintance does not ripen."

Hanna supported Foraker in his 1885 comeback and supplied him generously with needed funds. Much to Hanna's chagrin, Foraker after being elected governor appointed Cox oil inspector instead of the candidate he had recommended. And Cox on appointing his deputies did not even name Hanna's man. Relations between Hanna and Foraker were never the same, but their final break did not come until the national convention of 1888.[2] Hanna was by this time Sherman's campaign manager and his personal representative at the convention. Hanna, Foraker, and McKinley were again delegates-at-large. Foraker gave himself out officially for Sherman although there had been friction between them earlier in the year. Hanna maintained that he broke with Foraker when he learned that Fire Engine Joe was secretly trying to undermine Sherman and start a swing to Blaine.

Foraker's version of the break is more flattering to himself:

> A great many colored delegates from the South, as is their custom, had tickets to the convention which they desired to sell. They brought their tickets to our rooms at the hotel, and Mr. Hanna, in the presence of us all, bought them. I protested against such methods, saying that it would bring scandal on the entire delegation and hurt Sherman's cause. Mr. Hanna and I had a spirited discussion over the matter, and it resulted in my leaving the rooms.

The break between Foraker and Hanna resulted in one of the most extraordinary and extended political fights in American politics. Often partisans of the two men took to their fists in the primaries, state conventions, and the legislature. Yet neither faction felt strong enough to risk a final finish fight in which they might destroy themselves as well as their adversaries and open the way to a Democratic triumph. To Hanna venality was in the selling, not the buying, and he came to detest Foraker. Yet the exigencies of politics and fear of the Democrats would still at times bring them together on public platforms, bland and smiling, in a masked appearance of harmony. When McKinley, after having lost his seat in Congress, was with Hanna's support nominated for governor in 1891, it was Foraker who placed McKinley's name in nomination and made the eagle scream as he recalled the candidate's military record.

McKinley was elected, and re-elected two years later. Nevertheless, at the famous Zanesville Rout, the state convention of 1895, Foraker with Cox did indeed rout the McKinley-Hanna faction from control of the state organization. Foraker not only succeeded in having himself endorsed as the next United States senator but he even made his secretary, Charles Kurtz, chairman of the State Central Committee. Hanna, neglecting Ohio, had, with Colonel Dick, been devoting most of his efforts to securing the nomination of Governor McKinley in the national convention of June, 1896. Despite the Zanesville Rout, Hanna on a national scale—

[2] Hanna liked President Cleveland and he had considered Foraker's bombastic refusal of the President's request to return the captured Confederate battle flags to the southern states as "a stale gesture."

with much open assertion of the people's will and closed collecting of Southern delegates—managed to thwart Foraker and such bosses as Matt Quay of Pennsylvania and foxy Tom Platt of New York by getting McKinley nominated on the first ballot. With an irony apparent to the initiates, it was again Senator-elect Foraker who presented McKinley's name to that convention in one of his familiar rafter-shaking orations. The Republican party needed a man, he told the delegates (carefully holding back the key name for the traditional last phrase of his peroration), "the exact opposite of all that is signified and represented by the present free-trade, deficit-making, bond-issuing, labor-saving Democratic administration. I stand here to present to this convention such a man—his name is William McKinley." The vibrant conclusion brought the delegates to their feet in a wild, whooping, flag-waving demonstration that lasted twenty-five minutes and ended only when the band struck up "Hurrah for McKinley and Protection"—to the tune of "Marching through Georgia."

William Jennings Bryan's nomination as Democratic presidential candidate after his perfervid "Cross of Gold" speech was followed by his endorsement by the Populists. Bryan combined in his person the discontents that had been festering since the 1893 depression. During the summer and early autumn it looked as if the fiery and class-conscious young orator of the River Platte, in his furious speeches from coast to coast, might defeat the sedate stay-at-home McKinley. Bryan appealed to the dispossessed everywhere, to the galled mortgage-burdened farmers, the tattered remnants of Gen. Jacob Coxey's army of unemployed, to Coin Harvey and the silver dollarites. When he meant by his incandescent oratory was inflation; better to be buried under a mass of greenbacks than crucified on a gold standard.

While Bryan journeyed, McKinley remained in his homely angular house in Canton conducting what came to be known as his "Front Porch" campaign. Instead of going to the people, he let them come to him—and they came (on cheap excursion rates) in badged and beribboned delegations from all over the country. They trampled the McKinleys' green lawn into brown mud, they knocked down the grape arbor and the red geranium beds, picnicking in the litter while they waited for the starched presence to address them. With sedate graciousness he appeared at intervals on the symbolic porch—itself in danger of collapse from the many hands grappling the narrow columns—and spoke his few carefully primed words to each group.

In itself the Front-Porch campaign would never have sufficed. Hanna said afterward that if the election had been held in August or September McKinley would probably have lost. Bryan was setting the country on fire, but Hanna had the money for the fire department. As chairman of the Republican National Committee he raised $7 million from alarmed corporations and industrialists. The audits of the Republican National Committee accounted for over $3½ million, 3 million of which was raised in New York alone. Never before had there been so much money spent on a presidential election, nor would that sum be reached again until after World War I. Hanna conducted the first modern advertising campaign, selling his candidate like soap to the American people. Cartoons, posters, inscriptions were turned out by the carloads. Hanna set up twin headquarters in Chicago and New York, dispatched an army of 1,400 trained speakers, sent out over a hundred and twenty million campaign documents including circulars in German, French, Spanish, Italian, Swedish, Danish, Dutch, and Yiddish. "A born general in politics," Lincoln's old secretary John Hay remarked of him admiringly. By October Hanna felt that his exposures of the Bryan paper-money heresies and his slogan "the full dinner pail" had made their dollar mark and that the country was safe. Election day proved him right, for on November 2 McKinley defeated Bryan by eighty-five electoral college and half a million popular votes.[3]

"I would rather be senator in Congress than have any other office on earth," Hanna once told a friend. With McKinley in the White House and Sherman his secretary of state, Hanna saw his wish come true as he prepared to assume Sherman's Senate seat. It was an assumption that Senator Foraker and Governor Bushnell would have prevented if they dared—and they half-dared. Secretly Bushnell sent for Theodore Burton and offered to appoint the Cleveland congressman to Sherman's place despite Hanna. Burton was a man of aloof integrity whose chief interests in life were books and politics. A bachelor and scholar, a reactionary of rectitude, he would have been more at home as a Tory in the House of Commons than as a Republican in the House of Representatives, but for all his aloofness he had a singularly magnetic hold on his Cleveland congressional district.[4] Yet, although secretly he wanted to be a United States senator, although he did not approve of Dollar Mark, he was not willing to take his place in the Senate by the grace of Boss Cox. Even though Bushnell and Foraker promised him their further support in the senatorial election of the following year, he refused. Hanna, he told Bushnell, had the overwhelming support of the party and there was nothing to do but appoint him.

In spite of Burton's advice, Bushnell made no move to take it. For five

---

[3] Total votes: McKinley 7,111,607; Bryan 6,509,052.
[4] Burton served in Congress from 1888 to 1909 with the exception of two terms (1890–1894) when he was defeated by the reformist single-taxer Tom Johnson. He made a distinguished record as the chairman of the Committee on Rivers and Harbors. In 1902 he published his noteworthy *Financial Crises and Periods of Industrial and Commercial Depression,* and in 1906 a biography of John Sherman. In 1909 he was finally elected to the Senate.

weeks Ohio's vacant Senate seat remained vacant. But the White House and the chairman of the Republican National Committee were not to be defied by a mere governor, even with Foraker-Cox backing. Major Dick, who had ousted Kurtz and replaced him with Hanna's friend, Judge George K. Nash, told Bushnell bluntly that unless the Governor appointed Hanna to the Senate he himself would not even be renominated that autumn. Boss Cox told him even more bluntly: "Name Hanna!" Bushnell capitulated, delaying the signing of Hanna's commission, however, until the morning after the presidential inauguration so that Foraker would be the senior senator.[5] On that morning Foraker, glowing with affability, escorted his new colleague to the bar of the Senate—and to the untutored eye friendship prevailed.

Senator Hanna's interim appointment would expire when the state assembly convened in January, 1898. Senate and House in joint session had then to name a successor to fill the remainder of Senator Sherman's unexpired term and to elect a senator (not necessarily the same man) for the new six-year senatorial term beginning in March, 1899. The state Republican convention meeting in Toledo in June saw the Hanna and Foraker factions combine to renominate Governor Bushnell, while the Forakerites—with their fingers crossed—voted as well to recommend Senator Hanna for both the short and the long elected terms. Foraker himself presented Hanna's name to the convention. What was needed, Harding wrote approvingly from Marion, was "large chunks of harmony."

While Hanna relaxed in senatorial ease during the autumn months before the convening of the assembly in January,[6] Bushnell, Kurtz, and Foraker were working with mole-like industry to undermine his position. In this they were aided by another Hanna enemy, Cleveland's Republican Mayor Robert S. "Curly Bob" McKisson. In 1895 the tough, ambitious young Curly Bob had been elected on a municipal reform platform, but once in office he had shown himself more interested in building a party organization to challenge Hanna in his home city than in any bright banners of reform and progress. It was his ambition now to replace Hanna in the United States Senate.

The scheme was not as bizarre as it first seemed. Privately the Democrats agreed to support Bushnell for governor in the November election if in turn Bushnell and Foraker would throw their votes to the Democratic as opposed to the Hanna-Republican candidates for the assembly. Although Boss Cox had that year joined the Hanna camp, there was danger

---

[5] Although elected by the Ohio Assembly to the United States Senate in January, 1896, Foraker did not take office until March 4, 1897.

[6] At the end of September Hanna went on a five-week electioneering tour through Ohio, speaking to audiences that seemed more curious than enthusiastic. He had not yet developed as a speaker.

even in his secure bailiwick. For in Cincinnati a group of independent Republicans had joined with the Democrats to challenge his control.

By the time the assembly met on the first Monday in January, 1898, the conspiracy had begun to function. Hanna men found themselves deprived of chairmanships, places on important committees, and patronage. A Republican senator discreetly stayed away from the opening session to allow the Democrats to take control of the closely balanced Senate. Although the announced Democratic candidate for senator was the long-absentee John McLean, Democrats in the House promised the Bushnell group to give their votes to any Republican opposed to Hanna. For a time the anti-Hanna conspirators considered electing McKisson for the short term and Bushnell for the long term, but finally agreed on the Cleveland mayor for both terms. After the first session of the assembly it looked as if, when the balloting began the following week, Hanna's chair might soon be slipped from under him. The dust of battle was visible as far as Marion. Harding wrote placatingly in the *Star:*

No other caption will fit. The contest at Columbus is a senatorial fight. It dates from the Toledo convention, when Hon. Charles Kurtz was figuratively spit upon by Senator Hanna and Governor Bushnell was told he could accept the dictates of the dominant element or get off the ticket. For party's sake the rumpus was kept under cover and the campaign carried to a wonderfully successful finish.

Lamentable as it is, the outcome—the fight now on at Columbus—is a logical result. The fight is not so important in itself as the possible after results, made dangerous by the ill-temper and unwise criticism of the partisans that array themselves with one or the other contending faction.

The first essential thing to remember is that whoever is elected he will be a Republican, and whether it is Bushnell or Hanna, the Republican party and the great state of Ohio will be creditably represented. In sober judgment one man deserves quite as well of the party as the other. In the second place it is just to remember that the anti-Hanna Republicans are just as devoted as those who assail them. The test of party fealty in Ohio has never been a matter of devotion to one man. Charles L. Kurtz, Governor Bushnell, and the small army of Republicans who refuse to berate them for their contest are among the spartan Republicans of Ohio, who have led the way to pronounced victories in the past, and are not now threatening ruin if they fail.

The *Star* has never understood the opposition to be any disparagement of Senator Hanna's official career, but rather a protest against his political methods. . . .

Senator Foraker's part in the fight ended with the campaign. He made a grand canvas and aided in bringing victory to the Republican banner. He insisted that his obligation ended there, that while he personally preferred Senator Hanna for a colleague (the *Star* knows this to be true) he could not bring himself to apply a club to those of his friends who insisted on some rights of political liberty.

Hanna, when he belatedly saw his career threatened, reacted, as he always did, with ferocious energy. He stormed to Columbus, opened a command post at the Neil House, and began to send out his checks and his orders. Ohio was in an uproar. Delegations on railroad passes poured into the capital from all over the state. The hotels were packed. McKisson brought in strong-arm squads and Hanna sent out his own men among the legislators to threaten the recalcitrant and fortify the wavering.

From a political contest, the struggle became a primal application of force. As Hanna's biographer, Herbert Croly, wrote:

> Columbus came to resemble a medieval city given over to an angry feud between armed partisans. Everybody was worked up to a high pitch of excitement and resentment. Blows were exchanged in the hotels and on the streets. There were threats of assassination. Timid men feared to go out alone after dark. Certain members of the Legislature were supplied with bodyguards. Many of them never left their rooms. Detectives and spies, who were trying to track down various stories of bribery and corruption, were scattered everywhere. Much of the indignation was concentrated on the Governor. His inauguration was a ghost of a ceremony. The reception was over in twenty minutes, and out of the two hundred and fifty invitations sent to prominent people to be present, only twenty-five were accepted. A delegation of the Governor's own fellow-townsmen and neighbors went to see him in a body and asked him to explain his behavior. Finding that he could or would return no satisfactory answer to their complaints, they insulted him to his face. They threw his lithograph portrait on the floor in front of him, and spat and wiped their feet upon it.

So close were the opposing factions in the assembly that even the deftest political abacists could not be sure of the result. Even a single vote might swing the balance. Legislators were dragooned. Money was passed. There were bright promises of rewards and offices. One Hanna assemblyman, John E. Griffith, suddenly disappeared altogether. A Hanna posse finally located him, drugged or drunk, in the rooms of the Mc-Kisson men at the Southern Hotel, and brought him back to the Neil House.

On the day of voting the Hanna legislators trooped to the State House protected by armed guards. Desperate and determined men swarmed in the corridors. Hanna had arranged a system of signals to keep him in touch with the balloting. In the end three Democrats bolted their party's decision to vote for Hanna, and the combined balloting result of both House and Senate was 73 votes for Hanna to 70 for McKisson. As the figures were read off, a Hanna supporter darted out to the State House steps waving a handkerchief violently to give the Senator at his Neil

House window, the sign that he had won. His supporters massed in the square below cheering and shouting for him until the chubby, beaming victor finally stepped out on the balcony to wave to them, remarking under his breath that he was really too fat to play Juliet.

For the moment Hanna had Ohio in his pocket. The following year—in the same campaign that would bring Harding to the state assembly—he installed his personal candidate, Judge Nash, as governor. At the Republican nominating convention the ever-hopeful Harry Daugherty had emerged from the back rooms to challenge Nash, but had been flattened by Hanna and Cox.[7] Nash, a political hack of thirty years with a bald head and a walrus mustache, overwhelmed the Democratic candidate, the irrepressibly corrupt John McLean. As for McKisson, Hanna remarked that a baby in diapers would beat him if he tried to run for mayor of Cleveland again. McKisson did try, and Hanna produced the baby in the unlikely bulk of a Democratic boss known ironically as "Honest John" Farley.

To the junior senator from Ohio the new century seemed to mark the apex of his hopes and dreams. He had put his dearest friend in the White House and himself in the Senate. He had put Foraker in his place. He had thrown back the populist-Democrat Bryan and his greenback rabble, and would throw them back again even more emphatically in the 1900 election. Yet, though he could not see it—though in his few remaining years he would never see it—the country that he had helped stabilize was loosening. Once more in the grinding processes of history a synthesis of events was developing its inevitable antithesis.

"Some men must rule; the great mass of men must be ruled," Hanna had said as if he were pronouncing the Decalogue. "Some men must own; the great mass of men must work for those who own." For him it was of the nature of things that the prosperity of the country depended on the freedom of big business unhampered by petty legislators and such eighteenth-century anachronisms as the will of the people. Without this predatory freedom—the freedom to bribe and corrupt in order to have its way, buy legislators and sell states—the new industrialism that in its egocentric acquisitiveness had replaced the roads with railroads, the farms with factories, and the towns with cities might never have developed. The new imperial America could not have developed. Hanna sensed this, as the emergent reformers could not. For Lincoln Steffens the government had become "a government of the people by the politicians hired to represent the privileged class." What Steffens and the other reformers in their indignation did not grasp was that under the time spirit of the "gilded age" there had been no real alternative to this exploitation they

[7] Two years before, Daugherty had made an unsuccessful bid for nomination as attorney general. He would make two such empty tries for Congress.

deplored. What Hanna and Foraker did not, could not sense was that as the century came to its end the time spirit was moving on. Public opinion, so long dormant, was no longer willing to tolerate the complacent corruption of the gilded age.

Among the Democrats, Bryan in his fusion with the Populists had ousted the old silk-stocking conservatives from party control. In the year of McKinley's second triumph the anti-corporation candidate Robert M. La Follette defied the bosses to make himself Republican governor of Wisconsin. To the North, Minnesota elected the radical Gov. Samuel R. Van Sant, and a year later the trust-busting Albert B. Cummins became governor of Iowa.

Gov. Theodore Roosevelt in Albany was already troubling the sleep of Republican bosses. The unknown Charles Evans Hughes would shortly make himself nationally known by the insomnia he would bring to New York utilities magnates and the heads of insurance companies. Reform was the wave of the future, moving in on the shores of the old political-industrial complacency, self-righteous as each succeeding future wave always is before it crests and breaks.

In Ohio the reform time spirit was already flickering in some of the cities—damped though it was by the state assembly in Columbus. Samuel M. "Golden Rule" Jones had just been re-elected independent mayor of Toledo, a position to which he had been originally helped by Republican leader Walter Brown under the mistaken notion that Jones would help the street railways and electric-light corporations in securing franchises. Jones, from a bluff and genial manufacturer of oil-drilling equipment, had evolved into a Christian socialist of sorts who read (and quoted) Tolstoy, Emerson, and Whitman, and even more paradoxically took Christ's teachings literally. He announced that for his Acme Sucker Rod Company the one rule was now the Golden Rule, and he set up a Golden Rule Hall and Dining Room, a Golden Rule Park, even a Golden Rule Band. At municipal elections he became unbeatable—on his re-election as an independent he polled 70 per cent of the votes—and at his death he was succeeded in office by his young secretary, Brand Whitlock.[8] Even in Hanna's own Cleveland the time spirit had begun to glow. When Honest John Farley's term was up in 1901, he would be replaced by the dynamic Tom L. Johnson. A more practical man than Golden Rule Jones, Johnson had started out as a street railway magnate, with such spectacular success that Hanna had once offered to go into partnership with him. But in the midst of

[8] Whitlock was an Emersonian visionary who believed that his mission was to eradicate the brutality of the state. But the coarseness of the everyday world was too much for him, and he lived at home as much as possible reading and writing. After four terms as mayor he retired in disillusionment, eventually leaving America and settling in France.

making millions in traction, in steel, and in stock manipulations he became converted to the lay doctrines of Henry George, sold his holdings, and with a convert's zeal determined to apply the single-tax teachings to his home city. At the age of forty-seven years he was elected mayor of Cleveland on the issue of municipal ownership, "people against privilege." Outwardly he was a plump man with black unruly hair, almost classical features, and an almost permanent smile. His chief lieutenant and head of Cleveland's law department was Newton D. Baker, later Wilson's secretary of war. Hanna detested Johnson whom he called a "socialist-anarchist-nihilist."

The newly elected Senator Harding had no more use for Johnson and the unread Henry George than did Hanna. Yet, as he prepared to leave Marion for Columbus, he seemed for all his attachment to Fire Engine Joe more the young progressive than the young conservative. The spirit of the times—he had often used the Hegelian phrase in the *Star*—was on him. Foraker might say, as one correspondent wrote Harding, that "you was one of his people," but to Judge Nash's supporters the Marion senator-elect had announced his independence of "the C. L. Kurtz gang."

However the Crawfords and the Sweneys and the Klings might feel about it, the striking-looking thirty-five-year-old senator with the winning voice was now the leader of the party in Marion County. He was not a boss, backed by a ruthless and efficient machine, nor would he ever be one, for he lacked the unrelenting ambition, the vigor, the hot love of wealth, and the cold love of power. He would be most things to most men, a conciliator, in his own favorite phrase a "harmonizer," rather than a leader. Politics was a game he understood thoroughly—as a game. He had read little beyond the exchanges that came to the *Star* from other Ohio newspapers. His background in history and economics and literature had not progressed beyond the days when he sat on the hard benches of Iberia College. His mind accepted the world of Marion as he found it, and applied it to the world at large. Nevertheless, in his challenge to the Republican county elders, he appeared progressive, almost *a* progressive.

For years in the *Star* he had been demanding reforms in the Marion city government, improvements that improved rather than paid off political debts. As editor he had been non-partisan enough to support a union ticket that replaced a Republican by a Democrat on the school board. He even praised voters who were becoming "politically independent" in local affairs, and called this ticket-splitting tendency a safeguard against "corruptness," a lesson to both parties that the best men must be nominated. Every caucus, he wrote in an editorial, should be a mass convention to reduce "Bossism." Of Boss Cox he noted "the sober truth that politicians of his character are popular only amid victory." Although he was against the initiative and referendum, feeling that to have the voters directly originate or approve laws would reduce the legislators to errand boys, he had been enthusiastic in his support of Sen. James Garfield's civil service bill. "We shall take an immense step forward," he wrote, "when the public service is put beyond the control of designing politicians." Constantly he spoke of "rational" reform, "rational" progressivism.

On January 1, 1901, he became one of the 23 new senators to take his place in the austerely ornate senate chamber of the gray limestone capitol. That severe Doric building with the landmark of its truncated lantern dome built over sixty years before by convict labor summed up in its dimensions the more expansive, more urbane world into which Harding had now moved. The white Columbus landscape, on that chill New Year's Day, stretched before him still unknown, a blank sheet of paper on which the course of his political life was to be written.

[CHAPTER VIII]

State Senator

Of the 31 members of the Ohio senate assembled in the capitol on New Year's Day, 1901, 19 were Republicans, 11 Democrats, and 1 an Independent Republican. This seventy-fourth session was scheduled to end on April 16, and as the assembly met only on alternate years there would not be another meeting until after the elections of 1901. In session or out, the senators received $600 a year plus twelve cents a mile travel allowance.

To the neophyte senator from Marion the plush quiet of the square, high-ceilinged senate chamber came as a solemnly impressive contrast to the clatter of the Marion courthouse. From the crystal chandelier (now lighted by gas) to the marble dais—like an altar—supporting the speaker's desk and chair, the room had a continuity about it that suggested the parchment documents of the early republic in their copper-plate decorum. The carpeting was like moss underfoot, and the wide desks and solid leather chairs looked reassuringly opulent. Neo-classical statesmen could have spoken fittingly within the chambers of that neo-classic capitol. Of course they did not.

The Seventy-Fourth Ohio Assembly, if not more corrupt than most state legislatures, was certainly not less so. Reformers of the stamp of Ohio's Frederick Howe might cherish the ideal of elected representatives governed by an abstract concern for the public welfare, influenced not by pressure groups but by what was best for all Ohioans, all Americans. Such hypothetical legislators, if they were found anywhere, were not found in Columbus at the beginning of the century.

Behind the legislators, invisible but omnipotent, were grouped the Four Horsemen of special interests—the railroads, the public utilities, the building and loan companies, and (Ohio's unique contribution to American politics), the Anti-Saloon League. Through their lawyers and lobbyists they combined in intricate self-defense. Howe observed the scene with doctrinaire dismay:

133

Mark Hanna's law firm in Cleveland took a lion's share in the lobbying. It was said that no bill was permitted to come out of committee until Mr. Hanna's lawyers had first examined and approved it.

There was little venality in the assembly. Money was rarely used. It was not necessary. Some men were kept in line by being permitted to win substantial sums at poker. Others were compromised by prostitutes brought on from Cleveland and Cincinnati for that purpose. Indiscreet seekers after pleasure were made obedient by fear of exposure and blackmail.

Lobbyists were of every variety. Many of them had previously held State offices. The ex-clerk of the Senate was reputedly the representative of the Standard Oil Company. The lobbyist of the steam-railroads was an elderly man, religious in demeanor, cynical in conversation, who knew everybody who had ever been in Columbus. He spent his time playing cards in hotels, and knew how members of the Assembly could be reached. Newspapermen were involved in the system which was woven like a web in and out of the political and business life of the state.

Senator Hanna, Senator Foraker, and John R. McLean made a great part of their fortunes through the control of the political state. They legislated directly for themselves or they killed bills that would tax their property or regulate it. . . . When crises arose, Senator Hanna marshaled his supporters, Senator Foraker marshaled his, and the Democratic bosses delivered a sufficient number of votes to insure the desired results. The bosses were quite non-partisan.

Such social-worker animadversions would have seemed a good joke to the practical politicians bustling about the capitol on their affairs. Nor was the progressive streak in Harding stirred to any undue reformist zeal. He took Columbus as he found it, and he found it good. Coming there practically unknown, a junior senator among junior senators, he was before long—as a capitol reporter of the time later recalled—

the most popular man in the legislature. He was soon regarded as a coming man in Ohio politics. He was an excellent "mixer," he had the inestimable gift of never forgetting a man's face or his name, and there was always a genuine warmth in his handshake, a real geniality in his smile. He was a regular he-man according to the sign manual of the old days—a great poker player, and not at all averse to putting a foot on the brass rail.

A thorough good fellow was the bipartisan verdict on Harding, and a Columbus banker observed that he made a hit almost as soon as he arrived. He was equally popular in the capitol, in the corridors, in clubs, in social life, and even in certain pleasantly unmentionable places. Columbus brought out his soothing talents as an after-dinner speaker. Unlike Foraker, he did not stiffen his audience in their chairs with words of fire and ice. He was genial; as one man observed, his talk was "like a cordial—it always made the occasion pleasanter." He spoke whenever asked, at glee clubs and girls' industrial schools, before high-school graduating classes and builders' supply associations, hypnotizing the audiences with his mellow voice. "Patriotism!" he would tell them ringingly. "It is the soul of nationality and the energy of civilization." In the Senate he was always the harmonizer to calm flowing tempers and persuade stubborn opponents to get together and patch up their differences.

At the beginning of the term he had rented a parlor-bedroom suite in the Great Southern on hotel row, that labyrinth of buildings across from the statehouse known as "the little capitol" where so much of Ohio's business was done and undone. Often he held evening poker parties in his suite for fellow legislators, while the Duchess circulated trays of drinks and refreshments. The boys accepted her as a tolerant if somewhat formidable aunt. She liked to see her "Wurr'n" having a good time so long as it was with other men. It was she who sent him to a proper tailor, Paul Gettum—"Gett'em of Gettum!"—who specialized in making politicians look like statesmen. Harding bought his first dress suit and learned to wear it. From dinner speaker to dedicator of homes for "the boys in blue," he found himself more and more in demand. He was entertained and he entertained, both in Columbus and back at Marion. In February, when the Marion Elks put on the *Mikado,* Governor Nash and a number of legislators were his guests at the performance.

At this turn-of-the-century session there was no particular intimacy yet between him and Daugherty. Daugherty, by then realizing that it was easier for him to influence people than to win votes, had given up external political ambitions and was maneuvering backstage toward the Hanna wing of the party. After Harding's election he had written a note congratulating him and saying that he would consider it a compliment if the new senator would call on him during the coming session. Harding's closest and most durable friendship of the session was with the assistant clerk of the assembly, Malcolm Jennings. Jennings, a clever, wire-pulling careerist, was two years older than Harding and had been a legislative reporter since 1883. Affable, full of bouncy energy, with an aggressive jaw, long nose, and slightly bulging eyes, he had absorbed enough in his reporter's years for politicians and lobbyists to come to him for information. Harding would owe much to Jennings.

Membership in the abundant legislative standing committees was shared equally among senators of both parties. Harding was appointed to the committees on finance, ditches and drains, medical colleges and universities, privilege and elections, and public printings of which he was chairman. His most important committee was that of municipal corporations. The assembly passed hundreds of bills each session in the naïve legalistic conviction—so imbedded in the American tradition since the time of the Puritans—that the word is father to the deed, that in order to correct an error or right a wrong all that is necessary is to make a law.

Most of the enactments were vanity bills to carry a legislator's name self-importantly into a local paper or display it on the hustings, but without practical consequences. They became paragraph laws, buried away in the proliferating shelves of dusty unread statute books. Harding introduced fifteen bills in his first term as senator. With one exception they were the usual run of such vanity measures, parochial or inconsequential. Remembering his libel difficulties with Mary Lynn, he filed bill No. 46 to protect a publisher "who prints some things in a paper and believing them to be true." His bill No. 24 provided ostensibly for "the proper arrangements and preservation of certain pleadings and papers on file in certain probate courts." Its more practical aim was to force court clerks to buy a certain oversize legal typewriter that some of his friends were promoting. There were also Harding bills to raise the pay of various Marion County officers and to authorize a bond issue to build a schoolhouse in Prospect Township.

Much of the time and attention of the assembly were given to a bill backed by Boss Cox, and known as the "Cox Ripper," to reorganize the city government of Cincinnati. Such ripper bills were designed to take effective governing control of any too obstreperously progressive city and lodge it with the legislature. They popped up in the assembly whenever a Single Tax Johnson or a Golden Rule Jones showed signs of getting out of hand with civic reform. Two years before, a popular German Democrat in Cincinnati, Gustav Tafel, had scored a distressing political upset by defeating the Cox candidate for mayor. Although the Boss soon managed to suborn Tafel's henchmen and regain his old control of the city's functions, he was outraged at any such challenge to his monolithic rule. His ripper bill was his reply. The bill was rank even for a ripper, and many of the Republican senators objected to it privately, but Foraker and Hanna and Dick—who as Hanna's man had been elected to Congress in 1898—cracked the whip and insisted that the bill had to go through as a measure necessary "to restore the Republican party to power in Cincinnati." It first passed the Senate.[1] Harding admitted that the bill was "against my conscience," but as a party measure he felt it was his "duty as a Republican to vote for it."

His reaction to another bill sponsored by the Anti-Saloon League to extend local option was similarly ambiguous. During several days of hearings the Women's Christian Temperance Union packed the ladies' gallery with fanatical females while the Reverend A. P. Baker, superintendent of the League, let it be known that any senator who voted against the measure was digging his political grave. Many senators, including Harding, opposed the bill and tried to send it back to the House for reconsideration—in the hope that it would be killed there—but the grim

[1] The bill was afterward considerably amended in the House of Representatives, but from this time on Cox remained the boss of Cincinnati until his death in 1916.

females in the balcony and the grim organization behind them were too relentless for the lawmakers. The bill passed. Harding was one of those voting for it.

As chairman of the Municipal Corporations Committee Harding at the close of the session introduced bill No. 89 providing for "a general re-organization of municipal corporations." This bill, known as the Municipal Code Bill, was the only really important one that the senator from Marion sponsored, and in the transient glow of its liberalism he seemed briefly the aroused young reformer.

For two years a bipartisan commission composed of Judge David F. Pugh of Columbus and Edward Kibler of Newark appointed by Governor Bushnell, had been working on the code bill. In it the commissioners had drawn up an advanced, even a radical, plan for governing Ohio cities. Its chief provisions called for: executive power invested in the mayor and legislative power in a local council (rather than "ripper" control by the state assembly); a ballot without party designations; a civil-service merit system; municipal ownership of street railways and telephone services.

Such a bill allied the politicians in their distaste for the merit system and the non-party ballot with the public-service corporations in their opposition to any extension of public ownership. But reformers and editors throughout the United States saw the bill as a "sweeping and radical innovation . . . a most interesting experiment in the solution of the most important problem in this country, that of scientific and uniform ad-ministration of municipalities." Harding fought for his bill as, in his own words, "a remedy suggested by specialists" for an evil to be cured. After a long struggle he forced the measure through to a successful vote. "Senator Harding," wrote the *Ohio State Journal*, "led a great fight in the Senate yesterday afternoon in behalf of the people and in the interest of municipal reform and won a splendid victory in securing the passage of the Munici-pal Code Bill." Franklin Rubrecht, a Columbus lawyer who had attended the hearings, wrote Harding on April 11:

> While listening to the discussion this afternoon on the Municipal Code Bill, I was very much pleased to hear your eloquent and frank remarks in favor of the measure as reported by the Commission. . . . I am a Democrat, but it strikes me that, if you continue to advocate and practice the same candor and fair dealing as you have since I have noticed you, you will enjoy a political future not limited to legislative halls. . . . Your speech was con-vincing, sensible, frank, able, and logical, and created much favorable comment.

Harding's victory was premature. At the end of the afternoon he left for Washington, and no sooner was he gone than another senator moved to have the bill reconsidered. There were some protests by Harding's friends, "but much as the opponents of the bill liked Harding, as everyone likes him, they would show him no quarter on this occasion, . . . On Mr. Harding's return he will be condoled with by the friends of the bill as it is now as dead as dead can be." [2]

Four days later the session came to an end on its customary note of bibulous non-partisan hilarity. There was a truce to party feuding, while bottles passed from hand to hand in the cloakrooms. Any member who thought he needed the publicity could attach his name to a vanity bill, and scores of such bills were kited through unread. In Howe's strongly teetotal opinion many of the legislators clowning away the last hours were drunk.

Harding's health continued uncertain. During the Columbus session he suffered from ear trouble and at its close had to undergo a mastoid operation. Back in Marion, he was content to leave the everyday side of the *Star* to Van Fleet while he kept in touch with politicians and wrote occasional editorials. On mild spring afternoons his feet, propped up on the sill of his office window as he dozed in his chair, were a familiar sight to passers-by. He liked to sprawl there half-asleep after lunch in a digestive trance as the life of the town, *his* town, glided by. He was becoming a leading citizen. Men went out of their way—they did not have to go too far—to speak to him as he strolled from Mount Vernon Avenue to his office. Once a week he would drop in at Ralph T. Lewis's grocery store for his week's order. Lewis in his stained white apron would come from behind the pickle barrels to pass the time of day, and Harding would always end each order with six packages of Beeman's pepsin chewing gum for the Duchess.

Yet, although appearances were bland, the *Star* and its owner were not as secure as they seemed. Believing as he did in progress, Harding could never resist buying new machinery and equipment for his paper, no matter how much he had to stretch his credit with the local bankers. Kling's friend, the Republican county committeeman J. F. McNeal, who had never forgiven Harding for his defeat in the 1888 congressional convention, had, with Kling's connivance, systematically and secretly bought up about $20,000 worth of Harding's notes. Without warning he suddenly presented them for payment. For a few weeks, until Harding finally succeeded in borrowing money elsewhere, it looked as if he were going to lose his now-flourishing paper.

In Columbus the Marion senator might be one of the most popular newcomers to the capitol, he might entertain the Governor in his own house, but to the entrenched inner circle of Marion he was still a Harding,

[2] According to Professor Alderfer, who holds a uniformly low view of Harding and his motives, Harding deliberately left town to avoid conflict with the party leaders even though he was aware that his bill would be reconsidered and killed.

a suspect and unacceptable outsider, and they let him know it. Everything open to him he joined—the Sons of Union Veterans, the Moose, the Baptist Church. Happily he wore the black-cat insigne of the Concatenated Order of Hoo-Hoos. He would have joined Marion's Kosciusko Lodge of Odd Fellows if the Noble Grand had not been Amos Kling. But his longest-held wish was to become a Mason. Organized in 1840 by Marion's foremost citizens, aloof and quietly contemptuous of the other lodges, Marion Lodge No. 70 of the Free and Accepted Masons stood at the apex of the town's fraternal organizations. Harding, as senator and leader of the Republican party in Marion County, now felt he was worthy of being accepted by Freemasonry. Nevertheless, his first petition for membership, in February, 1901, was rejected. Two months later he again sent in his petition, as did his grocer friend Ralph Lewis, and this time they were both elected to receive the Entered Apprentice Degree—the first step to becoming a Mason. On July 26 Lewis was "passed" and admitted to the Marion Lodge as member No. 519. Harding was turned down after Eugene Sweney had stood up in the meeting, red-faced with anger, to announce that "Harding will never enter this lodge as a Master Mason when I am present!"

While Harding rose politically, the rest of his family remained at their old placid level. Tryon, serenely untidy, drove about the countryside in his buggy, scheming his little schemes between prescriptions, his frayed coat fastened with a horse-blanket pin. Phoebe held the family together both financially and morally, supporting her children in their education, closer to all of them than was the casual Tryon. Every Sunday Harding brought her flowers or, when he was away, arranged to have them sent her. Mother's Day was something he might have invented himself if a Sunday-school teacher from Philadelphia had not beaten him to it. Chat Remsberg had settled with her husband in California. Carolyn and Daisy were elementary schoolteachers in Marion, while living with their parents in the white frame house on Center Street. The flawed Mary continued her teaching in Columbus at the school for the blind. Daisy, the most bookish of the Hardings, had not been content with her course at normal school, and though twenty-four years old still nursed her ambition of attending one of the sedately named and to her almost mythical women's colleges in the East.

Deac would finish his medical studies at the University of Michigan in 1900, his ingrained piety untroubled by any dichotomy between Adventist fundamentalism and medical science. Hard working, morally rigid, close-fisted, he had no time at Ann Arbor for sport or girls or frivolities. Deac was, Harding admitted later, the only man he had ever known who would go to his marriage bed a virgin.

Quite in contrast to Deac was his step-cousin and—for one year—

fellow student, Marshall DeWolfe. Like his father before him, Marshall was nicknamed Pete, and in all other ways he seemed cut to his father's irresponsible pattern. While his grandmother Louisa was alive he had lived in the brick-and-plate-glass Kling mansion, protected by her from the temper lapses of his irascible grandfather. After Louisa's death in 1893 Amos sent the provocative Pete away to school for several years. In 1898, as Marshall Kling, he graduated from Marion High School.[3] Then in the autumn of 1899, once more a DeWolfe, he came as a freshman to Michigan's School of Literature. He remained in Ann Arbor for four years, although his scholastic progress was negligible, and he left finally without a degree. His infrequent letters home were demands for money. Like his father, he drank and gambled and wenched and drifted. When his grandfather refused him further funds, he wrote to his mother or directly to Harding whom he treated with raffish condescension, even as he dunned him for money. Jerry, he called him. In his lackadaisical way he liked his stepfather. It was Pete who had given Harding the puppy, Wedgewood Hub, as a Christmas present. The Duchess did her best to forget she had a son.

As the *Star* continued to run itself without further crises, Harding withdrew more and more from the role of editor to that of publisher. He continued to travel on any occasion, or on no occasion, with an aimless compulsion made possible by the largesse of the railroad lines. Except when the Duchess's health failed, she went with him, following her experience-tried maxim: "Never let a husband travel alone." In the summer of 1900 Harding arranged an "editorial" trip for himself and his wife to Halifax, Nova Scotia, sailing from Boston on the Plant Line. He also managed to secure other free transportation as required for the rest of his family and for many of his friends as well as for the boys on the *Star*.

When a penniless girl from one of Marion's side streets, Madge Fell, was taken with tuberculosis, Harding arranged for her to travel on a pass to Boulder, Colorado, and it was characteristic of his unassuming kindness that he paid her way at the Colorado Sanitarium for the year that she had to live. Possibly it was more the Duchess's shrewdness that caused the sanitarium director to let the girl stay for ten dollars a week—a third off the usual rate.

Harding, again ailing, took no very active part in the presidential campaign of 1900. During the autumn he made a certain number of local and county speeches. With the Jacobin Bryan once more running against the McKinley graven image, the election results were as easy to predict as

---

[3] He is listed in the high-school *Commencement Annual* as Marshall Kling, but on the actual program for the commencement exercises as Marshall DeWolfe.

snow in winter. This year it took Hanna as chairman of the Republican National Committee only $2½ million to beat the Great Commoner.

In October Theodore Roosevelt, impelled into the desuetude of the vice presidency by New York's Boss Platt eager to get him out of the state, spoke at Marion flanked by Senator Foraker, Governor Nash, and former Governors Foster and Bushnell. Harding was on the official welcoming committee but apparently he made little impression on his party's vice presidential nominee, for ten years later, when Harding was running for governor, Roosevelt, on a stump-speech tour of Ohio, had to ask who he was.

President McKinley increased his electoral majority by twenty-one and his popular vote by over a quarter of a million. In Ohio his plurality was the largest ever given a presidential candidate. Seventeen Republican congressional candidates were elected in the state, an increase of two from the 1898 election. "A cross between a landslide and a cyclone," the *Star* called the result, and Harding added: "It is an honest verdict from the sovereign people, who rule, and always will rule the best and greatest nation in the world today. . . . The day of pessimism is gone. Confidence, peace, and progress are proclaimed." The day after the election the *Mirror* admitted ruefully that "we met the enemy and we are theirs." Padgett from his uneasy editorial chair consoled himself a few days later with the thought that Hanna "declines to be the presidential candidate in 1904. He evidently thinks two terms enough."

As a result of the population changes recorded by the decennial census of 1900, many of the local Ohio political boundaries had to be withdrawn. This would increase the state senators by two in 1901 and alter a number of congressional districts before the national elections of 1902. Republican leaders in control at Columbus arranged to carve one safely Republican congressional district out of Morrow, Delaware, Union, Hardin and Marion counties. No sooner was the 1900 election over than there was talk of Harding as the first congressman from the new district. Grant Mouser was also mentioned as a candidate, as was Harding's old enemy and financial nemesis J. F. McNeal.

Politics could wait. Harding was more immediately concerned with securing "editorial transportation" to Florida before the snow set in. At Christmas time he and the Duchess gave their annual Tom-and-Jerry party for the closest circle of their friends, the Christians and their neighbor Charles C. Fisher who was also Harding's lawyer and a director of the Central Ohio Loan & Trust Company. "To meet Thomas and Jeremiah," read the invitation. A few days after the Hardings had put away the punch bowl they left for Daytona. An earlier Marion arrival had engaged a four-dollar-a-week front room for them at J. G. Brown's lodging house. Their meals they took down the street at the Parkinson House, paying six dollars a week each for their board. It was in these warm, idle weeks in Florida that Harding took up golf, before returning to Marion late in March.

When Harding had first become a candidate in the Thirteenth Senatorial District in 1899, Foraker's Kurtz had offered to stand behind him if he wanted a second term. Although 1901 was Logan County's year to nominate a candidate, Harding decided to run again. "I have just learned the ropes and I ought to go back," he told the county leaders, explaining that what was needed was a two-term rotation that would make use of a senator's experience, rather than an automatic jumping-jack shift every other year.

Re-election to the state senate was not common in Ohio, and in Harding's district no senator had ever been re-elected or even renominated in fifty-seven years. In spite of some doubts the Logan County committee finally agreed to endorse him, but in May Judge John E. West of Bellefontaine announced his own candidacy and brought out the embarrassing fact that some years earlier Harding had opposed Senator Plum when he wanted a second term. Nevertheless, at the Logan County convention at Bellefontaine on June 7 Harding managed to win 10 of the 13 Logan County delegates. In July Grant Mouser presented Harding to the senatorial convention, held in Marion, and this time he was nominated by acclamation.

McKinley's assassination in September by the half-mad anarchist Leo Czolgosz reduced the ensuing autumn elections to relative insignificance. Whatever the President might have been, the shock of his cruel passing numbed all political activity. A week after the murder Harding was the principal speaker at a memorial service held in Marion's new Grand Opera House. Nine days later he wrote to Hanna asking him if he would speak in the district before the election in November. Hanna, his high dreams shattered, replied perfunctorily that the little time he had for the campaign was at the disposal of the state committee and it was for the committee to decide. Late in October Hanna's train stopped for three hours at Marion en route from Sidney to Bucyrus, but the old Senator was reluctant to speak and would only agree to attend a municipal political meeting if someone else was to be the chief speaker.

Governor Nash, again nominated, was opposed in the election by the Democrats' Col. James Kilbourne. Tom Johnson, practical enough to see the futility of third-party gestures, had joined the Democratic parade while continuing to beat his drum for tax reform. Election day was mild and warm, Republican weather. Nash won easily, carrying 61 of Ohio's 88 counties; Republicans elected 21 of the 33 senators and 68 of the 110 representatives. Harding carried Hardin as well as Logan and Union counties, defeating the Democratic candidate, Doctor J. H. Criswell, by

3,563 votes—more than double his plurality of two years before. He still failed, however, to prevail over the stubborn combination of rural democracy and his old enemies in Marion, losing the county by 335 votes.

When Harding returned to Columbus for the convocation of the Seventy-fifth Assembly on January 6, 1902, he did indeed know the ropes, and there were not many others to manipulate them. Of the 33 senators, 23 were newcomers. And of the half-dozen re-elected Republican senators Harding was easily the most personable and promising. Foraker, whose term in the United States Senate expired that same year, wrote just after the autumn election to ask Harding to present his name to the assembly for re-election.

In the sisyphean struggles of the Hanna-Foraker factions, Hanna's men dominated the new House of Representatives while Foraker's supporters controlled the Senate. Harding's selection as Republican floor leader seemed a natural as well as a "harmonious" choice. As a party leader he became a party stalwart, yet with his genial nature and winning ways making Democratic and independent friends with equal ease. Nicholas Longworth of Cincinnati, the elegant and urbane bachelor who wore the gold pig miniature of Harvard's Porcellian Club on his watch chain, a graduate as well of Harvard Law School—just elevated from the lower house to the senate by the grace of Boss Cox—was one of his earliest and most convivial first-name friends of the session. Longworth's glittering bald dome, waxed mustache, and exclusive watch chain soon became regular features of the Harding poker evenings. Another close and permanent companion was Frank Edgar Scobey, the curly-haired, back-slapping, former Miami County sheriff with the bushy eyebrows, whose election as clerk of the Senate Harding had engineered.

The first act of the new assembly was to meet in joint session of Senate and House to re-elect Foraker. Harding, balancing delicately between the two factions, presented Foraker's name. "Senator Harding added much to his reputation as an orator," the *Ohio State Journal* noted with approval. "The speaker's address was rich in grace of diction, and his manner, earnest and forceful throughout, rose to the dignity of true oratory. He was heartily applauded when he rose, and he was repeatedly interrupted by the clapping of hands on both sides of the chamber and he was cheered to the echo when he resumed his seat."

It was Harding's mellifluous voice that his colleagues chose to grace the McKinley memorial service. As floor leader he was no longer just another small-town senator, to be retired at the end of his term to some dusty courthouse square. There were grander goals beginning to unfold vaguely before him. Already one heard backstage talk of Harding for governor in 1903. Even now Governor Nash complimented the Senate floor leader on his efficiency.

During the legislative interim a committee of five commissioned by the

Ohio Bar Association had been at work revising Harding's old municipal code bill, reducing it in size and, more significantly, eliminating the non-partisan elections and municipal ownership clauses. Harding himself showed no further interest in the remains.

From the opposite ends of the political spectrum, Tom Johnson and Boss Cox joined unwonted hands to oppose the measure. So desultory was its transit through the assembly that over two hundred amendments were added and the bill never came to a vote.

With the close of the 1902 session Harding, still apprehensive of his health, left with the Duchess for a trip through New England where he visited the Isles of Shoals off the coast of New Hampshire. He was back in Marion in June to entertain Governor Nash at Mount Vernon Avenue with a lawn lunch under the buckeye trees, attended by the Christians, the Fishers and their children.

In June, 1902, the whole ripper bill structure of special charters for special cities was suddenly demolished by the Ohio Supreme Court in a decision that, though it involved only Toledo and Cleveland, shattered the validity of every city charter in the state. Faced with this collapse, Governor Nash called on Senator Longworth and a committee from the Ohio Bar Association to prepare a new code bill for a special session of the assembly on August 25.

Longworth wrote to Harding, chaffing him on his good looks and asking if he would come to the capital to give him "advice and assistance" on the new code bill. After a week in Columbus, Harding and the Duchess left with the Fishers for an excursion to Norfolk, Virginia, the Fishers being supplied with Pullman passes as "employees" of the *Star*.

Four municipal bills were introduced at the special session, running the gamut from reform to anti-reform. Longworth's bill had certain reform features—by establishing a uniform law for all cities it would end the plague of ripper bills—but its provision for cumbersome, easily suborned elective boards of public works and public safety on the model of Cincinnati was tailor-made for Boss Cox and his satellites. Cox, Foraker, and Hanna endorsed the Nash-Longworth bill, made even more palatable to them by a "curative" addition that would have reinstated the fifty-year street railway franchise originally granted by Foraker's notorious Rogers Law.

The Senate passed the measure as presented, but the House of Representatives, although accepting the curative addition, under uncomfortable pressure by the reformers rejected the provision for elective boards. Governor Nash then appointed a House-Senate conference committee of nine Republicans plus one Democrat who had voted for the curative addition to iron out their differences. After much pressure from Hanna and the governor, the House members agreed to yield. Following a long talk with Hanna, Harding, as a member of the committee, played his usual deft role of harmonizer, persuading the dubious and easing the consciences of the reluctant by introducing some minor face-saving amendment which "was adopted after the author had explained its provisions in his charming and convincing way." Cox's Curative Code, as it became derisively known, passed in the House as a strictly party measure. Sixty-one Republican representatives and three renegade Democrats voted for it, to 35 Democrats against it. The vote was taken amid opposition shouts of "Slaves of the bosses!" and as the House adjourned the Democratic members derisively bellowed out a parody of the doxology:

> Praise Cox to whom all blessings flow;
> Praise him, ye people of O-h-i-o;
> Praise Hanna, Nash, and all the host
> But praise George B. Cox the most.

Whatever erring reformist fancies and wayward notions of progressivism may have lain leaf-like in the stray paths of Harding's mind, by the time he had finished his term as floor leader they had been blown away for good by the practical winds of politics. The phrase "stand pat," that Mark Hanna coined that year, would become his motto. Outside the Republican party, and party regularity, there was no salvation.

No twelve months could then elapse without at least one convention and one election, but 1902 was an off-election year with the only Ohio state vacancy to be filled, the office of secretary of state. In the election the Republican nominee, Lewis C. Laylin, easily defeated Tom Johnson's candidate, the clergyman-reformer and disciple of Henry George, Herbert Seeley Bigelow. Nationally the Republicans swept the state again, winning 17 of the 21 congressional districts.

Politics would keep Harding from the orange groves and the Florida beaches that winter. Before the end of 1902 he had decided to make a bid for the governorship. Governor Nash was retiring. The last Republican convention in Marion County had already resolved that Harding be the next candidate. Although it seemed for a while that Hanna's political chief of staff, Colonel Dick, might go after the governor's chair himself, Dick soon announced that he preferred to remain in Congress. Both Hanna and Foraker, agreeing to a temporary armed truce, let it be known that they were standing aside in the contest. In December Governor Nash at a Columbus banquet "bluntly declared" that he would be pleased to see Senator Harding as his successor.

Yet even politics could not drive thoughts of travel from Harding's mind. December found him writing from Marion to inquire about a group trip to Europe sailing from New York in June, 1903, to the Mediterranean. In November he had attended Nick Longworth's birthday dinner, and a

week later the impetuous bachelor was insisting that he and the Duchess
come to Cincinnati for a visit.

It was in 1902 that the *Star* began to review books, and although Harding found time to read little but the newspapers, he liked to glance at the
procession of best sellers that crossed his desk: Harry Leon Wilson, remembered for *Ruggles of Red Gap,* but not for *The Spenders* of that year;
George Carey Eggleston's *Dorothy South;* Max O'Dell's *'Tween You and I;*
and similar ephemeral titles and authors. One book, however, that came
to hand that autumn Harding read and kept with him for years afterward
as a kind of lay Bible. Some recollection of his McGuffey Reader days,
plus the vague awareness that Alexander Hamilton was (as he saw him)
the spiritual forefather of the Republican party, made Harding take up
Gertrude Atherton's *The Conqueror,* subtitled *A Dramatized Biography
of Alexander Hamilton.* Behind *The Conqueror's* somewhat starchy prose
was a background of solid research, and as a novel it read easily. Harding
used the book from then on as a quarry to piece out his set speeches.
When each season he would deliver his speech, "Alexander Hamilton—
Prophet of American Destiny," on the Chautauqua circuits, the Atherton
book was his unacknowledged source.

To an enterprising traveling man selling almost anything, Harding had
never been a difficult prospect. Now, in his rising dignity, he was an easy
touch for every book salesman. He scarcely needed reminding that it was
befitting a statesman to have a library. Soon the brown alcove at the rear
of his parlor at Mount Vernon Avenue filled up with sets of books—
Hawthorne's works; Bulwer-Lytton's works; the Encyclopædia Britan-
nica; *The Crown Book of the Beautiful, the Wonderful and the Wise;
The Complete Works of Ruskin;* twenty volumes of *Makers of History;*
Jared Sparks's *Life of Washington; The History of Our Country,* in eight
leather volumes, by Edward S. Ellis A.M.; stories from Homer, Herodotus,
Livy, Virgil. The unread volumes stared at each other from a tall mahogany bookcase with swinging doors on one side of the room and an expanding range of Globe-Wernicke portable shelves with leaded glass
fronts on the other. Fugitive best sellers by James Oliver Curwood, Gene
Stratton-Porter, Alice Brown, and Leroy Scott filled in the chinks between sets. Somewhere he got hold of and absorbed Edgar Saltus's purple-
paragraphed *Imperial Purple,* and added Caesar to his household heroes,
Napoleon and Hamilton.

Harding's sisters much admired his fine library. As he rose in the world
his family grew more dependent on him, and he aided them ungrudgingly.
Although never close to his father, he paid Tryon's office rent and, when
called on, met the mortgage payments of the Center Street house. In
September, 1902, Daisy with his help had achieved her dearest wish and

gone East to Vassar for a year as a special student. Deac, after receiving his medical diploma, had decided to specialize on mental cases and had taken his first job as an assistant physician in the Columbus State Hospital for the Insane. There the virginal doctor had met Elsie Weaver, a former Marion girl, whose father was a hospital gardener. Deac wanted to get married at once. Unfortunately hospital regulations required assistant physicians to remain single. Importunately he kept writing to his brother to get the regulations changed. When Harding first visited him in Columbus he found him shabbily dressed beneath his white coat and took him to Gettum's to buy him his first tailor-made suit.

Dick's withdrawal, if it opened the way for Harding, opened it for others as well. Ever since the summer of 1902, Myron Herrick the Cleveland banker, with the astute guidance of Congressman Burton, had been planning his own candidacy. Hanna and Cox at this early date favored Dick. Burton, whose admiration for Hanna was never excessive, helped Herrick prepare his formal announcement as a candidate, and in all the preconvention maneuverings Herrick followed the Congressman's advice.

Myron T. Herrick, eleven years older than Harding, had been born in a log cabin in Lorain County on land allotted his grandfather for fighting in the War of 1812. His father wanted him to be a farmer, but at the age of thirteen he read Henry Ward Beecher's novel *Norwood* and determined to go to college. By the time he was sixteen he had finished high school and managed to get an appointment as a rural schoolmaster in Brighton. Giving that up after a term, he drifted west to St. Louis, where alone and penniless he wrote a description of a new bridge and submitted it to the St. Louis *Globe Democrat*. So impressed was the editor by this little piece that he hired the unknown young author to travel about in Kansas and Texas and the territory of Oklahoma and write up what he saw. For eight months Herrick wandered through the Southwest, sending back stories of the towns and cattle ranches he visited and the people he met. Then, in spite of his success as a reporter, he returned to Ohio with his savings and entered Oberlin Academy. When his savings were gone, he paid his way by selling dinner bells to farmers, then became a salesman for Esty organs. After a year at Oberlin, he spent two years at Ohio Wesleyan College and managed to reach the junior class before his money gave out.

In 1875 he moved to Cleveland and became a student office boy in a law firm, with the chance to read law in his spare time. He was admitted to the bar in 1878. A beaming, wide-faced, shaggy-haired man, he early showed an extraordinary aptitude for making money. With a friend he bought property that was part of an estate and soon sold it at $100,000 profit. His touch was golden. He organized a hardware company, the Cleveland Arcade Building, and was elected secretary and treasurer of the Society for Savings. Later, with friends, he founded the National Carbon Company and the Cleveland Electric Illuminating Company and acquired control of the Western Maryland Railroad. In 1901 he was elected president of the American Bankers' Association.

McKinley was as dear a friend to him as he was to Mark Hanna, and when in 1893 Governor McKinley—a man of modest means—had lost $130,000 by signing the notes of a defaulting friend, it was to Herrick he went to save himself from bankruptcy. Herrick was a businessman in politics, yet, unlike Hanna, primarily a businessman and contemptuous of the bosses. A friend of presidents and of J. P. Morgan, Colonel Herrick— McKinley, while governor, had made him a colonel on his staff—moved in a larger world, cast a larger shadow than the small-town editor of the *Star*.[4]

On January 16, 1903, Harding officially if informally announced in a letter published in the *Star* that he was a candidate for governor. At the same time he let it be known that he felt there would be no packing of the convention this year, and that he as a friend of both Hanna and Foraker would cause no factional disputes. Governor Nash wrote him praising his loyalty and saying that although he did not wish to mix up in "this governorship matter," there was nothing in regard to Harding's candidacy with which he could find fault. McLean's Cincinnati *Enquirer* of the following day commented:

> It will be observed that the new candidate lays special stress upon the "seemingly" authoritative statement that the field is an open one, and dwells upon the fact that owing to the united support of Senator Hanna by all factions of the party there is no necessity for any organization mark upon the state ticket. . . . There is no disguising the fact that his entrance will greatly complicate the situation for Colonel Herrick. . . . Senator Harding is a thoroughly organization man, and because of this attitude has the confidence of the political leaders in various parts of the state. It is believed that he is more acceptable to George B. Cox than any other candidate named up to this time.

In contrast to the wealthy Herrick, Harding seemed to many the real man of the people. Heartened by Harding's announcement, a railroad fireman wrote him words of somewhat disconnected encouragement at the end of January:

> I see By the Papers that you are a Candidate for Gov and I Hope that you will get it—what we Laboring men of this and any other State wants is a Man of the People which *we all* know *Col Herrick is not* nor can not Be

[4] McKinley in his first presidential term wanted to make Herrick secretary of the treasury, and at the beginning of his second term offered to appoint him ambassador to Italy. Both these offers Herrick refused.

as He is to much intrested in *Trusts* and *Combines**. Now I am a RR man and a Member in Good Standing of the Brotherhood of Locomotive Firemen which I am Proud of. Now in My Humble opinion the Political Bosses dictates to Much as to Who should be the Nomanee which ought to Be Left to Duly Elected Delegates. Now By What I can asertain you are a Friend of the Common People. Now I want for to ofer a Sudgestion to you and that is that you Try and Get the Indossements of All the Labor unions in the State or—as Many of them as you Can. . . .

Have a Coppy sent to Mark Hanna and to Foraker Telling them Two Gentlemen in Plain English that you are the Choice of Organized Labor for Gov. . . . it will give Col Herrick something to think about Beside Banks RR Bonds and Stocks.

"It is humiliating to say so," Sen. David Moore of Morgan County wrote Harding in February, "but Republican politics in Ohio is gauged only by the Hanna standard so far as getting things are concerned." If Hanna stood aside, as he had indicated he would after Dick's withdrawal, Harding's chances of nomination were good. But against Hanna, Harding had no chance at all, and no one knew that better than Harding himself.

Hanna's term as senator was running out, and at the next meeting of the assembly he would have to present himself for re-election. Once more to take his seat in the Senate was a goal beside which all other political considerations and candidates were negligible. The threat of Tom Johnson, that "carpetbagger followed by a train of all the howling vagrants of Ohio," alarmed him. Johnson, by his smashing re-election as mayor of Hanna's own city, had seized control of the Democratic party of Ohio. The McLeans were forced to creep into their holes, and Johnson with the zeal of an evangelist was now touring the state in his high-speed red Winton, the "Red Devil," followed by eight wagon teams carrying a circus tent able to shelter 6,000 hearers. Johnson, tub thumping for reform municipal ownership, home rule for the cities, equal taxation, the referendum and recall, and the corruption of the Republicans seemed the successor to Bryan in the radical wing of the party. Crowds turned out by the thousands to hear him denounce the Hanna plutocracy, and the Great Commoner himself came to speak under the Johnson canvas.

Hanna was never so negligent as to underestimate an opponent. Johnson might steer his Red Devil right into the capitol and carry enough of the assembly with him to rob an old man of his senate seat. In April the Red Boss of Cleveland sent for the Black Boss of Cincinnati and told him bluntly that the Republicans needed a candidate for governor who could both fill the campaign chest and cut into Johnson's strength in Cleveland's Cuyahoga County. Harding was too tainted by Foraker. Herrick was the man. Boss Cox agreed, and a deal was made.

* Italic words underlined in original.

An anonymous caller reached Harding by telephone to tell him of the deal. Harding had suspected something of the kind. "There is not much to say concerning Mr. Cox's action," he admitted next day, "save that it puts all the rest of us out of it. Unless some exigency arises, Colonel Herrick will be nominated by acclamation, I think. While I confess a disappointment over the outcome, yet I am really pleased that the end has arrived."

With Hanna and Cox in agreement, the nomination for governor was a closed issue two months before the Republican convention. To the *Star* it was like going to a play one had already seen before, and the editorial column recalled wistfully the

> good old-fashioned convention, where, until the taking of the ballots, the result was in doubt and delegates ran about, wringing with perspiration and enthusiasm in the interests of their favorite candidate. Those are remembered as the halcyon days of the party in Ohio.

The Columbus *Dispatch*, with its alter ego the *Ohio State Journal*, carried more weight than any other Republican paper in Ohio, and the *Dispatch* approved of Herrick, pointing out that he represented the business interests in Ohio and that a "practical businessman" was what was needed in the chief executive's office. The *Dispatch* and the *Journal*, owned by Robert E. Wolfe, spoke with the same authority for the Republicans that McLean's *Enquirer* did for the Democrats. In both cases the papers had achieved a higher ethical level than their owner.

No Republican politician in Ohio could afford to disregard Bob Wolfe. His solid arrogance embodied his kind of success. He had run away from home at the age of nine, wandered and drifted to Washington, New York, New Orleans, Cuba, the Southwest. He had lived as a sailor, a cowboy, a tramp. There were stories about him that were only whispered in his home state. One was that he had served a term in jail, and that behind bars he had learned how to make shoes. In any case, while still a young man he had started from nothing and made his fortune as a shoe manufacturer. With wealth behind him, he turned to newspaper publishing and built up two of Ohio's outstanding papers. He knew everybody, and he was not a man to cross.

From Harding's political beginnings—and long afterward—Wolfe never thought much of him. Nevertheless, on April 23 the *Dispatch* came out for Harding for lieutenant governor and offered the slogan for the campaign: "Herrick, Harding, and Harmony," observing—it was the voice of Bob Wolfe—that a slogan was, after all, more important than issues.

In May Harding paid a propitiatory visit to the shrine above the Mecca saloon. Cox expressed his gratitude to the Senator for his work in the last legislative session. "I think we can make you lieutenant governor," he told him from the shadows. "Just sit tight and wait." But when Harding traveled to Cleveland to see Hanna, the Red Boss was evasive, not rejecting Harding out of hand but musing aloud as to whether it might not be politically wiser to have an old soldier in second place. What he mused on inwardly was the knowledge that President Roosevelt was considering Herrick for a running mate in the 1904 election. If Herrick were to move on to the vice presidency, Harding would succeed to the governorship, and state patronage would then be funneled through Foraker.

That spring the foxy Foraker had once more outwitted Hanna the aged lion, this time in the matter of the 1904 presidential election. To politicians everywhere it was clear that Theodore Roosevelt, now merely filling a dead man's shoes, would never be content until he was elected President in his own right. Foraker and Hanna both grasped the elementary political fact that the lusty young President with his thirty-two-tooth grin would be unbeatable. But as the election year began to cast its shadow, Hanna was in no hurry to commit himself to the Rough Rider. He and Roosevelt continued to maintain friendly relations, even though the President admitted privately that the chairman of the Republican National Committee was his one formidable opponent. What Hanna had in mind was to go to the convention with the favorite-son votes of the Ohio delegation tucked in his pocket. Roosevelt would need those and the other votes Hanna controlled, and he would have to bargain for them. Once aware of this scheme, Foraker determined to smoke the old lion out. He announced that he would favor a resolution at the June Republican state convention endorsing Roosevelt for the following year's nomination. Hanna said that he opposed such a resolution as premature. Nevertheless, Foraker's announcement placed him in an almost insoluble dilemma. If he seconded Roosevelt for 1904, he would lose his bargaining power. If he did not, it would seem to the President that the Senator was plotting to take the nomination for himself. Hanna tried to solve his dilemma by writing Roosevelt that although he felt a resolution a year in advance was premature, this did not mean he was in any way opposed to the President's nomination. Roosevelt replied, releasing his reply simultaneously to the press: "I have not asked any man for his support. I have nothing whatever to do with raising this issue. Inasmuch as it has been raised, of course those who favor my administration and nomination will favor endorsing both, and those who do not will oppose."

Belatedly Hanna found himself forced to declare for Roosevelt as "worthy of endorsement for his great service to the people." [5] Foraker

[5] A more subtle explanation, but one more worthy of Hanna's acumen, is that he outmaneuvered Foraker in an effort to force him on Roosevelt as a vice presidential candidate. If Foraker were out of the way, he could then claim his Senate seat for his own lieutenant, Congressman Dick.

could now put himself forward as the President's leading Ohio supporter and claim his consequent share of Federal patronage. With Foraker's triumph, Hanna was even less inclined to accept Harding. The candidate he had in mind for lieutenant governor was a former congressman from Williams County, Capt. M. M. Boothman, who had lost a leg in the Civil War and who with Capt. E. E. Nutt of Sydney claimed the old-soldier vote.

Officially Hanna continued to claim that he had made no choice of candidate for lieutenant governor, that his policy was "hands off," a slogan he had added that year to his earlier "full dinner pail," "let well enough alone," and "stand pat." In any case he was more concerned with his daughter Ruth's June wedding to the wealthy and debonair—if flighty-minded—Medill McCormick, an event so important that the date of the Columbus convention had been advanced a week to accommodate it. President Roosevelt and his Cabinet were expected to attend what the papers predicted would be "the most elaborate and distinguished wedding possibly of which there is record in the country."

Two days before the convention, on June 2, Hanna met Harding in Columbus and told him that he was not taking sides but that as an old soldier himself he could not oppose other old soldiers such as Boothman and Nutt. Harding with his delegates had taken the train that morning from Marion, accompanied to the station by the Citizens' Band playing "Onward Christian Soldiers." Once in Columbus, he had set up his headquarters at the Neil House—where Hanna also had a suite—with his friends Scobey and Jennings in charge. "I will not be put out," he told reporters after his talk with Hanna. "They may knock me down and drag me out, but I will not be put out."

The night before the convention Harding's headquarters were tense with swirling rumors. At midnight he still insisted to reporters that he was not an anti-Hanna candidate, nor would his nomination be an anti-Hanna victory. But Jennings told them that Harding was going to be nominated whether Hanna liked it or not. The mood grew more cheerful after the Republican Glee Club of Columbus arrived to serenade Harding. In the hotel rooms, amid the cigars and the clink of highball glasses, men in shirt sleeves bargained under the bare lights, told smokehouse stories, and bargained again. Just before 3 A.M. Boothman was seen limping into the Neil House. For those who could read the signs, something was up.

Cox, Dick, Herrick, and Hanna had argued about Harding until long after midnight. Hanna still did not want him but Cox pointed out that he had given his word and that a defeat for Harding would now be a personal defeat for him. In any case, the Boss felt that since Boothman did not have 300 votes and Nutt even fewer, to oppose Harding for anything as obscure as the lieutenant governorship was "peanut politics." At one point the four were interrupted in their arguments by an itinerant Adventist preacher who had been stalking the corridors all evening to warn stray delegates that the end of the world was at hand. "I want to save all you Republicans from hell," he announced as he walked into the room, his Bible clasped in his hand. "Get ready!" As he was being shown the door, Hanna observed that if the end of the world was that close, it might as well end with Harding as lieutenant governor. Dick and Herrick agreed. They then sent for Boothman and Nutt and told them of the party's decision. Both old soldiers agreed to drop out of the race. Harding was summoned. Hanna told him cheerfully that he was going to be the next lieutenant governor, adding that Boothman would place his name in nomination rather than Grant Mouser as Harding had planned.

Harding had not supplied himself with buttons or badges, but after hearing Hanna he bought up all the white carnations he could find in the nearby florist shops and began pinning them on his supporters. Word had got round, and by morning every other buttonhole seemed to have a Harding carnation in it. Hanna at breakfast—as was intended—could not help but notice the bobbing white flowers. The tale grew up afterward that it was the platoons of carnations that had made him change his mind.

The 900 delegates at the Columbus Auditorium, thoughtfully provided by the Hocking Valley Railroad with dollar excursion rates to Columbus, had spent the hour from nine to ten straggling into a hall "tastefully decorated" with potted plants, flowers, and red, white, and blue bunting, the usual band playing the usual tunes. More unusual were the numbers of women in the balcony. The air was languid. There was no suspense, no anticipation. Everybody knew that all the offices had been properly chosen long before. The business of the delegates was to approve the choice. One reporter thought that the undertakers' convention, taking place simultaneously at the Great Southern, seemed more lively.

Hanna, as temporary chairman, called the convention to order. There were cheers as he stood in mock harmony beside Foraker on the platform. Walking down the aisle, he had dragged his right foot. The more attentive delegates could not help but notice that the chairman of the Republican National Committee, the maker of Presidents, the shortly-to-be-re-elected senator, was coming to the end of the road. Since McKinley's death he had seemed to shrink within his skin. His clothes flopped on him as he walked. Even though his voice still carried as far as ever, its strength had gone. Foraker, for all his flowing white hair, looked indestructible as he took over as permanent chairman. He outlined the three main duties of the convention: to nominate Herrick; to nominate Hanna as senator; to endorse Roosevelt. Herrick appeared in the back of the hall and was escorted to the platform by a committee headed by Boss Cox. After the nominating speech a delegate moved to suspend the rules and nominate Herrick by acclamation. It was done with a labored shout. Herrick's acceptance speech was disappointing. He was not a good speaker. Captain Boothman, in gallantly nominating Harding, said that he and Nutt as old soldiers had decided to leave the race for the son of an old soldier. The nomination "went through with a whirl."

Rebuffed by Herrick, the delegates would have felt cheated without their ration of empurpled oratory and Harding gave it to them. It was party "harmony" as Harding had always preached it, and the convention broke up with an alliterative expansion of the Bob Wolfe slogan that delighted him: Hanna, Herrick, Harding, and Harmony. As Harding remarked afterward, even the Democrats would have to admit that Mr. Hanna had had a nice convention.

When Harding arrived home that evening the Citizens' Band was waiting to serenade him. A large crowd of his friends and neighbors, Republican and Democrat, had gathered in front of the house—the Fishers, the Christians, Doctor Sawyer, and his wife Mandy among the rest—with Grant Mouser as master of ceremonies. Already they were calling Harding "Gov." Only Amos Kling still held back. His reaction was to remark that he hoped he would never live to see a black man governor of Ohio.

Following his nomination Harding canceled the European trip he had planned. The rest of the summer, until the opening of the campaign in mid-September, he "bloviated" in Marion. There was time again for the languid Sunday outdoor lunches with the Christians under the buckeye trees, time enough on heat-heavy afternoons to doze in his office swivel chair vaguely aware of the pleasant, busy sound of the *Star's* printing presses on the floor below, and the not-so-pleasant sound of the Duchess's voice scolding the delivery boys. On the way back from the office he would stop in at Ralph Lewis's, not forgetting the six packages of Beeman's pepsin gum. Politically speaking, he was now Marion's first citizen. The newly-formed commercial club gave a ball in his honor. "I had hoped that Uncle Mark would keep his 'hands off,'" the Columbus banker, W. G. Neff, wrote Harding a few days after the nomination, "and in that case I think we would have made you governor this time. However, a good strong man will not be crippled in his career by holding the position of lieutenant governor."

Deac had planned to marry in January and start up his own private practice in Columbus. He wrote his brother that he had no ambition to be superintendent of a state hospital "but I do want to be intimately connected with the care and treatment of the state's insane so that I may thoroughly study the subject of insanity." Not until July 23, 1903, was he finally able to marry his Elsie. Twelve days later, with Deac and his bride in attendance, Carolyn married Heber H. Votaw, a sniffly Seventh-day

Adventist from Toledo. Votaw was then a traveling salesman, but planned to quit business that autumn to enter Adventist mission work either in Texas or Cape Colony. Mary, the dark and conscientious, wrote, too; one of those stiff, pathetic letters of half-printed characters that the blind write, enclosing the four-dollars-and-a-half interest payment on a hundred dollars that she had borrowed from her brother.

Harding the publisher still had his problems in spite of Van Fleet's editorial competence. One intrusive problem that autumn was Aylmer Rhoads whose weekend sprees were beginning to extend themselves through the week. When Rhoads took to pawning his overcoat and even his children's small possessions for drink, his wife appealed to Harding. Harding did his best, supporting the family while trying to cajole Rhoads back on his feet. But even on his feet Rhoads was still unsteady. Harding prided himself on never discharging anyone from the *Star*. He finally rid himself of Rhoads by getting him a one-way family pass to Cincinnati and a job on the *Commercial Tribune*. From time to time, as out of the distant past, Harding would receive a letter from another old neighbor, Kelly Mount, now in the state hospital for the insane in Columbus.

The Democratic state convention of 1903 was not held until August 25, but it was as much a rubber-stamp endorsement of Tom Johnson as the Republican convention had been of Herrick. Johnson had been campaigning in his Red Devil since May, covering every county in Ohio, speaking four to seven times a day, and holding a tent meeting every night. So rapidly did he move from place to place that he was finally forced to send his circus tent by rail. The crowds he drew were large and convinced.

The Republican Four-H campaign opened formally at Chillicothe on September 19 with Foraker, the ailing Hanna, Herrick, and Harding as the chief speakers. Harmony was not quite so conspicuous as the ubiquitous Foraker pictures that outnumbered those of Herrick by two to one. Harding had been doing his best for harmony. He, with the Duchess, had been a house guest of Herrick's in Cleveland, had visited Hanna—confined to his sickroom—and on August 23 had taken Hanna's place at a Republican club picnic at Scenic Park. On September 29 he went on a five-day speaking tour with Herrick and the still-ailing Hanna in Hanna's plushly ornate private railroad car. Johnson continued his swirling tours through Ohio in the Red Devil, like another Bryan lashing out at the "powers and privileges of incorporated wealth," demanding public ownership of street railways and denouncing the inequalities of the tax laws. But Hanna, in spite of his dragging leg and failing body, was a match for him. "Kill the attempt to flout the flag of socialism over Ohio," he told his audiences. To his mind and in his speeches, public ownership was socialism and socialism was the equivalent of anarchism, and he never failed to point out that "our late President, the honored McKinley, was a victim of that damnable heresy." Herrick alarmed his rural audiences with lurid predictions of what the single tax would do to farmers. The usually Democratic Catholics, fearful of seeing their churches taxed to the ground, turned against Johnson, and this in itself would have been enough to defeat him. Herrick carried the state by 113,812 votes, the largest plurality ever given an Ohio governor. Marion County remained Democratic, though with diminishing stubbornness. Harding lost the county this time by only 126 votes. His uncle, the now-retired Methodist clergyman, wrote him from Wisconsin: "I am proud to have my name-sake so highly honored. May yet higher honors come to you in the not distant future is the serene wish and confident hope of Warren Gamaliel Bancroft."

For all its triumph, the election left Harding as usual, nervously ex-hausted. After he had acknowledged the first round of congratulations, he left again on November 19 for the Battle Creek Sanitarium, taking with him his mother who was suffering from some kind of partial paralysis. But this time a few days of Doctor Kellogg's regime of grapenuts and stewed vegetables sufficed him, and in a week he was back in Marion. This was his last sojourn at Battle Creek.

Ohio's Seventy-sixth General Assembly that convened in Columbus on January 4, 1904 had a Republican majority of four to one in the house and seven to one in the Senate. Politically speaking, Harding was now the second man in the state of Ohio. In the Senate chamber he had entered diffidently four years ago for the first time, he now sat as presiding officer in the high-backed leather chair on the marble dais beneath the soaring gilt eagle. He loomed above the other senators at their desks as if he were again a teacher looking down on his schoolboys. The twenty years since he had bought the *Star* and announced with rash bravado that he would stay had brought him far, and the years to come would with luck bring him still farther. As a rule the office of lieutenant governor was given to elderly politicians of the second rank as an honorary climax to an insignifi-cant career. It had not been seen as a steppingstone to the governor's chair. Harding saw it differently. He was still young for political life, and he had already broken the one-man senatorial rule in the 13th District. The lieutenant governorship did not *have* to be the end of the line.

When Hanna appeared once more as senatorial candidate before the joint session of the legislature, it was Harding who escorted him to the speaker's chair. Hanna was elected to his old Senate seat over his Demo-cratic opponent, the Cleveland lawyer and Johnson backer, John Hessin Clarke, by a vote of 115 to 25, the largest majority ever given to an Ohio senator and a vindicating contrast to the three-vote margin of 1898. He did not falter in his acceptance speech, but the mark of death was already on him. In five weeks he would be gone.

It was still Hanna, Herrick, Harding, and Harmony on noon of January 11 when Governor-elect Herrick rode to his swearing-in before the capitol, escorted by the cavalrymen of Cleveland's famous Troop A of which he was a member. With him on the wooden platform were Harding, Hanna, and the outgoing Governor Nash, standing bareheaded as the Reverend Doctor S. S. Palmer of the Broad Street Presbyterian Church invoked, and the Republican Glee Club of Columbus sang "America."

The fourfold slogan did not last the session. After an attack of typhoid fever Hanna died on February 15, and in the political irony of things it was Foraker who delivered the memorial address to the United States Senate. Prompted by Herrick and Boss Cox, the Republicans of the assembly now unanimously chose Congressman Dick, the chairman of the Republican State Executive Committee and secretary of the National Committee, as Hanna's successor. Dick might indeed take Dollar Mark's place, but there was no one large enough to fill his shoes.

Herrick and harmony would soon part company as the governor began to discover that the businessman in politics is an amateur sailor on a very tacky sea. To make it more difficult for him, the governorship—until then a much more circumscribed office than in most states—had been strengthened and made more determining by giving the governor the veto power over bills passed by the legislature. Herrick had thought by efficient administration and sound financial practices to make himself a popular and successful governor. But he soon managed to stir up voting blocs that no politician in his senses would have troubled. The farmers turned against him when he refused to support a state agricultural college. Insurance companies complained of his interference in the state insurance department. After he had allowed a school code bill he approved to be altered to a "Cox Code" through pressure from Cincinnati, the reform element accused him of surrendering to Boss Cox. Sportsmen, gamblers, and horse breeders were furious when "on moral grounds" he vetoed the Chisholm Bill to allow betting at race tracks. Religious groups who opposed gambling were furious in their turn when the Governor threatened to veto the Brannock Bill, regulating the sale of liquor, unless its "unfair and unjust" features were removed. The bill provided for local residence option and dealt with such technical questions as whether or not the frontage of saloons should count as business or residential property and whether the population figure of residential districts should be set at 5,000 or 1,500. It had behind it the fundamentalist Protestant weight of the Anti-Saloon League. The League's adroitly fanatical superintendent, Wayne B. Wheeler, denied that the Brannock Bill was in any way unfair or unjust and demanded that it be passed without so much as a comma's change. When Herrick vetoed it, Wheeler denounced him for selling out to the liquor interests. The hard-shell rural vote turned solidly against him, making his re-election almost impossible.

With Hanna dead, with the reaction against the Governor growing, with Foraker waiting to strike back at Herrick and Dick, the governor's chair became a more sharply outlined object in Harding's mind. He said nothing as yet, but he quietly shared the opinion of the Reverend Doctor Frederick N. McMillin, president of the Dayton City Ministerial Association, who wrote him early in the year:

> The Republican Party in Ohio cannot afford to renominate Herrick either for the sake of its present nor for the sake of its future welfare. I hear that you will go for the nomination and if nominated there is no question about your election.

CHAPTER IX

Lieutenant Governor

While Herrick the businessman was embroiling himself with the state's pressure groups, Harding from behind his rostrum still managed to be most things to most men. He knew all the political leaders personally, and he knew how to evaluate and balance them—Dick, Kurtz, Boss Cox, Burton, Wheeler and the Anti-Saloon League, Charlie Taft, Bob Wolfe, the indestructible Foraker. His relations with Daugherty at this point were friendly but not particularly intimate. From the night poker sessions at the Great Southern to the reassuring pat on the back in the senate cloakroom, he expanded his friendships with effortless enjoyment. As presiding officer of the Senate he looked as imposing as the marble sarcophagus behind which he sat. Before the session was halfway over, he knew with his politician's sixth sense that the Governor was finished. No one with such a crop of enemies could hope to be re-elected. But if Herrick could be persuaded in the interests of harmony to step aside, Harding would be the harmoniously logical candidate to take his place. One did not need to be as astute as the senator from Marion to read the signs. By the time Herrick vetoed the Brannock Bill, disenchanted rural Republicans were calling him a drunkard, the tool of Cox, champion of the liquor interests.

In May the state Republican convention met, ostensibly to select the four delegates-at-large for the national convention in Chicago. Well before the convention the Big Four—Herrick, Foraker, Dick, and Cox—had already been picked. Harding was given the slick task of presenting these four "harbingers of harmony" to the delegates.

> The man who stepped into the breach today [wrote the *Plain Dealer*] was Lieutenant Governor Harding. To him had been set the difficult task of "bundling" into one united package Dick, Foraker, Herrick, and Cox.
>
> The skillful and most successful accomplishment of the task earned a genuine triumph for the speaker. By the use of a rare flow of words the L.G. for the moment made the delegates believe the word *harmony* had

been written with indelible ink. Roused from a condition of lethargy produced by the previous monotony of the convention the delegates vociferously cheered the name of each of the four men who will constitute the Republican Big-Four and at the end poured forth approval on Harding himself. If the enthusiasm this afternoon is any criterion, Lieutenant Governor Harding is destined to figure in an increasing extent in the future counsels of the party.

Carried away by the spell of his own words, Harding finally turned to the stolid figure of the boss of Cincinnati sitting beside him on the platform:

And next I want to name a great big, manly, modest, but mighty grand marshal of an invincible division of the grand Old Republican army of Ohio . . . modest, I say, but a man of ability, who is wise in council, trusted in advice, just in judgment, who places party above personality and success above selfishness. He has elevated his head high above the storm of calumny and abuse and has won his way to a trusted place in the party, and we yield deference and devotion to George B. Cox of Hamilton county.

Cox's coldly impassive features contorted at the warm flood of words and he buried his face in his handkerchief and cried. Harding's speech at the convention was "the hit of the day," according to the papers, but his praise of Boss Cox would come back to haunt him.

Attracted by Harding's reputation as a speaker, Harry P. Harrison, the manager of the Redpath Lyceum Bureau engaged him for the 1904 summer Chautauqua season to give a patriotic lecture on one of the early American statesmen. Harding chose Alexander Hamilton. With Gertrude Atherton's biographical novel as his source material, he prepared an hour's talk on "Hamilton, Prophet of American Destiny."

Five days a week during June and July, for $100 dollars a week plus his expenses, he toured the small Ohio towns of the circuit. It was the first of many summers that he would speak in the brown Chautauqua tents. Sandwiched in between Swiss yodelers, bell ringers, Princess Watawasa the full-blooded Penobscot Indian, and the Temple Male Quartet, he "preached the gospel of American optimism" under the flaring kerosene lamps.

Three men, he told his audiences, were the builders of the three great republics of history—Caesar, Napoleon, and Hamilton. And Hamilton constructed far more ably than the other two. More than that, the finger of divine purpose pointed the way:

God must have destined that the old world should learn of the new [he told the farmers and their families] and of its possibilities, of its availability for the setting of new lights, and the liberties that lead to real accomplishment. Later came the miracle of the revolution. The people were not trained for war, they were not equipped in any sense for the days of strife that fell to them, they were betrayed at home and abroad, but they won. Lofty statesmanship and unselfish patriotism were demanded. When it was most needed, there arose the greatest genius of the Republic, Alexander Hamilton. Without Hamilton there would be no American Republic today, to astonish the world with its resources and its progress.

Following the Atherton book, Harding outlined Hamilton's career from the obscure foundling in the West Indies to Washington's chief of staff. Hamilton was the "founder of what is now the Republican party." He stood for a nation, whereas Jefferson and his Democrats wanted merely a confederacy for self-protection—the issue that was decided finally by the Civil War. Hamilton was "the commanding figure that riveted the Union, laid the broad foundations which underlie our Federal government today, and laid the plans for the future development which his prophetic vision enabled him to see." And so on.

Beneath the billowing canvas the speaker's voice mesmerized. The withered record of what he said gives no key as to how Harding in the flesh was able to captivate his audiences. But even when he himself was tired, he could strike fire and send his hearers away glowing. Ever since Roosevelt had popularized the phrase, he liked to wind up his Hamilton talks with an allusion to the Square Deal. He believed in it, he told the earnest tiers of faces in the half-shadow, just as he believed in an honest day's work for an honest day's pay, and an honest day's pay for an honest day's work.

> The idler can expect little. The earnest toiler can expect the fruits of his toil. The solution to the entire problem of government is to raise higher the standard of American manhood and keep it there. Honesty is the great essential. It exalts the individual citizenship, and, without honesty, no man deserves the confidence of the people in private pursuit or in public office.

After the applause, the stir, and the clatter of wooden seats, the audience filed out into the cool air of the summer evening. No one was very sure of just what the speaker had said, but everyone going home under the stars remembered how well he had said it! Harding enjoyed such folksy audiences, enjoyed them even more when the Duchess's health kept her in Marion. Doggedly she traveled with him whenever she could manage it, perched by his side in the daycoach from one Chautauqua center to the next, her edged voice rasping at him all the way, querulous, persistent, while he sulked in his plush seat, a cigar wedged into his mouth, his frown growing deeper under her nagging until finally he would turn on her with "Goddammit, shut up!" and she would lapse into brief, offended silence.

The Chautauqua regulars disliked her. To the manager, she was meanly accurate in calculating expenses. Harding was, of course, popular. He liked the constant moves from town to small town. Often on those long, sun-hazed afternoons he would drop in at a local newspaper office and shake hands around the "back shop" and, to prove that he could do it, set a stick of type. As if to emphasize his dignity as a lecturer he carried a gold-headed cane, though this did not prevent him from walking down Main Street with his cane in one hand and an ice-cream cone in the other.

At the close of the Chautauqua season he visited the World's Fair at St. Louis, having arranged with the Wabash Railroad for free transportation for himself, the Duchess, and the Fishers. Doctor Sawyer and his wife joined them a day later, having been reduced to paying their own fare. From St. Louis Harding went on to Yellowstone Park and ended his summer travels with an eventless steamer trip on the Great Lakes. Votaw, now a full-fledged missionary, had been sent with Carolyn halfway round the world to take charge of the Seventh-day Adventist Burma mission at Kemmendine, Rangoon.

In the 1904 November election Roosevelt, with a united party behind him, was a triumphantly easy winner over the conservative Democrat, New York's Judge Alton B. Parker. To the emergent and as yet unnamed progressives, Teddy was their man, the dominant leader who three years before at the Minnesota State Fair had coined their phrase: "Speak softly and carry a big stick." [1] Conservatives had for a time been alarmed at this President-by-default who faced down J. P. Morgan, intervened in the coal strike, and wrote those rabid speeches attacking the trust. But the GOP platform was reassuringly free of any progressive heresies, and to reassure further, Roosevelt had chosen Elihu Root and Uncle Joe Cannon as presiding officers of the Republican convention, and Sen. Henry Cabot Lodge as chairman of the committee on resolutions. Three more unbending conservatives would have been hard to find.

To oppose the Rough Rider, the Democrats had nothing to offer but the colorless Parker's non-silver virtues. The result was so predictable that the campaign became a parody. Roosevelt carried every state north of the Mason-Dixon line. Harding joined the assigned party speakers, returning from his travels in time to campaign casually for Roosevelt in central Ohio. In October he went outside the state for the first time politically on a brief tour of rural Indiana, speaking at Peru, Dunkirk, and Union City.

He had hoped to spend New Year's with his Marion friends in Florida, but Ohio's political pot was beginning to boil at the end of the year and he felt he had to be there to watch it. Colonel Christian and his wife Coonie left for Daytona just after the elections. At Christmas Harding sent Coonie

[1] "Walk softly and carry a big stick; you will go far," was a West African proverb Roosevelt had first used as governor.

a china plate, scribbling coyly on a card that "everybody likes China including England and Russia and Japan." In a postscript he recalled the "glorious days" of Tom and Jerry and said he was sending the colonel a quart of "gold old rye."

Halfway through January, 1905, Ed Scobey wrote from San Antonio that he and his friends were reorganizing the Tri-Metallic Mining, Refining and Smelting Company to promote minerals and mines in Mexico, that they had just made Harding president, and hoped he would raise some money for them.[2] After two terms as Senate clerk Scobey had exchanged Ohio politics for Texas speculations, engaging in such varied activities as buying up San Antonio storage warehouses and prospecting in Mexico.

The Republican state convention to pick a candidate for governor would not take place until May, yet by January disaffected Republicans from all over Ohio were publicly protesting the prospect of Herrick's renomination. After Herrick's veto of the Brannock Bill, outraged Fundamentalist Protestantism had belabored him from pulpit and press. Month by month his reputation sank, as clergymen—astutely briefed by the Anti-Saloon League—denounced him. Those in Ohio who had a good word for him kept quiet. The Reverend Doctor E. L. Rexford, pastor of the Columbus Universalist Church, expressed the general mood when he wrote to Harding early in 1905:

> I have always been a Republican and have voted that ticket since the second election of Lincoln. But I certainly will not vote for Herrick again for Gov. of Ohio. I hope to see your name heading the next ticket. If Herrick's name heads it I fear the state will go to the Democrats. I think that would be an improvement over another Herrick term. He is the last of the Hanna bargains and it is time to put down a *period**. I would gladly vote for you, but no more Herrick for me.

The Richwood *Gazette*, the St. Paris *News-Dispatch*, the Warren County *Record*, and other county papers came out for Harding for governor. "Hail, Hip, Hip, Hurrah for Harding!" proclaimed the Van Wert *Republican*. William A. Braman of the Republican State Executive Committee urged him to enter the race, writing that the nomination of Governor Herrick to succeed himself would mean a Democratic victory. Harding received scores of such letters denouncing Herrick and urging the lieutenant governor to replace him. Scobey advised him to put Jennings in charge of a state headquarters in Columbus and go after Herrick in Cleveland with the help of the local boss there, Maurice Maschke, "the shrewdest manipulator of the bunch." On January 2 Harding leaked the news to the *Ohio State Journal* that he would allow his name to be pre-

[2] Harding remained president of the ephemeral company until May, when Scobey replaced him.
* Italic word underlined in original.

sented as a candidate for governor. "I've yielded to pressure enough to say that if the Republicans of Ohio in convention ask me to accept a higher position of honor than I now hold, why, I'll accept," he told a reporter. "I would not be honest to say otherwise. Of course I'd accept." Wheeler, that gray eminence of the Anti-Saloon League, wrote him two days later: "Your candidacy is spoken of with enthusiasm everywhere. The *Journal* and some of the Herrick henchmen are trying to belittle the whole affair, as is their business, but it does not work." Thoughtfully the Ohio Badge Company sent the lieutenant governor a few sample "Harding" buttons.

Though Harding was willing to allow others to float his name—without his approval, he still officially maintained—he hesitated at committing himself irrevocably. In November he had promised Herrick not to run against him, and though he wanted the nomination, he did not want the opposition of Herrick, Dick, and Cox. If they, as party leaders, would only realize that Herrick hadn't a dog's chance of being re-elected, if Roosevelt could be persuaded "in the interests of party harmony" to appoint Herrick an ambassador or to any other position that would allow him to resign gracefully, then Harding was available. Foraker conferred with Harding. The cagey old professional promised the lieutenant governor all the informal support he could give him, but balked at announcing his candidacy. Harding, he said, would have to do that for himself. On January 6 Harding took half a step by telling reporters that under no circumstances would he again be a candidate for lieutenant governor—and that was one bridge burned behind him.

To the apprehensive politicians who thronged to Herrick begging him to retire the Governor replied sharply that if he had to lose, he would rather lose the election than the nomination. He still remained on superficially pleasant terms with his lieutenant governor who continued the pose that he was not an active candidate. On January 15 Cox cut through the murk with his blunt announcement:

> Governor Herrick's administration was unanimously endorsed by the last Republican State Convention, and, in my judgment, will be by the next. . . . I see only one thing to do. Renominate Governor Herrick. . . . I think he is entitled to the support of all good Republicans. He shall have mine.

Harding was stung to reply editorially in the *Star* that "if nominations are always to be determined by Mr. Cox's attitude, as was Governor Herrick's in 1903, and it seems to be planned in 1905, then there is no longer need of conventions nor discussion of candidates."

Senator Dick in his capacity of chairman of the Republican State Executive Committee had already sent out a form letter to all the district leaders warning them that those organizing the opposition to Herrick—he did not mention Foraker by name—were trying to wrest control of the party organization from "the friends and followers of McKinley and Hanna." Two days later Cox and Dick reaffirmed their support of Herrick as the only possible candidate, even though Cox admitted privately that the Governor in vetoing the Brannock Bill had made "the biggest mistake of his life." The satellite figures then fell in line. Grant Mouser, recently elected to Congress and at odds with Harding over a post-office appointment, came out for Herrick, as did Maschke and former Mayor McKisson. "The jig is up," Jennings wrote Harding after the Cox pronouncement, adding that although something might yet happen, it looked to him as if they had been assigned to seats in the peanut gallery.

Harding left for Washington to confer with Foraker, still hoping to persuade his old leader to endorse him in the boom-ta-ra manner. The Senator refused, telling Harding that his boom was "sprung." Foraker was far too wise to back a loser against the Herrick-Dick-Cox triumvirate, and it was clear to his acute political vision that Harding would be the loser. The Senator had his own re-election to the Senate to worry about, and the concealed but still enticing will-o'-the-wisp of the 1908 presidential nomination. Harding never wholly forgave his chief for the refusal. There were rumors in the next few days, possibly initiated by Foraker, that the Lieutenant Governor would be appointed consul in Liverpool to get him out of the way unruffled. "Tommyrot!" Harding told the reporters who came to him with the tale.

If Herrick's spring nomination now seemed inevitable, his fate in the autumn was darkly obvious. Such a defeat, probably carrying the Republican state ticket with it, was nothing Harding wanted to share. Far better to retire to Marion with his present honors. He continued to insist that he would not be a candidate for lieutenant governor, and to demonstrate that he meant it, engaged passage on the United Fruit steamer *Alleghany* for a three-week cruise to Cuba and the Caribbean. A week before the *Alleghany* sailed he had to cancel his plans when the Duchess broke down with another attack of her old kidney ailment, this time so serious that she was taken to the Grant Hospital in Columbus. On February 24 she had a kidney removed, and for the rest of the year remained an invalid. Amos Kling, increasingly lonesome in his widowerhood, had for some time been making vague approaches to his daughter. When he heard of her operation, he took the large step of sending her a telegram from Florida: "Be calm cheerful and full of hope for you will surely be well again."

There were times enough when Harding wished that his wife were dead. Yet though he played with the idea, he could never assert himself to the point of leaving her. She was in her grim way part of him, a part he could not discard. Their dark and cluttered house represented home, with all the emotional overtones the word had for him. She, thick-ankled and withered, was no longer a sexual object, yet her illnesses distressed him. He had long been used to satisfying his physical needs elsewhere. She knew it, or at least sensed it, and was still woman enough to be torn with jealousy. In her fear of "loose women" she did her best to blinker his wandering eye. Wherever he went she tried to follow, watching him hawk-like. It did not occur to her to watch him within their own Sunday circle of Christians and Fishers and Sawyers and the scattering of other families that came to their lawn parties and played croquet on summer afternoons. Yet it was within that little circle that Harding in the spring of 1905 fell in love for the first time in his life. He had known Carrie Phillips for years as the smart and elegant wife of his friend James E. Phillips, the co-owner of the Uhler-Phillips dry-goods store on East Center Street. But until that spring he had seen nothing more in her.

During his first makeshift year running the *Star*, Harding had printed a local item on June 9, 1885, about James Phillips of John Frash's emporium at Huntington, Indiana, who "has come to Marion and will assist Wilfred Frash as a salesman in the new dry-goods store in this city." The following April the *Star* recorded that "Jim Phillips and Geo. Clermont have determined to become bachelors, and have fitted up a room in the Fisher block that rivals the Art Hall in beauty and splendor."

James Eaton Phillips was the same age as Harding, even to the month. He had been born and lived his early years in Kenton, twenty-five miles west of Marion, where his father was the local blacksmith. From a puny boy he grew into a thin young man, industrious rather than imaginative. He was not aggressive, and his mild, somewhat angular face was scarcely the kind that anyone remembered. At seventeen he went to work as a clerk in Metellus Thompson's dry-goods store and showed himself so trustworthy that after a year Metellus made him assistant manager of a branch store in Huntington, Indiana. After another year he left the Thompson store to take a job with another Huntington dry-goods merchant, John Frash. When in 1885 Frash opened a second store in Marion, Phillips moved on there. Frash was the first merchant in Marion to go in for advertising, the first to run half-page and full-page advertisements in the *Star*. He prospered at first, but later met with money-wise rivals, and in 1891 withdrew to Indiana. Jim Phillips and two other Frash employees, Ira and Edward Uhler, decided to form a partnership and take over the old Frash store on Center Street. The three young men opened their new store as Uhler, Phillips & Co., selling "dry goods, fancy and staple notions, cloaks, suits and infants' wear." Ira soon died, and the firm became Uhler and Phillips—later Uhler-Phillips—before long the largest dry-goods establishment in town. The partners were rising young men, charter members of the Marion Commercial Club. Phillips joined the Modern Woodmen of America, the Masons, and was one of the organizers of the Marion

Savings Bank. Full of civic zeal, he campaigned for such modern improvements as a sewer system and a Carnegie Library, and served for a while on the city council. On June 10, 1896, at the age of thirty, he married the twenty-one-year-old Carrie Fulton of Bucyrus.

Bucyrus, north of Marion and less than half its size, was the seat of Crawford County, and Carrie Fulton the town's most beautiful young woman. She was a head taller than her husband, high-breasted and her hair had the reddish tinge that the Greeks called golden. Her face itself, though full, was classical—or at least pre-Raphaelite—in profile. Although just a twenty-dollar-a-month schoolteacher, she seemed urbane by instinct, from the way she walked down the street to the way she dressed. And if there was something cold in her face, the lines of her body were warmly female. She looked much the Gibson girl arch-type that others were trying in vain to resemble. On her father's side she was related to Robert Fulton; her mother's people were descended from the sixteenth-century Swiss reformer, Ulrich Zwingli, and she herself was proud. Never would she let the bucolic town swallow her up while there was a world outside. She did not love James Phillips but she married him prudently because of all her suitors he had the best prospects and because he would take her away from Bucyrus and her classroom of gawky children. He loved her with a permanent devotion that was the more certain because he was never wholly certain of her.

First he bought a house for her, a gracious house with wide windows and small columns to its porch at 417 South Main Street on a rise of land known as Gospel Hill. And she made it more gracious. The year after her marriage her daughter Isabelle was born. Five years later, in May, 1902, she had a son, named after his father. The boy died in 1904. She wanted no further child to replace him. But her sorrow, instead of bringing her closer to her husband, drove them apart.

Jim Phillips had been Harding's friend for several years, writing to him as early as 1902 from Denver, Colorado, where he was visiting his tubercular brother. When Phillips himself was ailing in the spring of 1905, it was Harding who packed him off to the Battle Creek Sanitarium. The Hardings and the Phillipses often visited one another. Now, with Jim at Battle Creek and the Duchess slowly recovering from her kidney operation, Harding continued his visits alone. He, the lieutenant governor from the greater world of Columbus, exuding his maleness, was a man that Carrie may have turned to as a reaction to her grief over her child's death. With the Duchess in Columbus and Jim at Battle Creek, they became lovers. [- -
- -
- -
-]

Carrie Phillips was to be the love of Harding's life. Their affair lasted fifteen years, until it ended in sad recrimination at the time he became a candidate for President in 1920. She was for him a unique experience. For the first time he combined the enticements of mind and body in one person. Never before had he experienced physical desire and emotional release together. He fell in love with her, and remained in love with her, yet never completely certain of this charming and mercurial woman whom he possessed and yet did not possess.

When he was away he sent her doggerel poems, the verses spilling from his pen [- -

- - - - - - - - - - - -
- - - - - - - - - - - -
- - - - - - - - - -
- - - - - - - - - - - - -
- - - - - - - - - - - -
- - - - - - - - - - - -
- - - - - - - - -
- - - - - - - - - - -
- - - - - - - - - -
- - - - - - - - - - - -
- - - - - - - - - - - -
- - - - - - - - - - - -
- - - - - - - - - - - -
- - - - - - - - - - - - -
- - - - - - - - - - -
- - - - - - - - -
- - - - - - - - - - -
- - - - - - - - - - - -
- - - - - - - - - - - - -
- - - - - - - - - - -

- -
- -
- -
- -
- - - - - - - - - - - - - -]

Religion was for Harding like the Constitution, something to be honored and let alone. As a member of the First Baptist Church, he attended as often as a politician should, listening blankly to the sermon and shaking hands with the pastor on the steps afterward, but the religious preoccupation of his mother and brother and sisters had never touched him. There must be some reason for everything, he believed—in the odd moments when he thought about it—a God somewhere, an afterlife somehow in which one would not be judged too harshly for brass rails and poker games and the occasional midnight visits to the houses by the railroad station. But with Carrie his sensuality struck depths he was unaware of in himself.

[- -]

While Harding dallied, Herrick was shoring up his political fences for the May 25 convention in Columbus. Harding's reluctance to become a second-term candidate for lieutenant governor was shared even more sincerely by the triumvirate, unforgiving of his tentative challenge to Herrick. From the Democratic side, the *Enquirer* made the flattering comment:

> Mr. Harding is more than a considerable man. He has dignified a position which in the older times narrowly escaped being held in contempt. He has been so prominent and influential in the place that it appears to be not regarded by the leaders as wise to renominate him. It seems equally undesirable on the part of Mr. Harding to again lend his name to the stimulation of Republican state politics. He became a shining enough mark to be looked upon by those not quite in sympathy with the present State Administration as a person fit to be the Chief Executive of the state.

The qualities required in a lieutenant governor to balance the ticket in 1905 were not Harding qualities, according to Senator Dick. A man was needed who was a farmer, an old soldier, and from the south of Ohio. Fortuitously Dick had just such a candidate in Andrew L. Harris of Eaton. In 1861 Harris had joined the Union Army at the age of twenty-six, and four years later he had been mustered out as a brevet brigadier general. Not only that, but in 1891 and 1893 he had served as lieutenant governor under Governor McKinley. For all his seventy years, he was still as vigorous as when he had first served in Columbus. As a farmer, as a soldier, as a man from Preble County, he was the ideal compromise candidate. Herrick and Cox agreed.

The Republican state convention was one of the quietest, shortest, and largest—there were 1,196 delegates—ever held. Neither Foraker nor Harding was present. Dick had shaped a platform of deft platitudes that he hoped would bridge the reformist turbulence in November. Secretary of War William Howard Taft was the convention's keynote speaker, and the astute noted that his advocacy of granting the Interstate Commerce Commission the power to fix railroad rates was an indirect affront to Foraker and his railroad connections. Even with Taft's speech the convention did not last the morning. No ballots were taken. Harris was nominated, and Herrick and all the other candidates renonimated by acclamation while Wayne Wheeler and his Anti-Saloon League lieutenants smiled sardonically in the balcony. The convention was called to order at 10:10 A.M. and closed at twenty minutes before noon.

Nineteen hundred and five was the year that the Ricketts amendment went into effect, a law to cut down on the incessant voting by advancing the state and county elections a year so that they could be held simultaneously with national elections. After 1905 there would be no new state election until 1908, and the officers elected then would serve an extra year.

The convention had put Harding into cold storage. Though he still nursed vague political ambitions, he now had a three years' respite to think them over. And Marion in the leisurely spring weather was a pleasant place to think one's thoughts. Automobiles, although they still scared the horses at rural crossroads and furnished a stock supply of jokes for humorous magazines like *Judge* and *Life*, were by now a moving feature of the landscape. Not long after Harding was back at the *Star* office he bought his first car, an elegantly green Stevens-Duryea touring model with a high leather top and brass carbide lamps, for which he paid $2,750. He never learned to drive. After buying his car he hired a colored chauffeur, Frank Blacksten. The Stevens-Duryea soon became an impressively familiar object on the streets of Marion and the outlying roads. Harding often took Jim and Carrie Phillips on early-evening drives, and when the Duchess had recovered enough from her operation she made a fourth.

In June Harding went on another six weeks' tour of the Chautauqua circuit with his Alexander Hamilton speech. This year the Duchess could not follow him. There were weekends, however, when Carrie managed to slip away with him to the nearest city and the anonymous intimacy of a hotel room. Harding would later recall the passion of those summer nights in a frustration of longing. [- -
- -
- - - - - - - - - -
   -
- -
- -
- -
- -
- -
- -
- -
- -

------------------------------]

As the Duchess convalesced, there was much visiting between the Phillipses and the Hardings. The two families took picnic trips in the touring car. Yet for all the proximity, Jim and the Duchess, as if they were holding each other surety, suspected nothing. Harding continued to be awed by this capricious and sophisticated woman who deigned to be his mistress. After the clutter of his Mount Vernon Avenue parlor, her drawing room—she almost alone in Marion used the word—seemed spacious and cool in its tones of gray and green, its spare, simple furniture.

The summer idyll was marred by the brash reappearance in Marion of Pete DeWolfe, degreeless, jobless, and unconcerned. Goaded by the bedridden Duchess, Harding reluctantly took him on at the *Star* as a cub reporter. For a time Pete took to newspaper work and was full of big plans of being a journalist, of going on to Columbus or even Washington. But the amusements of life interested him more than gathering inconsequent items about church socials and lodge meetings, and he soon slacked off. [--] To be away from her made him restless, made the oppressive invalid presence of the Duchess even more oppressive. An undertone of sadness crept into his letters to his sister Carolyn at the Burma mission. "It seems a very long while since you went away," he wrote in September, "and it is a long while, but my time has been pretty fully occupied. Florence's long sickness has intervened. It is seven months now since she went to the hospital, and we have lived at home only two months of that time." He told of his new automobile and the trips he had been making and then concluded: "I just now heard that Florence's father is soon to be married. This information will 'fuss' her quite a bit, but it is no matter. She didn't marry to please her father, and must not expect him to remain a widower to please her."

With Theodore Roosevelt elected in his own right, the winds of change that had seemed to have died down in the Republican convention of 1904 now sprang up in 1905 with gale force. By whatever name one might call it, progressivism,[3] confident and persuasive, was on the march. From the White House came ringing phrases about "the dull purblind folly of rich men" and "corruption in business and politics," words that one could not have uttered in the presence of a McKinley or a Hanna and that shocked Foraker to his vested core. Lincoln Steffens now published his devastating article "Ohio: A Tale of Two Cities," in which, after praising Johnson's Cleveland, he excoriated Boss Cox and Cincinnati. A social worker, Henry C. Wright, wrote an equally savage and much more detailed exposure of Cox in a widely distributed booklet, *Bossism in Cincinnati*. The Cleveland *Plain Dealer* began a series of articles for its professional and middle-class readers exposing the boss-ridden Ohio cities. Following this the Scripps-McRae League—a chain of newspapers that included the Cleveland *Press*, Cincinnati *Post*, Toledo *News-Bee*, and Columbus *Citizen*—began to preach reform to a lower-middle-class and workingman audience. Brand Whitlock, running for mayor of Toledo as Golden Rule Jones's heir and successor, refused to affiliate himself with either party. In Cincinnati a group of college intellectuals and reform Democrats under the tall and aristocratic Harvard graduate, Elliott Pendleton, had organized with dissident Republicans to fight the Cox machine in the autumn municipal election. They chose a respected Cincinnati Superior Court judge, Edward J. Dempsey, as their candidate for mayor. Dempsey, a friend of Clarence Darrow's, was acceptable both to conservatives and radicals. To support him and attack Cox, Pendleton founded, financed, and edited the *Citizens' Bulletin*.

Reform had captured the Democratic party in Ohio. It was Tom Johnson who wrote most of the Democratic platform that year, a declaration of home rule for the cities; restriction of railroad passes; public expenditures and franchises to be submitted to the ballot; and a condemnation of the bosses. "The time is ripe for reform and revival," wrote the *News-Bee*. "The air is humid with the spirit of protest against political and financial corruption."

The Democratic convention, held in June, nominated an elderly Civil War veteran, John M. Pattison, for governor. Pattison, the son of a tenant farmer, had earned his way through college, served two terms in the state legislature and one in Congress, and had left politics to become president of the Union Central Life Insurance Company. In Congress he had been known as a Scripture-quoting dry, a liquor-law fanatic, and Lord's Day Observer who had successfully opposed the Chicago World's Fair's staying open on Sunday. Johnson's choice for governor had been Brand Whitlock, but Wayne Wheeler as state superintendent of the Anti-Saloon League

[3] The name Progressive, designating a party and a movement, came into use with Theodore Roosevelt's third-party campaign in 1912.

had intimidated so many delegates that he forced the nomination of his friend and fellow Leaguer, the Fundamentalist Pattison. Wheeler, a Republican but one of the most powerful men in Ohio with both parties, had earlier gathered over 100,000 signatures protesting Herrick's proposed renomination. When the Republican leaders defied him, Wheeler determined to use Pattison and the Democrats to defeat the wetcoat who had vetoed the Brannock Bill. Between the convention and the November election Wheeler arranged for 3,000 meetings for Pattison and Prohibition, and distributed over 75 million book pages of literature throughout the state. "We had a hard job making people see that they were not giving up their religion when they voted Democratic," Wheeler admitted afterward. "That was especially true in the rural sections, where they always voted a straight Republican ticket in honor of Lincoln. I used to tell them that Lincoln wasn't running this year."

With reform still a rising tide and the hard-shell anti-saloon vote turned against him, Herrick was doomed. Women stories began to circulate about him. Even that Gibraltar of Republicanism, the old Western Reserve, could no longer be counted on. "The enthusiasm that will obtain among the Republicans this fall will be among those who propose to vote the Democratic ticket," a disillusioned railroad lawyer from Delaware wrote Harding. "I see the Governor proposes to stump the state, and visit every county—in *his private car*—'tis well, the more speeches he makes, the smaller the number of votes."

Herrick's public career might be finished, the election settled in advance, but Harding's politic mind was already ranging ahead to 1908. Characteristically, he did his best to re-establish friendly relations with the eclipsed Governor. Several weeks after the convention Herrick wrote him:

> I appreciate more than I can express your frank and manly letter and know that you feel what you say—
> You know better than anyone else from our many talks how I feel on the whole situation and of my sincere feelings of friendship for you. That things should play at cross purposes seems to be one of the conditions of life at least political life. I am quite inclined to envy you the good chance to be your own man free from the cavil and criticism of those who do not agree with you—I wish you would come in when next in the city for I can not now write what [I] would like to say. With highest regards to Mrs. Harding and the hope that her recovery may be speedy.

The campaign opened September 23 at Bellefontaine, with Vice President Charles W. Fairbanks and Senator Foraker on the platform trying to turn talk and thoughts to grandiloquently vague national rather than embarrassing state issues. Senator Dick, hard pressed by Johnson and the reformist crew, found himself finally forced to come out boldly in defense of Boss Cox. Dick was thunderstruck a month later when Secretary of War William Howard Taft of Akron, trying to impress his audience with Herrick's independence of Cox, told them: "If I were able to cast my vote in Cincinnati at the coming election, I should vote against the municipal ticket nominated by the Republican organization." Taft then denounced the stranglehold of Cox on party nominations and elections that was driving young independent candidates out of politics.[4]

Dick persuaded Harding, "bloviating" in Marion, to take on some speaking assignments in the campaign, and Rud Hynicka on behalf of the Republican State Executive Committee arranged to have him appear at Cleveland on October 17. Scobey urged his friend to watch his step on Boss Cox's sidewalks. "Don't slop over," he warned him. Harding made about twenty-five speeches in all, but, as he admitted himself, they didn't count for much.

Pattison, suffering from Bright's disease, campaigned the counties under the banner of temperance and Sunday observance, and rural Republicanism got the message. Wheeler was seeing to that. In the combined state and municipal elections of November the old soldier, though jaundiced and faltering from the stress of campaigning, received 473,264 votes to Herrick's 430,617. Two years before, Herrick had beaten the barnstorming Tom Johnson by 113,812 votes; now he found himself losing by 42,647. Twenty-five "safe" Republican counties switched to Pattison. Yet for all their Wheeler-aroused discontent the rural counties were not yet ready to desert the Grand Old Party. General Harris defeated his Democratic opponent for lieutenant governor, Lewis B. Houck, 456,341 to 427,126, and all the other state offices from attorney general down were won by Republicans, with majorities of from 29,000 to 46,000. In the assembly the Democrats managed to tie the number of Republicans in the Senate, with one deciding seat going to a Golden Rule Independent from Toledo. But in the House of Representatives the Republicans salvaged a thin majority, with 62 members as opposed to 57 Democrats and 2 Toledo Independents. The real reformist triumph came in the cities. Cleveland re-elected Johnson by an increased majority; Brand Whitlock easily replaced his dead friend and mentor Jones in Toledo; reform mayors won out in Columbus and Dayton; and, most astonishingly of all, in Cincinnati the Cox machine lay in ruins following the victory of Judge Dempsey and the entire Fusion-Democratic municipal, county, and legislative tickets. So shaken was Cox that he—prematurely, as it turned out—announced his retirement from public life.

Back in Marion, Harding shrewdly analyzed the state results:

---

[4] Charles Taft refused to print or comment in the *Times-Star* on his brother's speech. But many felt that the Secretary of War was speaking not only for himself but for Roosevelt, and this was Taft's opening bid for the presidential nomination of 1908.

Herrick's defeat is chargeable to a dozen causes. He has been the unfortunate legatee of all the accumulated grievances of fourteen years.

Bossism was the chief point of attack, not Cox alone, but the unacceptable drift of the State machine toward having a chosen few names over State tickets. The temperance question embarrassed the Republican campaign and, while the Brannock bill could be explained, the open support of Governor Herrick by the liquor interests would not yield to argument. A dozen minor issues contributed, but the dictation of State leaders and the fear of Cox were the main things. . . . It is worth remembering, too, that we were in the path of a reform wave.

On January 8, 1906, in Columbus, the outgoing lieutenant governor greeted the incoming governor on the last occasion that Harding would ever hold state office in Ohio. Governor Pattison, yellow-skinned and feeble as he stood beside his wife in the Senate chamber receiving the hundreds of people who had come to greet him, was so obviously an ailing man that after two hours of shaking hands his doctor, E. J. Wilson, ordered him to bed. It was the only official function he would attend as governor. By February his relatives were trying to persuade him to resign, and there were rumors in Columbus that he had lost his mind. Doctor Wilson issued a statement that the Governor was sane but that "because of his bodily illness he is incapable of sustained attention to any subject." He was in fact a dying man, and though his doctors managed to keep him alive a few months longer, he died on June 19. Lieutenant Governor Harris succeeded him. "Aren't you sorry Dick wouldn't let you run for lieutenant governor?" the chairman of a county committee wrote Harding.

Whatever Harding thought of the whiskered old veteran now in the governor's chair that might have been his, he said nothing, not even when Dick gratuitously announced that he would support Harris for a second term. In Marion, Harding in his retirement had become the elder statesman. No one before in the town had risen so high in the state hierarchy, and he might rise even higher. As he walked along maple-shaded Mount Vernon Avenue on the paved walks for which the *Star* had fought so long, he felt the glow of assurance from his position, his financial security, and the inner confidence of himself as a man that Carrie had given him. He knew everyone he passed on both sides of Center Street, and everyone greeted him. Once it had been a casual "Warren," then "W. G.," then "Senator." Now they called him "Gov," and in their friendliness there was an undertone of deference. No longer would he be excluded from the inner circle of those who controlled Marion, and with his assumption came the local perquisites. The Marion Club opened its doors to him. He became a director of the Marion Lumber Company; the Marion County Telephone Company; the Home Building, Savings and Loan Company.

Harding the elder statesman was in demand. He was invited to be the honor guest at the Youngstown Foraker Republican Club's annual banquet. He spoke at McKinley and Lincoln banquets and other such events. The editor of the newly-founded *Ohio Magazine* asked him to write an article on Foraker. Even Amos Kling was beginning to have second thoughts about his son-in-law.

Preoccupied with the evolutions of politics, Harding did not tour the Chautauqua circuit that summer, nor did he so much as find time for the trip on the Great Lakes that he had planned. The long June days did bring their changes. On June 25 the seventy-three-year-old Amos Kling married Caroline Beatty Denman, the middle-aged but still not-too-faded widow of a Marion doctor. Though Amos became almost fatuously devoted to his Caroline, his autumn romance robbed him of none of his spring astuteness. In a pre-nuptial contract that he had his lawyer draw up he stipulated that his wife was to receive none of his property on his death.

Harding's periodic spells of "nerves" that sent him to Battle Creek or on his aimless travels were an inheritance that troubled the other members of his family as well. All of them seemed to collapse under pressure, as if they had only a limited reservoir of energy. Deac—by now the father of two children, George Tryon and Warren—had left Columbus early in 1906 to become superintendent of the Washington Branch Sanitarium in Washington, D.C. Within six months he was writing his brother that he must have leave of absence for a year's rest, and by autumn he had resigned. "It was hard to give up my work," he wrote, at the same time requesting a railroad pass, "but on the whole it is well that I did, for I need plenty of fresh air more than anything just now."

Daisy, too, living at home and teaching school, had had some kind of breakdown. Deac wrote on August 18:

> While it is probable that Daisy will feel very well by November, it is certainly advisable that she take a year's rest. I have tried to get her to see this, but she can not think of getting along a whole year without earning something. To plan to teach school during the coming year is a very unconservative thing for her in her present nervous state. . . .

The Hardings and the Phillipses still continued to see much of one another, and still in the small town there was no gossip, or almost none. Colonel Christian's sharp-eyed son George, among the few discreetly astute observers, wrote from Florida late in the spring that "learning that Jim Phillips might go to the farm, I tendered the prospective grass widow much affectionate interest." But any liaison between the carnal "Gov" and the regally aloof Mrs. Phillips was not something that would easily occur even to the most imaginative sewing circle. Secretly the two continued to meet, sometimes briefly at night in her garden, or more rarely in her bedroom when Jim was away. She urged him to try to plan a trip abroad for the four of them. That older world across the Atlantic of imperial cities and gray cathedrals and crowned heads of state was something she had dreamed of in Bucyrus. Now that her lover was free of Columbus he would have the time. Stirred by the thought, he wrote for a prospectus of the Bible Students' Oriental Cruise, sailing from New York on the White Star liner *Arabic* on February 7, 1907, to spend seventy days visiting Madeira, Cadiz, Seville, Gibraltar, Algiers, Malta, Athens, Constantinople, and Smyrna, with nineteen days in the Holy Land and Egypt and side visits to Naples, Pompeii, Rome, the Riviera, and Liverpool. According to the booklet the cruise offered "an unequalled opportunity for luxurious travel at moderate cost in high-class company of congenial people."

Reformers, jubilant in January when Pattison took office, were considerably more subdued by the assembly session's end in April. Nevertheless, the legislators were a more independent group than had been seen for a long time in the capital. Although Johnson and his newly-formed Association of Mayors of Ohio Municipalities were defeated by the lobbyists in their efforts to get the Municipal Code amended, the assembly did impose a two-cents-a-mile fare for the railroads, and passed a law regulating the fees of county officials—some of whom had been making up to $50,000 a year on a fee basis. The legislators also appointed a senate committee—the Drake Committee—to investigate the affairs of Boss Cox's Hamilton County. In a mixed assortment of unsavory facts they discovered that Rud Hynicka, when treasurer of Hamilton County, had pocketed $30,000 in interest on public funds from the banks he favored as depositories. Hynicka admitted it almost cheerfully, claiming—with truth—that he had been merely following a long-established custom.

Theodore Burton, although his gentility could at times be diluted by practical politics, was so disgusted by the Cox revelations that he demanded the end of party control by Foraker and Dick. In 1902 the Congressman had brought out his own plan for eliminating "bossism" from the county machine. Now he set about organizing a reformist group to oust the Cox-contaminated leaders at the September Republican convention in Dayton.[5] Specifically he aimed to remove Senator Dick as chairman of the State Executive Committee.

Beyond this factional struggle the convention itself was a minor affair in an off year. The only nomination of any consequence to be decided on was that of secretary of state. When, after Governor Pattison's death, Lieutenant Governor Harris became governor, the then secretary of state was advanced to the lieutenant governorship, leaving his old place vacant. Chief contender for the vacant position, and backed by Dick and Foraker,

[5] Charlie Taft nominated Cox as the chairman of the Hamilton County delegation to that convention.

was the vintage Republican Carmi A. Thompson of Ironton, the speaker of the House of Representatives.

Burton found practical if incongruous support in Harry Daugherty. Posing as the foe of the bosses and the people's friend, Daugherty arrived in Akron to help line up the delegates necessary to oust Dick. "Foxy Harry is playing them all," was Scobey's private comment. Harding led the Marion delegation and was a member of the committee on resolutions. To him Burton's effort seemed merely an attempt to substitute one machine for another. "The amiable and talented Mr. Daugherty shuddering about bossism is a spectacle to amuse all of Ohio," he wrote in the *Star*. "We like Daugherty, but he held a high seat in the bossing procession, when there was Hanna absolutism in this state, and never said a word." By the end of Harding's term as lieutenant governor any reformist tint that he may have had as a neophyte senator had long since been bleached out. He had developed into a regular of regulars, for whom the party came first. Party principle was the highest principle; the Republican party of Ohio needed Foraker and Dick and Daugherty and Burton and every other loyal worker, whatever his reputation.

> We want George B. Cox and the old guard in Hamilton County because they are Republicans, and are in better standing at home since Cincinnati has had an experience with the pretenders. We want the Republicans who carried the Pattison banner in honest belief that they were rendering a good service. . . . We want all the men who ever caught the Republican step and felt the thrill of victorious march.

The convention endorsed Dick and Foraker "without reservation" and nominated Thompson on the second ballot. Burton, the scholar, was overwhelmed; Daugherty left out on his usual limb. But even in the convention-held hall of the National Cash Register Company the winds of reform were blowing, for the delegates before they left endorsed a resolution for the direct primary nomination of United States senators.

The November election demonstrated that Ohio was not yet ready for Johnson or the Democrats. Thompson was elected by 56,390 votes over his Democratic rival, Samuel A. Hoskins, and in that mid-term year the Republicans won 17 of the 21 Ohio congressional seats. Harding made a few speeches in the campaign, including several—at Hynicka's request—in Hamilton County.

Following the election Harding remained desultorily in Marion until some weeks after Christmas. He wrote occasional articles for the *Star* and elaborated his Foraker article for the October *Ohio Magazine*.

> In the Senate [he wrote] a body yet to be matched as a deliberative assembly of great men by any nation in the world, he [Foraker] has won his

spurs, and stands today the most eminent legislator of the greater American Republic.

Harrison inquired from the Redpath Lyceum Bureau if he would lecture on the Big Stick that summer for Chautauqua, a subject suggested by the Lyceum's board of directors. Harding agreed to alternate the new lecture with "Alexander Hamilton." The year 1907 was an advertised political cipher and he might have left for Florida before the new year, but since his intimacies with Carrie the Ohio winters seemed less severe to him. Not until February were he and the Duchess finally in Daytona with the Marion colony.

Amos Kling and his bride, on a prolonged honeymoon, had preceded them by several months. The sunny weather and his youngish bride were mellowing Amos until he took to capering like a schoolboy. He and Caroline rode bicycles far up the beach, threw sand, and ducked each other in the water. Already he had approached his daughter, now on Harding's arrival he was willing for the first time to approach his son-in-law. Harding had the most to forgive, but he amiably and almost gratefully accepted the old man's overtures. Amos unbent creakily. After Harding had left Florida he wrote the old man, sending him a bundle of *Stars*, and on April 22 received his first letter from his father-in-law. "This is a duty as well as a pleasure on which I ought to have realized long ago," Amos wrote, "answering your nice letter upon your return home. You seemed to have had a rip-roaring time." He addressed the letter "Dear Sir" and signed it "Yours truly." Writing again in July, just after Harding had finished his Chautauqua tour, he still addressed his son-in-law as "Dear Sir" but enclosed several snapshots of himself and Caroline and suggested that Florence return to get some "respite from her social matters." Then, as if reluctant to loose himself from his honeymoon spell, he abruptly proposed that the two couples take a trip to Europe that August. As a gesture of reconciliation he himself offered to pay all the expenses.

On August 1 the Klings and the Hardings sailed from New York on the S. S. *Arabic* for Liverpool. Harding enjoyed the casual contacts aboard ship, the large and prolonged meals, the shuffleboard, the evening concerts and dances, and the late evenings in the bar. Europe meant little to him. To the boy from Blooming Grove, the man whose favorite painting was "Breaking Home Ties" and favorite music the "Barcarolle" from *The Tales of Hoffmann,* who could not tell the difference between a Gothic and a Romanesque arch, and did not care, the old world was a picturesque crowned anachronism inhabited by people who had not had the sense to come to America. England was for picture postcards, Germany for beer, Paris for lubricity, and art galleries and museums for women. Halfway across the Atlantic he wrote Colonel Christian:

Our English plans are pretty well fixed. We land at Liverpool Saturday, spend Sunday in Chester, visit Norwich, Derby, Stratford-on Avon, Oxford and Windsor on the way to London. Then the big town and its environs and Canterbury for a week, then to Germany. The Rhine section first, then Berlin, Dresden, Vienna, and back to Munich and Nuremberg and beer, then to Switzerland, and wind up with a good ten days in Paris and surroundings. We are going to be fairly good till we get there, but make no promises for our conduct while there. The delay in getting return passage increases our time in both Switzerland and France. It got to be a business proposition whether to buy a boat or spend a little extra time abroad, and we decided on the latter.

They sailed for New York on the *Kaiser Wilhelm II* on September 19, bringing back several trunks of souvenirs and a set of dinner plates bought in Dresden. By the end of the month Harding was once more in Marion, a traveler with the patina that only a European journey could impart. Europe, seen from the train window or hotel lobby, had been a peepshow. His world, the real world, lay just outside his office window under the shadow of Marion's silvered courthouse dome.

[CHAPTER X]

Leading Citizen

Not long after Amos Kling's second marriage, his grandson Pete DeWolfe became engaged to Esther Naomi Neely, a Marion girl ten years his junior. Pete was still attached by ties of blood if not of endeavor to the *Star*. Now, facing the responsibilities of marriage and anxious to impress the hesitant Esther, he made an unwonted effort to appear responsible, even taking on some minor political tasks for the paper under Christian's direction. The young Marion lawyer Alfred "Hoke" Donithen, having served two terms as city solicitor, had announced himself a Republican candidate for representative, and it was to Pete that Senator Foraker wrote asking the essential question: "Can he be nominated, and can he be elected?" Pete replied that he could, and added that Donithen was "for Foraker now and all the time." When Harding disembarked from the *Kaiser Wilhelm II* at New York he found a letter from Christian welcoming him home and bringing him up to date on what had happened while he was away. "Marshall has been quite a man," Christian concluded hopefully, "and all have noticed his admirable conduct and attention."

Harding arrived home to find a local political brush fire blazing, with Donithen opposed not only by the Democratic candidate, William T. "Silver Willy" Smith, but by a Bible-shouting Prohibitionist, the Reverend Doctor Clarence Hensel. Silver Willy was an admitted wet, for the bent elbow and against local option and any other kind of liquor control. Donithen, in trying to straddle the temperance issue, had turned the retributive anger of the dry Fundamentalists against him. Too late he announced that he was all for local option. In avid clerical eyes he was a "coward and trimmer . . . wholly insincere." As Harding explained the district situation to Governor Harris:

> The Democratic nominee is an unrepentent rebel, free silver shouter, who has declared against county option. The independent is a carpet-bagger minister, here only one year, talking nothing but temperance. We want your aid in appealing for Republican fidelity, and you can help us. . . . It

would be fine to have you call attention to all progressive, consistent, and effective temperance legislation coming from the Republican majorities in the General Assembly. . . .

While Harding was en route from New York to Marion, New York's Knickerbocker Trust Company closed its doors, setting off the financial panic that was the culmination of the 1907 depression. Its effects, like a spreading ripple, were felt all through the Midwest. Several Marion businesses failed, including the Marion Manufacturing Company for which Harding, Uhler, and Fisher had signed notes in the overoptimistic anticipation of producing tractors to compete with the Huber plant. Harding could still recall ruefully when he was president how much money he was then able to lose "without being wrecked." Tryon's perennial financial maelstroms were independent of business cycles, but with his son away he had not even been able to keep up the mortgage interest on the Center Street house. As he did periodically, he now spoke of quitting Marion and going back to the farm. To prevent the bank from foreclosing, Harding was forced to meet the back payments and take title to the house.

In the November election Silver Willy, despite all Harding's efforts, defeated Donithen by 660 votes. The Reverend Doctor Hensel, with 1,009 votes, polled several hundred more than was necessary to sway the balance. Outside the 13th District the results aroused no special interest. The sensation of the 1907 election was the comeback of Cincinnati's Boss Cox. Mayor Dempsey, like many a reformer before and since, had found victory easier than following it up. His coalition, forged in indignation's heat, fell apart in the tepid aftermath of day-by-day administration. Although he appreciated "the rottenness of things and the need of political betterment," he lacked the aggressive leadership necessary to hold his reform Republicans and Democrats together. He could not even hold the Democrats, for the Pendleton group soon broke away to form the City party. The result was that Cox's candidate, Leopold Markbreit, chosen for his German antecedents and his innocuous respectability, overwhelmed the Democrats and the City party. "The greatest victory for Republicanism ever known in Cincinnati," Cox pronounced piously.

At the Republic's very beginnings President George Washington had set the august precedent of the two-term tradition. But the question as to whether a vice president succeeding to the Presidency should count the remainder of his time as one term had remained unresolved. Theodore Roosevelt, approaching his first elective term in 1904, intended to settle the question for himself and the future when he announced:

> On the 4th of March next I shall have served three and a half years and this . . . constitutes my first term. The wise custom which limits the Presi-

dent to two terms regards the substance and not the form; and under no circumstances will I be a candidate for or accept another nomination.

Six years later he told a friend, pointing to his wrist: "I would cut my hand off right there if I could recall that written statement." But in 1907 any regrets he might have had were tempered by the prospects of a big-game hunting expedition to Africa and by his satisfaction in the man he was coming more and more to accept as his successor, his secretary of war, William Howard Taft. This hearty, willing man had hulked his 354 pounds about the world, faithfully and deftly running presidential errands in Cuba, Panama, the Philippines, Rome, Russia, and Japan and China. Roosevelt saw him not only as a loyal friend but—mistakenly—as an alter ego, smaller in stature if not in bulk, who could be counted on to carry out the Rooseveltian policies while their originator banged away at rhinoceros and elephant in Africa.

H. H. Kohlsaat, the Chicago multiple-lunchroom proprietor turned editor and politician, told of an evening in the White House library after Secretary of War Taft and his wife had dined with the President. Roosevelt playfully sat back in his easy chair, closed his eyes, and chanted: "I am the seventh son of a seventh daughter. I have clairvoyant powers. I see a man before me weighing about 350 pounds. There is something hanging over his head. I cannot make out what it is; it is hanging by a slender thread. At one time it looks like the Presidency—then again it looks like the chief justiceship."

"Make it the Presidency!" said the ambitious Nellie Taft.

"Make it the chief justiceship," Taft said.

Taft's father Alphonso, an earlier judge of the Ohio Superior Court, once remarked that to be chief justice of the United States was more than to be President. His son William inherited his father's belief. Roosevelt's magnetic persuasiveness, Nellie's urgings, and a fate that would later seem malignant were all pushing him toward the Presidency. His own deepest inclinations were always toward the Supreme Court. "It is the comfort and dignity and power without worry I like," he admitted a dozen years later when he had as chief justice at last attained his goal.

His had been a wide and easy road ever since Governor Foraker—not without self-serving political considerations—had appointed the twenty-nine-year-old lawyer to the Superior Court. Three years later President Benjamin Harrison was persuaded to make him solicitor general and, after two years, a judge of the Sixth Judicial Circuit. As a circuit court judge Taft established a reputation among lawyers with his bent for judicial reform. In 1899 he was mentioned for president of Yale. But he did not step into the national picture until President McKinley, the year before his assassination, requested him to head a commission to establish civil government in the conquered and turbulent Philippines. Reluctantly he resigned his judgeship to govern the far-off islands. So successful was his term in the Philippines, so engrossed did he become in his responsibilities as governor, that he could not be tempted away even when President Roosevelt in 1902 twice offered him a place on the Supreme Court. Roosevelt was only able to use his blunt persuasiveness in making him secretary of war because Taft felt in that position he would still have control over the Philippine affairs that had become his moral obligation. In 1906 Roosevelt again offered to appoint him to the Supreme Court, and again, preoccupied with the War Department, the Panama Canal, and the Philippine business, he declined. Roosevelt wrote understandingly of the "strength and courage, clear insight and practical commonsense and . . . very noble and disinterested character" of the man he had picked to succeed him. What the Rough Rider failed to understand was that his willing secretary of war was no Rough Rider but a conservative of conservatives.

On July 23, 1907, Taft wrote Roosevelt from his summer lodge at Pointe-au-Pic, Quebec.

> The situation in Ohio, with reference to the meeting of the State Committee, has become somewhat acute. Foraker is working as hard as possible, and pulling all the strings . . . to smooth out the situation for himself, and is very anxious, or I think his friends are very anxious, to secure an indorsement of me for the Presidency, accompanied by an indorsement of him for the Senate. Possibly he would repudiate such a wish, although I have no doubt that he really has it. . . . The last information I have is that Cox, who has always been close to Foraker, has notified Vorys that the two Hamilton County members of the State Central Committee will not vote for an unconditional indorsement of me at the meeting which takes place next Saturday. . . . I feel very deeply on the subject, and so deeply indeed that I haven't the slightest hesitation in saying that rather than compromise with Foraker I would give up all hope for the Presidency. I must explain to you that the Ohio brand of politics the last twenty years has been harmony and concession on the subject of principle to the last degree, provided it secured personal preferment and division of the spoil in a satisfactory way. Foraker has been the blackmailer in all Ohio politics. He blackmailed John Sherman into an agreement by which he was to go to the Senate and Sherman was to be supported for the Presidency, and then he played false with Sherman. He blackmailed McKinley and Hanna into allowing him to return to the Senate on condition of his support of McKinley, and then he worked against and thwarted McKinley in all his desires whenever opportunity came. Now he may beat me, but he won't beat me through any concession or compromise of mine. If he beats me he will have to beat me in a stand-up fight. You will observe that he is relying greatly on the proposition that we desire to eliminate him from Ohio politics. . . .

Roosevelt's desire was indeed to eliminate Foraker both from national and Ohio politics. But the hostility of the two men was inherent in their political personalities. Roosevelt, it was by this time clear, was intent on remoulding the Grand Old Party to his progressive, reformist pattern. For Foraker the old mould was sacrosanct. In 1905, Roosevelt, long outraged by the manipulations of the large railroad lines, demanded of Congress "some scheme to secure to the government supervision and regulation of the rates charged by the railroads." To Foraker this was an assault on the rights of public property, a "Socialistic first step in the direction of government ownership."

The railroad regulation bill endorsed by Roosevelt—known as the Hepburn Rate Bill—was introduced in the House of Representatives on January 4, 1906, by Congressman W. P. "Pete" Hepburn of Iowa and passed by a vote of 346 to 7. The Senate was another matter. Senator Nelson Aldrich, the Republican floor leader, was fundamentally opposed to the bill, as were such representatives of corporate business as Penrose, Platt, De Pew, and Foraker. Only Roosevelt's driving force, his tempestuous marshaling of public opinion and his willingness even to ally himself with the Democrats, if necessary, forced the bill through the Senate. In the sixty days of debate Foraker made eighty-seven speeches in opposition. "A more unnecessary law, or a more mischief-making law was never placed upon the statute book," he declared with the old fire. "My objection is to the government going into the rate-making business at all." But in the end even the most conservative senators recognized that it would be politic to vote for the inevitable—all except Foraker. He was the only Republican to vote against Roosevelt's bill, joined in his isolation by two eccentric states-rights Democrats.

Foraker's isolation grew to a bitter personal feud after Roosevelt's action following a shooting affray at a military post near Brownsville, Texas, in the summer of 1906. A battalion of the 25th U. S. Infantry, a colored regiment, had been sent to the Brownsville post to relieve a battalion of white soldiers. For several weeks there was brawling between the soldiers and disgruntled civilians. Finally, on a dark night, about twenty soldiers drew their rifles from the racks and shot up the town. Shots were fired into homes, saloons, and a hotel. One civilian was killed, two wounded. Gen. E. A. Garlington, the inspector general, interrogated the men of the 25th but all "uniformly and persistently denied guilt." Convinced that some were guilty and the rest shielding them, Garlington recommended that the whole battalion be dishonorably discharged. Many of the soldiers had served several hitches, and six had won the Congressional Medal, but Roosevelt followed his inspector general's recommendation.

Foraker sprang to the colored soldiers' defense with his old-time zeal, again waving the tattered remnants of the bloody shirt. He attacked Roosevelt with boom-ta-ra fervor and proclaimed that none of the soldiers of the 25th had been involved in any way in the shooting. The debate in the Senate on the Brownsville affair was the sensation of the hour. Roosevelt wrote his senatorial friend from Massachusetts, Henry Cabot Lodge, that everyone on the inside knew that Foraker was "not really influenced in the least by any feeling for the Negro, but that he acted as the agent of the corporations."

On January 26, 1907, Roosevelt and Foraker confronted each other across the tables at the annual dinner of the Gridiron Club. The impetuous Roosevelt, aroused by the sight of his sharp-tongued enemy, launched into a stinging attack on Foraker and his championing of the Brownsville soldiers. Samuel Blythe, the club president, was so taken aback that all he could think of saying was: "The hour of bloody sarcasm having arrived, I take the liberty of calling upon Senator Foraker for some remarks."

Foraker stood, white with controlled fury, and answered Roosevelt in such scornfully precise terms that the President had to be restrained from jumping up to interrupt him. From then on Foraker was to Roosevelt a "splinter of a splinter." He saw to it that the Senator, "one of the most unblushing servers and beneficiaries of corporate wealth within or without office that I have ever met," received neither patronage nor any say in Ohio appointments. Neither, if the President could manipulate it, would the Senate ever again see the aging Fire Engine Joe.

In the autumn of 1907 Foraker came out as a candidate for the Presidency, although he admitted to his friends that he knew he had no chance whatever of winning. The Brownsville aftermath, as he well realized, had destroyed any real chance that he might have had for the Republican nomination. But in 1909 he would have to face re-election to the Senate at the hands of the Ohio Assembly. If he could not control the Ohio delegation to the national convention as a favorite son, his control over the state would be gone; if Roosevelt should succeed in elevating Taft to the Presidency, Foraker's political eclipse would be permanent.

By the end of summer Boss Cox, sensitive as always to any shift in the political weather, was through Garry Hermann in cooperative communication with Charlie Taft. Charlie had taken a year off from all his other affairs to build up his half-brother as a presidential candidate, setting up headquarters in Ohio with A. I. Vorys in charge, and in New York with Charles D. Hilles who had worked for McKinley in 1900. Cox, by flashing the glitter of promised Federal patronage, now persuaded the Republican State Committee to endorse the man who had denounced him two years before, and from that point on became a solid Taft backer. Nevertheless, when the Advisory and Executive committees of the Ohio Republican League—about a hundred general officers from the 88 counties of Ohio—

met in Columbus on November 20, they endorsed Foraker with a whoop and clatter, after a speech by Harding presenting an endorsement resolution:

> The Republican League of Ohio, born in the enthusiastic devotion and patriotism of the young manhood of the Republican Party, pledges anew its fidelity to Republican policies and doctrines which have made the Republic prosperous and great. It avows its loyalty to that robust Republicanism expounded by its great leaders of the past—John Sherman, Marcus A. Hanna, and William McKinley; and as advocated today by their able and distinguished successor in leadership, Joseph Benson Foraker.

There were yelping shouts and cries of "Read it again! Read it again!" Harding continued:

> His record is one of unswerving devotion to his country and to his party.
> While distinguished for his loyalty to both, he is equally noted for his conservative judgment and the courage with which he maintains what, in his opinion, duty requires.
> Entertaining these views we send him greeting and assure him as he returns to his labors at Washington that he has our unqualified confidence and esteem, and we not only pledge him our loyal support for his re-election to the Senate, but we further declare that he is our choice as the Republican candidate for the President of the United States in 1908.

Above the shouts and clapping someone bawled out: "Hope that will hold you awhile!" Harding concluded in fireworks of applause:

> Gentlemen, in the name of the immortal Grand Army which saved to us the Union that we boast of and of which Army Senator Foraker is its most distinguished representative in public life; in the name of the humble black man; in the name of the believer in a "Square Deal," whether it is for the humble citizen or the distinguished statesman; in the name of that fighting band of Ohio Republicans who caught the inspiration as he bore the banner aloft twenty years ago and have marched with him to victory triumphant time and again; in the name of that Republicanism which we wish to make triumphant in 1908, I move the adoption of this resolution.

Foraker gratefully acknowledged the resolution and Harding's tested loyalty, but said that since he did not wish to appear as a candidate for two offices at the same time, he would therefore "with heartfelt appreciation" accept their support as a presidential candidate.

Harding had written Congressman Mouser that he hoped to be a Foraker delegate to the Republican national convention and asked his cooperation. Mouser replied two days after Christmas saying that although he loved to see such "unselfish loyalty and devotion to Foraker's candidacy," he himself was not for him. Through the New Year *Star* editorials beat the drum for Foraker.

On January 6 Harding upbraided Roosevelt for swearing to put Foraker
out of politics because of the Ohio senator's opposition to "two or three
great public questions in the light of his own conscience and loftier statesmanship," and suggested that the President should support Foraker out of
gratitude for what the Senator had done for him in 1903. The *Star* let
loose on Roosevelt's close friend and Golden Rule Jones's astute Toledo
opponent, the silken-mannered Walter F. Brown, who had come out
against Foraker. Brown was "the Judas of Toledo, the worst of the bosses,
who has driven the grand old elephant up a dozen alleys . . . and prosti-
tuted the great party to the purposes of the corporations in Toledo which
he represents." Harding jeered at Taft, leagued now with Boss Cox after
denouncing him in 1905.

It all seemed very emphatic, very final. However threatening the rising
Taft tide, Harding was sticking by the good ship Foraker. Then suddenly,
on January 22, he struck his colors. "Foraker is defeated and Ohio is for
Taft!" The *Star* announced:

> This is not a bandwagon climb; it is the calm recording of the trend in
> Ohio politics. The bandwagon is full anyway. The contest for presidential
> preference is at an end. The Buckeye state is for Taft. This is the plain
> truth. Senator Foraker may keep up a semblance of a fight for district
> delegates, but it will make no difference. Even granting that he is able to
> capture a few districts, which he must to impair the Taft candidacy when
> his own is a hopeless one, will not enlist the support of his friends, not the
> kind of support, at any rate, that counts in politics. . . . Licked—is the
> laconic way to put it, and in political honor his followers are prisoners of
> war, and will have to be good.

Foraker—though he might have remembered his own welshing in the
governors' contest of 1906—saw Harding's back-somersault in rather a
different light.

> Everything moved along so far as I had any knowledge for about sixty
> days [he wrote in his retirement] when suddenly, without the slightest
> notice or intimation beforehand, Senator Harding, in a double-headed
> editorial . . . withdrew his support from me and transferred it to Mr. Taft.
> He set forth a number of reasons that were satisfactory to himself, and
> no doubt conscientious and sincere on his part, which he repeated to me
> in a letter written contemporaneously with his publication.
> My friends and I were both surprised and chagrined. . . . It required no
> prophet to foretell that the result of such a defection would be disastrous,
> not so much because of his personal strength as because the same causes
> that occasioned the Hamilton County defection and now his defection
> would similarly affect others; but I excused him for sincerity and good
> intentions . . . for I recognized that it involved some sacrifice to stand by
> me with the National Administration and all its forces and influences
> arrayed against me in open and active hostility.

Under one of the new reformist laws that even the Republican Assembly was beginning to feel impelled to pass, county primaries had become optional as a means of selecting convention delegates. Foraker was much opposed to such primaries, feeling that they were destructive of "party discipline." Nevertheless, 20 counties held primaries in February for the Republican state convention at Columbus on March 3. Only in Knox County did Foraker enter candidates, and his list was buried. The Columbus convention was a Taft walkaway. Independent Republicans like James R. Garfield, the son of the assassinated twentieth President, and Arthur Garford joined their hands with the less fastidious ones of Rud Hynicka, Maurice Maschke, Walter Brown, Daugherty, and Harding. "The best man should win," Boss Cox declared affably, adding that Taft was of course the best man. Johnson's long shadow might be seen in the countermove by which the Republican platform recommended the extension of the merit system, competitive bidding for state purchases, the abolition of child labor, accident protection for workers, an effective primary law, control of public utilities, a referendum on franchises and the taxation of stocks, bonds, and other intangibles. Governor Harris, colorless though he might be, was renominated without opposition. From Cox to Garfield, everyone went away satisfied except Senators Foraker and Dick who were so ignored that they were never even mentioned.

The state Democratic convention, held in Columbus two months later, was not so harmonious. Tom Johnson, leading the reform Democrats, would personally have liked to see Brand Whitlock their candidate for governor. But, as an Independent was scarcely a practical political choice, he was willing to settle for Atlee Pomerene, an untried young lawyer with an obviously bright future. A graduate of Princeton and the Cincinnati Law School where he had won the prize as the best all-round debater, Pomerene had been twice elected city solicitor of Canton and once prosecutor of Stark County. It was not enough, even with Johnson behind him. On the second ballot the convention nominated the more conservative Judson Harmon.

Harmon, in his sixty-third year, was a commanding presence, tall and powerfully built with a ruddy complexion, cropped mustache, determined mouth, and eyes that challenged the crowd from under shaggy eyebrows. His erect bearing suggested more the soldier than the politician, yet his austere look could dissolve with gentleness when he smiled or laughed.

He was born in Hamilton County, the son of a Baptist preacher. After graduating from Denison University and Cincinnati Law School he had started to practice law in the town of Wyoming, and while still in his twenties was elected mayor. In 1876 he was elected judge of the Common Pleas Court of Hamilton County, and two years later elected to Cincinnati's Superior Court, where he was joined the following year by the rising young Republican, Joseph Benson Foraker. In 1883 he was re-elected by an even larger majority, but in 1887 resigned to take former Governor Hoadly's position in Cincinnati's leading law firm. On Harmon's recommendation Foraker, elected governor in 1885, then appointed the twenty-nine-year-old William Howard Taft to fill the remainder of his term. So notable was Harmon's career both as a judge and as a lawyer that in 1895 President Cleveland picked him for his attorney general.

Most of Harmon's support in the convention came from the rural members. Johnson had not wanted him, feeling that a lawyer who was getting $25,000 a year as receiver for Morgan's Cincinnati, Hamilton & Dayton Railroad would scarcely be sympathetic to the liberal Democratic platform—as indeed, in regard to municipal ownership and the initiative and referendum, Harmon was not. The Cleveland mayor was somewhat mollified when Harmon agreed to and the convention endorsed Johnson's candidate for attorney general, the square-faced second-generation Irishman, Timothy Hogan.

The delegates to the Republican national convention that met in Chicago's Coliseum on June 16 were as predetermined as the members of the Electoral College. Roosevelt had seen to that. There was not even the semblance of a contest. Taft was nominated on the first ballot by 702 votes to 68 for Philander Knox and 67 for Charles Evans Hughes. Yet in their uninstructed hearts the delegates longed for the Rough Rider with his big stick and thirty-two-tooth grin. The party managers guiding the delegates sensed the undercurrent of unrest, aware that one intemperate phrase might start a stampede for Roosevelt that would be impossible to check. When the Ohio delegation marched in carrying a large silk banner with Taft's portrait there were cheers, but at any mention of Roosevelt the cheers were louder. When the permanent chairman, Henry Cabot Lodge, referred to President Roosevelt as "the best abused and the most popular man in the United States today" the delegates jumped to their feet, uncontrollable, waving their hats, clapping, and shouting. The demonstration lasted forty-nine minutes, and as the sustained chant "Four-four-four years more" rose to the struts and rafters, it took all Lodge's deftness to keep the convention from bolting. When Taft's name was finally placed in nomination the applause, artificially stimulated though it was, lasted only twenty minutes—a discrepancy that Mrs. Taft noted and never forgot.

The Democrats, meeting at Denver, turned again to a this time chastened and subdued William Jennings Bryan who even talked of a "front porch" campaign. Gone was the Boy Orator with his cross of gold, his brave new world of paper money, and his raggle-taggle populist following. Bryan was now concerned with creating a stable image of himself as a moderate, almost as a conservative. It did him no good. In the November election, even though he garnered well over a million more votes than had the ultra-conservative Parker four years before, he lost by 6,407,982 to Taft's 7,677,788.

Although Taft carried Ohio by 70,000 votes, Harris, the faded old soldier, was not so fortunate. Harmon in a whirlwind campaign persuaded enough Republicans to scratch their ballots to elect him by a 19,372 majority. Charles Green, a Cox henchman running for treasurer, was the only other Republican state candidate to be defeated. The GOP elected 13 of the 21 Ohio congressmen. One of the Democratic newcomers to Congress was James Middleton Cox, a Dayton newspaper publisher, who campaigned on a low-tariff platform and was elected from the exporting 3rd District. The Republicans managed to keep their majority in the Ohio legislature, insuring the election of a United States senator in January.

That senator was not, however, going to be Foraker. On September 17, William Randolph Hearst, stumping the country for Thomas L. Hisgen, the presidential candidate of his splinter Independent League, appeared in Columbus and read a series of letters from John D. Archbold, vice president of the Standard Oil Company, to Senator Foraker. The letters, dating from 1900 to 1903, had been stolen from Foraker, and Hearst had bought them up. They revealed devastatingly that Foraker while a member of the Ohio Assembly and afterward as a United States senator had been the confidential legislative agent of the Standard Oil Company, a name that in Ohio and elsewhere had come to symbolize corporate ruthlessness and rapacity. Although Foraker tried to justify himself by explaining that his connection with Standard Oil had ended before his second term in the Senate, his voice was drowned out in the shrill aftermath of Hearst's exposure. Such phrases as "Here is still another very objectionable bill . . . I hope there will be no difficulty in killing it," tarred Foraker with Standard Oil pitch. Roosevelt, with some semantic confusion, wanted Foraker boiled in oil and at the same time thrown over by Taft "with a bomb." Stubbornly the Ohio senator insisted that he would still be re-elected.

Earlier in the year Congressman Burton had announced himself a candidate for Foraker's senate seat. Then, in order to gain the old Senator's still formidable support for Taft's presidential bid, he had been persuaded to drop out. But after Hearst's airing of the Archbold letters Burton, with Roosevelt's backing, revived his candidacy. Scarcely had he re-emerged as a candidate before he found himself opposed by Charlie Taft. Although Charlie's Cox-sponsored term in Congress was, to say the most, undistinguished, the prospect of his half-brother's almost certain election to the Presidency fired his old political ambitions. Through marriage and acquisition the richest of his family, an international art collector and patron of the arts, even the owner of a baseball club, the Cincinnati

Reds, Charlie's ultimate ambition was dynastic, a tribal dream founded on Will as President and himself as United States senator. Roosevelt, though friendly enough to Charlie, nevertheless felt that the one important thing was to eliminate Foraker and that Burton was the best man to do it.

Others than the family-minded Charlie were drawn to the Senate seat. There was now the tantalizing possibility that Foraker, Burton, and Taft might cancel each other out. The complicated maneuverings that followed were, like an iceberg, only an eighth visible above the surface. Harry Daugherty's low but perpetual moth-desire for political stardom was again stirring. The November days after the election found him making his friends aware of his availability. Much more seriously to be considered was Harding, the harmonizer who walked the straight-and-narrow path between Foraker and Burton, while nodding to Taft, friendly to all sides, hostile neither to Boss Cox nor Roosevelt.

On December 29, four days before the Republican caucus would make its choice for senator, Rep. George Wilbur and Sen. Richard Cameron of Union County issued a joint statement in favor of Harding as the "logical" candidate; the friend of Foraker, McKinley, Governor Harris, and President-elect Taft, who "for many years [has] fought for the principles of the Republican party as well as its candidates." Harding opened headquarters at Neil House, but before he could get his last-minute campaign underway, the whole anti-Burton movement collapsed. President-elect Taft sent word to Columbus that his brother must withdraw. Hiding his chagrin, Charlie obeyed, contenting himself with remarking that the party was more important to him than personal ambition. From Cincinnati Boss Cox announced that he was for Burton. Foraker attempted to prevent a caucus and throw the contest to the legislature where he hoped he might on a long chance pick up enough Democratic votes to win. But Roosevelt declared this treason to the party. Foraker, face to face with ultimate political reality, announced his retirement in bitter words. Harding, finding himself alone against the formidable weight of Roosevelt, Burton, and the Tafts, withdrew without bitterness and without discussion. Burton was nominated by the Republican caucus on January 3, and his election to the Senate ratified by the assembly nine days later.

Harding had looked on his Senate bid as a long shot, a spin of the roulette wheel of politics, nothing on this occasion to be taken too much to heart. "My candidacy was not old enough or conspicuous enough to be important," he admitted, "but I could utter no word of discord over the victory of Mr. Burton if I would."

Politics did not prevent him and the Duchess from holding their usual New Year's open house at Mount Vernon Avenue with the usual announcement to their friends:

By Special Permission of Eminent Authority
Messrs Thomas & Jeremiah Will Preside at
the Punch Bowl from Four 'Till Later.
You are expected.   284 Mt. Vernon Avenue.[1]

Shortly after Burton's election Harding reorganized the *Star* as the Harding Publishing Company with capital stock set at the par value of $80,000. Three-quarters of the stock he kept. The rest he offered to the *Star* employees, arranging that they could pay for whatever stock they bought in instalments out of their dividends. He had always liked to think of the *Star* as a family, and now he felt he could prove it. The profit-sharing scheme was one of the first in Ohio, as Harding liked to point out later with pride. He became president of the new company, with George Van Fleet vice president and Will Schaffner, the first teller of the Marion County Bank—son of the local furniture dealer and undertaker—coming in as treasurer. Harding managed to persuade his friend Malcolm Jennings to move to Marion and take over as secretary and general manager.

Since 1903 Jennings had been editor and manager of the Lancaster *Gazette* while for the last two years running an advertising agency as well. His appraising shrewdness saw an abounding future for the new company and for its president. Shortly after Harding's withdrawal from the Senate race, Jennings had written:

> As for your political future. You will make that yourself and on your personality. You cannot get your advancement by promotion through the grades as Dick did through long service as corporal, sergeant and lieutenant. You are young, have a good business which you cannot afford to give up. You are growing and are in an admirable position to wait. You like the game—and that is all there is in politics, for realization is often dead sea fruit and the fun is in the striving.

Carrie had been envious of Harding's 1907 trip abroad, the trip that she had wanted for herself. Ever since his return she had been at him to talk her husband into making a European tour, the four of them together. Both men could afford it. The 1907 depression remained no more than an unfruitful memory, and the Uhler-Phillips store was doing so well that it had opened a New York branch at 817 Broadway. The *Star*, too, was flourishing, and after its reorganization ran by itself with only an occasional paternalistic glance from the president-publisher. In Washington, Beveridge, and La Follette and the Senate insurgents might be preparing to harass President Taft on the tariff, but in Ohio the political air was quiescent, with the 1910 election a scarcely discernible cloud on the

[1] After several rows of new houses had been built, the street was renumbered and Harding's house became 380.

horizon. Harding's family affairs were in order. Deac had, with his
brother's help, bought an eight-room brick house on Douglas Street,
Columbus, from a Doctor F. C. Williams for $5,550. He had started his
own private practice and was using part of the house as a sanitorium.
Daisy, the only one still at home with her parents, continued to teach
school and run the Center Street house. Whatever Tryon's vagaries, the
house was now secure for her and her mother. Phoebe, as Harding wrote
Carolyn in Burma, was failing. She no longer delivered babies, but spent
most of her days now at home with her Bible and her Adventist tracts.
There was nothing immediate in her decline to hold Harding in Marion.
He and Jim Phillips agreed between them that a long cruise to a warmer,
more cheerful climate would be a better way of spending the winter than
in Ohio.

On February 4, 1909, the social column of the *Star* noted that Mr. and
Mrs. W. G. Harding and Mr. and Mrs. James E. Phillips had left for New
York, from which port they would sail on February 6 on the Hamburg-
American liner, S. S. *Deutschland,* for a tour of the Mediterranean
extending to and including Egypt.

Ten days after embarking Harding wrote to Coonie Christian:

> This is your Valentine, though it will necessarily arrive late. Well, we are
> now away ten days and it seems quite a month. Had a busy time in New
> York. The Duchess and Mrs. Phillips wanted to leave enough money in
> the shops there so they could do business until we get back and scatter
> more. . . .
>
> The voyage to Madeira was very fine, Sunday A.M. to Saturday A.M.,
> but we had two very rough days. All kept on their legs (i.e., all in our
> party) but the eating that we did for two days did not greatly diminish the
> ship's food supply. The big vessel tossed and rolled until our trunks
> waltzed about our stateroom, but we never surrendered, and we stayed
> on deck with our deck chairs lashed to keep them from dancing across the
> decks. The weather has permitted living on deck, day and night, but we
> have needed our heavy wraps and blankets. Friday night we had a dance
> on deck, but we didn't patronize it very freely. The Colonel [George
> Christian] would have been in clover.
>
> Saturday we stopped at Madeira, drank of the wine, bought of the
> embroideries, and sent a wave of prosperity over the island. Mighty pretty
> place. I could gladly stay a couple of weeks. Cannot say I greatly like
> riding on ox-drawn sleds over cobblestone pavements, but we tried it.
> Made the ascent of one of the mountains by cog-wheel railway and tobag-
> ganed [sic] down. Same stunt in another form. The tabog is an iron-shod
> sled, pulled, pushed, or held back by two Portuguese, and we descended
> over two miles of paved mountain roads and streets in that sled, with the
> two poor men pushing, panting, puffing, and pulling. I never gave anybody
> a fee so willingly in my life.

Most of the people in Madeira go barefooted. The poverty there is appalling. You chafe at your utter inability to relieve it. You would have been especially interested in the children—the cutest I ever saw. They all know how to seek gift money, and you could throw away the Marion County Bank and not go half way around among those you could meet in one day. The climate at Madeira is fine and the thing called race suicide is entirely unknown.

I had supposed Madeira was a Spanish possession, but soon found the mistake. The people and the government are Portuguese. The flowers are exceedingly beautiful and very profuse. . . . Children pelted us with flowers all the way up the mountain, hoping to be pelted with pennies in return. As far as the eye could reach, brilliant bloom was in sight. The straw-berries were ripe and exceedingly sweet.

All the time I have been trying to write, I have been confused by a continuous chatter by the Phillipses, the Duchess, et al. I couldn't fire them so I let them go on. Now they are at lunch. The eats on board ship are exceedingly good and appallingly plenty. There is no escape from the table d'hôte dinner, and on ship it is quite an affair. We have thus far eaten little enough to keep well, and ample enough to keep fat.

Well, enough of this. I will mail this at Gibraltar, and enclose with it our very warmest regards and best wishes. You will, of course, kindly remember us to the Colonel and Mildred and to Fred and Mamie, and to George Jr. and his family. If you want to drop us a line, you can make the Colonel do it.

Yours at sea,

W. G. H.

On those dreamy sequential days aboard ship time gave the illusion of standing still. It was a tribute to Carrie's self-possession that in such a narrowly enforced association the Duchess suspected nothing. Carrie herself was troubled. Sometimes when the Duchess and Jim had gone to bed, the other two would meet for a walk around the deck and a quick embrace in the shadow of the lifeboats. But there were moments when Carrie would feel her body yielding and then suddenly push her lover away from her. Harding, direct and importunate, could never understand her ambiguities or that the close shipboard association of the two men who loved her had come to seem a threat to her integrity. In the fragments of Carrie's surviving letters—letters that she never sent—she tried to explain her feelings to Harding. So long as the Duchess remained unsus-pecting, he had no complications of feeling.

Tanned, souvenir-laden, they landed at Naples in mid-March, then traveled north, stopping at Rome and Pisa and Florence before continuing on to Switzerland and Germany. At Naples, Harding bought a half-size marble bust of a female nude from Erico Brothers, one of the firms specializing in such objects for the more expensive tourist trade. In Pisa at the Galeria Andreoni he bought another marble of a naked dancing girl, the Duchess acquiescing on the plea that it was "art." She herself ordered a compensating marble-clothed statue of "Priscilla the Puritan Girl."

For Jim and the Duchess Europe was a more elaborate outing. For Harding it was a series of colored postcards. But for Carrie, even within her tourist insulation, it seemed a more rooted and more varied way of life than anyone could have conceived of in Bucyrus or Marion. Italy was unforgettably picturesque, but it was in Germany that she experienced a sense of coming home, as if this Germanic heartland with its glowing modern cities and its red-roofed medieval villages was part of her inheritance. Not England with its kinship of tongue, but Germany was where she belonged. On this trip she determined that she would go back, not for a few days or weeks but for months, years even. The language that she could barely decipher from her high-school German course she would learn. There she would one day live her life.

The two couples sailed for America on a nine-day boat, the *President Lincoln*, the third week in April, arriving in New York on the thirtieth. Crates of Italian statuary and trunkloads of trinkets followed them to Marion. Already in Ohio there were political whisperings of the coming year, the election year. While the *President Lincoln* was still in mid-Atlantic the editor of the Cleveland *Leader*, N. C. Wright, was writing to Arthur L. Garford, the Elyria industrialist and independent Republican leader, that Harding looked well ahead in the next nomination for governor and that President Taft would be in line for him.

Pete DeWolfe, now married to Esther Neely, still clung to the *Star*, but his good intentions had shattered against the harsh inevitability of a daily routine. Harding found him as idly insouciant as ever, haggard in appearance, and with a hacking cough. Tryon on examining him sent him to White Oaks Farm where Doctor Sawyer determined that his right lung was half-rotted with tuberculosis. Since the doctor said he could not stay in Ohio, he welcomed the relieving excuse for quitting the *Star*. Although Phoebe had not changed much in the three-month interlude, her decline continued. Carolyn, after receiving her brother's warning letter, left from Burma to pay her mother what would probably be a last visit.

The summer of 1909, sultry in Ohio, was ominous in Washington. During those sweltering days the insurgent Western Republicans in the Senate, led by Sen. Albert J. Beveridge, began their attack on the autocratic Sen. Nelson Aldrich's high tariff bill. While Taft vacillated, in the end to swing over to Aldrich and the spokesman of big business, La Follette, Dolliver, Cummins, and Bristow wore themselves out on the floor of the Senate in a bitter losing battle that foreshadowed the alienation of the Independent Republicans from Taft and the emergence of Progressives. In that summer of national dissension Harding resumed his Chautauqua tour, giving his familiar "Alexander Hamilton—Prophet of American Destiny," to new rural audiences. He had dropped the "Big Stick" lecture; with Taft in the White House, it had become too suspicious a symbol.

Murmurings about 1910 reached Harding in Marion from his county colleagues. The editor of the Marietta *Daily Journal* wrote to say that Harding's name sounded good to him for governor. Harry Kemmerer of the Carrollton *Free Press-Standard* asked Harding to come there to make a speech, and added that he looked forward to lodging and feeding him in 1910 when Harding had become "our candidate" for governor. Harding replied:

> If I were sure of my political intentions, I would write you and tell you how much I wanted you and any Carroll County friends I have to help me. A good many . . . are urging me to be a candidate, and [I] think all the signs favorable, and *I am willing*, but I am sure I do not wish to rush my friends into the thing until I can make what the medical men call "a favorable prognosis."

He was not capable of Daugherty's subtle and involved long-range manipulations. What must be, must be. He preferred to wait, letting events catch up with him while he took afternoon drives with the Duchess and the Phillipses. Carrie and he found each other alone when they could. She was now determined to go to Germany and send the fourteen-year-old Isabelle to school there. He did not take her seriously. When Jim Phillips asked his advice, he told him just to be patient, buy a car, and she'd forget about it. He played golf, for the first time seriously. And, as if consumed with restlessness, he made speeches all over the state. The annual field day of the League of Republican Clubs of Cuyahoga County, held at Luna Park, Cleveland, found him the principal speaker. He opened the Salem Homecoming Festival. He conducted the annual memorial service of the Coshocton Lodge of Elks. Group 8 of the Ohio Bankers Association asked him to speak at Wooster. "Preach the gospel of American optimism while preaching and practicing the gospel of Jesus Christ," he told the Ohio Christian Endeavor Union, adding that "pessimism never inspired an efficient endeavor or lighted a human pathway."

Carolyn arrived in the autumn full of Adventist zeal and tales of India and Burma. Whatever the course of his life, Harding always kept a deep and constant affection for his brother and sisters, and he rejoiced to see her. He rejoiced equally to see the last of Pete DeWolfe who left at the end of October for the Agnes Memorial Sanitarium in Denver, Colorado.

By January, 1910, postcards were appearing in Columbus with Harding's picture as Republican candidate for governor. Five counties had already endorsed him. He was by now committed, and sure of success. Herrick and Harris were out of it. If in 1908 he had replaced the old soldier on the ballot he was sure he would have beaten Harmon. This year he could do it! On January 22 he wrote to Carolyn, now on her way back to Burma:

> I have had the good intention to write you a letter ever since you left, but the pressure of things has prevented, speeches to prepare and deliver, and seeing people, make a very exacting penalty of trying to be in politics. About the only abiding consolation I get out of it all is that this time I shall attain the very distinguished honor or I shall henceforth and forever free myself from all public political participation—*and be much better off.* I almost envy you your stop at Hawaii and Manila and Japan. I should dearly love to visit these island countries and I surely intend to some day if I live and have no reverses. . . .

Even in an ordinary year the popular and successful Harmon would have been a difficult candidate to defeat, but 1910 was far from ordinary for the Republicans. With Taft in the White House entertaining Aldrich and associating with men of enormous wealth such as Frick and Morgan whom Roosevelt had called "the Enemy," the Grand Old Party was beginning to show the fissures that would lead to the split of 1912.

In spite of an "offhand" promise to his predecessor, Taft not long after taking office replaced Roosevelt's secretary of the interior, James Garfield, with Richard A. Ballinger. Garfield had helped his friend Roosevelt make conservation a national cause. Ballinger's idea of conservation was to distribute public lands and other national resources as quickly and cheaply as possible. Gifford Pinchot, the wealthy Pennsylvanian who had converted Roosevelt—one of his closest friends—to the idea of conservation and who in acknowledgment had been appointed Chief Forester in the Department of Agriculture, was so indignant at Ballinger's willingness to allow the richest coal mines in Alaska to go to the Morgan-Guggenheim syndicate that he publicly accused the Secretary of the Interior of being a traitor to Roosevelt's doctrines. In December, 1909, progressive Republican congressmen, with Democratic encouragement, forced an investigation of the Department of the Interior. A month later Pinchot admitted that he had been supplying confidential information from government files to aid in the attack on the Secretary. Taft demanded his resignation, but did nothing about Ballinger.[2]

---

[2] Pinchot, one of the most dedicated, powerful, and fanatic conservation leaders in the United States, eventually succeeded in hounding Ballinger from office. The Secretary had his liberal defenders. Harold Ickes considered Ballinger an "American Dreyfus" and in a 1940 article in the *Saturday Evening Post* defended Ballinger's Alaska proposals.

Two months after Pinchot had resigned, a coalition of insurgent Republicans and Democrats, led by Congressman George W. Norris, overthrew the crafty old czar of the House of Representatives, Speaker Joseph G. Cannon. "Sir," Cannon had once answered a questioning progressive, "the function of the Federal government is to afford protection to life, liberty, and property. When that is done, then let every tub stand on its own bottom, let every citizen 'root hog or die!' " Bills that threatened to exceed the Speaker's bottom specifications usually failed to see the light of day. He appointed the Rules Committee at his whim, and his was the dictatorial power to decide on all legislation. But now 46 Republican insurgents joined the Democrats to change the rules of the House and depose the arbitrary despot who had ruled them for so long. The insurgents had also combined to demolish the railroad bill written by Taft's attorney general, George W. Wickersham, much to Taft's anger. Insurgency was in the air. Progressivism—not to be spelled with a capital P for another two years—was becoming a common term as well as a common cause. One unanswered question poised over Washington in the early part of 1910: What would Rough Rider Roosevelt do when he returned from Africa in the summer?

Former Secretary Garfield had returned to Ohio to lead the progressive Republicans. Garfield had always traveled an independent course from the day when as a young lawyer he entered the Ohio senate in 1896. He had served two terms, his most notable achievement being to write a corrupt-practices law to limit campaign expenses. He opposed ripper legislation with such impracticable idealism that Hanna accused him of practicing "heavenly politics" and refused him Republican organization backing to run for Congress in 1900. Roosevelt, by contrast, appointed him a Federal civil-service commissioner in 1902 and made him secretary of the interior in 1907. In Washington he became a member of the "lawn tennis cabinet," one of the small groups closest to the President. His experiences as head of the Department of the Interior where he could see firsthand "the very inmost working of special privilege—of political influence metamorphosed into greed and chicanery," confirmed and hardened his progressive determination. From his law office in Mark Hanna's Cleveland he opened an attack on "special interests" and declared that "the progressives of today will win the battle." As spring moved into summer and the Republican state convention began to cast its shadow, he was seen as the progressive candidate for governor. From his Mecca shrine Boss Cox threatened to walk the Hamilton County delegation out of the convention if Garfield should be nominated. "A mad set of men," he said piously, referring to Garfield and his supporters.

The state Democratic convention met in Dayton on June 20, a month before the Republican convention at Columbus. Harmon's renomination was so taken for granted that it was not even discussed. He had shown himself a vigorous and successful governor. Though a conservative of the cut of his friend Grover Cleveland, he had managed to appeal to the progressive wing of his party in spite of the initial doubts of the Johnsonites. In his first three months in office he made appointments with painstaking care as to their fitness. Disregarding the outraged protests of the Democratic bosses, he had refused to discharge competent Republicans. As a conservative he was more interested in justice to the taxpayer than in any single tax redistribution of property. His standard was that "guilt is always personal," and he so judged his subordinates in office.

It had long been axiomatic in Ohio that a public office was a public bust, and never was the axiom more taken to heart than in the office of the state treasurer. Officials had come to consider it a perquisite of office to deposit large sums of collected taxes in their favored banks and keep the interest for themselves. Republican State Treasurer William S. Mc-Kinnon had told a financially-too-inquisitive legislator a few years earlier that it was none of his damn business either as a senator or as a citizen where the treasurer kept the state's money or how he ran his office. Actually McKinnon had been keeping surplus state funds in his own bank. State money had generally developed a way of sticking to the hands of the collector. The Ohio Republican image, chipped by the progressives, was shattered after Governor Harmon ordered the Republican attorney general, Ulysses G. Denman, to bring suit against a row of former Republican officials. McKinnon had died, but Denman's Democratic successor, Timothy S. Hogan, finally managed to recover $211,721 of misappropriated public monies from his estate. His deputy, Charles Green, and another former treasurer, Isaac B. Cameron, were indicted for embezzlement and eventually went to jail. A coalition of progressive Republicans and like-minded Democrats in the Ohio House of Representatives uncovered large-scale graft and bill-padding of the crassest sort in the office of the state printer, Mark Slater, a lieutenant of Dayton's former Republican boss, Joseph E. Lowes. In the Senate, on the other hand, reactionary Republicans leagued with similarly minded Democrats to block a program of tax reform sponsored by the progressives of both parties. It was a year of transition, of disintegration, a blurring of party lines as each party divided into its own regulars and insurgents, reactionaries and progressives. There were demands for a coalition of progressive Republicans and progressive Democrats. A poll by the Cincinnati *Enquirer* in June showed that a majority of those polled were dissatisfied with the Taft administration in general and the Payne-Aldrich tariff in particular. Governor Harmon, drawing increasing support from discontented Republicans, seemed certain of re-election. There was even talk of him as a presidential candidate in 1912.

Between January and June of 1910 Harding scoured the state, making over three hundred speeches, mostly in the country areas. The Chautauqua circuits had made his face and personality known. Rural ears were attuned to his oratory. County editor colleagues welcomed him. Though he lacked a boss-organized urban base, he was building up solid grassroots support. Foraker, even in his disgrace, could still be a potent help. There were friendly letters and signs of encouragement all along the way. In May, Ohio Northern University conferred its degree of doctor of laws on Harding. Optimistically he saw himself again as the harmonizer, the middle man between Garfield and the bosses. When he was first being mentioned as a candidate, a union organizer came to Marion and pointed out that anyone running for governor ought to run a union shop. Harding told him to go ahead and organize the staff, and when some of the older men balked he went down personally and told them to join. He himself carried a typographer's union card from then on.

Preoccupied with maneuvering for a still very problematical nomination, Harding did not go to Florida that winter. Amos Kling, still frisking on the sands of Daytona, wrote him from the Halifax River Yacht Club that they had formed an Ohio Society in Florida and that there was always "something doing" at the Kling bungalow. But now the old man had so mellowed that he was addressing his son-in-law as "Dear Warren" and signing his letter "Daddy." Pete DeWolfe scrawled a few lines from Colorado to say that his lung was improving and to ask for money. His wife Esther had joined him and he had rented a farm and was trying to raise sugar beets and potatoes. He complained of the drought.

On the hallway table of the Mount Vernon Avenue house stood a Harding wedding present, a plaster bust of a woman on a black pedestal labeled Diane. Harding liked to think that the vague features resembled Carrie's. [-] Their stolen weekends interjected into his political tours became fewer, but sharp small-town eyes were beginning to notice the frequency of his visits to South Main Street. The first light buzz of gossip had begun. But in the renewed spring weather the Phillipses and the Hardings continued their motor trips—to Caledonia or Bucyrus on a Sunday afternoon. Early in the spring Phoebe had had a fall, a gash in her hip had ulcerated, and she had been bedridden for several months. Late in May she died.

Before the funeral Harding wrote to Carolyn in Burma:

> Dear good Mother died this Sunday morning at seven o'clock. It was no surprise to us who had seen her daily since her fall, about March first. The failure was marked since the day the accident had sent her to bed. Father, Deacon, Mary, Florence, and I were at her bedside when the end came. We do not believe she suffered, that is she must not have been conscious

of it because in fact she knew nothing of us for 24 hours before. . . . She never complained, never feared. Before she lost consciousness, Deacon asked her if she was praying. "No, I am only trusting," she replied. She could and she had the right to trust . . . and surely, yea, surely, there are for her all the rewards in eternity that God bestows on his very own. I could not speak for myself, but dear, dear Mother will wear a crown if ever a Christian woman does—and I can believe in eternal compensations for such as her.

On June 18 Roosevelt arrived in New York Harbor aboard the *Kaiserin Augusta Victoria* to be met by an enormous naval parade. The whole country seemed ready to welcome him. Taft was amazed at the hold that the Rough Rider ex-President kept on the minds of the people, and said so. Roosevelt in turn was not reticent in letting it be known—unofficially but nonetheless effectively—that he was dissatisfied with Taft's conduct of affairs. Representative Miles Poindexter came to Oyster Bay, and Roosevelt promised to support him for the Senate against the possible candidacy of Ballinger.[3] He took no further notice of the President. No courtesies passed between Oyster Bay and the White House. In August Roosevelt left to attend the Frontier Celebration at Cheyenne, Wyoming. On that Western journey he traveled 5,000 miles through 14 states. Speaking at the dedication of the John Brown battlefield at Ossawatomie, Kansas, he came out for the graduated income tax, workmen's compensation, tariff revision, and other measures to curl the thinning hair of elderly conservatives. During his speech he coined the phrase "The New Nationalism," as if he were now prepared to start a new movement and take over from Taft. Privately he told his friends that he might be forced to run for President in 1912 to see that his policies were carried out. Not once on his Western journey did he publicly mention the President. Taft, much offended, wrote to his brother Charlie:

> [Roosevelt] allows himself to fall into a style that makes one think he considers himself still the President of the United States. In most of these speeches he has utterly ignored me. . . . His attitude toward me is one that I find it difficult to understand and explain. . . . He is at the head of the Insurgents, and for the time being the Insurgents are at the top of the wave. . . .

There was still no formal break between President and former President; they would even meet again on occasion with superficial cordiality, but to the White House military aide, Maj. Archie Butt, they seemed too bitterly apart ever to get together again.

---

[3] Ballinger had become a liability to Taft in his Cabinet and it had been suggested that a tactful way of getting rid of him would be to ease him into the Senate.

The June Democratic convention in Dayton that picked Governor Harmon for a second term conciliated the Johnson delegates by nominating Atlee Pomerene for lieutenant governor and Timothy Hogan for a second try at the attorney generalship.

The usually operative clockwork of the ensuing Republican convention had this year become disarranged. For the first time the 1,068 delegates had been nominated either by direct primary or by primary-elected delegates to their county conventions. Many of them were uncommitted. Although Garfield was the most popular candidate among the Republican voters of Ohio, and would have won easily if the nomination had been by direct vote at the polls, the convention was still another matter. All the influence of the White House was thrown to prevent the nomination of such an ultra-insurgent. To avoid Garfield, Taft was willing to accept much of his liberal platform if this could be tempered by an "independent" candidate. State Chairman Walter Brown favored Judge Reynolds Kinkade, a jurist who had achieved a reputation for upright independence by sending five prominent Toledo businessmen to jail for organizing an ice monopoly in defiance of the Ohio Antitrust Law. Kinkade received Taft's informal approval on a visit to the summer White House at Beverly, Massachusetts.

The direct primaries had made rigging the Republican convention in advance much more complicated. Gus J. Karger, head of the news bureau of Charlie Taft's Cincinnati *Times-Star*, writing to the President's secretary, C. D. Norton, summed up the Ohio situation as it looked in mid-July.

> We are still running around in circles. Cox says it will be O. B. Brown on the first ballot and everybody not immediately under his influence says he doesn't know what he's talking about. Burton's feet are still cold and he's backing away from the Cox agreement, at the same time praying for a case of dysentery or something equally as good that will furnish a good excuse to keep him away from the convention. Up in Cuyahoga County they are making certain that the solid vote of the so-called Burton delegation shall not be delivered to Brown, but unfortunately the fellows that are leaving Burton are going to Garfield, and Republicans of my stripe, for instance, would have to be dragged to the polls in a hypnotic state to vote for that high-minded gentleman. Cox wants to nominate Brown; Foraker grins with delight and says Harding is the only man he's interested in; Dick keeps plodding away and bringing the logic of the situation constantly 'round to Carmi Thompson; the President's disinterested friends don't like anybody that's been named, but don't know exactly whom or what they want; and the extreme radicals, many of them anti-Administration men, are lining up behind Garfield. Burton is sore about that White House conference that protested against "deals" and is at Hot Springs, trying to make the sphinx look like a garrulous old maid. But he has written some letters indicating his resentment, and if he gets real nasty I

wouldn't be surprised to see him take up Garfield, as that would be about the only way in which the Cuyahoga County delegation could be made to vote solid.

Alarmed by the reports of Taft's swing to Kinkade, Harding countered by writing the President ten days before the convention and committing himself irrevocably to the Taft camp:

> You will remember that before I permitted my name to be used in connection with the Governorship this year, *I journeyed to Washington* and sought from you the assurance that my candidacy would not be considered distasteful to you or in any way inimical to your interests. The assurance you gave me very cordially. I did not ask your help to secure the nomination, feeling that you should not be embarrassed by having to make choice between the Republicans of your own State, provided that all the aspirants were equally loyal to the Party and the administration. This was your own expressed view, and I am glad to say that you have maintained that attitude in the face of much urging to use your great power and influence to dictate a ticket in Ohio.
>
> My only object in writing at this time is to impress upon you the importance of maintaining your stand in this regard. I do not believe that it is possible for any man to be nominated by the Republican State Convention this year who is not your sincere supporter. That being so, there can be no reason why you should divide your strength in the State by making a discriminating choice between your friends and their adherents. I know that effort will be made by men not really in touch with the situation, but whose positions give them access to your private ear, to convince you that the Republicans of Ohio are floundering wildly about seeking a candidate and are in desperate straits. This is not true.
>
> Delegates have been selected to the convention by each county, either by direct primary or by conventions made up of directed elected delegates. The men selected compose a fairly representative body of men, with a full knowledge of the needs of the situation, and with capacity to do what is best for the Party.
>
> Speaking for myself, I may say that I have placed my candidacy unreservedly in the hands of these men. I have made no canvass, solicited no pledges, sought no alliances. I have felt that the people who are called upon to *elect* the candidates should be given the freest and fullest opportunity to *select* them with reference to their ability, availability and strength.
>
> I think this is your position as it is mine. Only the sort of a convention which this attitude implies will leave us in shape to go into a campaign without factional bitterness or soreness. I hope to be nominated, but if the convention, acting upon its own judgment, decides for another I would accept defeat without more than a passing personal regret; but this would not be possible should the nomination be the result of . . . interference of leaders in national affairs.
>
> Let me say that both as a public speaker and an editor I have been your

loyal supporter, not from a hope of securing your assistance in return, but solely because I believe you are right and doing a great work worthily and wisely. I acquit you of any obligation to me except the right to be treated fairly; and that right you have accorded me always.

I have not intruded suggestions upon you in the past with reference to this matter. I shall not do so again. I only felt that in view of representations which I know are being made to you by interested parties, I should thus explain my position.

Boss Cox had his own candidate in the field in the ostensibly liberal shape of Judge Orin Britt Brown of Dayton. Cox claimed that he had 450 votes sewed up for Brown, only 84 short of the majority necessary to nominate. Confidently he offered to bet $5,000 or any part of it that his man Brown would get the nomination; $5,000 that Brown would carry Hamilton County; and another $5,000 that he would be elected governor. With characteristic aplomb he notified Taft in Beverly that Brown would be nominated unless the President interfered, and this he must not do. The good-natured Taft reacted to Cox's insolence merely by remarking that "the state is lost if we accept any man of his dictation."

The week before the convention Taft held a conference at Beverly Farms with Burton, Dick, and the Republican State Executive Chairman Wade H. Ellis, a former Democrat who had seen the light and become associated with Boss Cox. Ellis was for Brown, Dick for Thompson, while Burton favored bringing in an inside outsider like Longworth. With not much enthusiasm they finally agreed with the President that if no candidate collected enough votes on the first two ballots, they would start a swing to Kinkade. Taft, in turn, agreed not to endorse any candidate personally even though he preferred Kinkade. Thompson and Harding were acceptable, but only as a last resort was he willing to accept Brown, and Garfield under no circumstances. Burton, controlling the Cuyahoga County delegation, promised that he would play neutral and divide his district's votes among all the candidates.

To the Cincinnati *Enquirer* the July 26 prospective convention resembled the Tower of Babel. And

> as at Babel, there will be standpatters, progressives, come-outers, conservatives, Forakerites, tariff-reformers, Dick shouters, liberals, dry detectives, Anti-Saloon Leaguers, Afro-Americans, Taftites, Garfield goo-goos, troublemakers, grafters, woman suffragists, referendum rooters, Sen. Theodore Burton, George B. Cox, Walter F. Brown, Harmon Republicans, corporation lobbyists, labor leaders, "Si" Allen, and Nick Longworth.

There were all of those predicted and Harry Daugherty as well, his old ambitions stirred by Dick's unpopularity, moving paunchily in the shadows as he buttonholed delegates to support him for Dick's seat in the United States Senate that the Ohio Assembly would be filling in January.

Shortly before the convention Kinkade withdrew, stating that he was neither an active nor a receptive candidate and that his decision was final. Dick, Burton, Wade Ellis, Republican State Chairman Walter F. Brown, and Taft's assistant secretary of the treasury, Charles D. Hilles, met secretly at 3 A.M., Cox not being present, and agreed that the choice was between Thompson and Harding. Garfield must not be nominated, Brown could not be nominated, and there should not be any dark-horse kicking over the traces. Though neither Thompson nor Harding had enough delegates to win on their own, their combined votes would come close to a majority. The politicians were astute enough to realize that the Republican nomination for governor in that fragmented year was a brass ring. And, as the newspapers pointed, Harding was everybody's second choice, possibly theirs, too. They decided to eliminate Thompson.

Harding arrived in Columbus on the evening of the twenty-fourth to confer with his chief lieutenant, Malcolm Jennings, already installed in the Neil House. With him came Grant Mouser, all old differences forgotten and ready to nominate his Marion neighbor. Ed Scobey had arrived from Texas, oozing confidence, to "take up his station" and apply his prestidigital political skill. Harding, he said, was the "strongest and most available man." Anchored with the conservatives, Harding in a public statement that aped Mark Hanna did his best to appeal to the progressives:

> I am standing for this nomination because a lot of Republicans—really a great lot of them—urged it, and I feel that it is not unseemly if one's best efforts in the party's behalf for ten or twenty years offered a passport to consideration. . . .
> This talk about candidates and platforms not harmonizing is mainly for diversion. . . . Platforms are the harmonized convictions of the majority in representative government, and the nominee is the commissioned standard-bearer of that majority.
> Speaking for myself, I "stand pat" when I know I am right and I "progress" under the conviction that new grounds are essential. . . . I believe that the Republican party has the conscience and the purpose to solve every problem attending our marvelous development.

Just before the convention opened, Cox conferred with the chairman, Senator Burton, in the hope of persuading him to make a deal for the Cuyahoga County delegates. Burton insisted that he would take no part in supporting anyone for the nomination. Privately he was considering Nick Longworth. In 1906 Longworth had married the impetuous and vivacious Alice Roosevelt. As Roosevelt's son-in-law and Boss Cox's political foster son he was the obvious compromise, even though Cox kept stubbornly to his prediction that Brown would get 450 votes on the first ballot and reach the necessary 534 on the second.

While the delegates were assembling, Garfield tried to seize the initiative by publishing a statement of principles in which he again attacked the special interests, and called for progressive planks ranging from the regulation of public utilities to workmen's compensation and the recall of both elected and appointed officials. When the resolution committee under the chairmanship of Senator Dick produced instead a platform praising Taft and defending the Payne-Aldrich tariff, Garfield withdrew from the convention, leaving his confused followers without even the satisfaction of a public protest.

Some of their anger they were at least able to relieve when Judge Brown's name was offered in nomination. "Cox's candidate!" a bulllike voice roared from the floor. As if on signal the Garfield men were on their feet shouting, pounding, hissing, and whistling. The speaker was finally driven off the platform. Cox sat through the din fanning himself with slow, even strokes of his straw fan, his face immobile. Only at the end did he smile slightly.

After the delegates had finally quieted to the balloting, it was found that Brown had only 413 votes to 485 for Harding. Longworth had 92 and Garfield, though not officially in the running, received 73. Chairman Brown, Ellis, Maschke, and Arthur Garford—a Republican leader and industrialist from Elyria—were inclining to Congressman Longworth as the one candidate to conciliate the outraged progressives. They arranged to release their reserve votes to him on the next ballot.

As the increasing votes for Longworth were announced, he looked off into space from his seat on the platform, either impervious to or unaware of his wife sitting in the balcony directly in front of him. She frowned and gave an emphatically negative shake of her head. Obviously the imperious Princess Alice did not see herself transplanted from her urbane Washington surroundings to become the first lady of Ohio. Near Mrs. Longworth in the press gallery the Duchess sat at a desk among the reporters, her pince-nez trembling slightly as she totted up the votes on a score sheet.

On the second ballot Harding increased his lead by 12, Brown dropped to 363 and Longworth jumped to almost double with 164. Cox's bid had failed, as he at once realized, Harding's was faltering and the boom for Longworth was under way.

Chairman Brown, Maschke, Crawford, and Wade Ellis now clustered around Cox like workers around a queen bee, begging him to release his delegates to Longworth. He told them tersely that there would have to be one more ballot for Brown.

At the start of the third ballot Longworth took the lead, after the 96 votes of Burton's Cuyahoga County delegation were shifted to him. When Hamilton County was called on, Cox stood up, his face a sardonic enigma. "Hamilton County casts 91 votes for"—he called out, prolonging the pause—"Warren G. Harding."

The delegates gasped. Rud Hynicka leaped to his feet, throwing away his fan and letting out a yell that echoed from the roof. Let the others fall in line how they would, Harding was nominated! Harding men shouting and whooping danced in the aisles and descended on Cox to wring his hand. Brown, Maschke, Garford, and the others stood stunned and speechless. Longworth still kept his seat on the platform but his face turned a dark red and his lips trembled. Princess Alice, fanning herself with as much aplomb as Boss Cox, looked down from the balcony with an expression of Rooseveltian contempt. In the press box the Duchess bent forward and shed tears onto the score sheet that she still continued to check until her husband's vote had reached the total of 746. Boss Cox headed the committee to escort the victorious Harding to the platform.

"I think Harding's nomination the best and strongest that could have been made," Foraker wrote next day from Poland Springs, Maine, where he had been avoiding the convention. At Oyster Bay, Roosevelt had nothing to say, "No, not one word." But he did write Garfield that the regulars had made "the average politician's platform and put on it the average politician's candidate."

Taft had been almost as fearful of Judge Brown as of Garfield. Harding's nomination was a great relief to him, although according to Archie Butt it was also a surprise. He sent Harding a warm message of congratulations in which he invited him and the Duchess for a visit at Beverly. Harding, writing that he hoped to be able to accept, replied:

> It is my belief that I will be elected, and I shall be very proud to be a party to Ohio's voted approval of your splendid administration. I have so genuinely believed in your administration that I can commend it in all honesty.

Nick Longworth, his vision possibly sharpened by his convention humiliation, told Taft darkly a few weeks later that the situation in Ohio looked more hopeless than it did before Harding's nomination.

It did not look hopeless in Marion. Republicans and Democrats joined in non-partisan pride to boost their leading citizen as their next governor. They planned a hero's welcome for him at the fairgrounds when he arrived back from the convention. Unfortunately an afternoon thunderstorm flooded the grounds and so strewed the highway from Columbus with trees and telegraph poles that not until after eight did the Stevens-Duryea pull into Marion. A patient crowd was still waiting in front of the courthouse, and the inevitable brass band burst forth with "Hail! Hail! The Gang's All Here!" Next day Harding responded from his front porch to another band serenade with the promise of a "clean, honorable, and courageous campaign." In the afternoon the delayed celebrations at the fairgrounds took place, with local notables of both parties extolling the *Star* publisher as "a man of the people, for the people, and raised by the people." The more exuberant even predicted that Harding would become President.

Jim Phillips had gone to Denver in July to take his tubercular brother to a sanitarium for treatment. "Gov," he called Harding, writing him that he himself felt "all shot to pieces" and that he had seen Pete DeWolfe. When Phillips returned after the nomination, he found Harding preparing his visit to the summer White House as part of an Eastern motor tour from Boston to the Isles of Shoals and back by way of Washington. Harding persuaded him without much difficulty to take his wife and come along. Jim and Carrie left with Harding and the Duchess on the eighth of August. Of their journey, only the bald account of the itinerary remains [- -]. Taft's secretary, Charles Hilles, arranged for them to be guests at the summer White House. The brightness of that summer, enhanced by Harding's pride in being able to introduce his [- - - - - -] to the President of the United States is unrecorded. But Harding's confidence in his political future grew. He told Taft that his prospects seemed brighter daily.

More detached observers saw little brightness. For all the attempts to paper it over in the interests of harmony, the cleft between the Republican regulars and the insurgents was widening. Taft and Roosevelt met with superficial amiability at a Yale luncheon in September, but Archie Butt thought them further apart than ever. "It would not surprise me," he wrote, "if he [Taft] did not come out openly and attack his predecessor, as many are urging him to do. But," he added ominously, "it will be the most fatal day of his life if he does." Garfield and his followers gave Harding a sullen and belated endorsement at the opening of the campaign in September, although most of them secretly intended either to vote for Harmon or not to vote at all. On October 22 Foraker, speaking for Harding at Marysville, turned on the progressives and denounced Roosevelt's New Nationalism as an insolent attempt to seize the powers of the states and transfer them to the Federal government. Garfield, making a belated opening speech for the Ohio Republican ticket in which he failed to even mention Harding's name, came back at Foraker, denying his right to speak for the party. The Republican State Committee—of which Malcolm Jennings had now become secretary—still trying to sweep dissension under the rug, requested the Senator to omit any further criticism of Roosevelt Republicans during the campaign. Foraker replied by canceling all his speaking engagements and suggesting that

> before Mr. Garfield reads anybody out of the Republican Party it might be well for him to make it a little plain that he is himself in the party. The newspapers report that Mr. Garfield was unable, after the nomination of Mr. Harding to tell whether he would support him for election or not

until he could think the matter over and confer with his friends. That took some time.

Harding did his alliterative best to sew up the ripped political seams. "Democracy has always been dominant in deploration," he told the faithful. "It has been grieving about privilege, which in reality is opportunity, and grumbling about favoritism which is meant to be encouragement, and in the gloom it never looked to the beckoning lights ahead."

In the opening rally held at Kenton, with Senator Dick and his would-be successor Daugherty sitting on the platform behind him, Harding tried to twine the party's progressive and conservative strands—along with the high-tariff skein—into a true lovers' knot:

> In deliberate and appreciative retrospection and gratifying contemplation, the American who fails to see a progressive Republican party is blind to the irresistible onward movement and deaf to the triumphant shouts of the all-conquering American people. . . .
>
> Why, my countrymen, it is no disparagement of the best intent of any political party to say that the Republican party of 1910 reflects the best conscience of the best civilization the world has ever witnessed. Our party represents that conscience because we are sponsors of the things accomplished.

Those who had been dismayed by the heights of the Payne-Aldrich tariff he asked to "forget any selfishness of spirit and to fix their gaze on the inspiring heights of surpassing accomplishment at home, and growing eminence in the marts of the world." As always his deepest conviction was of uncritical party loyalty. Weighed against loyalty, all other differences were superficial or at least reconcilable. Under the broad banner of the Grand Old Party, he told his audiences, they would all march together down the broad highway that led to victory, a brotherhood of Taft Republicans, Burton Republicans, Roosevelt Republicans, Garfield Republicans, and Cox Republicans.

The Democrats did not forget the Cox Republicans. Pomerene at the opening of the Democratic campaign in Canton labeled Harding the Cox candidate and reminded his hearers of the "deference and devotion" that Harding had paid to Cox in his 1905 convention speech.

Harding could not deny the recorded word, thrown up to him again and again. He granted that he *had* said some pleasant things about George Cox, and he would not now plead poetic license. He had meant what he said—that he admitted—but refused to say whether or not his "deference and devotion" still continued. And when he spoke in Cincinnati he spent his time with Cox. "Harding is a strong candidate," said the oracle of the Mecca, "and will surely be elected. Everything that I can do for him will be done with all my might and I hope that every Republican in the state

will join in, as he will make one of the best governors Ohio has ever had."
Governor Harmon took to campaigning with a dictionary in his hand, and
after asking rhetorically what "deference" meant, he would then read
Webster's definition: a yielding of judgment to the wishes or opinion of
another.

As, in the weeks before the election, the Republican bad blood kept
bubbling to the surface, it was clear to any impartial observer that
Harding had not the remotest chance of defeating the united Democrats
under the popular Harmon. "I feel that you have been put up to make a
'sacrifice hit' and I do not think it fair to you to have been put on the
ticket this year," a realistic friend wrote him from Columbus. But the
euphoric will to believe that encompasses candidates for office had taken
possession of Harding. "When I am elected, as I surely expect to be," was
a phrase he used constantly in his speeches.

Marion, too, in a burst of bipartisan enthusiasm expected that he would
be elected. "Warren G. Harding has put Marion on the map," the Boosters'
Committee announced. His photograph, flanked by American flags, was
in every store window along with signs reading Our Honored Citizen
WARREN G. HARDING. All the main streets were flagged, and telephone poles wound around with red, white, and blue bunting. The
Boosters were planning a gigantic night-before-the-election victory celebration with a parade and brass bands to be followed by a triple rally: in
the courtroom, on the courthouse steps, and finally at the Grand Opera
House.

During the last week of the campaign Taft sent several members of his
Cabinet to campaign in Ohio with the slogan "A Vote for Harding Is a
Vote for Taft." Colonel Roosevelt, tempted but not yet ready to make the
break official, was persuaded to take a one-day trip through northern
Ohio to round up straying progressives. The reluctant Colonel was not at
his best. Stopping off at Chicago on the way to Ohio, he had bluntly
refused to attend a banquet given by the Hamilton Club in honor of Sen.
William Lorimer, the "blond boss" who had been charged with engineering his election to the United States Senate by bribing members of the
Illinois legislature. After this high moral gesture Roosevelt next day met
Boss Cox at a reception given by Nick Longworth, shook hands with the
Boss, and chatted with Garry Hermann and Rud Hynicka. Garfield progressives were aghast. A defensive Roosevelt, loath to admit that his
son-in-law would not be re-elected to Congress this year without the
grace of Cox, spluttered that he would have made himself "utterly ridiculous" if he "had proceeded to set [himself] up as a censor and had declined to shake hands with anyone whom popular report accused of being
a boss." Roosevelt was equally unfortunate in the attack he made on
Harmon, when after a brief briefing by Republican politicians, he accused

the Governor of granting rebates and dodging taxes while acting as re-
ceiver for Morgan's railroad. Roosevelt harried Harmon for continuing to
receive his railroad pay while governor, and only as an afterthought did
he get round to mentioning the Taft-foresworn Harding at all.

> And now friends [he concluded perfunctorily] I speak for Mr. Harding for
> governor because, if without regard to any other consideration, he is
> elected governor you can count upon his helping to give your state a pub-
> lic utilities bill as that which Governor Harmon has prevented your having,
> because with the men around him and back of him, Mr. Harding is sure to
> do for you the things that Governor Harmon will not do for you.

Roosevelt, with his congressman son-in-law in mind, had made the
gesture, but it was not a gesture intended to convert the wavering.

Marion's victory parade for her governor-to-be on the night before the
election was the largest and most vociferous that the town had ever seen.
Three thousand marchers behind nine brass bands strutted past Harding
as he reviewed them in front of his Mount Vernon Avenue house, bareheaded, standing in an open carriage banked with an American flag. Led
by Marshal T. E. Andrews and the city police, with Baker's Band, the
ranks of the marchers cheered and the bandsmen thumped and brayed.
After the police came the First Voters Club; then a contingent from the
Huber Company in step with the Zion Band; the Prospect Band leading
delegations from Prospect and Bucyrus; a hundred marchers from Delaware carrying torches—also with a band; the businessmen and the band
of La Rue; the railway and the Houghton Sulky workers behind the
Mount Olive Band; the Marion Steam Shovel boys and the Waldo Band;
quarry workers, lumbermen, construction workers; the Claridon Band;
Harding's old Caledonia Band; delegations from Upper Sandusky, Harp-
ster, and Morral. Their faces ruddy in the torchlights, they carried signs:

Boost a Booster.
Vote for Harding, Marion County's Son.
Marion County for a Marion County Booster.

Above the martial music came the occasional sharp crack of explosives as
skyrockets arched in the autumn sky, sending out spangles of varicolored
stars.

The Opera House was a swirl of bunting and every one of its 600 seats
taken when Harding arrived to speak at nine o'clock, indisputably
Marion's first citizen. Grant Mouser welcomed the man "who has just
completed the most strenuous campaign in the history of Ohio for the
highest office within the gift of her people." In the intimacy of his home
town Harding's speech was less oratorical than usual, almost apologetic.
He complained that one had to pay a high price for political preferment,

said he was glad to be back home, and that he hoped to live so that he could tell anyone to go take a jump in the lake.

> Five hundred men in this audience [he continued] knew that the bosses had nothing to do with my nomination. No boss or big leader was for me. I was nominated in spite of the bosses, and said that in Cincinnati, too. I owe allegiance to only one boss—and she sits right over there in that box. She's a mighty good one, too.

He pointed to the Duchess, and at the applause that followed her face cracked into a smile.

The anticlimax came twenty-four hours later as the returns began to trickle in. Harding had buttered no progressive parsnips, in spite of Garfield's belated token effort. The result in Ohio was a Democratic landslide, the greatest since Hanna had streamlined the Republican party. Governor Harmon was re-elected by a 100,377 vote margin, carrying the entire Democratic ticket with him. Pomerene won by 45,531, and even Timothy Hogan was able to overcome rural Ohio's ingrained bias against Rome and the Celt with a 7,962 margin over the incumbent attorney general, Ulysses Grant Denman. The Democrats elected a majority of the assembly—insuring a Democratic United States senator to replace Dick— and 16 of the 21 Ohio congressmen.

In 1908 over a million Ohio citizens cast their vote for governor. In 1910 there were almost a quarter of a million fewer votes. In spite of Garfield's grudging plea, the progressive Republicans had simply stayed away from the polls. Harmon in his great triumph received 56,120 votes less than had his unsuccessful opponent, Governor Harris, two years before.

The Ohio trend was duplicated across the country. Republicans lost Blaine's Maine, Lodge's Massachusetts, Connecticut, Indiana, and New Jersey where a new governor appeared from outside the juggler's circle of politicians, one Woodrow Wilson, the president of Princeton. But, as Arthur Garford, the wealthy Cleveland manufacturer and amateur politician, wrote to a fellow insurgent, the progressive political disappointment was not very great.

It was Harding's first political defeat since his mock candidacy for county auditor in 1892, and he, unlike the progressives, was overwhelmed. He had not even managed to carry Marion County, losing there by 959 votes. Five days later he put a bolder face on things in a letter to Harry Kemmerer, his first booster in Carrollton. "I am serene and happy," he wrote, "if not quite so confident as I have been in the good faith of all people. I have the germ eradicated from my system, and can go ahead and do other things which please me more than hunting men of 'abiding honesty' to appoint to places, and listening to the appeal for the pardon of dishonest ones in the penitentiary. I will not in the future have to be either 'wet' or 'dry' or to shape my course within the lines of any faction." But to Hilles at the Treasury Department he admitted that it was not pleasant to stand in the path of a landslide, and that he was cured of any attack of ambition along political lines. To his *Star* readers he made his apologia in the form of an editorial, "Cost of Pursuit of Political Prefer- ment," in which he regretted his inability as a defeated candidate to repay the debt of gratitude he owed to his friends. Privately he told Van Fleet with Hamiltonian disgust that he was through in Ohio, that such things were bound to happen as long as every Tom, Dick, and Harry had the right to vote.

The following week he replied more buoyantly to a condoling letter from his friend F. F. Taggart in Massilon:

> Cheer up. Charles A. Dana used to say that the finest poem in the English language was the following:
>
> "We may be happy yet,
> You bet."
>
> Personally, I have lost nothing which I ever had except a few dollars which I can make again, a few pounds of flesh which I can grow again, a few false friends of whom I am well rid, and an ambition which simply fettered my freedom and did not make for happiness.

For consolation and reassurance he turned to Carrie. But she herself was troubled by the surge of gossip and small talk about them, some of which was coming back to her. She asked whether he was prepared to leave the Duchess and marry her, [- - - - - - - - - - - - - -] Rather than let the small talk grow larger, she let him know that she was planning to leave Marion, take Isabelle, and go to Germany and stay there! Placatingly he gave her his photograph at Christmas, [- -
- - - - - - - - - -
- -
- -
- -
- -
- -
- -]

CHAPTER XI

Two Women

Among the 600 boosters gathered in Marion's bunting-festooned Grand Opera House to welcome their home-town candidate for governor on the night before the 1910 election was a blond and chubby high-school freshman who, all unintentionally, in the years to come would be as much responsible as any one individual for the destruction of Harding's posthumous reputation. At fourteen Nan Britton had already developed rounded breasts and hips and an awareness of men. Her plump, half-pouting face was pretty, almost provocative. During that autumn campaign, with Harding's bland features staring at her from every store window on her way to high school, she had vociferously decided that she was in love with him. Expendable emotion seemed a characteristic of the Brittons, for Nan's older sister Elizabeth had earlier developed a "crush" on Carolyn Harding back on her visit from Burma the year before.

Nan's father Doctor Samuel Britton, a modestly successful horse-and-buggy doctor, had in 1899 come to Marion from Claridon, a village six miles to the east. After graduating from Kenyon College in 1880 he had read medicine in Claridon with his older cousin, Doctor J. W. Devore. In 1884 he received a degree from the medical department of Western Reserve University, then formed a partnership with his cousin. Five years later he was elected coroner, and two years after that he married Mary Williams, the district schoolteacher. When he first came to Marion he opened an office on East Church Street and bought a small one-and-a-half-story bungalow on East Center Street almost on the outskirts of town.

Although a Democrat, Britton had been friendly with Harding even before he left Claridon, dropping in at the *Star* office from time to time with some humorous sketch he had written about his experiences on his rural rides which the editor was always glad to use as filler. His happily infatuated daughter now decked the sloping walls of her little upstairs bedroom with Harding photographs cut from campaign posters and set in frames she bought at the five-and-ten-cent store. One picture she hung directly in front of her bed so that she could see her loved one the first thing in the morning and the last thing at night. In the margins of her schoolbooks she took to scribbling "Warren Gamaliel Harding—he's a darling." When the teacher was out of the room she would scrawl on the blackboard "I love Warren Harding," to the tittering amusement of her chums Ellen Lucille Mezger and Grant Mouser's daughter Annabel, tittering the more because Daisy Harding was their English teacher. On warm afternoons she would lurk in the doorway of Vail the Photographer's across the street from the *Star*, watching the soles of Harding's feet on the window sill as he "bloviated" in his office chair after lunch. When the feet disappeared, she knew that they were probably about to carry him home, and she would follow him, lagging behind at a distance until he turned up the concrete walk of the green Mount Vernon Avenue house.

Sometimes on Sundays the top-heavy Stevens-Duryea with the Hardings and the Phillipses and Isabelle and the dog Edgewood Hub would chug past her house on the way to Bucyrus, and she, sitting on the porch, would wave to them while they in turn waved back. Even as a high-school girl she had got wind of the stories about Harding and Mrs. Phillips that were beginning to stir, and the sight of the red-haired woman so like a fashion plate from *Vogue* made her tremble with jealousy. From her father's upstairs telephone she would often call the Harding house surreptitiously, hoping to hear *his* voice at the other end of the wire. To anyone who would listen she chattered about her hero, and to many who would not.

Nan's infatuation lasted through her high-school years. Inevitably in so small a town she, too, became a target of gossip. The members of the Twigs, the most fashionable older ladies' club of Marion, talked over the Nan problem when the Duchess was not present. Several times members suggested to Nan's mother that she try to calm her daughter down. Mary Britton did her best, disparaging Harding and his ways, returning home to tell how she had seen him standing on the corner spitting tobacco juice into the gutter. Nothing had any effect on Nan's elastic affections. Afternoon after afternoon she used to walk home from school with Daisy Harding, sensing even this as somehow a contact with the man she loved. Until her preoccupation with Harding, she had had daydreams of being a great actress or a great writer, dreams that would never be wholly eclipsed even in her later life.

So flaunting was she in her devotion that her father had finally gone to Harding's office to discuss his moonstruck daughter. Nan's antics even reached the Duchess's ears, she commenting acidly that as far as "Wurr'n" was concerned "distance lends enchantment." Harding, aware of her feelings, was not impervious to her premature charm. Once that winter he happened to meet her alone on the street as she was returning from an errand. With slightly more than his usual good nature he stopped to talk, and it was in that fluttering moment—as he admitted to her later—that he had first wanted to possess her.

Eradicated from Harding's system, the germ of politics left an antiseptic void. The *Star* earned a tidy sum—almost twenty thousand dollars a year. Van Fleet did a better job than the old editor could have done. Malcolm Jennings was more exacting and efficient running the business side than Harding ever could have been. Time stretched ahead of the ex-lieutenant governor like a gray fog. He had no hobbies but golf—that slack-minded substitute for a hobby. Almost never did he read anything beyond the newspapers, and they had a way of bringing him back to politics. There was Carrie—but he was not uxorious, even with a mistress.

There was always, of course, the last resort of travel. On March 1, 1911, the Hardings and the Phillipses left aboard the *Bermudian* for their "economy" trip to Bermuda. The island with its white beaches and pink stucco houses, even in the gaudy efflorescence of spring, made no recorded impression on Harding. Carrie and the Duchess shopped in Hamilton while he and Jim Phillips stared up at the great bulk of Government House or fished at the Devil's Hole. It was the last time that the Hardings and the Phillipses traveled together.

Harding arrived back in Marion in the mud season to find his perennial problem, Pete DeWolfe, still with him even at a distance of 1,100 miles. Aglow with transitory journalistic enthusiasm, Pete had leased a small weekly paper, the *Enterprise,* in Kersey, a town of 350, seven miles from Denver. Now the owner and former editor wrote to say that Pete had skipped town and demanded $51.75 that Pete owed him. Harding refused to pay it. Jim Phillips on his annual spring visit to his consumptive brother dropped in on Pete at Harding's request, and wrote back that Marshall had borrowed from everyone and was so "in bad" with all the business people of Kersey that none of them would advertise in the *Enterprise.* Phillips, after persuading Pete to have another try at editing the paper, told Harding that the boy looked much worse than the year before. Pete had a bad cough, and was not able to support himself, much less his wife and the daughter Eugenia that had just been born to them.

Tryon, too, was becoming a problem. After Phoebe's death he had lost interest in medicine, had sold the farm in Caledonia that he had always insisted on holding onto, and spent untidy days of doing nothing in his office. Then suddenly he began to shave mornings and put on his good blue suit. His buggy was often seen in front of a certain house where a forty-three-year-old widow from Indiana was visiting. She, Eudora Kelley Luvisi, had three half-grown children, and what she saw in a man old enough to be her father was, the neighbors thought, a meal ticket. But

Tryon had put his restlessness and loneliness behind him after taking up with her, and there was no arguing with him in his courting.

Roosevelt did not mind now how openly he said that Taft was hopeless, or that his remarks might be repeated. To those who, like Harding, had stood by Taft in spite of the Rough Rider, the President was enduringly grateful. Harding was always welcome at the White House. He and the Duchess were among those invited to the Tafts' silver wedding reception on June 19, 1911.

Taft might be "the unpopular and bewildered Man in the White House," but he did not intend to let this interfere with the elegance of his anniversary celebration. The 3,400 guests found the White House shrubbery twinkling with thousands of tiny varicolored electric bulbs. Paper lanterns hung from the trees, colored lights sparkled in the fountains, while above the White House searchlights illumined an American flag.

Mrs. Taft, wearing a diamond tiara—a present for the occasion—stood on the South Portico, leaning on the President's arm as she received her guests. Above her, embowered in smilax and palms, was an arch inscribed with the dates 1886–1911. At eleven o'clock the State Dining Room was thrown open for a buffet supper presided over by a giant anniversary cake with 25 crystal hearts embedded in scrolls. Turtledoves girdled the border, and cherubs rose from a frosted sea, while 25 small American flags plus the President's Flag topped off this confectionery marvel. For the former printer's devil and the wayward girl from the Marion roller-skating rink, to mingle with the diplomats in their court dress and the Army and Navy officers in their braid and summer uniforms, was a triumph, the apex of their social career. In the East Room the dancers were waltzing to "The Blue Danube" or "The Dollar Princess," then two-stepping to the "Grizzly Bear." From the South Porch came the strains of Mendelsohn's "Wedding March," reminding the dancers and the company why they were there.

Harding's return to Marion found him planning another trip across the ocean, this time with his Texas crony Ed Scobey, who had turned from politics to land speculation. He first suggested a visit to Iceland, but Scobey found the very sound chilling and insisted that they stick to Italy, Switzerland, and Austria. Carrie determined to leave with Isabelle for Germany at the end of the summer. Jim Phillips agreed—as he always did to anything she wanted. She had entered Isabelle for the September term in the Willard School in Berlin, run by an Englishman, Doctor Luce, mostly for the children of intermediate-grade English and American diplomats. Vaguely she agreed to come back the following August.

Scobey and his wife sailed on the *Laurentic* July 22. The Hardings left two weeks later to meet them in Switzerland. There would be no meeting

with Carrie on this trip. Faced with her willingness to accept an indefinite
separation, Harding grew panicky. [--------------------------------------
----

--]

The two couples traveled through Europe, as the Hardings had before,
an uneventful and somewhat boring tourist trip that brought them back in
September after several weeks in Scotland and Ireland. The changes that
Harding found in Marion on his return were more important to him than
anything he had seen abroad. According to the new census the popula-
tion had grown to 18,252. Not long after the election-night rally the
Grand Opera House, the pride of the previous decade, had burned down.
Now in the turn of progress it was being replaced by The Marion Photo-
Plays, "the home of the Pipe Organ." While Harding was away, George .
Padgett had sold the *Mirror* to Brooks Fletcher, an editor whom Harding
had known on the Chautauqua circuit. In spite of their desultory political
rivalry, relations between Harding and Padgett had remained agreeable.
When Padgett in 1907 decided to turn his Democratic weekly into a city
and county daily, Harding had lent him the money for the project.
Fletcher the following year changed the name of the *Mirror* to the
Tribune, "a newspaper with a conscience," although this was not intended
as a smear on the *Star.* The two publishers remained friendly and even
became friends.

Eudora had gone back to Indiana, and the love-struck Tryon bought
another farm, then followed her there. On November 23—forty-seven
years after his first marriage—he married her in Andersen, Indiana. Their
honeymoon journey was merely a child-encumbered trip from Indiana to
the house on East Center Street. When spring came Tryon moved with his
new family to the farm. But already his lineaments of gratified desire were
crossed by the wrinkles of age. Dora, he called his new wife, and sent her
picture to Carolyn at the Burma mission saying that she was a nice bright
woman but he never thought of comparing her to the "darling companion"
of his youth. Again he had to turn to his son for money. Daisy on a trip
away from Marion wrote indignantly to Harding:

> Now as to Dad and his late financial adventures. He told me that he had
> purchased that farm, but how I don't know. His finances always have been
> a mystery to me, but I know this that he will have his way if the heavens
> fall in his getting it. He has been possessed to live on a farm and I think
> Dora has encouraged him and so we might just as well let him get his fill.
> He won't stay long but I think his one reason for doing it is to be able to
> keep up and do it independently. He thinks that city life is too expensive.

We all feel deeply sorry for the financial scrapes he has gotten you into and we at present are unable to help you any so we feel that you had better do what seemeth best. Of course I've a certain amount of sentiment for the old place for I've spent nearly thirty years of my life there and I'd like to save it. . . . We know there is nothing left after the mortgage and taxes are cleared.

If Dad should want to go to the country let him go for he won't be satisfied until he has tried it. Had the house a good bath and toilet it might rent for $30 easily with so many more people in Marion now than heretofore. . . .

Carrie and Isabelle were living in a West Berlin pension at 39 Bayreuther-strasse, almost round the corner from the zoo and the Kurfürstendamm, a well-to-do residential section, the sort that the Germans would call "vornehm." In such select pensions one was likely to find modestly well-to-do pensioners, the eccentric English, German old ladies who talked of the Kaiser's grandfather, elderly professors, or the occasional retired army officer. From the Pension Polchow, left along the Tauentzien-strasse to the dominating bulk of the Kaiser William Memorial Church with its luminous mosaics, was not as far as from Gospel Hill to Marion's City Hall. To Carrie Phillips's eyes, removed from their Ohio blinkers, imperial Berlin with its Wilhelmine pomps and pomposities was a city of enchantment. She took German lessons each day while Isabelle was at school. And after the baffling intricacies of German grammar there were pleasant walks along the ordered paths of the Tiergarten in the mild autumn weather with the Victory Column looming up in the distance. There was the Brandenburg Gate topped by its prancing bronze horses; there was the wide and elegant sweep of Unter den Linden where the guards officers strutted past in their blue uniforms. One could take afternoon tea at the Café Görtner or Kranzler's or the Café des Westens. From the broad history-encrusted perspective of the Brandenburg Gate the life of Marion seemed meanly remote. And that a woman of Carrie's charm and presence could live for long in glittering prewar Berlin without getting to know officers and gentlemen was of course impossible.

Her letters—stamped with the square-crowned imperious figure of Germania and sent to the *Star* office—were brief and infrequent, and Harding's emotions stirred with uneasiness. Before she left they had worked out a code between them. He was "Constant," she "Sis." [--------
----

---]

Harding [-------------] that he had taken up politics again because he thought he had lost her. To a degree it was true; with her away politics was the only distraction he had left. For him the political was the most engrossing game of all, and it was inevitable that he should come back to it. Whenever he made speeches, whether before the Ohio Manufacturing Association or the Elks' Lodge of Sorrow, they had a way of turning political. Politics was like chess. One did not change the color of one's pieces; one was loyal to one's party because one was loyal to the game. Harding always tried to keep a friendly approach to his opponents. But the insurgents, the progressives, did not play the game.

Taft, halfway through his term was, in Roosevelt's opinion, "utterly hopeless . . . an entirely unfit President." But Roosevelt still vacillated between a desire to oust Taft and a feeling that it might be better to purge the party 'by letting the Republican standpatters go down to their inevitable defeat in 1912. Whatever his private hesitancies, the Colonel was still officially for Taft's renomination until October of 1911. It was then that Attorney General Wickersham announced that the government was initiating a suit against the United States Steel Corporation for violation of the Sherman Anti-trust Law. In the midst of the 1907 Panic, the dapper Judge Elbert Gary and Henry Frick of the Steel Corporation had come to Roosevelt one morning at breakfast to ask him what the government's attitude would be toward their buying up the shares of the Tennessee Coal and Iron Company. Thousands of these shares had been deposited in New York banks as collateral for loans, and now that the panic had driven the price of the shares below the value of the loans, the banks would soon be forced to sell. But the sudden dumping of these shares on the market would send the price still lower and force many banks to close. Frick and Gary were willing to buy the shares "out of a sense of public duty," if they could get some assurance that they would not be prosecuted for monopolistic practices under the Sherman Act. Roosevelt, after consulting his attorney general and his secretary of state, the lawyer Elihu Root, told them the government had no objection to the purchase. Later Roosevelt came to feel that Gary and Frick were not quite the pure altruists they made themselves out to be at that early-morning breakfast. Nevertheless, he believed that his decision had been right. He took Wickersham's action as a reflection both on his intelligence and his honesty. To the former President, Taft was responsible for the directed insult, and the open break between the two men dated from this suit. Politically it would have been more astute for Roosevelt to have helped Taft into his 1912 defeat in order afterward to remould the party in the progressive image and assure his own candidacy in 1916. But Roosevelt's anger was greater than his astuteness.

Progressive revivalism was beginning to produce some curious converts. By January, 1912, Mark Hanna's son Dan had come out for Roosevelt and was denouncing Taft in his two papers, the Cleveland *Leader* and the

Toledo *Blade.* Walter Brown, the iron-stomached clerical-appearing Toledo boss and Golden Rule Jones's old enemy, was another to see the progressive light. He, Garfield, and Pinchot took the lead at the Ohio Progressive Conference at Columbus in demanding the nomination for President of "Robert M. La Follette or Theodore Roosevelt, or any other Progressive Republican."

Brown's conversion to Progressivism was almost as startling as Boss Cox's announcement of his final retirement some time before the municipal elections of 1911. It had taken all the aging Cox's skill and pull to save himself from the new prosecuting attorney of Hamilton County, the reform Democrat Henry T. Hunt. A Yale graduate and a conservative, Hunt was picked as the non-partisan progressive candidate for mayor in the November election to overthrow the Cox machine headed, after Cox had stepped down, by Rud Hynicka. Hunt surprised even himself by overwhelming the shadowy Cox candidate, one Louis Schwab.[1] The progressive wave was still cresting. Brand Whitlock was chosen mayor for the fourth time in Toledo; Newton Baker, Johnson's lieutenant and Wilson's future war secretary, was elected in Cleveland. The three mayors became known as the "Holy Trinity." "Now all the larger cities are in hostile hands," Jennings wrote to Hilles, "and the organization in Hamilton County which gave us a large part of our majorities—and half of Taft's in 1908—is wrecked."

La Follette, the choice of the more extreme progressives, had collapsed mentally and physically in Philadelphia on February 2 while on a barnstorming tour. With the shaggy-maned senator from Wisconsin out of the way there could be no other possible leader for the progressives but Roosevelt. The week after La Follette's collapse, seven Republican governors— from Kansas, Michigan, Nebraska, New Hampshire, West Virginia, and Wyoming—arranged with Roosevelt to write a "cooked" letter requesting him to come out for the Presidency and assuring him that a large majority of Republicans favored his nomination and a large majority of voters his election. Two days later President Taft in a speech before the Republican Club in New York denounced the progressives as "political emotionalists or neurotics." Everyone knew that he meant Roosevelt and the New Nationalism, and the country waited for the Rough Rider's reply.

The reply came with Roosevelt's address, "A Charter of Democracy," that he delivered to the Ohio Constitutional Convention in Columbus on February 21. Passing through Cleveland, he found himself questioned by a reporter as to his political intentions and replied in an offhand phrase that would endure as one of America's most permanent political clichés. "My hat is in the ring," the Colonel told him.

[1] Even President Taft's arrival in his native city the Saturday before the election and his announcement that he would vote the straight Republican ticket failed to help the disintegrating Cox machine.

The Ohio Constitution of 1851 had provided for a mandatory constitutional convention every twenty years, the delegates to be elected directly by the people. Sixty years later the fourth Ohio constitutional convention opened in Columbus on January 9, 1912. Sessions lasted into the summer. Three-quarters of the 119 delegates were considered progressives and many basic reformist changes were expected in Ohio's laws. During the convention term the leading presidential candidates of both parties had been asked to speak to the delegates: Taft, Roosevelt, Governor Harmon, New Jersey's Gov. Woodrow Wilson,[2] William Jennings Bryan, and Hiram Johnson. For two of the speakers, Harmon and Roosevelt, the results were disastrous.

With his triumphant re-election in 1910 and his solid record of integrity in office, Governor Harmon was seen increasingly as a potential Democratic presidential candidate in 1912. Yet the basically conservative Harmon had always been more tolerated from political necessity than trusted by the Johnson reformers. When, appearing before the convention on February 8, he confronted the progressives with his own conservative scruples against the initiative and referendum, he destroyed any chance he might have had for the Democratic nomination.

If Harmon and Roosevelt had switched speeches, both might have been nominated by their respective parties! Roosevelt had come on to Columbus with progressive fire in his eyes. As the grinning Rough Rider planted his bulk in the domed hall of the state capitol, his supporters pinned "Roosevelt 1912" buttons on each passer-by. In his speech Roosevelt declared himself all in favor of the initiative and referendum and of recall of judicial decisions, defying the party regulars with such vehemence that he made his June nomination—which until then even Taft felt was inevitable—all but impossible. Henry Cabot Lodge, his old-guard friend, wrote him sorrowfully that although he could never oppose him, he could now no longer support him.

Disappointed with Roosevelt and disgusted with Taft, Bob Wolfe was using his evening *Dispatch* to support Harmon. His *Ohio State Journal,* that spokesman for Ohio Republicanism, was violently anti-Taft and opposed, though less violently, to Roosevelt. Harding was, of course, without doubts and disappointment. "Ohio for Taft?" he wrote just before he left for Europe in 1911. "Nothing surer in political life! And not only loyally for him but gladly and cordially."

The *Star* continued to give Taft its all-out support. With the Wolfe papers turned against the President, Harding decided to start a rival political paper in Columbus to fight the good fight for traditional Republicanism. After setting up a stock company, with himself as publisher, he sent Malcolm Jennings to the capital as editor. The Ohio *Star,* modeled after Marion's *Weekly Star,* would be the voice of the embattled Taftites.

[2] Wilson failed to appear.

Though edited in Columbus, the new *Star* was to be printed in Marion on Harding's presses there. He ran off his first edition of 50,000 copies. From his editorial office in the Harrison Building, Jennings—thanks to Taft subsidies—was able to keep the Ohio *Star* going for a little over a year, but the paper was never a challenge to the Wolfes and never a success.

Harding in Marion came out belligerently in the *Star* for Foraker as Ohio's next governor. The old ex-Senator, in spite of his private detestation of Taft, was willing to endorse him publicly. Harding himself was being mentioned as a repeat candidate for governor, an idea that he toyed with for several weeks until at the end of March he announced that he was not a candidate. "We are running a strong pro-Taft and anti-Teddy paper, without reservations," Jennings wrote Hilles from his editorial desk in Columbus, "and we get a wide range of return comment. . . . Harding is writing his friends everywhere . . . that his hat is not in the ring but is upon his head and that he has no ambition except to help preserve the party through the renomination of Mr. Taft." By April Harding was able to tell Hilles that things were going "so beautifully." Already he had come to a private understanding with the White House that he was to present Taft's name at the Republican national convention in Chicago. But not until Harding had been elected delegate-at-large in June did Taft make the request formally, writing that "it is a good deal of a task to do this, but I know your earnest support of me, and I hope that you will feel like assuming the burden. I know you can do it well, and I shall be delighted to be able to have it done by a man who represents the state so worthily as you do." This was to be Harding's first appearance on the national political scene and he was both flattered and awed. "I think I was more honored by that request," he wrote a decade later when he himself by the turn of fortune's wheel was occupying Taft's office, "than I was by my own nomination, in my own appraisal."

It is an axiom of American politics that a candidate for President must start off with the backing of his party in his own state. When Governor Harmon failed to rally the Democrats behind him, his bid for the nomination was over. Taft in the spring months before Ohio's election of delegates to the Republican national convention was determined to show that he was still his state's favorite son, as popular in 1912 as he had been in 1908. Up and down the state he traveled, on two trips of over three thousand miles, speaking to more than a hundred audiences, transforming his good-natured bulk into 350 pounds of rage as he called his predecessor in the White House a "flatterer," "demagogue," "honey-fugler," [3] "egoist," and "bolter." Roosevelt descended on Ohio, his jaws snapping like an angry bulldog, traveling about half Taft's distance with about twice the speed. He had proposed "to make the issue one of principle and not of

[3] A forgotten, but then fairly common midwestern term meaning mealy-mouthed wheedler.

personal abuse," but Taft's taunts were too much for him, and he was soon denouncing the President as "boss-controlled," a "standpatter," and worse.

The results of the election were a predictable disaster for Taft. Thirty-four Roosevelt delegates were elected, to eight for Taft, and Roosevelt's voting majority was almost two to one. If it had been a matter of popular choice Republicans all over the country, as well as in Ohio, would have picked the Rough Rider Colonel hands down. But popular choice has never been very popular with party politicians, and in Ohio the old-line conservatives of the State Central Committee—Burton, Dick, Harding, and Hynicka—were keeping their hands on the wheel. The progressives may have had enthusiasm and earnestness; the others had the needful shrewdness and skill.

The 758 delegates to the Republican state convention meeting in Columbus on June 3 had been selected by the time-honored caucus method according to the finer sensibilities of the party bosses. Sole purpose of the convention—a second convention to name the state officers would be held later—was to name the six delegates-at-large to the national convention in Chicago. For all its brevity the convention was a noisy portend of the Chicago meeting to come. Unhampered by the vulgarities of the Australian ballot, the old guard had corraled 349 delegates for Taft. Roosevelt delegates numbered 335, with 74 more uninstructed. The largest group of uninstructed delegates were from Cleveland's Cuyahoga County—53 in all, and more than enough to swing the balance—marshaled under their local boss, Maurice Maschke.

At the Columbus opening Walter Brown was re-elected chairman of the State Central Committee, the last gesture of reconciliation the regulars were to show. Taft and Roosevelt supporters snarlingly insisted that they alone had the right to the six delegates-at-large, and refused to consider splitting them. When the presiding officer, Senator Burton, long pledged to Taft, attempted to speak out against the progressives he was hissed and booed, and finally drowned out by catcalls. Roosevelt backers jeered the white-bearded Civil War general, J. Warren Keifer, presenting the report of the committee on resolutions favoring Taft, as a "back number." Since Cleveland and Cuyahoga County Republicans had given three-quarters of their direct vote to Roosevelt, Maschke promised Walter Brown to deliver his delegation's votes in that proportion. But, after a secret talk with Burton, Maschke stood up in the convention and announced that Cuyahoga County gave 48 of its 53 votes to Taft—insuring a majority. To shouts of rage and cries of robbery from the Roosevelt contingent, the convention by a 28 vote margin proceeded to elect six Taft delegates-at-large: Daugherty, Harding, Burton, Charlie Taft, Arthur Vorys, and one David J. Cable.

Any American President, however unpopular, is, through the influence of his office and his control of patronage and the national committee, in a position to force his own renomination or to designate his successor. This is as true of Roosevelt's 1908 choice of Taft as it was of Hoover's immolating self-renomination in 1932. It has been more true of the Republican party, to the extent that a third of its delegations came from the rotten boroughs of the South. Since the Civil War these for-the-most-part Negro delegates from Southern districts bereft of Republican voters were commonly regarded as bargaining counters at Republican conventions. Leaders like Blaine and Hanna took them venally for granted, as did Roosevelt himself in 1904 and 1908. Yet so dynamic was the force of Roosevelt's popularity and so diminished Taft's, that in the spring of 1912 the President himself was doubtful whether his control of the party machinery would hold back the former President. Roosevelt, in previous nominating conventions mutely acquiescent to the chicanery of the kept delegates, suddenly became the indignant reformer. To use the party machinery as Taft's manager, Frank H. Hitchcock, was doing to deprive the people of their choice, the Roosevelt choice, was robbery!

Before the Republican national convention met in Chicago on June 1, the credentials of over 200 of the 1,078 delegates had been contested and referred to the Republican National Committee. This Taft-controlled committee had chosen the elderly Sen. Elihu Root as the convention's temporary chairman, and if the delegates ratified their choice, Roosevelt would be pegged down like a political Gulliver by an intricate web of rules. Root could be counted on to apply the rules with a legalistic exactness that would cut the ground from under Roosevelt's insurgency.

Oddly enough Root had been one of Roosevelt's closest friends, ever since he had worked with him when Roosevelt was police commissioner of New York in 1897. A country boy from Vernon, New York, where his father—known as "Cube" Root—was professor of mathematics at Hamilton College, Root had come to New York to study law the year the Civil War ended. Without family funds, he supported himself by teaching at a girls' school while attending Columbia Law School. He had a sharp mathematical-legal mind and his success after graduation was rapid. In that corrupt and corrupting period of expansion after the war he became one of the most sought-after corporation lawyers in the country, specializing in banking affairs, railroad cases, suits over wills and estates, and matters involving municipal government. Like his father's, his mind worked in abstractions. The law was for him a thing in itself, and within his narrow ethics he was incorruptible. It seemed to him of the nature of things that man was made for laws, and not the other way around.

In 1899 McKinley had made this most unmilitary lawyer his secretary of war, persuading him that what was needed for the post was not a knowledge of Clausewitz but a legal mind sharp enough to direct the government of the newly acquired Spanish Islands. As war secretary Root showed a competence one would hardly have suspected from a corporation lawyer. The Spanish-American War had revealed the anachronistic stupidities and derelictions of the War Department, and Root shook it up from top to bottom. He reorganized the Army and broke the tenure of the elderly, incompetent staff officers. He established fair and legal dealings with the Philippines, Porto Rico, Cuba. He made his name and his mark.

After McKinley's assassination Root stood beside Roosevelt as the new President took the oath of office. He was chairman of the Republican convention that nominated Roosevelt in 1904. On the death of John Hay, Roosevelt made Root his secretary of state, a position he kept until Taft took office. "I shall never have, and can never have, a more loyal friend," Roosevelt wrote of him. Indeed the President would have preferred him to Taft as his successor, if it had not been for the bias against a corporation lawyer. Roosevelt remarked before he left office that, given the powers of a dictator, he would make Taft chief justice and Root President.

Root, in agreeing to become the Taft-sponsored candidate for temporary chairman, had considered it a "difficult and embarrassing duty," but as a regular of regulars, as president of New York's Union League Club, he felt he could not decline. Then, too, his mind, nourished for half a century on legalisms, was horrified at Roosevelt's Columbus speech advocating the recall of judicial decisions. Not even the oldest friendship could survive such heresy.

Ten days before the convention 37 members of the National Committee, dominated by the old-time boss figures of Senators Murray Crane of Massachusetts and Boies Penrose of Pennsylvania, and including Harry Daugherty, met in Chicago to rule on the disputed delegates, now whittled down to 92. Held behind closed doors, each session of the committee was tumultuous, sometimes verging on a riot. Delegation after delegation was accredited to Taft, while frustrated Roosevelt supporters shouted "liar" and "robber" in voices hoarse with impotent rage. No one could get the floor, according to one Roosevelt leader, but a "handpicked, machine-made crook." Of the 241 contested delegates, 233 were given to Taft and 8 to Roosevelt. Roosevelt headquarters announced bitterly:

> The saturnalia of fraud and larceny now in progress under the auspices of the National Committee took on a new repulsiveness today. . . . It was thought that the limit of folly and indecency had already been reached by this doomed and passion-drunk committee which in the last four days have issued the party's credentials to bogus delegates, reeking with fraud and straight from the cesspools of Southern corruption.
>
> Hitherto it was supposed that the National Committee was content with

the political emoluments of pocket-picking and porch-climbing. Today, however, they essayed the role of the apache and the garrotter.

Roosevelt arrived in Chicago the weekend of the convention in combustive good spirits and accompanied by a flying squad of relatives. Consciously, deliberately, he had shifted his personality from the attenuated Harvard-mannered East of his inheritance to that of the he-man Westerner. In his wide-brimmed black hat and wide belt that seemed as if it should still be holding a revolver, he looked the Rough Rider chief, the heir of the Populists.[4] "Fit as a bull moose," he described himself to reporters, tossing off casually the incandescent phrase that would give a slogan and a name to the new party. After all the years of backing and filing he had at last become the Progressive leader, almost a demigod.

From his headquarters on the third floor of the Congress Hotel he could hear the heartening shouts of "We want Teddy!" welling up from the street below. Pugnacious Roosevelt supporters with Teddy badges swarmed along Michigan Boulevard, among them former Rough Riders in their old uniforms, ready to crack heads and looking for wearers of Taft buttons. Illinois Congressman William B. McKinley—no relation of the late President's—in charge of the Taft campaign, had to house and guard Negro delegates to keep the more determined Roosevelt agents from buying them back. There were rumors that Roosevelt delegates were going to rush the hall as the convention opened and bar it to the Taftites; that Roosevelt delegates from Oklahoma were all armed with six-shooters. On the night before the convention Roosevelt spoke to a turbulently eager crowd that jammed the 5,000 places in the Auditorium and spilled over into the street outside. After accusing Taft and the National Committee of theft, he ended with the phrase that brought his audiences from their seats in a frenzy, "We stand at Armageddon, and we battle for the Lord."

The convention opened on June 18 at the Chicago Coliseum, that vast speech-ridden hall with its glassed-in roof and castellated outer walls erected piece by piece in 1888 from stones taken from the Confederate Libby Prison at Richmond where Union officers were kept during the Civil War. Built originally as the Libby War Prison Museum, it had been rebuilt in 1900 as one of the largest assembly halls in the country and had been used for the two previous Republican national conventions. Before the convention could organize to elect or reject Root as temporary chairman, Roosevelt challenged 74 of the Taft delegates already approved by

[4] He had indeed come a long way from the elegant young Porcellian Club undergraduate with the fluffy sideburns, who drove about Cambridge in a dogcart. Roosevelt managed to fashion a virile legend, and succeeded in believing it himself. Yet it is curious to speculate how the legend would have fared if the Rough Riders had kept to their original name of Teddy's Terrors!

the National Committee, demanding that they be replaced by his own or at the very least be barred from voting until the convention had been organized and the temporary chairman elected. By including these 74, the Taft forces would have had enough votes to elect Root as temporary chairman. Without the 74, Roosevelt would have been able to muster a majority and elect his own chairman, Gov. Francis McGovern of Wisconsin.

When the National Committee ruled that the 74 delegates could vote for the chairman even while their own status was in dispute, Root's election was inevitable. He was chosen by 558 votes to 501 for McGovern. With Root in the chair, it was clear to everyone that Taft would be nominated, with no irrelevancies about the people's choice. Any delegation disputes would be ruled on with precise and literal exactness according to the rules laid down by the National Committee—always in favor of Taft.

And so it happened. A committee on credentials elected by the Taft majority reported in favor of seating the disputed 74 as permanent members. The aloof chairman, with his close-cropped white hair brushed in bangs across his forehead and his high-pitched, querulous voice, was the master of the surly delegates below him. Weak in health, and suffering from dysentery, Root nevertheless kept a steady hand on the throttle of the Taft steam roller. "Railroading" was what the Roosevelt partisans were calling the proceedings, and the galleries had taken it up. Each Root ruling in favor of Taft was greeted with derisive shouts of "Toot! Toot! All aboard! Choo Choo!" Some of Roosevelt's supporters brought in pieces of sandpaper and rubbed them together to imitate more exactly the sound of a steam engine.

After Root's election, Roosevelt ordered his delegates to sit tight and refuse to vote. The air in the close-packed auditorium was like that before a thunderstorm, sullen and heavy, unrelieved by the vain efforts of the band to enliven things in the intermissions, unsoothed by a Mrs. Flo Jacobson's rendering of "Moonlight Bay." When Harding appeared on the platform to put Taft's name in nomination, he was booed before he opened his mouth. Never before had the Marion orator, the Columbus harmonizer, the reconciler of unreconcilables, faced such a hostile audience. Standing there in a new Gettum cutaway with a geranium in his buttonhole, he could scarcely make himself heard beyond the first rows of seats. A storm of hisses, hoots, groans, and boos drowned out his eulogy of Taft. The people, he tried to tell the convention, "a plain people and a sane people are ruling today." As a rude voice bellowed "Where?" he spluttered and went on, "ruling with unwavering faith and increased confidence in that fine embodiment of honesty, that fearless executor of the law, that inspiring personification of courage, that matchless exemplar of justice, that glorious apostle of peace and amity. . . ." "Choo-choos" and sandpaper echoed in the balcony and cries of "We want Teddy!" Before Harding could say "William Howard Taft," a Roosevelt and a Taft delegate from South Dakota had started a fist fight on the floor. At the other end of the hall a Pennsylvania delegate dropped to the ground after a punch in the nose. In such an atmosphere, to mention Washington's "declination" of a third term, to compare Taft to Lincoln, was like pouring water through a sieve. Even alliteration failed to sooth the Progressive beast, though Harding did his soothing best:

> Progress is not proclamation nor palaver. It is not pretence nor play on prejudice. It is not the perturbation of a people passion-wrought, nor a promise proposed. Progression is everlastingly lifting the standards that marked the end of the world's march yesterday and planting them on new and advanced heights today. Tested by such a standard, President Taft is the greatest Progressive of the age.

At this such a whirl of angry voices welled up that it seemed as if Harding might be driven from the platform. Finally, amid a clatter of wooden seats as delegates quit their places, and with the derision of the balconies, Harding "for one hundred millions of advancing Americans," named for renomination "our great President, William Howard Taft."

Following Harding's speech, Henry J. Allen—later to be governor of Kansas—stood defiantly before Root and bade ironic farewell to the Taft majority telling him that

> . . . no radical in the ranks of radicalism ever did so radical a thing as to come to a National Convention of the great Republican Party and secure through fraud the nomination of a man whom they knew could not be elected.

And with those final words the fire went out of the convention. There followed the dreary mechanical routine of reading the platform and nominating Taft. The President received 561 votes; Roosevelt, 107; La Follette and the minor candidates, 60; while 349 delegates remained present but not voting. After the artifact victory, Allen led the Roosevelt delegates from the hall while the balconies hooted.

Nick Longworth, as a delegate, found himself in the unfortunate position of a tightrope walker in a gale. Not to have been for Taft would have forfeited him the support of the Cox organization, that, however battered, was still indispensable in electing him to Congress. His family was solidly for Taft. On the other hand, he was married to the Rough Rider's equally rough-riding daughter. Harding, anxious as ever to conciliate, had made his way to where Longworth was sitting and offered to support him for governor in the second session of the state convention. Princess Alice, sitting haughtily behind her husband, announced with cold contempt that "one could not accept favors from crooks." Her enduring distaste for Harding, so she wrote in her autobiography, began at that moment.

Meanwhile the Roosevelt delegates, "like a mighty army," marched off with a self-righteous fervor as evangelical as it was militant to Orchestra Hall a mile away where they held a rump convention of their own. The Rough Rider Colonel in a fierce and fiery speech, eyes narrowed and jaws snapping, gave his heart to them and promised to run for President as a Progressive if they would confirm him in a regular convention.

Convention followed convention that summer, each treading on the heels of the next. Ohio's state Democratic convention, preceding the national convention, picked Congressman James M. Cox as candidate for governor. The national convention, a sweaty politician-logged interlude in Baltimore, took 46 ballots to nominate New Jersey's Gov. Woodrow Wilson.[5]

The second session of the Republican state convention on July 3 opened in the bleakness of Columbus's Memorial Hall to scant attendance and skimpy decorations. The uneasy Taft majority was willing to compromise, even to nominating Garford for governor, if only the dissenting minority would endorse Taft. Walter Brown for the Progressives refused. When Harding pleaded for Taft and harmony, the Roosevelt men tried to shout him down. "I wouldn't want to belong to any party that wouldn't endorse its standard-bearer," he told them in a low, aggrieved voice, and they hooted in reply. The majority, of course, endorsed Taft, and on the fifth ballot Harding engineered the nomination of the weakly neutral Judge Edmond B. Dillon of the Franklin County Court of Common Pleas as default candidate for governor.

The Judge's pride was soon succeeded by sobering autumnal thoughts, and before the month was out he had formally withdrawn. Now the choice lay with the Taft majority on the Republican State Central Committee, and there was talk of again nominating Harding. Foraker, from the malice of his retirement, let it be known that he was all for it, that his friend Harding might well win and in any case could not be worse defeated than he had been two years before. A more sincere friend wrote Harding privately warning him not to let himself be made the "goat."

Harding had no such intention. Taft's coming defeat was writ large, and though Harding was willing to go down with the regular ship, he had not forgotten his lifeboat drill. The Bull Moosers might throw this election to the united Democrats; there would be other elections. Taft himself had considered that his defeat this year might be followed by a Progressive collapse and his vindication in 1916. Of Harding's nominating speech he wrote in thanks that it was "a masterly address . . . magnificent." And

[5] Harmon received 148 votes on the first ballot, 29 from Ohio, and 90 from New York. When the New York delegation left him, his modest boom collapsed.

Harding, receiving the President's thanks, had not forgotten that, no matter who was elected, there were choice plums on the patronage tree that would ripen between the November election and the March inaugural. The Central Committee finally found its goat in a Zanesville publisher, Robert B. Brown, whose chief claim as a candidate had been his violence in denouncing Roosevelt in his newspaper.

On August 5 the Progressive party convention met in Chicago in the same Coliseum that had seen Taft's sullen nomination the month before. It was an extraordinary gathering, more a conventicle than a convention. Not since the first Republican convention denounced slavery in 1856 had moral fervor burned so fiercely at a national political gathering. Liberalism had found its voice. To applause and laughter the square-faced ebullient Hiram Johnson—slated to be Roosevelt's running mate—led the California Progressives into the hall carrying a banner:

> I want to be a Bull Moose
> And with the Bull Moose stand,
> With Antlers on my forehead
> And a Big Stick in my hand.

Oscar Straus, the Jewish philanthropist, marshaled the New York delegation down the aisle singing "Onward, Christian Soldiers." That most belligerent of Protestant hymns was to become the Bull Moose national anthem. The Bull Moose delegates both in their appearance and in their passion for a social-service world resembled more alumni of Bronson Alcott's School of Philosophy than they did paunchy politicians. They were dissenting small businessmen, farmers, professors, social workers, professional plain-livers and high-thinkers, women like Jane Addams (who would most appropriately second Roosevelt's nomination), and of course what Roosevelt himself had called "the lunatic fringe." Beyond the fringe lurked the professionals, men like Walter Brown and Dan Hanna and Henry H. Timken of the Canton roller-bearing firm, who felt that, since "the dear old Republican party is gone forever," standing at Armageddon would not be too perilous for the business structure of the community. Hanna and Timken would be the chief financial backers of the Bull Moose in Ohio.

The Ohio Progressive convention that met on September 4 in Columbus was a small-scale repetition of the Chicago convention even to the evangelical atmosphere, for it opened with the recitation of the Lord's Prayer in unison and ended in a flourish of trombones and the singing of "Old Hundred." With James Garfield as chairman, the convention endorsed Roosevelt and Johnson with heady enthusiasm and named Arthur Garford as the Bull Moose candidate for governor. The split with the Republican regulars was complete. Walter Brown had resigned as chairman of the

State Central Committee, taking 10 of the 21 committeemen with him to the Bull Moose. When the chairman and the more important members of the State Executive Committee followed, the Republican party of Ohio seemed as broken in organization as it was in spirit. In spite of the appeals of the fragmented Central Committee, no one at first would touch the vacant chairmanship. But for Harry Daugherty, the also-ran, the party's disaster was his opportunity. What dismayed others, exhilarated him. Intrigue and back-stairs maneuverings were in his blood. Newton H. Fairbanks, the Springfield leader, begged Daugherty to take over the chairmanship of the Executive Committee "for the benefit of the party," appealing to his combative spirit even while admitting that it was "a most uninviting and herculean task." Daugherty did not need to be persuaded. Once installed as chairman of the Executive Committee—whose members still included Charlie Taft, Hynicka, Harding, and Malcolm Jennings— while at the same time becoming the solitary member-at-large of the inner-circle Central Committee, he demanded and received absolute control of the party for the campaign. He was, and only just in time, Ohio's Mr. Republican.

Seventeen of the 88 county organizations had gone over to the Bull Moose, and the others were still engaged in a chaotic civil war. Daugherty dropped his legal practice to give all his time to the job of reviving the state Republican party. With ruthless energy he drummed up funds for a new war chest, laid down the law to the waverers, determined "who were for the flag and who had it under their feet," and drove out "the traitors." Some of the Bull Moose candidates were planning to run on both the Progressive and Republican tickets. Daugherty squelched that by obtaining a ruling from the state Supreme Court that no candidate could appear under two-party designations. Roosevelt supporters never forgave Daugherty for this coup that deprived them of the double shelter of the Republican party label. In forcing the Progressives from the county committees, Daugherty was brutally efficient. During those conflict months he saw more of Harding than he ever had before, but their relationship, though cooperative, was still casual. Daugherty did not yet call Harding by his first name.

If there were some—usually from a higher cultural and intellectual level—who disliked Harding on meeting him, there were not very many. Alice Longworth might describe him in his crudities as "just a slob," but most people were instinctively and uncritically drawn to his warm and easy personality. His friendliness went beyond party barriers. Henry Timken, meeting him at the Coliseum in July at the parting of their political ways, offered to bet a thousand dollars that Roosevelt would carry Ohio. Yet, for all that Timken was taking the Bull Moose road, he was so attracted to Harding that he begged him to join him on a hunting trip after the election, no matter who won. On August 21 we find Harding going to a picnic at La Rue with the Democratic attorney general, Hogan, who congratulated him on his convention speech, adding that as an Ohioan and a Democrat he was proud of him.

Since Harding's appearance at the Chicago convention his reputation among the regulars had expanded beyond the boundaries of Ohio. Gerrit J. Dickens, the head of the speakers' bureau of the Republican National Committee, asked him to go on a speaking tour outside the state in October. Harding agreed to spend twenty days barnstorming. On October 2 he opened the campaign with a speech in Indianapolis. The next day found him in St. Louis where he addressed the Civic City Club, somewhat to his political embarrassment, for he told a Jewish dialect joke that backfired and subjected him to embarrassing criticism afterward from the local rabbis. On the fourth he spoke in Kansas City, on the seventh in Omaha, on the eighth and ninth in Des Moines and Dubuque, and ended his tour with three days in Michigan.

Meanwhile the chastely framed Creed of the *Star,* with its eleven journalistic commandments, had been turned to the wall for the duration. Roosevelt had repudiated his party, and Harding reserved for him the venom that the faithful generally reserve for the apostate. To be a Democrat was understandable, if regrettable. Some of Harding's best friends were Democrats. But to attempt to shatter the party of one's birth and inheritance, the Grand Old Party, that was the ultimate sin. Roosevelt was the buncombe man, the champion of the Bull Moose has-beens and want-to-bes, "Theodore, Rex with his tail of disappointed, disgruntled, distanced followers." The liar Hiram Johnson was his "black-guardly running-mate."

The *Star* of September 4 parodied the Roosevelt vigor:

> I am by nature truthful; all other men are liars. . . . We are bound to win. I have just begun to fight; look at my teeth. I stand at Armageddon. How's that for a slogan? Taft's out of it. I used to like him, but he would stand in my way. I am a progressive—from one term to another. My defeat would be a fatal calamity. Anything that contradicts anything I may say, might, or could or would say, is a liar. So there! Bully!

On October 14, at Milwaukee, Roosevelt was shot by a madman as he stood in his car facing a cheering crowd. The bullet, deflected from any vital part by a steel eyeglass case, lodged in his rib, but in spite of a considerable loss of blood he insisted on making his scheduled speech. On the news of this assassination attempt the *Star* backed water furiously:

> No matter what we think of the political attitude of Colonel Roosevelt, we sincerely deplore the attack upon his life, and we hope it is even less harmful than the hopeful reports suggest. We should deplore a madman's

assault or an assassin's attack on any human being, and we deplore it all the more on Colonel Roosevelt, because he is a great personality, and a great factor in the shaping of our American civilization, just now at a crucial test.

In the heat of partisanship the crime will be variously regarded. Already we have heard it referred to as a piece of rare good luck, to advertise and create sympathy. We have heard it declared a deliberate design to thwart his political ascendancy. These are extreme, and both wrong. The assault on Colonel Roosevelt is that of a man insane, and probably made insane by the political strenuosity of the day. He is of the type of Guiteau, who had no possible reason for shooting the lamented Garfield, except an insanity that was born of the political stress of that time.

We trust Colonel Roosevelt will have a speedy recovery and be able to resume his campaign.

Roosevelt recovered speedily, as did the *Star*. By the end of the month Harding was writing from his old editorial chair that "the entire Roosevelt party campaign has been based solely upon selfishness, false pretense, envy, and spite." Roosevelt's personality was "selfish, intolerant, unstable, violently headstrong, vain, and insatiably ambitious of power, . . . the most dangerous agitator who has ever threatened the perpetuity of government."

Harding, of course, realized that Taft was doomed, but even if it should aid Wilson and the Democrats he was out to ruin the Bull Moose party and its leader "unfitted in every way to be President." Roosevelt, he observed to his tepid comfort on election night, might wreck the Republicans but he could not wreck the Republic.

The election brought as arrant a repudiation of a President in office as had been seen in modern times. Taft carried only two states, Utah and Vermont. Roosevelt won in Pennsylvania, Michigan, Minnesota, South Dakota, California, and Washington. Wilson swept the rest, winning 435 of the 531 electoral votes. In the popular voting he was, nevertheless, a minority winner, with 6,300,000 votes to 4,100,000 for Roosevelt and 3,500,000 for Taft.

The national trend was duplicated in Ohio, though with a certain lassitude that indicated a surfeit of politics, for there were 85,000 fewer voters than in 1908. The devious Daugherty, shoring up the breached party walls, had at least scored a minor triumph in repelling the Bull Moose. Cox was elected governor with 439,323 votes, but Robert Brown, the Republican regular, led the Bull Moose Garford 272,500 to 217,903. Ohio Democrats elected 18 of the 21 district congressmen as well as one congressman-at-large and the majority of state senators and representatives. Nick Longworth, in spite of the backing of the gear-stripped Cox machine, lost his seat in Congress by 97 votes. Timothy Hogan's Celtic Catholic inheritance seemed no longer a handicap in the 437,532 votes he received to 285,690 for his Republican and 201,025 for his Bull Moose opponent.

"Contemplating The Result," the *Star* headlined its post-election editorial, a result it admitted alliteratively was more a disappointment than a surprise:

> Torn through ingratitude, rended by the rule or ruin faction, the Republican party could not successfully appeal to a people grown restless in the reign of good fortune. . . . The Republican party . . . had made conscientious effort to early inaugurate so-called progressive measures, and it had to defend that record of surpassing accomplishment, or see promise held more alluring than patriotic performance, etc.

For President-elect Wilson, Harding had words of surprising good will:

> [Wilson] is a clean, learned, honorable, and patriotic man, and the country had better risk the dangers of the economic policy for which his party stands than return to power "the great personality" insane with ambition and heedless of traditions or the lessons of history. . . . The result is more a disappointment than a surprise. It was difficult to see how a divided Republican Party could win. . . . Republicans who made the fight this year may treasure the consciousness of a duty performed. . . . Harry M. Daugherty made a gallant fight where one of less courage would have surrendered before the fight was begun.

As for that "great personality":

> Well, the mad Roosevelt has a new achievement to his credit. He succeeded in defeating the party that furnished him a job for nearly all of his manhood days after leaving the ranch, and showed his gratitude for the presidency, at that party's hands. The eminent fakir can now turn to raising hell, his specialty, along other lines.

With the campaign over, Harding could relax in the cozy satisfaction that he had not let himself be roped in as a candidate for governor. But there seemed little political future for him now in Democratic Ohio. The repudiated Taft administration still had four months to run, and in that time there was still the plum tree with its fruit for the deserving. Harding considered himself among the more if not the most deserving. For some time it had been known that Charles Bryan was retiring as ambassador to Japan. Why should not Taft appoint his most assiduous Ohio backer to the interim vacancy as a reward for loyal support of a lost cause? Though Harding's career in politics might be finished, after serving a few months in Japan he would for the rest of his life have the status of an ambassador. The possibility that Wilson might let him stay on in Tokyo for a time may have been one reason for the *Star's* cordial references to the President-elect.

The week after the election Harding wrote to the assistant secretary of the interior, Lewis C. Laylin, whom he had known in Columbus as Ohio's secretary of state, asking if he would sound out Taft on the possibility of his being appointed Japanese ambassador. Unfortunately for Harding's dreams, Taft had already picked a career diplomat, the Minister to Belgium, Larz Anderson, as Bryan's successor in Tokyo. Anderson was a fellow Cincinnatian, from a family of great wealth, who moved easily and naturally in Washington and international society. In the last twenty-five years he had risen through all the grades of the diplomatic corps up to the level of ambassador. These last few months in Japan before his retirement were to crown his career. At the time of the Civil War the senior Tafts and Andersons had been close friends. Taft's sister-in-law had married Anderson's brother Charles. Beyond such close family ties and Anderson's obvious fitness, it is doubtful if even Taft's vast good nature could bring itself to reward a small-town ex-lieutenant governor with an ambassadorial post as a reward for a nominating speech and a few months' billingsgate against the Rough Rider. On November 14 Laylin replied:

> As soon as possible I arranged an interview with President Taft. He at once told me that the . . . place [was] promised to Larz Anderson, whose promotion from Belgium to Japan is announced today. The President in the strongest terms commended your loyal support and stalwart Republicanism and expressed regrets that these obligations, incurred some time ago, prevented your appointment as Ambassador to Japan. He wished me, however, to assure you of his cordial appreciation and to suggest that if other vacancies or changes occur in the diplomatic service during his administration it may be possible to give you some other appointment that would be satisfactory to you.

No such vacancies or changes occurred. Harding, still hopeful, printed an editorial in the *Star* calling on Wilson to appoint Taft to the Supreme Court. Then, stirred by his old restlessness, he left for Texas on a shooting trip with Timken and Scobey, warning them in advance that he did not like to take the lives of small creatures. Timken had already paid up his $1,000 bet, lost when Taft beat Roosevelt in Ohio. The three men met at Houston where the Mayor had invited them to sail down the Gulf of Mexico in his yacht. The Duchess did not go. She was again ailing, her kidney trouble aggravated by a heart condition. Early in 1913 Doctor Sawyer, who had taken charge of her, told Harding that he did not expect her to live out the year.

Harding was in Marion for Christmas. But the town of his triumphs had become an empty network of streets. With politics in abeyance, with Carrie in Berlin, there was nothing really to fill his time, no outlet for his loneliness. Daisy had left in September for a year, traveling westward by way of Japan to visit Carolyn in Burma and to escape the discord of Tryon's second marriage. Tryon's farming venture had failed, and he was back in the Center Street house, with Eudora turned shrewish, badgering him for his lack of enterprise and lack of funds. Harding spent his days at the *Star* office, writing the occasional editorial. Always when he walked up the concrete walk of the Mount Vernon Avenue house at the end of the afternoon and opened the front door there was the thin, querulous voice from the upstairs bedroom.

When Carrie left for Germany, she told her husband she would be back the following summer. He had even engaged passage for her in June. During the spring she went with Isabelle on a cruise along the Dalmatian coast. Isabelle sent Harding a card saying that they were reading *Greek Lands and Letters* and sending her love to the Duchess and Hub. Then Carrie wrote him that she was not coming back, not that summer or the next, or perhaps ever. She no longer talked about any marriage. Berlin, she let him know, was where she belonged, and she mentioned casually the things and places she had seen, the men she had met. He sent her a subscription to *Vogue* and a series of current popular novels from Brentano's—*The Inside of the Cup, A Hoosier Chronicle, My Love and I, The Lonely Queen,* and an English translation she had asked for of *Wilhelm Meister.* Sometimes he sent her money. [- -

----

--]

The spring of 1913 came slowly, at least in Marion, a void and un-
political season. In Columbus Governor Cox had concluded one of the
most ambitious programs of social welfare and reform ever presented to
an Ohio assembly. Laws that the Progressives had been demanding for a
decade now found themselves on the statute books. Cox himself, looking
back, felt that the major contributions of his administration had been a
workmen's compensation act, a rural school code, and the reform of the
penal system; but the Democratic legislature under his direction had
taken a hand in regulating everything from the lobbyists to the length of
the ballot. Some there were who doubted the sincerity of Cox's progressivism, pointing to his own quick rise to wealth in the newspaper business,
his long and close association with the Dayton political boss Edward W.
Hanley. A. D. Fairbairn, the publicity director for Cox's 1912 campaign,
described him privately as an "opportunist . . . a human welfare fakir."
Nevertheless, in his confidence, energy, and ability he seemed in the spring
of 1913 unchallengeable.

Marion's ways were not those of Columbus, and Harding's venture with
the Ohio *Star* had not proved a success. After Taft's defeat Jennings stayed
on at the Columbus office, but his goal was merely to liquidate the paper,
sell it to a syndicate if possible while in the meantime setting up his own
newspaper service bureau. Soon he would put newspaper work behind
him to become permanent secretary and lobbyist for the Ohio Manufacturers' Association. Arthur J. Myers, who ran a grocery business with
his brother-in-law, took over Jennings's place as secretary of the Marion
Star.

Harding played golf, occupied himself restlessly with trifles, and arranged to go on the Chautauqua circuit again in the summer. As a Marion
booster he had headed a local committee to try to persuade the Willys-
Overland Automobile Company to relocate in Marion. Although the
company finally chose Toledo, Harding felt that his efforts entitled him to
a car at the wholesale factory price and spent several weeks arguing
vainly about it. In the end the company suggested that the local dealer
might give him a 10 per cent discount. Daisy wrote from Burma that she
would be sailing back in May. The house on Center Street, with Eudora
in it, was no longer a home and she thought rather than live there again
she would teach at the Ohio State School for the Blind where she could be
with Mary, and the two of them could have a little apartment together in
Columbus. Amos Kling, now eighty years old, had planned to spend most
of his days in Florida, but early in May he suddenly returned from Daytona overwhelmed with homesickness. In an unspoken way he seemed to
be trying to reach out to people, walking in his yard, driving, going out of

his way to greet his old business associates. When Harding returned from his Chautauqua tour he found the old man yellow and withered though still talking of another winter in Florida. On October 20 Kling died of the same kidney ailment that was wasting his daughter.

He left an estate of $637,179. To his son Vetallis he gave the income from $35,000, the principal to be paid at Vetallis's death—if he did not marry—to Florence and Clifford. His daughter received $35,000 and a lot. Pete DeWolfe and two other grandchildren each inherited $25,000. True to his marriage contract, Amos left his second wife Caroline nothing but a token hundred shares of preferred stock of the Columbus Railway Company. The residue of the estate went to Clifford.

Just a week after Kling's death Mary Harding died of a stroke. Harding was overwhelmed, as he always was at anything that touched his family. On October 29 he wrote to Carolyn at the Burma mission:

> Dear, good, noble, big-hearted sister Mary died last night. . . . Death came suddenly from a hemorrhage of the brain. Deacon was at her bedside. It seems she was taken with a bad attack last Friday, but was then seized again last night. . . . We are all deeply grieved. A better, dearer soul never lived. The thing that grieves me most is that I was in Columbus for a special engagement yesterday afternoon, and not knowing of her illness I never called on her. I was in a hurry to get back because of Florence's illness. Florence has been in bed for nine weeks with a bad heart and a nervous breakdown. She is in bad shape. Deacon thinks she will recover, but there is no chance of her getting out before Christmas. Added to Florence's woes, her father passed through a long, serious illness and died early last week. You can imagine the effect of all that on a daughter nervously broken down, and with a wobbly heart. It has all been very trying. Mary was in to see Florence a week ago Sunday, just before her father died. She dined with me, and visited with Florence a couple of hours. . . .

He went on to say that as soon as Florence was better they were planning to go on a world cruise that would include a visit to Burma, and he explained how he had taken over the mortgage of the Center Street house and paid off Tryon's accumulation of debts. At the same time and in almost the same words he wrote to his sister Charity in California. Daisy, on her return journey, was visiting Chat when the news of Mary's death came.

> Poor Daisy feels so lonely since Mary's death [Chat replied]—she had expected to make a home for Mary when her eyes failed entirely.
> And so poor Father is going to be out of debt. It surely can't be, he couldn't live through it—or after it I am sure for he has never been out of debt since we moved to Caledonia, but I certainly do hope and wish he could before he leaves this world. I feel he has a burden though now on his shoulders that he can never unload and that is his wife and those youngsters, the support of which should have gone toward Mary. . . . She

often wrote lamenting because she had no home. It didn't seem like home to her when she went to Marion—her things scattered everywhere and with her sensitive nature she surely felt it. . . . I can't see what Father meant—but it can't be helped, so it is best to let it drop.

For Pete DeWolfe his grandfather's death was his own opportunity. Now for the first time in his life he could get his hands on some real money, instead of the few dollars his mother and Harding doled him at Christmas. He wrote to Harding, ordering him to send him $1,000 at once so that he could clean up his debts and clear out of Kersey. By December he was announcing his retirement from the real-estate and insurance business. He thought he would drift awhile "to get straightened around" and told his stepfather to hurry up with the next $10,000 due him.

Daugherty had written to Harding in the spring enclosing an old speech he had found from the 1910 campaign in which he had described Harding as never dodging, never scratching, never sulking, a "manly man." Ever since that long-ago morning meeting in the yard of the Globe Hotel in Richwood, Daugherty had been drawn to Harding. Beneath the Columbus lobbyist's fly-blown exterior there was a sentimental streak that came out in his feeling for his wife and the few friends that he managed to keep. In curious contrast to the legend, it was always Daugherty who sought out Harding. "Love my friends more and more every day," he wrote as an accompaniment to the enclosed speech, "and see more good than bad in every man who does not agree with me. Regret some things, among which is the fact that I don't see you oft times."

After the November débâcle Daugherty wrote again in a similar vein, only now calling Harding by his first name:

> One great thing resulting from this war we have had and that is that we
> are better friends than ever and understand each other thoroughly and
> will hang together through thick and thin.

Since Carrie refused to consider leaving Germany, Jim Phillips late in the year decided to visit her in Berlin. Unsuspicious as ever, he continued his friendly relations with Harding. When he was getting ready to leave, Harding even came over to help him pack. [- -
- -
- -
- -
- -
- -
- -
- -
- -]

242 The Shadow of Blooming Grove

It was during these interlude love years that Harding's closer relationship with Nan Britton began. How close the relationship was, whether it went beyond clandestine correspondence, no one now knows but herself. In her confessional account of their affair, *The President's Daughter*, Nan admitted that she had become Harding's mistress when she was twenty. Unadmittedly she was receiving surreptitious letters from him when she was sixteen or seventeen. Even at the time she was thirteen both Harding and his wife were aware of her persistent infatuation. In *The President's Daughter* she tells of a summer afternoon when she and her older sister Elizabeth drove by the Mount Vernon Avenue house and spotted Harding and the Duchess sitting on the round colonnaded porch. They stopped for a visit, and while they were sitting on the porch Elizabeth roguishly remarked that Nan had her room papered with Harding's campaign poster pictures. Harding smiled at Nan, saying he moved that she have a *real* photograph of him for her wall. The Duchess neither smiled nor spoke, and as the girls left her manner was frigid.

In June, 1913, Doctor Samuel Britton died, leaving an almost penniless wife and four children—the two girls, a boy Howard two years younger than Nan, and a baby, John. Mary Britton, the mother, turned to Harding for help and advice, and since she had taught school before her marriage he helped her get a job as a substitute teacher. Elizabeth had graduated from school and took a job as piano player at the Columbia Theater on Center Street. Nan went back to her last year in high school. Her mother had said that whenever she visited Harding, he had asked after Nan. And he had promised that he would "do something for her." Nan was determined to see that he did!

CHAPTER XII

Senator I

For a dozen years the political trend had been Progressive—culminating in the 1912 election. Much of what the early insurgents had demanded had become law, accepted for better or worse by both parties. It seemed a generation ago, rather than merely a decade, since McKinley's frock-coated presence in the White House. Even the frock coats were disappearing. With the inevitability that is as invariable as it is surprising, the reaction followed. Whether one called the shifting moment the turn of the tide, the climate of opinion, or saw it in the Hegelian sense of thesis breeding antithesis, the astute were becoming aware that the Progressive movement had passed its prime. Feminine, irrational, impatient, the mood of the electorate—to the wondering dismay of the reformers—had begun to change. The terms left and right as applied to politics had not yet come into use in the United States but in a metaphor—that would later become a cliché—the political pendulum was swinging to the right.

The Ohio trend first became apparent in the municipal elections of November, 1913. In Toledo the regular Republicans came back at last to oust Brand Whitlock's Independents. Columbus repudiated a reform administration. Most spectacular of all was the return to power of the Boss Cox machine in Cincinnati where a Hynicka-sponsored and controlled nonentity, Frederick Spiegel, defeated the young reform mayor, Henry Hunt. Governor Cox's reforms had brought Ohio national interest and in some cases emulation,[1] but Ohioans themselves were becoming restive. Conservatives were appalled at the more than three hundred bills passed by the Legislature. The Anti-Saloon League resented state—as opposed to local—control of liquor licensing. Businessmen claimed that new regulations and labor laws would drive industry from the state. Labor unions, on the other hand, felt they were not being favored enough. Farmers saw, or thought they saw, their freedom hampered by increasing controls. The

[1] Ohio's new budget system, one of the first among the states, preceded the Federal budget bureau by eight years.

Bull Moose was showing signs of going into hibernation. "Home Rule!" as a slogan had begun to undermine Cox's administration.

Even as early as the 1913 Ohio legislative session there had been talk of the Republicans and the Progressives settling their differences. In January, 1914, the leaders of the two parties held a "Get-Together Meeting" at Memorial Hall in Columbus where they listened to a belligerently ringing address by Congressman Frank B. Willis, reputed to have the loudest voice in northern Ohio. Pragmatic Progressives like Dan Hanna were all for a merger. But most of the Progressives, fortified by a favoring wind from Oyster Bay, still felt that they alone were the party of the future. The Columbus get-together, ending with a harmony dinner, was not a success. So outnumbered were the Progressives by the Old Guard that a wit referred to the dinner as "the embalmed beef banquet." All doubts about the durability of the Ohio Progressive party ended on Lincoln's Birthday when Garfield and Garford announced themselves as candidates respectively for governor and for United States senator.

Nineteen fourteen was the first election year in which the Seventeenth Amendment, providing for the direct election of United States senators, came into effect. Senator Burton, as the regular Republican candidate for re-election, found the prospect disenchanting. During the spring he was overwhelmed by a depression that he could not shake. His 1908 supporters, the Scripps-McRae papers—the Cincinnati *Post,* the Cleveland *Press,* the Columbus *Citizen,* and the Toledo *News-Bee*—refused to support him further; he was increasingly at odds with his party in the Senate; and he feared more intra-party conflicts in Ohio. Expecting to be renominated without opposition, he found himself opposed by the bitter-mouthed Foraker and by Congressman Ralph D. Cole. Republicans, he remarked, were ungrateful. He told his friend William Tyler Page, the clerk of the House of Representatives, that the thought of making a strenuous state-wide campaign for the nomination and following it with a low-hitting election struggle was too much for him, and that he had decided to withdraw from public life. On April 8 he issued his statement:

> I am averse to becoming a candidate for re-election to the Senate and shall not be a candidate unless circumstances arise which I do not antici-pate will occur. While, on some accounts, I should be glad to continue in Congress, where I have been actively engaged for more than twenty years, I have no importunate desire to return to the Senate.
>
> But more important than this, my chief anxiety is for the success of the Republican Party in the State of Ohio at the coming election. The pros-pects are extremely favorable. Yet it is possible that someone who has been less involved in the factional dissensions of the last two years would be more favorably regarded. . . .

With Burton on the shelf, with only token opposition from a nonentity like Cole, the way seemed open to Foraker. But the angry old man was not to achieve his hoped-for vindication so easily. Dan Hanna, moving back into the Republican circle, saw him as "a peril to the party" and joined Maschke in trying vainly to persuade Burton to change his mind. That aging political bridesmaid, Harry Daugherty, felt his heart again flutter with hope. The day after Burton's withdrawal Daugherty let it be known that he was receiving so many letters and telegrams urging him to run for the Senate that he might be forced to accede. It took Dan Hanna to explain the facts of popular arithmetic to him and several days for him to absorb them.

Meanwhile Burton and Maschke, sorting through the diminished store of Taft-true Republicans, came up with Harding as the harmony candidate. Harding was coy. In spite of his earlier promise not to oppose Foraker, he agreed to run if Hanna would support him, while at the same time expressing the pious wish that Hanna would stop his personal attacks on Foraker. He still held to his role of the Marion Cincinnatus, reluctantly available. "I am not seeking any nomination," he wrote. "I have, however, never declined to honor any draft made upon me by my party and would not do so now." In Cincinnati he visited Foraker and told him he had decided to enter the primaries against him. Although the surprised Foraker had counted on his rival's support, he wished Harding well, and on May 27 Harding, "with genuine reluctance," announced his candidacy. Foraker on the same day stated that he had "no objection to others becoming candidates."

Burton's black mood passed, and a few weeks later he began to wonder if he had not acted prematurely, if it would not have been perfectly possible, would in fact not still be possible, for him to be re-elected to the Senate. He called in Maschke, reminding him that he had qualified his withdrawal by saying "unless circumstances arise." Circumstances could now be considered to have arisen. Maschke told him that it was too late, that the leaders in their conference had already and finally pledged themselves to Harding. It may be then that the scholarly Burton expressed the unscholarly opinion of his successor attributed to him: "That goddamned, honey-fugling pussyfoot, Warren Harding."

The two months' campaign preceding the August 11 primaries was lusterless. Daugherty, once he had resigned his own ambitions, worked beneath the surface for Harding with mole-like industry. Harding, always in awe of the man he had so often extolled, never attacked Foraker directly but fell back on the "exigencies of the contest," implying that the old ex-Senator, even if nominated, had too many enemies to be elected. The less reticent Dan Hanna let go at Fire Engine Joe, calling on Progressives and regulars as well to eliminate "a man so out of date, so tainted by reactionary activities."

From childhood Harding's self-confidence was never more than skin deep, and although his skin had grown thicker with the years, he still had ambiguous moments when he was overwhelmed by a sense of his own incapacity. A few weeks after he had announced himself a candidate Daugherty met him in Columbus on a rainy afternoon, bedraggled and discouraged, convinced that he could not win. Daugherty, with contagious brashness, bet him two suits of clothes—choose the tailor and the goods, he told him—that he would beat Foraker. Always Daugherty had the knack of cheering up Harding, of encouraging him when his friend's own courage was ebbing. Later Daugherty in his retirement, straining to vindicate himself, would exaggerate the closeness of that early friendship and even try to claim that it was he who had propelled Harding into the Senate race.[2]

Foraker, although eager for vindication, wanted it on his own terms and felt it beneath him to campaign actively for a seat that he had already twice occupied. Only once, at Cleveland's Luna Park in July, did he make a public appearance, sitting with Cole and Harding on a flag-draped platform "like so many pumpkins at a county fair." Each candidate then made his pitch; in Foraker's opinion an "undignified, ridiculous, cheap, and unworthy performance." Astute enough to be aware of the surreptitious activity for Harding, Fire Engine Joe discounted it, feeling—as he wrote to Newton Fairbanks a week before the primaries—that it would not do him very much harm. He was confident. In Cincinnati he had the solid backing of Hynicka's renovated Cox machine. Unfortunately for his chances, he had come out in the spring against a national prohibition amendment and not only Dan Hanna but the Anti-Saloon League was after him. Harding won out by 12,000 votes, the final results being Harding 88,540, Foraker 76,181, and Cole 52,237.

The bull-voiced Congressman Willis became the party's nominee for governor, defeating David Tod, an inconspicuous former state senator. Willis had employed his voice and glib affability to get himself elected to Congress from the 8th District in the Republican famine years of 1910 and 1912. A big-boned rural boy, he had worked his way through Ohio Northern University and had even taught law there for several years, although his booming manner, evangelical oratory and gesticulations he had learned from Billy Sunday were scarcely professional. He had scored his first political triumph at the age of twenty-seven in 1899 when as a Republican candidate for the Ohio Assembly in Democratic Hardin County he had

---

[2] "I found him like a turtle sunning himself on a log, and I pushed him into the water," Daugherty told Mark Sullivan. Daugherty's colloquial vividness—a quality quite lacking in Harding—often set the seal on what would in time become a legend.

scorched the roads on his bicycle, canvassing each house and holding forth on each doorstep. In the tempered days before public-address systems his voice was a real, and in fact his chief, political asset. He liked people, laughed his way through each day, and never took public service very seriously. Campaigning was a lark for him, and in 1910 he had campaigned lustily for Harding. Although he himself was closely tied to the Anti-Saloon League, the party's platform on the liquor question was as equivocal as the wet city bosses could make it, and political wits soon labeled him the "highball" candidate—part booze, part water.

Nine days after the nomination Harding wrote fulsomely to Foraker:

> While I am experiencing the elation that attends a victory in the contest for nomination, I cannot resist writing you the one regret that is in my heart, that is—I had to acquire it in a contest against you. My admiration for you, ever growing for nearly 30 years, is no less today than when I enrolled for a contest in 1908, which I *knew* at the hour of enlistment would end in failure.
>
> Now that the primary contest is all over, I want you to know that I entered the race hoping you would incline to retire. I could not and would not ask it, but I hoped for it. I knew the drift of Republican sentiment. It would gratify you, it would compensate you for your distinguished public service, to know how highly you are esteemed, how much you are admired and how many loyal friends you have in every county in Ohio. I write it because you ought to know it. . . . At the same time, I knew the widespread feeling of inexpediency under existing conditions, a thing your ardent admirers could not or would not tell you. It was because of this that I entered, and hoped for your voluntary retirement. I said a number of times in the campaign, in personal interviews, that I would gladly appoint you if I had the power. More, I said nothing for which I need offer explanation or apology.
>
> I tried to silence the one big gun of hostile criticism [Dan Hanna] and would have succeeded had not the fact that I asked it gotten in the daily press.
>
> All of this, my dear Senator, because deep in my heart is the regret that you are not to go back to the Senate. By this I do not mean that I did not seek to succeed with my own candidacy, for you know I did not "stalk" to aid you, but I can truly say I would have rejoiced to acclaim your return to the Senate as a fit vindication to your noble and admirable career. Feeling this, I must write it, and, in the flush of a primary victory, tell you my admiration has not waned, nor my esteem grown less. My one regret is that my own victory had to be won in your defeat.
>
> I do hope you will not think yourself retired, that you will continue to inspire and encourage Ohio Republicans, and give them the benefit of your counsel and assistance. I do not believe I am consumed with ambition, indeed my most earnest hope is for a Party rather than a personal victory in which we can equally rejoice. You can wonderfully help. . . .

Foraker's reply was prompt and distant, thanking him for his "kind expressions," giving the conventional assurance that he would work for Harding's election, and promising a Republican victory in November.

In the Democratic primaries Governor Cox defeated an injudicious newcomer two to one. Attorney General Hogan, the leading candidate among several for United States senator, won by a plurality of 37,661 over his nearest opponent, but significantly failed to poll a majority of the votes. The Governor and the Attorney General had not been on the best of terms ever since Hogan had opposed Cox's short-term ballot amendment—one of the Governor's most cherished objectives—as "another novelty, another nostrum." Cox in 1913 had tried to get rid of him and get possession of his office by appointing him justice of the Ohio Supreme Court, but Hogan had refused the appointment.

Like Harding and Willis, Hogan was born an obscure Ohio country boy. He attended Ohio Normal University at Ada and then taught school for fourteen years at Wellston near his birthplace. After a fellow teacher had given him a copy of Blackstone, he read it with fascination and turned to studying law in his spare time until in 1894, at the age of thirty, he was admitted to the bar.

Hogan had curly hair, a jutting jaw, and a quick Celtic mind. As attorney general for two terms, he had made a brilliant record prosecuting frauds and had secured the first indictment of grafting state officials in half a century, sending former Treasurer Cameron and Deputy Treasurer Green to jail, and recovering several hundred thousand dollars' worth of stolen funds from the estate of Treasurer McKinnon. In his last election campaign his Catholicism had seemed a dead issue. Unfortunately for him, it was merely dormant.

To Ohio politicians, as to Americans in general in that languid summer of 1914, the course of events overseas, from the murder of the Archduke Franz Ferdinand in June to the outbreak of the war at the end of July, seemed unreal, remote, part of the endless and tragic dynastic struggles of the Old World that Washington had warned against in his Farewell Address and that their ancestors had crossed the ocean to escape. Columbus, torpid in the heat-heavy days, was more concerned with the August primaries than with the frenetic bustle of European chancelleries and the muffled tread of mobilizing armies.

To Carrie Phillips in Berlin the war's outbreak meant the end of her German life. She had watched the capital transform itself into a pulsing barrack city. Under the green linden trees just past their flowering, along the great boulevard from the Brandenburg Gate to the Royal Castle, the crowds surged in a delirium of emotion; soldiers in the new field-gray uniforms, students in the massed colors of their corps caps, civilians of all age and class intermixed, arms entwined, as if age and class differences no longer mattered in the unity of the Fatherland. They sang: "Deutschland über Alles"; "The Watch on the Rhine"; and the gray columns marching away, the glitter of the spiked helmets concealed by a cloth covering, thundered out "Wenn die Soldaten durch die Stadt marschieren"—"When the soldiers march through the streets." Leave Germany she must, this country and this life she had so loved; but her feelings, her sympathies, her heart remained behind. She and Isabelle sailed from Bremerhaven aboard the American steamer *New York* on August 24.

While waiting for her and for the opening of the political campaign in September Harding went on another Chautauqua speaking tour. Moving from county seat to county seat with the ornate silvered domes of the courthouses glistening in the sunlight, driving along the die-straight roads where the now-gathering swallows dipped over the wheatfields in the pellucid air, he could not connect that headlined turmoil overseas with any aspect of his Ohio country. To be neutral in thought as well as in action *was* the only way for Americans—even if the Democrat Wilson had said it.

During the summer of 1914 Harding began writing to Nan Britton, although it is probable that at that time their affair went no further than an emotional exchange of letters. Nan graduated from high school in June. Her picture in the graduation number of *The Quiver* shows a dimpled, half-petulant face beneath a frizzy blond topknot. "We all know 'Nawn'," her classmate-editor observed. "Talking she knew not why and cared not what." Her senior oratorical piece had the strangely prophetic title of "What Every Woman Wants." After graduation Nan spent the summer with her mother at a cottage on Brady Lake while they both took a teaching course at Kent State College. Seven of Nan's classmates, also hoping to be schoolteachers, boarded at the cottage while taking the same course. Unknown to Mary Britton, Harding and her daughter kept up a fervid and frequent summer correspondence. Nan's classmates used to slip down to the post office and bring back the letters in their fat blue envelopes secretly to prevent Nan's mother from learning about them. But Harding was not then indiscreet enough, so far as is known, to have had a rendezvous with Nan.

For all his quickening anticipations on the Chautauqua tour, his meeting with Carrie after three years was not a happy one. He found her distant, resentful, pro-German, contemptuous of Marion and brown Chautauqua tents and sweaty political meetings. Isabelle she sent to Mrs. Dow's school at Briarcliff Manor on the Hudson, but she herself was bored by the petit-point world of the sewing circle and the Twigs and such social events as the Tally Wag Club's Mutt and Jeff Dance. She and Harding again became lovers without, however, being able to bridge the gap of the European years that lay between them. She belittled his political strivings, his "mad pursuit of honors," and he told her that he had gone back into politics to try to get her out of his mind.

If he had been certain of her, he might have put her in some secondary place in his life, but the very fact of his uncertainty bound him to her, intensified his feelings that he tried to relieve by writing. By Christmas he was again sending her verses:

The Republican election campaign that opened in Akron on September 26 was strenuous with the possibility of victory, promised by the tally of the Maine election nine days earlier where the Republicans had increased their strength by 125 per cent from 1912. Although the Democrats just barely managed to elect their candidate for governor, the popular mayor of Portland, they increased their vote by only 18 per cent, and the fading Progressives lost dismally. The Republican elephant was on the road back. At the Akron opening Harding and Willis reviewed a monster parade, then spoke at a rally afterward under the alliterative banner of Willis Will Win. New York City Comptroller William A. Prendergast, who had presented Roosevelt's name to the 1912 Chicago convention, joined them like a convert on the platform and told the assembled Republicans that he now believed "the best interests of the State and Nation would be conserved by a united front under the Republican banner."

Two years before, when Hogan was re-elected attorney general, race and religion had been dormant, almost negligible. But the war overseas, emphasizing once more the difference between Europe and America, was giving a new impulse to latent anti-foreign feeling all over the country. In Ohio the prospect of an Irish Catholic representing the state in the United States Senate stirred the rural nativists to their fundamentalist depths. Crass Protestant propaganda sheets like *The Menace* or *The Defender* sprang up, splashing their pages with lurid warnings that Benedict XV through his Knights of Columbus was about to take over the Buckeye State. Everywhere, on fences and walls and billboards and freight cars, was chalked or painted the terse couplet:

> Read *The Menace* and get the dope.
> Go to the polls and beat the Pope.

Zealous Protestants called Harding's attention daily to the "insidious political Roman policy" of the "Knights of Columbus" candidate. Anti-Catholic letters poured in on him. The Supreme Vice Chancellor of the Knights of Pythias wrote that Hogan—undoubtedly prompted by the Pope—was planning to cancel the tax exemptions of all Pythian, Masonic, and Odd Fellows homes. Another correspondent warned him that 80 per cent of all Wilson's appointments had gone to Catholics and that Romanism in the United States was not a religion but "a vast p-o-l-i-t-i-c-a-l m-a-c-h-i-n-e." "Give us a straight reply or we go to the Socialists," Harding was told. "If you are a toe kisser to the holy humbug we don't want you." The editor of *The Menace* urged him to send the paper en masse to Protestant Democrats and appeal to them to keep "Romans" out of the United States Senate.

Hogan was an old picnic friend, and never once in the campaign did Harding directly attack him or his religion. Nevertheless, to those who did, he gave his silent encouragement. William Long, the editor of *The Accuser*—a "Socialistic–Anti-Catholic" paper carrying on its masthead the motto *Romanism Is the Rock in the Road of PROGRESS*—wrote outlining his paper's campaign against Hogan and "all the candidates of Rome," and asking Harding to speak to his "order" at Casino Park, Mansfield. Harding replied with great cordiality that he would unfortunately be away then but that he was "very much interested in your campaign activities." He suggested that Long call on him the next time he was in Marion.

So intense did anti-Catholic feeling grow during the campaign that many of the Democratic leaders wrote Hogan off and even tried to persuade Governor Cox to avoid appearing on the same platform with him. Catholicism became the burning issue, one in which Harding could enjoy the flame without tending it. Prohibition and women's suffrage, those potent swingers of the balance, were not to be engaged. Harding, as a juggler of irreconcilables, had always done his best not to face issues squarely. Garford and the Progressives had come out flatly for prohibition, as had Willis—to the approval of the Anti-Saloon League. Counterattacking, the big brewers had deducted 1 per cent from all their bills to set up a slush fund. Since Harding could scarcely hope to straddle both camps, his solution here was to "leave it up to the people." In regard to women's suffrage he followed Jennings's hedging advice to recognize the intellectual equality of women but to question whether giving them the ballot might not mark a change in the relations of the sexes.

The genial surface relations between Harding and Hogan did not extend to Garford, outraged at Harding's suggestion that now was the time for the waning Progressives to rejoin the old party. On October 14 the former bicycle-saddle manufacturer, looking the Kipling of politicians with his jutting jaw, heavy eyebrows, and thick mustache, addressed a Progressive rally at Mount Vernon. Peering angrily through his oval spectacles, he scored Harding as "the greatest exponent of standpatism the state ever had":

> Mr. Harding had much to do with wrecking the Republican party because he was not true even to his own associates. He went against Myron T. Herrick, former Senator Foraker, Ralph Cole, and others of his own political faith, and forfeited the confidence of nearly every man who worked with him. He participated in the stealing of the Cuyahoga delegation for Taft when Cleveland was three-and-a-half to one for Roosevelt. Not in his entire political career has he ever taken an open stand for Progressive measures, nor has he ever struck one blow in the interest of the people or popular government.

In the feverish last weeks before the election Harding campaigned strenuously, speaking from one end of the state to the other two or three times a day, hailing a return to Republican control "and the onward march to the fulfillment of our highest American destiny." After him came the whisperers, flaunting the sinister machinations of the Pope. The Marion lawyer Hoke Donithen managed Harding's campaign. Daugherty for the most part stayed in his Columbus office tending to his non-political concerns, now and then talking with other members of the Executive Committee and dropping the occasional encouraging note to Marion. He made no speeches during the campaign, and shortly before the election went on a week's vacation.

The Menace, The Defender, The Accuser were stronger voices than Garfield's. At the election on November 3 Harding defeated Hogan by over a hundred thousand votes,[3] carrying the rest of the party with him though by much smaller pluralities. "This is the zenith of my political ambition," he happily told the Marion crowd that had gathered in front of the Mount Vernon Avenue house to serenade and congratulate him. Willis reached a 30,000-vote margin over Cox, while the Progressives, Garfield and Garford, received a mere 6 per cent of the vote. The reconstituted Grand Old Party elected all the other state officers, a majority of both houses in the Ohio Assembly, and 13 of the 21 congressmen—including, this time, Nick Longworth.

Taft, who had in the campaign described Harding as "a man of marked ability, of sanity, of much legislative experience, and . . . a regular Republican of principle," wired his congratulations, concluding: "You will have a great future before you." Roosevelt wrote meditatively to Garfield from Oyster Bay that "the people are sick and tired of reforms and reformers." The Colonel had much to meditate on, for across the country

---

[3] The final figures were: Harding 526,115; Hogan 423,748; Garford 67,509.

the Progressives had polled less than 2 million votes, to the 6 million each amassed by the Republicans and Democrats. The die-hards had not died in 1912, and now, hard and living, they returned to the Capitol led by Uncle Joe Cannon. Cannon joined Penrose, Gallinger, Lodge, and Smoot to take complete conservative control of the Republican party. Assuming the rapid demise of the Progressives, Harding wrote to Garfield a week after the election urging him to return to the regular fold. "I trust," he observed with a politician's trust, "that nothing has been said in this campaign which has in any way tended to mar our pleasing personal relationship."

Carolyn, half a world away, was astonished at her brother's successful re-emergence. "I thought you were done with politics," she wrote him, then added as a pious postscript that "Mother had a firm conviction that God had a special work for you to do." This letter she sent from London between the nomination and the election. Votaw had become restless in Burma, and in spite of an industrial school for sixty boys that he had started, his missionary zeal was abating. His health, he was sure, was being undermined by the climate. With his knowledge of Burma and India, he wrote Harding, he felt he could lead a much more interesting and useful life by giving lectures on the Far East in America than by rotting away in Kemmendine. He and Carolyn had left Burma in July, sailing back around the world from east to west.

Meanwhile in Colorado Pete DeWolfe's affairs seemed to be reaching a climax. The spring had found him living in Denver and negotiating to buy a weekly newspaper there which he planned to make "state-wide in scope." He wrote that it was a wonderful opportunity and he demanded $1,000 at once, another $1,000 after he had returned home, and $3,000 "as soon as you folks can." "I am not blowing my money as you have concluded," he told Harding. "May have spent more than you would desire but not blowing it. I must have some money this week or give up further attempt until some does come." By August that notion had evaporated and he was back at Kersey, a justice of the peace, and doing job printing for political candidates. After Harding's nomination he wrote his step-father congratulating him. At about the same time Harding received a note from H. E. Klinefelter, the Main Street merchant, that Marshall DeWolfe had owed him $33 since June, 1909. On September 30 Pete's son, George Warren DeWolfe, was born. Pete wrote Harding several peremptory notes in the autumn. He spoke only of money and said nothing of his health, but apparently it was declining rapidly, for on New Year's Day he died. Soon afterward his widow Esther returned to Marion with her two children. The Duchess showed little concern at her son's death. About her grandchildren she showed no concern at all, and seldom saw them. The very fact of their presence was an irritation. At fifty-four she had become coy about her age, and did not like to be reminded that she was old enough to be a grandmother.

Shortly after the election the Brittons broke up their Marion home. Mary went to Martel, a village east of Marion between Caledonia and Iberia, to become the district schoolteacher. Her daughter Elizabeth had gone to Chicago and was working her way through the music school there. Nan moved on to Cleveland where she lived at the YWCA and worked as a salesgirl for six dollars a week at the George H. Bowman Company, a china store on Euclid Avenue. Before leaving Marion, she dropped in at the Hardings' one afternoon to congratulate the senator-elect. The Duchess in a pink linen dress came to the door, and her stiff marcel grew even stiffer as she looked at the impish blonde schoolgirl. Harding was in the library alcove playing poker with his regulars. He came out into the brown hall, thanked Nan, and held her hand just a little too long and a little too tightly, until the Duchess harrumphed that the others were waiting for him.

Jim Phillips kept dropping in to ask Harding's advice about an idea he had had for some time of selling out his interest in Uhler-Phillips and starting up a new business in Elyria. Harding advised him not to go. [-] They quarreled, she sullenly unreconciled to the county center so far removed from the European metropolis, he abject in his uncertainty of her. [-] If she had remained in Berlin, she would no doubt by this time have shaken loose from him completely, but within the narrowed limits of Marion her choice was limited. Each still needed the other, and their cross-purposed relationship continued, turbulent and frenetic. Not only were they limited by Marion but by the Duchess's returning health. In spite of Doctor Sawyer's prognostication, she was up and about again at the end of 1914.

When Carolyn was still in Burma, Harding had promised the Duchess a voyage round the world that would include a visit to the Kemmendine mission. But with Carolyn and Heber back in the United States he gave up the idea of any such long cruise. Instead, now that the Duchess could travel again, Harding took her with him to pay a visit to his crony Scobey in Texas. That irrepressible good fellow had become one of Harding's best friends. An Elk, a Knight of Pythias, an Odd Fellow, a member of the Royal Arcanum, and a Knight Templar, he was even to his poker playing the kind of man Harding liked best, always politically informed, always ready with shrewd advice.

As a United States senator-elect, Harding was discovering that his publicity value had grown. On January 19 Scobey arranged for him to speak on the Mexican question at a dinner given by the San Antonio commercial organizations. To Texans the civil war raging in Mexico since the overthrow of Diaz was of more consequence than the European war. Venustiano Carranza and Pancho Villa were reducing the country to chaos, and Villa was talking of setting up a North Mexican Republic. No foreigner's life was safe, no title to property valid. The only real solution was for the United States to step in and clean up the mess, Harding assured the approving San Antonio businessmen. "The magnificent resources of Mexico will never be given to mankind," he told them, "and that country will never come into its own until it is brought under the civilizing influences of the American flag."

Harding spent several more days relaxing with Scobey, playing golf and poker and swapping what they called "parlor stories" of a moderately indecent flavor, some of which were contributed by Scobey's second wife Evalina. His first wife had died in 1905, his Mexican mining flings had turned out badly, and in discouragement he had left Texas for a time, ending up in Brooklyn, New York, where he had gone into the dump business as sales agent of the Troy Wagon Works. Cheered by his second marriage, he returned to Texas to new and more successful land speculations. "Lower Rio Grande Valley Lands a Specialty" he had printed on his letterhead. Always he kept in touch with Harding. "My three genuinely devoted friends," Harding considered him, Jennings, and Colonel Christian.

Immediately following the Texas trip Harding had arranged to visit the Hawaiian Islands in order as a senator, and on his new senatorial expense account, "to get firsthand information in regard to the production and distribution of sugar." On the way back he planned to see Chat and other relatives in California. The last week in January Harding left with the Duchess and the Sawyers for the West Coast, taking with him as his new private secretary young George Christian, the neighbor's boy who long ago in his best knickerbocker suit had opened the door of the new Mount Vernon Avenue house for Harding's wedding guests. The angular beetle-browed George, with his unruly black hair and flashing eyes, would continue until Harding's death as his secretary, friend and confidant. Although Christian, like his father, was a Democrat and had even been his party's unsuccessful candidate for the legislature in 1901, Harding set more store on neighborly friendship than party labels, and in the end George was even destined to become converted to Harding Republicanism.

The Harding party sailed from San Francisco on the *Matsonia*, arriving in Honolulu on February 3. Harding was speaker at an Ad Club luncheon, after-dinner speaker for the Bar Association of Hawaii, guest of honor at a Chamber of Commerce banquet, guest of the Buckeye Club. The troops of Fort Shafter held a review in his honor. Charlie Forbes, appointed by Wilson to direct the construction of the Pearl Harbor naval base, was one of the most assiduous callers at the Harding suite in the Beach Hotel. Harding took an instant liking to the handsome, hand-shaking Forbes. Most people did like him. No one meeting this plausible go-getter would possibly have suspected that just fifteen years before he took control at Pearl Harbor he had been an Army deserter.

On March 2, 1900, Charles R. Forbes had enlisted in the United States Army at Boston, Massachusetts, and was assigned to the Signal Corps. Two months later, at Fort Myer, Virginia, he had gone over the hill from the Army and his wife, and nothing was heard of him for four years. He was apprehended in April, 1904, and for some reason restored to duty without a trial. By 1907 he had become a sergeant, first class, and was honorably discharged in January, 1907. Eight chancy years had finally brought him the control of the construction of the great naval base. Harding found his poker first class, his persuasive charm irresistible. The Duchess was equally taken with his second wife, Kate Marcia. Charlie Forbes showed himself diligent in entertaining the new senator and his party, taking them round Oahu, to the Marconi wireless plant at Kahuku, and even arranging for Harding to take a trip on a submarine. Charlie and Kate then planned a cruise for them to Hilo on the central island of Hawaii and a visit to Mauna Loa. By the time Harding left the islands he had come to consider the astute poker-playing Forbes as one of his favorite companions. The Harding party embarked for California on the U.S.S. *Sierra* on February 13. Harding and the Duchess left the others to spend a few days with Chat in Santa Ana where Elton Remsberg, now manager of the local athletic club, had just acquired a free quarter section of government land. Chat and he had three daughters, the eldest, Nelle Marie, being twenty-five. After his visit with Chat, Harding stayed with some cousins in Los Angeles long enough to go out to Universal City and watch the movie, *The Stool Pigeon*, being filmed.

The senators elected in 1914 would not take their places until the new session of December, 1915. In preparation for his six-year Senate term Harding shortly after his return to Marion bought a large brick duplex house that had just been completed at 2314 Wyoming Avenue in Washington. Neo-Georgian in style, separated from the street by a sedate terrace, it stood in sophisticated contrast to the open frontage and fur-beloved lumpiness of 380 Mount Vernon Avenue. The new house was expensive, almost $50,000, but Harding could afford it. Besides the pay and perquisites of his new office, the *Star* was bringing him in $20,000 each year. His campaign expenses in those open-air-rally days had been a mere $6,000, of which only $1,885 had been his own money. And the other apartment in the house would pay the interest on the mortgage and the upkeep.

Much of his time in this interim year was taken up with the multiplicity of ephemeral letters that afflict politicians in office and that most turn over to their secretaries. He did not forget Marion. But the metaphorical toga of a United States senator became a magic cape that carried him beyond the boundaries of Ohio and even into the inner pages of the metropolitan papers that he had touched fleetingly in 1912. In May *The New York Times* in an editorial on "Favorite Sons" for the 1916 Republican presidential nomination mentioned Ohio's Burton, Herrick, Willis, and Harding. From speaking at county Elks' dedications and Grand Army of the Republic memorial exercises, he had moved up into the national world. On May 27 he was in New York as one of the speakers with former President Taft before the National Association of Manufacturers. Unlike Roosevelt, who after the sinking of the *Lusitania* in May, 1915, had begun his crusade for American preparedness and intervention on behalf of the Allies, Harding still saw the war as brought on by commercial rivalry—at a cost of $50 million a day—and continued only through the wealth accumulated by the industrial development of England and Germany. From this sober deduction one might assume that industrial development was a doubtful blessing. But the non-sequitur quality of Harding's mind shone out in his rhetorical conclusion that "from the dawn of civilization commerce has been the inspiration of developing nations and it will continue until the millennial day." As for preparedness itself, he announced in October that he "heartily favored it," while at the same time doing his best to harmonize with those who thought otherwise:

> It is not wise to rush militarism and we will not do it. We do need an army double the present force, with some practical method of providing trained officers for the available volunteers.

During June and July he again cruised the dusty back roads on the Chautauqua circuit with his set lecture on Hamilton. Most of the time the Duchess went with him. Carrie remained aloof, petulant that he was so occupied with other matters than herself, then sulking and refusing to see him when he came to her or upbraiding him for his "mad pursuit of honors." In August, as if to show his independence of her, he went on a fishing trip to Quebec. But it was an independence that did not last.

Even in death Pete DeWolfe was still causing his stepfather trouble. Posthumous bills kept arriving like homing pigeons. Pete's lawyer in

Colorado, Hamlet J. Barry, wrote that he was besieged by creditors, and that there were over $1,500 worth of claims against the estate with the only assets 80 acres of farmland not worth seven dollars an acre. Pete's body was brought back secretly and on November 23 buried in an unmarked grave beside his father's unmarked grave.

Tryon, his son's second domestic worry, had taken to sleeping in his office out of the way of Eudora's nagging voice and shrewish ways. His life brightened when in October, after obtaining a legal separation, she returned to Indiana with her children.[4] He and Daisy now remained alone in the Center Street house, she continuing with her schoolteaching, a pre-destined old maid. Heber Votaw, after a summer of finding out that no one was interested in hearing him lecture on India, took a job teaching at the Adventist Missionary College in Washington. Deacon George, in Columbus, felt that he was flourishing, with a new office and sanitorium at 78 South Third Street where he already had two house patients "plus enough business appointments to insure $10 a day." His son Charles, the fourth child and third boy, had just arrived that summer.

When Harding left for Washington in November, he left his family, at least and at last, in order. Never again would he be more than a vaca-tioner, a visitor, in "the bulliest town on earth." During the lonely few weeks in the Wyoming Avenue house before the Senate session opened, and even in his more occupied days afterward, he missed the intimacy of Marion. "I think I am going to like the work down here," he wrote Jennings, "but I confess a longing every afternoon to get a whiff of the hurly and bustle of the newspaper shop at home."

If the wheel of fortune had not carried Harding to the White House, if he had merely served out his Senate term—or even a second term—his name, embalmed in the yellowing pages of old congressional directories, would have been as forgotten today as the names of most of those senators who gathered in the club-like atmosphere of the Senate chamber on De-cember 6, 1915. Who remembers Moses E. Clapp, Henry F. Hollis, LeBaron B. Colt, Carroll S. Page, Francis E. Warren, Furnifold McL. Simmons? Perhaps a few elderly neighbors, a scattering of relatives to recall with vague pride that Grandfather or Great-uncle was once a United States senator.

There were no Clays, or Websters, not even a Hanna in the Senate of the Sixty-fourth Congress. Lynn Haines in *The Searchlight on Congress,* written in 1916, considered the Senate time-serving, "indefensibly politi-cally," with service to the public "secondary to self-service—to prerequi-sites, to the playing of politics for the Senate's sake. Its whole atmosphere

---

[4] Tryon filed suit for divorce on the grounds of Eudora's "gross neglect of duty," and was granted the divorce a year later. Eudora retained his name and did not marry again. She died in Union City, Indiana, on July 24, 1955.

has become partisanly and personally political. It has descended from the plane of intellectual combat to the level of election deal and dicker. Pork is king."

Harding saw nothing to complain about. He was content to be an accommodating member of this wealthy, undistinguished club. Talleyrand's *"pas de zèle"* he would have approved of—if he had ever read Talleyrand. For all his amiability he possessed neither the knowledge, training, nor energy to be a good debater. Never in the seven sessions that he served did he champion any measure from the Senate floor. He preferred instinctively the middle way, better known in politics as sitting on the fence, although he was always an adroit mender of fences. As in Ohio, the two issues that caused him the most problems in his fence-sitting were women's suffrage and prohibition. When in the summer of 1916 he found himself badgered by militant suffragists to take a stand, he admitted that up until his election as senator he had been indifferent to the question of votes for women. "Believing as I do in political parties and government through political parties," he told them, "I had much rather that the party to which I belong should, in its conferences, make a declaration, than to assume a leadership or take an individual position on the question." Not if he could help it would he assume a leadership or take an individual position.

During Harding's five Senate years he introduced 134 bills, of which 122 were local Ohio affairs, bills to change the name of a lake steamer, secure a Civil War veteran's back pension, and such. None of his twelve public bills were of any national significance but concerned such ephemeral matters as encouraging the teaching of Spanish, celebrating the anniversary of the landing of the Pilgrims, authorizing the loan of tents to relieve the 1920 housing shortage, providing for the investigation of influenza and other diseases, amending the McKinley Memorial Birthplace Association Act, and giving discarded army rifles to duly-accredited camps of the Sons of Veterans Reserve. On roll calls he was absent 43 per cent of the time—a low average even for the Senate—and he usually managed to be somewhere else when a vote was taken on any measure that might antagonize a minority group in Ohio. With bills affecting labor, for instance, he voted seven times in favor of labor, eleven times against, while ten times he was not present to vote.

Shortly after the opening of the new session the lank-mustached Vice President Marshall—immortalized by his prescription: "What this country needs is a good five-cent cigar"—called Harding to the rostrum. Sen. Francis G. Newlands of Nevada, notorious for his long-windedness, was about to launch into a speech. "You are to be hazed," Marshall whispered as he handed over the gavel to Harding. "We usually call on a new senator when Senator Newlands makes a speech. You are to remain in the

chair until the close of his speech, whether tomorrow or next week!"
When Newlands at last finished his speech to an almost empty chamber,
Marshall returned and told Harding: "You have served your sentence.
Hereafter you will be considered a full-fledged senator."

By the New Year Harding was settled in his new house. The cellar was
well stocked with cases of everything from bourbon to champagne, and
at a 10 per cent discount, through his Columbus liquor-dealer friend,
Sam Ungerleider. Nick Longworth, happy at returning to official Washington, frisked over to act as Harding's mentor and renew their old
Columbus poker sessions in larger surroundings. No longer did Harding
need to be troubled by the effort and uncertainty of biennial elections.
This was indeed the zenith of his political ambition, and yet having
attained it he was tormented by the self-doubt, compounded by frustration, that always lurked just below the surface of his Roman exterior. [- -
- -
- -
- -
- -
- -
- -
- - - - - - - - - - - - - - -]

Once accustomed to Washington, Harding became a frequent poker
visitor at the Longworths'. Whenever the Duchess felt well enough, she
went along, too, never taking a hand herself—as did Princess Alice—but
fluttering in the background ready to mix drinks or scramble eggs, always
with a guarding eye on her "Wurr'n." For all the times that the Hardings
visited the Longworths during those Senate years, Princess Alice never
once set foot inside the Wyoming Avenue house. The Duchess felt the
full impact of the slight, though Harding did not. In her first contacts with
official Washington society she sensed that she was unequal to mingling
in this urbane, uncertain world, and longed for the certainty of Marion
where she was looked up to by the rest of the town not only as a United
States senator's wife but as the daughter of Amos Kling.

It was at a Longworth poker party that the Hardings met the rich,
harebrained Ned McLean and his equally rich, unpredictable wife Evalyn
with whom they formed a quick, incongruous, and permanent friendship.
Evalyn, the daughter of an immigrant Irish carpenter, Tom Walsh, who
after twenty years of prospecting had discovered the fabulous Camp Bird
gold mine in Colorado, was still, at the age of thirty, one of the wealthiest,
most spoiled, and willful adolescents in the United States. Yet beneath
her willfulness lay a kindly heart, and sensing the loneliness of this

estranged and aging woman tending the drinks in the background, she did her best to be friendly to the Duchess. Harding she at once found fascinating, even to his gaucheries, as he sat behind a pile of poker chips, oblivious of his suspenders and biting from a plug of chewing tobacco that he was equally willing to lend or borrow.

One more generation than the Walshes separated the McLeans from poverty. Washington McLean, the grandfather, had started out in the early days of Cincinnati as an apprentice boilermaker. After serving his apprenticeship, he and a workmate started a boiler shop of their own, most of which they built with their own hands. By the time "Wash" was thirty-five he was rich and had come to know every important politician in Ohio. In 1852 he bought the Cincinnati *Enquirer*—the principal organ of the Democratic party west of the Alleghenies. Moving to Washington, he expanded his fortune in real-estate investments. It was his son John who had had to leave Cincinnati in a hurry after the riots of 1884.

John McLean, educated not in the school of hard knocks but at Harvard and Heidelberg, increased the family fortune if not the family reputation. He had, in his daughter-in-law's words, an acid stomach and an acid heart. What he cared most about, what he used his money and papers to obtain, was power over other men. Politically he exercised this as an Ohio member of the Democratic National Committee, even though after the riots he lived in Washington in his vast mansion on I Street, designed by John Russell Pope, that covered half the block. After leaving Ohio he bought the Washington *Post*, but in spite of his exile and his other interests he still had occasional illusory visions of manipulating himself into the Ohio governor's chair or the United States Senate. At the time his son met the Hardings John was dying of cancer and jaundice, racked with endless hiccoughs, his mind corroded by paranoid mistrust. He was estimated on his deathbed to be worth $100 million, although actually his wealth amounted to between $10 million and $15 million.

If John lacked character, his only child, Edward Beale McLean, lacked intelligence as well. With a dapper mustache affixed to a long, empty face, he looked exactly what he was—a playboy, a joker; behind his dapper mustache a loose-lipped, undisciplined fool. As a spoiled child he had had everything he wished, his mother even bribing other boys to let him win at games. His two concerns in life were drinking and driving custom-built motorcars. Alcohol he had discovered so early that at the time of his marriage—when he was twenty-two—he often had to wear his right arm in a sling to keep his hand from shaking as he held a cocktail glass.

Tom Walsh before his death was worth as much if not more than John McLean. From a one-and-a-half story wooden shack on a shabby street in Ouray, Colorado, he—the Colorado Monte Cristo—had come to live in an exposition-like palace he had built at 2020 Massachusetts Avenue,

Washington, D.C., with sixty rooms, a four-story reception hall (lighted by stained glass), a library fit for a university, and a Louis XIV ballroom. And with his rise in the world he became the easy friend of statesmen, presidents, and kings.

His daughter, Evalyn, was a wild, gay child with an early developed taste for alcohol. Her small face with large houri eyes framed by dark hair—if she had not been dyeing it pink or some other color—was wistfully pretty until the years ravaged it with dissipation. Although undisciplined, uneducated, semi-literate, her mind—unlike Ned's—was sharp and alert, a quick if malformed intelligence. Ned had wanted her so much that he had even promised to stop drinking if she would marry him. They were engaged half-a-dozen times before they eloped. John and Tom each presented the casual newlyweds with $100,000. For the young couple money was like water in a well that could be drawn up with a bucket while the well level remained the same. On their honeymoon journey Evalyn in Paris stopped off at Cartier's for a wedding present and bought the Star of the East Diamond, the pear-shaped 92½-carat brilliant that was one of the famous stones of the world. The price was $120,000. By the time the pair returned to the United States their combined $200,000 was gone.

Evalyn's son Vinson Walsh McLean was born on December 18, 1909, and at once referred to in the press as "the hundred-million-dollar baby." The one worry and fear of his scatterbrained parents was that something might happen to the child. Never was Vinson left without a bodyguard, never could he appear in public. He could not so much as go to the circus. The circus would come to him.

Within months of Vinson's birth his grandfather Tom died of cancer, leaving half his fortune in trust to Evalyn. On another European trip that consisted of driving madly from one gambling casino to the other, Ned and Evalyn stopped in Paris long enough to buy the Hope Diamond from Pierre Cartier. For that blue 67-carat stone of baleful reputation, that may or may not have once belonged to Marie Antoinette, they paid $154,000. There were no two such fools in the world, Cartier told them with Gallic frankness, who would not only possess this unlucky jewel but actually pay for its possession. Later Cartier refused to allow them to return it, and Evalyn on second thought took it to a priest to have it exorcised.

On their reappearance in Washington in 1912, Ned and Evalyn gave a dinner party for the Russian ambassador, Ned's uncle by marriage, the first dinner at 2020 Massachusetts Avenue since Tom Walsh's death. Major Archie Butt, Taft's military aide, was there to describe it afterward in his diary:

> Everything was gold. It looked like the reign of gold. The table ornaments were gold and stood so high that no one could see the person opposite him or her. They sent to England for yellow calla lilies, which do not grow

here, and from each urn or vase yellow orchids fell like waterfalls. . . . Beside the big round table there were four smaller tables with huge umbrellas over each made up of orchids and lilies, with wonderful electric effects interlaced in the ribs of the umbrellas.

After dinner the famous Metropolitan Opera singer, Madame Gluck, sang, and there was a tenor, Signor Martin. Evalyn wore the Star of the East—the Carafe Stopper, one wit had called it—in a bandeau just above her forehead. Around her neck hung the Hope diamond. The dinner for forty-eight cost $40,000.

Following that evening meeting of the McLeans and the Hardings, an unlikely intimacy sprang up between the willful Evalyn and the ailing, withered Duchess. When Evalyn was again at the Longworths' a week or so later and asked why the Hardings were not there, Princess Alice told her that the Duchess was ill and possibly dying. Evalyn called at Wyoming Avenue next day. She found the Duchess lying flat in bed, her complexion blue, the room in a litter, and a rack of neckties hanging on a chandelier near the bureau. Evalyn's impetuous sympathy stirred the isolated woman's confidence and she began to talk, the harsh voice reduced to a whisper as she told the story of her life. Once released, the tenacious memories tumbled out: her father; her elopement with the ne'er-do-well Pete; her son who had died; Amos Kling's early hatred of "Wurr'n," and the years her father would not even speak to her; the Masonic Lodge that had rejected her husband; those years she had worked so hard at the *Star,* herding the delivery boys and even scrubbing the floors; Harding's nervous breakdown.

For a few days after Evalyn's visit it seemed that the Duchess might really be dying. Doctor Sawyer—the only man, the Duchess insisted, who could keep her alive—arrived from Marion with his wife, Coonie Christian, and Amos Kling's widow. After he had once more taken charge of her she began slowly to improve. During her recovery Evalyn kept sending her flowers, called on her, took her away when she was convalescing, and after her recovery introduced her to the haphazard social world of her Washington acquaintances. "What did they say of me?" was always the Duchess's question, after the two of them had been together in a group of the "smarter set."

As a newcomer to the Senate Harding was assigned to the routine and insignificant committees reserved for freshman senators: Claims; Coastal Defenses; Commerce; Expenditures in the Treasury Department; Investigation of Trespasses on Indian Lands; Sale of Meat Products. He was, nevertheless, among the best known of the freshmen, well remembered by the regulars as the man who had stood on the burning deck of the 1912 convention. Obliging, easy-mannered, ingratiating, his greatest concern in the Senate was, as it had been in Columbus, to be accepted and to make no enemies. A friendly flask of bourbon remained a fixture of the desk drawer in his office. He was always ready for a round of golf or an evening of poker. With Democrats he was as genial as with Republicans, making friends with old-liners like John Sharpe Williams of Mississippi and Wilson's former floor leader in the house, Oscar Underwood. The assistant secretary of the navy, of the obscure Democratic branch of the Roosevelt tribe, Franklin Delano Roosevelt, was one of the administration officials who occasionally played golf with Harding. Roosevelt found him "most agreeable, a good sport, whether he won or lost." Secretary of State Josephus Daniels considered Harding "one of the most agreeable men with whom I ever came in contact, courteous and cordial." Even the Secretary of War Newton Baker, Tom Johnson's friend and successor as mayor of Cleveland, cherished "a grateful and affectionate memory" of the Senator who, he wrote, "sought to be helpful in every possible way, and refrained from any partisan criticism at a time when partisan feeling ran very high."

Seated next to Harding in the Senate's back row of newcomers was New York's James Wadsworth, Jr., the diminished son of the old-guard congressman who had fought Theodore Roosevelt on the pure food and meat laws and whom Roosevelt had driven from public life. Harding and Wadsworth became such good friends that, when with time and the election attrition of other senators they moved their desks forward, they insisted on moving together. "So I was his neighbor during those six years," Wadsworth wrote of Harding. "I was very fond of him. He was essentially an honest man. He disliked sham and was deeply concerned over the influence of demagogues in American public life." As chief demagogue Wadsworth undoubtedly had the Rough Rider in mind.

Also seated near Harding, also to become his close friend, and of far more concern to his career and to the posthumous demolition of his good name, was the hard-faced senator from New Mexico, Albert B. Fall. Pugnaciously erect, with mustache and goatee, gambler's bow tie, black, broad-brimmed Stetson hat, and a mean little cigar the size of a lead pencil clamped in his jaw, he looked the incarnation of the West. His eyes were a disconcerting blue, and he had been known to carry the six-shooter of his frontier days even on the floor of the Senate. His beliefs were as much of the frontier as his appearance. He believed that northern Mexico should be annexed by the United States, that conservationists were akin to Eastern bird-watchers, and that public lands should be disposed of immediately and without restrictions.

For all Fall's frontier challenge, he had actually been born in Frankfort, Kentucky, just a year before Harding's birth in Blooming Grove. There, as an orphan, he had been brought up in poverty by his grandfather, a Campbellite preacher, and his first ambition was to become a clergyman, although he also dreamed even as a boy of owning a fine farm in Kentucky. When he was fifteen he took his first job as a schoolteacher in the Bald Knob district near Frankfort. Here, like so many country boys before him, he borrowed a volume of Blackstone and began to read law. But always the West drew him on. In 1879 he made a fugitive trip to Texas and worked for a while on a farm near the Red River. Two years later he borrowed $100 and with two companions again set out for Texas. For a time he worked as a bookkeeper in Clarksville until, finding his health and eyesight affected, he joined a "drive" of steers on the way from San Antonio to Kansas. He worked as a cattle hand, even as a chuck-wagon "boss" or cook, before returning to Clarksville where he once more took up clerking and reading law. He became especially interested in Mexican-Texan land titles and soon opened an office specializing in insurance and real estate. In 1883 he went on a prospecting trip through eight states of Mexico, ending up in Zacatecas where he worked as a miner, timberman, mucker, and mining foreman. Besides learning the technicalities of mining, he also learned to speak fluent Spanish.

He had married Emma Garland Morgan, the daughter of a Texas member of the Confederate Congress, and in 1886 he and his brother-in-law invested all their money on a prospecting trip to Silver City in the territory of New Mexico that ended up in the booming, brawling mining town of Kingston. So rich were Kingston's veins of silver and other ore, that any poor prospector might start out with his pick in the morning, "strike it rich," and return a millionaire by evening. Fall was not like Tom Walsh, one of the lucky. His money ran out and the season's end found him living in an earthen dugout near the Grey Eagle Mine while working as a hard-rock miner for $3.50 a day. There, in the same mine, he met another "broke" hard-rocker, Edward Doheny, and they became close and lasting friends.

After several grubbing months Fall wandered 70 miles south to Las Cruces on the banks of the Rio Grande. The majority of the citizens in that blooming and irrigated valley were more concerned with politics than mining or agriculture, and Fall's knowledge of Spanish and his easy contacts with Spanish Americans gave him his start. At first he busied himself with real estate and reading law, and he was soon joined in Las Cruces by his wife and two children, and then by his father, mother, sister, and brother. He was formally admitted to practice law before the territorial courts in 1891 and much of his practice derived from the Spanish-speaking majority and concerned matters of citizenship, water and mineral rights, land titles, and the legality of Mexican marriages. Cattle-rustling cases were his specialty. He became a familiar figure in the New Mexican courts, and as his law practice developed he represented railroads, coal-mining developments, lumber concerns, and other interests.

His introduction to the violence and bloodletting of territorial politics came when he as a young Democrat bought a struggling weekly newspaper and dared oppose the controlling Republican boss, Thomas Benton Catron, and his so-called Santa Fe Ring. Fall organized a fusion ticket to oppose the Republicans and raised a group of armed cowboys to fight off the deputies Catron sent to "guard" the polling places. Under Fall's leadership the Democrats gained power in Las Cruces, while the rivalry of the two armed factions grew more fierce. Fall and the county's deputy sheriff one day shot it out on the main street, Fall—himself unhurt— shattering the sheriff's left elbow.

Fall was first elected to the lower house of the territorial legislature, and when the Democrats won control he became floor leader. In 1892 he was elected to the territorial council or upper house as an "independent" Democrat. Cleveland after his interval re-election appointed him to the territorial Supreme Court, although Fall resigned after two years. For two brief periods he was the territory's attorney general.

During the Spanish-American War Captain Fall raised a company of volunteers to justify his military title, but they and he, as an anticlimax to the Rough Riders, got no farther than "the peanut fields of Georgia." With this prosaic episode behind him, he became associated with the flamboyant Col. William C. Greene, a multimillionaire mining promoter with vast Mexican holdings in Sonora and Chihuahua, supervising a staff of lawyers and thousands of Mexican laborers. By 1908, when Greene went bankrupt, Fall as his general counsel and manager had acquired an intimate knowledge of Mexican law, government, and society. He also acquired a remnant of Greene's Mexican gold and silver mines.

In 1906 Fall became a Republican. His realization that when the New Mexican Territory became a state it would elect two Republican senators helped to persuade him, but already in 1902 he was running for the territorial council on a combination Independent-Democrat and straight Republican ticket. New Mexico's constitutional convention met in Santa Fe in 1910, and Fall, revolver in belt, was one of its most influential members. After the convention he spent some time in Washington talking over New Mexican affairs with President Taft. In 1912 he and Catron were elected to the United States Senate by the new state legislature.

The overthrow in 1910 of Porfirio Diaz, Mexico's aged dictator, and the revolutionary turmoil that followed, caused Fall considerable financial loss. Because of his knowledge of Mexico, he spoke often and with authority in the Senate on Mexican affairs. He urged Taft to take more active measures to protect American rights and property in Mexico, and Wilson's policy of "watchful waiting" stirred him to sulphurous criticism. In 1913, because of American property losses, he demanded the annexation of all the northern Mexico states. After the rebel leader Pancho Villa's raid on Columbus, New Mexico, he called for intervention with an army of half a million.

Fall had not joined the Bull Moose in 1912, and he was always opposed to Roosevelt's conservation policies, but from 1914 on the Rough Rider's growing belligerency and his animus against Wilson brought him closer to the senator from the Southwest. Fall in the Senate became spokesman and adviser for Roosevelt on Mexican affairs, "on the whole the man," Roosevelt wrote, "with whom I have been most cordially able to co-operate among all the people at Washington. He has done capital work in the Mexican business." In 1916 Roosevelt called him "the kind of public servant of whom all Americans should feel proud."

Fall was a lusty poker player, forming with Harding a small group of senators who "associated socially three or four evenings a week—always at homes of those in the group who kept house, because, primarily, the object of these gatherings was to get good home cooking." After these dinners they would play poker, always breaking up, by agreement, exactly at midnight.

The new year that saw Harding settling into his back-row Senate seat was a year of decision in a United States moving relentlessly forward under the vast shadow of the European war. Following the sinking of the *Lusitania* in May, 1915, the mood of the country had hardened. By the summer Roosevelt was calling for American action as a debt owed not only to humanity but to national self-respect. Speaking at a campfire of Gen. Leonard Wood's businessmen volunteers at the Plattsburg Military Training Camp in August, the Rough Rider had scorned Wilson's "high-sounding words unbacked by deeds," without bothering to conceal his contempt for a President who even after the torpedoing of the *Lusitania* had used the phrase about being "too proud to fight." Although still the Bull Moose leader, Roosevelt privately had come to consider the Progressive party a "dead horse," and as early as January, 1915, had written his son Kermit that he did not think it humanly possible that the Progressives would make another national campaign. His hatred of Wilson kept nudging him toward a united front with the Grand Old Party. In the spring of 1916 he even wrote a conciliatory letter to Foraker, commending his "absolute Americanism." On March 31 he met Root again at a luncheon given by Robert Bacon. General Wood and Senator Lodge were also present, and according to Wood's diary they had an enjoyable mealtime "cussing out Wilson." Roosevelt's most devoted Progressive followers were trying to persuade the Republican leaders to unite on him as the strongest presidential candidate, the only one who could defeat Wilson in the election that autumn. But Hilles declined to eat moose. Roosevelt himself was convinced that there was no chance of his being nominated by the Republican convention that year, and he announced publicly in March that he did not wish the nomination, that he was not in the least interested in his own political fortunes or anyone else's.

With war-hawk sentiment flourishing mostly in the urban East, the rural South and West—long convinced of the iniquity of Europe—were ready to respond to Wilson's campaign slogan "He Kept Us Out of War"—with the implication that Wilson, if re-elected, would continue to keep the country out of war. Wilson himself had turned about and, if not for war, was at least for preparedness, even symbolically leading a Preparedness Parade carrying an American flag over his shoulder.

Ohio in its rural areas was what would later come to be called isolationist, and in its cities there were heavy German minorities attached by language and sentiment to the fatherland. Harding could not afford to indulge in the Eastern sport of castigating the Hun. As for preparedness, he neatly balanced his announcement that he favored an army double the present force with the placating warning that "it is not wise to rush militarism and we will not do it."

As politics came out of hibernation with the spring, politicians' fancies again turned to the thoughts of the summer national conventions. The gap left by Roosevelt's announcement that he was not a compromise candidate, and the surly determination of the old-guard Republican leaders in any case that the Bull Moose would not get his nose into their tent, left the Grand Old Party in a leaderless fog. William Boone, the New York boss and national committeeman, after unsuccessfully suing Roosevelt for libel in 1915, had ever since been going over lists of prospective delegates with a fine-tooth comb to make certain that those selected would be stampede-proof, Roosevelt-proof. In Columbus there was back-stairs talk of Burton, of Herrick, and even of Harding as dark-horse candidates. The affable senator whom everybody liked, the easy orator, seemed a fair-weather harmony possibility, if a remote one.

But in the spring of 1916 Harding was still scarcely at ease as a senator, and the thought of presidential responsibilities was more frightening than flattering. When the talk reached him in Washington he wrote to Jennings in Ohio, revealing himself to his trusty "Mac" as he did to no one else:

> Of course [he wrote on March 29] the advancement of progressive forces would tend to put me out of business at the end of my first term, but I shall not greatly grieve. I came here with the intention of being senator to the best of my ability for six years and though I may grow to be very fond of the position and enjoy life at the capital, as I feel now I could retire without serious grief. Indeed I would want to retire unless the forces in the Senate are very much strengthened, particularly on our side.

A month later he was again confiding in Jennings. After complaining of the "destructive tendency" on the part of the radicals he concluded with his own unvarnished opinion of himself as a presidential candidate and President:

I think you know me quite as well as anybody in Ohio, and you know I am unsuited to the higher position if it were possible for me to attain it, and you know that I am truthful when I say that I do not desire it and most sincerely want to escape the responsibilities that a candidacy alone would bring and the greater anxieties that would attend an election in times like these. Honestly I would not have the place if I could reach out and grasp it, and I really do not want any of my friends to promote it in any way. Of course I am human enough to enjoy having friends who think well enough of me to suggest me for that position, and I confess some pleasure in knowing that events have so broken thus far that I should attract some favorable mention, but when it comes down to serious consideration I am wholly truthful when I say that I had rather no mention were made whatever.

Of the Ohio dark horses, Burton was the only one who showed any real inclination to make the race. Herrick, back from Paris where he had taken up semi-permanent residence, let it be known that he preferred to be a candidate against Senator Pomerene, up for re-election that November, and opened his campaign with a barrage of letters to local politicians. The venerable former Senator Dick was also toying with the idea of a vindicating reappearance in the Senate. Harry Daugherty, that political bridesmaid still yearning for a nomination bouquet, announced that the United States Senate was now *his* goal. When Herrick, busily soliciting his old associates, wrote in February to Newton Fairbanks as chairman of the State Central Committee, asking for his support, Fairbanks declined, writing that after the "herculean" efforts in 1912 Daugherty should be nominated unopposed for his "more than thirty years of hard, unselfish, loyal, and unrewarded service in the ranks of the party." Charles E. Hard, the publisher of the Portsmouth *Daily Blade* and a former state executive committee chairman, replied in a similar vein. Harding was more circumspect. At a Republican banquet in Columbus he praised Daugherty at length as a "loyal and devoted Republican" who deserved consideration, but carefully stopped short of saying he intended to support him. Following his speech, he wrote to Dick and Fairbanks, playing down his banquet enthusiasm for Daugherty by letting them know that he favored no candidate and that he would take no part in the senatorial campaign. He informed both Herrick and Daugherty that he was neutral between them. "I think Daugherty is somewhat annoyed because I have not come out in an interview or an editorial in favor of his candidacy," Harding wrote to Jennings in midsummer. "He has had my sympathy all along, but I have not felt at any time that I could take an open and conspicuous part in his behalf."

Burton as Ohio's ostensible favorite son remained unopposed in the April presidential primaries, and among his four delegates-at-large, Harding was picked to lead the list in spite of Hynicka's opposition. Governor Willis, his popularity as governor sagging, was also named, as were William Cooper Procter, the floater of Ivory Soap, and the chastened Bull Moose errant John J. Sullivan. The unanimity for Burton was, however, only a few ballots deep. Burton, the cold intellectual, had never been popular with the state party leaders. As a candidate he assumed an air of aloof indifference, as if he felt that the nomination for the Presidency should seek him out rather than the reverse. There was still muttered talk in Columbus of ditching him for Harding. Foraker was wily enough to see that Burton had no chance. Reluctantly the old man decided that Roosevelt was probably going to sweep the convention. Charles Kurtz made no bones about his pragmatic determination to back the Rough Rider.

As anxious for the old-time harmony as they were fearful of the "ferocious Teddy," the members of the Republican National Committee, with Taft's old secretary Charles Hilles as chairman, met in April to pick Harding as the temporary chairman and keynote speaker of the June national convention. Harding had shown he was on the side of the conservative angels by voting against Louis Brandeis's confirmation as justice of the Supreme Court. In his first formal Senate speech, on the question of granting more independence to the Philippines he had trailed rhetorical clouds of glory while eulogizing McKinley as "the great kindly soul that . . . literally went to war for humanity's sake." [3] The committeemen, given a taste of his generalized oratory, were counting on Harding to knit up the Progressive-raveled sleeve of the Republican party. Harmonizer Harding was soon writing Garford, his jaundiced Progressive opponent of two years before:

> I carry no bitterness in my heart which dates from 1912 and have a very earnest desire to see things done and things said which shall enthusiastically call to our ranks all who believe a Republican restoration will be the most helpful thing for our common country.

Whoever they might be, all the restorative candidates seemed eclipsed by the shadow of the lost leader of Oyster Bay. A die-hard minority of regular Republicans wanted Root, but to nominate the executioner of

[3] Harding piously maintained that the Philippines were not ready for independence and that the "consent of the governed" was no more applicable to those islands than it had been to the Louisiania or Gadsden Purchase, the Mexican cession, or the acquisition of Hawaii, Alaska, and Puerto Rico. "It seems to me," he concluded, "if it has been our privilege and our boast that we have established and developed that best popular government on the face of the earth, that we ought to go on with the same thought that impelled Him who brought a plan of salvation to the earth. Rather than confine it to the limitations of the Holy Land alone, He gathered His disciples about Him and said, 'Go ye and preach the gospel to all the nations of the earth.'"

1912 would be to drive the Progressives into the arms of the Democrats and make Wilson's re-election inevitable. The most likely candidate to bring the Republicans and the Progressive rump together seemed to most Republicans to be the former reform governor of New York—since 1910 Supreme Court Justice Charles Evans Hughes. But the fastidious Hughes with his clipped, aristocratic beard and clipped manners was not a candidate, nor was it certain that he would accept the nomination even if offered to him. He was not in any case a man to stir the galleries or the public. "A bearded iceberg," Roosevelt called him.

The Republican convention that opened in Chicago's turreted Coliseum on June 7 was a lackluster assembly of carefully culled anti-Roosevelt delegates. By prearrangement the Progressive convention was meeting close by at the Auditorium; Garfield and his group still hoping to bargain for a double Roosevelt nomination, the more practical politicians like Walter Brown ready for merger with the Republicans whomever they might nominate. Although they represented a dying flame, the rank-and-file Progressive delegates burned with the old Bull Moose glow. In the drizzling rain of the night before groups of militant Progressives wearing resurrected Bull Moose badges invaded the lobby of the Congress Hotel, the regular Republican headquarters, to shout for Roosevelt and sing "Teddy, You're a Bear," a song written by Ring Lardner. Among the extraordinary visitors wandering around on the loose that wet evening was Diamond Jim Brady with his many-carated stickpin. Among the characters was a plump, self-important dry-goods merchant from Boston, Frank W. Stearns—known to his intimates as Lord Lingerie—who bustled through the hotel lobbies proclaiming that the best compromise candidate would be the lieutenant governor of Massachusetts, someone named Calvin Coolidge.

By Wednesday morning the nighttime drizzle had turned to a driving rain, with gusts of wind blowing umbrellas inside out as sodden delegates made their way along Michigan Avenue. The inside of the Coliseum was decked out in the spurious gaiety of red, white, and blue bunting, with a flag-draped painting of Lincoln behind the rostrum, but the mood of the floor and balcony was as dismal as the weather. Reporters were referring to the prison-stone building as the Mausoleum. To William Allen White, the Progressive Kansas editor, the massed delegates seemed cold with hatred for Roosevelt.

Harding, from his temporary status, had been confirmed as permanent chairman. As keynote speaker he was going to appear for the first time as a national figure on his own. Lodge and some of the other leaders were secretly concerned lest Harding stampede the convention with his electric oratory. White remembered him on that morning standing on the rostrum beside the speakers' table, a tall, well-built man, just turning fifty, vigorous, self-contained almost to the point of self-repression, but not quite; handling himself, as to gestures, the tilt of the shoulder and the set of the head, like an actor. His clarion voice filled the hall and he was obviously putting on a parade with the calm, assured, gracious manner of the delegate from some grand lodge exemplifying the work to the local chapter. When he smiled, he knew he was smiling. When he frowned, it was with a consciousness of anger. His robust frame was encased in well-tailored clothes, creased and pressed for the high moment. His eyeglasses were pinned elegantly to his coat. He used them in his gestures—histrionically. His statesman's long-tailed coat, of the cutaway variety, and his dark trousers were of the latest New York mode. Fifth Avenue was tailoring Senator Harding in those days. . . . Full, fair notice was served, with Harding in the chair, that the old crowd would have no fusion, was ready for no armistice with the soldiers of Armageddon. Harding stood there on the rostrum, the well-schooled senatorial orator, with his actor's sharply chiseled face, with his greying hair and massive black eyebrows, with his matinee-idol manner, tiptoeing eagerly into a national limelight; which—alas! he was to catch and keep from that day until he fell in tragedy.

As chairman Harding needed no more than his ingratiating manner and mellow voice. But thrust forward as the keynote speaker, suddenly alone, spokesman for his party to the entire country, he found that alliterative generalities sonorously spoken were not enough. What was needed was not the molasses of rhetoric, but words that would strike sparks and kindle a response in those humid faces. Fire Engine Joe could have managed it in his prime, the absent Roosevelt could still have done it. Harding, with his singsong appeals for harmony, merely increased the sullen spirit of his audience. He spoke from eleven-fifteen to one-ten, starting out with a confidence as glowing as the red McKinley geranium in his buttonhole; but his voice soon grew flat and monotonous with the strain as he begged his unresponsive hearers to "bury party prefixes," to confirm "the glory of our progress, the answered aspirations of a new-world civilization." No gleam of interest or curiosity flickered in the faces below him. Routinely he used the half-dozen stock gestures he had learned years ago from Wiley's *Elocution and Oratory*, raising his arm to heaven, shaking his finger, drawing his arm back behind him, flinging up his hand in a double swing. And when he had gone through the whole bag of gestures, he went through them again in the same sequence. The rattling of chair seats as delegates wandered toward the exits began to sound as loud as his voice. There was only the most perfunctory courtesy applause when he finished. "A convention of oysters probably would compare to advantage with the animated churchyard that listened to Harding's keynote speech," the correspondent of the *New York Times* wrote.

There had been talk of . . . Harding setting the convention aflame with his oratory so that the lightning would strike him when the moment came, if it ever should, to name a dark horse. But nobody could stampede this convention, and Harding could not stampede any convention.

Another reporter felt that even if Harding had been Daniel Webster, Robert G. Ingersoll, Demosthenes, and Billy Sunday rolled into one he could not have stirred a quiver in the "Little Neck Convention." Lodge need not have had any mixed-metaphor worries about dark-horse Harding setting the convention aflame. After his keynote speech Harding received just one presidential vote, and that from New Jersey on the second ballot.

The nominating speeches followed in all their traditional floridity. Gov. Charles S. Whitman of New York led off in naming Hughes; Nicholas Murray Butler, president of Columbia University, nominated Root; the names of old-guard Sen. John W. Weeks of Massachusetts, Fairbanks, and the rest followed. As each candidate was named, his pledged delegates responded with self-imposed zeal, spinning their wooden rattles, marching up and down the aisles with signs and banners, trying to imitate the antics and enthusiasms of other years. But the demonstrations were so lackadaisical, so obviously spiritless, that one reporter concluded that the whole bunting-tinsel buffoonery was a dying tradition. The balcony spectators were as sullenly silent as the delegates. Governor Willis, starting out with his hog-caller's bellow to place Burton's name in nomination, found himself stopped short by the frozen response. Taking the Burton badge from his lapel, he pinned it on a toy elephant that he had carried with him to the platform, but the gesture that would have brought the roof down in Sandusky failed to stir even the dust motes on the rafters of the Coliseum. The only time the convention quivered was when Senator Fall named Roosevelt. At that magnetic name a woman among the spectators ripped out a Rebel yell, and the balconies erupted with shrieks of "Teddy!" "Teddy!," while from the floor came some hissing and scattered cries of, "Throw him out!" Fall's speech was staccato, concerned mostly with the direct action he promised the Rough Rider would take in Mexico. But it was the one speech that stirred the rafters.

On the first ballot, on Friday, Hughes the unannounced candidate received 253½ votes to 103 for Root, 105 for Weeks, 77½ for Burton, 74½ for Fairbanks, and 65 for Roosevelt. With the second and final ballot for the day Hughes had climbed to 328½ with 98½ for Root and 81 for Roosevelt. The convention was adjourned to give the leaders time to talk things over and make whatever deals they could. On Friday night a "peace committee" from the Progressive convention, that included George W. Perkins, the International Harvester Company director, Hiram Johnson, and Roosevelt's old attorney general, Charles Joseph Bonaparte [4] met with the regulars, Sen. Reed Smoot of Utah, Butler, Borah, and the desiccated Yankee boss from Massachusetts, W. Murray Crane. Until three in the morning they conferred secretly in a smoke-filled room in the Auditorium, the Republican Old Guard still stubbornly holding back from Hughes, the Progressives refusing to consider Hughes unless he was a unanimous choice. After the peace conference had broken up, Butler talked to Roosevelt at four in the morning over Perkins's private wire. From Oyster Bay Roosevelt asked if the delegates were in a sufficiently "heroic mood" to stampede to him. Butler said they were not. Roosevelt, long cool to Hughes, suggested Lodge as a compromise candidate. Perkins told Butler that this was impossible.[5]

Hilles, Butler, and the inner circle of the Old Guard would have preferred Root, but they knew now he was out of the question. After Butler's telephone conversation the regular leaders shuffled the delegates in their pockets and quickly decided on Hughes. At another peace committee meeting at 9 A.M. Perkins agreed to go along with them.

Hughes swept the convention on the first Saturday morning ballot with only token opposition.[6] Frank Hitchcock, Taft's postmaster general, had in those early-morning hours offered Burton the vice presidential nomination, but Burton's proud and eager secretary, Granville Mooney, refused it, and second place on the ticket went to Fairbanks.

Meanwhile the delegates to the Progressive convention had spent three days in the Auditorium whistling in the dark. They wore the badges and sang the songs of 1912. They marched out of the hall to a chorus of "We want Teddy! We want only Teddy!" They kept up the pretense—though they knew it was pretense—of being the wave of the future, heartened by their chairman, Raymond Robbins, the social-worker friend of the maverick Harold Ickes. They explained away the low-ebb negotiations going on with the Old Guard. When Perkins came back from the peace conference with his Hughes proposal, they turned on him and nominated Roosevelt by acclamation. Then, when the shouts had died down, Robbins, his face white and his voice quivering, read a telegram from Oyster Bay declining the nomination and recommending Henry Cabot Lodge, a man of "the broadest national spirit" and one of the "staunchest fighters for different measures of economic reform in the direction of justice." Stunned by the

---

[4] Bonaparte was the grandnephew of Napoleon I.
[5] Merlo J. Pusey in his life of Hughes has pointed out that the astute Roosevelt knew perfectly well that Lodge's nomination was impossible, and that the reaction to his suggestion would probably make Hughes's nomination inevitable while absolving him from having any hand in it.
[6] After the legend of the smoke-filled room of the 1920 Republican Convention, it is curious that almost nothing has been said of the smoke-filled room of 1916 where the nomination of Hughes was arranged.

name of the reactionary from Massachusetts, the delegates sat for a few seconds in silence. Then a crosscurrent of voices rose to an angry buzz, as if someone had kicked a hive of bees. At a signal from Robbins the band struck up "America," but no one attempted to sing it. In rage and frustration men tore Roosevelt badges and pictures from their lapels and trampled them underfoot. As the last of the delegates struggled from the Auditorium, they and everyone else knew finally that the Progressive party was dead.

Harding's private disillusionment was almost as great as the public humiliation of the Progressives. For whatever his other doubts about himself, he had always been proudly confident of his ability as an orator. Then, in the moment when he stood as the spokesman of his party on the national stage, he had failed. As chairman of the convention he had seemed to be moving up into the ranks of national leaders, those men he had so long admired—Foraker in his heyday, Hanna, McKinley. After his keynote speech he had been reduced to the rank of a small-town senator. The metropolitan papers had all either derided or deplored him. "Since the roasting I received at Chicago," he admitted to Jennings, "I no longer harbor any too great self-confidence in the matter of speechmaking."

Two weeks after the convention Harding in his somewhat battered role of harmonizer wrote to Oyster Bay expressing his "very great satisfaction" at Roosevelt's declining the third-party nomination and at his pledge of support for Hughes. Hoping that Roosevelt would regard his earlier attacks in the Pickwickian sense, Harding praised the sincerity of the Rough Rider's opposition to Wilson and his unselfish desire "to serve our common country," assuring him that his support of Hughes would "re-enlist the devotion of thousands of Republicans who have never been lacking in their personal esteem, but were arrayed against you for a considerable period because of party differences. I believe you will have your reward in the high opinion of your fellow countrymen."

So began the curious rapprochement between the man from Marion and "Theodore Rex . . . the buncombe man, . . . the most dangerous agitator" of 1912.

[CHAPTER XIII]

Senator II

The results of the Ohio state primaries on August 8 were predictable. On the Democratic ballot Senator Pomerene had only token opposition, while James Cox was given another chance for the governorship. The Republicans renominated Governor Willis whom they had endorsed in their June convention. Weeks before the primaries Dick had been persuaded to drop out of the senatorial race, but Daugherty—so realistic about politics where others were concerned—still could not face the fact that he himself was a ballot-box spinster. His name stayed on the ballot, and Herrick overwhelmed him, carrying 85 counties to his three. "Daugherty's defeat did not surprise me," Harding wrote to Jennings. "I thought I saw it coming and feel a very sincere personal disappointment on his account. It strikes me that his defeat means his complete retirement and in many respects he deserved a kindlier political fate."

With the collapse of the Bull Moose movement the Progressives began to drift back to the two old parties, the rank-and-file majority—if not the leaders—turning to the Democrats. After the August primaries Garford and his financial backer, Henry Timken, surrendered and agreed to accept membership on the Republican State Central Committee.

During most of August and September Harding was either in Washington or on the Chautauqua circuit, but he was in Marion on September 16 for the opening of the campaign. He took a moderate part in the drive for Hughes, speaking within but not outside the state. The Democrats campaigned with the magic slogan: "He kept us out of war!" Hughes tried to make an issue of military preparedness and of Wilson's failure to protect American citizens in Mexico. As an approach it was too belligerent. Whatever their sympathies for the Allies, most Americans still did not want war. "You are working, not fighting," Wilson speakers told their audiences, and then asked them rhetorically which they preferred: Wilson with peace and honor; or Hughes with Roosevelt and war? The German government's agreement of the previous May to restrict submarine warfare to the limits Wilson insisted on—"the general rules of international law concerning visit and search"—seemed a tangible assurance of peace. Yet, even as Democratic speakers equated a vote for Hughes with a vote for war, Wilson himself had to face the fact that war was moving inevitably and relentlessly closer. Shortly before the November election he had been privately informed by the Kaiser's secretary of state that German public opinion would soon force the Imperial government to give in to demands for unrestricted submarine warfare. Such a resumption would, Wilson knew, mean war for the United States.

Maine, with Yankee stubbornness, always insisted on holding its state election six weeks before the November national election, giving rise to that old political chestnut: "As Maine goes, so goes the nation." It had been true the year of Wilson's election, and both parties while predicting victory were watching Maine apprehensively in 1916. In the September election Republican Carl E. Milliken corraled the strayed Progressives to defeat Maine's Democratic Gov. Oakley C. Curtis by 13,800 votes, and the Republicans elected the two United States senators as well as the three congressmen. "It looks good," was Hughes's comment. "I don't see how we can lose now." But it was a victory too narrow to give much credence to saws and proverbs. Roosevelt's belligerency could rally the East for war, but the South and the West in their rural isolation wanted peace. The heavy German vote of the Midwest had swung to Wilson. The election would be close.

As it turned out Hughes threw away the election by a political gaffe on his campaign trip to California in August just before that state's primaries. Progressivism was still a force in California, and Gov. Hiram Johnson— who had left the Chicago convention announcing that he was "too mad to be tired"—was now running for both the Republican and Progressive nominations for senator. The entrenched Old Guard, backed by the unsavory Southern Pacific machine and headed by Republican National Committeeman William H. Crocker, was ready to undercut Johnson at any opportunity. Hughes, the New York visitor who felt he had no right to take sides in an out-of-state nomination struggle, did not grasp the intensity of the hate between the two factions. Once he had crossed the state border he let Crocker arrange his tour, expecting him to make joint arrangements with Johnson. Crocker's arrangements were to exclude the proud and irascible governor. The culmination of misunderstandings came when Hughes on his return from Pasadena to Los Angeles stopped off for a few hours' rest at Long Beach's Virginia Hotel. It so happened that Governor Johnson had registered at the same hotel an hour earlier. Hughes was unaware of Johnson's presence, and though some of his entourage learned about it, he was not informed. Johnson, well aware of Hughes, waited for an invitation that never came. He himself refused to take any step toward a meeting at Long Beach, saying that he did not wish to break through the cordon to bask in Hughes's reflected light.

Hughes, angry and dismayed when he learned of what had happened, sent the Governor an apologetic telegram. It was too late. Johnson and his supporters never forgave Hughes for this slight or for his close if involuntary association with Crocker and "the foul regime which had governed California prior to 1911."

The election was in fact so close that it took three days to determine definitely who had won. At first, on the Tuesday election night as the returns from the East began to come in, Hughes seemed an easy winner. A huge electric sign on the roof of the Hotel Astor on Times Square blazoned HUGHES to the crowds below. He carried every Eastern state north of the Potomac except Maryland and New Hampshire, and every Midwestern state except Ohio. Wilson had to be dissuaded by Tumulty from wiring his congratulations to Hughes that night. Then, as the returns from the South and the far West began to register their Wilson totals, the balance swung slowly back, and Wilson took the lead. So hair's breadth was the contest in California for the state's 13 electoral votes that the completely tabulated figures were not ready until three days later. With California still undetermined, Wilson had accumulated 264 electoral votes to Hughes's 254. Finally, on Friday morning, the tabulators were able to announce that Wilson had won California and the election by 3,775 votes. Hiram Johnson, running on the same ticket with Hughes, had carried his state by the enormous majority of 296,815. The Long Beach non-meeting had been fatal.[1]

Wilson, backed by the anti-war sentiment of rural Ohio, carried the state with 604,161 votes to 514,753 for Hughes, the first Democratic presidential candidate to win a majority of Ohio's votes since 1856. Senator Pomerene defeated Herrick by a 36,097 vote margin—the only Democratic senator elected between New York and the Mississippi north of the Mason-Dixon line. Cox barely managed to squeak through, beating Governor Willis by 6,616 votes. The Democrats also won 13 of Ohio's 22 congressional seats as well as a majority in the state assembly.

With Hughes's defeat, Roosevelt stood out like an oak around which all the other trees had been leveled, the obvious and only Republican candidate for 1920. Possibly the astute politician in Roosevelt had foreseen the

---

[1] Wilson's popular margin was almost 600,000. Burton was convinced afterward that if he, with his knowledge of West Coast politics, had been the party's vice presidential candidate, the California fiasco would never have taken place, and Hughes would have won. Even without California, Hughes would have been elected if Ohio had given him its usual Republican majority.

1916 débâcle. In December Harding was one of the Ohio politicians to help organize a state advisory committee "to advise, encourage, and cooperate, in mutual purpose and for party success." He had been writing occasional political letters to Roosevelt since June. Now Roosevelt invited him to a conference to make plans for revivifying the Grand Old Party. "We did not dwell on the differences of 1912," Harding wrote, "for that was an old story. He thought his course was justified and we jointly deplored the results. But he did insist we must all get together and save the country to a Republican restoration; that the Republican party was the one agency to give the highest service to our country, and the compact of council and co-operation was made then and there."

The President who had kept us out of war knew at the time of his re-election that the odds were against his keeping us out much longer. But his chances turned sharply better on December 12 when the Kaiser startled the world by proposing peace negotiations with the Allies rather than "to continue the war to the bitter end." Two days later Wilson issued his own proposal, asking that all the belligerents declare their terms for concluding the war. On December 26 the German government replied, urging "the speedy assembly on neutral ground of delegates of the warring states." The Allied answer to both Wilson and the Kaiser was "No." On January 22 Wilson appeared before the last session of the old Senate and, speaking "on behalf of humanity," demanded "a peace without victory" and for the first time mentioned a League for Peace as the necessary prerequisite. But his sensible view that "only a peace between equals would last" seemed to the inflamed belligerents a repudiation of what they had been fighting for, the lives they had lost, and the sacrifices they had made.
  Eight days after Wilson's speech the Imperial German government announced that on February 1 all approaches to the British Isles, the French coast, and the Mediterranean would be in a state of blockade, that the German Navy would resume unrestricted submarine warfare, and that "all sea traffic will be stopped with every available weapon."
  The German declaration came to Wilson as an "astounding surprise." After several days of anguished inner debate and a grim and hesitant meeting with his Cabinet, he reluctantly made up his mind. On February 3, a resolved President appeared before Congress to announce the breaking off of diplomatic relations with Germany. He still insisted that this was not war and that he was not "proposing or contemplating war or any steps that may lead to war," but few believed him, nor did he any longer really believe himself.
  As America's inevitable entry into the war became clearer, and public opinion rallied to the Allies, Carrie in Marion grew more strident in her championship of the lost fatherland. The day after Wilson's speech Hard-

ing did his best to warn her indirectly in a three-page letter on Senate stationery that he obviously wrote in the expectation that the still-un-suspicious Jim would read it: "Sis" he called her, but signed it "Sincerely Yours" and with his initials:

[- -
- -
- -
- -
- -
- -
- -
- -
- -
- -
- -
- -
- -
- -
- -
- -
- -
- -
- -
- -
- -
- -
- -
- -
- -
- -
- -
- -
- -
- -]

Her reply was savage. If war with Germany should come and he should vote for war, she would expose him, let her husband know how his old friend had betrayed him, make the letters he had written her public, drive him from office. If war should come, he would find other things than politics to reckon with!

Time itself seemed to accelerate in the weeks following the diplomatic break with Germany. On February 24 the British Secret Service managed to intercept a code message sent by Under Secretary Alfred Zimmermann of the German Foreign Ministry to the government of Mexico, promising to restore Mexico's lost territories in Texas, New Mexico, and Arizona, if Mexico would back Germany in the event of war with the United States. Wilson realized that the Zimmermann note had severed the last thin alternatives to war. On March 3 the Sixty-Fourth Congress had come to an end with a Senate filibuster by La Follette and his "little group of wilful men" —as Wilson called them—determined to prevent the arming of merchant ships. The following week the President on his own authority ordered guns and gunners placed on American merchantmen and summoned a special session of the new Sixty-Fifth Congress to meet on April 16.

In a sharp resumption of their attacks German submarines had begun to sink three-quarters of a million tons of shipping a month. Then, on March 18, three American merchant ships, the *City of Memphis,* the *Illinois,* and the *Vigilancia*—American built and armed, with American crews—were torpedoed. "Seven weeks have gone by and he has not done a thing," Roosevelt wrote in fury. Even as early as the invasion of Belgium the Rough Rider, ever emotionally drawn to "the discipline of war," had toyed with the idea of an eventual Roosevelt division commanded by himself. By January he was even making tentative lists of the men he would take with him. After a year of rounding up his old Cuban comrades-at-arms and unblooded younger militants, he had written to Secretary of War Newton Baker on February 3, 1917, offering to raise a division of volunteers and have them ready for the trenches in France within six weeks if war should be declared. Baker replied to the fuming Roosevelt that no such action could be taken without the consent of Congress. Finally, in an empty interview, the War Secretary told Roosevelt that his request would be "carefully considered"—which, they both knew, meant filed and forgotten. Meanwhile, the war declaration crept closer. Wilson advanced the date of his special session of Congress to April 2 "to receive a communication by the Executive on grave questions of national policy."

On that damp and climactic evening Wilson, the war leader, appeared before the Congress to deliver his message in the chamber of the House of Representatives. Everyone knew it would be a war message. The curb-standers who had waited along the boulevards holding American flags as the presidential car passed knew it as well as the members of the

Congress and the diplomatic corps who filled that packed room. In the front row sat the Supreme Court justices, though not in their judicial robes, led by Chief Justice White. Next to them were the members of the Cabinet, and behind them on the floor of the house—for the first time that anyone could remember—the foreign ambassadors. When the senators filed in they wore or carried small American flags, with the exception of La Follette and Norris.

As the slim, poised President entered the House chamber, everyone rose and the room echoed with cheers and applause. It was the most dramatic moment in American history since the Civil War. La Follette, conspicuously alone, stood apart from the cheering, his arms crossed, his head bent so that his features were hidden under his flaring thatch of gray hair.

Wilson, deft as a duelist, thrust with the phrases that he was so adept at turning as he recited American grievances against Germany and called on the Congress to declare war:

> The present German submarine warfare is a warfare against mankind. . . . There is one choice we cannot make, we are incapable of making; we will not choose the path of submission.

At those electric words Justice White dropped his wide-brimmed hat as he clapped his hands together and rose to his feet. He stood there, the tears running down his cheeks, while everyone else stood up as if at his signal. Wilson spoke for just over half an hour, looking beyond war to "a universal dominion of right by such a consent of free peoples as shall bring peace and safety to all nations and make the world itself at last free." He spoke of the "pride of those who know that the day has come when America is privileged to spend her blood and her might for the principles that gave her birth and happiness and the peace which she has treasured." And he ended with a sonorous paraphrase of Martin Luther: "God helping her, she can do no other."

Even Theodore Roosevelt was for once satisfied. "The President's message is a great state paper," he told reporters, "which will rank in history with the great state papers of which Americans in future years will be proud. . . . I, of course, very earnestly hope that I may be allowed to raise a division for immediate service at the front."

To command that division in battle was now his single-minded and ultimate object. He had been a leader of men; soldier, President, Progressive. He had known the heads of nations, crowned and uncrowned. He had been a big-game hunter in Africa, an explorer in the wildernesses of South America. He had seen his four sons grow to military manhood. Now almost sixty years old, blind in one eye, plagued still by the poison of fevers he had contracted on the Amazon, he had one last demand to make of life—to die in combat.

When the Senate met on the noon following the President's War Message, Sen. Gilbert Hitchcock, the ranking member of the Committee of Foreign Relations, asked for an immediate consideration of the war resolution. According to the inflexible Senate rule, when any senator objected, a resolution could be held up for twenty-four hours. La Follette objected, and to the fury of the majority and hoots from the galleries the Senate adjourned.

Next day, on April 4, from ten in the morning until almost midnight the senators debated the war resolution. In the hothouse fervor of patriotism that followed the President's speech, each senator was given the opportunity to bay for war, wave the flag and display a vicarious spirit of sacrifice for the benefit of the *Congressional Record* and his constituents back home. Before the resolution was voted on, 17 senators spoke in favor of it, among them Harding. But this time Harding was more circumspect, more restrained than the others. He who had orated so fully at Fourth-of-July celebrations and on Decoration Days, who had made the eagle scream at county fairs and GAR reunions, could never have stood aside when his country—as he phrased it—unsheathed the sword. No one could have imagined him, nor could he have imagined himself, folding his arms with the willful minority of faded Populists and Progressive left-overs. Every impulse of conforming patriotism, reinforced by his deeper levels of self-doubt, urged him on to the Gadarene rush of chauvinism. But anxiety and affection held him back. When he spoke he was speaking not only to the Senate but to a wide-windowed house on Gospel Hill in Marion. Vote for war he must; perhaps, hopefully, Carrie would understand if he explained.

> It is my deliberate judgment that it is none of our business what type of government any nation on this earth may choose to have [he told his colleagues]; and one cannot be entirely just unless he makes the admission in this trying hour that the German people evidently are pretty well satisfied with their government, because I could not ask a better thing for this popular government of the United States of America than the same loyal devotion on the part of every American that the German gives to his government.

Being Harding, he could scarcely on such an occasion have avoided bringing in Julius Caesar and Napoleon, or ending in a rhetorical Catherine wheel, though even his pyrotechnic conclusion contained a warning assurance for Carrie:

> World domination is not of man. That is of God, the Creator. It has become the fortune of this Republic to cry "Halt!" to a maddened power casting aside the obligations of civilization and the limitations of that which we look upon as highest humanity. I know that the task will be undertaken by the American people not originally committed to the cause of war, but a people who will understand that when the Congress speaks

after due deliberation, after the patience which this body and this government have exercised, the voice of the United States Congress is the voice of the nation, and one hundred millions of people will commit themselves to the great cause of the maintenance of just American rights—a thing for which the nation can well afford to fight, and while fighting for it put a new soul into a race of American people who can enthusiastically call themselves truly and spiritually and abidingly an American.

Only five senators spoke against the resolution: La Follette, Nebraska's die-hard Progressive, George Norris; the radical farm leader Asle Gronna of North Dakota; William J. Stone, the chairman of the Committee on Foreign Relations; and James Kimble Vardaman, the old rabble-rousing Populist and Negro-baiter from Mississippi. Vardaman in string tie and with hair almost to his shoulders seemed a revenant from Calhoun's day, but this time he eschewed his usual oratory, merely stating in a few sentences that "plain, honest people" had no interest in this foreign war. Stone, the Democratic leader, destroyed himself politically when he told the Senate that he would gladly lay down his life "to prevent this mistake." Gronna read the petitions and telegrams he had received protesting against war, and Norris spoke with great bitterness of putting "the dollar sign on the American flag."

When La Follette began to speak at four in the afternoon, the galleries filled, and the air of the chamber was tense and silent. He spoke for three hours, scoring Wilson for false neutrality and challenging him to submit the war resolution to the vote of the people. In La Follette's opinion the war was a commercial struggle between two great rivals, and he found no moral difference between them, between English sea mines and German torpedoes. He closed by recalling "the poor . . . the ones called upon to rot in the trenches," who had no press to voice their opinions but who would in the end be heard for peace.

Not until an hour before midnight did the war resolution finally come to a vote, with only 6 votes against it to 82 in favor. When the clerk called La Follette's name, his "No!" vibrated through the hushed chamber. As he strode out of the room following the vote his colleagues avoided him, and he stalked to his office through corridors filled with snarling faces.

The next morning debate began in the House of Representatives and ran through until 3:12 A.M. the following morning when the congressmen voted 373 to 50 for war. Jeannette Rankin, a social worker from Montana and the first woman to be elected to Congress, voted No, explaining in a breaking voice that she wanted to stand by her country but she could not vote for war.[3]

[3] Curiously enough Miss Rankin, who then quit politics for a generation and was elected to a second term only in 1940, was the sole member of the Congress to vote against war after the Japanese attack on Pearl Harbor. Following her 1941 vote, she hid in a telephone booth in the Capitol to avoid reporters.

On April 10, restively smelling the battle afar off, Roosevelt pocketed his pride and came to the White House to plead for his division with the man he had described as a "trained elocutionist," a "logothete," a "pacifist," "neither a gentleman nor a real man." Now he begged Wilson to put aside their old hostilities "as dust on a windy street." Wilson was graciously noncommittal, and the Rough Rider came away from his interview convinced that his division was a certainty. Pausing on the White House steps, he explained to a group of reporters that, while he supported Wilson's demand for universal military service, he planned to raise his division for front-line combat from men over the proposed twenty-five-year age limit or from those otherwise exempt from the coming draft. Wilson, however, had no intention of giving his impetuous rival any command whatsoever. He felt and said that this was a scientific and professional war with no room for flamboyant amateurs. Roosevelt's Rough Rider charge up San Juan Hill in Cuba in 1898 was a romantic and overpublicized gesture. To give Roosevelt a division would, in Wilson's opinion, have been like indulging a spoiled child. Also, Wilson, when crossed, was vindictive— and Roosevelt had crossed him many times. What Wilson would not see was the magic of the Roosevelt name as a rallying point for his own crusade "to keep the world safe for democracy."

Over a month before Wilson's War Declaration, when he reluctantly concluded that war was inevitable, he instructed Secretary Baker to prepare a plan for conscription that would be as acceptable as possible to the public. Wilson knew well enough that the only fair, the only possible way to enlist the millions of men needed for the Army was to draft them. But most Americans still clung to the vague consoling notion of free men springing to arms—in the tradition of the Minute Men and the Rough Riders. And there were still the old and bitter memories of the draft riots during the Civil War. An army of sullen conscripts seemed un-American. Since there would be far more opposition to a conscription bill in Congress than there had been to the declaration of war, Wilson and his war secretary planned deftly "to create a strong patriotic feeling and relieve the foreboding which remains to some extent in the popular mind against the draft."

When the draft bill was at last being debated in the Senate, Harding on April 23 introduced an amendment that would allow the President to raise not more than three divisions of volunteer units. Although Roosevelt was not mentioned by name, everyone understood that the amendment was his amendment and that the divisions would be his divisions. Roosevelt had already written to Harding early in March thanking him for recent friendly references and adding that "what you say is exactly true! We have invited war by our feeble, timid, shuffling course!" Having moved cozily close to Roosevelt, Harding with his unoffending regularity was recognized by the Republican senators as the most suitable go-between to bridge the narrowed gap between the Rough Rider and the Old Guard and unite the two wings of the party in a common emotion. The bill with his Roosevelt amendment attached passed the Senate, opposed by only eight recalcitrants led by La Follette. Senator Lodge wrote to his old and long-since reconciled friend at Oyster Bay that the result was "a very great pleasure to me and the deepest sort of personal satisfaction." No action of Harding's could have moved the impatient Rough Rider more than the sponsorship of the Roosevelt amendment. When on the following day the House passed the draft bill 397 to 24, but at the instigation of Wilson and Baker struck out Harding's amendment, Roosevelt wired him from Oyster Bay:

> I deeply appreciate your patriotic work. As both Houses have passed the obligatory service bill there is now no shadow of excuse for rejecting your amendment and those who vote against it will record themselves as being hostile to the immediate and efficient use of the men in America peculiarly fit to be used as General Joffre has asked. Will you not show this letter to Lodge, Johnson, Kellogg, and our other friends and get them to exercise their influence in the House? Opposition is of course merely political. This ought not to be made merely a political war.

On April 28, when the truncated draft bill was returned to the Senate, Harding was ready with a renewed Roosevelt amendment, this time to permit the raising of four divisions of volunteers for service abroad. "An immediate force of American volunteers," Harding told the senators, "would put new life in every Allied trench and a new glow in every Allied campfire on every battlefront in Europe."

Meanwhile Roosevelt, convinced that the President, whether he liked it or not, would be forced by public opinion to approve of the Roosevelt division, had opened recruiting headquarters in New York. By May 7 he was receiving over two thousand applications a day, headed by sons and grandsons of such history-encrusted names as Phil Sheridan, Fitzhugh Lee, Stonewall Jackson, Simon Bolivar Buckner, and Nathan Bedford Forrest.

Roosevelt followed his telegram with an expansive note to which Harding replied on May 7:

> I beg to acknowledge your appreciative note of May 3rd. On the very day of its receipt, I had a personal call from both your daughter and your son, and the latter very cordially expressed your sincere appreciation of my part in seeking to make provision for your armed expedition to Europe. . . .
>
> I am sure that you can accomplish more than any other American could ever hope to undertake, and that you would give most gratifying proof that American sentiment is heartily in favor of vigorous action which is in full accord with our utterances of American ideals. . . .

On May 13 the House reversed itself and passed the draft bill, conscripting all men between twenty-one and thirty, with Harding's Roosevelt Amendment attached. Four days later the Senate gave its final approving vote and the bill was sent to the President for his signature. Wilson signed, but announced as he did so that in spite of the authorizing amendment he did not plan to create any such amateur divisions.

It would be very agreeable to me [he wrote], to pay Mr. Roosevelt this compliment, and the Allies the compliment of sending to their aid one of our most distinguished public men, an ex-President who has rendered many conspicuous public services and proved his gallantry in many striking ways. Politically, too, it would no doubt have a very fine effect and make a profound impression. But this is not the time nor the occasion for compliments or for any action not calculated to contribute to the immediate success of the war. The business now in hand is undramatic, practical, and of scientific definiteness and precision.

Privately Wilson remarked that same day at luncheon that the United States was wholly ignorant of modern war and that it would be dangerous to send over someone like Roosevelt who would no doubt try to show Europe how to manage its own affairs. On the passage of the draft bill Roosevelt had wired Wilson requesting immediate permission to raise two divisions. Wilson refused, replying that his decision was based on "imperative considerations of public policy, not open personal or private choice."

Even Georges Clemenceau's appeal from France to allow Roosevelt "the right to appear on the battlefield surrounded by his comrades" failed to move the President.[4]

On May 25 Roosevelt disbanded his paper divisions, issuing a bitter address to the 200,000 men who had volunteered to serve under him. Privately—and not so very privately at that—he referred to Wilson as "that skunk in the White House," and on May 28 burst out to William Allen White that the President was "an utterly selfish, utterly treacherous, utterly insincere hypocrite."

On May 8, in the midst of his struggle in the Congress for the Roosevelt Amendment, Harding received a letter from Nan Britton. Obviously bear-

---

[4] Wilson's flinty rationality failed to grasp how valuable the patriotic impact of the Rough Rider commander would be in reconciling the opposition. When the more astute Franklin Roosevelt set out to rearm a reluctant country in the summer of 1940, one of his first gestures toward the Republicans was to recall Colonel Theodore Roosevelt, Jr., to command his old World War I regiment, the 26th Infantry of the First Division. Colonel Roosevelt was later promoted to brigadier general and commanded the division until the early setback in North Africa made it clear that a war of professional command had no place for zealous amateurs.

ing in mind that the letter would be read by secretaries, she had written it with feigned impersonality:

> I wonder if you will remember me; my father was Dr. Britton, of Marion, Ohio.
>
> I have been away from Marion for about two years, and, up until last November, have been working. But it was work which promised no future. . . .
>
> I have been reading of the imperative demand for stenographers and typists throughout the country, and the apparent scarcity, and it has occurred to me that you are in a position to help me along this line if there is an opening. . . .
>
> Any suggestions or help you might give me would be greatly appreciated, I assure you, and it would please me so to hear from you.

Nan had written from New York where, as she told Harding, she was attending secretarial school. Chicago had not suited her. A life of selling china and glassware was not what she had daydreamed for herself in Marion, and she had written to two of her father's Kenyon classmates asking if they would advance her enough money to go to business school in New York. In such matters Nan would always remain the perpetual schoolgirl, breathless in her belief that it was the obligation of men to look after her. From her fixed adolescent point of view it seemed only natural that her father's classmates should become ersatz fathers, ready to finance a young girl like herself in her schemes. Not that she was avaricious or mercenary in the later golddigger sense. Merely she felt she needed, would always need, a sugar daddy to supply her with attention and money. That was what men were for. Her first polite dun was characteristic of her. From then on she would always be turning to men for money, with buoyant ingenuousness taking for granted that she would be given what she asked for. Usually she was. Neither qualms nor any sense of obligation ever troubled her.

Her father's classmates sent her to New York. There she lived with the family of one of them, whom she called in her book Grover Carter, in a small town house on Sutton Place near the Queensboro Bridge while she attended the Ballard Secretarial School at the YWCA. Halfway through her course she even managed to earn some extra money by part-time typing for Paderewski's publicity manager. Three weeks before graduating from Ballard she did what she had long planned, and wrote her letter to the "Hon. Warren G. Harding, United States Senate." The letter was of a common enough type in any politician's mail, but in this ordinary and innocuous request for employment Harding's male instinct grasped at once the key phrase "it would please me so." In the midst of the draft bill debates he scribbled her a note from his Senate desk.

Within three days Nan, sitting on the window sill of her third-floor bedroom in the shadow of the great bridge, was reading his reply. Yes, he remembered her . . . "you may be sure of that, and I remember you most agreeably, too." Although he had no position in his office, he would do all he could to help her and he would be willing to "go personally to the War and Navy Department to urge your appointment." Ten years later, when Nan wrote *The President's Daughter,* the 439-page book about her relations with Harding, she recalled that spring afternoon, the sparrows chirping, the voices of the children playing in the streets heard like an echo as she read and reread his last paragraph. There was "every probability," he wrote, that he would be in New York the following week. If he could reach her by telephone or "becomingly" look her up, he would do so, and "take pleasure in doing it." "You see, I do remember you," he concluded. She replied in hot haste:

> It was good to know that you remembered me; and I appreciated your kind interest and prompt response. . . .
> I am hoping that you will be in New York next week and that I can talk with you; I am inclined to believe that an hour's talk would be much more satisfactory. There is so much I want to tell you; and I am sure that I could give you a better idea of my ability—or rather the extent of my ability, for it is limited—and you could judge for yourself as to the sort of position I could competently fill. . . . In case you are able to see me for an hour it would please me immensely to make an appointment—provided it does not interfere with your plans.

Four days later his answer came, a longer letter handwritten on Senate Chamber stationery. He said he might have to break down civil-service barriers to secure a place for her, then continued archly, "I like your spirit and determination. It is like I have always imagined you to be." He added that he would be in New York within the next ten days and that it would be a pleasure to look her up. "Always know . . . of my very genuine personal interest in your good fortune," he concluded.

Early the next morning, before she could reply to his second letter, he telephoned from the Manhattan that he had arrived in New York and asked her to meet him as soon as possible at the hotel. She hurried over, trembling with excitement. He was standing on the steps waiting for her and smiling, just as she had remembered and imagined him. Arm in arm they went inside to the reception room and sitting together on the settee they talked, intimately and exactly, of the old days in Marion. At last she was able to tell him freely of her schoolgirl feelings for him. He suggested that they go up to his room so that they could continue to talk without anyone's interrupting them. Because of some convention, he explained, the only room he had been able to secure was the bridal suite.

"We had scarcely closed the door behind us when we shared our first kiss," she wrote in her palpitant high-school prose, the rosy moment undimmed after a decade. "The bed, which we did not disturb, stood upon a dais, and the furnishings were in keeping with the general refinement of atmosphere. I shall never, never forget how Mr. Harding kept saying, after each kiss, 'God! . . . God, Nan!' in high diminuendo, nor how he pleaded in a tense voice, 'Oh, dearie, tell me it isn't hateful to you to have me kiss you!' And as I kissed him back I thought that he surpassed even my gladdest dreams of him."

Holding her in his arms, Harding admitted now that he had come from Washington solely to see her. He needed a woman. And after the battering Carrie had given him he needed uncritical consolation. For him this almost-schoolgirl had the dimpled charm of her youth, the charm of novelty that he had never been able to resist, and an uncalculating affection so relievingly different from Carrie's contemptuous vagaries. Nan claimed she was still a virgin, but the "lovely mystery," as she phrased it, she was not yet ready to explore in spite of his urgings. Becoming practical, he asked her to let him find her a job in New York rather than come on to Washington. They had lunch at the Manhattan, then went to the offices of the United States Steel Corporation where he said he could find a place for her. En route in a taxi he asked her suddenly how fast she could take dictation and suggested he try her out on a letter. "My darling Nan," he began, putting his arm around her, "I love you more than the world and I want you to belong to me. Could you belong to me, dearie? I want you . . . and I need you so . . ."

"I remember," she wrote, "the letter did not run into length because I silenced him with the kisses he pleaded for. He would tremble so just to sit close to me, and I adored every evidence of his enthusiasm."

At United States Steel offices he introduced her to Judge Gary, the head of the corporation, and arranged for her to take a position after she had returned from a visit to her sister in Chicago. Then he took her back to the Manhattan, the taxi pulling up somewhat far from the curb at the Forty-third Street entrance. As he got out, he tripped and fell. His face reddened for a moment, then he recovered himself and whispered to her ardently: "You see, dearie, I'm so crazy about you I don't know where I'm stepping."

Back in the bridal suite, she cuddled into his lap in the big armchair, he fondling her and telling her: "We were made for each other . . . I'd like to make *you* my bride, Nan darling." Yet, on that first glowing day she insisted there were "no intimacies in that bridal chamber beyond our very ardent kisses." Before they parted "Mr. Harding, having been acquainted with my plans for going to Chicago . . . tucked $30 in my brand-new silk stocking and was 'sorry he had no more that time to give me.' "

He came to New York once more to see her before she left for Chicago, but not until she was staying there with her sister Elizabeth did she receive her first real love letter from him—a rambling letter of forty in-coherent pages, scribbled on scratch-pad paper and enclosing a snapshot of him standing on the Capitol steps. Thrilled though she was, she was practical enough in her loving reply to make her first incidental request for money. He sent her $42, an odd amount, as he explained, that might appear as payment for some possible work.

Within a week she received another letter asking her to meet him at Indianapolis where he had been asked to speak. He was at the station when she arrived, and as she walked through the iron gate she took his hand and noticed that he was trembling. In the taxi on the way to the Claypool Hotel they continued to hold hands. He registered her under the name of Harding, as his niece. Although they had separate rooms, they spent most of the night together. The next night Harding was to speak near Connersville, a small town fifty miles to the east. There they stayed at the McFarlan Hotel, Harding suggesting that it would be "a good joke" for Nan to use his secretary's name. She registered as Elizabeth N. Christian. Yet for all their close contact and Harding's urgings, she still coyly withheld what she referred to as "love's sweetest intimacy."

While they rode in the taxi from the McFarlan to the Connersville station to catch the midnight train for Chicago, he kept whispering to her over and over, "Dearie, 'r y' going t' sleep with me? Look at me, Nan: goin' to sleep with me, dearie?" He had reserved a section in the train, and they spent the night in each other's arms. She let him touch her exploringly, but no more. The next morning, just before they arrived at the Englewood Station, she remarked that he looked a bit tired. "God, sweetheart!" he bleated at her, "what do you expect? I'm a man, you know." In a Chicago hotel he registered her for the first time as his wife. The sardonic desk clerk remarked under his breath that if Harding could prove he was really married to the young lady, he could have the room for nothing!

Nan returned to New York from their "kissing tour" still technically virginal. Not until the end of July did she and Harding reach their "climactic intimacy." He had arrived suddenly from Washington one sultry afternoon and had taken her to the Imperial, a second-rate hotel on Lower Broadway that had been recommended by friends of his for such "unconventional circumstances." Nan, looking more girlish than usual, was wearing a pink linen dress. Harding registered as Hardwick. They did not speak going up in the elevator. Their room was a long one with two large windows which the bellhop opened before leaving them alone. Below they could hear the muted noises of Broadway. "I became Mr. Harding's bride—as he called me," Nan wrote, "on that day."

As they lay in bed together in the slack aftermath the telephone rang. Harding answered it roughly, saying, "You've got the wrong party." But almost as he said it there was a sharp rap, the door was unlocked from the outside, and two men—apparently detectives—stalked in on the cowering pair. The first man to enter demanded Nan's name and address, and when she turned to Harding, he—his nerve gone—told her: "Tell them the truth. They've got us." The second man wrote down what she said in his notebook. Harding sat disconsolately on the edge of the bed, his naked feet dangling just above the floor while in a flat, ingratiating voice he tried to explain that they had disturbed no one, and he begged them to let Nan go. But to all his pleadings the man with the notebook replied, "You'll have to tell that to the judge," and he intimated that a patrol wagon was on the way. Then the second man picked up Harding's hat and noticed the name, W. G. Harding, stamped in gilt on the sweatband. On seeing the senatorial name, the two "detectives" dropped their bluster, becoming "not only calm but strangely respectful, withdrawing very soon." Harding and Nan—all passion spent—dressed and packed, and the now obsequious detectives took them out by way of a side entrance where Harding gave one of them a twenty-dollar bill. "Gee, Nan," he told her afterward with explosive relief as they settled down in the safety of a taxi, "I thought I wouldn't get out of that for under a thousand dollars."

On July 1 Nan began work as a stenographer in the Safety, Sanitation and Welfare Bureau of the United States Steel Corporation. At least once a week Harding would come on from Washington to spend the night with her. She used to meet him at the Pennsylvania Station as he arrived on the Congressional Limited, handbag in hand. Although they registered as man and wife at various nondescript hotels, there were no more badger-game incidents. He liked to take her to musical comedies like Fred Stone's *Jack o' Lantern* or to the Winter Garden to see Al Jolson in *Sinbad the Sailor*. Over their dinners in discreet shaded places like the Churchill they would moon at each other in anticipation. "I used to love those dinners with Mr. Harding," Nan wrote.

> They were so sweetly intimate and it was a joy just to sit and look at him. The way he used his hands, the adorable way he used to put choice bits of meat from his own plate onto mine, the way he would say with a sort of tense nervousness, "That's a very becoming hat, Nan," or "God, Nan, you're pretty!" used to go to my head like wine and make food seem for the moment the least needful thing in the world.

From Washington he sent her money regularly and five-pound boxes of her favorite Martha Washington candy, and on her twenty-first birthday a gold wrist watch. Back in the Senate Chamber during the tedium of debates he often wrote her thirty and forty and sixty-page letters, scribbling them in pencil on a memo pad, pages such as he had written to Carrie, with the same mixture of banal tenderness and crude flesh longing. Every Sunday morning a special-delivery letter arrived from him. Nan replied in ardent kind. Harding liked to say that "nowhere except in French had he ever read anything comparable to the love letters we used to write one another."

On a Memorial Day address in Columbus Harding complained of the government's drum-beating, tub-thumping campaign to sell Liberty Bonds as "hysterical and unseemly," although he added with quick caution that he did not wish to hinder the campaign itself. Again he was speaking beyond the crowd to a certain house in Marion: "I might say in passing that it is none of our business what form of government any nation has so long as it respects international law."

Carrie did not carry out her threat to expose him after his vote for the war resolution but her anger flared up, and [- -] Like a juggler, he managed to keep her and Nan separate in a common orbit. Though Nan was pliable and satisfying, the enigmatic Carrie still bound him fast. Before the war ended she, the pro-German, would cause him much trouble. The hysteria of wartime America embarking on its crusade to keep the world safe for democracy did not touch her. Sousa might replace Wagner, state legislatures might pass laws forbidding the teaching of German, boys might stone dachshunds on the streets, sauerkraut might be renamed liberty cabbage; she viewed the star-spangled scene with contempt. In spite of the slogans and the parades and the ever-recurring poignancy of young men in uniform marching away, her heart still remained in the imperial city of William II that would never again be imperial as she had known it. Wilson had asked that the usual summer Chautauqua program be continued as an aid to popular morale. With this as an excuse, Harding, restless in the tension of Washington and eager as always to travel, left his place in the Senate for another tour in August. Back in a seedy hotel room after his Hamilton lecture in some rural Ohio county seat he would write his pages to Carrie [- -]

Harding's Memorial Day remarks on the "hysterical and unseemly" Liberty Bond campaign and his hint of "certain things that had been stated in executive session that would startle the American people" that he could not divulge, brought a stinging rejoinder from the sharp-tongued Sen. James A. Reed.[5] Reed declared that Harding's innuendo was much more damaging than any hidden fact could be, and bluntly invited his colleague to put up or shut up. Harding after his early *Star* years was

[5] Reed's tongue could be grossly sharp. At about this time he was accusing Herbert Hoover of grafting as the head of the Commission for Relief in Belgium.

never one to respond to direct attack, and he did his best to divert the issue, declaring that he was no knocker, that his remarks had been no more than sallies of partisanship, and that in fact it was time to halt such "unseemly talk." Reed asked if he meant by such sallies that Americans loved their freedom less than the Germans did their chains. Then with a backlash of sarcasm he accused Harding of slandering the great country of America over which "the Senator was ambitious to preside as Chief Executive." It was at the time a comic accusation, stirring the senators to chuckles. Harding protested that he had no such ambition. "I should like it said," he added, "since this question has been raised, that I think too well of my country to wish one of such incapacity in so exalted a position." Reed had the last biting word. "Mr. President," he declaimed, to the laughter of the chamber, "the humility of the Senator doth most become him."

At the beginning of the new session Harding, with increased seniority, had been assigned to the Naval Affairs Committee, the Committee on the Philippines, and the Committee on Standards, Weights and Measures. But whether it was a question of battleships or avoirdupois, his committee attendance was scanty and he never took his assignments too seriously. It was neither in his temperament nor his intellect to make himself an expert in any field, as Burton had done while serving on the Rivers and Harbors Committee. His interest in the mechanics of government, either in committee or as he sat at his Senate desk during debate penning letters to Carrie or Nan, was as slight as his part in winning the war. Yet off the Senate floor, with his now well-recognized smile, he was always ready to help any senator of either party. When Herbert Hoover returned from his famine relief work in Europe to take over as Wilson's food administrator, Harding appeared at the Food Administration office to offer his help, asking no patronage of Hoover in return. The gesture was typical of the man. It flattered Harding's inner uncertainty to be of service in small ways to others. Cordell Hull found him "one of the most charming persons in a social way one would ordinarily meet."

In the first sloganeering war months Harding, too, was willing to "stand by the President." "I will vote for food and fuel control," he wrote Jennings in July, "will thank God if industrial paralysis does not follow and will also ask him to forgive me my official sins." Characteristically he was willing to go even further and give Wilson complete responsibility for events. Just before he left for his Chautauqua tour in August he was interviewed by Richard Barry of *The New York Times*. Flattered by being singled out for a feature article by the country's foremost paper, Harding said for once what he really thought, without any qualifying obfuscations. What the country needed, he told Barry, was a supreme dictator, and by the logic of events it would be sure to have one before the war went much

further. Alexander Hamilton "in his matchless vision" had seen the necessity of such a crisis dictator and had influenced the drafting of the Constitution accordingly. As for Wilson, Harding concluded

> I must say that he is not my choice but the people of the country have
> chosen him. . . . Why quibble with events which are already accomplished?
> Mr. Wilson is our President, duly elected. He is already by the inevitable
> force of events our partial dictator. Why not make him complete and
> supreme dictator? He will have to answer to the people and to history
> eventually for his stewardship. Why not give him a full and free hand, not
> for his sake, but for our sake?

Harding's blind and restless urge to move about never left him. He
returned from Chautauqua in September; then, as soon as the Senate
session ended on October 6, he left for New Hampshire's White Mountains
to fish and chop wood and tell stories with a congenial Senate group in a
lodge belonging to Massachusetts Senator John W. Weeks. On the way to
New Hampshire he stopped off at the Belmont in New York and spent the
night with Nan. Usually he managed to slip away from Washington to
see her once a week. To make things more discreetly easy for him she had
left the Carters and was now living in a room on West 136th Street. He
came to her ardently; she believed that "his pangs seemed virginal in their
intensity and surpassed any longing he had ever experienced in his life."

No sooner was Harding back from New Hampshire than he was off for
a visit with the Scobeys in Texas. The Duchess had all but recovered from
her crisis of the spring, and he took her with him. Scobey, his bushy eyebrows turning gray above his double chin, met them at San Antonio. From
San Antonio they went on to the fishing village of Point Isabel near the
mouth of the Rio Grande where they were entertained by Scobey's friend
R. B. "Gus" Creager in his summer cottage on the water. "The best pal I
have in the South," Scobey wrote of Creager who was soon to become
Harding's "pal." The red-haired Creager—an oil and land speculator
known as the Red Fox of the Rio Grande Valley—had once been Texas's
Republican candidate for governor, and was one of the most influential
Republicans in the state. Harding had met him first through Scobey at the
1916 convention. As much the life of the party as Scobey, enjoying with
the same gusto fishing, driving, poker, and "parlor stories," he had taken
an instant liking to Harding. These were the easy shirt-sleeved people
Harding felt most at home with, and he stayed on in Texas almost to the
opening of the Senate session on December 3.

So relaxing was the Texas weather in that bluff, congenial circle that
Harding wrote neither to Nan nor Carrie. Nan finally sent him a prudently
worded telegram and to avoid more from her he replied in prudent kind.
Just before Christmas he sent each woman a five-pound box of Martha

Washington chocolates. On December 19 he made one of his rare appearances on the floor of the Senate to offer a resolution for inquiring into the Shipping Board in which he deplored the delays in the government's shipbuilding program and wanted to know why more ships were not being built. Ten days later he came out for Wilson's take-over of the railroads while repeating his earlier objections to state and Federal regulation. "The big thing is to win the war," he told his colleagues, "and since this is the decision of the Chief Executive, charged with main responsibilities, it must be the accepted one."

In spite of the monitory Espionage Act of June, 1917, Carrie continued to flaunt her German sympathies. Anti-German feeling had reached the point where La Follette was being burned in effigy in Wisconsin, and Harding was hard put to it to protect her. Already, as he knew, she was being shadowed by Secret Service agents. He tried to warn her but she answered him furiously, and her anger, as always, brought him helplessly back to her. On New Year's Day, 1918, he wrote her at impulsive length, [--] She replied with scorn, belittling his hang-dog passion. He answered [--

----

------------------]

The German spring offensive and the first American casualties added alarm to American hate, and a spy scare swept the United States, receiving its statutory recognition in the Sedition Act of May 6, 1918. In his public speeches Harding was denouncing the "miserable spies among us" and indicating that their place should be "against the wall." He told the National Security League of New York in April that "if America did not do its full part to end the German peril once for all, then it was not fit to live." [--

------------------] she not only continued to prefer the Imperial red, white, and black colors to red, white, and blue but belittled the Third Liberty Loan and entertained German-Swiss visitors in her home. Early in the year, when Harding had invited her and the guileless Jim and the "admirable and adorable" Isabelle for a Washington visit to talk over the situation, she had refused. After she had again replied to him with defiant pro-German sentiments, he wrote desperately to Jim on April 22:

Several days ago I wrote to Carrie along the lines you suggested, relating to the bond campaign, and got a reply which in substance said you ran your own affairs. I rather felt my appeal very futile.

I wrote her again yesterday, very seriously and earnestly, warning her of impending dangers. She is under the eye of government agents and it is highly urgent that she exercise great prudence and caution. I know, of course, that she is not deserving of surveillance, but feeling grows intenser, and prejudices are more pronounced as the casualty list grows, and I could beg of her to be prudent and above the impassioned prejudice of passing days.

I don't mean to add to your worries, but it is too serious to remain silent. She may tell you of the letter. Hope she shows it to you. Then you can add your bit. I can't appeal very effectively, though I have earnestly tried. I wonder if you could command her. Frankly I doubt it.

Perhaps you can appeal. It takes more than tact. But it is really serious. It is too bad, but she is under suspicion—all because of imprudent speech. She forgets we are in war—hellish war—and she forgets how Germany treats those who are against the government.

It is time to *think*. If she is loyal and prudent, the cloud may pass. She must be. If she isn't, there is certain humiliation and distress and annoyance and embarrassment in store. I dislike to write this, but I feel I must.

On May 1 Harding had received Jim's reply and was again writing:

I was glad to have your letter. . . . I know most of the stuff said about Carrie is all rot. . . . I know she is no German informer—couldn't be. Yet these things have been reported.

I never have doubted her ability to square herself with a reasoning government agent, but I haven't wished her to undergo the annoyance of such a visit.

The greater peril is some unheeding, impassioned, self-appointed sponsors of justice and patriotism, who might humiliate or harm her. It is a pity that there can be such danger, but War is Hell, and Sanity does not always prevail. Hence the need of extreme prudence, caution, wisdom, and tact.

She and Isabelle ought not to come to Washington NOW. Nor ought they to go to New York. I had some inquiry made about things said, and the Washington trip last year led to suspicion about acting as an informer (ridiculous, of course) and the suspicion was confirmed by the long stay at the naval base at Port Jefferson. Any call I made, any call they made, would be watched.

This War Problem has distressed me infinitely more than you guess. I believe I know Carrie is loyal and helpful. But Passions and prejudices are not at my command.

I am delighted that she is working as she is. Of course, she excels—she always does. Hope it is kept up. The "hostess" appointment would be fine, and she would do that well. I think it is under Red Cross auspices. Go to Judge Mouser. It ought not originate with me. It would be impolitic for me to ask him. But I feel sure he can suggest the way—then let me know and I will help at Ohio headquarters or at national headquarters.

After these warnings and the shock of being interrogated by Secret Service agents, Carrie said less about Germany and spent more of her time in Red Cross work. It made things patriotically easier for the Phillipses when Isabelle became engaged to a soldier, William H. Matheé, Jr. Matheé had been born in Aachen where his father had been acting United States consul, and the fact that he knew Germany and spoke German made him welcome to the homesick Carrie. As a private in the Army Air Service Matheé was stationed with the 47th Flight Training Squadron at Randolph Field, Texas, too far for any immediate marriage plans.

Harding's family, encouraged by his rise in the world, continued to rely on him. Heber Votaw of the flashing smile and unctuous voice had not found a teaching career at the Adventist Missionary College to his taste —or possibly to the college's. December, 1917, found him writing to Harding that a pension of $12 a week was not enough to live on, and asking his brother-in-law to help him find some new job. "When one has been fourteen years in one line of work," he wrote, "it takes a little time to become adjusted to the thought of doing something entirely different. . . . I had a brief experience as a traveling salesman before taking up the ministry and had reasonable success."

In May, 1918, Heber was helping Deac—recovered from his heart attack—to get his new sanitorium, the Hartman Farm Home, established in Columbus. Deac—never a man for extravagances—paid him $60 a month and his keep. After three weeks Heber was again writing Harding complaining about his back and nerves and other ailments "that cannot be diagnosed" and asking for a job in government service. Harding promised him one and meanwhile offered to build him up at Battle Creek, but Heber preferred to relax his nerves by drinking the water at nearby Magnetic Springs. While he was away Carolyn took a civil-service examination for state charity work.

Harding, solicitous and true as always to any promise to his relatives, arranged to bring Votaw to Washington as one of his senatorial assistants. For Carolyn he wangled an appointment on the women's bureau of the Washington District Police Department as a police officer, second class, at a salary of $1,650 a year. Tryon was of course by this time his permanent pensioner.

Early in 1918 the Duchess had joined a war sewing circle made up of senators' wives who met in a suite of rooms in the Senate Office Building.

With her improving health, her mindless energy returned. The release she had earlier found in bossing the newsboys at the *Star* she found again in stitching clothes for war orphans. She who had never touched a sewing machine in her life now spent six or seven hours a day, several days a week, busily sewing and chattering.

The second session of the wartime Sixty-fifth Congress ran for almost a year, from December 3, 1917, to November 21, 1918. Harding, always more conspicuous for his senatorial appearance and easy manner than for anything he ever did or said on the Senate floor, had the effect on legislature of a comma or a semicolon. Silently he voted for the Espionage Bill, for food control, and for the war revenue bill although he opposed the 65 to 75 per cent tax on war profits since "if you strike at excess profit you reduce incomes and are likely to hinder our industrial development." Claiming that he was a temperance man rather than a prohibitionist, he called the Prohibition Amendment "unwise, imprudent, and inconsiderate" but nevertheless voted for it—as he explained—so that this agitating question could be resolved by submitting it to ratification by the states. He, on behalf of the drys, was the easy-mannered go-between to persuade the wets to accept the amendment with a six—later seven—years' time limit for ratification in return for a year's grace for the liquor trade to wind up its affairs. Privately he hoped, with the wets, that after half-a-dozen years a third of the states would still be holding out. The Women's Suffrage Amendment he was still giving his "very earnest and thoughtful consideration." But as an old newspaperman he opposed government control of newsprint as "socialistic" and expressed fear that under such a measure our republic would be "heading straight for State Socialism and control by the 'Bolsheviki.'" He considered that he had fulfilled his duty as a member of the Commerce Committee by inspecting with four other senators the new shipbuilding facilities—now the largest in the world—at Hog Island in the middle of the Delaware River.

Nine months after Harding's *New York Times* summons for a wartime dictator, Senator Overman of North Carolina introduced a measure to give the President such unlimited power to organize and direct the country's resources that the Democratic majority leader Sen. Thomas S. Martin of Virginia refused to introduce it. Harding now viewed the authoritative Overman Bill through more partisan spectacles. "I am not willing," he told the Senate, "that Congress surrender the functions so as to create a smoke screen for the President for retreat from our established form of government to dictatorship."

Most of the time he attended Senate sessions he was silent. "I do relatively little talking in Congress myself," he wrote to Bob Wolfe in Columbus. Many of his ardently voluminous letters to Nan he composed during senatorial debates. Yet though he cut no debating figure, he was a Senate survivor of the 1916 débâcle, chairman of the State Advisory Committee, the leading figure in the Republican party of Ohio. The drys, prompted by the hog-calling Willis, might have their doubts, Hynicka and his Cincinnati wets might be sharpening their knives, nevertheless as the off-election of 1918 approached there was inevitable small talk in the state of Harding as a dark-horse presidential candidate in 1920. Ohio was a political superstition as well as a state. Every Republican President who had entered the White House by the votes of the people since the Civil War had come from Ohio or been born in Ohio. Yet, ever since the days of Vallandigham, Ohio had had a strong Democratic counterbalance. It could never be considered thick-and-thin Republican like Vermont. Ohio's 24 electoral votes could have elected Hughes, and a Republican native son could have garnered those votes. So, according to the political haruspices, an Ohio candidate in 1920 would be a logical choice, and Harding was the one Ohio party leader still intact in high office. This was clear enough to a semi-professional soothsayer like Scobey who, wetting his finger to the November winds, wrote him at the end of March:

> Now, take the present situation—you are going to keep your hands off on Willis. In the first place, I do not have to tell you anything about Willis. You know he is a fourflusher and double-dealer, and I know if he is nominated the chances are greatly in favor of his defeat. I think he is the weakest man Ohio can nominate. But should he win he will be against you, either for the Presidency or for the Senate. You know Willis will run for anything—he will be against you even for justice of the peace. So why let a man like him try for power? On the other hand, suppose he is defeated; and if he is nominated the chances are Governor Cox will be a candidate. If he is elected for the third time, with all the prestige he will have, he might make a formidable candidacy against you for the Presidency, or for the Senatorship. Heretofore you have always told me you did not want to be a candidate for the Presidency—but no man is too big for this job, if he can get it. You might have to fight for your real life to remain in the Senate if Cox should be elected for the third time. My notion is that as Senator from Ohio, holding the position you do in relation to your party, you ought to name the ticket. Go out and fight for it and win at the polls.

No visions of political plums danced in Harding's head as he replied a few days later.

> It is very comforting and satisfying to have a good many people think well of one for the big office but none of this has any strong appeal for me. I am inclined to think I should like to stay in the Senate but I am not letting the matter worry me to a sufficient degree to keep me awake nights.

To his closest friends, like Scobey and Jennings, Harding always insisted that even if some curious combination of political chances should make him a possible presidential candidate, the responsibilities of the Presidency were more than he ever wanted to consider. He told Nan the same thing. But another term, or possibly two, as senator began to seem less and less objectionable as his social milieu in Washington expanded. He had become a member of the Chevy Chase Club and was planning to join the Washington Country Club. Marion receded to a remote if sentimental reference point. He even considered selling the *Star*, offering it to a publishers' representative at what he considered the steep price of $140,000, and explaining to Jennings that since he was away so much of the time he would not mind being "free of the responsibility attending the ownership."

In spite of the enlarged Washington surroundings where Blooming Grove cast no shadow, he was still troubled by his health, physical and mental. He put on weight—he was over two hundred pounds now—and for all his golfing, his breath grew shorter. His heart trouble was real enough. "I had a serious spell of it covering a period of two or three years," he wrote Scobey. "As a matter of fact, I have never gotten wholly free of it." On May 5 he left to join one of his more recent senatorial cronies, the slab-faced, flag-waving Joseph S. Frelinghuysen of the dynastic New Jersey family, for a week of "fishing and loafing" at the Adirondack League Club in the Adirondacks "to do what I can to put my nerves on an even keel." He stopped over in New York and spent a routine night with Nan. Once a week he managed to see her, though sometimes for only a few hours, returning to Washington on the night train after arriving in the late afternoon. He supported her, by both their standards, generously enough. Though her demands were never very large, they were constant.

Beyond the borders of Ohio any mention of Harding in 1918 as a dark-horse presidential candidate in 1920 was the smallest of small talk. Theodore Roosevelt stood out as the unchallenged and unchallengeable leader of the Republican party. Taft was now far happier as a law professor at Yale than he had ever been as President; Hughes had turned his back on political life; Foraker was dead—the last of his generation. Senator Boies Penrose—incorruptible in his corruptibility as Republican boss of Pennsylvania—squatting like some vast toad in his apartment at the Wardman Park Hotel in Washington, told a group of House and Senate leaders attempting to read the 1920 Republican political horoscope: "There is but one candidate. He is the only candidate. I mean Theodore Roosevelt. . . . I don't like him. I once despised him. But that doesn't alter the fact that Theodore Roosevelt is now the one and only possible Republican candidate in 1920. He will surely receive the nomination."

In February Roosevelt had been in the hospital with an abscess in the thigh and abscesses in both ears, an aftermath of his jungle fevers. Taft sent him a telegram of sympathy. It was the beginning of a reconciliation between the two. When Roosevelt was out of the hospital he sent Taft an advance copy of one of his speeches and even accepted Taft's suggested alterations. Although now permanently deaf in one ear and troubled by other ailments, Roosevelt was reinvigorated by his hatred of Wilson. He even expressed the fancy of being shut up alone in the same room with the logothete President, both of them with boxing gloves on. His long ambition was to ride down Pennsylvania Avenue with the defeated Wilson on Inauguration Day, 1921. His short ambition was to elect a Republican Congress that November. In May Roosevelt made a Western tour to speak for the war effort, for unhyphenated Americanism, and the Third Liberty Loan. Passing through Chicago, he met Taft in the dining room of the Blackstone and the two men, after eight years, happily shook hands again. A month later Roosevelt was able to say that he and Taft were absolutely united in their views on present needs and their opposition to the Wilson administration.

On his Western trip Roosevelt put himself in touch with all Republican regular leaders and old Progressives, using as his contact man the Indiana lawyer-politician Will Hays who had just been elected chairman of the Republican National Committee. In spite of an inherited Hoosier Sunday-school superintendent manner, Hays was an astute and adaptable young man, a manager of applied politics rather than the saurian boss type of Cox or Penrose. When Roosevelt spoke briefly in Columbus on his way to Cleveland, Hays arranged a meeting with Daugherty to talk over the Republican situation in Ohio. Daugherty gave a dinner for Roosevelt at the Columbus Club, and following it the two men talked confidentially. Roosevelt made it quite clear that he was after the Presidency in 1920, and told Daugherty that he had Harding in mind as his vice president.

Roosevelt had continued to be overwhelmingly grateful to Harding for having sponsored the Roosevelt Amendment and seen it enacted into the law that Wilson had seen fit to disregard. So close to Roosevelt's heart was his namesake division and so stirring to his blood the thought of commanding troops in action on the Western Front, that anyone who sponsored his cause would have been seen forever after through the distorting lens of gratitude. But, beyond that, for Roosevelt to have the man who nominated Taft in 1912 as his running mate would be a solid and visible indication that the breach between the party's conservative and progressive wings had been finally healed. Vice President Harding would be the very symbol of harmony. In itself the Vice Presidency was considered a sterile honor, a cubbyhole for unwanted politicians. Wilson's Vice President Marshall was so obscure that most people were not sure he existed. Marshall was not always sure himself. Roosevelt, when planning for Harding as his vice president, had no thought of advancing him further.

Like all men of action, he never expected death to interfere with his plans. And so great was his hatred of Wilson that to defeat and humiliate him Roosevelt would have been willing to have Benedict Arnold on the ticket.

The Rough Rider still saw war for all its mechanized butchery as the Great Adventure. His four sons were in France, Ted a major in the 1st Division, Quentin an aviator, Kermit and Archie commissioned officers. He found a Spartan pride in the fact that Archie had already been wounded. But on July, 1918, the news came to him that his youngest, Quentin, had been shot down in an air battle over the Western Front. Although the old Rough Rider would have the iron fortitude to make a previously scheduled speech that very afternoon, although he would in the autumn months campaign with venom and vigor for a Republican Congress, nevertheless with his boy's death the fire of his ambition had been extinguished. The Presidency might be his for the reaching in 1920, but in the grief that he concealed so bravely he no longer had the desire to reach. As soon as Harding heard the news he wrote to Oyster Bay from Washington:

My dear Colonel Roosevelt:

I am sure the whole country is thinking of your home today, because of the report of Quentin's death on the battlefront in France, and millions would join in sharing the sorrow which you and Mrs. Roosevelt must feel. But I am sure the sorrow is tempered with pride, because Quentin proved the metal [sic] that was in him and gave the highest manifestation of that Americanism which ever must be the hope of the Republic.

Harding was only briefly in Washington when he wrote his condolence letter. During that time Scobey and H. H. Timken visited him, but most of his summer was spent on an extended Chautauqua tour that began at Niagara Falls on June 28 and ended in Auburn, Maine, on September 5. Wilson in December had again given his blessing to the Chautauqua as a morale booster by issuing a *Call to Service* to the Association of Chautauqua Managers in December. Harding, Sen. William S. Kenyon of Iowa, and the evangelical Bible-belter Doctor S. Parkes Cadman planned to alternate on a fixed list of dates so that the two senators would be able to get back to Washington any time their vote was required. Harding never tired of being on the Chautauqua circuit; the traveling, the friendly small towns, the declamatory ease with which he gave his Hamilton lecture, the freedom from his Duchess who became the more watchful as her health improved, and the chance of weekends alone with Nan. Although the money was not a primary consideration, he was now getting $600 weekly, speaking once a day six days a week through northeast New York, Vermont, New Hampshire, and finally Maine. On August 3 he was giving his Hamilton lecture at Oswego. There he found a Washington letter from his secretary, George Christian. "I have been having an unusual week," Christian wrote. "Emily Daugherty blew into town on her way to visit Draper's wife at Martinsville. As soon as she struck the Willard, no Martinsville for Emily." Christian sent for Daugherty and did his best to sober her up, but he admitted she was "not in very good condition."

Harding spoke at Gouverneur, Potsdam, and Massena. From Massena he replied to another of Carrie's arbitrary letters. More than ever fed up with the complaisant Jim she, forgetting her earlier rages, demanded that Harding get a divorce and marry her. [-] Finally, on Saturday, August 17, he arrived at Plattsburg on Lake Champlain. Some days before, he had written Nan asking her to arrange to come to Plattsburg to spend the weekend with him at the New Witherill Hotel and enclosing "ample funds" for the trip.

Nan at least never disappointed him. Friday night she took the train from New York to arrive at the Witherill just before breakfast. She registered as Elizabeth Christian, went first to her room, and then to his. At her knock he came to the door eagerly in his pajamas, and always afterward she remembered how the morning sun was streaming through the windows. "Gee, Nan," he told her, his arms around her. "I'm s'glad t'see you!" He was to speak at the training ground that afternoon and he would not be able to see her from lunch until evening, but that morning he had saved for the two of them. He took her quickly. They met outside the hotel half an hour later in a small grove and walked from there along Main Street and out into the country to a secluded meadow that Harding had prudently reconnoitered in advance. Nine years later Nan recalled the sunny meadow:

> It sloped gently down to a winding stream, and on one side there was a thick wood. The ground was soft and the grass high. It was sweet to hold his head on my lap and have him just lie there looking up at the blue sky.

Lying there he talked of a speech he was to make in Marion in December, and spoke of the Duchess, and of his friendship with the Freylinghuysens. Nan prattled of her new dress and hat and shoes, and what she had paid for them.

During his afternoon speech Harding was suddenly struck by an attack of dizziness and barely managed to finish. Afterward, but before he again saw Nan, he scribbled Carrie a letter. Nan's easing of his physical desire seemed to turn him back to the older woman. [-

----

----------]

By the time Harding was back at his desk in Washington, the final and most desperate German drive had been stopped, and victory—whether for that year or the next—was at last in sight. Ludendorff with his great spring offensive had come close to winning, might in fact have won if he had had the reserves to exploit his early victories. Green American troops rushing forward along the poplar-lined roads in that fateful spring to stem the German onslaught passed despondent peasants trudging with their belongings in the other direction and calling out hopelessly "*La guerre est finie.*" But the tide turned with Foch's great July victory in the Second Battle of the Marne—in which nine American divisions took part. German morale had at last snapped. On August 8 the British broke the German lines at Amiens in what Ludendorff himself called "the black day of the German Army."

Although the fighting went on stubbornly, by the end of summer it was clear to both sides that the Germans could not hold out much longer. The Americans were advancing slowly through the Argonne Forest, the British had taken St. Quentin and Armentières. On September 29 Ludendorff in a panic demanded that Berlin initiate peace negotiations. Five days later the German and Austrian governments appealed to Wilson for an armistice on the basis of his Fourteen Points that he had set forth as peace terms in January, 1918, to counteract Bolshevik propaganda that the war was merely an imperialist struggle.

Although the war's momentum continued and men still died from trench to trench, its dynamism had gone. A few weeks, more or less, and it would stop. With victory so near, America's propaganda-whipped national unity began to disintegrate. Critical voices were no longer stilled by slogans of standing by the President. During every war there is the common bond of the great goal fought for, and after every war the common disillusionment that—if given a chance—expresses itself by the ballot. Always there is the emotional reaction of the people against the party in power that ineluctably becomes associated with restrictions, short supplies, and regimentation. So it was in the United States in the months before the congressional elections of November, 1918. Already the mood of the voters had begun to show signs of shifting.[6]

Even without this subtle shifting, the loss of a certain number of mar-

[6] One could sense a similar mood in England in the spring of 1945. This emotional reaction against wartime austerities, this turning away from the party in power because it was in power, brought about the Labor party victory in the general election of July, 1945, far more than did any ideological feelings.

ginal Democratic seats could be expected.[7] Wilson in the exultation of
the coming victory expected no such loss. "No peace," he replied on
October 14 to German appeals for an armistice, "'till Kaiserism ends."
Harding applauded alliteratively from the wings:

> This is more like the real spirit of America. Germany is called upon to
> yield to a civilization unafraid. It is a role of reaction and redemption, with
> America looming in the eyes of the world and confident and self-respecting
> at home. . . . The people of Germany . . . will now have their lesson, their
> penitence, and their penalty—because all Germany must pay now.

Then, with his European peace demands, Wilson demanded that Americans elect a Democratic Congress to carry out his will. The Republican
leaders had been loyally pro-war, but Wilson warned that "the return of
a Republican majority in either house of Congress would be interpreted
on the other side of the water as a repudiation of my leadership." Wilson
Cabinet members stumped the country on behalf of "Wilson and Democracy." Even the shy and politically negative food administrator,
Herbert Hoover, was pressed into going to New Hampshire to urge the
voters to elect a Democratic senator and congressmen. The Republican
reply to Wilson was a joint appeal by Taft and Roosevelt for a loyal
Republican Congress. The Rough Rider, stifling his grief, undertook a
speaking campaign in which he accused Wilson of asking support for
himself and not for loyalty to the nation.

In Ohio the old internecine warfare was still being waged within the
Republican party, but on a diminished scale and by smaller men. Instead
of Foraker with his rapier, Hanna's broadsword, or Boss Cox swinging his
bludgeon, there were Willis, Hynicka, Wolfe, and Daugherty sharpening
their pocketknives. The dry Republicans had managed to nominate Hog-
caller Willis for another term as governor, and the Hamilton County wets
were preparing to butcher him. Harding, trying to appear the elder statesman standing above the battle, wrote confidentially to Scobey that Willis's
"self-seeking friends are very zealous in his behalf. The cities do not warm
up to him and wish some other candidate." Daugherty, nursing his perennial hatred, was maneuvering to have Hynicka removed from his position
as national committeeman from Ohio. Harding refused to let himself in
for such back-stairs maneuverings. His relations with Daugherty at this
time were not close. Willis, with the Anti-Saloon League behind him, felt
that he could take Harding or leave him, and was inclined to leave him.
The Democrats, without dissent, had again nominated Governor Cox.
Privately, Harding did not believe that Willis could win.

[7] The so-called "mid-term reaction" usually follows when the presidential candidate
is not on the ballot to command the waverers by his charismatic leadership.

The great drama overseas dwarfed the petty political drama of an American mid-term election, and the campaign was further diminished by the spread of the influenza epidemic in October. That sudden reincarnation of the Black Death would in its silent East-West orbit kill more people in a few months than had the war in its four years. With death lurking in every quiet corner, with schools and churches and assemblies closed, there was no place or audience for political rallies.

Wilson was confident that the country would sustain him. Democratic leaders predicted they would have a majority of 10 to 12 senators and from 15 to 30 congressmen. The day before the election the Austrian government signed an armistice, and the headlines on election morning announced that ALLIES FIX TERMS THAT GERMANY MUST MEET.

The election, though no landslide, was a bitter personal affront to Wilson. The Senate's Democratic majority of eight was turned into a Republican of two. In the House of Representatives the Republicans, outnumbered by five in the last Congress, took control with a 33 vote majority. Ohio's 13 Democratic and 9 Republican congressmen were now replaced by 14 Republicans and 9 Democrats. Only Willis failed to be carried along by the Republican upsurge. If he had been able to carry Hamilton County, he would have defeated Governor Cox; but there he found the Hynicka knife was in his back and he lost by 18,000 votes. The week before the election Roosevelt had written and then telegraphed Senator Fall, running in New Mexico for a second term:

> No American representative in either House of Congress during the last five years has a more absolutely straight American and war record than yours. . . . You have won the right to the support of all loyal and true-hearted American patriots and I earnestly hope that the good people of New Mexico will return you to the Senate with practical unanimity.

After Fall's re-election and his letter of thanks to Oyster Bay, Roosevelt again wrote him that "you are an American after my own heart."

Harding had returned to Marion to vote. While there he talked for some time with E. B. Conliss of Toledo who had arranged to meet him to discuss the purchasing of the *Star*. For all his sentimental attachment to the paper, Harding could still prefer a large cash settlement to sentiment. With the Republican revival Harding was beginning to look forward to another Senate term in 1920, and he had come to feel that his permanent home was now Washington. He told Conliss that he could no longer give the *Star* his "intimate personal attention" and felt he ought to place its control in the hands of someone who could.

In the few days he spent in Marion he managed to make up with Carrie. There is indeed no record of their patched lovers' meeting, but a week later Harding wrote [- -

The election itself was forgotten five days later in the swirling delirium of the armistice that followed on November 11. It seemed easy to believe, it was believed, that the world had really been made safe for democracy as Wilson the war leader announced the peace. Everyone in Congress had his subsequent say, including Harding.

> The terms of the armistice are in every way ample [he announced to the back pages of *The New York Times*]. They mean the final end of the war. They announce a dictated peace. It is not so spectacular as a march to Berlin but it proclaims the collapse of German autocracy and the dawn of a new era in the world. Surely all American aspirations are met.

The echo of the armistice celebrations had scarcely died down before more party warfare flared up in Ohio. Willis as long ago as June had called the "Dry Republican Convention" for his own renomination and with the idea of whittling at Harding's party leadership. A group of old Roosevelt Progressives under Walter Brown combined incongruously with the Hynicka-revived Boss Cox machine to fight Willis for party control and for control of patronage in the new assembly. Daugherty, convinced that Hynicka had marred his chances for the senatorial nomination, was still out to "bump" him from his place on the Republican National Committee. As a member of the State Executive Committee Daugherty, in his spite against Hynicka and his associates, was even showing signs of sidling up to Willis and the Anti-Saloon League. For Harding it was a time of strained relations with Daugherty. Even before the election he was writing to Jennings that in certain political matters he was going to have to take issue with "H. M. D." The Ohio imbroglio was the kind of party disharmony that Harding had always disliked and that could now even threaten his senatorial career. He told Daugherty in a private meeting that some things Daugherty was committed to "could not be." As chairman of the State Advisory Committee he urged Newton Fairbanks, chairman of the State Central Committee, to arrange a joint meeting with a view of reorganizing the Advisory Committee, settling present differences and—Harding maintained—allowing him to retire from the unwelcome responsibilities of the chairmanship. Fairbanks declined, preferring to keep his own post and to let the Harding-controlled Advisory Committee die of inanition. Harding suspected Daugherty's clenched hand in the refusal. "Wholly because of our very intimate and agreeable, personal, and political friendship, I am impelled to write you this letter," he began an admonition to him on November 29, and after his cordial beginning proceeded to tell off the ever-ready feudist.

> We cannot have a successful Republican party in Ohio [he wrote], if we map our course with a view to taking reprisals and everlastingly baring to the public view the grievancies [sic] of campaigns which have passed. . . . I cannot agree with you that we are to have everlasting warfare in Hamilton County. I can sympathize with your feeling in this matter, but I cannot accept your judgment. . . . You know my personal attitude as well as anybody in Ohio. I am always seeking to harmonize and think a great deal more of party victory than I do of the promotion of my personal ambitions.

Harding assured Daugherty of his belief in his friendly attitude and his "high appreciation" of his political friendship, but concluded that "in a petty fuss about organization control we can only endanger party prospects in the future."

Daugherty's reply to Harding's "unfortunate letter" was more outrage than innocence. "I thought you knew me well enough," he wrote, "to know that I never play any cards under the table in politics or anything else." He explained why he had felt a combined meeting should not take place, but now said he was willing to go along with Harding for an immediate meeting. As for Hynicka and his Hamilton County cohorts, he did not propose to pursue them "for what they have done to the party or me. I am not in the fertilizer business and do not consider it profitable to pursue or puncture dead horses." He insisted that he had not influenced Fairbanks in any way and said that he would regret the loss of Harding's good opinion.

Harding answered with conventional assurances of personal friendship, but the tone was cool. "The trouble with you, my dear Daugherty," he wrote, "in your political relations with me, is that you appraise my political sense so far below par that you have no confidence in me or my judgment. Pray do not think because I can and do listen in politeness to much that is said to me that I am always being 'strung.' "

When Charles Hard suggested a pact with Daugherty, the still-nettled Harding refused.

> I will make no arrangement of any kind in the future with Daugherty [he declared]. I felt myself under very great obligations to him and have highly valued his political friendship. He is a brilliant and resourceful man but his political hatreds have come to a point where they bias his judgment and I do not always think him a trustworthy adviser. More than that, he was not frank and open with me in discussing the situation, though I was perfectly sincere and open with him. . . . All this has destroyed my confidence and I would not consider a deal under any circumstances.

Daugherty's further letter to Harding on December 30 was a bid for reconciliation. In it he admitted that Harding's political judgment was as good as his own, denied that he had been sidling up to Willis although it might be "impossible" for him to oppose the ex-Governor. "I do not cry over spilled milk in politics or business," he wrote; "I follow the plan of looking out for a fresh cow in some convenient pasture." He was willing to stand by Harding if Harding would let him, whether Harding aimed at becoming Ohio's favorite son in 1920 or delivering the state to Roosevelt.

In mid-November the Duchess came down with another attack of her old kidney ailment.

> She has what the doctors call "hydro-nephrosis," [Harding wrote Scobey on November 18]. In other words, it is a swelling of the kidney, due to secretions of the organ which do not find an outlet through urinary channels. As a result her kidney is swollen to eight or ten times its normal size and is far more painful than you can imagine. She has in attendance part of the time, Dr. Carl Sawyer, who is stationed at Camp Meade, and has the constant attendance of Dr. Hardin of this city.

Tied to Washington by his wife's illness yet daily out of range of her watchful eye, Harding took to bringing Nan to Washington, parading her in public with extraordinary indiscretion. In the pride of having this desirable young woman on his own he seemed to forget caution, strolling with her down Pennsylvania Avenue as he chewed gum and pointed out the sights. She registered at various hotels—the New Ebbitt, the Raleigh —still as Miss Elizabeth N. Christian. Sometimes evenings he took her to his office in the Senate Office Building and made love to her there. It was in that somewhat statutory atmosphere, late in January, 1919, that she conceived. Harding had long been convinced that he could never become a father.[8] "No such luck!" he used to tell Nan, and had become increasingly careless about using contraceptives. "And of course," as Nan put it, "the Senate offices do not provide preventive facilities for use in such emergencies."

On December 4 Wilson, still self-righteously confident in spite of the election results, sailed with his peace delegation for France on the *George Washington* accompanied by five destroyers. It was, he told Congress before leaving, his duty to go to Europe to do his part in realizing the ideals our soldiers fought for. Harding was not yet ready to disagree. "A fine tribute to the soldiers and sailors of the Republic and the country's patriotic support of the war," was his comment on the President's message. But he added that the message "was not revealing so far as peace terms were concerned." The blunter and more irreconcilable Hiram Johnson remarked that he did not know what Wilson wanted at the peace conference. To Theodore Roosevelt, Wilson—after, as during the war— was "a silly doctrinaire at times and an utterly selfish and cold-blooded politician always."

On the day of the armistice the Rough Rider had returned to the hospital with an attack of inflammatory rheumatism, staying there until Christmas Day. But even on his sickbed he was recognized as the undisputed postwar leader of his party, the only possible presidential choice of the 1920 Republican national convention. "I am indifferent to the subject," he told his biographer, Joseph Bucklin Bishop, in the hospital. "I would not lift a finger to get the nomination. Since Quentin's death the world seems to have shut down on me."

He would not need to lift a finger this time, and the nomination would still be his. Mindful of the lost Roosevelt division, he still thought of the innocuous Harding as a balance to the ticket, a party regular flattered to take the supernumerary job that a more vigorously ambitious independent like Hiram Johnson would have scorned. It would be in 1920 as it was in 1904 when he had picked Charles Fairbanks, the conservative senator from Indiana, as his running mate with the quip: "Who in the name of heaven else is there?"

Harding as vice president fainéant, would have reached beyond the height of his Marion ambitions presiding with affable ease over "the most exclusive club in the world," and having little else to do. The job would have suited him even better than that of senator by removing him from

[8] As a boy he had had a severe attack of mumps with swelling of the testicles, and doctors at Battle Creek believed that he was probably sterile, since he had had no children by the Duchess. After his death Marion defenders have used the medical argument that he could not have been the father of Nan's child.

the importunities of constituents. And a vice president under Roosevelt needed never worry about being overburdened with responsibilities.

Then at Oyster Bay, early on the morning of January 6, 1919, the Rough Rider died in his sleep of a blood clot in the heart. Wilson proclaimed thirty days of official mourning, and Vice President Marshall appointed Harding a member of the Congressional Committee to attend the funeral. Daugherty with his ferret nose for politics had already wired Harding "suggesting" that he attend.

Roosevelt was buried two days later in the spot he had picked for himself in the hillside country graveyard near the village of Oyster Bay. Fifty political figures—among them Harding—attended, and an equal number of local school children. Some four hundred close friends stood by in the snow to watch as the American flag was removed and the plain oak coffin lowered into the grave. With the leader gone, the future of the Republican party—so brightly obvious a month ago—was shattered. Harding and the others picking their way downhill through the snow could see no pattern in the fragments, but the enigmatic question remained. Who would be the Republican presidential candidate in 1920?

CHAPTER XIV

Candidate

Roosevelt's death, as Daugherty noted exultingly, made a big change all over the country. "I have some ideas about this thing now which I will talk over with you," he wrote Harding the day of the funeral. Daugherty was not the only one who could see the political sun shining through the Oyster Bay cypresses. Scobey wrote at once from Texas as soon as he heard the news. "It looks to me like if you want to be President now, here is your opportunity. Ohio is a pivotal state and they know that you can carry it. If you are going to be a candidate you ought to start soon."

Faced with even the most distant prospect of the Presidency, Harding found he had little taste for such a circumscribing elevation. Brought up in the little-red-schoolhouse tradition, he had a rustic awe of the office. The greatest thing that might happen to a boy born on a farm or even in a log cabin would be to end in the White House—as Lincoln had done. But that American dream had never haunted Harding's nights as a senator. Again and again in his conversations and his letters to his friends he refused to consider the awesome responsibility. To his Kansas City supporter, the young newspaperman E. Mont (Emmett Montgomery) Reily, one of the few Republicans allied with the Democratic boss T. J. Pendergast, he wrote:

> Truly, my dear Reily, I do not wish my friends to make any effort to make me a candidate. I do not want to be considered in that connection. Without discussing the question of availability, particularly that availability which is based on geographical location, I must assert the conviction that I do not possess the elements of leadership or the widespread acquaintances which are essential to the ideal leadership of our Party in 1920.
>
> I think I owe it to the Party to say these things, because I know better than some who over-estimate both my ability and availability. Apart from these things I cannot avoid the feeling of utter reluctance to permit my friends to enlist a campaign for a preferment which does not appeal to me and to which I do not consider myself essential. . . . I do not wish to be considered in connection with the nomination for our Party.

The Senate, he told Reily, he much preferred to the White House.

Five pleasant and none-too-taxing years had given him a sense of belonging in the nation's capital; to continue those pleasant years by re-election to the Senate was goal enough. Between sessions, golf, poker, travel, convivial associates, and the occasional dalliance consumed his days. He liked to entertain his cronies at Wyoming Avenue, though anything like the scale of living of the McLeans, or even the Longworths, was far beyond him. Nevertheless, the earnings of the *Star* gave him an income large enough to play the good fellow. In one month in 1919 his liquor bill was $529. The editor who had never really been accepted in his Ohio small town had here become the accepted senator—no firebrand like Hiram Johnson, no defiant challenger like La Follette, but a regular Republican acceptable. Marion had become a mirage. Washington was now his home town. Several times he was again on the point of selling the *Star,* but his old inner doubts—this time expressed in the uncertainty of his re-election—held him back. The protuberant house on Mount Vernon Avenue he would have sold except for the Duchess.

A week after Scobey's urgings Harding replied in one of the most ingenuous letters he was to pen:

> I expect it is very possible that I would make as good a President as a great many men who are talked of for that position and I would almost be willing to make a bet that I would be a more "commonsensible" President than the man who now occupies the White House. At the same time I have such a sure understanding of my own inefficiency that I should really be ashamed to presume myself fitted to reach out for a place of such responsibility. More than that, I would not think of involving my many good friends in the tremendous tasks of making a Presidential campaign.
>
> There are some people who discuss the availability of my name and I am frank to say I am human enough to rejoice that there are people who think well enough of me to mention me in that connection. More than that, it is a mighty gratifying thing to know that one has friends who are willing to give up their time and their means to back a candidacy, but I should be unhappy every hour from the time I entered the race until the thing were settled, and I am sure I should never have any more fun or any real enjoyment in life if I should be so politically fortunate to win a nomination and election. I had much rather retain my place in the Senate and enjoy the association of friends and some of the joys of living—not the least of these is an occasional trip to Texas.

Scobey was not to be put off so easily. He replied with cheery assurance that he had heard from the clerk of the Senate in Columbus that there was already a movement to start a Harding boom in Ohio. The boom would result in a solid Harding delegation to the Republican national convention and what had started in Ohio would gain strength all over the country.

Harding answered with even blunter frankness:

> Really, my dear Scobey, the winning of such an undertaking is not worth the work and anxiety involved. I do not mean by this that I am utterly lazy and unwilling to shoulder my share of the burden, but I cannot for the life of me see why anybody would deliberately shoulder the annoyances and worries and incessant trials incident to a campaign for nomination and election to the Presidency. . . .
>
> I can say to you what I would not care to say to anybody else in the whole country. There have been many tenders of strong and ample financial support to undertake any sort of a campaign and these tenders came from sources that one would need have no embarrassment in accepting them. Nevertheless, I have turned them all down because I cannot bring myself to accept the sacrifices of means and time on the part of friends and the involved activity that would go with a campaign for such high preferment.

Just after he had written to Scobey, Harding attended a Lincoln Day dinner in Toledo given by Lucas County Republicans where—with the adroit Daugherty in the background—Chairman Fairbanks and the members of the State Central Committee endorsed him as Ohio's favorite son presidential candidate. Afterward, on the train from Toledo to Columbus, he sat with his friend the old State Committee chairman Charles Hard. Hard had been using both his paper, the Portsmouth *Daily Blade,* and his political connections to drum up Harding presidential sentiment. Harding begged him to drop such efforts, since he was not and would not be a candidate. When Hard tried to insist that he owed it to Ohio (Mother of Presidents!) to add one more to the list, Harding snapped at him that he "didn't know a damn thing about it." He told Hard he would not be a candidate because he did not feel that he was big enough to fill the office; there were many Republicans much better qualified and better known who would be glad to be presidential candidates in 1920. He was not going to be a candidate—and that was that!

When Jennings, fired by the booming news reports, wrote predicting a brave presidential future, Harding reacted as he had to Scobey. "It is good to read your political assurances," he wrote, "but I harbor no delusions or designs. I should like to be kindly esteemed, but the pretence that seems to be necessary to popularity is not agreable [sic] to my nature—or something of the sort."

Late in January Harding delivered a Roosevelt memorial address before the Ohio General Assembly in Columbus. With yeasty eloquence he extolled "one of the most conspicuous figures in all American history . . . inseparably linked with the finding of the American soul, with the great awakening and conservation." And he did not neglect to add that the Rough Rider was "less radical than he ofttimes appeared." Harding had been particularly inspired by the sight of the flag on Roosevelt's coffin:

> My own ears were deaf to the reading of the ritual and the recital of his
> favorite hymn, I was thinking of the flag and the soulless form it draped
> in jealous sorrow. Great citizens had passed before. Beloved executives,
> heroic soldiers, and far-seeing statesmen—all had come to the inevitable,
> either too soon or in the fullness of distinguished lives—and the nation had
> mourned, and peoples sorrowed, and potentates had sympathized, but
> there was a distinct conviction that the flag lost its bravest defender when
> Theodore Roosevelt passed from life to the eternal. A flaming spirit of
> American patriotism was gone. A great void had come, and there was
> none to fill it.

While a haggard Wilson at the Paris Peace Conference was beginning
to break under the strain of defending his Fourteen Points from the Tiger
Clemenceau's rapacious cotton-gloved hands, Harding in Washington was
observing that the President's efforts could be better directed if he were
home. When Wilson cabled that the starving European nations must be
fed to stop bolshevism, Harding on one of his infrequent appearances on
the floor of the Senate suggested that Wilson conclude a peace treaty and
give more thought to the American taxpayer and less to feeding Europe.
"I don't agree with the President," he told the senators, "that we must
establish a new internationalism paralyzed by socialism," and he attributed a large part of the growing menace of bolshevism—so apparent
now in Spartacist disorders overseas—"to the policies and utterances of
the Chief Executive of the United States." When he had concluded, the
patrician John Sharp Williams crossed over from the Democratic side to
shake his hand.

In February Wilson sailed from France to spend a few days in his own
country defending his policies in person. His face twitching and old age
upon him, he arrived in Boston on February 24, in spite of his physical
deterioration still full of fiery challenge in behalf of his League of Nations. "I have fighting blood in me," he told a New England audience.
Defying his critics, "ignorant of the sentiment of America," he sailed back
to France on March 5 after announcing at a New York meeting in the
Metropolitan Opera House the night before that he was going to stay in
Europe until the peace treaty and the League were settled, and reassuring
his hearers that the League was now an integral and inextricable part of
the treaty. The chairman of the Senate Foreign Relations Committee, the
implacable Henry Cabot Lodge, had prepared a bon-voyage gift for the
departing President in the shape of a round robin signed by 39 senators
notifying him and the world that they would have none of his League.
Harding was one of the signers. "I don't think there is anything in it for

the United States . . ." he wrote Scobey while Wilson was still in Paris. "I have not said anything much in a public way but I have made up my mind privately that I intend to oppose it no matter what the political result may be."

As soon as the session ended, Harding left with a group of senators for Augusta, Georgia, as members of an informal club known as the Little Mothers. Nicholas Murray Butler and President Lincoln's son Robert were charter members of the club that had been formed a dozen years before. Each night they met in the lower rooms of the Hotel Bon Air, sitting about a table drinking and talking over political questions. In Harding's time the members included Sen. Frederick Hale of Maine, Frank Hitchcock of Nebraska, Frank Brandegee of Connecticut, Willard Saulsbury of Delaware, and Speaker of the House Frederick Gillett. There were even occasional Democratic members, such as Ohio's Governor Cox. The convivial Little Mothers were finally brought low by the Eighteenth Amendment, but it was a measure of Harding's social acceptance that the Hoo-Hoo from Marion was able to fit into this more sophisticated atmosphere.

After a few days at Augusta, he went on to St. Augustine for a week of golf. At the weekend the Duchess—now well enough to travel—joined him at the old Marion eyrie in Daytona. Daytona was a family reunion. Deac, still convalescing from his heart attack, was there with his family and even opened his wallet cautiously enough to buy six acres and a cheap bungalow at Burbank. Tryon had come along with them, and was frisking in the sunshine "like a boy." Harding bought a new Cole six touring car, motoring over 1,500 miles before returning North at the month's end. The Duchess's health had so much improved that she gained fifteen pounds.

At the end of February Nan had written Harding that she was pregnant. He wrote back in concealed alarm that he was sure her trouble was not so very serious and that it could be handled. They met in her room at the New Willard. The thought of having a child by him, far from dismaying her, filled her with romantic excitement. Not so Harding. He was so upset when he came to her room that his forehead was wet with perspiration. "We must go at this thing in a sane way, dearie," he told her, "and we must not allow ourselves to be nervous over it." Then he left her for a few minutes, to come back with a bottle of Dr. Humphrey's No. 11 tablets which, he said, Mrs. Harding used to take. Nan said she knew they would do her no good. He shrugged his shoulders: "No faith, no works, Nan!" Obliquely he suggested to her that if he had to choose between medicine and an operation he personally would prefer "the knife." She preferred the child. Her relentless enthusiasm was bound to prevail over his soberer judgment. If the pregnancy of this girl became known, he knew he would be ruined politically to say nothing of having to face the Duchess. She would "raise hell," her special variety. Yet he felt forced to pretend, to go along with Nan's romantic dream. He humored her, called her "the perfect sweetheart and perfect mother." She was his "shrine of worship." Enshrined was a word he loved to use. She daydreamed to him that their child must be a boy. "The young lieutenant," she named him. Harding said it was "grand." In her self-absorption, she disregarded and dismissed his hesitancies. The afterglow of that meeting persisted, eight years later, diffused in the lavender of her prose.

The room in the Willard was as full of promise as her little room in Marion papered with campaign posters. So that meeting remained in her mind when she came to write about it. They were talking of the place in the country that might be theirs one day, with dogs and horses, chickens and pigs, books and friends.

> As he talked [she wrote] his voice grew tense. His hands trembled visibly. I took one of them in mine and held it tightly. His gaze was directed out of the window and he spoke as to himself. I had to blink very hard to keep back my tears. I had never seen him so moved, so shaken. . . .
> ". . . and I would take you out there, Nan darling, as—my—wife . . ." He freed his hand with sudden force and grasped both my arms tightly. "Look at me, dearie!" he cried. "You *would* be my wife, wouldn't you? You would marry me, Nan? Oh, dearie, dearie," brokenly, "if I only could . . . if we could only have our child—together!" This last came as a hushed exclamation, almost a prayer, scarcely audible. The yearning of a heart laid bare! I nodded wordlessly. The very air seemed sacred.

Once Nan was in Chicago her more practical sister urged her to have an abortion. Harding's letters kept guardedly suggesting the same thing. Elizabeth even brought her some "bitter apple" medicine which she refused. Wrapped in her dream, she was deaf to any tentative suggestion that she might get rid of "the young lieutenant."

Harding kept her well supplied with money. Yet although he did not show it, he was dismayed. Nan in her cloying way could be as demanding as Carrie or the Duchess. This girl, without meaning to, could, in an indiscreet moment, bring the whole structure of his career about his ears.

He said nothing beyond warning her to be cautious. When she returned to New York he set her up in a small apartment at the Hotel La Salle Annex on 136th Street. Whenever he visited her now, she noticed how worried and preoccupied he seemed. In June he spoke at Carnegie Hall on "The Land of Opportunity." She, who usually loved to hear him orate, thought he spoke badly as he rambled on about the farmer's son who had become a banker, Jim So-and-So whose father owned a quarry in Marion and who had worked his way through school, etc. When they were alone afterward, she said he had not spoken as well as usually. He admitted it.

"Why, dearie," he said, "I was so tired. I thought I couldn't even speak at *all!*"

They continued to make love as usual, once even indiscreetly in a secluded part of Central Park. Just before she left her job at the end of her fifth month, he gave her a ring. She had been after him for some time to give her one. He himself wore a large diamond on the third finger of his left hand that she had long admired. He would gladly have given it to her, he said, if it were not for Florence. As a surprise he bought her a sapphire ring surrounded by diamonds, and slipped it formally onto her finger. "We performed a sweet little ceremony with that ring," Nan recalled, "and he declared that I could not belong to him more utterly had we been joined together by fifty ministers."

In July, with her signs of pregnancy becoming obvious, she left New York for the seaside resort of Asbury Park, New Jersey. "Milk," she wrote, "of a lovely richness was already coming from both of my breasts." At Asbury Park she went under the name of Mrs. Edmund Norton Christian, her story—arranged with Harding—being that she had married a Lieutenant Christian of the United States Army who had been sent to Europe almost at the close of the war, and that her mother had disapproved of the marriage. The first few days at Asbury Park she stayed at the Hotel Monmouth, then moved to a rooming house and finally found two front rooms in a box-like brown-shingled cottage on Bond Street.

When the new Sixty-sixth Congress met on May 19, Harding's seniority had moved him halfway down the Senate aisle. The new majority leader, Senator Lodge, now took him from Naval Affairs and installed him as a cooperative member of his Foreign Relations Committee. He continued on the committees on Commerce, Expenditures in the Treasury Department, Pacific Islands and Porto Rico, Public Health, Weights and Measures, and even reached the dignity of chairman of the Committee on the Philippines.

He was away when the Senate voted on the Women's Suffrage Amendment, though he would have voted for it if he had been there.[1] But he was present on July 10 when Wilson—two days after his return from Europe—personally presented the Siamese-twin documents of the Peace Treaty and the Covenant of the League of Nations for ratification by the Senate. The President looked more the gaunt and determined schoolmaster as he stalked into the chamber with the bulky volume containing the treaty under his right arm. He was escorted to the rostrum by a senatorial committee that included his natural enemies, Lodge and Borah. Although the Republican senators were mute and two irreconcilables even refused to stand up when Wilson entered, his appearance brought cheers

[1] He arranged to have his vote paired with another senator's who was against the resolution.

and even a rebel yell from the massed galleries. He read his speech from small typewritten cards, hesitantly at first, speaking not so much to the senators as beyond them to his countrymen all over America. The League of Nations, he told them, was the hope of the world. In that glowing instant it seemed that he might be right. Most Americans, regardless of politics, still clung to the belief that some such league was the alternative to what they had just endured in war. Regular Republicans like Taft and Burton and Root and Hughes thought so. They were as solidly behind Wilson's league as were conservative non-politicians like Harvard's President A. Lawrence Lowell and his staidly liberal predecessor President Emeritus Charles W. Eliot.

"America First" had always been and always would be a ready slogan in Harding's mind. He commented that the President's address was the appeal of the "internationalists" and "utterly lacking in ringing Americanism." He admitted he agreed with what Wilson said about America's "moral leadership" but did not "regard it necessary to write leadership into a covenant such as that of the proposed League of Nations." His opposition to the League had immediate and unforeseen repercussions in Ohio where pro-League Republicans began circulating unharmonious petitions in its favor. Even Doctor Sawyer in Marion was on a local advisory council favoring the League.

After two weeks of Senate debate on the combined Versailles Treaty and League of Nations, Harding was one of a group of four Republican senators—William P. Dillingham of Vermont, Bert M. Fernald of Maine, and Irvine L. Lenroot of Wisconsin—selected to call on Wilson and inform him that there must be reservations attached to the Treaty before it could be ratified by the Senate, in particular there must be reservations to Articles X and XI of the Covenant. These articles as they stood would give the League of Nations the power to mobilize American troops for service in any part of the world without the consent of Congress.

The President lectured the four senators, as if he were a professor trying to make his point with a group of slow-witted freshmen, explaining that the United States must enter the League under the same terms as all the other countries. In Paris he had signed his name as President and given his word in the name of the American people, and he could not go back on his signature or his word. Amicable but impervious, the senators listened to him while nodding their disagreement.

With party leaders of the stature of Taft and Hughes in favor of the League, Harding had no mind to join the irreconcilables around Borah and Hiram Johnson. What he looked for was a way to sit on the League fence, as he wrote to Jennings, "to preserve all of the League proposal which we can accept with safety to the United States, in the hope that the conscience of the Nations may be directed to perfecting a safe plan of cooperation toward maintained peace. But there will be no surrender of things essentially and vitally American."

Indefinably, nudged on by his statesman's appearance and his easy, sociable ways, and without doing much about it, Harding was becoming if not a Senate presence then at least a fixture. At the McKinley Day banquet in Dayton on January 29, 1919, the chairman of the Republican County Executive Committee had hailed him enthusiastically as "our next President!" Talk and newspaper gossip continued about him as an Ohio dark horse. A measure of his increased prominence is the long feature interview granted him by *The New York Times* at the beginning of the session in which as spokesman for his party he claimed that the new Republican Congress would bring speedy and complete repeal of the war powers granted to the President; return the railroads, shipping, and telephone and telegraph companies to private hands; cut taxes and government spending; put the Army and Navy on a peace-time basis; and pass new immigration laws. And he predicted a great fight over the peace treaty.

During July Harding had a visit from the Scobeys and Gus Creager. Before their arrival Harding had written Scobey that he would like to take a "flyer" in an oil venture if Scobey and Creager could recommend one. "I need somehow to make some easy money," he admitted. The pals apparently had a boozy time of it in Washington, for Scobey's departure found him writing an apologetic letter about the effect of Senator Elkins's hospitality on their visit to the Capitol. "The liquor was all right," he admitted; "the time was all right, but the place was bad. I really would have enjoyed letting my light shine if it had been at your house and in your company." Harding replied consolingly:

> It was not necessary for you to address to me any word of apology. . . .
> You are a joy to me when you have the candles lighted but you do not fit
> the Marble Room of the Capitol appropriately under a complete lighting
> up, and it was for that reason I felt it necessary for both you and me to
> send you into retirement into the Committee Room. Hale, Elkins, and
> others rather enjoyed the diversion.

With her recovery the Duchess saw more of Evalyn McLean. Harding had continued to meet the McLeans at the Longworths' poker evenings. They now occupied John's I Street mansion, but from the spring of 1919 spent most of their time at their country house, Friendship, in Georgetown that they had just repossessed after lending it for the winter to house convalescent soldiers. Friendship had once been a monastery, and the McLeans had made it over in their fashion, spending as much for roses for their conservatory as Harding had spent for his Wyoming Avenue house. Even Evalyn had to admit it was a mad sort of place. One might arrive to find a llama on the lawn, a monkey in the bathroom, and donkeys, goats, and ponies on the terrace. The corridors were shrill with the cries of a parrot that had belonged to a diplomat and had learned to curse in several languages. The kitchen with its French chefs was a cross between the Ritz and Maxim's, and the cellars were stocked with wine and spirits like those of a wholesale liquor dealer. If Vinson and his brother Jock—now three years and three months old—wished to play in the stables there were midget horses for them and a brightly painted coach that had once belonged to Gen. Tom Thumb.

Late in May it was the turn of the Duchess to console Evalyn, for what the McLeans feared most—the baleful influence of the Hope Diamond, if one believed in such things—came to pass. Vinson the hundred-million-dollar baby, in spite of all his guards and guardians, was killed in an accident. Ned and Evalyn had gone to Louisville, Kentucky, for the Derby, leaving old John's valet, Meggett, at Friendship to look after Vinson. On Sunday morning Meggett and Vinson took a walk under the trees and when they reached the gate the boy wanted to go outside. Once beyond the gate, he darted across the road to snatch some ferns from a gardener's cart that was passing, and on running back was struck lightly by a Model-T Ford coming in the other direction. At first Vinson seemed unhurt if a little dusty, and walked back to the house hand in hand with Meggett. But in the afternoon he became paralyzed and by evening he was dead.

The first session of the new Congress ran until November 19, but the intricacies of the peace in the dislocations of that turbulent year made no great demands on Harding's Senate presence. Although Senator Lodge's Foreign Relations Committee spent the summer holding hearings and debating the Versailles Treaty and the League of Nations, the end of July found Harding once more escaping from the Duchess to the familiar Chautauqua road. "It is always a delight to me to be on the Circuit," he wrote, "quite apart from the joy of the income which is incident thereto and quite apart from the hardships and annoyances of bum hotels and the animal life that one encounters in many of them." He had tried to persuade Theodore Roosevelt, Jr., back from Europe with a chestful of medals, to join him on the tour for three weeks. The new Colonel Roosevelt declined, but Harding was joined without persuasion by Willis who was soon "whooping it up with the old-time vim."

While Nan remained at Asbury Park, Harding prudently avoided seeing her, although he gave her all the money she needed or might later need. He kept sending her a hundred or a hundred and fifty dollars at a time, and sometimes as much as three or four hundred dollars for her confinement and the baby's clothes. Late in September she paid him a brief, surreptitious visit in Washington. Separated from her, depressed by the inevitability of his approaching fatherhood, he found himself thinking again of the elusive Carrie. She at least was a woman and not a girl; she would never have led him into the Asbury Park predicament. On September 27 her daughter married William Matheé, just discharged from the Army. Harding telegraphed Isabelle:

> Hope your wedding day is as beautiful at Marion as here. So sorry I am not able to be present. Most sincere congratulations and unlimited good wishes.

Meanwhile he continued to write Nan: quick, penciled letters, cheering her as best he could in his mangled prose. Kindness, prudence, fear, affection, weakness—his motives were a compound of all these, but she knew rightly that he would never abandon her. The days passed idly, summer giving way to autumn, the cottages shuttered, the beach becoming deserted. Nan took walks, read books, wrote letters. Early in the morning of October 22 she felt her first labor pains. At two in the afternoon "the young lieutenant" was born. He turned out to be a girl. She decided that she had really wanted a girl all along and named the baby Elizabeth Ann Christian. Doctor James Ackerman, "the society doctor of the Jersey shore" who had attended Nan, by mistake recorded her name on the birth certificate as Emma Eloise Britton.

Six weeks later, leaving Elizabeth Ann with a nurse, she went to New York where she at once telephoned Harding in Washington. As soon as she heard his voice, she began to cry. She wanted to see him, she must see him, right away. Evasively he told her that although in fact he was coming to New York, he thought it unwise for them to be seen together while she was in the weakened condition that she said she was. She went back to Asbury Park.

The turbulent autumn that marked the anniversary of the war's end marked a year turned sour. Europe remained shell-shocked, hungry, half-ruined, threatened with revolution. The mood of the people of the United States had shifted from the enthusiasm of the war-imposed slogans to a probing resentment like that of the returning soldiers now being discharged with two months' pay and a ticket home and left to shift for themselves. Wilson the academic, isolated in the self-righteousness of his mission, did not sense the change. In spite of those stubborn, puny-minded senators intent on holding up and emasculating his treaty, he was convinced that the people of the country still stood behind him. To appeal directly to them he left Washington on his special train on September 3 for a twenty-seven-day tour of the country. Ten thousand miles he planned to travel in his blue car, the *Mayflower*, from Takoma, Washington, south almost to the Mexican border, making addresses at 26 major cities and at least 10 whistle-stop speeches daily from the *Mayflower's* rear platform.

Like hounds baying on his trail, three anti-league senators pursued him from city to city. Johnson's square, assertive features, Borah's heavy eyebrows and pitted, fighting face, came to haunt Wilson's dreams. With James Reed—the isolationist English-hating senator from Missouri, still outraged by Britain's Stamp Act of 1765—they followed after, speaking where the President spoke, answering his defense of his Peaceable Kingdom with savage diatribes. "I have come to fight a cause and that cause is greater than the U. S. Senate!" Wilson told the crowds in a hoarse and failing voice as the hounds ran him closer to earth. They cheered him, but—as he could read in the papers each morning—there were greater cheers for his pursuers. For the President, his nervous energy already sapped by the Paris Peace Conference, the trip was a disaster. His face twitched more markedly, he suffered from blinding headaches and insomnia, he grew forgetful; and his tears came easily. Passing through Pueblo, Colorado, on his return journey the night of the twenty-third, he was struck down. He had staked everything on bringing his League of Nations to the people, and he had lost.

During the summer and while Wilson was on his ruinous tour, the gray autocrat from Massachusetts deftly maneuvered his Senate Foreign Relations Committee toward the destruction of Wilson's League. The hearings that Lodge held were intentionally fruitless, prolonged to give the country's growing anti-League sentiment a chance to expand. Harding, when he was present, remained for the most part a strikingly inconspicuous figure at the hearings, but when Wilson in his anger sent back word to the recalcitrant senators to put up or shut up, Harding replied for Lodge that they would not shut up until they had relieved their country of participating in entangling alliances. Senator Lodge's amendments and reservations to the Peace Treaty, according to Harding, "echoed the conscience of the Republic."

In ironic recollection of Wilson's Fourteen Points, Lodge's committee attached 14 reservations to the proposed Peace Treaty. By the reservation to Article X the United States would not be obliged to defend any other country at the bidding of the League unless Congress first approved; but the wily Senator knew that Wilson in his dogmatic stubbornness would never accept such a Lodge reservation. After the committee had submitted its report to the Senate, Lodge let Harding lead off the debate before the final vote was taken.

The applause from the galleries during Harding's speech was an indication of how far public opinion had already turned from the once hopefully acclaimed idea of the League. "A venture," Harding now referred to it, and told the cheering balconies that to accept it unaltered would be a betrayal of America. He announced that he could never vote to ratify the Treaty without the Lodge safeguards, that if European countries insisted on bartering peoples and territories, it was not for the United States to underwrite their actions. He concluded, to more balcony demonstrations that Vice President Marshall was unable to control:

> It is my deliberate conviction that the League of Nations Covenant as negotiated at Paris either creates a supergovernment of the nations which enter it or it will prove the colossal disappointment of the ages. I cannot believe this republic ought to sanction it in either case.
> It will not break the heart of the world to make the Covenant right, or at least free from perils which would endanger American independence. But it were better to witness this rhetorical tragedy than destroy the soul of this great republic.

Harding was so proud of his League of Nations speech that later he had it recorded on a phonograph record with "Beautiful Ohio" on the other side.

The peace that was so little like its sloganed promise had spurred the high cost of living—as inflation was then known—had brought proliferating strikes, unemployed ex-soldiers, race riots, bombings by Reds and hysterical actions against them, a crime wave and prohibition. Wilson, a remote and silent invalid, inaccessible in his White House seclusion, became the subject of wild rumors. There was spreading dissatisfaction among ordinary, inarticulate Americans, the longing for a father figure to lead them out of the morass of the present to a prewar past that existed more serenely in the imagination than it ever had in fact. The one such father figure who loomed larger with each month as Wilson's shadow diminished was Theodore Roosevelt's old friend and comrade in arms, and in a sense his political heir, General Leonard Wood.[2]

Wood with his grave, solid khaki figure, the dog-headed riding crop under his arm, gave a sense of assurance and stability in times of trouble just by his appearance. However ill-defined the qualities of a natural leader, he had them, with an authority too innate to require its assertion in the martinet manner of a Black Jack Pershing. No returned doughboy would ever vote for Black Jack, but Wood's soldiers had always been ready to cheer in the ranks as he passed. His military career was unique, for he had joined the Army medical corps in 1885 and twenty-four years later had become chief of staff and the Army's ranking general.

[2] A similar longing for a father figure to deal with the dislocations and disillusionments following the Civil War and World War II resulted in the ineptitudes of Presidents Grant and Eisenhower. General Wood was more capable and intelligent than either.

He was one of those seemingly stamped by inheritance with success. The mark was on him when as an overgrown tow-haired boy of twenty he left the wind-swept isolation of his Cape Cod home, in a "seersucker" suit several sizes too small for him, to enroll at the Harvard Medical School. The medical school, under such men as Doctor Oliver Wendell Holmes, had given him knowledge and moulded him into a more urbane form. After a brief fling at private practice in Boston, he joined the Army in the only position then available to him, that of a civilian contract doctor. His first post was the ramshackle Fort Whipple in the Arizona Territory where almost at once he took part in the campaign against Geronimo, the Apache chief. On long marches through the wild and mountainous regions of Arizona and northern Mexico, enduring heat, dust, and great fatigue, fighting the occasional small engagement, the young medical assistant became by necessity a troop commander, the civilian a soldier. Later Wood was awarded the Congressional Medal for his part in this campaign that brought him a commission and began his real Army career. In 1897 Wood, by then a captain, met Roosevelt and the two men were instantly drawn to each other. At the time of the Spanish-American War they organized the volunteer regiment of the Rough Riders, with Wood as colonel and Roosevelt as second-in-command. By the war's end Roosevelt had captured the headlines as the hero of San Juan Hill, but Wood had become a major general. As military governor of Santiago, then as military governor of all of Cuba, he served as America's first proconsul, ruling with such temperate efficiency that he became as popular with the Cubans as he was with his own soldiers. From Cuba he was sent to the Philippines, to become equally successful as governor of the Moro Province and then commanding general of the Philippines Division. In 1908 he returned to the United States and in 1910 the contract doctor became the Army's chief of staff.

Even before 1914 Wood had begun to preach preparedness, speaking to young men in colleges across the country and arranging volunteer summer camps. In 1915 he organized the first Business Men's Training Camp at Plattsburg where the younger members of the Eastern business and social world—"millionaire rookies," the papers called them—spent a month at their own expense under canvas learning the elements of soldiering. He and Roosevelt were the country's foremost advocate of preparedness, still looked on with disfavor by Wilson as an incitement to war. Although the President, as the war drew closer, would come to accept some military preparation as necessary and would himself carry a flag in a Preparedness Day parade, he never forgave Wood for his "premature" agitation. When Wilson finally did make his War Declaration, he kept the Army's senior general at home, reducing him finally to training a division of recruits at Camp Funston, and then—with the petty spite that sometimes overcame his judgment—refusing to let Wood take his 89th Division overseas when its training was complete. Wood bore himself through all his wartime disappointments with professional silence, but public resentment against Wilson's action grew, and when the mood of the electorate began to swing away from the party in power, Wood's name was thought of first as the Republican candidate for 1920.

For the Roosevelt family Wood was seen as the Rough Rider's worthy successor. Several months before his death Roosevelt had told his friend and 1912 Republican convention floor manager Henry J. Allen that if he was unable to run for President he hoped they would back Leonard Wood. Shortly after the Colonel's funeral, his sister Corinne asked the General to take over the leadership of the Roosevelt forces. "It would seem," Taft muttered, "as if the funeral bake meats had furnished forth the feast for the heir." Wood remarked later that he felt he was traveling along the line Roosevelt himself would have traveled if he were alive. It was not the line that ended in the 1912 Armageddon, but it was not the reactionary branch that Wood's critics tried to make it appear.[3] Essentially Wood was a progressive conservative, with more emphasis on the conservative, a Republican with a distaste for politicians, and with the loosest of party ties, not to the fancy of either dogmatic liberals or party bosses.

Wood's first need, if he were to be a candidate, was for an astute political manager. Roosevelt supporters urged him to take John T. King, Republican national committeeman from Connecticut, associate of Sen. Boies Penrose, the boss of Pennsylvania, and from 1916 Roosevelt's liaison with the ratholes of politics. "I like John King," the Rough Rider used to say. "We have a perfect working arrangement. John supplies the efficiency, and I supply the morals." (If Roosevelt had lived, King would probably have been his campaign manager in 1920.)

King was a blandly tough, curly-haired Irish boy who had first grown rich collecting garbage in Bridgeport and then made himself the scarcely more savory political boss of the city. Suaver than Daugherty, with the same beady (if more regular) eyes, more manicured, with more inherited Celtic charm, he was of the same tribe. Roosevelt, the master politician, knew how to handle such types, but Wood was a neophyte. Corinne Roosevelt warned the General to be careful of King's slipperiness.

It was King's conviction that nominations were made, not in heaven but through terrestrial agreements with bosses and political managers. Col-

[3] Wood suffered from being quoted out of context to make him seem the military autocrat that Oswald Garrison Villard accused him of being. He had in one speech attacking communism quoted a Protestant clergyman who had said of the alien Reds: "Send them away in ships of stone with sails of lead, with the wrath of God for a breeze and with hell for their first port." Although such denunciations were infrequent in his speeches, this particular garish example has often been used against him.

lecting delegates was an old Celtic custom with which he was long familiar. For him the room over the Mecca Saloon would always be as much of a beacon as it would be for Daugherty. Even as Daugherty had begun to circulate quietly through the Ohio political back alleys in the interests of Harding, so King began to angle for Wood delegates. He consulted Penrose, and the Pennsylvania boss, although no Wood enthusiast, did not bar the possibility of coming to an agreement with him. King's strategy was to negotiate with the various state political managers "without fuss or feathers" and follow this with back-room deals at the convention. The idea of such undercover dealings was repugnant to Wood and his friends, enthusiastic amateurs who felt that the will of the people— stimulated by large-scale advertising and publicity—should suffice. These zealous amateurs, for the most part former rookies of the Plattsburg camps—young lawyers, writers, businessmen, most of them veterans of the AEF—now formed the Leonard Wood Non-Partisan League with the same zest with which they had earlier sponsored the Military Training Camps Association. Root and Roosevelt's old protégé Henry L. Stimson who had become Taft's secretary of war, came out early for Wood. J. P. Morgan's son-in-law became his chairman for New York City. Even the Senate oligarch, Henry Cabot Lodge, offered to nominate him. In Ohio Dan Hanna and Walter Brown were rounding up the old Progressives for the General.

The Leonard Wood League within a month had over sixty thousand members, and branches in every state. In October Col. William C. Procter, the Ivory Soap king from Cincinnati, became the League's chairman. It had been his gift of half a million dollars to Princeton's graduate school that had set off the great controversy there between the university's Dean Andrew F. West and its President Wilson that had in the end lifted Wilson from Princeton to the White House. Now he was ready to spend at least another half million to replace Wilson by Wood. The League formed a committee of 50 to raise money. William Loeb, Jr., of New York, who described himself as a clearing house for Wood funds in the East thought $1 million would be needed. Loeb, the steelman Col. Ambrose Monell, and two friends of Wood's, George A. Whalen and Rufus Patterson, each pledged a quarter of a million. Procter pledged an initial quarter of a million, and Dan Hanna promised to raise $600,000. The Standard Oil executive H. H. Rogers, and James B. Duke the tobacco king, showed their interest.

The scholarly and almost ascetic but politically naïve Procter determined to sell Wood to the public like Ivory Soap. Under his direction the national organization of the Wood campaign assumed giant proportions. He established elaborate headquarters in New York and Washington, and an even more elaborate central headquarters with himself in charge at

Chicago. Two-thirds of the money spent was for publicity, the rest for speakers and other work. Procter contributed at least three-quarters of a million dollars in unsecured loans to the campaign which was waged in every state but California.

Procter campaigned for Wood because he believed in him, and like his soap, he felt that his candidate should be ninety-nine and forty-four hundredths per cent pure. For manipulators like King and Daugherty, he had nothing but contempt. King left to his own devices might indeed have been able to sew up the nomination for Wood by commitments to the delegate-controlling bosses. If Wood was willing to show himself reasonable, as the Old Guard leaders like Boss Penrose defined reason, they might be willing to accept him. Neither Procter nor Wood would consider such deals. For some months Stimson managed to keep an uncertain peace between the contemptuously idealistic Procter and the scornfully practical King.

> Every day's events are contributing to the irresistible strength of the Wood boom [William Allen White noted in November]. Wood epitomizes safety from all the dangers that beset the land. He is incarnate law and order in a world drifting toward anarchy. "Other refuge have we none. Hangs our helpless soul on thee" sings the country to Leonard Wood. It doesn't ask how he stands on the tariff; it isn't interested in his attitude toward the farmers' land bank nor does it care where he stands on the Initiative, Referendum, and . . . Unless the situation changes, no other candidate will be mentioned in the Republican Convention. . . . But today Leonard Wood is the political man of the hour. More than any other American he represents the need of the times. One reads this in Washington, one reads it in the Middle West, and in the South, and in a score of places high and low. He is the epitome of the need of America today.

The wheel horses of the party, the pros, the Old Guard of the Mc-Kinley era wanted no such independent. What they looked for was "the good old stuff of the good old days, to be taken care of by the good old boys." "Inconceivable?" asked that astute political observer Samuel Blythe in March, 1919. "Wait and see!" [4] Senator Penrose, the ailing boss of Pennsylvania, put it even more bluntly when he later told a friend of Wood's that the "fellows here in the East" were not going to make the mistake they made in nominating Roosevelt in 1900. This time they—the Senate oligarchy of Penrose and Knox of Pennsylvania, Wadsworth and Calder of New York, Watson and New of Indiana, Smoot of Utah, Brandegee of Connecticut, Lodge of Massachusetts—were going to put in a man who would listen. If Wood would not listen, they would find someone with ears better attuned.

The problem for Penrose and the Old Guard was to find a candidate to

4 The *Saturday Evening Post* of March 22, 1919.

stand up to the Wood boom. Whatever their capacity for listening, there seemed to be a dearth of candidates, a distinct possibility that the nomination would go to Wood by default. Hughes was through with politics; Root and Lodge were too old; Hiram Johnson would undoubtedly be a candidate, but it was out of the question for the Republicans to consider a man who had bolted the party in 1912 and undercut Hughes in 1916. Frank O. Lowden, with a brilliant record as a reform governor of Illinois, was much more than a dark horse, and by the autumn of 1919 seemed second only to Wood as a popular candidate. His independent spirit was, however, not one that would make him welcome to the party stalwarts.

With the alarming disregard for politicians being shown by Wood, Penrose began to mull over a candidate more willing to "go along." If he could have had his way nationally, as he had in Pennsylvania, he would have picked his Senate friend from Indiana, Jim Watson, as the Republican nominee in 1920. But Watson was a Senate newcomer, besides being too much of a senatorial caricature with his string tie and his wide hat and his hair fluffing over the collar of his cutaway. Harding in the summer of 1919 looked a possible alternative, and Penrose from his unofficial headquarters in Washington's Wardman Park Hotel sent for him. He arrived at Penrose's suite on a humid afternoon in August and the boss told him to take off his coat and sit down. Then suddenly he sprang the question at him: "Warren, how would you like to be President?"

Harding in his surprise replied that he had no money, that he had his own troubles back in Ohio, and that he would be glad enough just to get back to the Senate. Imperiously Penrose told him that he didn't need any money. "I'll look after that," he explained to the uneasy Senator. "You will make the McKinley type of candidate. You look the part. You can make a front-porch campaign like McKinley's and we'll do all the rest."

Harding was still dubious. But as the Leonard Wood League members increased their tumult, and Procter's rather inept advertising campaign blanketed the country with *civilian* pictures of the General, Penrose more and more talked up the Senator from Marion in party inner circles. Although a senator who had outlived most of his earlier colleagues, the fifty-eight-year-old Penrose was still the single most powerful Republican boss in the country, dictator of Pennsylvania for a generation, a ruler in the Republican council of elders. Unlike most bosses, he had been born to wealth and position and had fought his way down rather than up in the world. His forebears belonged to the inner circle of old colonial Philadelphia families, his father was a respected doctor and teacher, his fortune came to him through inherited real estate.

Penrose graduated from Harvard the year before Theodore Roosevelt. As an undergraduate he had been the largest man in the college—six feet four inches tall—brilliant, lazy, insolent. From Harvard, after a desultory fling at reading law, he went back to his patrician home at 1331 Spruce Street and entered ward politics via the swinging doors of the nearest saloon. The power of politics was the only thing that really engrossed him, the corrupt feudal politics of Pennsylvania that dated before the Civil War when Simon Cameron—with the help of Penrose's grandfather —had bribed his way into the United States Senate. A gutter Nietzschean, Penrose's guiding force was a cold love of power. At twenty-four he became a member of the Pennsylvania legislature, and not too long afterward the partner of the aging big boss of Pennsylvania politics, Matthew Stanley Quay. When Quay retired to the United States Senate, Penrose, having learned the technique of control, became Pennsylvania's boss of bosses. Scornful of democracy and the people, he believed in a ruling oligarchy. Corporation heads doing business in Pennsylvania—the Fricks and the Carnegies and the Rockefellers—would pay him, and he in getting what they wanted done would pay off the ward heelers. He was a man of his word. In his dishonesty he never personally took a dishonest penny, but he found a delight in finding other men corruptible. After he elected himself to the United States Senate in 1897, he spent $150,000 a year of his own estate to keep his Pennsylvania machine running smoothly.

Unlike Quay, Penrose was no hypocrite. Low company was his by aristocratic choice. From the day he arrived at the state capital in Harrisburg, he held open orgies. His framed photograph graced the best brothels of Harrisburg and Philadelphia. A gross feeder, he could eat seven pounds of steak at one sitting and wash it down with a quart of bourbon. When not carousing or politicking, he liked to read and to watch birds. The floor of his bachelor quarters was littered with new books. He knew every species of warbler in Pennsylvania by its song.

In his Senate years he expanded to 350 pounds, so vast a bulk that a sofa was installed for him in the rear of the Chamber. There he sprawled during the sessions, toad-like with bulging eyes and thick neck indistinguishable from his chin. But by the end of the World War his debauched body was in rebellion, the flesh beginning to melt.

Even after his interview with Penrose, Harding still kept insisting privately that he had no ambitions for the Presidency.[5] He told Jim Watson that he was happy just to stay in the Senate, play a little golf, and have a good time. Confidentially, he let Watson know that his blood

[5] Andrew Sinclair in his political biography of Harding, *The Available Man,* tries to make out that Harding's presidential ambitions dated from 1912 and that his repeated assertions of the contrary were merely oblique maneuvers toward the White House. But a reading of his private correspondence, particularly the Phillips letters, makes it clear that he had no such early ambition, that he was never sure of himself, and that he dreaded responsibility. As Senator Watson said of him, "The simple fact is my dear old friend just did not like to work.

pressure was at 185, he had traces of sugar in his urine, and he did not want the burden of being President. A short time later he wrote to Hard, repeating his insistence of the previous February:

> I have been honored with many cordial tenders of support for a nomination for the presidency, and confess that I have been pleased at such evidences of confidence and esteem. To all of these I have said as becomingly as I knew how that I do not aspire to such distinction, but that I do believe the Senate offers the best opportunity for such public service as I am capable of performing and is most agreeable to my own preference. On that account I have had it in my mind to ask to be re-elected to the Senate, provided, at a fitting time for decision, my record shall have justified such approval on the part of the Republicans of Ohio.

The intricacies of Ohio political warfare had not become easier to comprehend since Roosevelt had found them incomprehensible. With the Wood boom rolling, the old Roosevelt Progressives led by Walter Brown, Dan Hanna, and Garford looked forward to taking over the Republican party in the state. Foraker's memory was still green in Cincinnati, and Hynicka was ready to throw the potent weight of Hamilton County against his enemies. Fairbanks and Hard and the Taft stalwarts of 1912 needed a favorite son to harvest the Ohio delegates before the Wood scythes reached them; and this, too, the subtle Daugherty had foreseen, pleading inevitability against Harding's reluctance. If the Wood forces captured Ohio, Harding's seat in the Senate would no longer be safe. To maintain his political power in his party he might have to come out as Ohio's Republican favorite-son presidential candidate.

In mid-October the Republican State Advisory Committee met in secret session and, guided by Brown and Garford, named a subcommittee to smoke out Harding as to his intentions. The old Progressives made it bluntly clear that they did not favor Harding for President "because he has not shown himself to be the type of man needed for the place." They were for Wood, with Lowden as vice president. They would, however, support Harding for another term as senator.

Harding wrote to the committee that he was not a presidential candidate but would be gratified for its support for another term in the Senate. Four days later he was spluttering to Scobey with considerably more boldness than he had shown in his letter to the committee:

> The little bunch of former Progressives, led by Walter Brown and probably with the approval of some others who ought to be my friends, attempted to stand me up in a corner and tell me to decide what office I wanted and thereby close the door to any possible future action. So far as I was personally concerned, I had no particular objection to closing the door on the Presidency, for I never intended to seek a nomination for that place, but

I could not consent to allow those fellows to dictate the course I should pursue in Ohio, and I told them so as politely as I could in a letter. . . .

The first armistice anniversary found Harding writing to H. H. Kemmerer, his old friend and booster in Carroll County: "I have never taken myself sufficiently seriously to entertain a presidential aspiration and I really prefer to have a career in the Senate than to be considered for any other position. . . . I myself incline to look very favorably on General Wood."

At about the same time he was writing to Jennings:

> I needn't recite to you again my own feelings relating to the entire political situation. I could be happy without even returning to the Senate. I grow so weary of the conspiracies, insincerities, and petty practices of politics that I have moments when I am inclined to make a sweeping gesture and tell all of them to "go to hell." However, that doesn't seem to be the prudent course to pursue and I mean, therefore, to move along, without seeking the limelight excessively, and ultimately take such a course as seems to be the becoming one to pursue in order to exercise the highest influence of the party in Ohio in the important political events of next year. You have known me a long while and have known me pretty intimately. I think you know as well as anybody that I do not take myself excessively seriously and do not think my participation in public affairs utterly essential to the continued existence of sane government. I really do not care a rap about higher political honors and do not mean to aspire to them.

Daugherty had other ideas that he confided privately to George Christian:

> Now I think we should without Harding knowing about it canvass and keep in touch with the big field. He need say no more that he would not be a candidate for the Presidency. He will of course not say that he is. He don't have now to do much talking or know much. Presidents don't run in this country like assessors, you know. He had at home the same troubles as McKinley and Hanna and Taft had. In a way at the right time I will make this clear.

Daugherty, feeling that the time was ripe, now began to turn his full persuasive powers on the reluctant candidate. Harding, after the close of the congressional session in November, was spending a few days in Marion on a local speechmaking tour. Daugherty telegraphed that he must see him at once, and he replied by going to Columbus that evening. He arrived about eight o'clock and the two men went to Daugherty's library where they talked for the next six hours. For all Daugherty's urgings, Harding could not bring himself to give up a Senate seat for a long chance at something he did not want and for which he maintained he was not even fitted.

Daugherty persisted. "What would you do in my place?" Harding finally asked him lamely.

Writing with flamboyant defensiveness in his apologia a dozen years later Daugherty recalled the scene as he debated with Harding:

> "I'd go into the big circus." . . .
> "And you think I have a fighting chance?"
> "I think you have the best chance."
> "How do you figure it?" he asked.
> "On this line," I answered. "Neither one of the leading candidates can win. General Wood is backed by a powerful group of rich men who wish a military man in the White House. . . . But there's not enough money in the world to buy the nomination for a man who wears epaulets in 1920."
> "Lowden's a power to be reckoned with," Harding suggested.
> "Sure. The best man on the list, too. I like him. He'd make a fine President. But he'll never have the prize of a nomination."
> "Why?"
> "He's too rich."
> "Nonsense."
> "Besides, he married Pullman's daughter. No party will name a railroad magnate for the office of President." . . .
> "Come down to brass tacks," Harding ordered. "Am I a big enough man for the race?"
> "Don't make me laugh! The days of giants in the Presidential Chair is passed [sic]. Our so-called Great Presidents were all made by the conditions of war under which they administered the office. Greatness in the presidential chair is largely an illusion of the people."

According to Daugherty's recollection he finally persuaded Harding that night to make the race and the two of them walked back through the early-morning darkness to Jennings's house where Harding was staying.

"We had it out," Daugherty told Hard a few days later. "I can't say when he will announce. I had all I could do to overcome his will. We had one hell of a time. But listen! While Harding did not absolutely promise, I say to you and you can rely on it—*he will be a candidate.*"

As a further step to overcoming the Senator's will, Daugherty arranged for Fairbanks, his 1916 successor as chairman of the State Central Committee, to make a public declaration for Harding. Some time earlier Harding had told Fairbanks that no man in his right mind would want to take on a President's responsibilities. Nevertheless, on December 1 at a banquet given by the Roosevelt Club of Toledo, Fairbanks made the first public proposal of Harding as Ohio's candidate. Harding, who was present, had no inkling of what Fairbanks intended to say. Next day the Ohio papers carried the news in streamer headlines.

Harding did not make his own official announcement until December 16, and this he did, with the politician's conventional oblique coyness, in a letter to the chairman of the Miami County Republican Committee who had urged and endorsed his candidacy. He expressed his gratitude for the endorsement, said he had been reluctant to have his name used but declared that his first obligation was to the Republicans of his home state. He would accept, but would leave platform and policy up to the convention. Following the announcement Harding tactfully left to spend a golfing Christmas at Pinehurst, North Carolina, with Speaker Gillett and Massachusetts Congressman Alvan T. Fuller. Gillett had a football with him and whenever the train stopped at any stations on the trip South, they got off and kicked it.

Two other favorite-son senators, Hiram Johnson and Miles Poindexter of Washington, had already announced their candidacies. Lowden had taken his first step on December 17, by entering the South Dakota primaries. Wood's candidacy had been launched officially on December 7 when Procter let it be known that he had accepted the chairmanship of the Leonard Wood National Campaign Committee.

On December 11 in Washington at a meeting of the National Association of Republican State Chairmen, National Chairman Will Hays issued a call for and set the date of the 1920 Republican convention. For the Republican Old Guard leaders gathered there, the chief and urgent topic of conversation was how to stop the boom for Wood. Harding and Lowden were the two candidates most frequently mentioned. And again the pivotal position of Ohio was brought up, the key state that had gone Democratic in the last two elections and that might have carried the Republicans to victory in 1916. A candidate was needed to guarantee Ohio in 1920, and this gave Harding the politician's edge. He would be easy to picture as another McKinley. That was the way Penrose had pictured him. That was the way both Fairbanks and Hard saw him. Hays and the other chairmen felt that the best tactic would be to discourage instructed delegates to the convention.

Daugherty, of course, took care to be at the Washington chairmen's meeting, circulating among the professionals, putting in a wary word for his man. He was accompanied by a blubbery shadow, Jess Smith, whom he had acquired at Washington Court House some years back. Smith had taken to filling in for Daugherty as a secretary, greeter, go-between, valet, odd-job man, and foil. Rigidly uncommunicative about his own domestic disasters, Daugherty, burdened with his ailing wife and his alcoholic son Draper, had in the course of their association developed a need for Jess's uncritical companionship. On his political trips he liked to have a hotel suite with Jess in the next bedroom, and in time he could not sleep unless the door between their two rooms was open. Whenever he rested up from politics in his bachelor's shack on Deer Creek a few miles from Washington Court House he took Jess with him.

Although a compulsively snappy dresser Jess, big-framed and flabby, was no great advertisement for the clothes he wore. His bulging brown eyes were gentle but the rest of his face was pulpy—pink, loose-hanging cheeks, and a black mustache above moist, thick lips. When he talked he had an unfortunate way of spraying his hearers with saliva, so that it had become a saying around Washington Court House: "Here comes Jess. Get out your umbrella." He liked to loll on the courthouse square, any courthouse square, his favorite expression as he buttonholed a passer-by being: "Whaddaya know?"

Jess was twelve years younger than Daugherty and had been baptized Jesse, although everyone called him Jess and he later signed his name without the second "e." His father, Cicero Smith, had been a clerk in a dry-goods store opposite the courthouse at Washington Court House, and had died when Jess was three. His mother remarried, again a Smith, though unrelated to the first. The second Smith became sheriff of Fayette County —a high-paying job in the days when Ohio sheriffs were allowed to pocket their fees. Jess was never cramped for cash. When he graduated from the Washington Court House High School, he was the local sport, a snappy dresser even then, yet never quite one of the boys. He disliked athletics of all kinds, avoided quarrels, and showed little interest in the girls of his class.

On graduating from high school he spent four years clerking in a dry-goods store belonging to relatives of his in Bristol, Tennessee. Then he returned to Washington Court House where his mother set him up in business with a half-interest in a ladies' and gents' furnishings emporium. (Daugherty took care of the legal matters in helping him get started.) On hot summer afternoons people liked to drop in from the sun-baked court-house square to the cool store interior, more often women than men. Jess liked the Main Street gossip and the gossipy companionship of women as much as he loved the feel of silks and satins. It was said that whenever a baby was born to a local newly married couple, he led all the rest in counting fingers. To the tobacco-chewing loafers on the courthouse steps who greeted him amiably enough he was always a bit of a joke. He feared any kind of physical combat and he was afraid of being alone, and although his only reading outside of the newspapers was detective stories, he had a mortal dread of firearms. His mother became a widow for the second time. Jess continued to live with her, under her thumb. His store prospered. Everything he touched turned to money, his business, his prudent investments in stocks and bonds.

Then in his mid-thirties Jess surprised everybody in Washington Court House by falling in love. The object of his late-blooming affections was Roxy Stinson, daughter of a widow who had come to Washington Court House and set up a small music conservatory over the emporium with an adjoining apartment. Roxy, a tall, willowy girl with reddish hair, had a stylish way of wearing her clothes and a sharp mind. In her mother's opinion she was much too good for Jess Smith, and she sent her to Europe for a year to study music. Roxy returned, a cosmopolite by Fayette County standards. Still Jess pursued her with his intentions, following her even into the dining room of Mrs. Tuttle's boardinghouse, across the street from the Cherry Hotel, where she and her mother took their noonday meal.

After turning Jess down for some months Roxy finally agreed to marry him, much to the dismay of Jess's mother, who felt he was too young. Roxy was twenty-four years old and Jess was worth over a hundred thousand dollars when they were married in November, 1908. The idyll did not last. In a little over a year she was suing to divorce him on the grounds of his extreme cruelty in humiliating her and refusing to give her money. Everyone knew that the real reason was her mother-in-law, although it was also whispered that Jess had been unable to fulfill his duties as a husband.

After the divorce Roxy and Jess remained strangely good friends. She went back to live with her mother in the flat over the store, and he squired her about as he had when he was courting her. After his mother's death he continued to live in the family house, but could not bear to be alone in it overnight. He moved his colored chauffeur in with him, and whenever the chauffeur happened to be away Jess would take home one of the clerks from the store. With the wartime inflation his store made him wealthy, and his wealth made him known and brought him a countinghouse respect. He busied himself with fraternal organizations, became head of the Elks in Ohio. Although overage, asthmatic, and too fearful of firearms to make a soldier, he whooped it up during the war with belligerent zeal for the Red Cross and in the Liberty Bond drives. Such was Beau Jess of Washington Court House when he attached himself to Harry Daugherty and his fortunes and from a purveyor of velvet and gimps became Daugherty's trusted political errand boy.

Some time during December, 1919, Daugherty took over as Harding's political manager, although this was not announced officially until a month later. Compared to Wood's almost unlimited funds Daugherty had to operate on a shoestring. Scobey and Jess Smith gave $500 each. An independent oilman, James G. Darden, sent in $6,000. Daugherty himself gave $12,500.[6] Carmi Thompson, with $13,950 was the largest single contributor. Through Harding's friend Finley Peter Dunne, the bibulous creator of "Mr. Dooley," the oil refiner Harry Sinclair and Harry Payne Whitney each agreed to lend—but not give—$7,500. Sinclair told Dunne he was for Wood and that Harding hadn't a chance in the world. Daugh-

[6] Before he had finished Daugherty spent $50,000 of his own money on Harding's campaign.

erty's goal was $100,000. Many of Harding's Ohio friends made small donations, and approximately a third of the total came from citizens of Marion.

Prudently Daugherty stayed away from Ohio, leaving Hard in charge there to try to secure a solid slate of favorite-son delegates. Daugherty himself opened a two-room headquarters in a shabby Washington hotel and, with Jess Smith and the Columbus political hanger-on Howard D. Mannington as his assistants, began his country-wide undercover campaign. In several Washington press interviews he received some favorable comment from his remark that the next President should be one who "would take counsel from the legislative branch of the government." His headquarters instructions were to offend no other candidate or possible candidate except Wood. He arranged for 50 Ohio Republicans to come to Washington, paid for their rooms at the Willard, saw to it that Harding gave them a flattering reception, and persuaded them to sound out the members of the National Committee on Harding as a candidate. He himself got in touch with every member of the National Committee, trying to get each to agree to consider Harding, if not for first, at least for second or third choice.

Without Daugherty's unscrupulous energy Harding knew that his campaign would be no more than the vanity gesture of a favorite son. He still felt dubious. To a Marion real-estate agent writing to inquire if the Mount Vernon Avenue house was for sale, he replied that it was not, since there was always the possibility that he might be returning to Marion for good after the next election. To Scobey he wrote on December 30 about the approaching campaign:

> There does not seem to have been a ripple on the surface except in opposition to Daugherty. I am not sure but that is more frequently made an excuse than it is a genuine reason for complaint. He is vastly much the smartest politician in the bunch and the only one with vision and acquaintances to carry on a nationwide campaign. More than that he is the only big fellow in Ohio who doesn't find his system more or less tinctured with jealousy of me.
>
> Things seem to be going along fine. Daugherty was here yesterday and made the most gratifying reports. More than that, reports are exceedingly good from many other sections of the country.

From the moment Daugherty took over as Harding's manager his strategy was simple, however complicated his tactics might become. Wood, he felt, had enough natural enemies among politicians to make his nomination impossible. He felt this even more strongly in January when the feud between King and Procter at Wood's headquarters reached a climax. To King, Procter was an "impossible political animal" and his advertising campaign a costly failure; Procter objected to King's "bartering and manipulation." When in the final showdown King demanded complete control of the Wood campaign, the General dismissed him. The bosses drew their own moral from King's fate. Wood had now cut himself off from the Old Guard. Lowden, though Progressive within his own state, had taken pains not to antagonize the party organization, and many of the regulars were willing to turn to him as the strongest candidate to block Wood in the convention. Yet, in Daugherty's long-term reasoning, Lowden had even less chance than Wood of winning a majority of the delegates. The two would cancel each other out, and when the convention had blundered into an impasse, some less conspicuous candidate would be accepted as a compromise. This compromise candidate, to Daugherty's mind, could and should be Harding. For the next six months the prescient manager would devote himself to praising favorite sons and collecting second- and third- and fourth-choice pledges for Harding. Such a long-odds possibility stirred his gambler's blood.

> Harding's campaign from the beginning was a one-man-managed campaign, carefully planned, if I know what it is to plan a campaign [Daugherty wrote in his retirement]. Without his knowing it I traveled all over the country to get the situation at first hand. I did this at my own expense. . . . Harding did not know much about what I was doing; I never bothered him, just went ahead, and when I learned what the situation was I told him about it. . . . The real work was done months before the convention when the pins were set up all over the country for second, third, and fourth choices for Harding among the delegates and influential men of the various communities. . . . The simplicity of his campaign was so pronounced that nobody knew about it until we began to collect the second, third, and fourth choice votes when we got the convention tied up. This was part of the game and we nominated Harding by the use of these second, third, and four choices in the tie-up.

In his devious travels Daugherty managed to corral a scant scattering of delegate pledges, most of them from the Southern states—one each from Alabama, Arkansas, Florida, and Mississippi; two from Louisiana and Kentucky. Mont Reily had collected five Missouri delegates openly for Harding plus eight concealed ones. From Texas Scobey promised five delegates, plus three or four more in reserve. Harding's own political correspondence in the pre-convention months is voluminous. It has been held that Daugherty, operating on his own and seldom in Washington, was unaware of the wider ramifications of Harding's campaign, and that he claimed too much in claiming the responsibility for Harding's nomination. Harding, in fact, was not the passive figure that Daugherty, intent on his own vindication, tried to make him. Nevertheless, without Daugherty's Mephistophelean energy, Harding alone would never have stumbled forward to the nomination. Hard, to whom Harding had entrusted his business affairs in Columbus during the senatorial years, wrote in 1959, long after Daugherty's death: "Again, and again, and again I say Harding would never have been nominated but for the leadership of Daugherty."

For all Daugherty's adroitness, his leadership was bound to draw fire in Ohio, for his idea of achieving cooperation had often been with a knuckle-duster, and the state was full of his enemies. Harding with his cherished concepts of harmony had moments of doubt about his pugnacious no-holds-barred manager.

> Timkin and Wolfe and others have made a great outcry against Daugherty [he wrote to Scobey in mid-January]. You know, of course, that Daugherty does not own me in any way and I am under no particular spell in my relationship to him. He does have one appealing attribute, namely, that he is cordially for me in the open, and I would rather go to hell and defeat with an outspoken friend than ascend to the seats of the Mighty by coddling those who are friendly to my face but ready to stab me when I am not looking.

By January Hiram Johnson, the stalker of Woodrow Wilson and his League, had become the most obstreperous challenger to Wood. His dynamism was still potent with the old Progressives of the West not only in their populism but in their isolationism and suspicions of the financial East. Wood might stand for the League of Nations with reservations, Johnson would have no part of it under any conditions. Intense and combative, eager to enter any state contest, Johnson drew the crowds. Though he had served as his party's pallbearer in 1912 and its gravedigger in 1916, there seemed a chance that in 1920 in the reaction against Wilson he might be his party's standard-bearer. His chief backers were William Wrigley, Jr., of spearmint gum, and the advertising wizard and assistant chairman of the Republican National Committee, Albert D. Lasker. The many-sided Wrigley was himself running as a Lowden delegate while contributing to Wood's as well as Johnson's campaign. The Senate Old Guard, who did not believe in Johnson's chances, nevertheless encouraged him as a means of cutting into Wood's inherited Roosevelt-Progressive support.

Harding's immediate problem was to secure his still wobbly hold on his own state. Ohio had a peculiar ballot law—the only one of its kind in the country—in which candidates for delegate to a national convention were forced to indicate their second as well as their first choice. In December Hynicka on behalf of Procter approached Harding with the suave suggestion that the Wood forces would agree to have any of their delegates file for Harding for second choice if he in turn would instruct his delegates to make their second choice Wood. It seemed reasonable enough to Harding, and, as he wrote to Carmi Thompson, a harmonious way to put an end to the guerrilla warfare between Daugherty and Hynicka. The deviousness of Hynicka's proposition was at once apparent to the equally devious Daugherty. He and Harding had several conferences with Dan Hanna and Procter. Procter now made the ostensible concession of offering to support Harding for first choice on the nomination ballot, if Harding would support Wood for the second. But Daugherty pointed out to Harding that this would mean turning over the state to the enemy. After favorite-son Harding had received Ohio's 48 convention votes on the first ballot, his delegates would then be marshaled aboard the Wood band wagon. Far from stopping Wood, the Hynicka-Procter maneuver would have given his bandwagon a sturdy push forward.

Harding let Hanna and Procter think he was "thinking over" this proposal, but with Daugherty at his elbow he had never really considered it. Finally in a public announcement in mid-January he openly challenged Wood, declaring that he wanted only the support of those delegates who would stand by him to the end. If there was any doubt about Ohio's choice, he added, let it be decided at the primaries. As insulating second choice for his delegates he picked the eighty-five-year-old General Keifer. Daugherty he named as one of his candidates for delegate-at-large, the other three being Herrick, Willis, and—as a concession to Hamilton County—Cincinnati's Mayor John Galvin.

Procter took up the challenge, announcing that since Harding had refused to concede the Wood forces second choice, they would fight him for first. After King's dismissal the Wood committee had felt the lack of a seasoned politician's directing hand, and brought in Frank Hitchcock who had managed Taft's campaign in 1908 and stood on the regulars' burning deck in 1912. Hitchcock, a close-mouthed, imperturbable professional, specialized in rounding up Southern delegations. He and Procter were to have equal authority. Wood's managers planned to enter their candidate in every state holding a primary contest for delegates except California. Harding's meager funds allowed him no such expansive and expensive gestures. Only in Indiana did he plan to make a primary contest outside Ohio. There Gov. James N. Goodrich had withdrawn as favorite son, and the Wood, Johnson, and Lowden forces were all campaigning for the state delegates. Daugherty was openly confident not only that Harding would get a solid Ohio delegation but that he would also beat his wealthier rivals in neighboring Indiana. His exuberant confidence for once got the better of him while he was talking over campaign prospects with two reporters in his room at the Waldorf-Astoria in New York:

> I don't expect Senator Harding to be nominated on the first, second, or third ballot [he admitted], but I think about eleven minutes after two o'clock on Friday morning of the convention, when fifteen or twenty men, bleary-eyed and perspiring profusely from the heat, are sitting around a table some one of them will say: "Who will we nominate?"

At that decisive time the friends of Senator Harding can suggest him and can afford to abide by the result. I don't know but what I might suggest him myself.[7]

With the gratuitous addition of cigar smoke by later commentators, the "smoke-filled room at 2:11 A.M." became metonymy for cynical political manipulation.

Harding's old Columbus friend, Judge David Pugh, whose municipal reform bill he had introduced in the Ohio Assembly in 1900, protested that the statement gave him "the blind staggers." "In plain vernacular," he wrote "you are to be nominated by 15 or 20 bosses." Harding was upset by the "unseemly" statement. He replied that Daugherty was misquoted, but that it was a "very unfortunate publication."

Harding's own confidence was growing as well as his self-assurance. He remarked that if he did not start off in the convention with 150 votes plus the 48 from his own state he would be "terribly grieved." To Daugherty, his candidate still seemed to act as though his heart was not very much in it, "but he got it into his system when we got on the battleground." Following Daugherty's strategy, Harding solicited his political acquaintances all over the country for their second or third choice. Writing to San Francisco's political leader John H. Rossiter, he congratulated him on California's "cordially" backing Johnson, then asked "if it would not be possible to have at least some men on the California delegation who would think kindly concerning me in case there comes a time in the convention when the nomination of some one other than Senator Johnson may seem likely." Rossiter replied that he had talked with the closest friends of Johnson, and that the major part of the California delegation would be strong for Harding as second choice.

To Charlie Forbes, returned from his self-admittedly heroic exploits with the American Expeditionary Force and now living in Spokane, Washington, Harding suggested that it might be the prudent thing to cooperate with Senator Poindexter's friends and secure a claim on his delegates after they became convinced that Poindexter had no real chance of being

[7] Charles Hilles, writing Mark Sullivan years later, charitably explained Daugherty's gaffe. "Daugherty was hastily packing his bag in a Waldorf-Astoria Hotel room when two reporters called. He expressed regret that he had not time for an interview. One of the reporters insisted in asking questions. Daugherty indifferently uttered a few laconic sentences and started for the elevator. The reporter, trying to provoke Daugherty into talk, followed. He said that he presumed that as Daugherty could not support by an authentic table of delegates his boast that Harding would be the nominee, it followed that Daugherty must expect to win by manipulation—probably in some back room of a hotel with a small group of political managers reduced to pulp by the inevitable vigil and travail. The reporter went on to say to Daugherty that he presumed the conferees would be expected to surrender at 2 A.M. in a smoke-filled room. Daugherty, unaffected by the taunt retorted carelessly, 'Make it two eleven.'"

nominated. "Personally, I am not counting on anything in California in the way of a first-choice vote," he explained, "and do not expect very much from Oregon, Idaho, or Montana, but I think we can count on the friendly attitude of Borah to help things come our way if it is apparent that Johnson cannot succeed."

To make himself better known, his face more familiar, Harding set out on a campaign tour through New England where there was a certain amount of sentiment bubbling up for Gov. Calvin Coolidge of Massachusetts. Six months before Coolidge had been a nonentity in the Republican succession of governors, but had emerged as a national figure since the Boston police strike of September, 1919, in which—to those outside the inner Boston circle of those who knew the facts—he assumed the role of "the pilot that weathered the storm." Fairbanks, writing to L. K. Torbert of the Union League Club of Chicago, felt that Harding was growing stronger every day and added "The ticket you suggest, 'Harding and Coolidge,' would sweep the country like a whirlwind, and re-establish an American government at Washington." Harding, challenging no one, used his tour to impress his Roman presence, his silver voice, and friendly manner on the forgetful electorate.

He was in Washington on February 3 telling the National Press Club that "no nation was ever eminent except in the high tide of commercial supremacy," and a week later was on his way to Marion. Mont Reily, his self-appointed Western manager—"a queer duck," Daugherty thought him—had mapped out a tour of several weeks through Kansas, Oklahoma, Texas, Colorado, and Nebraska. On February 28 Harding started off with the Duchess and Daugherty, being joined by Reily at Kansas City. He opened his campaign officially in Dallas, the first Republican presidential candidate ever to speak in Texas. He also spoke in Fort Worth and at Beethoven Hall, San Antonio. At Denver he spent two days and appeared before an enthusiastic audience of over three thousand. While in Colorado he had a friendly visit with Brooks Fletcher, the editor of the Marion *Tribune,* and thinking of running for senator on the Democratic ticket if Harding was not going to run. Harding said he could not yet commit himself. On March 12 he was the guest of the Ohio Society of Omaha.

Scarcely was he back from the West before he started on his much more strenuous campaign trek through Ohio and Indiana. The Indiana primaries came a week after those in his own state. Both were vital to him. He opened his Indiana campaign on March 27 at a luncheon at the Columbia Club in Indianapolis, referring to himself as a rather unwilling but very confident candidate. He spoke in Anderson, Muncie, Kokomo, Huntington, telling his audience that what was wrong with America was that we were getting away from government by political parties. We needed more "honesty in life" than we needed a League of Nations.

The Wood forces counterattacked. After Wolfe had warned Harding to drop Daugherty, the *Dispatch* ran a pointed editorial denouncing the political manipulations of favorite sons. Procter then gave Harding what he considered a last chance, offering Wood's support to help re-elect him senator if he in turn would withdraw from the presidential race, and threatening to run someone else against him for senator if he did not. Following Harding's vote for the anti-strike clause of the Esch-Cummings Bill returning the railroads to private ownership, the workers started a Railway Men's Anti-Harding Club which so fired George Christian that he wrote to a Marion friend to bring a quart in his valise for an "indignation party." Procter and Hitchcock—working together none too harmoniously, and reportedly calling each other "false alarm" and "Ivory Soap bubble" —were still keeping the headquarters in Columbus humming stirring up the railroad workers, persuading an Ohio United Mine Workers' convention to condemn Harding for his labor record and unofficially support Wood.

These setbacks were more than balanced when Walter Brown, forsaking the last remnants of his Progressive past, abandoned Procter and pledged Harding his unqualified support. Harding expanded in euphoric confidence. "If things fall down in Ohio the whole structure will crumble," he admitted to Scobey, but "I do not think there will be any disappointment. . . . If my correspondence and personal files are dependable, the great rank and file of the state is very cordially behind me."

While Harding barnstormed from state to state, he still continued his
[- -]
Yet even as the two approached the breaking point, as she wrote ridiculing his political ambitions, accusing him of having affairs with other women, and as she flaunted her own past, he found himself drawn back to her. [- - -
- -
- -
- -
- - - - - - - - - - -]

Although with the Duchess's sharp eye on him he made no attempt to see Nan, he sent her money regularly, a hundred or a hundred and fifty dollars at a time, sometimes as much as three or four hundred. Nan had gone with the baby to Chicago where she was living with her sister Elizabeth and her brother-in-law Scott Willits, a musician with the Chicago Opera Company, in a small four-room apartment at 6103 Wood-lawn Avenue on the corner of 61st Street. After putting Elizabeth Ann out to board about a block and a half away where she could see her daily, Nan had taken a job as a secretary.

Some time in April Jim Phillips learned of his wife's affair with his old friend. Possibly he may have found out for himself, more probably she had told him in her fury after Harding again refused to consider marrying her. The break was now complete, and Constant—she specified the amount with cruel emphasis—would have to pay. When he delayed his answer, she wrote again. Finally he replied:

[--

--------]

There was still to be an aftermath, but this was his last letter to his beloved and adored Carrie.

The presidential primaries—in the 20 states having them—were held at the erratic whim of state legislatures any time between March and June. For the most part they developed into a straight contest between Wood and Johnson, with Lowden making only token entries. Lowden's major effort was in South Dakota where both he and Wood spent vast sums of money for the 10 electoral votes of that sparsely populated state. Over King's objections, Procter had insisted on this symbolic confrontation. Wood toured the state in the worst of weather, speaking to the farmers and their wives, at one point using a handcar to get through a blizzard for a meeting at Watertown. He carried South Dakota by 31,625 votes to Lowden's 26,981. Johnson, attracting the large German vote and the increasing numbers of Americans who rejected Wilson's League, received a surprising 26,301.

In Michigan Johnson managed to defeat both Wood and Lowden, taking the state with the help of Anti-League Irish- and German-Americans and the remnants of the Progressives. Johnson also carried Nebraska against Wood. Here General Pershing had made a ballot test of his own presidential ambitions, but Black Jack's scanty vote total had left his ambitions as private yearnings.

Contrary to Hitchcock's advice and to the political amenities, Procter insisted on contesting Lowden's home state. There Lowden was viciously opposed by the mayor of Chicago, William H. "Big Bill" Thompson, who had made a name for himself by threatening to "punch King George in the snoot" if that unwary monarch should ever set foot in his city. In spite of the third of a million dollars that Procter spent in Illinois, Lowden defeated Wood by 236,802 to 156,719 votes, with Johnson an inconspicuous third. Nevertheless, Big Bill delivered Chicago's Cook County to Wood. The contest left a bitterness between Lowden and Wood that made any later cooperation almost impossible.

In New Jersey Wood confronted Johnson alone in what the business East considered a crucial contest. Wood won as expected, but contrary to expectations he squeaked through with a mere 1,300-vote margin in a total of over a hundred thousand, leaving Johnson in his defeat with the prestige of victory.

The day of the Ohio primaries—April 27—showed a different state of affairs from the optimistic anticipations of Harding's files and correspondence. The not-so-favorite son carried his home state by a mere 15,000 votes over Wood, his total of 123,257 being less than the combined totals of Wood and Johnson. Nor could he even claim a solid slate of delegates, for Wood had managed to capture nine of the 48, plus three or four more ostensibly for Harding but controlled by Hamilton County. With Dan Hanna's support, the General had swept Cleveland. In Cincinnati Hynicka, in spite of pre-primary expressions of cordiality, had passed the word down to his ward captains to "knife" Daugherty as delegate-at-large. So thoroughly did the carvers do their job that a Wood candidate, William A. Boyd, won out over Daugherty by 959 votes. Wolfe's *Ohio State Journal* concluded that Harding was eliminated as a presidential candidate and Daugherty discredited as a politician.

Daugherty by manipulating his political abacus tried to prove that Harding had after all scored a victory, but other leaders felt that he might not have enough political resources left to be renominated for senator. Both Brown and Willis had been eyeing the Senate seat, and in fact Willis's blustering support for Harding as a presidential candidate had been not so much loyalty to the man as longing to replace him.

If Ohio had been a misfortune, Indiana the following week turned out a disaster. Harding and the Duchess had gone to Indianapolis to watch the returns at the home of Sen. Harry New. By early evening the trend was clear. In the state that Daugherty had so confidently claimed, less than one voter in ten had marked his ballot for Harding, and the Ohio Senator trailed far behind Wood, Johnson, and Lowden.[8] He could not claim a single Indiana delegate. New advised him on the spot to give up the contest and get himself re-elected to the Senate while he could still manage it. The despondent Harding agreed and picked up the telephone to notify his Ohio headquarters. Before he could get the operator, the

[8] The final Indiana tabulation was: Wood 85,776; Johnson 79,829; Lowden 31,118; Harding 20,819.

Duchess crossed the room, her eyes blazing, and snatched the telephone out of his hands. "Wurr'n Harding," she shrilled at him, "what are you doing? Give up? Not until the convention is over. Think of your friends in Ohio!"

Penrose, reading the Indiana results in his Spruce Street den, struck Harding off his list of possibles and began to consider refurbishing Philander Knox. The Pennsylvania boss had promised Harding his support if he could "make good," but Harding had shown he could not even make Ohio. Penrose's enthusiasm had in any case diminished since Harding's speech to the Manufacturer's Association of Philadelphia on February 22 which Penrose's secretary, Leighton C. Taylor, had taken down in shorthand and read to him. "Harding isn't as big a man as I thought he was," was Penrose's comment. "He should have talked more about the tariff and not so much about playing cymbals in the Marion brass band."

Harding's first reaction to the twin disasters of Ohio and Indiana was one of passive despair. Threatened as well by Carrie, he wanted to quit before anything more could happen, would have quit if his manager had let him.

Mid-May found him traveling to Boston with Senator Lenroot to speak at the annual dinner of the Home Market Club. In the club car during the journey he told Lenroot that he considered himself wholly out of the presidential race and that he was glad of it. He said the same thing less directly in his Boston speech when he predicted that Massachusetts' Gov. Calvin Coolidge might receive the nomination. It was in this speech that he was first quoted as using the word "normalcy," a word he is commonly supposed to have then coined and one that he subsequently used with pride again and again, including it even in his inaugural address. Falling back on the alliterative sequences that were his oratorical stock in trade, he told his Boston audience that "America's present need is not heroics but healing; not nostrums but normalcy; not revolution but restoration; . . . not surgery but serenity." [9]

If adversity could have crushed Daugherty, he would have been flattened in McKinley's day. Setbacks only steeled him to his purpose. With his own tough confidence, he revived Harding's spirits, persuading him that he had still won a victory in Ohio, that Indiana mattered much less than the second and third and fourth choices. He trotted out the old

[9] Harding did not coin "normalcy" although he did bring it into common use. It first appeared in 1857 in Davies & Peck's *Mathematical Dictionary*. Indeed reporters claimed that Harding did not even revive the word, that in his script he had written "not nostrums but normality." In reading the speech he mispronounced this as "normalty," to the concealed amusement of reporters who were later kind enough to change the gaffe to "normalcy" in their copy.

arguments. Wood and Lowden would cancel each other out. Johnson was too radical, for all his showing in the West and in New Jersey. Root and Knox were too old. In the end the delegates would still turn to Harding if he played his cards right.

Daugherty kept busily at his subterranean contacts. One essential meeting he had long been trying to arrange through his circus friend John Ringling was with the Oklahoma oil multimillionaire Jake L. Hamon. It had just cost Jake $120,000 to tuck 18 of Oklahoma's Republican delegates in his pocket, and he was thought to have an oily interest in some 30 out-of-state delegates. Such a bloc, as Daugherty well realized, if thrown in at the psychological moment might be sufficient to start a convention stampede.

Most of Jake's fellow townsmen in Ardmore thought of him, fondly or otherwise, as the last of the Oklahoma bad men. With gold-plated smile, uptilted cigar, derby on the back of his square head, and as likely as not his mistress Clara on his arm, he was one of the fixtures of that booming oil town, a bold man and a hard drinker.

Born in Kansas in 1875, he made a name as a prankster at the University of Kansas law school. He married one Georgia Perkins in 1898 and in 1901 came to Oklahoma to start a law practice of sorts in the old Indian town of Lawton. He speculated in real estate, swindled the Indians of their remaining land, and when oil was discovered about 1911 in southern Oklahoma he took leases on wells in the Healdton Field near Ardmore and became rich overnight. He gobbled up oil wells, gas wells, and townships along the Oklahoma, New Mexico, & Pacific Railroad line which with John Ringling he had built from Ardmore to Healdton in 1913. His ambition was to extend his railroad to Lawton so that he could ride into his old home town in his own private car on his own tracks.

When he moved to Ardmore he left his wife and two children behind him and took up with Clara Barton Smith, a seventeen-year-old clerk in a dry-goods store. After sending her to school in Kansas, he made her his confidential secretary as well as his mistress. Since his wife refused him a divorce, he arranged a fictitious marriage for Clara with his nephew Frank so that she could take the name of Hamon. For eight years Jake lived in Room 28 of the Ardmore's Randol Hotel and Clara lived in Room 29. The more dependent Jake became on Clara, the more independent, the more capable of taking his measure she became. Theirs was a turbulent and quarrelsome relationship.

In 1906 Jake entered politics as chairman of the Republican Territorial Central Committee. When Oklahoma was admitted to statehood the following year, he became the chairman of the first Republican State Committee. At the beginning of the 1920 campaign Procter picked him as the leader of the Wood forces in Oklahoma, but then switched to the then

National Committeeman James J. McGraw. The switch caused a state-wide fight. Jake spent thousands to defeat the Wood delegates in the primaries as a first step to defeating McGraw for re-election as national committee-man. Ostensibly the 18 Hamon delegates were for Lowden, but there was talk of their giving Jake a complimentary vote on the first ballot.

For Jake politics was an exuberant adjunct of business. As an oil opera-tor he had long had his eye on government lands, the reservations that conservationist mollycoddles and old women of both sexes wanted to fence off from private enterprise, keep the public from getting the fuel it needed, and incidentally keep people like himself from making money.

Ringling finally brought Hamon to Washington where Daugherty met him at his hotel dining room for breakfast. Hamon, tucking his napkin into his vest, ordered *"three* eggs and plenty of ham." The dyspeptic Daugherty, who had never eaten three eggs at once in his life, ordered the same. "You live among tenderfeet but you know how to order a real breakfast," Jake complimented him. Daugherty managed to finish his breakfast, and the two men spent a cordial day together. Jake promised that if the time ever came that Lowden could not carry the convention, he would throw his Lowden votes to Harding. For Daugherty that was better than a first choice.

Three weeks before the convention Harding had recovered sufficiently from his Ohio-Indiana setback to assure Scobey that he expected approxi-mately 115 votes on the first ballot. Scobey replied that even if Harding never should be President he still looked like one, and nothing had really happened "to preclude your nomination." But even the approach of the convention could not still Daugherty's relentless determination to oust Hynicka from the National Committee. Walter Brown protested to Hard-ing in the interests of harmony, but the vengeful Daugherty insisted that Hynicka was a traitor who had never wanted to see Harding President. In spite of Brown, he was resolved to punish the Cincinnati boss. Brown, trying to act as an ameliorating go-between, was accused by Daugherty of also having traitorous intentions.

Harding in his distress wrote Brown that he felt they could accomplish nothing in the spirit of reprisal, and he begged Brown to understand that he was not influenced by Daugherty, and that he himself had had a satis-factory interview with Hynicka and was willing to come to terms with him.

As the June convention date neared, some of the bloom seemed off Wood's candidacy. Observers like William Allen White were beginning to have second thoughts about military men. The Lowden boom con-tinued to flourish. Though Penrose and the Old Guard considered him too independent, too much the farmer's friend, he had not shown Wood's contempt for politicians or outraged the state and local leaders. Lowden had political intelligence, charm, and goodwill, and a sterling record as governor—enough, his manager, Illinois's Secretary of State Louis L. Emmerson felt, to offset his Pullman connection.

Beyond the big three of Wood, Lowden, and Johnson there were numerous dark horses besides Harding being groomed in the Republican stable. As well as Poindexter there was that rufous atavistic Yankee, Calvin Coolidge. Frank Stearns, the fussy Boston dry-goods merchant who was Coolidge's original backer, was planning to mail copies of a book containing Cautious Cal's speech platitudes, *Have Faith in Massachusetts,* to every prospective delegate. The able and popular governor of Pennsylvania, William C. Sproul, seemed a distant possibility—Penrose willing. Even more hopefully distant was Columbia University's president, Nicholas Murray Butler, who combined a high taste for learning with a low taste for politics. When Gov. Henry Allen of Kansas was mentioned it was mostly through courtesy of his friend William Allen White.

If the inglorious electorate had been given the free choice that is so seldom offered it in politics, many of the voters of both parties would have chosen Herbert Hoover as their next President. As chairman of the Commission for Relief in Belgium in 1914, as Wilson's food administrator, as the man most responsible for feeding starving Europe directly after the war, Hoover commanded a non-partisan respect that was almost veneration. During the war his name was such a household word that "hoover-ize," came to mean to save food. When he returned to the United States in September, 1919, after almost a year of directing European postwar famine relief he, in the words of the *New Republic,* clearly outclassed "any other conspicuous American citizen." Politically he looked like "a Providential gift to the American people for the office of pilot during the treacherous navigation of the next few years." The only difficulty was that no one knew for certain whether he was Republican or Democrat, or if he was anything at all. In 1918 he had campaigned for Wilson's Democratic Congress. With the tide turning so sharply against the·Democrats, it would take a glamorous non-political name like his to bring the party to victory in 1920. Wilson's prewar ambassador to Germany, James W. Gerard, came out for him. As late as January, 1920, Assistant Secretary of the Navy Franklin Delano Roosevelt was writing wistfully of Hoover to Hugh Gibson, the first American ambassador to the revived Poland: "He certainly is a wonder and I wish we could make him President of the United States. There could not be a better one." The chairman of the Democratic National Committee, Homer S. Cummings, was still considering Hoover in February. Democratic delegates pledged to him were elected in New Hampshire, and he received more Democratic votes in the Michigan primary than any Democratic candidate. Finally Hoover broke the spell by announcing that he was a Republican.

As a supporter of the League of Nations Hoover entered the May California primaries against Johnson, as he explained, to give Progressive Republicans there a chance to vote for the League. The irreconcilable Johnson, tremendously popular in his own state, defeated Hoover by 370,000 to 210,000; but that over two hundred thousand voters had chosen this a-political newcomer was remarkable, the more because Hoover neither campaigned in nor even visited California. Since, however, the convention would scarcely reject Johnson for his defeated opponent, the California results seemed to put an end to the Hoover candidacy.

The conclusion of all the primaries gave Wood 124 instructed delegates; Johnson, 112; Lowden, 72; and Harding, 39. Chairman Hays and the Republican National Committee had been working to secure as many uncommitted delegates as possible from the non-primary states, and the course of the convention seemed unpredictable. Whoever was nominated by the Republicans would be elected, and that was about all that could be said. Bryan, the three-time loser, jokingly remarked that the Democratic prospects were so poor it would be perfectly natural for them to draft him again. Mulling over the dilemma of the Republican interregnum, Henry Cabot Lodge met with Senators Wadsworth and Calder shortly before the convention and agreed that after the vanity votes for the favorite sons had been cast, they would throw their influence behind Hughes. Through their emissary, Judge Meier Steinbrink, they let Hughes know of their tentative decision. Earlier that spring Hughes's daughter Helen, a brilliant young Vassar graduate, had died of tuberculosis contracted following a period of war work for the YMCA. "Since our daughter died Mrs. Hughes and I are heartbroken," Hughes told Steinbrink. "I don't want to be President of the United States. I request that my name be not even mentioned in the convention."

Even Mark Hanna would have raised a tufted eyebrow at the amounts that Procter was spending for Wood in the pre-convention campaign. Though Procter would not stoop to bribery, no other caution restrained him and he blanketed the country with posters, pamphlets, buttons, books, and billboards. Scornful as ever of the professional politicians, he was convinced that he could sell Wood to the public and to the convention with the same insistent energy that had made his floating Ivory Soap cakes a national institution. But, as one professional observed, "all the ivory did not go into the soap." Procter's campaign by its very lavishness overreached itself. In February Hearst's *New York American* had run an "exposé" of Wood's rich backers. Later in the spring Johnson in several bitter speeches accused Wood of spending vast improper sums that gave him undue advantage. Several weeks before the convention Daugherty got "the right man" to give Senator Borah some private details about the easy Wood money. Borah, Johnson's friend and backer, was one of the master orators of his day, so unbending that Washingtonians seeing him on his daily horseback ride in Rock Creek Park marveled that he would consent to go in the same direction as the horse. The anti-League Senator was soon condemning Wood's "saturnalia of corruption" and announcing that a plot was on foot to buy the Presidency. At his insistence the Senate Committee on Privileges and Elections on May 27 appointed a subcommittee, known as the Kenyon Committee from its chairman Senator Kenyon, "to inquire into the campaign expenditures of various political candidates of both parties and any related facts that would be of public concern."

The committee, meeting the week before the convention, failed to show that any sinister group was trying to buy the Presidency, but it did bring out that the Wood forces had spent on the record $1,773,303, and probably several times that off the record. For the Republican regulars the Kenyon investigation was a happy means of putting a crimp in the maverick Wood; and branding him the rich man's choice did him lasting damage.

If Wood's candidacy was hurt by the Senate investigations, Lowden's candidacy was almost destroyed. Lowden's campaign had cost $414,984, all but $35,000 of which he had supplied out of his own pocket. Clean on contributions, he was tripped up by "related facts" when the committee brought to light that Emmerson had paid the Lowden manager, E. L. Morse, in Missouri, $32,000 "to create Lowden sentiment." Seventeen thousand of this, Morse had paid to Missouri National Committeeman Jacob L. Babler. Among his disbursements Babler had paid two uncommitted St. Louis delegates, Robert E. Moore and Circuit Court Clerk Nat Goldstein, $2,500 each "for nothing in particular but to create sentiment for Governor Lowden." Enough sentiment was created for Moore and Goldstein to announce themselves Lowden delegates. Such sentiment, although created without Lowden's knowledge, cut down his boom and came close to ruining his chances at the convention.

Johnson's expenses were $194,393, Harding's a modest $113,109. Although Wood, and Lowden even more, suffered from the Kenyon report, the revelations backfired on Johnson, drawing on him the combined enmity of both Lowden and Wood supporters. No compromise could be foreseen with either of them and the Senator from California. Wood and Lowden between them mustered a majority of the delegates. Either one of them by combining with Johnson could have created a majority, but such hypothetical combinations were now practically impossible. Once more there were stirrings in the dark-horse stable. And if none of the steeds were conspicuous, was any more so than Harding? Daugherty admitted afterward that but for the work of the Kenyon Committee Harding's nomination would not have been possible.

Not until December, 1919, did the Duchess—fortified by Daugherty—

become reconciled to the idea of her "Wurr'n" as a presidential candidate, but once she accepted it, the idea obsessed her to the exclusion of most other thoughts. It was like the old days at the *Star*. "Wurr'n" would be President and *she* would see that he was.

One rainy afternoon in February, with three other senators' wives, she visited Madam Marcia, the fashionable Washington clairvoyant. The plump and matronly Madam Marcia exuded a well-mannered conviction of the future that seemed as real as the string of pearls she always wore. Plotting the zodiac—with the help of the *Congressional Directory*—she managed to make some surprisingly accurate predictions to the credulous great and near-great who in turn had made her prosperous. And if certain predictions of high fame had not always been followed by the fact, at least it was flattering to the client and helped build up good will.

Madam Marcia had seen enough of the world in its grubbier aspect to be able to judge it shrewdly. As a child she had grown up in a Brooklyn tenement, sold papers on the streets at the age of eleven, and picked up card-reading from hanging round a fortuneteller's dingy parlor. At sixteen she ran away from home to dance in pink tights in the chorus of the Frank Deshon Opera Company. Meeting a young doctor, Horace Marion Champrey, she married him. After two children were born, he left one Thanksgiving to buy a turkey and never returned.

Marcia ended up with her children at Coney Island where she worked for Gipsy Oliver telling cards and reading palms. Her career as an astrologer began on the day when she came across the Great Man of the Zodiac on the cover of *Dr. Janes' Vermifuge Almanac*. After absorbing this astral knowledge she became an ordained minister of the Spiritualist Church—something one could then do by paying three dollars—and moved on to Washington. There she advanced shrewdly from the cheaper to the better streets to become Madam Marcia, seen at 1509 R Street by appointment only, the friend and adviser of the great.

Of the four women visiting Marcia that February afternoon the Duchess alone said nothing. Early in May she returned by herself incognito and asked Marcia to cast the horoscope of someone born November 2, 1865, at 2 P.M. Jupiter being in his own sign of Sagittarius in the tenth hour, and the *Congressional Directory* being within arm's length, the sagacious and informed Marcia was able to tell her unknown visitor on her next visit that the man in question would rise to great eminence, that he was "sympathetic and kindly, intuitive, free of promises and trusting to friends, enthusiastic, impulsive, perplexed over financial affairs. Many clandestine love affairs; inclined to recurrent moods of melancholia."

Though this cut close to the bone, the Duchess returned for more. This time Marcia revealed to her that if the man born on November 2 was running for President, nothing on earth could stop his being nominated and elected. "But," she added darkly, "he will not live through his term. It is written in the stars. . . . Following the splendid climax in the House of Preferment, I see the Sun and Mars in conjunction in the eighth house of the zodiac. And this is the House of Death—sudden, violent, or peculiar death."

How much the Duchess believed in Madam Marcia's planetary insight she did not know herself—but she did not disbelieve. She chattered about the shadowed prediction obsessively with all her friends. It even came to William Howard Taft's ears that Mrs. Harding had been much distressed by a visit to some fortuneteller. Nursing this apprehension, she watched the June days roll by to the convention with a nervous excitement that was half fear.

[CHAPTER XV]

The Dark Convention

On June 5, the last Saturday before convention week, the *Literary Digest* released its final poll of the candidates, reflecting the most accurate survey yet devised of Republican opinion across the country.[1] Wood still headed the list, but followed much more closely by Johnson than had been anticipated. Hoover in third place was the biggest surprise. The final figures were:

Wood	277,486
Johnson	263,087
Hoover	240,468
Lowden	120,391
Hughes	59,719
Harding	36,375
Coolidge	33,621
Taft	32,740

The second choices were in the same order, with Wood leading and followed by Johnson, Hoover, Lowden, and Hughes.

From the first of June delegates, alternates, and supporters had been arriving in Chicago, and by the weekend of the sixth they were spilling into the Union and LaSalle Street stations by bannered trainloads. An early heat wave had struck the Midwest, and they arrived in their badges and stiff straw hats, sticky and cinder-caked, to a humid, sweltering city.

---

[1] The *Literary Digest* polls were considered authoritative, almost institutions. But as they were drawn mostly from middle-class subscribers to the magazine they reflected a cross section of that group rather than of the country at large. This became devastatingly apparent in the election of 1936 when the *Digest* predicted that Alfred M. Landon, "the Kansas Coolidge," would defeat Franklin Roosevelt by 320 to 161 electoral votes. Roosevelt's victory in every state but Maine and Vermont not only marked the end of the *Literary Digest* polls but also of the *Literary Digest*. Yet in judging the nomination sentiments of the Republican voters in 1920 the *Digest* poll had reached a representative cross section of party members and was undoubtedly accurate.

Every room in town was occupied, and they angrily discovered on registering at their hotels that the management had doubled and tripled the rates. To make matters worse, there was a waiters' strike.

It was, politicians agreed, the queerest convention anyone could remember. It lacked focus. Of the 984 voting delegates, 125 were pledged to Wood, 112 to Johnson, 72 to Lowden, and 39 to Harding. Seventy-two were pledged to various favorite sons, and 508—over half—had not made up their minds (or their minds had not been made up for them). "You wanted an unbossed convention," New York's eighty-six-year-old former Sen. Chauncey M. Depew told a group of newspapermen in the lobby of the Blackstone. "Now you have it, what are you going to do with it?"

Depew with his bald pate, rapacious nose, and sideburns that sifted over his choker collar, was as much a Republican fixture as Uncle Joe Cannon. A corporation lawer-courtier for the railroads, Commodore Vanderbilt's trusted public servant, Depew had been to every Republican national convention since 1856, had helped nominate Lincoln in 1860, and five years later had ridden on his funeral train. In the 1896 convention he had moved that McKinley's nomination be made unanimous. Witty, voluble, rich enough no longer to be actively venal, he was still in demand as a Republican speaker. In his sardonic view the 1920 candidates were a three-legged bunch of dark horses and no one could tell which might run best.

Once the rank-and-file delegates had checked in, they wandered in aimless shirt-sleeved curiosity along Michigan Avenue from one headquarters to another, listening to Lowden's brass band, collecting a red and green feather emblem stamped "Wood," lining up to try Hiram Johnson's "Teddy" handshake, or perhaps while looking for a drink finding themselves serenaded by the Republican Glee Club of Columbus. But the evangelical mood of other years, with torchlight parades and spellbinders and flag wavers, was lacking. Some blamed the general listlessness on the drying-up effects of the Volstead Act in this first Prohibition convention. Whisky had not altogether disappeared, but at six or eight dollars a pint conviviality tended to become a measured item. Even the old five-cent schooner of beer, though it still sold briskly across the street from the Coliseum, now cost a quarter.

The most expansive bustle was at the Wood headquarters on the ground floor of the Congress. There the McKinley-Tudor Elizabethan Room opening on Peacock Alley had been partitioned off in a series of small cubicles into which arriving delegates were taken for a confidential chat before being presented to the General. A grotesquely large bust of Theodore Roosevelt stood on a table in the room's center. Pretty girls were pinning Wood feathers on everyone who entered. Wood was wearing his olive-drab field uniform—over his protests Procter had insisted on it—with the azure, white-starred Congressional Medal ribbon conspicuous above the other decorations on his chest. No delegate could help but be impressed by that sternly avuncular figure. Wood might not have his Rough Rider friend's thrusting magnetism that could bring a crowd roaring to its feet, nor could he capture the passionate partisanship of the galleries that long ago in the Minneapolis convention had stamped and chanted for James G. Blaine, but he was still the outstanding leader at the convention. Senator Lodge, though most of the Massachusetts delegates were for their favorite-son Coolidge, told the Boston financier Clarence W. Barron that there was no reason why Wood could not be nominated.

Lowden's less elaborate headquarters were in the Congress's Gold Room although his own private suite was in the Blackstone. Where Wood's lieutenants gave out feathers and small talk, his gave out small talk and badges. Johnson, wearing a wide-brimmed Rough Rider hat, had pitched his standard in a huge room at the Auditorium. Beneath a blown-up photograph of himself holding his small son in his lap with the family collie leaning against him, he pumped the hands of those he hoped would feed him votes. Pictures of Theodore Roosevelt, as if to indicate the succession, flanked Johnson's own. Something of the revivalist fervor of the 1912 Progressives still clung to the Johnson headquarters. It was, as someone remarked, as if Billy Sunday had entered politics. Eight floors above, Herbert Hoover's friends had hired the hotel's ballroom with a view of the lake. Here the atmosphere was more that of a college seminar where thoughtful and earnest non-politicians like Oscar Straus discussed the issues of the day. Bob Taft, the former President's elder son, was one of the fixtures of the Hoover room. He was, he announced, for Hoover "first, last, and all the time." Five months after such a situation had occurred to Daugherty, the Hoover enthusiasts were struck with the thought of a deadlocked convention in which the delegates might rise from their political selves to better candidates.

Senator Poindexter's headquarters at the Congress were for those who preferred solitary meditation or a quick nap with no one to disturb them. Daugherty had secured the elaborately carved Florentine Room for Harding at the same hotel, the very room where the defiant Roosevelt had pitched his standard in 1912. Heroic likenesses emphasizing Harding's Roman features covered the walls. It was rapidly becoming a standard joke for visitors from other headquarters to drop in and ask: "Who's Harding?"

Harding had engaged his personal suite at the LaSalle Hotel, some distance from the Coliseum. He and the Duchess left Washington for Chicago in a group that included Nick Longworth—now through time, luck, and attrition Speaker of the House—Princess Alice and her sharp-tongued friend Senator Brandegee, the future Vice President Charles W. Curtis of Kansas, and Sen. George H. Sutherland of Utah whom Harding would later appoint to the Supreme Court, as part of a "trainload of insects streaking out to merge with the convention anthill." In the club car Harding again gave way to his doubts, saying that he had no show for the nomination and that he felt like withdrawing even if it did leave Daugherty out on a limb.

He had planned to travel alone and have Nan meet him Saturday at the Englewood Station but the Duchess with her uncanny intuition had upset his plans and he had resigned himself to the Republican special. As soon as he could slip away after his arrival in Chicago he went to the Willits' apartment, and it was there that Nan—after an empty wait at Englewood—found him. Her sister Elizabeth, knowing that he was coming, had arranged for the rest of the family to be away. Nan led him into the minute parlor and he sat down in an overstuffed chair and took her in his lap. She chattered, as she had back at school, that he would be President, and he scouted the idea. For several hours they clung to each other. She tried to persuade him to meet her soon in the park when she was taking Elizabeth Ann for a walk so that he could see his child, and he told her he was "crazy to do it." Yet to her puzzlement she could never get him to appear there and catch a glimpse of Elizabeth Ann.

While Harding dallied, Daugherty was making his preparations with solicitous energy. Besides the Florentine Room's headquarters he had taken forty additional rooms, at a cost of $750 a day for ten days. Since the LaSalle was distant, he obtained another private suite for Harding at the Auditorium through Gus Creager who had arrived with Scobey as a member of the Texas delegation. From the headquarters in Washington, New York, Columbus, and Indianapolis he brought in his best workers until he had a staff of 500 that would expand to 2,000 before the convention was over. George Christian had come on from Washington, and Malcolm Jennings from Columbus. Daugherty set up a complete roll of all delegates, their hotels, and even the numbers of their rooms, their candidate choices from first to fourth. Every hotel in town had its Harding lookouts, every headquarters was infiltrated by at least one Harding man. In anticipation of Dale Carnegie, Harding workers were instructed to "smile, keep in good humor," and make no enemies. They met each incoming train with Harding badges, made themselves useful to arriving delegates wherever they could. Daugherty had brought along the Republican Glee Club of Columbus—founded in 1872, and of which Harding was still an honorary member. Each midday its 75-man chorus entertained the public on the mezzanine floor of the Congress. Evenings Daugherty sent the 75, wearing dress suits in spite of the heat, from one headquarters to another to build up good will by serenading the various candidates.

As soon as Jake Hamon arrived in town, Daugherty went to his suite in the LaSalle to sound him out on a possible Harding-Lowden alliance. Jake, by the judicious expenditure of another $100,000, had just succeeded in persuading the Oklahoma delegation at its caucus on June 6 to elect him national committeeman in place of McGraw. Since McGraw was vice-chairman of the Wood campaign, Jake was keeping his 18 delegates in line for Lowden, but the idea of an alliance interested him and he arranged for Daugherty to have a talk with Lowden's manager, Emmerson. Daugherty offered Emmerson the loan of as many Harding votes as he could give on the early ballots without making Harding look too small. The aim of their alliance, he admitted, was to beat Wood, and once the General was beaten the alliance was at an end. Emmerson with great friendliness agreed. Harding and Hamon met several times before the actual opening of the convention. Jake was interested in the Senator just as he was interested in oil. He offered Harding his friendship, donated $25,000 to the campaign, promised him second choice on the Oklahoma votes.

Over the weekend Big Bill Thompson came to Daugherty offering his 21 convention votes for an alliance against the hated Lowden. Daugherty adroitly sidestepped, did not commit himself, but offered to take over Thompson's expensive rooms in the Congress for Harding's Women's Headquarters. Big Bill accepted, and they parted friends even though Daugherty had made him no promises.

In the annex of the Congress the new national chairman, Will Hays, and his Credentials Committee were beset with the quadrennial problem of contested delegations from the rotten boroughs of the South. A deft reconciler, toothy, with rabbit ears that were a gift to caricaturists, this thin, dark, energetic man with luminous eyes and a singularly sallow complexion embodied a new managerial type that was beginning to replace the portly old-time boss. Hays, it was said, preferred pasting heads together to knocking them together.

He had grown up in Sullivan, Indiana, a friendly young man who read law in his father's office and joined everything joinable, making speeches at old settlers' picnics, churches, lodges, on Labor Day, and the Fourth of July. In 1896, when he was seventeen, he saw McKinley nominated at the St. Louis convention, and that was the beginning of his fascination with politics. Before he was old enough to vote he had become Republican chairman of his precinct in Sullivan. He advanced to county chairman, chairman of the Republican Speakers' Bureau, member of the Republican State Executive Committee. In 1912 he refused Roosevelt's offer of state chairmanship of the Progressive party. Two years later he was elected Republican state chairman and organized his state so thoroughly that in the national Wilson sweep of 1916 Indiana elected a Republican governor, both United States senators, and all its congressmen. In recognition of this Hays was elected national chairman in 1918. He described his own deepest beliefs as "faith in God, in folks, in the nation, and in the Republican party."

The paper organization that was the Republican party in the South existed for two reasons: to absorb patronage, and to supply delegates at the going rate to the national conventions. Wary managers such as Hitchcock always knew the rate. One of Wood's lieutenants told Samuel Hopkins Adams that the 1920 price had run as high as $5,000 a delegate. It was Hays's job as a regular to thread his way through conflicting venal claims, to build up Lowden as much as possible without outraging Wood. Sometimes he compromised, allowing each contesting delegate a half vote. And for the first time in recent convention history he let in the reporters. He and his committee apportioned the disputed seats: 88 to Lowden, 34 to Wood, and 7 to Johnson. Sen. George H. Moses of New Hampshire, Wood's Southern manager, loudly denounced such "steamroller tactics" until Wood, who at that point wanted no quarrel with the National Committee, muzzled him.

The convention was to open in the Coliseum Tuesday morning, June 8. On Monday Harding again slipped away to see Nan. Several times he went to Woodlawn Avenue during the week, and once she rode back on the elevated with him. As they were riding side by side she caught him glancing at something in a neighbor's paper and asked him what he was looking at. He said he was "just trying to steal the baseball score." On Thursday, the day before the balloting began, she met him in the lobby of the Auditorium and he gave her a convention ticket. But she could never persuade him to see Elizabeth Ann.

All day the sweaty crowds—mostly men, mostly in shirt sleeves— milled about the hotel lobbies. They grouped and dissolved kaleidoscopically as the temperature rose and the heat waves shimmered along the lake front. Aimlessly the delegates wandered, like yokels at a fair. Weaving through them with unknown aims, the fixers and manipulators circulated. "Everywhere," wrote Wood's biographer, Herman Hagedorn, "there was a sense of smooth, sleek little animals slipping noiselessly to and fro; politicians conferring, carrying messages, making alliances."

Breasting the anonymous tide were the leaders, the candidates themselves, the senators from left to right, from the grim-jawed Borah to the supercilious gray-curled head of Henry Cabot Lodge. Unobtrusively but confidently in view was Wilson's "group of willful men" who had led the Senate fight against his League: Senators Edge and Frelinghuysen of New Jersey; Wadsworth and Calder of New York; Curtis of Kansas, the future Senate leader and vice president; Brandegee of Connecticut; McCormick of Illinois; Phipps of Colorado; Knox of Pennsylvania. William Jennings Bryan, bald and relaxed, observed the eddies with detachment as a correspondent of the United Press. The votes of the New York delegation like counters in his pocket, Nicholas Murray Butler surveyed the scene with the urbanity fitting to a university president and former professor of philosophy. Uncle Joe Cannon, a quid of tobacco in his ancient jaw, was there as a delegate, as he had been to every convention but two in the last sixty years. Chauncey Depew, with his sideburns, drew the eyes of the crowd as he passed. So did that gaudy revenant from another era, Diamond Jim Brady, wearing a jeweled stickpin in the form of an American flag. There were still others who had outlived their political day, like Boss Barnes and the frail fading former Sen. Murray Crane of Massachusetts, the captains of 1912 and 1916 now wandering like lost children in their second childhood. Then there were those leaders-to-be whose day had not yet begun, like Joseph W. Martin, Jr., the former state representative from Attleboro, Massachusetts, present not as a delegate but as an observer. Several times a day Jake Hamon passed down Michigan Avenue with his brassy crew, his loud mouth flashing a gold-plated smile, triumphant as the new national committeeman from Oklahoma, trailing boasts of the thousands he had already spent. Equally strident was the passage of the flabby-lipped Big Bill Thompson, a Penrose on a municipal scale, the wealthy oaf with the common touch and the bull voice. More apparent in their very inconspicuousness were the silent background figures, the men of power who did not need to speak since their money spoke for them: Samuel Vauclain of Baldwin Locomotives; the oilmen Harry F. Sinclair and Edward L. Doheny; Ambrose Monell of metals; Henry M. Byllesby of public utilities; William Boyce Thompson of copper; Dan Hanna and Elbert M. Gary of steel; Cornelius Vanderbilt, whose wife considered Depew their forensic butler. Among them, T. Coleman DuPont, the munitions maker, with the six votes of Delaware in his pocket appeared as his own favorite son. George Harvey, the owlish-eyed editor of the *North American Review*, huddled behind the arras at the Blackstone with four J. P. Morgan partners, determined to unmake the Wilson he had so long ago made governor of New Jersey. From his high-minded Kansas-Progressive point of view, Wood-delegate William Allen White thought he had never seen a convention "so completely dominated by sinister predatory economic forces."

Crosscurrents of rumors floated along Michigan Avenue. Odds were quoted: 7 to 5 against Wood; 8 to 5 against Lowden; 3 to 1 against Johnson; 4 to 1 against Hoover; 5 to 1 against Hughes; 8 to 1 against Harding. Johnson was said to be slipping. It was being whispered about that most of his delegates were merely waiting for the second ballot to desert to Wood. Harold Ickes, the testy Progressive now back in the fold as a Lowden delegate from Illinois, met with Roosevelt's sons, Ted and Archie. Sharing their sister Alice's contemptuous view of Harding, the two

Roosevelts foresaw his possible nomination and wanted to know what could be done about it. Ickes suggested that they publicly denounce Harding in their father's name and declare that no true Rooseveltian would support him in the convention or afterward. They refused. Ted wanted to protect the ambition he had developed to follow in his father's footsteps. As Lieut. Col. Theodore Roosevelt, Jr., a war hero, he saw the next steps emerging—the Navy Department, the governor's chair at Albany, the White House vista. If Harding did have a chance, Ted could not afford to offend him.

By way of warning, Johnson and Borah held a large anti–League of Nations rally at the Auditorium Theatre, the scene of the 1912 bolt. Johnson spoke for fifty minutes to a demonstrative isolationist-Progressive audience. Borah roared in his leonine manner for two hours, telling the audience that he would riddle the League in the convention. Both Borah and Johnson insisted that the Republican party had but one choice—to repudiate the League of Nations unconditionally.

While the delegates and alternates immune to Johnson's isolationist blandishments steamed and sweated in their rooms, the Republican inner circle disputed over the convention's permanent chairman. Former Senator Beveridge had been the original choice and had even prepared his speech. But Johnson insisted that he wanted Borah. Nor had the regulars forgotten that Beveridge in 1912 had been chairman of the Progressive convention. Finally the Committee on Arrangements by a vote of 22 to 9 gave the permanent position to the temporary chairman, Senator Lodge.

The Republican Glee Club of Columbus might harmonize its collective voice in the enervating darkness, but Harding's name was scarcely heard on Monday night. Wood was still *the* candidate to beat, the one question being whether the Borahs and the Penroses could combine incongruously to stop him. There was some talk of Chairman Hays as a dark horse—a prospect that Daugherty, who distrusted Hays, secretly feared. Hughes and Knox were again mentioned as compromises. "The Republican party will begin its convention here tomorrow under conditions of uncertainty unparalleled in recent political history," a reporter wrote, desperately grasping at such gossamer strands of talk and rumor to make up his morning article. "Unbossed and largely unorganized, the delegates were asking one another tonight in what direction they were straying and when a master would arise to lead them out of the wilderness of their own indecision." Senator New of Indiana, a former chairman of the National Committee, had attended every Republican convention since 1880 and he had never seen such uncertainty. He thought there was little real enthusiasm for any candidate and that it would take considerable balloting before anyone could "see the light."

The night brought little relief from the heat, and while most of the delegates were having breakfast on Tuesday before the official opening, the thermometer had already begun to climb. Since the last convention the seating capacity of the Coliseum had been enlarged to 13,289 seats. Postwar high wages had doubled the cost of getting the building ready. No carpenter would so much as hammer a nail for less than $1.25 an hour!

From half past nine on delegates were beginning to emerge from their hotels, and a straggling but steadily increasing crowd drifted up Michigan Avenue toward the Coliseum. Inside the amphitheater massed flags hung from the girders, veiling the glass hothouse roof. On the south wall behind the speakers' platform was displayed (hopefully) a huge presidential flag, an eagle on a blue background flanked by four white stars. The platform itself ran forward beyond the rostrum and into the body of the auditorium like a flying bridge. A white circle had been painted at the very edge of the bridge and a sign directed the speakers to "stand within the circle and speak slowly." Behind the circle a huge sounding board curved up, above which the telephone company had installed a "newfangled" amplifying attachment. As the first delegates made their way through the maze of empty seats the telephone technicians were testing the amplifier by playing a record of a soprano singing "My Old Kentucky Home." The balconies were beginning to fill, the earliest arrivals being a phalanx of Johnson supporters whom Big Bill Thompson had sent to drown out the others. Three hundred police and firemen were on duty, ready to deal with anything from fist fights to smouldering cigarettes.

The morning shadows grew shorter and the sun lighted up the improbable mixture of rough-cut ashlar and yellow brick that was the Coliseum's façade, touched the castellated turrets and the Gothic arch topped by a gilt American eagle. Before the main entrance several dozen suffragettes from the National Women's Party were picketing the convention in protest against the refusal of the Republican governors of Connecticut and Vermont to call a special session of their legislatures to ratify the Women's Suffrage Amendment. Thirty-five of the required 36 states had already ratified this nineteenth Amendment, and the militants with their purple, white, and gold banners were going to stay there until the Republicans conceded them the one necessary addition. The eldest suffragette, the Reverend Olympia Brown—a tough, stringy little woman in a sunbonnet hat—was as old as Chauncey Depew and considerably more combative. When asked which candidate she preferred, she replied grimly: "None of 'em!"

As a concession to the suffragettes and the looming nineteenth Amendment, 27 women were included among the 982 delegates making their way to their places in the echoing hall where the dust motes were beginning to rise and the temperature was already ninety. The two bribed delegates from Missouri had been banished. More noticeable than the presence of the women was the absence of the men in blue, the veterans of the Grand Army of the Republic whose uniforms had formed a solid mass of color at so many Republican conventions in the last fifty years. Even twenty years ago they had huzzaed en masse to see their own Major McKinley renominated. The few bent old men now scattered in the balconies in their brass-buttoned blue tunics and their black wide-brimmed hats with the gilt cord and GAR badge had fought in their youth, and in their lusty middle age had rallied to Grant and Garfield and Harrison. They had listened to Fire Engine Joe with the blazing eyes and imperious white head and the voice that brought to mind a war horse crying among the trumpets, until even the most desk-ridden veteran of the Quartermaster Corps had the vivifying conviction of having fought with cold steel at Gettysburg. Now they were part of the sentimentalized past. When one said "the War" in 1920 one meant another war. Here and there, as a gesture to sentiment, one of the boys in blue sat among the delegates and the alternates. Addison G. Proctor, the only delegate present from the 1860 convention that nominated Lincoln, was one of the 30 Michigan delegates, "without preferences this time."

The Grand Army of the Republic had passed. Even the music had changed. Opposite the presidential flag Johnny Hard's band, perched on a platform like a choir loft just under the girders, thumped out a succession of toe-tingling ragtime tunes. No longer were they tenting tonight on the old campground or hanging Jeff Davis to a sour apple tree as they had from Grant to Roosevelt. Instead, there was Mr. Zip, Zip, Zip, with his "hair cut just as short as mine." If no one else noticed, the old men in blue did.

On the floor the delegates grouped in their numbered sections around the standards of their states with the alternates in a compact mass behind them. By eleven o'clock, the time scheduled for opening, the balconies were jammed and every seat on the floor taken. Still the speakers' platform remained empty. Overhead the massed and looped American flags hung down damply. The buzz of talk, the clatter of seats, the shuffle of feet by degrees unified into the sound of the crowd. One became aware of it as an entity. Hard's band played a medley of patriotic songs and the audience stood up. Then the band switched to "Columbia, the Gem of the Ocean," and the delegates waved little flags that had been placed on the seats, waving them "conscientiously but by no means furiously." The band played "Dixie," and the indentured delegates from the South managed a cheer. For all the bunting, an uncertain apathy hung almost visibly over the assembly. Old-timers thought that most of the delegates needed a livening drink.

At 11:34 there was a bustle at the back of the hall and Chairman Hays, lean and stooping, strode down the flying bridge, smiling his ferret smile, then stepped within the painted circle. Again the new era was apparent. The McKinley frock coat had some time ago given way to the cutaway and striped trousers, but Hays was wearing an ordinary dark sack coat with plain but lighter-colored trousers. The applause flickered up to him. Rapping for order with an oversize gavel that had been carved from a rafter of Independence Hall, he announced that the Republican national convention of 1920 was in session. The Right Reverend Charles E. Woodcock, bishop of Kentucky, gave the opening prayer. With the well-bred Episcopalian distrust of spontaneous intercession, he read from manuscript:

> Leave us not to our own courses we beseech Thee, but so direct us by Thy mighty power that we may be led in the way that makes for unity and peace, . . . that we may make no compromises of duty for fear of consequences. Let not strife divide us nor grief corrupt us. . . .

When the Bishop concluded, there was no evangelical amen from the floor. But as if in answer to the prayer a man leaped to the front of the platform with a surge of energy like an uncoiling spring to lead in the ritual singing of "The Star-Spangled Banner." This bounding presence was Albert Edmund Brown, professional pepper-upper, ex-director of community singing at Camp Devens, now attached to the Republican League of Massachusetts. As the band blared in the loft and the assembly mumbled and stumbled through the two stanzas of the unsingable anthem, Brown's arms and legs flailed like a Catherine wheel at his impossible task. He at least knew the words! There was a buzz of relief as the final chords faded. Then Brown's voice cracked out like a pistol shot.

> Now give three cheers and a tiger for the greatest country on earth—the United States of America!

Obediently they replied, with self-conscious effort, each cheer louder than the last.

> Hurrah for the United States!
> Hurrah for the United States!
> Hurrah for the United States!
> And a long-tailed T-I-G-E-R!

Within the magic circle Hays, informal and smiling, announced that the next order of business would be the reading of the call for the convention. After a pause, while the official photograph was taken, he gave his report:

> The Republican party has met in this open and free convention to accept from the American people a mandate for the government of the United

States. As chairman of your National Republican Committee, I report progress. . . . In November the Republican majority should exceed three million. In spirit I report more than progress; I report fulfillment. The great party of the Union has become a unit. It shall so continue. There will be no bolt from this convention.

Hays had measured his last sentence carefully, with the Johnson-Borah threat in the background. The expected applause followed. He then presented Henry Cabot Lodge to act as temporary chairman.

As Hays concluded his hopeful warning, Senator Lodge was escorted to the platform by Chauncey Depew, Myron Herrick and Mrs. J. B. Hume of California. Lodge, in his black cutaway, white waistcoat, tight gray curls, and beard, resembled a reactivated mummy. "A degenerate son of Harvard," that university's pro-League president, A. Lawrence Lowell, had called him after their League of Nations debate in Boston's Symphony Hall. He had been a convention delegate in 1896, 1900, 1904, 1908, and 1916. He had been permanent chairman of the conventions of 1900 and 1908, chairman of the Committee of Resolutions in 1904 and 1916. His name had been whispered more than once for President. As he made his way forward, Hays called out: "Three cheers for Henry Cabot Lodge!" Spotlights—twenty-one of them—beamed down from every corner of the building to pinpoint the aloof figure and dazzle the eyes of the delegates. Above the cheers for Lodge were shouts of "Turn out the lights!"

The convention was now in charge of the crisply withered Boston Brahmin. He spoke with a slightly nasal drawl that was his caste mark— the broad A and the prolongation of the vowel sounds—and the sounding board with its amplifier gave a metallic ring to his voice. His keynote speech lasted an hour and twenty-one minutes, a savage attack on Wilson but delivered so coldly that it struck no sparks from his audience. H. L. Mencken, that connoisseur of platitudes, brought to Chicago to report the convention, was more appreciative. "Bosh," he called the speech, "delivered with an air."

Lodge warmed up with an attack on the government's lack of firmness in dealing with Mexico. He moved on to the League of Nations with its Article X which was "not a guarantee for the world's peace but a breeder of war and an enemy of peace." Everything else was merely an overture to his attack on the hated Wilson:

> Mr. Wilson and his dynasty, his heirs and assigns, or anybody that is his, anybody who with bent knee has served his purposes, must be driven from all control, from all influence upon the government of the United States. They must be driven from office and power not because they are Democrats but because Mr. Wilson stands for a theory of administration and government which is not American.

To laughter and applause he concluded that

> in 1916 Mr. Wilson won on the cry that "he had kept us out of war." He now demands the approval of the American people for his party and his administration on the ground that he has kept us out of peace.

As he ended, the delegates and alternates stood up and gave three cheers "for Senator Lodge and the Grand Old Party."

Some time in the autumn Chairman Hays had set up a harmony committee of 160 under New York Congressman Ogden L. Mills to try to work out a platform acceptable to both the Progressive and conservative wings of the party. Hays wanted Mills as chairman of the convention's Committee on Resolutions to introduce this platform. Instead, the Old Guard on the committee elected Senator Watson. For two days and nights the members hacked away at a party platform. The Progressive crowd— as they were still known—White, Borah, and McCormick, managed to win endorsement for Federal highways, conservation, equal pay for women, and the prevention of child labor. But conservatism carried through in the body of the platform which endorsed "rigid economy," a "more business-like" government, a high protective tariff, and exemption of American ships from Panama Canal tolls, exclusion of all Asiatics, the registration of aliens and withholding of citizenship from them until they became "genuinely American." Further, no one should be permitted to advocate "resistance to the law or violent overthrow of the government"; education should awaken "a sense of patriotic duty"—the usual claptrap that remained unread and unheeded.

The rest of the platform might be mere words, but the hidden reef threatening to wreck the Republican ship was the plank on the League of Nations. Ironically the very idea of such an association of nations was a Republican notion, derived from Taft's League to Enforce Peace which he had founded with Harvard's A. Lawrence Lowell, in 1915. Wilson took the conception of his League of Nations from Taft's Peace League. Taft, along with such elder Republican statesmen as Root and Burton, was unreservedly for Wilson's League even with the disputed Article X, which Burton maintained was no more than the Monroe Doctrine applied to the whole world. Wilson had incorporated three of Taft's amendments into the second draft of the League Covenant. The most eminent of those eager to have the United States join the League with reservations was Hughes who felt that such reservations would still leave its main provisions unimpaired. Convention spokesman for the mild reservationists was Murray Crane. Businessmen and financiers of the East belonged to this group—"international bankers," in Johnson's sneering words. Harding had at first seemed to belong with them. In his speech at a McKinley Day banquet in Dayton in January, 1919, he had said:

> I am not opposed to the League of Nations, a world court, anything else that you may wish to call it. I think that something of the kind can be worked out, not as a guarantee against war, for that is impossible, but some sort of system of deliberation among the nations before resorting to war as a means of settling their differences. If President Wilson can do that, I say Godspeed to him in his efforts, but I am opposed to anything that smacks of the surrender.

Harding's Godspeeds had toned down since the shift of the wind from the internationalists. His point of view at the time of the convention was more that of Lodge's, and Lodge was for reservations as a dodge to thwart Wilson. Beyond Lodge lurked the irreconcilables, led by Johnson and Borah, demanding the complete repudiation of the League and threatening if they did not have their way to bolt the convention and form an isolationist-Progressive third party in the pattern of 1912.

Faced with this dilemma, Senator Watson, as chairman of the Resolutions Committee, appointed a subcommittee of 13—of all ranges of opinion, from William Allen White and Ogden Mills to Borah and Reed Smoot—to evolve by some legerdemain a League plank that would be equally acceptable to the Tafts and to the Johnsons. The subcommittee met at Crane's suite in the Blackstone, but after three long and futile sessions adjourned at 1:20 A.M. without agreeing.

Boss Penrose, slowly dying in his Philadelphia house, nevertheless had a special wire running from his bedroom to the Pennsylvania delegation in the Congress. On June 5, and without believing it, he had announced that the convention's best bet was Governor Sproul. John King, still at outs with Wood, had come to Chicago to look after Penrose's interests and to see that the 76 Pennsylvania delegates stayed in line for Sproul. Without an iron controlling hand, Penrose knew that most of them would drift to Wood.

Before the convention the papers had referred to the Big Four—Wood, Johnson, Lowden, and Harding in that order. By Tuesday night they had switched to the Big Three, and Harding seemed out of the picture for good. General Pershing on Monday had asked Secretary of War Baker to place him on the retired list, and again there was speculation about him as a dark horse. Wood supporters were heartened in being able to claim as delegates the chairmen of the two most important committees—Senator Watson and Edward Duffield of the Credentials Committee—as well as the prospective permanent chairman Henry Cabot Lodge. Wood, they predicted, would get 347 votes on the first ballot and clinch the nomination with 688 on the second.

The Wednesday-morning convention session lasted only fifty-five minutes, its principal business being to appoint Lodge permanent chairman and to amend the rules so that the platform, if the League plank still was lacking, could come up as unfinished business *after* the nomination of the candidate. A more unctious Protestant than the Episcopalian variety, the Reverend Doctor John Timothy Stone of Chicago's Fourth Presbyterian Church, gave the opening prayer. Then a song leader tried to get the delegates to sing "The Long, Long Trail," but the voices kept trailing off. Community Singer Brown leaped forward into the breach to lead in "The Battle Hymn of the Republic." The voices mumbled through the verses but came out roaring at the chorus. Lodge announced that the Committee on Resolutions was not yet ready to report and there was no further business. In the interlude of ruffled silence that followed a few voices cried out for Chauncey Depew, seated within eye range of the chairman, his bald head glistening. Always ready to respond, speaking easily with extemporaneous wit, he was used to being called on for a few odd-moment words. In 1916 he had entertained the convention for over an hour while the leaders were carrying on back-stage discussions. Lodge beckoned him forward, and to much applause he made his way to the platform, an ancient cherub, his railroad serfdom forgiven and forgotten. In his choker collar and Edwardian four-in-hand he resembled John Quincy Adams in his old age—except for the anguished eyes, for Depew's eyes were smug. Lightly mocking, the old courtier ridiculed Wilson as the vain and self-opinionated world saver, the American innocent, too fatuously stubborn to realize he was being taken in by the European sharpers.

> He was dealing with the ablest men in the political game [Depew told them with a Pickwickian twinkle], in the diplomatic game, in the international game, there are in the world. And he was a babe confident of himself. And what happened? Why, those great gamblers in international politics said to him: "What do you want, Mr. President? You are the greatest man in the world; what do you want? You represent the greatest nation in the world, and you speak for every one of your people; what do you want?" He said: "I want a League of Nations which will put us like a heaven on earth, reproduced on this round globe, of which I will be the recording angel."
>
> Those astute old players said to him: "All right, Mr. President, that is the most magnificent proposition ever offered since Calvary two thousand years ago." Said Lloyd George: "I would like to have the German possessions in Africa just to settle the Negro question there." "All right," said the President. It was larger than all Europe. And that little Irishman from Australia, I know him very well, Hughes, said: "Mr. President, it is a luxury for a man from the Antipodes, way the other side of the world, to meet such a great man as you. That scheme of yours for a League of Nations is simply magnificent. But Australia wants Guinea, belonging to

Germany, but close to us." And Wilson said: "Take it." And then came forward Clemenceau and he said: "We need coal; we need iron; we need the Saar Valley and we need the Ruhr Valley." The President said: "Take them."

And then came Sonnino, and he said: "We want Fiume." Precisely what there was in the mentality of the Chief Executive of the United States that made him object I do not know, but he said: "You can never have Fiume." It so happened that nobody there had ever heard of Fiume. Nobody knew where Fiume was, whether one of the Sandwich Islands or a fixed star. . . .

There were much laughter, shouts, claps, and whistles when the smooth, aged voice finished. Other voices now began to call for Uncle Joe Cannon, but Lodge had had enough and, after allowing newsreel cameramen to take a few shots, adjourned the session. A thousand cars were waiting outside, provided by Mayor Thompson, to take the delegates and alternates to a luncheon at the plant of the Illinois Steel Company.

All through Wednesday the resolutions subcommittee, meeting in Murray Crane's suite, continued to founder over the League. Crane tried to offer a temporizing pro-League platform, but Borah, McCormick, and Brandegee—shedding tears—threatened to denounce the party if it were adopted. The solution—a simple one—was finally provided by the absent Elihu Root who submitted his suggestion as he was on the point of sailing for the Hague to help organize the League's Permanent Court of Justice. Realizing that even a mildly pro-League plank would split the party, the internationalist Root provided a text so ambiguously worded that it meant nothing at all except that it meant nothing. Everyone from Taft to Borah could read it to his comfort. The Republican party stood for "agreement among the nations of the world to preserve the peace of the world . . . without the compromise of national independence" and without involving the American people "in a multitude of quarrels, the merits of which they are unable to judge." Wilson was given his ritualistic denunciation, while Root's real object lay hidden—still to leave the door ajar for America to join the League. Taft was satisfied that the vague verbiage had said "the things that would lead the party into the League." Johnson was triumphantly convinced of the opposite. With only one dissenting vote the subcommittee adopted Root's plank.

Thursday's convention session lasted only ten minutes. At eleven-nineteen Lodge presented Cardinal Gibbons, the head of the American Roman Catholic hierarchy, in all the eminent splendor of his scarlet cape. With more urbanity than his Episcopalian predecessor, the Cardinal had not only written but memorized his prayer. So overcome was one of the delegates at its conclusion that he burst into applause. Lodge then announced that the Committee on Resolutions working through the early morning had at last achieved a League plank. He dismissed the delegates until nine Friday when the presentation of the candidates and the actual balloting would begin.

The white-haired Mark Sullivan, dean of Washington correspondents and friend of Presidents, and as judicious an observer as might be found at the convention, was one of a dozen guests that noon at a lunch given by the New York banker, Fred W. Allen, at the Blackstone. His table-mates were all political sophisticates who, Sullivan felt, should have known who the nominee would be if it were possible to know. Allen after lunch proposed that they each put a five-dollar bill in a sealed envelope together with the name of the candidate they predicted as a winner. Whoever guessed right, the total would be given to any institution he picked. Sullivan put down Harvard as his institution and Wood as his candidate. Some weeks later Allen returned Sullivan his five dollars, writing that none of the guests had picked Harding.

At midday the Columbus Glee Club gave its usual concert in the Blackstone's mezzanine:

> We sing with hearts on fire
> O Harding, salute!

A passing reporter, observing the sparse reaction, thought that "when you get hearts on fire for Harding, you have generated enough heat to set Lake Michigan boiling and turn the Chicago River into a pot roast."

On Thursday afternoon the Harding headquarters at the Congress were almost empty except for three young couples holding hands. A reporter from the *World* found it "a vast vacancy into which has been thrown a mass of decorations." But the Duchess had not lost confidence in her stars, in Jupiter reaching "a trine aspect to the Moon in the sign Aries," as demonstrated by Madam Marcia in May. "I am content to bask in my husband's limelight," she told another reporter searching for any kind of filler on that blank afternoon, "but I cannot see why anyone should want to be President in the next four years." Then, as if she had recalled the sun and Mars in the House of Death, she suddenly exclaimed: "I can see but one word written over the head of my husband if he is elected and that word is 'Tragedy.'"

Harding, oblivious to any star-conjunctured doom, was not so sanguine about the moon's trine aspect. Wilted, unshaven, hung-over, he had long since lost his Daugherty-instilled confidence. Jacob Meckstroth, a Colum-bus newspaper friend, observed that he had not smiled the whole week. According to an Ohio law—which Harding's Columbus friends had tried unsuccessfully to alter—he had until midnight Friday to file his declara-tion and petition for renomination. But to file for the Senate would be an admission that he was out of the presidential race. Some time Thursday afternoon he sent his Cleveland friend, George B. Harris, to Columbus to wait at the Deshler Hotel Friday evening for instructions. Even the Duchess's star-inspired confidence was giving way to thrift. "I don't know why we're keeping the headquarters," she told Wood's friend Albert Brunker. "It's simply a needless expense. We haven't a chance. But Mr. Daugherty felt that since the Senator had come out for the nomination, it would be the dignified thing to have headquarters here." The gloom in the Florentine Room deepened.

Meanwhile the shadow of Blooming Grove, that had darkened every political campaign of Harding's, spread to Chicago as a tall man with gray hair parted in the middle, bushy eyebrows, and rimless spectacles moved unobtrusively from one headquarters to the other distributing flyers. The man, with the soft-spoken manner of a teacher and the glare of a fanatic, was William Estabrook Chancellor, Professor of Economics, Politics and Social Sciences at Wooster College, Ohio. Married to a niece of Henry Ward Beecher's, a Democratic admirer of Wilson and the League of Nations, author of books on education, sociology, and history published by such reputable firms as Harpers, Century, and Houghton Mifflin, Chancellor was nevertheless dominated by white-supremacy obsessions to the point of his own mental stability. Sometimes he would stop his lectures to rant against the blacks. Not only did he believe in the strictest segregation, but he advocated the disenfranchisement of Negroes. His flyers, printed crudely on cheap paper, stated that Harding had inherited colored blood from several ancestors, that his father had always been considered a mulatto, and that his great-grandmother, Elizabeth Madison Harding, born in 1799, was a Negress. Harding's candidacy in this view was an attempt to create a Haitian-type United States. Since Harding at this time was considered out of the running, no one gave much attention to the pamphlets. Later much attention would be paid to them.[2]

Among the rumors and counter-rumors of Thursday evening was one that Harding might be willing to take second place. There was renewed talk of trying to push Lowden through to the nomination on the fourth ballot. Penrose, temporarily improved, spent some time on the telephone with McCormick, Sproul, King, and Grundy, warily insisting that the Pennsylvania delegation stick to Sproul. As the hour of decision grew nearer, it was still the General against the field. It was possible—the thought of it had been troubling the dreams of the Old Guard for months —that Wood might indeed sweep the convention with a flying start, that the lackadaisical and uncommitted delegates might suddenly be drawn to him like iron filings to a magnet. Mark Sullivan felt on that sultry evening

[2] Curiously, a Negro delegate from Chicago's 1st District was named George F. Harding.

that Wood was gaining "not only delegates but loyalty and prestige. . . . He can be defeated, but it is harder for his enemies to beat him than it is for him to win."

The wise insiders were already predicting the first ballot:

Wood	249
Lowden	232
Johnson	112
Butler	88
Sproul	76
Harding	58
Coolidge	50

Another night had brought no cooling. When the convention was ready to open Friday morning at nine-thirty, the temperature was ninety inside the Coliseum. The delegates massed restlessly behind their state standards, the packed galleries gibbered, and thin ragtime music echoed from Hard's band sweltering in the loft.

Not until ten did Chairman Lodge appear on the flying bridge, the official stenographer trailing behind him, pencil and notebook in hand. A perceptive sergeant-at-arms had provided a large new pounding board for the chairman's oversize gavel. This morning the prayer was by Pastor Johnston Myers of the Immanuel Baptist Church who invoked the God, not of Abraham and of Isaac, but of Washington, Lincoln, and Roosevelt. Lodge then announced that the next business was the nomination of candidates for the Presidency.

With the savage, unappeasable ritual of an American political convention, the nominating and seconding speeches now began. They would go on all day in spite of the temperature and even though none of them would alter a single opinion or a single vote. Governor Allen of Kansas, the first speaker, had been chosen by Wood to nominate him. Allen had already written three nominating speeches, and all of them had been rejected by Hitchcock and the Wood board of strategy as too specific. Privately Hitchcock suspected Allen of angling for the vice presidential nomination at the hands of the Old Guard.

Lodge introduced Allen to the convention as the man who would present the name of Maj. Gen. Leonard Wood. Convention etiquette had always demanded that a candidate's name be held back to the last sentence of the nominating speech, and Lodge's gaffe destroyed Allen's chance of building up suspense to that resolving point. His speech presenting Wood as governor of Cuba, preparedness leader, and citizen-soldier was dull and unconvincing. Nevertheless, at its conclusion Wood delegates trudged damply up and down the aisles in a forty-two-minute demonstration shouting "It's Wood: let's go!" while the brasses blared and the drums thumped. From the rafters Wood workers loosed bags of red and green feathers, startling a white pigeon from its perch and sending it flapping and soaring above the tiered seats. When Lodge had again pounded the convention to order, Roosevelt's sister, Mrs. Corinne Roosevelt Robinson, was deferentially escorted from the rostrum to the most advanced point of the bridge to make the seconding speech. Dressed in black—for she was only recently a widow—speaking with clipped clarity, she time and again brought the applauding delegates to their feet in homage to her brother, the dead leader who still remained the choice of most of the delegates in their hearts.

> He [Wood] was my brother's devoted friend [Mrs. Robinson told the delegates] and my brother was his true friend. But I want Leonard Wood for President, not because he was my brother's friend but because he was my brother's type.

Speaking for Lowden, Congressman William A. Rodenberg of East St. Louis, a big man with a big voice, stirred the Illinois Governor's supporters by declaiming that he stood for "law and constitutional government" with "sound and practical business principles." The demonstration that followed took care to be as noisy as Wood's and to last three minutes longer. Delegates paraded up and down the aisles with lithographs of Lowden, proclaiming "A Business Man with a Business Plan." Lowden's name was seconded by a Mrs. Fletcher Dobyns. In a tactful gesture to the emergent women's vote the managers of Johnson, Butler, and Coolidge also had their candidates seconded by women.

In what the humorist Irvin S. Cobb called "the worst speech that ever was" Charles S. Wheeler presented Hiram Johnson's name to a chorus of boos when he condemned excessive campaign expenses and called on Southern "hand-picked delegates" and Northern "political slaves" to revolt and "scourge" the bosses from the party. "What did California do in 1916?" a delegate shouted, and there were taunts about Johnson's backer, William Randolph Hearst. Johnson's alienation from the majority was complete. His demonstration lasted twenty-five minutes, his supporters waving I AM FOR HIRAM placards, while anti-Johnson delegates booed and hissed. In the heat and after four rancid days any spontaneity had long since vanished.

Nominating and seconding speeches then followed for Coolidge, Judge Jeter C. Pritchard of North Carolina, Butler, and Hoover. The one spontaneous outburst came from the balconies when Judge Nathan L. Miller of New York spoke of Hoover as "the man possessing the qualities, the equipment, and the ability to deal with the problems which are confronting us." Then the penned masses stirred and shouted and cheered their man, impotent to affect the sullen delegates but at last able to express their will.

Some weeks before, Harding in a gesture of conciliation had asked the hog-calling Willis to present his name to the convention. Willis was popular with the delegates and they applauded his vociferous appearance. He endeared himself still further by making the briefest speech yet:

> The record of Ohio's candidate is the record of the Republican party for the past fifteen years. . . . Long before the voices of other statesmen rang out in favor of an American merchant marine this stalwart son of America was battling for a system that would give to us an American merchant marine that would carry, under the American flag, the commerce of this republic to all parts of the earth. . . .

Then, noticing the women delegates, in a sudden inspiration he interrupted his rotund periods and Billy Sunday gestures to lean forward over the flying bridge and ask with colloquial intimacy, "Say, boys—and girls, too—why not name as the party's candidate . . . . ?" There was laughter in the interrupting applause and responding cries from the floor of "That's right! We're all boys and girls! The girls are in politics now, too!"
Willis continued:

> What we want is not brilliant maneuvers but safe and sane seamanship by a captain who knows the way, by a captain who as he walks the deck working with the officers and men in these troubling times can say, "Steady boys, steady." That is the type of man Ohio is presenting today. McKinley was a great President because he understood Congress, and could cooperate with it. This man understands the viewpoint of Congress and can cooperate with it.
>
> My friends, in the name of the Republicans of Ohio I present for your deliberate consideration this great stalwart American-thinking Republican; not a professing progressive but a performing progressive. He delivers the goods. He is a man of sane statesmanship with eyes fixed on the future, a great typical American citizen. Ladies and gentlemen of the Convention, I name for the office of President of the United States that stalwart son of Ohio, Senator Warren G. Harding.

Although the demonstration lasted only ten minutes and consisted mostly of members of the Ohio delegation standing on their chairs, waving flags and giving three cheers for their man, it left a pleasing impression of Harding as the good-will candidate. Gus Creager, in his Texas drawl, seconded the nomination. Through the heat of the fading afternoon there followed in diminuendo the names of Sproul, Poindexter, and Sen. Howard Sutherland of West Virginia. "After reading these nominating speeches," the correspondent of the Boston *Transcript* concluded, "Washington, Lincoln, Grant, Roosevelt, Julius Caesar, and Napoleon feel like pretty small potatoes this morning."
During the morning, while the nominating speeches rolled inexorably on, Harding sat in his rooms at the Auditorium with Nicholas Murray

Butler. Unshaven, fanning himself in his shirt sleeves, his coat and waist-coat tossed on the bed, he told Butler that he could not afford to keep his headquarters or rooms any longer and was giving them up that evening. "This convention will never nominate me," he said, locked in discouragement. "I do not propose to go back to the Senate. I am going to quit politics and devote myself to my newspaper."

Wood was still ahead. His manager, Hitchcock, driving for victory in the first or second ballot, was demanding that the complimentary vote for favorite sons like Coolidge and Butler be omitted. There were no deals, no obvious shifts in strength behind the curtain of speeches. Hitchcock's attempt to come to an understanding with King failed. King himself had been told by Penrose that if there seemed a danger of Wood's sweeping the convention in the early ballots, the Pennsylvania votes were to be thrown to Lowden. According to *The New York Times* the anti-Wood forces planned an "inconsequential test of strength" on the first three or four ballots, "then a long recess during which the 'elder statesmen' may repair to the secret council chamber and select a candidate."

"Nobody is talking Harding," reporters wrote, "not even considered as among the most promising dark horses." The nominating speeches dragged on until five o'clock. Inside the Coliseum the temperature reached one hundred. Finally Lodge announced to relieved applause that the convention would proceed to the nomination of candidates. The slack atmosphere grew tense as the secretary began to call the roll of the states. Wood led on the first ballot. The totals were:

Wood	287½
Lowden	211½
Johnson	133½
Harding	65½
Butler	69
Sproul	83½
Coolidge	31
La Follette	24
Pritchard	21
Sutherland	17
Poindexter	20
Hoover	5½
DuPont	7

Just as planned, the floor managers were still holding back their reserves, masking them among the various favorite sons. Daugherty had 30 or 40 undercover Harding votes on loan to Lowden. Yet even with these he had less than half the number he had so buoyantly predicted in the spring. Many of Lowden's delegates were on such a temporary loan basis, deposited with him to hold Wood and until some other trend was definable. Lowden's floor manager, the cherubic and astute Alvin T. "Toby" Hert of Kentucky—manager of the Western Republican headquarters in 1916—felt that he had a reliable core of only about 150 delegates. Wood's strength showed in the New England states, New Jersey and Maryland, part of the South, and in about half the Far West. Lowden's support was concentrated in the Middle West and South, while Johnson had the other half of the Far West, Nebraska, North Dakota, and Michigan. Outside Ohio Harding had one vote each from Alabama, Arizona, Arkansas, Colorado, Florida, and Utah, one and a half from Mississippi, two from Kentucky, Louisiana, and New York, three from Wyoming, and five each from Mont Reily's Missouri and Ed Scobey's Texas. But on the next ballot he lost Arkansas, Florida, Louisiana, and Wyoming, and his vote total dropped from 65½ to 59.

Determined to defeat Wood under all circumstances, the Senate leaders brought their "flying squadron" into action on the second ballot to make the trend to Lowden seem irresistible. Senator Wadsworth, squadron leader and chairman of the New York delegation, planned to use his delegates as the major instrument of this strategy. Wood had counted on Wadsworth, even at one point asking him to be his floor manager, and when Wadsworth begged off he gave no hint of any secret opposition. As Nicholas Murray Butler admitted the following week, the first task of the flying squadron was

> to bring the vote of Governor Lowden at least up to the Wood vote. Owing to local and state complications there were very few sources from which new strength for Lowden could be drawn so early in the balloting. Pennsylvania could not help, because if it left Sproul, twenty-five or thirty of its votes would go to Wood. Massachusetts could not help, because if it left Coolidge, there would be an increased vote for Wood in that state. Ohio could not help because Harding had but thirty-nine of the forty-eight votes and could spare no more. Michigan could not help because if it broke up the solidarity of its Johnson vote, more votes would go to Wood than to Lowden. It was clearly necessary, therefore, for New York to become the Belgium of the war, and I cheerfully gave my approval to the plan to turn New York votes to Lowden in increasing volume.

On the second ballot Wood gained two votes, Johnson 13½. Butler's release of 10 New York delegates combined with an influx of colored delegates from the Southern rotten boroughs gave Lowden an increase of 48 votes and brought him to within 30 of Wood. If on the third ballot he could push his total past Wood's, he would eliminate the General. For, as Mark Sullivan explained, there are two basic rules of the game at political conventions. A dark horse can slip a little in his obscurity on the early ballots, but a leading candidate must make some gain at each tally. And a candidate in the lead must stay in the lead, for once he drops behind, he is out.

The flying squadron mustered its strength in the third ballot to give Lowden 23 additional votes, including 16 from New York that Butler released through an agreement whereby he added two to every one from North Carolina. But 13 upstate New York delegates shifted to Wood, as did 9 from Massachusetts, giving him a total of 303 to Lowden's 282½. Johnson gained two votes, Harding lost a half. The discouraged senators, backed by the Johnson supporters, were looking for a temporizing adjournment, but most of the delegates vociferously insisted that they wanted "to get on with it." When a delegate offered an adjournment motion, instantly seconded by Wadsworth, he was shouted down. On the fourth ballot Wood rose to 314½, 177 votes short of the nomination but almost two-thirds of the way there. Lowden, gaining a mere 6½, reached 289. Johnson was down to 140½ and Harding had 4 votes less than he had on the first ballot.

While the balloting progressed, there was a conference of senators at the back of the platform. Smoot and McCormick were seen whispering together, each with an arm on the other's shoulder. Then, as the results were announced, Smoot—a lugubrious man who looked more like an undertaker than a senator—moved down the bridge to the edge of the platform.

"I move," he croaked, "that the convention do now adjourn until tomorrow morning at ten o'clock."

A surprised silence was followed by Lodge's prim voice: "Those in favor of the motion to adjourn will signify it by saying 'Aye.'"

There were a few vague "Ayes."

Again he intoned "Those opposed, 'No.'"

A great thunder of Noes rose up. With an aloof wave of his gavel he turned away indifferently as he ruled that "the 'Ayes' have it and the convention is adjourned until tomorrow morning at ten o'clock."

As the delegates shuffled and elbowed their way through the now-gaping exits, Mark Sullivan caught up with Smoot and the two rode downtown together in a taxi. Sullivan asked him why he and Lodge had forced the adjournment. "Oh," said Smoot, "there's going to be a deadlock and we'll have to work out some solution; we wanted the night to think it over." Sullivan asked if Wood would go on gaining in the morning, and Smoot, with all the authority of an apostle of the Mormon Church, replied that he would gain on the first ballot and then stop. After leaving the Senator, Sullivan dropped in at the Wood headquarters and put the same question to Hitchcock. Hitchcock said he expected Wood to gain on the first and all following ballots and pointed out just where he anticipated the additional delegates were coming from.

With the adjournment a discouraged Harding had given up any further hope of a continuing deadlock between Wood and Lowden. William Allen White met him in a hotel elevator, boozy, with bloodshot eyes and a two days' beard and looking "like the wreck of the *Hesperus*." Daugherty, on the other hand, exhilarated by the rising tension, was buoyant as a gambler sold on his run of luck. All the afternoon he had been making his contacts at the Coliseum, or buttonholing key figures around the hotels or on the streets. He had his workers spread everywhere, talking Harding, meeting the delegates after the adjournment to find out where they were located, and assigning Harding supporters to every group. During that portentous evening he sent the Columbus Glee Club serenading from headquarters to headquarters. He put out a new set of Harding portraits. "We made it a Harding night," he wrote. "Of good cheer and friendly gestures for every candidate." And everywhere Daugherty passed the word along that the way to break the deadlock was to nominate good old Harding.

At eight o'clock Harding had so far recovered his political spirits that, deciding not to withdraw from public life, after all, he telephoned Columbus and told Harris at the Deshler to file his name for senator. The early evening he spent in his hotel room reminiscing with a friend about his boyhood and his school days in Blooming Grove.

While he reminisced and the delegates sweltered and the sleek little animals came and went on their private missions at the various headquarters along Presidential Row, Borah in the role of a political Gabriel sent out men with megaphones to announce an immediate meeting in the Assembly Room of the Auditorium Hotel "to consider the danger of nominating a candidate who did not have a clean record." At the meeting Borah, with his usual vehemence, said he would not support men such as Lowden and Wood who had been shown to have indulged in the lavish use of money to get the nomination. Again there was the implied threat of a Johnson bolt.

After abruptly adjourning the convention, Lodge had dinner with his friends Brandegee and Harvey, and Senator Curtis, the leader of the Kansas delegation. Curtis had started out in life as a boy jockey and a farmer, and ended as a merchant, postmaster, and eight-term congressman before being elected to the Senate as a regular of regulars. Wholly a Westerner, his beady eyes were part of his Indian inheritance, as was the blood of French trappers. It was said of him that he was moved only by the crack of the party whip or the sound of its dinner bell.

The Old Guard representatives spent the dinner hour talking over the stalled convention, and then adjourned to the suite in the Blackstone that Harvey shared with Will Hays. That suite, 404, 5, 6, on the thirteenth floor consisting of two bedrooms and a reception room, became the famous "Smoke-filled Room" of American political folklore. From 8 P.M.

until 2 A.M. senators and party leaders wandered in and out of Suite 404 at random, poured themselves drinks, and talked indecisively through the perfecto smoke. In all the comings and goings there was neither plan nor order. This unplatonic symposium became a clearinghouse for divided viewpoints. Among the senators dropping in during the course of the long evening were Watson of Indiana, McCormick of Illinois, Lawrence C. Phipps of Colorado, Selden P. Spencer of Missouri, Calder of New York, and New Jersey's Frelinghuysen, former Senators Crane and Weeks of Massachusetts, and Senator-to-be Joseph R. Grundy of Pennsylvania.

The discussion threaded its way among the looping strands of cigar smoke. Only Reed Smoot seemed to have any decided opinion, and he talked up Harding to anyone who would listen. The others groped vaguely for some way out of the day's deadlock. Various participants came away with various impressions of the Smoke-filled Room, precisely because of the vagueness. To Senator Wadsworth, who left early, fed up with "listening to a lot of footless conversation," the alleged President makers were "as futile as chickens with their heads off!"

In a probing effort to find out what the different state delegations would do on the next morning's ballot, the senators sent out a call for Indiana's National Committeeman Joseph B. Keating—reputed marshal of the floating delegates—and Lowden's manager, Toby Hert. Somebody remarked that the room looked like the Senate Chamber in epitome, with the non-Senator George Harvey in the vice-president's chair. Senator Lodge, the eldest of the elders, sitting back in his chair and swinging his foot, reviewed the facts in his thin, clipped voice. Joe Grundy recalled that Lodge began the discussion by remarking that although he had come to the convention as a Wood supporter, it was now "impossible and undesirable" to nominate either Wood or Lowden. Somebody else would have to be picked in the morning, for the heat and the financial exhaustion of many of the delegates made it practically impossible to hold the convention together over the weekend. "It will be Lowden or a dark horse," Hert tipped off a reporter some time before midnight. A number of the senators still favored Lowden, but Borah, on his arrival after his speech denouncing financial depravity, told them that Lowden had been too tainted by the bribed Missouri delegates. Nominate him, and Johnson would bolt! Borah suggested Knox as a compromise candidate with Johnson as his running mate. Some time that evening an emissary was sent to the Johnson headquarters with that tentative suggestion, but the answer came back that the ticket should read "Johnson and Knox" not "Knox and Johnson." [3]

[3] Sullivan records the long-current oral legend that the emissary hinted to Johnson that Knox had heart disease and would probably not live out a four-year term. Johnson replied indignantly: "You would put a heartbeat between me and the White House!" and refused to consider anything less than Johnson and Knox. Knox died October 21, 1921.

In the Smoke-filled Room's seesawing small talk, the names of all the other candidates were reviewed, to the darkest of the dark horses. Months before, Lodge had told Coolidge that a President should be at least ten or, better, twenty years younger than he himself was. When someone mentioned Lodge's name, the old man shook his head ruefully and remarked, "Seventy, a month ago!" He shook his head with more emphasis and less rue at the mention of Calvin Coolidge. Later, certain Eastern Republican leaders came to feel that Coolidge might have emerged as the dark-horse candidate if Lodge had pushed him hard enough. But the patrician Senator felt no inclination to push the plebeian Yankee Governor with the twanging Vermont voice who was already challenging him for political leadership of the state. "Nominate a man who lives in a two-family house!" Lodge had remarked earlier in the week to Henry L. Stoddard, the editor of the *New York Evening Mail*, at a dinner in the Chicago Club. "Never! Massachusetts is not for him!"

The smokers continued to ruffle through the names of possible candidates like a deck of soiled cards. Sproul would be labeled the Pennsylvania Railroad candidate. Hughes in his personal sorrow had already declined, and the New York organization was in no mood to draft him. Knox was old and ailing, and besides he had voted against both the Prohibition and Women's Suffrage amendments. Lenroot was from La Follette's treacherously Progressive Wisconsin. Allen had made a botch of nominating Wood, and in any case he was too closely connected with the Court of Industrial Relations. Harvey nursed a latent thought of making a coup with Hays, but Hays himself had declared that as chairman of the National Committee he could not bid at his own auction.

However many times the political cards were shuffled and dealt and discarded, somehow the Harding card always remained. As Lodge pointed out, no Republican candidate for President had ever been elected without Ohio's electoral vote. This year the Democrats might well pick Governor Cox of Ohio for their nominee. "For these reasons," Grundy recalled, "he [Lodge] believed the availability of Senator Harding to be so outstanding as to justify the convention nominating him on the following day." It seemed so logical a solution to the deadlock that "all present heartily joined in the nomination of Harding." According to Calder, Lodge, even though personally pledged to Wood, was "the leader and moving spirit" in bringing about Harding's selection.

During that enervating evening of debate Wadsworth was in and out of the Harvey suite at least three times. When he left for good, just before one o'clock, the attendance was dividing and nothing definite had been decided. Walking along one of the upper corridors of the Blackstone, he ran into Harding, quite alone but aware of the discussion in Harvey's suite and anxious to know if there was any news. Wadsworth told him there was none, and went on to bed.

Between dinnertime, when White had seen the stubble-chinned, hung-over Harding in the elevator and Wadsworth's meeting with the shaved and renewed Senator in the Blackstone corridor, Daugherty had been able to transfuse something of his own gambler's blood into Harding's slacker veins. In spite of Daugherty's quoted prediction, he had been unaware of the gathering in the Smoke-filled Room. Early in the evening he had got wind of a plot by Hynicka to capture the Ohio delegation. Secretly controlling his four or five ostensible Harding delegates, Hynicka had been trying to persuade the rest that Harding was done for, that with a united Ohio vote for Wood they might start a Saturday-morning stampede to sweep the convention.

Daugherty got the reluctant Walter Brown to call a caucus of the Ohio delegates, and at midnight Harding spoke to them, using all his easy charm to persuade them to stick to him, not to rob him of his big chance. Shortly before that meeting Jacob A. Meckstroth of the *Ohio State Journal* had glimpsed a jaunty and beaming Harding coming out of Ohio head-quarters with Myron Herrick, and was amazed at the transformation from the crumpled man he had seen just after the adjournment. "You can say," Herrick airily told Meckstroth, "that Senator Harding will be nominated on the first ballot tomorrow."

A little after 1 A.M. the remaining shirt-sleeved stalwarts of the Smoke-filled Room decided by a "standing vote" that "it would be the wise course to nominate Harding just as soon as this could be brought about." Lodge still dominated the room. McCormick, Calder, Curtis, Smoot, Brandegee, and Watson were among those present. The decision for Harding was not, as it was later depicted, a plot by a group of Old Guard senators to foist a pliant tool on the convention, but more the recognition of a psychological development that seemed to have made the Ohio Senator the most available candidate. Many of those cigar-smoking senators would continue to give their personal pledged votes to Lowden or Wood, and their decision for Harding was still tentative. During most of the night they would arrange to pass the word to the undercover delegates in the Lowden camp and to the favorite-son delegates they controlled to shift to Harding. Harding would have his chance, and if after four or five ballots he failed to show sufficient strength, then they would turn to some even darker horse.

Once the tentative decision was made, Harvey telephoned for Irvin R. Kirkwood and Henry J. Haskell of the Kansas City *Star.* As the two news-men entered the suite, someone called out through the smoke: "Kirkwood, tell us whom to nominate!"

"I will not!" Kirkwood replied. "That's your job, thank God!"

Harvey led the reporters into a bedroom, then returned with Brandegee and another elder statesman. In a quick resumé the senators explained that as Lowden and Wood were deadlocked and Johnson impossible, they had turned to Harding among the secondary candidates as the "logical" man, the one who had the least marks against him. He was from a strategic state, he was experienced politically, he was popular in the Senate, his appearance was presidential, and he could be trusted to "go along" with Congress. Haskell objected that Harding was scarcely known outside Ohio. Brandegee said disdainfully the convention would make him known; then, for all his Yale background, he rasped in the vernacular: "There ain't any first-raters this year. This ain't 1880 or any 1904; we haven't any John Shermans or Theodore Roosevelts; we got a lot of second-raters and Warren Harding is the best of the second-raters."

Senator Smoot, the Harding enthusiast, was perhaps as responsible as anyone for the spread of the Smoke-filled Room legend. Meeting a reporter of the *New York Telegram* in the elevator just after leaving the Harvey suite, he told him expansively that the senators had decided on Harding and that he would be nominated in the afternoon after enough ballots to give Lowden a run for his money. Toby Hert was sent to break the news at Lowden's headquarters.

About two o'clock—close enough to Daugherty's 2:11 A.M. prophecy to accommodate the legend—Harvey sent for Harding. The owl-eyed Harvey, his pompous air of destiny reinforced by alcohol, received Harding in one of the bedrooms.

> We think [he told the already alerted Senator in his slow and self-consciously impressive voice] you may be nominated tomorrow; before acting finally, we think you should tell us, on your conscience and before God, whether there is anything that might be brought up against you that would embarrass the party, any impediment that might disqualify you or make you inexpedient, either as a candidate or as President.

A rather stunned Harding asked for a little time to mull this over, and Harvey left him alone. What things Harvey might have heard, what caused him to make this bizarre query have remained as unknown as the thoughts that transpired in Harding's mind. But after ten minutes Harding opened the door and told Harvey there was no impediment.

An effusive Harding emerged from Harvey's suite and went directly to Johnson's rooms several floors below. Johnson and Albert Lasker and several others were there when he arrived. Harding said he wanted to talk to Johnson alone. They went into an adjoining bedroom and when they returned Johnson's square, solid face was livid with anger. "I like Harding," he spluttered to Lasker after Harding had left. "I like him very much, but I can't conceive of his being President of the United States. He's done nothing to deserve it. He tells me they have just agreed upstairs to make him President, and *he* came down here to ask *me*, wouldn't I run as vice president. Of course I indignantly refused."

At 3:30 A.M. the Kansas reporter Raymond Clapper, waiting in the corridor outside the Harvey suite, caught Senator Curtis as he was leaving and asked him who it was going to be. "I might as well give a fellow Kansan a break," Curtis told him. "We are going to try to put Warren Harding over. We'll try him out for a few ballots tomorrow but if he doesn't show strength we'll switch to Governor Sproul."

While the debate was ebbing and flowing in Harvey's suite to the systaltic rhythm of cigar smoke, while a relentless and unsleeping Daugherty tracked down his second- and third-choice delegates, the political tides still surged around the Wood headquarters. Hitchcock kept urging the delegates to stand firm. Wood still had reserves. In Pennsylvania alone he had 16 partisans who were committed to vote for Sproul until Wood came within 96 votes—20 plus Pennsylvania's 76—of the nomination. Then Sproul had promised to deliver the entire Pennsylvania delegation to Wood. And at the adjournment Wood had come within 82 votes of that goal. All 30 Michigan delegates had voted for Johnson on Friday but most of them planned to go over to Wood after the first ballot on Saturday. The remaining votes could easily be obtained by an alliance with Johnson. Wood sent Governor Allen to Johnson's manager, Angus McSween, to offer an alliance with Johnson as vice president, but Johnson would no more consider it than a similar offer from Lowden.

The sticky night was like the fateful one before a battle, with surreptitious marshalings of forces, the tenseness of the still-uncommitted future. "Nineteen hundred twelve was a Sunday-school convention compared with this," Johnson remarked as he observed the predators and the jackals on Presidential Row.

Penrose, the absent leader of the Pennsylvania delegation, had had a relapse and all Friday his doctors had forbidden him to have anything to do with the convention. Nevertheless, between 9:30 and 10 P.M. the telephone rang in Wood's headquarters and a voice said that Senator Penrose wanted to speak to the General. John Latimore Himrod, Wood's confidential secretary, who took the call, put his hand over the mouthpiece and relayed the message to Wood. Wood, standing across the room with Gen. E. F. Glenn, refused to speak to Penrose but told Himrod to take any message the Philadelphia boss wanted to give. "You may say to General Wood," Penrose told Himrod bluntly, "if he were nominated tomorrow would he give us three Cabinet members?" On hearing this Glenn turned to Wood: "Now, General, one word will make you President of the United States!" Wood told the waiting Himrod: "Tell Senator Penrose that I have made no promises, and am making none." Penrose answered that he was sorry but that "we" intended to have a Republican President and insisted on the privilege of naming three members of the Cabinet.

There were other offers and hints of offers. Albert Beveridge recalled being at Wood's headquarters when two Republican elders arrived with a proposal similar to Penrose's and with similar results. "Shady business, gentlemen," was Wood's reply, "and I'll have nothing to do with it."

Perhaps the most bumptious arrival in the Elizabethan Room that evening was Jake Hamon. Bombastically he explained to Wood's old Cuban quartermaster general, Chauncey Baker, that the 50 Southwest delegates he controlled would be enough to conclude the bargain for the Pennsylvania delegation, and he offered his delegates to Wood in exchange for being allowed to name the Secretary of the Interior and the ambassador to Mexico. When Wood heard this he for once lost his temper, and striding toward Jake shouted at him: "I am an American soldier! I'll be damned if I betray my country! Get the hell out of here." [4]

At three in the morning the Massachusetts industrialist and inventor John Hays Hammond and two of Wood's former military aides, Maj. Halstead Dorey and Maj. George T. Langhorne, sprawled grotesquely in the leather armchairs, were wakened by a burst of hilarious laughter from Wood standing in the doorway watching them. But the General's laughter soon faded as he warned them that the opposition was combining against him. Hitchcock, an old hand in managing Southern delegates in 1908 and 1912, observed: "There is only one thing. We can pull something off by bribing some of these delegates. That," he added, mournfully, "you wouldn't allow."

No, Wood told him, he would not.

Harding did not go to bed that night. In the first light of morning a reporter caught a glimpse of him sitting motionless in his hotel room. At 6 A.M. Joe Martin, out for an early-morning walk along Michigan Avenue, met his Massachusetts neighbor, former Senator Weeks, emerging bleary-eyed from the Blackstone. Joe asked about the conference in Harvey's room. Weeks said they had been debating all night—that no real decision had been reached when they broke up. Lowden, Johnson, and Wood would be given another chance to break the deadlock, but he doubted if they could. On leaving he told Joe almost under his breath, "I think it will be Harding."

Joe headed back for the Congress. In the Florentine Room he found a janitor taking down Harding pictures and asked if he might have a button of the next President of the United States. The janitor offered him a hand-

---

[4] Later in the evening Jake told a former convict friend that the nomination would go to Harding and that it had cost the Hamon interests a million dollars. After Hamon's death his son is reported to have told lawyers that Jake had been promised a third interest in the Teapot Dome lease for his support.

ful. "Any man who thinks this man is going to be President," he told Joe, "can have all that's left!"

The early release of the Associated Press reported that "Harding of Ohio emerged this morning from all-night conferences of Republican chieftains as the man with whom they hoped to break the imminent deadlock. Delicate relationships were involved . . . but most of the leaders . . . appeared agreeable to trying Harding first among the large field of dark horses." According to *The New York Times,* "when the conservative group finished its conference at an early hour this morning a sort of tentative understanding existed among its members that Senator Harding fitted into the complex situation better than any other candidate."

Harvey, after his night's vigil, had breakfast with Alice Roosevelt Longworth in the Blackstone dining room and gave her the news.

> He told of countless "conferences of elimination" [Princess Alice wrote in her memoirs]; he said that he, Lodge, Smoot, Crane, Watson, Brandegee, to name but a few who had "conferred" with Borah, if not acquiescing, at least not offering ponderable objection, had determined on Harding. . . . I sputtered and asked why, if "they" were strong enough to put Harding over, could they not have selected some "dark horse" such as Knox who would seem to have higher qualifications for the Presidency. The reply to that amounted to saying that Harding could be counted on to "go along." In other words, he could be controlled.

Another breakfast was taking place at the LaSalle where the sleepless but rejuvenated Harding sat at the table with the Duchess, his brother Deac, and Deac's two boys—sixteen-year-old George and fifteen-year-old Warren Harding II. Several Columbus men wearing feathered Wood badges came over to the table and spoke to Harding. After they had left Deac asked him: "Do you really think you have any chance of getting the nomination?" "Deac," Harding answered him with great assurance, "it looks like I might get the nomination on the seventh or eighth ballot." And he explained to his nephews that since the three leaders, Wood, Lowden, and Johnson, could not win, there would have to be a fourth man. That man he now expected to be. The boys were wild to go to the Coliseum to see their uncle nominated, but Deac refused to allow it. Even such an honor coming to the family was not, in the Deacon's eyes, a justification for profaning the Seventh-day Adventist Sabbath.

Word was getting round, carried like a smouldering torch by Daugherty's messengers. The odds that on Friday had been 10 to 1 against Harding had dropped to 5 to 1 before the convention opened. Just after breakfast Curtis called on his Kansas delegates to let them know that "it had been decided" to give Harding a play after trying for a ballot or two to nominate Wood. The delegates for the most part were glad enough to

hear that something, anything, had been decided. Like the other swelter-
ers, they were wearied, impatient, short of money and shirts and tempers,
and their impelling thought was to wind up the convention and get out of
Chicago by Saturday evening. Only Delegate William Allen White protested: "If you nominate Harding you will disgrace the Republican party.
You will bring shame to your country." Another delegate hissed across the
room to him: "Ah, White, you are a dreamer. Try to be practical for
once." White finally and reluctantly agreed that when the time came he
would go along with the rest of his delegation and vote for Harding, but
on condition that if Harding failed the Kansas vote would go then to
Herbert Hoover.

On that Saturday morning the early sun seemed pitiless. The concrete
pavement was still warm underfoot along Michigan Avenue, and the night
had not been cool enough to lower the temperature of the giant convention hall. Delegates had earlier shed their coats to sit in their shirt sleeves.
Now, as they gathered in the Coliseum, they began to undo their neckties
and peel off their stiff collars. As the floor and the galleries filled, the
temperature began to climb from the high ninety's to the one-hundred
mark. Even the band sounded weary. Again the convention was late in
starting. Not until 10:23 did Senator Lodge appear under the arch of the
sounding board. Methodist Episcopal Bishop Thomas Nicholson took
charge of the prayer for the day.

> Oh God [he intoned], help us to have done with all falsehood, all pretense,
> all hypocrisy. . . . May we here so act that the future historian must write
> a record of even nobler achievements. . . . Impress these delegates with a
> due sense of responsibility to Thee, to the Republic, to the other nations of
> the world, and to all mankind as they frame the platform and choose the
> standard-bearers of this party for the coming national campaign.

And, as Daugherty remarked, every floor leader made his own interpretation of the prayer. Before the opening of the convention he had spirited
Harding away to a rented room on a side street a few blocks away and
unknown to anyone except Daugherty. He insisted that Harding stay
there for the fateful morning, promising to join him after the first ballot,
and from time to time sending a trusted friend like Weeks to keep him
company.

While Harding sat in the discreet isolation of his bay-windowed
lodginghouse, the morning's balloting began, the fifth ballot of the convention. As intended, it was not decisive, but more a vane to indicate the
first shift in the political weather. Wood's total dropped 15½ to 299.
Sixteen more New York delegates switched to Lowden, leaving Butler—
who had started with 69—only 4, and carrying Lowden 4 beyond Wood

to 303. Johnson, still in thin third place, lost 8 votes. Daugherty continued to hold his reserves in line for Lowden, but other scattered votes began to drift to Harding—4 from Kansas, 3 more from New York, 6½ from Missouri, a few more from Texas. As Daugherty had feared, when the Ohio roll was called there was an attempt at a coup by Hynicka. One of the Hynicka-controlled delegates, Thomas F. Turner, climbed on a chair and shouted that Harding had refiled for the Senate and was out of the presidential race. There were cries of No! No! and Shame! among the Ohio delegation. For a moment it looked as if there were going to be a free-for-all, until Turner was howled down. At the end of the fifth ballot Harding had 78 votes, a gain of 16½ over the last ballot on Friday and 12½ above his previous high. The weather vane was swinging round: Wood had passed his peak; Lowden's ostensible delegates would not hold; Johnson, unexpectedly weak Friday, was slipping further; Sproul, by Penrose's order, still held his 75 Pennsylvania votes; Pritchard and Sutherland had long been eliminated; and the still-vague outline of the Ohio dark horse was growing.

On the sixth ballot Wood's floor leaders, desperately calling all their reserves, could barely manage to tie Lowden with 311½ votes. Johnson lost another 23½ votes. Daugherty learned that Hynicka on this ballot was planning a swift and secret demonstration that Harding's hold on his home state was slipping, and he sent couriers to every delegation warning of an Ohio switch. Sure enough, when the clerk called Ohio, its national committeeman stood up and cast the four Cincinnati votes pledged to Harding for Wood. The convention was in an uproar, floor and galleries turbulent with boos, catcalling, and hisses, but Daugherty's protective action had robbed Hynicka's gesture of its surprise effect and turned sympathy toward its intended victim. Harding gained another 11 votes.

As the sun approached the zenith, the temperature in the Coliseum rose to 100, 101, 102. Delegates sweated and stank and fidgeted and tried to fan themselves with programs and newspapers. On the seventh ballot Wood just managed to top Lowden by half a vote, 312 to 311½. But Harding was now in third place with 105 votes to Johnson's 90½.

It was close to one o'clock when the eighth ballot began. Daugherty now withdrew a few of his Wood delegates that he had been hoarding and 4 from Lowden. Wood with 290 votes lost 22, Lowden was down from 311½ to 307, and Harding had surged ahead to 133½. "That half vote may be a mascot," Harding remarked when he heard the figures. Delegates in their restlessness were leaving their seats to throng the aisles. Some were munching sandwiches. The whisper spread across the floor that Harding was "going over the hill," and Thompson's gallery boys were instructed to whoop it up. To Daugherty it seemed that the next ballot would be the breakaway on which he had gambled all his chips. He sent his orders flying to marshal every available Harding vote, all the delegates that had been hidden or held back. "It looks more like Harding," the Connecticut delegate Frederick Ullman telegraphed William Howard Taft. "Connecticut will go to him on the next ballot."

Yet, even as the weather vane pointed fixedly at Harding, senatorial second thoughts were proliferating, not the least behind Senator Lodge's unapologetically supercilious façade. From the press gallery H. L. Mencken watched that small presiding figure with delight.

> He presided over the session [wrote Mencken] from a sort of aloof intellectual balcony, far above the swarming and bawling of the common herd. He was there in the flesh, but his soul was in some remote and esoteric Cathay. . . . It was delightful to observe the sardonic glitter in his eye, his occasional ill-concealed snort, his general air of detachment from the business before him. For awhile he would watch the show idly, letting it get more and more passionate, vociferous, and preposterous. Then, as if suddenly awakened, he would stalk into it with his club and knock it into decorum in half a minute. I call the thing a club; it was certainly nothing properly describable as a gavel. . . . Supporting it was the Lodge voice, and behind it the Lodge sneer. That voice seemed quite extraordinary in so slim and ancient a man. It had volume, resonance, even a touch of music; it was pleasant to hear, and it penetrated into that fog of vaporized humanity to great depths. . . . His delight in the business visibly increased as the climax was approached. It culminated in a colossal chuckle as the mob got out of hand, and the witches of crowd folly began to ride, and the burlesque deliberations of five intolerable days came to flower. . . .

Lodge, disdainful of Coolidge and his two-family house, must have been equally disdainful of the malapropian tobacco-chewing Harding. The Massachusetts Senator had declared that he had no taste for President making; what he wanted to do was beat a President. But during the eighth ballot he sent for Walter Brown and asked him if the Harding forces would object to a recess. Brown said they most emphatically would. Nevertheless, at the ballot's conclusion Lodge recognized Toby Hert who at once moved to adjourn. New York and California seconded the motion. With a bull-like roar Willis leaped onto a chair and bellowed for a roll call. Lodge beckoned Willis and Herrick to the platform to assure them that there was no plot against Harding, but that the nomination should not be forced and Johnson should be consulted. Willis signaled his agreement to the Harding delegates. To another chorus of Noes, Lodge pronounced the motion carried and at 1:40 P.M. recessed the convention until four o'clock. Daugherty was not so easily appeased. Stumping his way toward the stage, red-faced and furious, his good eye flashing, he shouted at Lodge: "You cannot defeat this man this way! This motion was not carried! You cannot defeat this man!" Propitiatingly Lodge took him aside, trying to fob him off with the devious explanation that they wanted a united party and needed the recess to swing Johnson's followers over to Harding by offering Johnson the vice presidency. "A fool's errand," the unappeased Daugherty told Lodge.

Harvey and a few of the senators even, if briefly, nursed the belated second thought of nominating the National Committee chairman. Brandegee during the recess sent for the leader of the Connecticut delegation, J. Henry Roraback, and told him to cast Connecticut's next ballot for Hays. Roraback refused, saying that Connecticut was now for Harding. Brandegee and Harvey told him that was foolish since 600 Hays votes had been absolutely tied up. Roraback still refused. William Howard Taft always maintained that the recess was an attempt by "bitter-ender" senators to "spring" Hays on the convention. According to Butler, this Harvey-Brandegee coup was foiled only by "the stubborn independence of the Connecticut delegation."

A few minutes after the Coliseum had cleared for the recess, Lowden telephoned Wood from his Congress headquarters to tell him that the rumors of a senatorial cabal intriguing to force Harding's nomination were true and to ask for a conference. Shortly after 2 P.M. Wood drove with his chauffeur to the side entrance of the Congress where he found an unnerved and frightened Lowden waiting. Lowden told the General that delegates elected through his own financing were now being used against him. The two agreed that Harding's nomination would be a disaster to the party and that their only way out, while they still had time, was to form a coalition and stop the now-rolling Harding bandwagon by an adjournment over the weekend. Lowden said he could count on a loyal core of 150 delegates, Wood estimated that his numbered at least 250. If Johnson could be persuaded to go along, they would have the majority to force an adjournment.

They decided that the details could be looked after by their managers, and Wood, after dropping Lowden at the Congress, went at once to see Johnson. The old Progressive, contemptuous of the thought of Harding as President, agreed at once to cooperate for an adjournment. Meanwhile Procter hurried over to Lowden's headquarters where he found the Governor with Toby Hert. Hert said that only an immediate coalition of the Wood and Lowden forces could forestall Harding's nomination, and he wanted to know if Wood would accept second place. Procter said that Wood and his managers felt that the General, more than any other man, deserved first place, but they would be glad to have Lowden in second place. Both Lowden and Hert refused to consider this.

While Procter was reporting back to Wood on his inconclusive interview, a discouraged Lowden again telephoned to say there were rumors that the Kentucky and Iowa delegations were going over to Harding, and he was now thinking of formally withdrawing. Wood begged him to "sit tight."

Procter dashed back to the Congress to find Lowden with Hert and the national committeeman from Michigan, Charles B. Warren. Vehemently Procter told them that the issue was now far more than Wood's candidacy, since it concerned the fortunes of the whole party. Lowden must not withdraw. Once they had managed to adjourn the convention until Monday, they could work out some plans over the weekend to prevent Harding's nomination. The other three agreed.

Wood had also sent his Illinois manager, MacChesney, to get hold of Hays at the National Republican Committee headquarters in the basement of the Coliseum. There, in those three spare but somewhat cooler rooms, MacChesney found the national chairman bustling from one room to the other as nervously as—and with a toothy resemblance to—the White Rabbit. "If you'll tell me which room you're likely to stay in long enough for me to get in a word," MacChesney finally managed to say to him, "I'd like to talk to you." Hays settled down and MacChesney told him of their plan to hold the reopening of the convention until after four o'clock and then move for an adjournment. Hays was in favor. "It can be done," he announced dramatically. "It shall be done!"

Hays hurried to the Lowden headquarters to find Lowden, Hert, Warren, and Procter waiting for him. Certainly, he told them, an adjournment was advisable for the good of the party. They arranged that Hert would make the motion. But as the others left the room Hert turned to Procter and remarked that since Wood and Lowden were out of it, they could decide on an alternate before Monday morning. Procter was not willing to agree that Wood was out of it. Hert persisted: "Wood and Lowden are out of it, are they not?" Procter told him that was something to be decided between then and Monday morning. Hert did not reply. What Procter did not realize was that Hert was far more interested in defeating Wood than in electing Lowden or any other candidate. Hays returned to the Coliseum to delay the opening until they could make final arrangements for adjournment.

Daugherty, in the meantime, had borrowed a car from the National Committee treasurer, Fred Upham, and sent Harding back to the LaSalle where he had him installed in a larger suite with a private elevator. For the rest of the recess Daugherty was in and out of the various headquarters, no longer hanging on the coattails of events but approaching the stature of a President maker. At the Pennsylvania headquarters he talked directly with Penrose, recovered at least temporarily from his relapse of the day before. The Pennsylvania boss, convinced that Harding was going to be nominated, had prepared a statement for the press which he read to

Daugherty. Harding was a great Republican and would make a great President! Daugherty, fearful that if the statement appeared in the afternoon papers before the next ballot there would be an outcry that Harding had been nominated by the bosses, begged Penrose to hold off. Penrose agreed, and told Daugherty to release the statement whenever he saw fit.

At four o'clock the delegates were in their seats and growing restive at the sight of the empty rostrum. Yet, in spite of the heat, there was an electric change in the atmosphere. The word had been passed that it would be Harding, and the delegates acted as if a great weight had been lifted from them. Even the band sounded livelier. Those with sharp eyes might have noticed the odd persuasive figure whispering here and there unobtrusively among the delegates. Wood noted that evening in his diary that one politician was reported to have been offered $1,000 to swing his delegation, another five thousand. Less venally but equally unobtrusively, various senators circulated on the floor, pointing out that Harding was the quick, the simple solution for winding up before the weekend. The astute Walter Brown and Myron Herrick with his great political prestige carried the news sagaciously from group to group.

The minutes ticked by and the tense Coliseum masses grew increasingly unruly. Someone shouted, "Play ball!" and others took up the cry until it echoed from the rafters and drowned out the band. Sweaty delegates were climbing on their chairs to bawl for Lodge. Hert had agreed to meet Procter at the Coliseum and settle the matter of adjournment, but at half past four he had not appeared, and Procter sent out a messenger to search for him. Lodge warned that he could not hold the convention back any longer. Hays begged for another ten minutes "in the name of party harmony." At four-fifty there was still no sign of Hert. Lodge stalked to the rostrum and directed the secretary to call the roll for the ninth ballot.

At the very moment that the messengers were searching for Hert, he was within earshot distance in one of the Coliseum's small rooms in back of the speakers' platform, huddled with Lowden, Warren, Daugherty, and Harding. Shortly before the end of the recess Daugherty had picked up Harding and driven to Lowden's headquarters only to learn from Emmerson that Lowden had already left for the Coliseum. When Daugherty and Harding finally found him there, he told them with resigned cordiality that he was out of the contest and had just released his delegates, most of whom he expected to go to Harding. Then he congratulated Harding on his imminent victory. Daugherty admitted afterward that his most crucial help came from Lowden, "who, with his friends and delegation, was with us in the windup."

The roll call of the ninth ballot progressed with alphabetic inevitability. Alabama, Arizona, Arkansas, and California registered no change. Then, suddenly, the Connecticut delegation, which had been giving 13 of its 14 votes to Lowden, switched to Harding. Six of Florida's 7 votes followed. Illinois continued to cast 41 votes for Lowden, and the 17 that were Thompson-controlled for Johnson. The big break came with Kansas. Curtis had notified the delegation on the floor that Wood could not make it and the time had come to break for Harding. The dismayed William Allen White remembered "sitting there sweating, fanning myself with my twenty-five-dollar Panama, with my coat over the back of my chair, in a blue-and-white striped silk shirt of great pride, red-faced, perturbed, and most miserable in body and spirit. I didn't want to vote for Harding."

Daugherty had conjured up a fresh supply of banners, streamers, and portraits, and had sent his men up to the Coliseum skylights with hundreds of Harding postcards which they now showered down on the crowd. After Allen had called out that Kansas was casting her 20 votes for Harding, a delegate seized the state standard, raised it in the air with an attached photograph of Harding, and started a jubilant Kansas march around the hall to the yelled approval of the galleries. White toddled along after the other 19, "ashamed, disheveled in body and spirit, making a sad fat figure while the bands played, the trumpets brayed, and the crowd howled for Harding." His striped shirt and red necktie stained with sweat, he found himself wishing that he had sulked in his seat, and wondered if the long chance of Hoover was worth the feigned enthusiasm of this mock parade.

As Kentucky was called, following Kansas, Hert emerged from his back-room hideout into the convention floor to throw his state to Harding. Procter pounced on him in the aisle and demanded to know about the adjournment. "It's off," Hert told him. "You damned liar, aren't you going through?" the livid Procter demanded. "No," said Hert, heading toward his delegation.[5] When Kentucky's 26 votes went to Harding, everyone in the Coliseum realized that Lowden had capitulated.

Louisiana with its 12 kept votes now followed Kentucky. Missouri offered its 36 votes to "that stalwart American senator, Warren G. Harding." New York gave Harding 66 of its 88, and after that vote was announced Herrick jumped on a chair and blew kisses to the New York delegation. Jake Hamon now threw in all his Oklahoma and Southwest strength. But Pennsylvania still held to Sproul. There was silence when Ohio was called. Defiantly Hynicka and his stalwarts still cast their 9 votes for Wood, to the fury of the other Ohio delegates and the hoots and jeers of the gallery. Harding led the field on this ballot with 374½ votes—still 119 short of majority—but the end was obvious. Wood held at 249, with Lowden down to 121½ and Johnson 83. Maschke then walked over to

[5] Hert later told Procter: "Why, you knew we were out to beat Wood." Wood never forgave Allen for leading the break.

Hynicka and told him ominously: "If Harding is not nominated on the next ballot, you will always be blamed."

The balconies, in the enthusiasm of mob excitement, were taking up the chant of Harding! Harding! Harding postcards fluttered down from the rafters like snowflakes. Harding supporters tramped up and down the aisles with banners and streamers, exhorting the doubters to climb aboard the band wagon while there was still time. The relief of the convention was like a sudden clearing after a thunderstorm. At last the die had been cast; and that it had been loaded mattered less to the delegates than that they had avoided another weekend in that broiling, expensive city. "The delegates would not listen to remaining in Chicago over Sunday," wrote James Morgan in the Boston *Globe*. "The temperature of the hall had stayed not far from 90 for four days and the President makers did not have a clean shirt left. On such things, Rollo, turns the destiny of nations."

Harding himself remained in the back room with Lowden where they were now joined by the delegate-less Nicholas Murray Butler. The Duchess was sitting in a box in the front balcony just to the left of the flying bridge. Daugherty from the floor had just sent a message to the manager of the Pennsylvania delegation asking for all their votes on the next ballot, when he looked up and saw her. She had taken off her hat and was sitting humped forward, her puffed arms tightly folded. In her right hand she gripped two enormous hatpins. Daugherty made his way to the balcony and sat down beside her. Something, he told her, was going to happen in this next ballot. They had the votes and her husband would be nominated. At the word "nominated" she gave a sudden start, almost leaping from her chair to drive the hatpins deep into Daugherty's side. He swayed as if he were going to faint, as if he were smothering. Above the pain he felt the blood beginning to run down his leg into his shoe and wondered if the pins had pierced his lung. As he moved unsteadily from the box, he could hear Lodge calling the tenth ballot. He groped his way to the floor and listened to the roll call with a vertigous sense of detachment.

Far back in the steamy recesses of the balcony Nan watched her lover's certain progress to the nomination. In the midst of the whistling and cheering and waving of banners she remembered how as a high-school freshman she had written in the margin of her books: "Warren Gamaliel Harding—He's a darling.'" It was all Harding now—Arkansas, Colorado, Illinois, Indiana, Maine, Massachusetts. Even Hynicka's Ohio holdouts now switched to Harding. By the time Pennsylvania was reached, Harding had 440 votes and needed only 53 more to give him the nomination. Daugherty as he padded along the aisle could hear the queer swish of blood that filled his shoe. He wavered and caught hold of a chair, felt he was smothering again, and sat down to steady his nerves. From somewhere off in space he heard the clerk call out Pennsylvania, and then the deep-voiced reply: "Pennsylvania casts 61 votes for Warren G. Harding."

The balconies broke loose with yells. Harding had won! Daugherty tottered to an anteroom and discovered that his lung had not been pierced after all. When he took off his shoe he found it full not of blood but of perspiration. William Allen White, in sad isolation, had cast his vote for Herbert Hoover—one of the nine that Hoover received on the last ballot.

At six-fifteen Harding was still sitting in the back room with Lowden and Butler as the balloting progressed. Suddenly there was a great roar from the convention, and in an instant Warren burst through the door shouting. "Pennsylvania has voted for you, Harding, and you are nominated." Harding stood up solemnly, took Butler and Lowden by the hand. "If the great honor of the Presidency is to come to me," he told them, "I shall need all the help that you two friends can give me." A few moments later a recovered Daugherty arrived to send the new nominee back to the LaSalle. The figures on the tenth ballot were: Harding, 692½; Wood, 156; Johnson, 80⅕; Lowden, 11. Belligerently the 24 Wisconsin delegates continued to vote for La Follette, to the accompaniment of jeers and hisses. Senator Frelinghuysen's offer of the customary motion to make the nomination unanimous brought the frowzy-headed Harold Ickes to his feet bellowing "No!" Amid a few more Noes, Lodge ruled that it was unanimous.

The Coliseum echoed briefly to the Harding victory shouts, but the noise was more of relief than delirium, with none of the hat-smashing frenzy that a Blaine or a Foraker or a Roosevelt could arouse. About two-thirds of the delegates were on their feet, perhaps a hundred stood on chairs, and a few women waved damp handkerchiefs. Lodge, hoarse-voiced and weary, in announcing that Harding had the necessary majority, by a slip of the tongue said Lowden—and raised a howl louder than that at the nomination.[6]

As the delegates in little groups were beginning to saunter out of the auditorium, Hert, McCormick, Borah, Weeks, Wadsworth, and several other senators were meeting in a timbered open space under the platform to pick a vice presidential candidate. Hastily they chose the progressive Irvine Lenroot of Wisconsin as a sop and balance to Harding's conservatism. Amid the clatter and bang of folding seats McCormick presented Lenroot's name to the waning convention. Hert and Herrick seconded it. Lodge had withdrawn, leaving Willis as presiding officer. Lenroot's nomination seemed indifferently routine when suddenly an unknown

[6] Harvey wrote: "There was no popular explosion for Harding. There was little spontaneity. He was nominated because there was nothing against him, and because the delegates wanted to go home."

delegate from Oregon, Wallace McCamant, bellowed for recognition and with a voice like Willis's placed Calvin Coolidge in nomination. Somehow the name of the mousy governor of Massachusetts, the pseudo-hero of the Boston police strike, struck off an unexpected spark that neither Willis nor the senators could extinguish, and in a sudden blaze of enthusiasm and before the leaders knew what was happening Cautious Cal had stampeded the convention. There were two more token nominations—Governor Allen of Kansas and Henry W. Anderson of Virginia—but they were only token, and while their brief nominating speeches were going on the Coliseum echoed to the cries of "We want Coolidge!" Cautious Cal received 674½ votes on the first ballot to 146 for Lenroot, and this time no one objected when the nomination was made unanimous.

Wood in his first fury had been ready to storm onto the convention floor and denounce the "theft." But later, composed and even gallant in his defeat, he stood squarely on the threshold of the Elizabethan Room, amid a litter of red and green feathers, his military boots glistening, dog-headed riding crop under his arm. His wife by his side, he received the condolences of his friends, with a smile for each and a composure that seemed almost jovial. At the LaSalle the crowds thronged in waves round the new candidate—supporters, well-wishers, the hopeful, the curious, the sycophants, reporters, and photographers. The beaming Duchess had forgotten Madame Marcia and the thoughts of nemesis. Harding's own volatile temperament soared. With a bad poker hand he had taken the pot. "We drew," he remarked, "to a pair of deuces and filled."

[CHAPTER XVI]

President-Elect

Before leaving Chicago Harding managed to dodge photographers and reporters, borrow a ride in a friend's car, and sneak away for a few hours to meet Nan at the Willits's apartment. She prattled on about Elizabeth Ann—whom he had still avoided seeing—and inevitably about financial arrangements, and he warned her that she might find herself shadowed from then on, but told her not to worry about it. She let him know that she felt "greatly worn" and needed a six- or eight-week vacation "to bring back the roses" to her cheeks. He agreed to send her to the Eagle Bay Hotel at a small lake in the Adirondacks. Then, after their love-making, she walked to the elevated station with him and watched him disappear behind the turnstile. She had one more glimpse of him as he came out on the upper level and waved to her briefly from the railing of the platform.

While Nan stayed at Eagle Bay she received a visit from a slight, soft-spoken young stranger with a ruddy complexion who met her in the lobby, handed her a bulky envelope but refused to give his name. The envelope, containing $800, was from Harding, and the ruddy-complexioned stranger turned out to be a Secret Service man attached to the new Republican nominee. She later knew him as Jim Sloan.[1] Aware of Nan before the election, Sloan would become afterward Harding's most trusted go-between.

From Chicago Harding returned to his flower-decked office in Washington to find himself one of the tourist sights of the capital, pointed out by guides, besieged for autographs. Tryon, stunned out of punctuation by his son's prominence, wrote from Marion:

> Since you have gone into the ring I am getting more anxious than I was at first as I was not anxious at first for you to try for the Nomination as there are so many anarchists and traitors and agitators it seems like taking your life in your hands I will hope for the best anyhow.

James Sloan, Jr., had spent twenty years in the Secret Service.

Two weeks after Harding's nomination the Democrats held their convention in San Francisco, a somewhat better lubricated affair than the Republicans since the Democratic National Committee managed to get hold of forty barrels of whisky. Wilson's son-in-law, William Gibbs McAdoo, and his rough-on-Reds attorney general, A. Mitchell Palmer, were the two leading candidates. It took eight days and 44 ballots before the exhausted delegates, with political geography in mind, at last turned to Ohio's Governor Cox and a straight pro-League of Nations platform. Harding wired his congratulations at the honor shown "our great state of Ohio." For vice president the convention chose the debonair thirty-eight-year-old Assistant Secretary of the Navy Franklin Delano Roosevelt. "A well-meaning, nice young fellow," Lodge commented, "but light."

All the factory whistles in Marion shrilled the news of Harding's nomination. The boy riding into town on a balky mule, the young editor dodging out the back door as the sheriff came in the front, the shadowed man whom Kling had cursed in the courthouse, the still somewhat uncertain leading citizen, had become a world figure, Ohio's pride. "The proudest moment in our history," the *Morrow County Sentinel* called the nomination and added: "Harding is worthy. He is just plain folks." In Marion his boyhood chum Dick Crissinger, twice the Democratic nominee for Congress, organized a bipartisan Harding-for-President Club with Herrick and Willis as vice presidents. Harding, it was announced, would stay home and run a McKinley Front Porch campaign from his bandstand-like porch. Marion in 1920 would be another Canton of 1896!

From the Union Depot the Marion Civic Association set up a "Victory Way" extending over a mile to the Harding home. White columns topped by gilt eagles marked both sides of the road at twenty-yard intervals, from West Center Street to the courthouse, from South Main Street to East Church, and finally to the house on maple-lined Mount Vernon Avenue. Arches of flags and bunting shaded each crossing, and blown-up Harding photographs stared from every window. Store fronts bloomed with red, white, and blue bunting. Frosted cakes in the bakery windows spelled out HARDING, and John Jolly the Center Street barber had daubed the same capital letters on his window in shaving soap. To deal with the expected crowds two new patrolmen were added to the police force.

On the weekend of June 27 Harding, now inevitably shadowed by Jim Sloan, left for Bound Brook, New Jersey, to stay with Senator Frelinghuysen at the Hill, his nine-hundred-acre estate. Senators Hale of Maine and Kellogg of Minnesota—his old Chevy Chase golf companions—had come to make up a foursome at the adjoining Somerset Country Club. On Sunday Harding attended the Third Dutch Reformed Church, of which Frelinghuysen was an elder. He left the Hill on Tuesday. Back in Washington he made the phonograph recording of his earlier League of Nations speech. The first of the 15 million Harding buttons were now ready—there had been some difficulty with a celluloid shortage—as well as 5 million Harding-Coolidge posters.

At the end of the week Harding and the Duchess left Washington with Harry Daugherty for a three-day motor trip to Marion. On arriving in the middle of the afternoon they found several hundred townspeople waiting in front of 380 Mount Vernon Avenue. Clifford Kling and his wife, unconscious of irony, had made the house ready and were there to welcome them. News of Harding's arrival spread quickly and in a short time 3,000 people had crowded onto the grass around the projecting bow of the porch. Harding stepped out, all smiles and homely satisfaction, while the Marionites shouted in their pride. After reading a speech, he put aside the manuscript and presented the Duchess to them, "a good scout who knows all my faults and yet has stuck to me all the way." Then he held out his hand to "another loyal friend, one of the best scrappers in the world—Harry Daugherty!"

Although the campaign would not formally open until August, the informal Front Porch campaign began on Harding's return. The poster artist Howard Chandler Christy arrived to paint Harding's portrait. Colonel Christian's house next door had been taken over as a political headquarters, and its small dining room became Harding's office. Under the apple trees in the rear of the Harding house a portable bungalow held the newspaper correspondents. From Canton the McKinley flagpole was sent on and erected in the new McKinley's front yard. The flag-raising at seven each morning always attracted a crowd. Sometimes Harding himself did the raising. Each day barefoot urchins lined the curb before the unfenced front yard waiting to catch a glimpse of "the next President." The bulbous front porch never seemed unoccupied. Little girls came there with their dolls. Neighbors brought over their knitting and sewing. Parading on the porch for the photographers, the Duchess held a succession of babies in her arms, while Harding admitted that he would "rather have a houseful of kiddies than anything else in the world." Nevertheless, Pete DeWolfe's children, the ten-year-old Eugenia and the eight-year-old George, never appeared in the family setting, since the Duchess preferred to avoid even the appearance of being a grandmother. For some time now she had taken to wearing a velvet-banded brooch round her neck to conceal the wrinkles.

Harding was to be officially notified of his nomination by Senator Lodge at special ceremonies on July 22. A few days before, the Harding front yard had been covered over with crushed limestone to prevent its becoming a quagmire. Before the encouraging photographers Tryon in his suspenders trundled several barrows of the gravel as it was being spread. Coolidge in Vermont was making similar folksy gestures, having himself photographed while ploughing in his grandfather's smock.

For Notification Day, Marion—its population now numbered 28,591— was prepared for 150,000 visitors. Crissinger, in charge of arrangements, planned to feed 100,000 for two meals and threatened that any place in town caught raising prices would be closed down. The hotels were all full, but private rooms were available from 75 cents to $1.50.

The great day was warm and sunny. From early morning until noon delegations appeared with bands and banners before the Front Porch. First to arrive were the 75 members of the Hamilton Club of Chicago, beribboned, carrying canes, and wearing gray top hats, as the official escort of Senator Lodge and the Notification Committee. Through the business district and up the Victory Way they marched, four abreast, accompanied by a band and an honorary escort from the Marion Marching Club. Reaching the Mount Vernon Avenue house they broke into their notification anthem, "Good Morning, Mr. Har-Har-Harding"—to the tune of "Mr. Zip, Zip, Zip"—and continued to sing as they swept past the McKinley flagpole and across the gravel-coated yard to come to a halt in front of the curved porch. In the afternoon there was a reception for Harding and the Republican higher-ups at the Marion Club.

Governor Cox earlier that week had with Franklin Roosevelt visited Wilson at the White House and standing before the crippled President declared with tears in his eyes that he was a million per cent behind him and the League. The President, in a wheel chair and with a shawl covering his paralyzed left arm, whispered, "I am very grateful." Lodge in waspish riposte was ready to accept the League as the issue of the campaign. "Wilson's League," he told his notification audience that evening to cries of "Give it to 'em!" from the crowd, "ought never to be accepted by the American people." And he referred to unworthy persons who, for an unfortunate period, had seized the reins of power.

Some 2,000 had gathered in the Chautauqua Auditorium at Marion's Garfield Park for the ceremonies. While the Republican Glee Club of Columbus sang

> We'll throw out Wilson and his crew,
> They really don't know what to do,

30,000 of the less favored had to content themselves with milling about outside. Harding read his homemade acceptance speech under a spluttering arc lamp, holding fast to his glasses which kept slipping down his nose. Taft, on seeing an advance copy, had begged him to make pro-League changes, and Crane and Root also forwarded their objections. Harding mentioned all the things he had to mention—the railroads, labor, law enforcement, the tariff, the sound dollar. He called for "preserved nationality as the first essential to the continued progress of the Republic." Looking beyond the Eighteenth Amendment, he saw America as the appealing voice to sober the world. Then, spurred by Lodge, he rejected even League reservations and came out flatly for a peace by declaration to be followed by a newly negotiated treaty divorced from the League. Normalcy made its by now inevitable appearance as something we must "stabilize and strive for." (Hoover decided privately that "normalcy" was a "leave-me-alone" feeling after a fever.) Finally Harding turned almost diffident as he spoke of his awareness of his own limited abilities. But "in a hopeful spirit and with a hymn of service" in his heart he pledged fidelity to God and country in accepting the nomination. Hays, sitting on the platform in a new cutaway, wiped away a tear. Mark Sullivan thought the atmosphere one "usually associated with churches."

Along the bunting-decked Victory Way from the Union Depot up Center Street blossoming in red, white, and blue, the three-story Uhler-Phillips Building alone stood out in the starkness of undecorated brick. Here Jim Phillips, the complacent cuckold, had taken his bitter, passive revenge. Every correspondent, every outside politician in town for the notification who stopped to wonder at the buntingless structure soon found out the reason. William Allen White observed and asked, and recorded his observations—without recording names—in his book *Masks in a Pageant*. Harding's primrose-path detours became a genial topic for the reporters in the shack under the apple trees. No one was yet aware of Nan, but other incidents cropped up. Raymond Clapper, as an eager young reporter assigned to Marion to cover the campaign, had brought his wife with him. She recorded one such incident when

> three newsmen, invited to dine at the home of one of Harding's widow neighbors, were, during the evening, taken upstairs by an innocent eight-year-old member of the woman's family and proudly shown Harding's toothbrush. Said the child, "He always stays here when Mrs. Harding goes away."

The capricious Carrie still caused talk, for in spite of the bitterness of her last letter she had achieved a reconciliation of sorts with Harding. Often she would stroll along Mount Vernon Avenue past the Front Porch, to the outrage of the Duchess. Prof. Arthur Hirsch, the head of the history department at Ohio Wesleyan University, on a chance visit to Marion during the campaign happened to be an observer of one such incident:

> I stood some distance back one forenoon when Mrs. Phillips was standing only a few feet away, on the Harding front lawn, talking to Mr. Harding who sat on the porch corner that he used as a campaign headquarters. With one eye on him and the other on the front door of the residence, she would take one cautious step, then another, toward the porch. Suddenly,

Mrs. Harding appeared. A feather duster came sailing out at Mrs. Phillips, then a wastebasket. Mrs. Phillips did not retreat. Next came a piano stool, one of those old, four-legged things with a swivel seat by which it could be lowered or raised. Not until then was there a retreat. She tossed him a kiss and left quietly. Mrs. Phillips was then an attractive woman, with a neat, conservative hair-do, a house dress, and attractive shoes. Her face was especially attractive in contrast with that of Mrs. Harding. And she was well mannered and, in a neighborly way, congenial. I saw her several other times at rallies. At one, in the Marion fairgrounds amphitheater, she sat quietly in the crowd, while Mrs. Harding was on the platform with her husband. The latter had on a big hat with long feathers that kept bobbing this way and that, for Mrs. H. was a nervous creature, excitable and restless. While he was speaking, she would get up and shake her fist at, I suppose, Mrs. Phillips, get all excited, and sit down again. He seemed not to notice her.

The scandal was too open for the Republican National Committee to tolerate. Hays sent Albert Lasker to take care of the Phillipses. Lasker had formed his own opinion of Harding at their first meeting when Harding asked him to agree at least not to fall out if they should disagree. That was not the way Lasker saw life. Harding, he felt, was soft. But as the campaign's publicity director his job was to "humanize Harding as an old-fashioned, sage, honest-to-the-core Middle Westerner who could be trusted never to rock the boat." For the man who had put the film in Pepsodent, that would be easy.

Lasker himself was the son of a German-Jewish pedlar who had come to Texas and established himself as a merchant and trader. The father's bitter memories of Europe had left the son a fanatic isolationist. At the age of eighteen Lasker had gone to work as an office boy in the Chicago advertising firm of Lord & Thomas. One of his first duties was cleaning the cuspidors. In five years he was making $52,000 a year, and before he was forty he owned the firm and was taking a million a year from it. Besides filming Pepsodent he created Puffed Wheat from Puffed Berries, gave Palmolive its Schoolgirl Complexion, and set women to smoking Lucky Strikes. He had the advertising man's sixth sense for the popular mood. By the massive use of all the modern advertising techniques he was going to streamline Hanna's methods, to replace "wiggle and wobble" by Harding and Coolidge. With a dozen picked advertising specialists he set up headquarters in New York. His secret concern was that Harding was not isolationist enough.

With Carrie Phillips, Lasker was blunt. In his one interview he agreed to pay her $20,000 plus a monthly sum as long as Harding held public office. In addition she and her husband were to take an expense-paid trip round the world via the Orient where Jim would investigate "the raw silk trade." Only, they must leave Marion before the election and stay away. Jim and Carrie left for Japan at the summer's end.

Blooming Grove, too, began to cast its long shadow. The legend of Harding's Negro blood was again whispered all over Ohio, as it had been so persistently whenever he had run for office. Through the state single-sheet flyers made their appearance carrying the old dubious scandal. No one knew, no one was ever to know who paid for them or distributed them, but in most cases they bore Chancellor's name. *The Right of the American People to Know* gave the Harding family tree with its dark embellishments as:

Amos Harding (Black) West Indian Negro	Wife—Huldah Harding (colored)
Issue	
George Tryon Harding 1st (colored)	Wife—Ann Roberts (colored)
Issue	
Charles A. Harding (colored)	Wife—Mary Ann Crawford (pass-for-White)
Issue	
George Tryon Harding 2nd	Wife—Phoebe Dickerson (White)

This marriage was objected to by the brother of Phoebe Dickerson for the reason that George Tryon Harding, the second (the father of Warren G. Harding), had Negro blood.

The above is verified by Elias Shaffer, 804 Holloway St., Akron, Ohio, who has known Mr. Harding for fifty years. He went to school with Dr. Geo. Tryon Harding, the second (father of Warren G. Harding), knew his father Charles Harding and Charles Harding's two brothers who were uncles of George T. Harding, the second, and says that they had the color, features, and hair of negroes and were so considered and accepted in the community. Mr. Shaffer is 73 years of age, a member of the Grand Army Post at Marion, and a Republican in politics.

Issue	
Warren Gamaliel Harding (colored)	Wife—Florence Kling (White)

This marriage was objected to by the father-in-law, Mr. Amos H. Kling, a prominent Republican and one of the wealthiest men in Marion, who spoke out publicly and openly denouncing this marriage and said his daughter had disgraced herself and family by marrying a man who had negro blood in his veins. This statement can be verified by a hundred people in Marion, Ohio.

Senator has not publicly or privately denied this statement. All denials have been made by unofficial announcements.

Authority: Professor William E. Chancellor, Wooster University, Wooster, Ohio.

"You have no conception of how the thing is flying over the state," George H. Clark, the chairman of the Ohio Republican State Committee, wrote to Daugherty. "It is everywhere. *It is affecting the woman vote.* We cannot get Hays and the National Committee fixed on any questions of policy with respect to the matter. I wired Hays this morning demanding the fixing of policy. I am not alarmed about the matter, but it is incident in the campaign and must be taken care of. We have fought this thing through before, and we must fight it out again."

Hays at first preferred not to reply to or even regard the charge, but Lasker sent out elaborate Harding genealogies to the press and issued a lily-white Harding family tree prepared in part by Pennsylvania's Wyoming Historical and Geological Society. "No family in the state," declared Daugherty publicly as Harding's personal manager, "has a clearer or more honorable record than the Hardings, a blue-eyed stock from New England and Pennsylvania, the finest pioneer blood, Anglo-Saxon, German, Scotch-Irish, and Dutch."

Nan picked up the story in Chicago. As a "friend" of Harding's she had managed to get herself a clerical job in the Republican National Committee headquarters at the Auditorium Hotel. Much of her time was spent in mailing out Harding lithographs. The day after the story reached the headquarters she found her office and the corridor outside stacked with large piles of genealogical sheets that traced Harding's ancestry back to Stephen Harding in the seventeenth century. *The New York Times* ran a Harding genealogical history. Ned McLean in his indignation wanted to publish a front-page denial in his Cincinatti *Enquirer,* but Daugherty managed to persuade him that to mention the story directly would only spread it further.

Cox, in the euphoric isolation that surrounds a candidate, was convinced that although the campaign was an uphill struggle he would still win. Wilson still believed that the American people would support Cox and the League of Nations. Few other prominent Democrats had any hope. Wilson's Secretary of the Navy Josephus Daniels admitted privately that "of course" Cox had no chance. Postmaster Gen. Albert Burleson felt that Cox was going to take the worst beating in years. Stockton Axson, the brother of Wilson's first wife, tried to prepare the invalid President for the inevitable defeat.

To the discouraged Tumulty the story of Harding's mixed blood came like a flash of sunlight. As soon as he got hold of one of Chancellor's flyers he hurried over to the White House from the executive offices, waving it in his hand like a flag. Wilson was in his wheel chair on the South Portico, his wife beside him. The colored butler had just arrived with a tray of crackers and milk, and Tumulty could hardly wait for him to leave. "Governor," he burst out gleefully, "we've got 'em beat! Here's a paper which has been searched out and is absolutely true, showing Harding has Negro blood in him. This country will never stand for them!" Wilson slowly finished his glass of milk. Then he said firmly: "Even if that is so, it will never be used with my consent. We cannot go into a man's genealogy; we must base our campaigns on principles, not on back-stairs gossip. That is not only right but good politics. So I insist you kill any such proposal." Tumulty wilted, Edith Wilson wrote, "like a little boy who has been caught robbing a bird's nest."

Despite the vague if lengthening shadow of Blooming Grove, the Republican candidate—seen from Marion or seen from Washington— seemed unbeatable. In two years all the resentments engendered by the war and the frustrations and dislocations since the Armistice had become objectified. Irrationally, inevitably, Wilson and the Democrats were held to blame—for controls and high prices and strikes, for a world *not* kept safe for democracy, for the twistings of the Paris Peace Conference and the League of Nations, for ungrateful allies, for the barred White House occupied (it was whispered) by a lunatic. All the hyphenated Americans —so deplored by the Rough Rider—had turned with vindictive joy against the Democrats; the Germans because of the war, the Irish because Wilson's self-determination stopped short of Ireland, the Italians because of the loss of Fiume. The demand for change was overwhelming. Richard Washburn Child, Boston lawyer, literator, and ex-Progressive, after organizing groups of authors and journalists to support Harding, became a Front Porch confidential adviser and wrote some of Harding's more literate campaign speeches. Even a life-long Progressive like Brand Whitlock could not escape the time-spirit. After Harding's nomination he wrote with satisfaction in his *Journal:*

> I am more and more under the opinion that for President we need not so much a brilliant man as solid, mediocre men, providing they have good sense, sound and careful judgment and good manners. All these Harding has. He is . . . more honest than McKinley, not so much of a hypocrite and poser, but human and attractive personally.

The feeling was latent in the air: the government had to be changed; those in the seats of authority must come out, and those out must replace them. Whatever else it might be, the election of 1920 was going to be an anti-vote, a vote against Wilson and war.

Each morning on Mount Vernon Avenue at seven thirty the flag fluttered self-assuredly up the McKinley flagpole. Each day bore its quota of celebrities—Pershing, Hughes, Taft. The brass bands blared and thumped from the depot along the Victory Way. The delegations gathered before the jutting hemisphere of the Front Porch, paused and waited until the big smiling iron-gray man in the pencil-striped serge jacket and the white flannel trousers stepped forward to meet them. The chairman of the delegation would then stumble through his address, and Harding would reply from his prepared script. He tried to be more careful now of what he said. Mencken-like comments about his oratory were beginning to get under his skin.

Between delegations he patted children on the head, pitched horseshoes with reporters or the policeman on duty, dropped in at the shack under the apple trees for a stogie or quick drink out of range of the Duchess's restricting eye. She had laid it down that, for publicity reasons, he could not smoke or play cards until the campaign was over. The most she would allow was an occasional chaw of tobacco—since it didn't show up on a photograph. Daniel A. Poling, visiting him at the *Star* office, remembered watching in fascination as Harding punctuated his conversation about public and personal affairs with shots at one or the other of two brass cuspidors located at either end of his flat-top desk.

Daily the bass drums thumped. Grand Army veterans of a hundred posts trod the path to the Front Porch, to be followed haphazardly by members of the Ohio State Dental Association, veterinary associations, Elks, Moose, Knights of Pythias, Republican marching clubs from near and far. The federated Indian chief, Red Fox Skiuhushu, adopted both Hardings into his tribe and gave the Duchess the name of Snow Bird. In Long Beach, California, the Reverend Doctor George M. Rourke of the First Presbyterian Church remarked from the pulpit that the Front Porch Campaign was nothing new, that the Apostle Paul had organized the first front porch campaign in the two years he spent in Rome. In the latter part of August the mammy singer and self-appointed president of the Harding and Coolidge Theatrical League, Al Jolson, arrived in Marion on a special train from New York to organize a "jazz" Front Porch campaign. With him came Texas Guinan, Blanche Ring, Lew Cody, and forty other actors and actresses, to march up the Victory Way behind a hundred-piece band. Harding posed with them for photographs, then, in a mood of theatrical nostalgia, confessed that the two plays that had most moved him were *The Passing of the Third Floor Back* and Mansfield's "superb production of Shakespeare's *Charles the Fifth.*" He particularly remembered "a camp scene on the night before a crucial battle and, as I recall it now, the King put aside his regal garb and, clad as a simple soldier, went among his armed forces to learn their feelings, their confidences, their fears, and ascertained on terms of equality and intimacy what a monarch might never have learned in any other way." Although, as Harding pointed out, there was no kingship in this republic, he was able to draw the parallel that "thoughtful Americans are wondering about tomorrow."

After Harding's speech, Jolson led his leaguers in singing the official Republican campaign song that he himself had written, "Harding, You're the Man for Us:

> We think the country's ready
> For another man like Teddy.
> We need another Lincoln
> To do the country's thinkin'.
> Mist-ter Hard-ding
> You're the man for us!

Marion boomed with Harding. Ralph Lewis, having abandoned his pickle barrels for real estate, was raising money in town for a new 150-room hotel that the backers now decided would be named after their presidential candidate.[2] Harding himself subscribed $2,000. He found himself in the role of community uncle. When on Notification Day Doctor Thomas H. McAfee, the pastor of Trinity Baptist Church, was disabled by a stroke, Harding pledged the salary for a new pastor so that Doctor McAfee could keep his title of minister and still receive his salary. Ed Scobey came on for a visit, as did his golf mates Joe Frelinghuysen and Davis Elkins of West Virginia. Often they would make up a foursome at the Marion Country Club. The Duchess and Evalina Scobey sometimes went along to watch.

All during the decades since Eugene Sweney had blocked his membership in the Masons, Harding had nursed the old hurt and the old ambition. Now, as a potential President, that long-banned emblematic door was at last unbarred to him. Sweney refused to go back on his vow that Harding would never enter the lodge while he was present, but he agreed to stay away from the crucial meeting. On August 13 Harding was passed, and received his Fellowcraft degree from the Marion Lodge. Two weeks later he was raised to the Sublime Degree of Master Mason. On receiving his degree he told his brother Masons:

> You know that I have longed to be a Mason for twenty years and you know why I have not been. There is not an atom of hatred in my heart. I am glad that my ambition has been fulfilled.

During the sunny days of the Front Porch campaign and through October right up until the election, the League of Nations issue caused Harding more obvious trouble than anything else. So occupied was he in trying to balance between the isolationists like Borah and Johnson and Lasker and the pro-League Taft and Root and Hoover that he never really knew from one day to the next how he himself felt. He had no more than "passing opinions," William Allen White wrote, after sending a letter to Marion asking for support of the League and receiving an equivocating

[2] The Harding Hotel was completed in 1924.

reply. "My whole job as President," Harding said in one of his harmony efforts, "will be first to get people of the United States together in better understanding, and then to get the nations of the world to a friendlier understanding of a workable world league." After his Notification Day speech, the pro-League group bore down on him. Hoover telegraphed that it should be made clear that the issue was not no League against the League, but a League better calculated to save this country. Harding then told Yale's pro-League Prof. Irving Fisher that he was as much in favor of the League as Fisher was, but proposed to embody the Lodge reservations into League amendments.

So wobbly had Harding's League position become by late August that George Harvey hurried to Marion to keep him on the straight and isolate path. *Harvey's Weekly* was already ticking off the days of the Wilson administration, announcing gloatingly each week: "Only 237 days more!" "Only 230 days more!" For the next nine days Harvey all but slept with Harding, working with him on an address to be delivered to the Harding and Coolidge Club of Indianapolis on its pilgrimage to the Front Porch on August 28. Harding had Harvey sternly behind him when he told the Indiana pilgrims that although Wilson's League was "an unworkable device to which we must not delegate our national conscience,"

> I believe humanity would welcome the creation of an international association for conference and a world court whose verdicts upon justifiable questions this country in common with all other nations would be both willing and able to uphold. The decision of such a court or the recommendation of such a conference would be accepted without sacrificing on our part or asking any other power to sacrifice one iota of nationality.

Taft wrote in disgust to Burton that "Harding is weakly anxious to secure a patent on a new device to rid himself of Wilson's claim of earlier invention."

In spite of their close Senate friendship, Fall had never given any serious consideration to Harding's dark-horse chances at the convention. He expected that Wood would be nominated, but was not a delegate and did not even go to Chicago. Harding, always impressed by Fall's intricate knowledge of Mexican affairs, wrote him in August:

> I would like exceeding much to have you here so that I may avail myself of your counsel and advice. Really, I very much need to be surrounded by some of the friends whom I trust most fully. I don't want you to do this at any sacrifice but I do not hesitate to tell you that I should very much like to have your advice and cooperation through some anxious moments of speech preparation and determination of foreign policy. Of course, I think a candidate ought to have very little to say about foreign policy but I find

questions are pressing from time to time and I want to be becomingly prudent at every stage of the campaign.

Fall went to Marion and helped draft some of Harding's speeches but described himself afterward as merely "a confidential scout."

In June the inflationary war boom had belatedly collapsed. Industries cut back production, in many cases ran half-time. Wholesale prices fell. Particularly hard hit were the farmers. Where wheat had sold for $2.15 a bushel in 1919, it now sold for 88 cents. Unemployment climbed to over four million, and everywhere in the country the longing, the clamor for a change in government grew. The odds in favor of Harding moved up from three to 4 to 1. From the serene vista of the Front Porch the prospect seemed almost too good to be true. Republican politicians, with an occupational awareness of the relationship between pride and falls, felt there must be a catch somewhere. Governor Cox, conducting a whirlwind tour across the country, was beginning to make them nervous.

Sometimes Cox spoke as many as twenty-six times a day. In his tour of a month he traveled or would travel 22,000 miles through three-quarters of the states to give 394 scheduled speeches. Angrily he charged that the Republicans were raising a $15 million "corruption fund" from powerful interests attempting to buy control of the government, and he warned of a business plot by those who wanted "the bayonet at the factory door, profiteering at the gates of the farm, the burden of government on shoulders other than their own, and the Federal Reserve System an annex to big business." In the fervor of his campaigning he later raised his corruption fund estimate to 30 million.[3]

Franklin Roosevelt with his wife Eleanor traveled almost as far and made almost as many speeches as his running mate. He would, he announced, drag the enemy off the Front Porch. Through the rural West he found he was often mistaken for Theodore's son by horny-handed Bull Moosers who shouted out at whistle stops: "I voted for your old man an' I'll vote for you!" So often did this happen, so great was Franklin's charm, that Hays put Theodore, Jr., on the trail to set matters straight. At Sheridan, Wyoming, the young Colonel explained away the Roosevelt Democrat. "Franklin," he told the crowd, "is a maverick. He does not have the brand of our family." At first Harding refused to be pushed off his comfortable porch by the whirlwind Cox. But soon letters of protest and warning began to arrive in Marion. Jake Hamon wrote from Oklahoma that the West was in danger and urged Harding to go on a speaking tour. More weightily, Boss Penrose told Daugherty that the Front Porch would have to give way to the rear platform.

[3] The Republicans spent $6,022,678 in their campaign, the Democrats, $1,349,477. Both parties ended up with deficits.

The first week in September Harding spoke at the Minneapolis State Fair. On the way he had paid a courtesy call on General Wood in Chicago and the two of them had spent an afternoon at Fort Sheridan visiting wounded soldiers returned from France. Wood, though genial, made no offer to take part in the campaign. Except for this trip Harding had clung to his Front Porch. However, a week after his return he announced that late in September he would make a whirlwind tour of the large cities of the East and Middle West.

In spite of the contradictory results of 1916, the early barometer of the Maine state election—on September 13—was still considered a potent political indicator. Such forceful speakers as McAdoo, Roosevelt, and Secretary of the Navy Daniels stumped the state for the Democrats, predicting that they would win the governorship and two of Maine's congressional seats. Privately they admitted they had little chance, but hoped to hold the Republican victory to less than 20,000. In 1896 the Republicans had carried the state by a record 48,000, and in this first postwar election they were out to better that mark. On an election day of deluging rain they succeeded, winning the governorship by 65,877 votes and all three congressional seats. Daniels tried to make out that the Maine election was on local issues and indicated no national trend. But the Republicans, with Harding, gleefully repeated: "As Maine goes, so goes the nation!"

The Front Porch campaign thumped to an end on September 25 with 2,500 traveling salesmen marching up the Victory Way behind half-a-dozen hired bands. Cox some years before had referred to traveling salesmen as "parasites and public nuisances," and the marchers had not forgotten. Defiantly they had inscribed the words on their Harding banners. Following their reception Harding released a pair of carrier pigeons with a good-will message to the convention of the United Drug Company in St. Louis. The close of the day brought a delegation of former newsboys of the *Star*, some of whom had come from as far away as California. With selective sentimentality they recalled the past, and there was a burst of laughter when the Duchess, standing with Harding on the porch, asked: "How many of you boys have I spanked?" Half a dozen of the old boys raised their hands.

The next day Harding and the Duchess with a large party that included Daugherty, Jess Smith, and the McLeans left on a special train of three private cars for a three-day speaking tour of Maryland, West Virginia, and eastern Kentucky. To the Hardings' private car, the *Superb*, the Ned McLeans had attached their own car *The Enquirer*. Although the McLeans had always been Democrats and the Cincinnati *Enquirer* and the Washington *Post* had traditionally supported the party, Ned was so enthusiastically for Harding that he wanted to give him the papers' endorsement. Harding advised him not to break the tradition, but Ned saw to it that nothing adverse to Harding appeared in his papers. Campaigning for the Republican candidate was giving Ned a purpose in life that he with all his money and power had never felt before. For once he truly busied himself, neglecting his dissipations. Evalyn began to hope that his engrossment with Harding might save him from himself. She had brought her fabulous jewels on the tour, scorning to substitute paste. Even the two hatpins on her large feathered hat were tipped by huge glittering diamonds. Wherever she went, a bodyguard followed.

By October 1 Harding was back in Marion, ready again to leave on the fifth for a Midwest speaking tour. In spite of the elaborations of his verbiage, the League of Nations issue refused to lie down and be harmonized. Vague as Harding's notion was of an association of nations to "give utterances to the conscience of the world"—as opposed to the League's "internationality of force to suppress the freedom of the world" —it was still too specific for the isolationist old Progressives. Johnson remained ostentatiously out of the campaign. Borah declined to speak further and returned his expense money to the National Committee. Harding talked of making the Hague Tribunal the "framework" of his association of nations, then admitted in a moment of indiscreet frankness that he was "without a single program constructive in character" about such an association.

On October 7, in Des Moines, Iowa, he gladdened the hearts of Johnson and Borah by announcing that he was not for clarifying or interpreting Wilson's League, but for rejecting it. Wilson "favors going into the Paris League and I favor staying out." After Des Moines Harding's language against the League grew stronger, although he still talked of his "association of nations." Privately he tried to reassure both factions. Hoping for the best, Root persuaded Hoover, Hughes, Butler, Stimson, White, Harvard's A. Lawrence Lowell, and 24 other well-known Republicans to sign a "Declaration by Thirty-One Pro-League Republicans" declaring that the Republican party would take the United States into the League with a modified Article X. Some pro-League Republicans declined to be reassured. Herbert Parsons, former national committeeman from New York and a Taft supporter in 1912, denounced Harding's speech as "mush" and came out for Cox. Irving Fisher formed the Pro-League Independents in Cox's support, and Henry Noble MacCracken, the testy Republican head of Vassar, announced that for the first time in his life he was voting Democratic.

From Des Moines the *Superb* moved across Iowa and Missouri, stopping frequently if briefly at sun-baked little towns for Harding to make a rear-platform speech to gawking farmers. Late in the afternoon of October 9 the special train arrived at Oklahoma City. There Jake Hamon had arranged the most tumultuous demonstration Harding was to find on his tour. Flanked by the Duchess and a pallid Daugherty just recovering from influenza, Harding joined a motor cavalcade, passing triumphantly along streets where thousands had been waiting for hours to get a glimpse of "the next President." Jake gave him a banquet at the Huckins Hotel, attended by more than three hundred Oklahoma party leaders and editors. Afterward there was a torchlight parade to the fairgrounds where Harding spoke to a huge, exuberant crowd. It was, according to the *Daily Oklahoman,* "the noisiest, gladdest, maddest day" the Republican party had known in Democratic Oklahoma for years.

From Oklahoma City it was a continuous run to Marion. Harding at one point accepted the engineer's invitation, donned a peaked railroadman's cap, and took the throttle of the locomotive, holding it at sixty-five miles an hour for twenty miles. After a day of rest in Marion he left once more for a circuit of Tennessee, Kentucky, and Indiana. At Chattanooga on October 13 he toured the battlefield of Chickamauga, visited Lookout Mountain, and made a speech asking the South to abandon its one-party rule. The tour ended at St. Louis. There at the Coliseum Harding was interrupted by a heckler from the gallery who wanted to know: "How about the League of Nations?" There were shouts of "Put him out!" but Harding shunted the shouts aside and brought his audience to its feet when he protested: "Please, please, don't put him out. Let's put the Democratic administration out!"

Harding was on his Front Porch again for First Voters' Day on October 18. More than twenty-five thousand first voters trekked to the Front Porch that day from all over the state, among them undergraduate delegations from all the Ohio colleges. These gave their college cheers on Harding's appearance. Mixed with the undergraduates was an elderly group, alumni of Iberia College come back to honor their most famous graduate.

Except for a one-day trip to Buffalo and Syracuse, Harding would not leave Ohio again until after the election. Within the state he wound up his campaign with a huge burgoo [4] ox roast at Jackson and a luncheon given him at Cleveland by Carmi Thompson with Herrick and Burton present, a torchlight parade in the drizzling rain in Akron under damp banners bearing the slogan America First! and a windup in Cincinnati before the chastened Hynicka. He closed the campaign in Columbus's Memorial Hall the Saturday before the election. As the special train passed through Dayton, copies of the Dayton *Journal* were thrust aboard with the flaring headlines THE VILE SLANDERERS OF SENATOR HARDING AND HIS FAMILY WILL SEEK THEIR SKUNK HOLES ERE TODAY'S SUN SHALL HAVE SET! Under his own name the editor, E. G. Burkam, wrote:

---

[4] Burgoo is a local term for a gravy or stew.

Thousands upon thousands of typewritten, mimeographed and even printed statements usually under the heading of "Harding's Family Tree," have been distributed in Dayton and Montgomery County, at first in cowardly secrecy and in the last few days openly and boldly by men low down in the Democratic party, unprincipled heelers and men high up in the Democratic party who have sunk their standards to the very sewers of depravity.

The time has come for plain language. These vile circulars declare that Warren G. Harding has Negro blood in his veins. The ugly details you have no doubt read.

This is the vilest plot and conspiracy in the history of the worst epochs of American politics.

Unless there is no such thing as truth in the world, unless there is no such thing as honesty in the world, unless there is no such thing as decency in the world, if our moral standards are not a sham, then the perpetrators of this outrage will suffer the everlasting condemnation of public opinion within the sacred precincts of every home in America.

The answer to this conspiracy, this plot, is that its base allegations ARE A LIE.

Warren G. Harding has the blood of but one race in his veins—that of the white race—the pure inheritance of a fine line of ancestors, of good men and women. That is sufficient!

The whispers had become a roar, the story was out. Burkam's plain language had spread it far beyond the limits of the circulars. Wild with rage, Harding stormed through the train to Daugherty's car with a copy of the *Journal* in his hand, accusing his manager of being responsible for the headlines. Daugherty had never seen him so angry, but finally managed to convince him that he had nothing to do with it, that his instructions had always been never to mention the subject.

It was a grim ride to Columbus. Several anonymous letters had arrived in advance threatening that Harding and Daugherty would both be shot that night. Daugherty, driving from the station, thought that the atmosphere of the city seemed sullen and brooding. By contrast the vast packed hall was buoyant with enthusiasm. Daugherty introduced Harding, closing with the words: "No lip of libel nor tongue of slander can harm your cause or you." Everyone in Memorial Hall knew what he meant. That was the only direct campaign reference by Harding or his managers to the Blooming Grove shadow.

While Harding had been barnstorming through the Southwest and West, Professor Chancellor had been plodding through Blooming Grove, Galion, Iberia, Steam Corners, Caledonia, and Marion, searching for any scrap of gossip that might validate his obsessive conviction of the Hardings' mixed blood. In his researches he took down notarized statements from a ninety-three-year-old Marion farmer, a former city treasurer, a carpenter formerly of Blooming Grove, and a Galion resident, all of whom swore that Tryon and his father before him had always been regarded as colored. These affidavits Chancellor now affixed to a broadside which he himself signed, *To the Men and Women of America—An Open Letter.* In it he maintained that the colored Hardings were descendants of a French-speaking West Indian Negro, Amos Harding, and that Tryon as a mulatto had never been able to compete with white doctors.

> When one citizen knows beyond the peradventure of doubt what concerns all other citizens but is not generally known [Chancellor wrote] duty compels publication. . . .
>
> Warren Gamaliel Harding is not a white man; he is not a creole; he is not a mulatto; he is a mestizo, as his physical features show. Anyone who hears or reads his public utterances is free to pass upon his intellectual and moral traits. Anyone who knows the quality of his public record in various offices is free to pass upon his mind and character as indicating his several race origins.
>
> Are we ready to make the experiment of entrusting the Presidency of this Republic to this hybrid man? To be silent now might be to permit the extending of the interesting local race evolution of the Galion-Blooming Grove-Bucyrus-Marion countryside throughout this land. Shall America be a white man's land? For one, I believe that red man, yellow man, black man, colored man, one and all, are better off under the social control of the white man.
>
> I might cite the names of scores of persons who have always considered Warren Gamaliel Harding a colored man and who resent his present masquerade as a white candidate upon the ticket of a hitherto honorable and dignified party. . . .
>
> Of hundreds of persons interviewed of those who knew him as a rural school boy and as college student, everyone without exception says that Warren Gamaliel Harding was always considered a colored boy and nick-named accordingly. . . .
>
> It is for us to decide what the Capitals of Europe and Asia and all the rest of the world shall think of us as represented in the person of our President on and after March 4, 1921. Let us have neither Hayti nor Russia here! May God save America from international shame and from domestic ruin!

Chancellor also prepared a broadside, signed by himself, on Harding's family tree in which Tryon was described as having "thick lips, rolling eyes, chocolate skin. . . ."

The pamphlets blanketed not only Ohio, but the country. Although Cox and the National Committee repudiated the slander campaign, somewhere eager anonymous Democrats were paying for and directing this mass distribution. Tens of thousands of pamphlets were being slipped under doors.

Distributed on commuter trains running to Chicago, they caused fist fights. In the corridors of a New York hotel strangers handed out small pictures of the White House captioned "Uncle Tom's Cabin." The Post Office Department in San Francisco, by Wilson's order, confiscated a quarter of a million of such flyers. Notice of the whispering campaign crept into the papers, even into the all-the-news-that's-fit-to-print columns of *The New York Times*. To one who had not seen the pamphlets, the press uproar was a mystery, for no paper gave any hint of what Chancellor's accusations were. Most papers rang the changes on Harding's blue-eyed pioneer Anglo-Saxon ancestry without further explanation. But alumni and others who had read the signed pamphlets blamed Wooster College. Its president, the Reverend Doctor Charles F. Wishart, found himself besieged with protesting telegrams and telephone calls, reporters, excited graduates and undergraduates, and politicians of both parties. Hastily he called a special meeting of the board of trustees and summoned Professor Chancellor.

Chancellor, nervous, voluble, and highly excited, denied having written or printed the broadside but admitted that he had made a study of the Harding family and had supplied the genealogical "proofs" in the pamphlet material. He told the trustees in a trembling voice that Harding's nomination was a plot to achieve Negro domination in the United States. Wishart said that he did not wish to know the truth as to whether Harding was colored or white. All he and the trustees wanted was a written denial by Chancellor that Harding was colored. When Chancellor refused to give this, the trustees unanimously requested his resignation and voted him four months' salary. Speaking to the students next day, President Wishart tried to play down the pamphlets as due to Professor Chancellor's "misguided zeal rather than evil intent."

The "whispering campaign" and Chancellor's dismissal made the headlines of the *Times*, still with no indication of what was being whispered. Only the *New York Herald* was bold enough to admit editorially that "in the closing hours of the campaign a dastardly conspiracy is put on foot to steal the election through an insidious assertion that Warren G. Harding, Republican candidate for President of the United States, is of Negro ancestry. . . . In all of our political history," the *Herald* continued, "there is nothing comparable to this foul eleventh-hour attack on a presidential candidate solely for the purpose of defrauding the Republican party of its impending victory." Scott C. Bone, the Republican National Committee's publicity director, denounced "conscienceless Democratic partisans."

Chairman Hays speeded up the distribution of more thousands of whitewashed Harding genealogies. When Boss Penrose was asked what should be done, he replied pragmatically: "Don't say a thing about it.

From what I hear we've been having a lot of trouble holding the nigger vote lately." In Washington Evalyn McLean learned to her dismay that Carolyn Votaw—now a welfare director in the District of Columbia Police Department—was about to address a colored meeting. Calling long distance to inform the Hardings, Evalyn heard "harsh and grating sounds" as the Duchess ground her teeth at the news. Then the nasal peremptory voice rasped over the wire from Marion: "Get that sister of Wurr'n Harding to come out to Friendship—if you love us. Keep her there! Do not let her make that speech if you have to lock her in your cellar." Harding himself called Ned a few minutes later and begged him to keep Carolyn from the meeting. Cooperatively Ned and Evalyn enticed Carolyn to Friendship, forced her to stay there while the meeting was going on, and shipped her back to Ohio.

Yet for all the flurry the shadow of Blooming Grove was at this time no more than a cumulus puff momentarily darkening the election landscape but quickly passing. Over the weekend the whispering campaign faded away, dropped by the press. Odds on Harding rose to 10 to 1. Only Cox, closing his campaign with the pipe-dream conviction that his election would show America willing to enter the League, kept his optimism intact among the downcast Democrats.

Election day, November 2, broke gray and chill. Harding had a leisurely late breakfast—his favorite, of waffles with chipped beef and gravy—then drove with the Duchess, his chauffeur Frank, and George Christian to their precinct polling place, held in the private garage of their neighbor, J. A. Schroeter. They arrived at ten minutes past ten to find a line of over a dozen voters preceding them. Harding, wearing a heavy winter overcoat, refused the invitation to go to the head of the line but stood with the others for fifteen minutes. When he finally handed in his ballot, photographers focused on him with still and moving-picture cameras. He had to repeat the gesture of handing in the ballot, and when some photographer made a joke about his voting twice, everyone laughed.

After voting he went back to Mount Vernon Avenue, changed to his golf knickers, put on an old red sweater, and with Harry Daugherty drove to Columbus for a day of golf at the Scioto Country Club. By the time they left Columbus in the late afternoon it had begun to rain and Harding urged the chauffeur to "step on it." Ten miles outside Marion the car skidded, veered off the road, and almost hit a telegraph pole. Somewhat shaken, chilled, and hungry, Harding arrived home to find himself the center of a surprise birthday party, arranged by the Duchess. The Christians were there, as were Carolyn and Tryon. After dinner Inez the cook proudly brought in a white birthday cake with fifty-five pink candles.

While Harding was still at table a delegation of Star employees—everyone from Editor Van Fleet to the youngest printer's devil—arrived at the Front Porch to be the first to congratulate their editor. Remembering the smooth-worn 13-em make-up rule that Harding still carried in his pocket as a lucky piece, they in their confidence had had a "golden rule" facsimile designed at the local jeweler's with the date of the election engraved on it and a blank space to inscribe Harding's re-election in 1924. As he appeared on the porch, his napkin still in his hand, the white-bearded Lew Miller stepped forward with the ribboned box containing the golden rule and spoke his carefully memorized piece:

> We wish to present you this make-up rule, the emblem of the printer's trade. We trust that the future "make-up" and building up of this great country will be as easily and efficiently accomplished by you as when you were "make-up" man on the *Star*.

Harding's mouth twitched, his face puckered as he tried to speak. Then, with tears spreading down his cheeks, he told them in a choked voice:

> Fellow members of the *Star*. You and I have been associated together for many years. I know you and you know me and you know I wouldn't cheat you. I am coming into a position of great responsibility if the present returns are interpreted correctly. I have been on the square with you, and I want to be on the square with all the world.

Then he glanced at Miller directly in front of him, and overcome by the sight of that familiar eccentric whom he had acquired with the flickering *Star* for a hundred borrowed dollars a third of a century ago, he continued:

> There is my old friend Miller, the oldest employe of the *Star*. Thirty-six years we have been together and sometimes those years have been thorny. Sometimes Miller has drawn his pay that I had to borrow from my own mother. Sometimes next morning I have had to borrow back from Miller the pay he drew the day before.

He was too overcome to say more.

The fellow members of the *Star* may have been premature, but the early returns soon confirmed their optimism. By ten o'clock it was clear to Harding, sitting in a mission-oak rocking chair and chewing on a stogie as he jotted down the returns, that he had won. The Duchess in her confidence had already picked a quarrel with the newsreel cameramen, informing them that once she got into the White House they never would. Midnight showed a Republican landslide. The news spread, and few people in Marion went to bed before morning. Through the early hours the gravel yard before the Front Porch and the leaf-strewn avenue beyond were choked with Harding's friends and neighbors blowing horns and waving rattles, for everyone in town was his friend and neighbor now. They cheered his grinning figure as he appeared, stogie in hand, and he waved back at them, the Duchess beside him radiant beneath her wrinkles.

In the press shack under the apple trees the atmosphere was more arid. Several dozen correspondents and their wives had gathered there, and when the news of the victory was assured, the Hardings had sent over two bottles of champagne. Much joking followed about the Harding stinginess, and to enliven the evening's dryness the tales of Carrie Phillips, the merry widow and her toothbrush, and other "primrose detours" were burnished up. In Wooster a belligerent group of Harding supporters decided to celebrate his election victory by tarring and feathering Chancellor and riding him out of town on a rail. For all his race obsessions the Professor was always popular with his students, and they secreted him in a college dormitory. Four recklessly loyal undergraduates then barricaded themselves in the Chancellor house and when the mob gathered outside with torches and tar buckets, the boys poked rifle barrels through the windows and threatened to kill the first man who came up the walk.[5] At the sight of the rifles glinting in the torchlight, lynch-law enthusiasm dwindled and the mob soon dissolved into individuals slinking away into the darkness.

Even Hays and Daugherty at their most optimistic would not have dared predict the Republican sweep that was apparent by the following morning. Harding had carried 37 of the 48 states, with 404 electoral votes to Cox's 127, for the most overwhelming electoral victory since that of James Monroe just a hundred years before. His popular vote was 16,152,200 to 9,147,353 for Cox, the highest percentage ever recorded by a successful presidential candidate.[6] Cox carried only the states of the Solid South, and not all of those, for Tennessee swung to Harding. South Carolina—representing the deep South—went for Cox by 64,170 to Harding's 2,244, but the border state of Kentucky with 918,711 votes cast came within a few thousand of choosing Harding. In Congress the Republicans increased their Senate majority from 2 to 20. The old House of Representatives after the 1918 election had 233 Republicans and 191 Democrats. Now the Republicans had carried the new House by over 2 to 1, 289 to 142 for the Democrats.

[5] One of the four, Howard F. Lowry—later to become American editor of the Oxford University Press—recalled that evening in a *New Yorker* article in 1939: "I honestly don't know what would have happened if that crowd had really rushed the house. My own guess is that we would probably have shot ourselves in the confusion."

[6] In itself the voting was not heavy. Less than half the eligible voters went to the polls, partly because the results seemed foregone, partly because the new women voters showed no great eagerness to vote. Eugene Debs, the Socialist candidate, although still in the Atlanta Penitentiary for his anti-war activities, received 919,799 votes.

As soon as the inevitable became apparent, Cox wired the usual congratulations "in the spirit of America," and Harding replied in kind. The morning *Star* hailed the Republican victory as "a mighty rebuke to slime." Tumulty thought that the landslide was more like an earthquake, and Franklin Roosevelt consoled his political advance agent, the former Associated Press reporter Steve Early: "Thank God, we are both comparatively youthful." Garford sent his congratulations to Daugherty, rather than Harding, calling him "the man behind the gun."

While the first morning papers announcing the Republican triumph were pouring from the press, Nan Britton lay in an upper berth on the midnight train from Chicago to Marion. At half past six she waked and asked the porter who the new President was. "Harding's the man, Miss," he told her, and she could feel her heart thump. She arrived at the Union Depot at seven to find a Sunday-like quiet over the city after the celebrations of only a few hours before. Registering at the Hotel Marion, she telephoned her old neighbors, the Scofields,[7] who insisted on taking her home. But before she left she called Jim Sloan and arranged to meet him that evening in front of the post office.

Sloan was waiting there in an official car, alone, silent and discreet as ever. He drove her out East Church Street and Mount Vernon Avenue to a small house a block beyond the Hardings' that had been used by the campaign clerical forces and was now empty. Quickly he let her into the sun parlor, still full of desks and papers, and watched outside the front entrance until Harding arrived a few minutes later. He slipped the door open for the President-elect, then closed it; and Harding and Nan were alone. Taking her hand, Harding led her through the dining room—where the shades had been drawn—and into the kitchen. Except for a shaft of light from under the swinging door, the room was dark. He groped his way to a chair, sat down, and took her in his lap. That penumbral moment she transfixed in her true-confession prose:

> After affectionate greetings, I exclaimed softly, "Oh, sweetheart, isn't it *won*derful that you are President!" He held me close, kissing me over and over again. Our eyes were now becoming accustomed to the darkness and I could see his face dimly outlined. He looked at me some time before he answered. Then his "Um . . . . say, dearie, do you love me?" showed me that the glories of a victorious hero were submerged in the grander glories of a lover's delight in being with his woman. "*This* is the best thing that's happened to me lately, dearie!" he whispered.

He left ahead of her, and on leaving gave her three five-hundred-dollar bills. The next day Nan paid a visit to her old teacher, Daisy Harding, showed her a picture of Harding, and persuaded her to go with her to

---

[7] Will Scofield was judge of Marion's Common Pleas Court. His wife knew the Duchess and belonged to the Twigs.

the Mount Vernon Avenue headquarters to have it autographed. When the startled Sloan glimpsed Nan through the front window of the Christian house, she caught the apprehensive look in his professionally impassive face. She and Daisy went round the porch to peek in the office window where they could see Harding at his desk talking to Will Hays. They managed to attract his attention, and he came out the side door, shook hands with her formally, and then autographed his picture. Nan thought he looked slightly annoyed.

As President-elect, Harding could make a virtue of his restlessness, his unexamined urge to travel, and soon after the election he announced that he was going on a month's vacation by way of Texas to inspect the fortifications of the Panama Canal Zone. First he planned to get together with Scobey and Gus Creager in Texas at the Red Fox's Point Isabel cottage where they could play golf and poker, fish for tarpon, and swap parlor stories over the highballs. Then by way of New Orleans he would sail for Panama. When Wilson learned that Harding was planning a trip to Panama he offered through Secretary Daniels to put the government yacht *Mayflower* at his disposal, but Harding declined even though the offer was renewed several times.

The presidential special, with most of the reporters from the back-yard shack, left Marion at 7:30 A.M. on November 6. Harding and the Duchess took with them in the *Superb* Doctor Sawyer and his wife Mandy, the Jenningses, George Christian, and—to make sure of a golf foursome— Harding's Senate playmates, Frelinghuysen, Elkins, and Hale. Senator Knox observed that Harding must have taken those three for "complete mental relaxation." Ned and Evalyn McLean had their own private car attached. A third car contained the reporters, cameramen, stenographers, and Secret Service agents.

Across the flatlands of Indiana and Illinois thousands waited to see the President-to-be, and Harding made almost as many whistle stops and rear-platform speeches as he had on any day of his campaign tour. At St. Louis, Daugherty with his shadow, Jess Smith, boarded the McLean car. The train lay over in San Antonio where a noisily exuberant Scobey and Creager held their post-election reunion with Harding. In a more earnest mood Senator Fall was waiting to see Harding at Brownsville, accompanied by Elias L. Torres, the first secretary of the Washington mission of General Alvaro Obregón's new Mexican government that had overthrown the Carranza regime in the spring. Wilson had refused to recognize the Obregón government, fearing that it intended to expropriate all American properties in Mexico. Torres and Fall had come to Brownsville hoping to arrange a meeting of Obregón with Harding.

After his talk with Fall, Harding left for Point Isabel. Since the narrow-gauge railroad then was more like a roller coaster, the party drove the twenty miles by car. Creager's cottage was large enough only for Harding's immediate circle. Even the McLeans could not be fitted in. Creager had fitted out an abandoned brick hotel with army cots for the others. The only place to eat was a lunchroom across the road whose menu consisted solely of ham and eggs. While the Hardings, Creager, Scobey, and the senatorial trio fished from the only two available launches in the brightness of the gulf, the others drank, grumbled, played cards, and fought off the still-abundant mosquitoes. Then, after several days of sunshine, a blizzard swept down from the North blanketing them in chill misery. The McLeans played poker all day with the morose reporters whose daily stories soon became back-page news. Finally, with the stinging weather, Harding called a retreat. Since the roads were now too muddy for travel, press and party, wrapped in blankets, took the roller coaster back to Brownsville.

On November 18 the *Superb* left Brownsville for New Orleans where Harding, piped aboard by the steam calliope of an excursion steamer, sailed on the United Fruit Company's *Parismina* across the Gulf of Mexico for the Canal Zone. As the *Parismina* approached the green hills and the silhouetted buildings of Colón, Cristobal, and Coco Salo, Harding had his first taste of presidential pageantry. An escort of submarines met the *Parismina* while United States planes flew over in battle formation. By now he was becoming more used to the formal deference given a President-elect, and his basic self-doubt gave way more and more to a fatalistic confidence. Evalyn McLean's sharp eyes recorded the change:

> The constant adulation of people was beginning to have an effect on Senator Harding. He was, more and more, inclined to believe in himself. He cherished an idea that when a man was elevated to the presidency, his wits, by some automatic mental chemistry, were increased to fit the stature of his office.

The Harding party disembarked and spent a few days in the pseudo-Moorish confines of the United States-owned Hotel Washington in Colón. Harding played several rounds of golf at the Brazo Brook Club near the Gatun Locks while the Duchess shopped. After two days in Colón they continued through the fifty-mile length of the Canal on the United States mine-layer *Graham*, stopping at Quarry Heights Army post for a Thanksgiving dinner, with a turkey provided by the Camp Fire Girls of Texas. At the Pacific end of the Canal President Porras of Panama gave a dinner for Harding at Balboa Heights, the antiseptic American enclave above Panama City. And in Balboa the foreboding news arrived from Oklahoma of the violent death of Jake Hamon.

Jake had been shot by Clara Smith after a drunken quarrel in his room in the Randol Hotel. Although he lived for four days after the shooting, he sensed he was dying and sent for his friend Bill Nichols, the taciturn former police chief of Oklahoma City. Two days before he died he gave Nichols a sealed note addressed to Harding and begged him to deliver it as soon as possible. Nichols set out directly after the funeral. When he caught up with the President-elect, the magic of Hamon's name brought him a private interview at once. Harding read the dead man's note with the tears running down his cheeks, then tore it to bits. "What a wonderful fellow he was!" he said to Nichols. "Too bad he had to be taken out. Too bad he had that one fault—that admiration for women."

Harding's Panama visit concluded with a farewell banquet at the Washington Hotel. He and his party sailed from Colón on the *Pastores* the last day of November, cruising leisurely across the Caribbean to Jamaica. As the *Pastores* docked at Kingston the President-elect was greeted with viceregal formality by an honor guard of the West Indian Regiment while a military band in Zouave uniforms drawn up at the dockside played "The Star-Spangled Banner." The Royal Yacht Club was decked with flags. Meeting Harding at the gangplank, the mayor of Kingston, after a tropical breakfast at the Myrtle Bank Hotel, drove with him to King's House for an official reception by the governor. On leaving King's House, Harding was given the famous Jamaican souvenir, an inscribed good-luck nut. After an eighty-mile tour over the island's winding mountain roads, saluted by sugar-cane workers in the fields with machetes, Harding and his party re-embarked, arriving at Norfolk, Virginia, on December 4. The captain's dinner on the last night was like a carnival. The Duchess remembered the menus as "triumphs of art" and the shipboard festivities, with more aptness than she realized, as "a scene from Cinderella." Following the dinner Harding sat in the heat of his cabin behind layers of cigar smoke, the sweat dripping from his face as he autographed the menus of the guests aboard.

The *Pastores* reached Hampton Roads shortly before sunrise. Seaplanes, Army airplanes, and naval blimps swooped over the water and encircled the ship. At her approach the flagged vessels anchored along the channel dipped their ensigns amid a din of whistles. Several planes looped the loop and nearly grazed the *Pastores's* masts as they dropped bundles of morning papers on the deck.

On landing Harding made a short nautical speech in which he advocated a government-aided merchant marine to make the United States "the greatest maritime nation on the face of the earth." After receiving a silver loving cup from the Newport News Lodge of Elks he and the Duchess—she had just shaken hands with several hundred members of the American Legion Women's Post—attended a luncheon at the Warwick

Hotel. Then at the old Jamestown Exposition grounds "to the strains of inspiring music and song," he watched a review of 10,000 bluejackets just back from naval exercises. "The Navy," he told the sailors, "is the first line of American defense." After inspecting the Navy Yard and the Army base he ended the afternoon at the Billy Sunday Tabernacle where before 8,000 pious civilians he paid his respects to God.

Harding and the Duchess reached Washington on Sunday afternoon to be whisked away by the McLeans to their town house on Fifteenth and I streets. That Edwardian palace, inherited from Ned's father and covering half a block, had been fashioned into its vastness by the architect John Russell Pope from the inner core of a small old-fashioned house of crumbling brick. Barberini tapestries hung along the walls of the enormous ballroom where at formal dinners the gold services of the Walshes and the McLeans competed in conspicuousness. Evalyn and Ned were out to capture the new President. Ned by now forgot the death of the million-dollar baby. Evalyn was beginning to forget.

On Monday, December 5, the opening day of the "lame duck" session of the old Sixty-sixth Congress, Harding appeared for the first time in the Senate as President-elect. As he entered the Senate Chamber, his Ohio Democratic colleague, Senator Pomerene, grasped his hand, and there was much applause from the galleries. Evalyn, the Duchess, and Alice Roosevelt Longworth were sitting in the front row. As the roll was called, Harding answered resoundingly "Here!" and again the galleries applauded. Vice President Marshall told the senators that for the first time in the history of the country one of their colleagues had been elected President, and Senator Lodge pointed out somewhat superfluously that the President-elect was "here with us today." When he suggested that Harding be recognized by the chair, Marshall rushed to Harding's desk and after pumping his hand conducted him to the Vice President's platform. Harding, in making his brief farewell, asked the cooperation of the Senate "to find a common ground in the spirit of service."

On learning that the Hardings were in Washington, Wilson's wife asked the Duchess to tea that same afternoon, suggesting that the housekeeper, Mrs. Jaffray, could then show her through the White House and help her make her plans. Edith Wilson sent her note to the McLean house. The Duchess replied with thanks that she would bring Evalyn McLean with her. In a second note the President's wife informed her that she had better come alone.

At five-thirty the uneasy Duchess, in a feathery blue hat, rouged cheeks, and a tight black-net veil, was shown into the Red Room where Edith Wilson was waiting for her. In any circumstance the two domineering women would have disliked each other. The outgoing hostess scarcely bothered to conceal her sense of superiority, the newcomer refused to admit her uneasiness even to herself. In her memoirs Edith Wilson wrote of the Duchess on that afternoon:

> Her manner was so effusive, so voluble, that after a half-hour over the tea cups I could hardly stem the torrent of words to suggest I send for the housekeeper so she could talk over her desires as to the house. . . . I said Mrs. Jaffray would take her through the house, except the President's own room where he was resting. Otherwise I hoped she would feel free to look at everything.

After ringing for Mrs. Jaffray, Edith Wilson explained coldly that she had an outside appointment and that she would leave the two of them alone. "Mrs. Harding, this is Mrs. Jaffray," she said as the housekeeper entered, and without saying good-by left the room. The Duchess turned on Mrs. Jaffray. "Well," she told her bluntly, "I won't want you any more, for I have already made other arrangements." With vindictive thoroughness the Duchess inspected her future residence. On seeing the Lincoln double bed in the Wilsons' bedroom she gave orders to have twin beds installed for her arrival. When Edith Wilson returned several hours later, she was surprised to hear the Duchess's nasal, peremptory voice far down in the kitchen querying the cook.

On the way to the station for his return to Marion Harding left a card for Wilson at the White House but did not attempt to see him. His home city, he discovered on arrival, had renamed the high school the Harding High School. The shares in the Harding Hotel were sold out. No sooner had he settled down in Mount Vernon Avenue than talk of his prospective Cabinet began to expand. There were rumors and counter-rumors; that he would appoint Wood Secretary of War, Lodge or Root Secretary of State, "Hell 'n Maria" Dawes Secretary of the Treasury, that he would find places for Harvey, Lowden, Hoover, and Theodore Roosevelt, Jr. Faced with making appointments, Harding was divided between his awe of the Presidency and his wish to reward his friends. With the passing weeks his awe grew stronger. "I am just beginning to realize what a job I have taken over," he wrote Jennings. "The man who has a Cabinet to create has one tremendous task. I find I am called upon to be rather impersonal about it and put aside some of my very intimate views of men and give some consideration to the public estimate of available timber."

At Point Isabel he had announced loudly that Ed Scobey was going to be the new Director of the Mint. Dick Crissinger, the barefoot boy of years ago with whom he had raided watermelon patches in Caledonia, he had slated as Comptroller of the Currency. George Christian would remain his private secretary. Since the Duchess was convinced that only Doctor Sawyer could keep her alive, Harding insisted on him as the

White House personal physician. For the back-slapping Charlie Forbes, who had moved from Hawaii to campaign for him in the state of Washington, Harding was considering a job on the Shipping Board or else the governorship of the Territory of Alaska. Forbes, in spite of his earlier tarnished record, had since become a military hero. Commissioned in 1917, he served in France as signal officer of the 33rd Division, maintaining communications so intrepidly and efficiently under fire that he won the Congressional Medal of Honor and ended the war a lieutenant colonel. "I have always rejoiced in your friendship," Harding wrote him, and am grateful for all you have done for me."

In selecting his Cabinet and in the field of foreign affairs Harding let it be known that he was consulting the country's "best minds." After his return to Mount Vernon Avenue the best minds began to gravitate to Marion—Hoover first, followed by Butler, Hughes, Root, Harvey, and even Bryan. To Hoover, Harding offered the choice of the Interior or Commerce departments. Although it seemed the lesser post, Hoover preferred to become Secretary of Commerce—with the condition that he have Harding's support in reorganizing the department. Hoover had let it be known that he disliked "such Republican phenomena as Senators Penrose, Watson, Knox, Lodge, and their followers," and the Old Guard in turn were opposed to Hoover for anything. Brandegee wrote that "Hoover gives most of us gooseflesh," to which Harding replied that he did not share "the hostile opinion which many entertain concerning him, and I think there is very much of political significance involved in considering him."

The weightiest choice that fell on Harding was of his Secretary of State. His first thought was Butler, his second, Fall. When Butler refused to consider the offer, Harding remarked that the best man he could then see for the post was Senator Fall. The dismayed Butler told him that Fall's reputation in Pueblo before he ever left Colorado for New Mexico was such that he should not be considered in the Cabinet. "You are entirely mistaken," Harding replied. "You have listened to rumors circulated by jealous enemies of his. Fall is a very able man. I sat with him on the Committee on Foreign Relations and he is the best-posted man of the whole lot, particularly as to all Latin-American matters."

Party elders finally managed to divert Harding's choice from his quick-draw Senate colleague to the austerely urbane Hughes. Once Harding had decided on the bearded iceberg, he began to feel he had never really considered any other choice. When Hughes came to Marion, Harding assured him that he had not offered the position to anyone else—as strictly speaking he had not. In the light of Fall's later demolished reputation, it is ironic that Hughes then thought as highly of him as had

Theodore Roosevelt a few years earlier. Harding's long-time Marion friend and state campaign manager, Hoke Donithen, was to recall an incident of Hughes's Marion visit:

> One rainy night, just as I was preparing for bed, the phone rang. I answered. It was Harding. Would I do him a favor? Judge Charles Evans Hughes was visiting him and wanted to go on to New York that night. The next train East on the New York Central did not stop at Marion. Would I call the Division Superintendent at Bellefontaine, arrange to have the train stop in Marion and then drive over and take Judge Hughes to the station?
>
> Of course I would, and gladly. An accommodating railroad official was only too glad to stop the train in Marion as a favor to the President-elect and the arrangements were soon made. At the appointed time I went to the Harding home to get Judge Hughes.
>
> I found Harding and Hughes standing in the front hall and the Senator was helping the Judge with his overcoat.
>
> Harding introduced us and then added, "I have asked Judge Hughes to become Secretary of State and he has agreed to do so, if he can complete certain litigation against the government in which he represents some California vintners."
>
> I made some remark to the effect that the entire country would applaud the appointment and then Hughes, who was in a very serious mood, cut in to say this to Harding: "Senator, before I leave I want again to speak to you about Albert Fall. In my opinion he is the greatest international lawyer in the country. He is the man you should appoint Secretary of State and I again urge you to do so."
>
> "But that's all settled," Harding replied. "You have agreed to take it and you are the man I want."
>
> As they shook hands and bade each other good-bye, Hughes again said "Remember, Mr. President, what I have said. Fall is the best man for Secretary of State. I have promised you that I would take the post, and I will keep my promise, but if this legal matter we both know about should prevent it, don't fail to appoint Fall."
>
> After a word of farewell, Hughes and I went to the car and I drove him to his train.
>
> As the years have passed and events have unfolded, I have heard much criticism of Warren for putting Fall in his Cabinet as Secretary of the Interior. I have never found it in my heart to blame him, for I heard Charles Evans Hughes urge him to make Fall Secretary of State. It's a strange world.

Whatever advice Harding was willing to take from the assorted "best minds," one thing he was stubbornly determined on, and that was to make Harry Daugherty his Attorney General. Senators New of Indiana and Wadsworth of New York came to Marion just before Christmas to discuss appointments and party organization in their states. After dinner at the Harding house, at about nine in the evening, they went for a walk with Harding in order to get away from the interruptions of telephone calls and visitors. As they walked down Mount Vernon Avenue in the darkness, New expressed his objections to Daugherty as a politician with far too many enemies, and said that his appointment as Attorney General would be a disappointment to members of the bar generally who would expect something a great deal better. Wadsworth chimed in that he thought Daugherty's appointment would not only be a mistake but dangerous. Harding stopped on the macadam walk, then said with deep feeling: "Harry Daugherty has been my best friend from the beginning of this whole thing. I have told him that he can have any place in my Cabinet he wants, outside of Secretary of State. He tells me that he wants to be Attorney General and *by God he will be Attorney General!*"

Directly after the election Bryan, who had always been personally more friendly with Harding than with Cox, wrote him a private letter of congratulations. In it he urged him to announce that he would not be a candidate for re-election, since (he felt) a President could only exercise his tremendous power if he had purged himself of further ambitions. Bryan had refused to campaign for the Democrats because of Cox's evasion of the liquor question. The day after the election he had appealed to President Wilson to resign and allow the newly elected President to take office immediately.[8] After accepting Harding's post-election invitation to Marion, he told reporters that the new President "would stand for international cooperation in the interests of peace."

The portly Taft arrived in Marion for a breakfast appointment with Harding the day before Christmas. He, Harding, and the Duchess had a waffles-and-chipped-beef breakfast at seven-thirty in the oak dining room. Although Taft would have preferred eggs, he was too tactful to say so. They talked first of social arrangements in the White House. The Duchess, still smarting from Mrs. Wilson's superior airs, announced that she was getting rid of Mrs. Jaffray. Taft advised her not to. He explained that the housekeeper was from Canada, knew her place, and was quite unobtrusive. He also put in a good word for Arthur Brooks, Wilson's valet and factotum. Harding broke in to say that when he was in the White House he wanted to "chuck" ceremony. The Duchess objected, and Taft tried to convince Harding that she was right. When Harding left the room briefly, Taft took the opportunity of explaining more about the social life

[8] If Wilson resigned, Vice President Marshall would succeed him. Bryan's plan was to have President Marshall appoint Harding Secretary of State and then resign in turn. Harding as next in succession would then become President. After President Hoover's defeat in 1932, President-elect Roosevelt made the same demand for Hoover's resignation. In 1946, following the Republican mid-term election victory, there were similar demands for President Truman to resign.

of the White House, concealing his surprise that the Duchess knew so little. He tried to impress on her that—no matter how Harding might dislike it—his friends must now call him Mr. President for the sake of the dignity of the office and to avoid excessive familiarity.

When Harding returned, the Duchess left the men alone. At once, and to Taft's surprise, Harding plunged into Cabinet matters, saying that he had offered Hughes the State Department. Taft thought Hughes would prefer going to the Supreme Court as Chief Justice, and urged Root as Secretary of State. Harding thought that Root was too old. Taft recommended Hilles for the Treasury, but Harding said he had decided on Dawes. He added that he had wanted Hoover for the Secretary of the Interior but might have to make him Secretary of Commerce. Taft thought that a Cabinet with Hughes, Dawes, and Hoover in it would be a great Cabinet. Harding said he had others as good. He was hoping to persuade New to resign as senator from Indiana to become Secretary of War, and have Hays replace him in the Senate. Daugherty would be his Attorney General. Taft did not balk at Daugherty. He thought Harding was entitled to have one such friend in the Cabinet. Hays he considered a lightweight.

> He [Harding] rather demurred to this [Taft wrote his wife]. He said he [Hays] was the man to whom the Senate Oligarchy had turned to beat him, Harding. He said "You know because you furnished the evidence." . . . I said I understood that it had been arranged at a luncheon of the National Committee . . . at which Hert of Kentucky was present, and that Hert declined to carry out the plan in the Convention. He asked what I knew of Hert. I said I knew very little, that I knew Hilles liked him but I had been told he had made his money in a questionable way which ought to be looked into if he was to be appointed. He said the Kentuckians were pressing him hard. Indeed he said he knew that Harry Daugherty wanted him appointed very much, but Harry was sly and had not said a word directly in his favor. He said he could see through Harry when Harry did not suspect it, but he said Harry was loyal and a good lawyer.

Finally after talking about more prospective appointees, the sorry state of the Philippines and a possible Governor General (Taft suggested Forbes), Harding turned directly to Taft. "By the way," he said, "I want to ask you, would you accept a position on the Supreme Bench? Because if you would, I'll put you on that Court." Taft was dumbfounded. It had always been the ambition of his life to be a Supreme Court Justice, he told Harding, but since he had already declined it twice, and since he had been President and appointed three of the present bench as well as three others, and since he had opposed the appointment of the present Justice Brandeis, he felt he could accept nothing less than the Chief Justiceship

That might soon be available, since deaf and ailing Chief Justice White, whom Taft as President had appointed,[9] had long considered resigning. Harding listened reflectively but did not reply, and Taft tactfully changed the subject to politics, advising Harding to "appoint no Negroes south of the Mason-Dixon line, because it did neither the Negroes nor the whites any good to make appointments in communities where the leading element was white. Harding said sarcastically that this was a matter he must of course give attention to because of his reputed ancestry. . . . He said he believed in a Lily White Republican party and not a Black and Tan."

Taft left before lunch, sensing that Harding did not want him to stay into the afternoon. Just before leaving he posed with Harding for a photograph, and met Doctor Sawyer and some of the reporters from the shack. He thought Harding looked tired, and suggested that he try to get three hours' exercise every afternoon.

Harding spent Christmas quietly at Mount Vernon Avenue. In the hall, under a large Christmas tree topped by an American flag, lay a jumble of presents, from the bizarre to the valuable, from Texas pecans to Georgia possum hides, with which Americans make a habit of showering their Presidents. The Duchess had invited the newspapermen still in Marion to Christmas dinner. In the afternoon the Sawyers and the Christians arrived, sensing that this would probably be the last Christmas in the golden-oak house and with that vague feeling of foreboding at doing something for the last time. At dusk Daugherty turned up with Jess Smith and his Roxy. The whole party, except for the Duchess, then left for a late supper at the Sawyers'. Harding was Roxy's partner in the White Oaks Farm dining room and she noted that he was "very attentive."

Early in January Elizabeth Willits had gone to Marion for a showdown talk with Harding. They met in the temporary office at the Christians'. Harding admitted his affair with her sister and his responsibility as the father of Elizabeth Ann. He agreed to provide for Nan and offered to pay the Willits $500 a month if they would adopt the baby legally.

Already he had made his late January plans to visit the Frelinghuysens in Florida where he intended to sun himself until his inaugural. Now that the excitement and the tension of the election were over, his mood vacillated from pride and optimism to his old feeling of self-doubt and distrust. On January 7, when he received his red fez as a member of Columbus's Aladdin Temple, Ancient Arabic Order of Nobles of the Mystic Shrine, he told his fellow Shriners:

[9] When Taft signed White's commission he remarked: "There is nothing I would have loved more than being Chief Justice of the United States. I cannot help seeing the irony in the fact that I, who desired that office so much, should now be signing the commission of another man."

I wonder if you know the feeling of a man who has been called to the greatest office in the world. There is an aloofness of one's friends, and that is one of the sad things; and in me there is a deepening sense of responsibility. I have found already that there is intrigue and untruth that must be guarded against. One must ever be on his guard. This everlasting on one's guard spoils a man.

With the long-barred paths of Masonry at last opened to him, he now made the spangled and be-medaled ascent with pride. Two days before becoming a Noble of the Aladdin Temple, he had in the Scioto Consistory received all the Scottish Rite degrees. On January 11 in Marion he received the Mark Master and Most Excellent Master degrees, and on January 13 the Royal Arch Degree. Three days before he became President he received the Order of the Red Cross and the Order of the Knights of Malta and Knights Templar.[10]

Harding had delayed his resignation from the Senate until the new Republican governor, Harry L. Davis, could replace Governor Cox. In the nomination struggle for Harding's Senate seat—with Harding determinedly keeping "hands off"—Willis had beaten out Walter Brown and was easily elected in the Republican election sweep. Cox offered to appoint Willis as interim senator for the lame-duck session whenever Harding should resign, but Harding wanted no favors from a Democrat and prepared to wait until Governor-elect Davis took office. On January 9 Harding sent in his letter of resignation, and Davis appointed Willis to replace him.

The rumors continued to swirl about Harding's future appointments; still talk of Root as Secretary of State and Wood in the War Department, more talk of Toby Hert being rewarded for his convention double-cross with the Navy Department, of Pershing being sent as ambassador to France. Harding announced that he would not make any Cabinet decisions known until after his second vacation when he planned to take a twelve-day cruise along the east coast of Florida in Senator Frelinghuysen's 88-foot houseboat *Victoria*. Just before this trip he gave an inspirational address to the pupils of the renamed Harding High School. The Mount Vernon Avenue house had been rented to a building contractor, Millard Hunt, and the Harding furniture taken to a storage warehouse. When Harding left in the *Superb* for St. Augustine, the Duchess had already gone on to New York. Daugherty and Christian were aboard with Harding as the special train pulled out of the Union Depot.

Frelinghuysen was waiting on the platform at St. Augustine, and the

[10] In September, 1922, at Boston, Massachusetts, Harding was elected a member of the Supreme Council of the Sovereign Grand Inspectors General of the 33rd and Last Degree, but because of the Duchess's illness was unable to attend the Council rendezvous to receive the degree which can be conferred only in person.

two men played a round of golf while the last preparations were being made on the *Victoria*. Trim, with sparkling white paint and the glitter of polished brass, shipshape and unseaworthy, the *Victoria* cast off the next morning on its sheltered voyage down the Indian River and to Miami. Senator Fall, that "star of a fellow," had joined the voyagers the evening before. Harding had written Frelinghuysen just after Christmas asking that he be included. "He would be fine company for the indoor sports," Harding wrote, "and it would be wholly pleasing to me for him to be one of the party. He would not be good at golf, but when it comes to making up an evening party he would be a joy. I am very fond of him."

The idyll of summer February days in the tropical landscape along the wide and placid river was broken by the *Victoria's* unfortunate tendency to get stuck in the mud. Time after time the voyagers had to take the launch ashore to resume their travels by car. At one point Harding considered abandoning ship. At Daytona he dropped in at the old Marion colony and saw Clifford Kling, then, after a night at Palm Beach with a dinner party given by Daugherty at the Everglades Club, sailed on to Miami where he had an effusive visit with William Jennings Bryan, now converted from Northern climates to the fundamentalist conviction that Florida was the new earthly paradise. From Miami Harding left with Fall for a two days' fishing trip on the yacht *Shadow* off the old pirate lair of Caesar's Island where he caught a four-foot barracuda and a six-foot sailfish. On February 4 Fall wrote to his wife Emma:

> After being with Harding for two days, he made me the direct tender of appointment as Secretary of the Interior and urged my acceptance, stating that, among other things, he knew he could count on my advice and assistance should I remain in the Senate, but that he would feel much freer to have me as one of his official advisers, associated with him direct. I finally told him I would accept the appointment.

On their return Fall went back to Texas. Daugherty left at the same time for Ohio on two special missions. Though Daugherty did not tell anyone as yet, the first mission concerned the shadow of Blooming Grove and a threat on Harding's life.

Professor Chancellor, after his dismissal from Wooster College, had been heard to boast that Harding would never enter the White House. After Daugherty learned of this he left Florida and notified Attorney General Palmer. Palmer despatched Secret Service agents to Wooster warning Chancellor to stay away from Washington. Meanwhile the ex-Professor, immobilized in his house by hostile public opinion, was preparing a limited autographed *Illustrated Life of President Warren G. Harding* and mailing out circulars that announced its publication "immediately after March 4, 1921." Features of the book would include "an account of the ethnological experiment at Blooming Grove, a main Ohio station in the underground railroad, formerly called Harding Corners, and of the six months' investigation into the ancestry of the President including a report as to whether his parents were ever married; and if not why not." Reservation coupons with five dollars (eight dollars after March 31) were to be sent to William Estabrook Chancellor, member of the City Council of Wooster, Ohio, and "for twelve years connected with the Presbyterian College of Wooster." On learning of this project, Daugherty called the United States attorney for the Cleveland District, Edward S. Wertz, to try to find some way of suppressing the book. Secret Service agents arranged to put pressure on Chancellor to have it destroyed. Daugherty returned to Florida on February 15 to let Harding know and to talk over what further action should be taken. Two weeks later in his home, in the minatory presence of Secret Service agents and Post Office Inspector C. S. Zimmerman, Chancellor was forced to burn his manuscript—although, as Zimmerman wrote Daugherty—it might have been a "fake bonfire." Following the bonfire Chancellor drew his $1,200 savings from the bank and slipped away to Montreal.

Finley Peter Dunne, attending Daugherty's Everglades Club dinner, had thought Harding much changed from the pleasant, convivial companion he had earlier known. The President-elect complained to Dunne of the jokes the newspapers were making about his drinking and his poker playing. Dunne tried to reassure him by saying that every President had been treated in the same way. But Harding had other worries unknown to Dunne. Several sportive letters that he had written as a senator to a Washington woman of clouded reputation were now being offered for private sale in New York at an asking price of $1,000. Daugherty's second mission was to undertake to get back the letters. Eventually they were recovered and destroyed, but Harding could not conceal his uneasiness during the negotiations.[11]

On the sluggish return from Miami, Harding still stayed with the *Victoria*. The voyage ended on February 7 on a mud bank in the narrow-channeled Mosquito Lagoon just below Daytona. After being rowed ashore and making his way along a path through swamp growth, Harding took the train to St. Augustine. There, in the Ponce de León Hotel, in an endless chain of visitors and conferences, he settled down between sessions on the golf links to completing his Cabinet.

---

[11] Samuel Hopkins Adams talked with a lawyer and a Washington correspondent who had seen the letters, but as the woman was still alive when he wrote his book he did not reveal her name. Daugherty's negotiations at first merely succeeded in raising the price to $5,000. "At this point," Adams writes, "it was discovered that the bargainer was politically vulnerable through a member of her family. Counter-pressure was brought into play and the documents were surrendered without price."

Piecemeal he released his selections to the press. Three qualifications he listed as necessary: fitness for public service; the attitude of the public toward the appointment; political considerations. "This," Harding announced, "is going to be a Republican Cabinet." Although his Secretary of State would be his most important choice, and although he had determined on Hughes before Christmas, he had delayed any announcement because of the hostility of Penrose and Lodge to the "whiskered Wilson." Nevertheless, he was determined to have this man of whom he was so much in awe. "I have simply got to have Hughes in my Cabinet as Secretary of State," he wrote to the Reverend Doctor William F. McDowell. "There is nobody else who is in the same class with him." Hughes came on to St. Augustine to be at Harding's side when Harding presented him to the press correspondents and, in indirect reference to Wilson's domination of foreign policy, told them that "the Secretary of State will speak for the State Department."

Harding was equally in awe of and equally determined to have Hoover in his Cabinet, but the objections to Wilson's food administrator were even sharper and more extended. Borah and Johnson for the irreconcilables, Smoot and Curtis for the regulars, Boss Penrose for himself, wanted none of the man who had campaigned for the Democrats in 1918. Daugherty wrote that "a great many prominent persons in Washington" were opposed to the appointment. Harding was not to be dissuaded. Hughes, Hoover—such men he must have if he were to have a great Cabinet, if his administration were to make a "seemly" mark.

> I am sorry [he wrote Daugherty] that so many people impress you as hostile to Mr. Hoover to a place in the Cabinet. Of course, I do not want the administration to start out with a quarrel with the Senate or any considerable faction in the Republican party. I do hold him in very high esteem and think his appointment would appeal to the cordial approval of the country. The more I consider him the more I do come to think well of him. Of course, I have no quarrel with those who do not think as I do, but inasmuch as I have the responsibility to assume I think my judgment must be trusted in this matter.

Daugherty was sent to tell Penrose and Lodge that it was to be Hoover and Mellon—or no Mellon. Penrose had what was left of his heart set on the Pittsburgh financier as Secretary of the Treasury, and after an eloquent burst of profanity, grinned and told Daugherty: "All right. You win." After Dawes had refused the Treasury post, Harding did not need to be pushed to appoint Andrew W. Mellon, for Mellon was second only to John D. Rockefeller as the world's richest man and Harding's feeling for him was sacerdotal. "The ubiquitous financier of the universe," Harding termed him and was easily persuaded that this frail, retiring, and unimaginative Midas with the sad, dark-circled eyes who moved in an abstract world of figures and quotations and funds, would be the greatest Secretary of the Treasury since Alexander Hamilton, the financial wizard necessary to conjure away wartime extravagances and reduce taxes and the national debt.

As for Daugherty, Harding's insistence on making him Attorney General did not waver in the face of the inevitable protests. When at St. Augustine he received a letter from Ohio's Methodist Bishop William F. Anderson tactfully suggesting that Root would make a better Attorney General than Daugherty, he replied: "I would not want the country to think me so much of an ingrate that I would ignore a man of Mr. Daugherty's devotion to the party and to me as an aspirant and candidate. I very much wished to make some recognition of his incalculable services and asked him to accept a post for which I think him ably qualified."

As Secretary of Agriculture Harding picked the competent if temperamental Iowa farmer, conservationist, and editor, Henry C. Wallace.[12] Wallace was a farmer's farmer. After graduating from Iowa State Agricultural College in 1892, he had then become an assistant professor of dairying. In 1894 he and his brother and his clergyman father took over the rural paper they called *Wallaces' Farmer*. Through this paper and the Cornbelt Meat Producers Association, of which he was secretary for fourteen years, Wallace exerted a large influence among the various farm organizations and became a recognized leader of the agricultural interests. For the farm belt he seemed a promise that the Republican platform pledges of farm relief meant something. Although he considered Harding "sporty" rather than steady he thought he "seemed willing to listen to reason in the farm cause."

It was Wood's ambition to end his military career as Secretary of War, but it was an ambition Harding was determined to do nothing to further. With the happy thought of removing him from the scene altogether, he wrote the General from St. Augustine:

> I wish you to have it from me and understand through direct communication how very anxious I am that you consent to accept the Governorship of the Philippine Islands. I should like to make your appointment the very first one of the new administration.

A "damned insult," Root termed the offer. Wood refused it. Harding gave the War Department to the wealthy Massachusetts broker-turned-politician of respectable mediocrity, John W. Weeks, a plump and fatherly-looking man who had been defeated for re-election to the Senate and to whom the Republican party was much indebted for campaign financing. It was Weeks who recommended Edwin N. Denby for the relatively

[12] Father of Franklin D. Roosevelt's Secretary of Agriculture and later Vice President Henry A. Wallace.

minor post of Secretary of the Navy after Lowden had turned down the job.

From his double war record Denby seemed a popular choice, for he had enlisted in the Navy as a seaman in the Spanish-American War, and in World War I—though overage and overweight—he had joined the Marine Corps in May, 1917, as a private and had risen to the rank of major. Denby had served three terms in Congress. After his discharge from the Marine Corps he had made a million dollars as an automobile dealer in Detroit. Outwardly he was an impressive man with a determined bald head and stiff jaw that gave the impression of power, poise, and dominance. But behind his virile façade, although it took a little time to realize this, was neither sense nor commonsense.

Hays had hoped to become Secretary of Commerce, but finally agreed to the politician's choice of the Post Office. Virtuously he wrote Harding early in February:

> I am willing to undertake the Post Office department. This is done with the fullest cognizance of the confidence evidenced by the offer and the responsibility incident to acceptance. I have felt and still feel that I could give you more ultimate service and benefit in the Department of Commerce, but the fullest consideration of the whole subject matter brings me to an inevitable conclusion exactly squaring with my first opinion and that is that I must take hold of the load and help lift wherever you yourself decide I can lift the most.

When Harding left St. Augustine for Marion on February 27 all the members of his Cabinet had been announced except the Secretaries of Labor and the Interior. For the Labor Department he wanted a union man—or a reasonable facsimile—and James J. Davis, the director general of the Loyal Order of the Moose—a man whose goal was never to offend anyone—seemed to fill the bill. Davis had been born in Wales and when he was eleven years old had started working in a mill. At nineteen he had been a puddler in a steel mill in Elwood, Indiana, and though his laboring days were long behind him, though he had made his particular million in reorganizing the Moose, he still held his union card. Later a ghost writer of more than usual talent would write Davis's autobiography, *The Iron Puddler*, a book which would even attain a mild literary success. "I have been a puddler of iron," Davis—or his ghost—said of his proposed appointment, "and I would be a puddler of men!"

The expected announcement of Fall as the new Secretary of the Interior was not made until Harding reached Marion. Curiously enough Fall had been among those urging the appointment of Hoover as Secretary of Commerce. "I don't love him any better than you do," he wrote Harding, "but what do our small grievances amount to compared with the prosperity of millions of people? . . ." The collective membership of the assembled Cabinet was estimated by the *New York World* to own or contro' more than six hundred million dollars.

Since the Mount Vernon Avenue house was rented, Harding stayed the last few days before the inauguration with Tryon and Daisy among the bamboo whatnots, horsehair sofas, and creaky Morris chairs of the East Center Street house. On March 2, after a breakfast with the Sawyers at White Oaks Farm, he spent half a morning at his old desk at the *Star*, inspected the new Harding Room at the Marion Club, and in the evening underwent his initiation into the Knights Templar. The next day he said his farewell to his home town from the Front Porch of the now empty house. At ten o'clock Marion closed down for an honorary hour—banks stores, and schools—to see the President-elect off and to hear his last speech. Hundreds stood ankle deep in the mud before the curve of the Front Porch railing while the stroke-crippled Reverend Doctor McAfee presented the Hardings with a silver plaque "with God's blessings."

Accompanying the Hardings on the *Superb* as it left the Union Depot were Daisy, Tryon, and Deac with his two sons, young George and young Warren. Pointedly not included, although living in Marion, were Pete DeWolfe's children, Eugenia and George. With his Cabinet picked, his inaugural speech written, a huge congressional majority behind him, Harding was content to watch the snow-streaked Ohio landscape slip past him. Congress would again legislate—as the Constitution intended—and the executive branch would execute. He, as the Chief Executive, would never go down in history as a great President; he knew himself better than that. What he wanted, what he hoped to be far more than that was America's "best-loved" President.

[CHAPTER XVII]

President I

With the departure of the Wilsons, the White House lost its remoteness. No longer did locked iron gates bar the public from the grounds. The Duchess on entering the building after the inaugural as its mistress found the servants drawing the curtains in the East Room, as they told her, to keep the people outside from peering in at the reception. Some of the curious were already crowding round the windowpanes. "Let 'em look if they want to," the Duchess rasped. "It's their White House!" After the reception she mentioned to Alice Longworth that she had a little red book in which she had written the names of all those who had not been civil to her and "Wurr'n" Harding since they came to Washington. Those people were now to realize that she was aware of their behavior!

In the White House Wilsonian decorum gave way to Harding folksiness. Once more the lower floors as well as the grounds were open to casual visitors. After a lapse of four years, children again took part in the traditional Easter-egg rolling on the South Grounds. Harding revived the old custom, fallen out of use since John Quincy Adams's time, of having Marine Band concerts on the lawn. Any and everyone who could pass the hurried Secret Service inspection for respectability and harmlessness was free to come to the White House and shake hands with him at the open reception held each day between twelve-thirty and lunch. Even in bad weather seldom less than a hundred visitors appeared, and often more than two thousand showed up to shake the presidential hand—schoolteachers, students, high-school graduating classes, club and lodge members, tourists, hikers, hitchhikers, foreigners, Boy Scouts, Girl Scouts, religious groups, Indians in costume, baseball and football teams, theatrical and moving-picture stars, children of all ages. For at least fifteen minutes a beaming Harding pumped hands, made impromptu pleasantries, and patted little children on the head with "Look who's here!" Sometimes the Duchess appeared with him—for a Girl Scout delegation she even wore her own Girl Scout uniform. Sometimes he was accompanied by Laddie Boy, his shaggy and inquisitive Airedale, presented to him by Charles Quetschke, the owner of the Caswell Kennels of Toledo. During his time in office he is estimated to have shaken a quarter of a million hands. When Christian objected to these mass greetings as taking up too much of his time and energy, Harding insisted that they never tired him. "I *love* to meet people," he told his secretary. "It is the most pleasant thing I do; it is really the only fun I have. It does not tax me, and it seems to be a very great pleasure to them."

With no niggling afterthought about why he had not been asked sooner, Harding now joined the Rotary and Kiwanis clubs as well as the Marion Aerie of Eagles. He became a prophet of the Order of the Veiled Prophets. To the hundreds of organizations that now solicited him he was always willing to accept honorary membership—from the Borrowed Time Club and the Pittsburgh Motor Club to the Platonic Literary Society of Rutherford College.

On second and less self-assertive thought the Duchess had kept the adroit and efficient Mrs. Jaffray on as housekeeper. In time the housekeeper would achieve a certain qualified affection for the mistress, though always with genteel amazement at the Harding manners. Harding liked to have private stag dinners of a dozen or fifteen men, and his idea of a suitable menu—to which Mrs. Jaffray would reluctantly consent—was wienerwurst and sauerkraut. Not long after the Hardings had moved in, the colored head butler came to the housekeeper to tell her that the President had ordered toothpicks on the dining-room table. She told him he must have misunderstood. "No," the butler insisted, "he asked me as plain as anything for toothpicks." She said to forget about it, but the next day he came to her again and said that the President had demanded his toothpicks "real forceful like." From then on toothpicks appeared on the White House table.

After Harding had settled on his Cabinet, he felt free to reward his friends in his lesser appointments. "God," he remarked, "I can't be an ingrate." As he had promised, he gave the unexacting Ed Scobey the technically and legally exacting post of Director of the Mint. Dick Crissinger he translated from the Marion County Bank to Comptroller of the Currency as a step to promoting him to the highest banking office in the country, that of Governor of the Federal Reserve System. The Duchess insisted that only Doctor Sawyer knew how to handle her kidney stoppages, and he was tempted from White Oaks Farm by a commission as brigadier general in the Army Medical Corps Reserve to become the Hardings' personal physician and chairman of the Federal Hospitalization Board. One of the perquisites of his office was a large cavalry horse, "Turco"; and to see the wispy doctor-general in his high-collared uniform with its starred shoulder straps, a Sam Browne belt slapping against his hollow chest, his little pointed beard bobbling in the wind, as he cantered through the park, soon became one of the sights of Washington. Ironically or otherwise, everyone now called him General.

Heber Votaw, as a former lecturer at the Adventist Missionary College, found a secular haven for his evangelicalism as superintendent of Federal Prisons after Harding had removed that office from the Civil Service list by executive order. One of the Duchess's old *Star* delivery boys, red-haired Ora M. "Reddy" Baldinger, a Senate page for whom Harding had secured an appointment to West Point and who during the war had risen to the rank of major in the Army Air Service, was appointed the President's military aide. Since that jovial Hawaiian acquaintance Charlie Forbes, now a partner in the Hurley-Mason Construction Company of Tacoma, was cold to the thought of the governorship of Alaska, Harding made him director of the much-criticized Bureau of War Risk Insurance, and when Forbes said he knew nothing about insurance Harding told him that *that* was an advantage. The Kansas City go-getter, E. Mont Reily, he appointed governor of Porto Rico, a place Reily had never been but where he could be counted on to wave the flag and stand for no nonsense. George Harvey, after closing down *Harvey's Weekly*, received his reward as ambassador to England, where he would grace the Court of St. James as the first American ambassador to make his appearance in knee breeches. Richard Washburn Child—later to develop into an enthusiastic apologist for Mussolini—became ambassador to Italy. Herrick, long a resident of Paris, achieved his heart's desire as ambassador to France. Ned McLean achieved his in receiving a code, a card, and the starred badge of a special agent of the Department of Justice at a salary of a dollar a year. Harding had planned to make Jess Smith Commissioner of Indian Affairs and, after Western senators objected to that, even considered making him Treasurer of the United States. But Jess was content to settle for entrée to the White House and an unofficial desk of his own near Harry Daugherty's office in the Department of Justice Building.

Most of Harding's first month was spent in taking care of the hundreds of job hopefuls pressing him from all sides. Among his secondary appointments he made Theodore Roosevelt, Jr., Assistant Secretary of the Navy, a young man so intent on following in his father's footsteps that he took no notice of Harding's offer at almost the same time to pay Colombia $20 million damages for the Panama Canal affair—even though this assuaging offer was tantamount to admitting that Father Roosevelt in his eagerness for a canal had acted improperly in 1903.[1] St. Louis politicians had per-

[1] When the Colombian Senate failed for venal reasons to ratify the treaty which would have allowed the United States government to construct the Panama Canal, President Roosevelt subsidized, supported and later recognized the insurgent group that broke away from Colombia and proclaimed the canal site region the independent Republic of Panama. Roosevelt never had any doubts about the rightness of his action.

suaded Harding to appoint Nat Goldstein as collector of Internal Revenue for his vote-juggling services at the convention, but so great was the outcry against the easy-money delegate that Goldstein finally withdrew his name. Harding wrote him a letter of thanks for getting him off that particular hook.

To settle the complications of German property confiscated in the United States during the war, Harding selected the director of the Republican National Campaign Committee, Thomas W. Miller, as Alien Property Custodian. Though Miller would later haunt Harding, he seemed at the time a reasonable selection, coming as he did from an upper-class Eastern background, with membership in the Union League Club of Philadelphia, the Yale Club, the Bankers of America, the National Republican Club of New York, the National Press Club, the Racquet Club of Washington, the St. Elmo Club of New Haven, and the Wilmington Country Club. Later he had moved outside such staid Eastern circles to manage a ranch in Nevada and afterward to work for the Bethlehem Steel Corporation. From 1915 to 1917 he was a congressman from Delaware. Then at the outbreak of the war he enlisted as a private, served eleven months in France, and rose to the rank of lieutenant colonel. As one of the original incorporators of the American Legion, he drew vociferous support for his appointment from the ex-soldiers.

With the passage of the Eighteenth Amendment, Wayne B. Wheeler, as the triumphant leader of the Anti-Saloon League, had probably more influence and authority over governmental affairs than any elected official. In fact, he liked to boast of the graves he had dug for elected officials opposed to his League. Wheeler's tenacious political roots in Ohio forced Harding to pay attention to him, and Wheeler never hesitated in giving opinions that were veiled orders to congressmen and senators and now even to a President. For Wheeler, a man was measured solely by his alcoholic content. Four days after the election he let Harding know that there were objections to Root as Secretary of State since Root might select wine-bibbing diplomats to represent dry America overseas. Mellon was even more objectionable for having been interested as a banker in a number of distilleries. Of Daugherty, Wheeler took a more kindly view, feeling sure that "he would stand squarely for the enforcement of the Prohibition Law as well as others." When Wheeler wrote to Harding that he wished to see him before the new Prohibition commissioner was appointed to replace Wilson's John F. Kramer, the wish—with Harding's memory of Wheeler-dug graves stretching back to Herrick's in 1905—was in the nature of a command. Wheeler's "choice" for commissioner was an Ohio editor and former schoolteacher, Roy A. Haynes, the mayor of high and dry Hillesboro in Highland County where the temperance crusade had originated in 1873.

Walter Brown as chairman of the Joint Congressional Reorganization Commission assumed the complex burden of working out a plan of departmental organization and simplification for the Federal government.[2] Lasker took over a Shipping Board then foundering in a chaos of waste and inefficiency consequent on the heedless wartime rush to build ships. Wilson, in the Southern tradition of his party, had barred Negroes from government positions. The scattering of colored assistant attorneys general and United States attorneys that he had inherited he replaced by whites. Harding, in the tradition of the Republican party as the black man's friend, made a number of lesser Negro appointments: assistants to the attorney general, collectors of internal revenue, and even a minister to Liberia.

Behind all other appointments lay the suspended question of Taft's appointment to the Supreme Court. Creaky Chief Justice White had many times said that he would retire when he could do so in favor of the man who had appointed him. But now that the time had arrived, the Chief Justice—though failing in sight and hearing—stuck to his post with senile stubbornness, as deaf to persuasion as he was to small talk. Even Daugherty's Ohio glibness had no effect, though the Attorney General visited the Chief Justice several times and noted hopefully that he looked very feeble. Rumors sprang up that when the President could get White out of the way he would appoint Hughes Chief Justice and make Fall his Secretary of State. As the weeks drifted by, White's tenacity increased. He once told a questioning associate querulously that he had no intention of resigning. Meanwhile Harding's crafty campaign adviser, Senator Sutherland, let it be known that he was "crazy" to become Chief Justice. Tentatively Harding promised him the job, then tried to assuage the protesting Taft by telling him that Sutherland "could wait."

Taft had never really cared about being President and he had always longed to be Chief Justice, and he had seen himself appointing another to the one place he really coveted for himself. "Presidents come and go," he had said in 1916, "but the Court goes on forever." He had long felt that a Federal judiciary reform was needed and that the impetus should come from the Supreme Court. It was his ambition to provide the impetus as Chief Justice. From that high seat he was convinced that he could make judicial administration prompt, modern, and efficient. Behind his disinterested aim lay the more interested one of vindicating his defeat of 1912. And now through an old man's senile stubbornness his most cherished goal was going a-glimmering.

Harding, as Brandegee explained, "hates to offend anybody. His nature is to arrange compromises and ways by which everyone can be pleased."

[2] Brown later became Postmaster General in Hoover's Cabinet.

In this case Harding's idea was to persuade White and either Justice William R. Day or Oliver Wendell Holmes to resign. Then he could appoint both Taft and Sutherland to the Court. Taft suggested that Holmes be sidetracked to the Disarmament Commission, and added that "the bench would be well rid of him."

Suddenly on May 19 White died. Harding's first compromising reaction was temporarily to make the aging Justice William R. Day Chief Justice, but Daugherty insisted that, with the congestion of the courts and the lack of additional judges on Federal circuits, Taft was needed at once. Late in June Harding at last told Taft's old campaign manager Gus Karger he could let the "Big Chief" know that it would be "put over" about the first of July. Taft heard the news while he was traveling with his wife in Bermuda. On June 30 he was appointed the tenth Chief Justice of the United States.[3]

Two days after the inaugural Secretary Weeks sent for Wood to point out how urgently he was needed again in the Philippines. Under a complacently indolent governor the islands had become riddled with graft, extravagance, and wild finance, and were now faced with economic collapse. Although still set against accepting the governor generalship, Wood agreed to go to the Philippines on a mission of investigation and prepare a report on the conditions there. "Such corrupt incompetent management I have never seen or heard of," he wrote after his inspection tour. "Losses run into the many tens of millions." After finishing his report he finally though reluctantly agreed in July to go back as governor general.

The year and a half between Wilson's stroke and Harding's inauguration had been an interregnum, marked by closed gates and drawn curtains in the White House, with brief glimpses of a stricken old man in the tonneau of a swiftly passing car. Technically, the United States still remained at war with Germany and Austria-Hungary. Administration had ceased to administer. Government was at loose ends, and the ends were becoming frayed. But now as the White House gates swung open, the new leader emerged, confident, handsome, virile, and no less the symbolic leader because it was contrary to his nature to lead.

Congress proposes, the President disposes. That was how Harding felt it should be. His Cabinet chiefs, his experts like Hughes and Hoover, were on their own, beyond his direction. It was up to them to administer. To take up the slack of the interregnum and end the formal state of war, Harding summoned a special session of Congress for April 12.

[3] Harding was finally able to place Sutherland on the Supreme Court on September 5, 1922, after the Wilson-appointed Justice John H. Clarke resigned. Clarke had been Hanna's unsuccessful opponent for the Senate in 1903.

From Washington's to Wilson's administration the United States had never had a formal budgetary system to coordinate its haphazard and often conflicting financial activities, and Harding in his special session message demanded and received the authorization for a Bureau of the Budget. Prompting him, steering him to make this request was the Ohio banker and public-utilities consolidator Charles E. Dawes, McKinley's old Comptroller of the Currency. Dawes's genuine financial talents, though they had impressed Harding, were masked by the flamboyance of his self-cultivated eccentricities. He smoked a trick pipe with an apparently upside-down bowl that brought a flurry of jokes in the papers about the need for asbestos suits; his favorite and much-repeated epithet was "Hell 'n Maria!"; his thin hair parted just off center and his pugnacious jaw jutting over a stiff collar were a gift to caricaturists second only to Hays's ears. During the World War he had organized a board to coordinate Army purchases overseas and later as purchasing agent for the American Expeditionary Force he received the substantive rank of brigadier general. After the war he still continued to use his military title. Knowing nothing of finance, Harding was in awe of those who did, and since Dawes the budget advocate had already turned down the Treasury Department, the President begged him to head the new bureau. "In view of the many duties imposed," Harding wrote him, "I do not suppose there will be so important an office in the administration. I do not know whether you would consider it." Hell 'n Maria Dawes did consider it. Taking a dozen dollar-a-year men with him, determined to reorganize the United States financially, he became the country's first Director of the Budget.

During his early spring weeks in the White House Harding showed an obvious awed delight in having, like a McGuffey Reader hero, reached that pinnacle of American political ambition. According to Ike Hoover, the head usher, he "reveled" in his position. Judson Welliver and Charles Hard—imported from Ohio—functioned smoothly as his political secretaries, George Christian took care of the more personal matters. "Being President," Harding remarked, "is an easy job." Criticism of his appointments soon nettled him. Daugherty was of course the chief target. Herrick had refused a Cabinet post with Daugherty in the Cabinet and had warned Harding that Daugherty as Attorney General would wreck his administration. A friend wrote to the old Roosevelt campaigner Frank Knox that it would not be long before Harry was selling the sunshine on the front steps of the Capitol. *The New York Times* saw Daugherty as a "best friend" rather than a "best mind" and the *World* felt that he was a lobbyist, unfit for any high office. Fall's appointment caused no marked comment, being objected to chiefly by Pinchot and the conservationists who rightly recognized him as their unrelenting enemy. Within Ohio resentment flared up over appointments like Crissinger's and over General Sawyer, "the suddenest brigadier general in all history." "It isn't fair," Harding complained testily at the stormy reaction to his Attorney General. "This premature criticism is a serious menace to popular government. . . . I don't like it. It amounts to jumping on a man before he has had an opportunity to demonstrate his ability or intention. After there has been malfeasance in office, then go after that man. Go after him hard. But don't make any imputation in advance of action."

The routine of Harding's day began with breakfast at eight, no matter what time he might have gone to bed. Lying in bed late, he said, was for women. A typical morning was that of June 24 when after a session with his secretaries he had an appointment at ten with Senators Curtis and Capper, at ten-ten with Senator Bursum, at ten-fifteen with the Hon. C. W. Swisher of West Virginia, at ten-thirty with Milton H. Florsheim of Chicago, and at ten-forty-five with Col. Theodore Roosevelt and the national commander of the American Legion. At eleven o'clock came his Cabinet meeting, and, following the meeting, after Congressman Mondell had led in a committee to present him with a cowboy hat, the relaxation of mixing with the anonymous collection of sight-seers, tourists, and stragglers gathered outside the White House offices to shake his hand. A day's callers might include Pershing, Samuel Gompers, the old hermit of journalism E. W. Scripps, Booth Tarkington, Mary Roberts Rinehart, Harry Lauder in a kilt come to breakfast and to play golf, or Will Rogers—to whom Harding said as he shook hands: "This is the first time I ever got to see you without paying for it."

Each day Harding had a yellow-bound book of press clippings made up for him which he glanced through in the oval sitting room on the second floor while the Duchess's canary Pete "that sang like a nightingale" chirped in the cage near him. Beyond the clippings he read almost nothing. He liked to have Laddie Boy beside him, and publicity photographs often showed the two of them together. When a press agent penned Laddie Boy's answer to a performing dog Tige, whose owner had written inviting Laddie Boy to a performance at the Plymouth Theatre in Boston, the answer with its "cordial wag and friendly sniff" touched the hearts of animal lovers and sentimentalists all over the country. Laddie Boy, wearing Washington License Plate No. 1, led the parade in Be Kind to Animals Week. According to the proliferating news stories he brought the President his paper in the morning, had breakfast and lunch with him, sat in on Cabinet meetings, and on the golf course barked reproachfully whenever Harding stubbed an approach or missed an easy putt. A New York dog, haled into court for street fighting, tried (through its owner) to influence the judge by claiming Laddie Boy as his father. On his birthday Laddie Boy received a dog-biscuit cake from his own father.

At least two afternoons a week Harding played golf, and nothing but a downpour could keep him from the course. Yet, though his golfing was given much publicity, he actually spent less time on the links than had Wilson before his stroke. When he kept his score in the nineties he was enthusiastic, but 101 was his average for the game. With a handicap of 22 he almost won the Washington Newspaper Golf Association tournament, and would have if clicking cameras on the home green had not made him look up on a short putt. To commemorate his interest in the sport he presented the President Warren Harding Cup as a perpetual trophy for the National Public Links champion. Usually he played at the Chevy Chase Club. The florid Frelinghuysen was his most intimate golfing partner in a group that included Speaker of the House Gillett, Senators Hale, Hitchcock, Kellogg, and Edge, Secretary of Agriculture Wallace and George Harvey (before he went to the Court of St. James). Once on the links, he played as if his life depended on every shot, and made so many bets that sometimes he was betting against himself on individual shots and holes, on low score against his partner, or with his partner six dollars Nassau against their opponents (meaning six dollars out, six dollars in, and six dollars across). Colonel Starling of the Secret Service detail, following discreetly in the rear, kept the accounts.

Any well-known professional or sportsman who happened to be in Washington might be asked to join a Harding foursome, though Will Rogers found himself excluded after his vaudeville skit on Harding talking golf during a Cabinet meeting. Ring Lardner was introduced to presidential golf by an old Harding acquaintance, Grantland Rice. On his first afternoon at Chevy Chase with Harding he sliced a drive, knocking a branch off a tree which struck the President. Instead of apologizing, Lardner remarked that he was just trying to make a President out of Coolidge. Harding liked the joke, and Lardner liked Harding. On their way to the President's House, a bungalow that the club had built for the nineteenth hole, Lardner told Harding that he wanted to be appointed ambassador to Greece. When the President asked why, his lugubrious hound-dog face grew even longer as he answered: "My wife doesn't like Great Neck."

When at an afternoon's end the President and his golfing friends dropped in at the President's House, Colonel Starling unlocked the desk drawer where three or four bottles of Scotch or bourbon were stored, a colored attendant brought in setups, and while the players were drinking highballs, Starling toted up the bets. Harding usually took only one drink, and when this was finished and the bets settled would tell Starling: "Telephone the Duchess that I am on my way home."

On more intimate afternoons Harding would golf with his old Senate pals Frelinghuysen, Elkins, and Hale—with George Christian as a replacement—on Ned McLean's nine-hole course at Friendship. With Harding in the White House, Ned was taking golf more seriously than he took most things, and had hired a professional, at $10,000 a year, to help him reach Harding's 101-stroke level. Evalyn even managed to persuade the cautious Coolidge to play a few rounds, although the desiccated Yankee in his high-waisted trousers held up by galluses was an incongruous sight mincing behind the portly foursome in their plus-four knickers and bright Argyll-patterned socks. Harding seemed to feel freer at Friendship than anywhere else. Evalyn thought it was a kind of sanctuary for him.

When Harding first came to the White House he rode horseback on the horse "Arizona" provided for him by the cavalry, but Starling noticed that he had a worse "seat" than Wilson and after a few rides he confined his exercise to golf. He was on hand to toss out the traditional ball for the opening of the baseball season at Griffith Park and often attended the games, switching his allegiance from the Cincinnati Reds to the Washington Senators. In fact, it became a joke that he spent more time on the record of the Senators than he did on the *Congressional Record*. Babe Ruth was several times a White House guest. For Harding the sports page was the most interesting section of the paper. He followed, if he could not attend, all boxing matches and prize fights. The day after heavyweight champion Jack Dempsey had knocked out the Frenchman Georges Carpentier at Boyle's Thirty Acres in Jersey City, films of the fight were rushed to Ned McLean where they were shown at his I Street house. Eleven years before, after the Negro Jack Johnson had defeated the white Jim Jeffries, Congress had passed a law forbidding the interstate transportation of prize-fight moving pictures, this to spare the South the spectacle of a black man beating a white. Though still in effect, the law was a technicality to the I Street audience that included Harding, Daugherty, Hughes, and others of the Cabinet, Christian, Smith, and several foreign ambassadors.[4]

Two evenings a week Harding held a poker session at the White House. The regular members of what he called his poker cabinet included Daugherty, Weeks, Fall, Cummings, Hale, Lasker, Henry Fletcher, Ned McLean, Jess Smith, Charlie Forbes, George Christian, Doc Sawyer.

[4] A New York film entrepreneur, F. C. Quimby, had made the fight films by arrangement with the promoter Tex Rickard. The oddly named though non-Oriental Jap Muma, general manager of the McLean papers and supplier of McLean entertainment, had picked them up in New Jersey and brought them to Washington. Quimby and Rickard had not intended to show the films outside of the state, but to Muma on his way to Washington they seemed a potential gold mine if there were some way round the law so that they could be exhibited all over the country. Muma spoke to Daugherty after the showing who told him to take up the matter with a Washington lawyer friend of his, Albert R. Urion, "one of the greatest little men you ever met in your life." And Daugherty added: "If you put this across you ought to get a big cut, no less than fifty per cent."

Among the associate members were Speaker Gillett, Secretaries Wallace and Mellon, Senators Frelinghuysen, Edge, Brandegee, Knox, Curtis, Newberry, McKinley, Phipps, Kellogg, General Dawes, Generals Pershing and Harbord, Nick Longworth, Ted Roosevelt, Ed Scobey, Fred Upham, and Dick Crissinger. It was Upham's secondary duty as treasurer of the Republican National Committee to keep the White House supplied with liquor. Out-of-town members who dropped in when they could included Harvey, Gus Creager, Wrigley, Harry Sinclair, and Charlie Schwab. Harding was on a first-name basis with most of them—Harry, Ned, Will, Albert, Charlie, Doc, Jess. But Hughes, Hoover, and Mellon he always addressed as Mr. Secretary. Hoover and Hughes appeared only once and unsuspectingly at such an evening. When Hoover saw the long poker table laid out in the President's study, the Quaker in him was offended at having gambling going on in the White House. Neither he nor Hughes played that evening, and neither was asked again.

Just as she had done years before in the shirt-sleeved atmosphere of Columbus, the Duchess fluttered in the background chattering and mixing drinks. "Ma," Daugherty called her; Ned McLean, "Boss"; Charlie Forbes, "Duchess."

Forbes recalled one of those poker evenings in the White House library half-a-dozen years later, and after his own disgrace:

> We played at a rectangular table in the north end of the room. On this particular occasion the President sat at one end and Will Hays, who was then Postmaster General, at the other. The others were Albert Lasker, at that time chairman of the Shipping Board; Harry Daugherty, Ned McLean, Mrs. McLean, and Mrs. Harding. Mrs. Harding did not play—she often sat with us at poker games but never played. I remember that it was very hot and that Albert Lasker took his coat off, displaying red suspenders two inches wide. I won $397 and Will Hays won. The losers all paid up promptly.
>
> During the game Ned McLean announced that Jack Johnson, the prize fighter, was to be discharged from the Federal Penitentiary at Leavenworth, and either Ned or Lasker exclaimed, "Why, his old mother used to work for me and he has a fine of $1,000 hanging over him and can't pay it." Ned McLean said: "Albert, I'll give $500 and you give $500 and we will pay his fine." The President spoke up: "Don't let that worry you; I'll remit the fine." And the game went on.

The sessions lasted from after dinner until twelve-thirty or one o'clock. Though the Stradivarius-playing Nick Longworth [5] was a Harding intimate, Princess Alice recorded her contempt for the plebeian President and his poker sessions.

[5] Longworth was an accomplished violinist, owned a Stradivarius, and when he was not playing poker with Harding, enjoyed playing in string quartets.

> No rumor could have exceeded the reality [she wrote]; the study was filled with cronies, Daugherty, Jess Smith, Alec Moore, and others, the air heavy with tobacco smoke, trays with bottles containing every imaginable brand of whisky stood about, cards and poker chips ready at hand— a general atmosphere of waistcoat unbuttoned, feet on the desk, and spittoons alongside.

At least once a week the poker cabinet met outside the White House, sometimes at the McLeans' I Street mansion, sometimes at Friendship. The Hughes and the Tafts, and the Wilsons, too (if he dared admit it to himself), impressed Harding to silence. Only with the McLeans of this world could he really relax. Occasionally he spent a poker evening at the Massachusetts Avenue town house of the witty Mrs. Louise Cromwell Brooks, a woman cut from the same cloth of gold as Evalyn McLean but to a slightly more sophisticated pattern. Stepdaughter of Edward Stotesbury, one of the wealthiest men in America, she had divorced her first husband in France in 1919 and returned to the United States with her two children, shuttling between Washington and her country estate, Rainbow Hill at Eccleston, Maryland. She was said to have a collection of love letters written her by General Pershing. During the latter years of her marriage she had met Harding when the Senate elevator they were both riding in had broken down. His roving eye had spotted her, and she had responded affably to his egregious maleness. On one of their poker evenings Louise won a set of White House china when Harding suddenly challenged her to a cold hand, "just the two of us—winner names the stakes." She won and demanded a set of White House dishes. Next day a barrel of china stamped with the mark of the Benjamin Harrison administration arrived at her door.[6]

Harding continued the same restless side bets during his poker sessions that he made on the golf course. The Washington correspondent Louis Seibold on calling one evening to see the President was shown a pearl stickpin that he estimated must have been worth four or five thousand dollars. Harding said that he had won it at a poker game. "I got this spading with the man on my left," Harding told Seibold. "He took it out of his pocket and said, 'I'll put this up against a hundred dollars.' It looked good to me, so I took him up. I won with a four of spades."[7]

If, among the members of his Cabinet, Harding felt the most respect for Hoover, Hughes, and Mellon, he felt closest to Harry Daugherty. A private

[6] On February 14, 1922, Mrs. Brooks became the wife of Brig. Gen. Douglas MacArthur.

[7] Spading consists in betting that one's hand will contain a spade higher than one's opponent's. Samuel Hopkins Adams, to whom Seibold told this story, wondered if anything more was implied in Harding's receiving odds of forty or fifty to one on a side bet.

line ran from the White House to the Attorney General's office and Harding made a habit of calling Daugherty several times a day. The Attorney General was in and out of the White House at all hours, often staying the night. Mrs. Jaffray recalled that at table he eschewed all other dishes and always asked the chef for poached eggs, spinach, and milk. Ned McLean had lent him the little house at 1509 H Street—halfway between the White House and the Department of Justice—that John McLean had used for an office, and Daugherty on his arrival in Washington moved in there with Jess Smith.

When it had first been rumored that Daugherty would be Harding's choice for Attorney General, Mark Sullivan commented on Daugherty's unfitness and added that if Daugherty were as good a friend of the President-elect's as he maintained, he would turn down the offer. Just after Harding in St. Augustine had announced that Daugherty was his choice, Sullivan saw the Attorney General-designate coming down the steps and offered his hand in congratulation, remarking, "Well, you are going to be Attorney General." "Yes," said Daugherty taking the proffered hand with serene good humor, "no thanks to you, Goddam you."

The shadow world of the Ohio lobbyists, the back-room maneuvers of Columbus politicians, though engrossing in themselves, were hardly a preparation for the duties of Attorney General of the United States. At first the prospect of such an exacting routine made Daugherty hesitate. He was of two minds about the job. His practical mind did not want it. He said so then, and he was to continue to say so in his apologia a dozen years later, writing that he had urged Harding not to appoint him and concluding that when he did accept the post it was the most tragic blunder of his life. But his second, vanity-impelled mind, overweighing his doubts, saw the honored office of Attorney General as a vindication for past slights and political defeats, a justification and a triumph. He told his Ohio friends that he wanted to be Attorney General so that he could walk down Columbus's Broad Street and tell Bob Wolfe to go to hell. Sullivan, who wrote at the time that Daugherty was not fit either as a man or a lawyer to become the country's Attorney General, nevertheless always remained convinced that Daugherty in spite of his deficient ethical sense did not want the Attorney Generalship or any other relation to Harding for the purpose of corrupt advantage to himself. "I know Harding," Daugherty explained to Sullivan, "and I know who the crooks are and I want to stand between Harding and them." Such high-mindedness would not of course interfere with the standard operation of rewarding one's friends and punishing one's enemies. Yet Louis Seibold of the *New York World*, Daugherty's most persistent journalistic gadfly at the time, shared Sullivan's opinion. "I have always believed," he wrote fifteen years later, "that Daugherty really wanted to protect Harding but that he was unable to stand off the other fellows who were also demanding rewards which he felt Harding could not refuse."

Daugherty's borrowed house, to be remembered in capital letters as the Little House on H Street, became a social as well as a patronage center. "The love nest," Daugherty called it. Walter Miller, a fifty-year-old colored servant of the McLeans had been dispatched by Ned to take charge as "valet, butler, chambermaid, and everything." Ned also sent a cook, Emma Parker. Armour & Company donated provisions, and liquor needs were supplied by Bill Orr, former secretary to the governor of New York, former fund raiser for the Front Porch campaign and now a wholesale bootlegger. The liquor was stored in John McLean's old wall safe in the front room that he had used as an office.

Although the house was small, with only the office, dining room, and kitchen downstairs, and two bedrooms upstairs, the entertaining was large. Jess Smith told Roxy that it cost him and Daugherty $50,000 a year, divided between them, for household expenses. Shortly after the inaugural Daugherty gave a dinner there for the Hardings and the McLeans. Ned and Jess hit it off very well. "He [Ned] and I think very much alike about a great many things," Jess wrote Roxy. Among the most frequent visitors to the intimate poker evenings were Fall, Doc Sawyer, Charlie Forbes, Harding's new alien property custodian Thomas W. Miller, Daugherty's associate in the Morse pardon case Thomas B. Felder, Harry Sinclair, and Daugherty's Front Porch publicity agent Howard Mannington. Among the occasional visitors were Will Hays, John Ringling, and Carmi Thompson. Daugherty estimated that he had between 50 and 500 visitors daily. They came while he was eating breakfast, at lunchtime, during dinner, and late into the evening—senators, congressmen, regulars from Ohio, those with claims, those with hopes, the insistent, the obsequious.

The lesser claimants Jess took care of, grading their importance, giving some a mere handshake or clap on the back, treating others to luncheons, dinners, baseball games, and shows. For Jess life was beginning at forty-nine, with gold threads among the silver. Although not officially connected with the Justice Department he had an office on the sixth floor close to Daugherty's with the use of an official stenographer and official stationery. Senators called him "Mister" Smith. He, the dry-goods merchant from Washington Court House, had been asked to join the exclusive Metropolitan Club and was even listed in the *Social Register*. Men came to him hat in hand for his yes or his no. He was known, a fixture at Friendship and at I Street. To him Washington seemed no more than a larger Washington Court House. Press pictures of the President opening the baseball season at Griffith Park would show a grinning Jess in the background but *there*. Sullivan remembered seeing him standing at the Shoreham Hotel at the corner of Fifteenth and H streets, then the great crossroads of Washington, "his head up, his features eager and happy, his coat lapels spread back, his thumbs in the armholes of his vest." Spotting an acquaintance across the street, he would call out, "Hey, there, come on over." Always he used his Ohio courthouse greeting: "Whaddaya know?"

"We are all very much better off than we have ever been before," he wrote his Roxy. Divorced in fact and freed from impossible sexual obligations, his relations with her became closer, more intimate. He wrote or telegraphed her almost daily, confided to her the details of his new-rich world. Sometimes he gave her cash, sometimes stock certificates to cash in her name, boasting of the money "we" expected to make on the Dempsey-Carpentier fight films or some other scheme. Every three or four weeks he visited her. His absence always distressed Daugherty who kept sending Jess telegrams saying that he was lonesome without him and asking him to hurry back.

To Jess the White House had become an open house. When Harding was not available, the Duchess was equally glad to see him. She consulted him on clothes, and happily he gave her his expert advice. He had even taken a pre-presidential trip to New York with her to help pick out her inaugural gown.

As First Lady the Duchess grew increasingly testy. Mrs. Jaffray thought she had about as little reserve as any person the housekeeper had ever met. Although it was quite unprecedented, she demanded her own personal Secret Service agent. Colonel Starling assigned Harry Barker to her, and she used him as an errand boy, factotum, and for keeping an alert professional eye on "Wurr'n." Such odd jobs fell to Barker as noting the visitors to Harding's office or bringing Marcia secretly to the White House for an astrological consultation. Having a household staff of 27 made the Duchess suspicious. Some of them, she was convinced, were spying on her. She pored over the monthly bills in detail, complaining to Mrs. Jaffray among other things that the cooks were using too much coffee. On mislaying a diamond sunburst that Harding had given her as an inauguration present and that she wore on her wrinkle-concealing velvet collar, she stormily accused the servants of stealing it, and kept the White House in an uproar until a Secret Service agent found it under a pile of letters. Coolidge and his family she disliked, undoubtedly resenting Grace Coolidge's quiet charm. Harding had broken precedent by inviting his Vice President to his Cabinet meetings. The Duchess was not so magnanimous. When the widow of Sen. John B. Henderson of Missouri wanted to present her stately house and grounds on Sixteenth Street as an official residence of the Vice President, a bill was introduced in Congress to accept it and make an appropriation for the upkeep of house and grounds. "Not a bit of it, not a bit of it!" the Duchess almost shouted at Nicholas Murray Butler when she heard the news. "I am going to have that bill defeated. Do you think I am going to have those Coolidges living in a house like that? A hotel apartment is plenty good for them!"

In Washington the Hardings attended the Reverend Doctor William S. Abernathy's Calvary Baptist Church. On his first Sunday in the White House Harding had skipped church to play golf and the papers had duly noted it. The Duchess did not let him try that again. She kept a tight rein, even in small things. Whenever he felt the need for a chaw of tobacco he had to dodge upstairs. Sometimes when the craving overwhelmed him he would secretly crumple a cigarette and chew it. "She says cigars are all right, but it's undignified to chew," he told Louis Seibold regretfully.

For the Duchess, surrounded by servants and secretaries, it was an effulgent thing to be the First Lady of the United States, to have new varieties of sweet peas and roses called after her, to give her name to the color "Harding blue." Yet there were uneasy recurring moments in the White House when she felt she was tempting fate. She wrote to her former delivery boy Norman Thomas that now she and her husband had reached the summit of ambition she was very much afraid. Never did she forget her old boys at the *Star*. In such natural relationships she was at her best. Weekly she visited disabled soldiers and sailors in the hospital, moving among them on her swollen ankles with crusty good humor, more than welcome, for once fulfilling her matriarchal role with dignity and without harshness.

For Harding, pomp soon gave way to circumstances. With only his meager Ohio background in history, economics, and law to enlighten him on public questions, he faced them with bewilderment, and his self-doubt expanded. Coming back from the Chevy Chase golf course one afternoon with Judge John Barton Payne, he told him: "Judge, I don't think I'm big enough for the Presidency." In the same deprecatory mood he admitted to the newspaper columnist David Lawrence that he was a small-town man of limited talents. "Oftentimes, as I sit here," he said, pointing to his desk, "I don't seem to grasp that I am President." Tariff, taxes, foreign affairs blurred in his mind. He announced that he was for a "two-cent tariff," whatever that was. He told a speechlessly astonished Bruce Bliven that "the United States should adopt a protective tariff of such a character as will help the struggling industries of Europe to get on their feet." When Arthur S. Draper, the foreign correspondent of the *New York Herald Tribune*, called at the White House after an extended tour of Europe, expecting an interview, Harding begged off. Beckoning toward his political secretary, Judson Welliver, he told Draper plaintively: "I don't know anything about this European stuff. You and Jud get together and he can tell me later; he handles these matters for me." Following the interview Draper and Welliver had a long lunch together, the secretary complaining how difficult it was to get the President interested in foreign affairs. Harding now let Welliver write most of his speeches. He had been surprised and hurt at the sneers about his oratory on which he had always prided himself and which Mencken had labeled "Gamalielese." Now he was beginning to doubt even his own voice. "I really never thought much about 'style,' " Harding admitted in May, "until the critics got after my nomination for the Presidency. I suppose I am too old to materially change it now."

The crowds that came each day at noon to share his presence and shake his hand were a reassurance to him, and he expanded in their presence. He devoted much time to answering his unsolicited private correspondence, often working late at night to reply personally to the juvenile or crackpot letters that should have been handled by some third assistant secretary, if at all. He promised to buy tickets from an eleven-year-old boy raising funds for a swimming pool, and recalled the Caledonia creek he used to swim in. To the maker of Dodson's Bird Houses and Famous Sparrow Trap, who wished to convert the White House grounds to a bird sanctuary, he replied with thanks, asking the inventor to postpone his project "for the present." He declined a silver Persian kitten born on Inauguration Day. A female schoolteacher begged him "in the name of Jesus" and as his body was "the Temple of the Holy Ghost" to quit the use of tobacco and "let me know when you quit." He complimented her sincerity but did not "look upon the habit with quite so much horror as you do and think you attach over-much importance to my moderate use of it." Harding's files became clogged with such correspondence and his hundreds of replies. Nicholas Murray Butler, coming to the White House one evening, found him in his private office staring at a huge pile of letters which he had not had time to examine and which he said with a groan that he must go through. Butler asked if he might look at some of them, and Harding told him to take any he pleased. Those Butler glanced through he found trivial, and protested that it was ridiculous for a President to spend his time answering them. He himself would never have bothered. "I suppose so," Harding said, "but I am not fit for this office and should never have been here."

Harding's developing conception of the Presidency was more that of a ceremonial office like the French President's or the King of England's. He felt himself most a President on such formally martial occasions as when he stood under the shadow of the flagship *Pennsylvania's* fourteen-inch guns and told the massed bluejackets that the United States wanted only "that which is righteously our own, and, by the eternal, we mean to have that!" He saw the office of Chief Executive as a presence that should embody the nation, without needing to be concerned with such mundane problems as tariffs, railroad strikes, and the fall in farm prices. As a ceremonial President he would have found fulfillment and a release from his restlessness in traveling about the country to officiate at formal and dedicatory exercises, review the fleet, and inspect Army posts. His first official trip from Washington he took in April when he left for New York with a caravan of ten automobiles to dedicate a statue of Simon Bolivar—a journey that caused Colonel Starling a dismaying moment when New York's Mayor "Red Mike" Hylan managed to horn in on the procession and persuade Harding to plant an unscheduled tree just below Columbus Circle.

In May the freighter *Wheaton* brought back the bodies of 5,212 soldiers, sailors, marines, and nurses who had died in the war to the Hoboken Pier, and Harding arrived on the *Mayflower* in an early-morning fog for the dock-side service. On the voyage down the Potomac he had composed his funeral address. Such neo-Periclean orations he still preferred to write himself. At the huge and cavernous dock shed he, with the Duchess beside him, walked silently past the rows of flag-draped pine boxes while a muffled band played Chopin's "Funeral March" and the relatives of the dead stood in the background. After a moment of silence and a prayer, Harding, his face pale and set, stepped forward to speak. There were tears in his eyes when he looked at the massed coffins, and his voice choked as he read his short address:

> These had served [he concluded], which is the supreme inspiration in living. They have earned everlasting gratitude, which is the supreme solace in dying. . . . One's words fail, his understanding is halted, his emotions are stirred beyond control when contemplating these thousands of beloved dead. I find a hundred thousand sorrows touching my heart, and there is a ringing in my ears, like an admonition eternal, an insistent call, "It must not be again! It must not be again!" God grant that it will not be, and let a practical people join in co-operation with God to the end that it shall not be.

Harding was more than proud of this particular speech, and later recorded it for the Victor Phonograph Company.

School children holding flags lined the streets near Brooklyn Bridge as Harding crossed to Manhattan later in the morning in a fog that had turned to rain. In the evening he was the guest of honor at a banquet given by the Society of Political Science. "Some may complain of my style of grammar," he remarked rather plaintively at one point, "but I guess you understand me." Afterward, still in evening clothes, he went with a party to the new offices of the *Herald Tribune,* and to demonstrate that he was still a newspaperman, peeled off his coat in the composing room and made up three columns for the morning edition.

He made other ceremonial addresses: at Valley Forge; before the National League of Masonic Clubs; at the Elks' memorial service; on Memorial Day at Arlington National Cemetery. His warm and reassuring presence inspired confidence that normalcy was indeed about to return—normalcy, that awkward coined word that nevertheless so well described the general longing for the days before 1914.

Two and a half years had elapsed since the Armistice, and the United States—having rejected the Versailles Treaty warp with the League of Nations woof—was still technically at war with Germany and the disintegrated Austro-Hungarian Empire. Two and a half years of growing disillusionment followed the herd unity of the war years with its artificially sustained apocalyptic belief that we were fighting "to keep the world safe for democracy." The slogan had become like a last year's circus poster, faded and tattered on a crumbling wall. So far the postwar years had brought only change and unrest. Behind the other phenomena lay the malaise of inflation, the pervading psychological uneasiness that accompanies a fluctuating currency.

In 1914 the national debt had been a little over a billion dollars. By 1920 it had risen to 24 billion. The average annual wage of a steel worker was $925 in 1915. By 1920 it had risen to $2,173. Retail prices continued to climb after the war, reaching their peak in November, 1920. The value of the dollar had declined to forty-five cents. Nevertheless America, on the gold standard, would remain on the gold standard.

Sitting in their mahogany-paneled room in New York, the national directors of the Federal Reserve Bank had decided by formal resolution to deflate the currency. Such a drastic economic policy was still politically possible after the first World War as it would not be after the second. Deflation as the classical remedy for wartime inflation and distortion of production meant cuts in wages as well as prices. It meant a period of unemployment, of business malaise, a situation that in the innocence of those pre-Keynesian days seemed unavoidable, if hopefully—as indeed it turned out—temporary. After the wartime rise in farm prices and agricultural products, the optimistically-mortgaged farmers were particularly hard hit by deflation, above all the cattle farmers of the Middle West. Small-town merchants were teetering on bankruptcy. Workers who saw their wages cut were not reconciled by drops in prices, nor were the unemployed. The actual average income was declining.

To meet these gathering events, domestic and foreign, Harding felt compelled after his inauguration to call a special session of Congress for early April. The League issue still refused to be harmonized, the voices of the irreconcilables ringing as loudly as ever. Knox was ready to by-pass the Versailles Treaty and had prepared a separate resolution that would have merely repealed the 1917 declaration of war. Hoover and Hughes and Root still continued hopeful of America's accepting the Treaty along with the League reservations. In preparing his first message to Congress Harding again attempted to appease both sides with his vague notion of "an association of nations." The night before he delivered his speech, the Duchess and Daugherty on going over the text had insisted on deleting a paragraph they considered might commit the United States to the actual League by inference.

On April 12, in a new dark cutaway that his tailor had deftly designed to conceal his increasing paunchiness, Harding addressed the special session in the House of Representatives Chamber under the matriarchal eye of the Duchess in the balcony. Her marcel glittering under her aggressively feathered hat, she sat in the front row with Evalyn McLean and Judson Welliver, where they were soon joined by Doctor Sawyer, diminutively splendid in his blue dress uniform. The President looked vigorous, assured. His voice was not as precise as Wilson's, but it was warmer, and he brought cheers from the floor and galleries when he proclaimed that "in the existing League of Nations, world-governing with its super-powers, this republic will have no part." There was considerably less applause when he announced that "we make no surrender of our hope and aim for an association to promote peace in which we must heartily join." Increasingly sensitive to his own prerogatives—and undoubtedly to the surprise of his old colleagues—he told the senators and congressmen that he was willing to accept Knox's peace resolution only if a clause about treaty making was omitted, since for the Senate "to assume the function of the Executive" in foreign affairs would be as objectionable as was "the failure of the Executive" under Wilson.

As a message it was the expected declaration of Republican administration policy, containing no surprises. Harding called for a cutting of government expenditures, lowering of taxes, and the repeal of the excess-profits tax, "mature consideration" of permanent tariff legislation, a lowering of railroad rates and promotion of agricultural interests. One of his most important requests—several times rejected by earlier congressmen—was for the national budget system. His most personally cherished projects were a "great merchant marine" and a Department of Public Welfare. There was applause, then silence when he told the legislators that "Congress ought to wipe out the stain of barbaric lynching." Even the *New York Times*, no enthusiast for Harding, admitted that his address "where it is definite is sound." And where the *Times* found it indefinite it left room for the belief that "wise counsels will prevail."

Unfortunately for Harding's solacing conviction that legislative initiative should come from Congress, neither the House nor the Senate in spite of their top-heavy Republican majorities was capable of demonstrating more than a haphazard inclination for leadership. The leaders themselves were going or gone. In the Senate the fading autocratic Lodge in bringing down the League had shot his own bolt. Knox was ailing. Penrose, his clothes hanging scarecrow-like on his wasting body, had the mark of death on him. A babble of Western insurgent voices echoing the Progressive past contradicted the suaver tones of the Hanna and McKinley-derived Easterners. There was even less applied direction in the somewhat more conservative House of Representatives. Speaker Gillett lacked his old power, and Nicholas Longworth on the way up to replace him, for all his old Ohio associations, was not politically a Harding man.

In the disintegration of congressional leadership Harding—if he had been anyone else but himself—could have seized the reins of government as the unchallenged leader. A Wilson would have brandished the whip, a Teddy Roosevelt would have cracked it over congressional heads. But to Harding the reins themselves were for other hands. As Welliver admitted plaintively to William Allen White, Harding "never appreciated the extent or the effectiveness of the moral force he might have wielded." Another of his secretaries, William H. Crawford, felt in the spring of 1921 that the President had voluntarily allowed the power of the executive to fall lower than it had for the last twenty-five years.

Few American Presidents have personally occupied themselves more than Harding with questions of postmasterships and such minor patronage. After eight years of Democratic rule there were indeed a quarter of a million jobs available, but there were also 4 million overeager aspirants. And the President who had always hated to say No became all too glumly aware that patronage created ten times the number of enemies that it did friends. Among the millions of requests were thousands from unsuspected kinsmen all over America. "I never knew how many Hardings there were until I was elected to the Presidency," Harding wrote to Harvey in London. "I think there are about 8,334 in the United States who are available for public service. Up to the present time I have not named any of them." Daugherty and Hays were the administration's chief patronage dispensers. Wilson, after replacing Republican by Democratic postmasters, had prudently placed his new appointees under civil service. Harding by a presidential order now removed civil service restrictions from 13,000 postmasterships.[8] Hays in spite of, or perhaps because of, his preoccupation with patronage came to feel that the whole spoils system was "not a party asset but a party liability." He announced that he would "humanize" the postal service, and in fact conducted it in an efficient and non-political manner. In the Cabinet Hughes, Hoover, Mellon, and Wallace stood for the merit system, with Daugherty, Davis, and Fall opposed. Daugherty persuaded Harding to appoint Elmer Dover, a Columbus regular and Hanna's old secretary, as Assistant Secretary of the Treasury in charge of Custom Service and Internal Revenue. Taking up Hays's slogan in reverse, Dover swore that he would "Hardingize" the Custom and Revenue

[8] For "greater efficiency" Harding arranged to allow the selection of postmasters from any one of the first three on a qualified civil service list.

Service, and did so with such gusto that the decorous Mellon threatened to resign if the bombastic Assistant Secretary remained. Fall's Department of the Interior still managed to retain a comparatively high percentage of men trained in specialized fields. It was in the Prohibition Department that the spoils system really came into its own, for Wheeler as lobbyist for the Anti-Saloon League had managed to exempt the Bureau from civil service rules and to have it included in the Treasury rather than the Justice Department. Through his hold on Prohibition Commissioner Roy Haynes, Wheeler personally checked all appointments to his pet preserve. The 1,500 prohibition agents and all other employees had to be cleared through him.

If Harding had imagined that the Republicans in both houses of Congress would work harmoniously with him, his special session soon showed him otherwise. The top-heavy majority at once split into regional groups. "Now, Bob, be good," he had begged La Follette on his last visit to the Senate before his inauguration. "I'll be busy making you be good," La Follette warned him. At the start of the session Fighting Bob and Norris with Kenyon of Iowa and Arthur Capper of Kansas organized a farm bloc of 27 senators that held the balance of power in the Senate. Raising the old populist cry of exploitation by Eastern bankers, backed by Secretary Wallace, they demanded that the government come to the farmers' financial rescue. Their angry voices were opposed by Hoover and Mellon, and at one more remove by Harding himself. "The farmer," he said optimistically, "requires no special favors at the hands of the government. All he needs is a fair chance."

"America should put its house in order," Harding told the new Congress, meaning by this a reduction in government spending and wartime taxation, a lowering of prices, and a similar—if less publicized—reduction in wages. But the "normalcy" Congress showed little inclination to put anything in order. Lacking in intelligent and determined leadership, the session drifted into summer. Recommendations of Harding and his Cabinet—"wise and urgent" the *Times* called them—were shunted aside or postponed. Insurgent Westerners, denied aid for their farms, were in no mood to repeal the excess-profits tax or reduce the income surtax of the wealthy and the tax revision was delayed again and again. A makeshift tariff bill was passed, obviously temporary; and a temporary immigration bill, obviously permanent, to cut the admission of the homeless and tempest-tossed to a fraction and eliminate Orientals altogether. Harding's Department of Public Welfare and his request for an expanded merchant marine were rejected out of hand. The Congress did not even manage by the time of its vacation adjournment in August to bring an official end to the state of war with Germany and disintegrated Austria-Hungary. Congressional talk and delay, representatives and senators with one eye on the main chance and the other on the next election, appeared in a different light to President Harding than to Senator Harding.

In simple truth [he wrote to Jennings at the year's end in a mood of despondent frankness], I get discouraged sometimes about the stability of popular government. I come in contact with the abject surrender of public men to what appears to be about one-half of one per cent of the voters to whom they look to their commission to public service. What the country needs more than anything else is a House and Senate for ten years which gives (sic) at least as much thought to the welfare of the Republic as is given to individual candidates for re-election. Nothing so disheartens me as to have an extended conference with men in responsible places, hear them admit of the correctness of a policy or position, and then frankly say it is impossible to go through with the policy or maintain the position and be assured of re-election. I have concluded that I would vastly prefer a limited career with the consciousness of having done the right thing than to hold on to the constitutional limit by playing to the favor of those who do the fake work under our political system. My own disappointment with the public estimate of me lies in the fact that so many seem to think I can take a whip and show Congress where to head in.

Averse though he might be to cracking whips or twisting arms, he continued to show himself jealous of the prerogatives of the Presidency and determined to defend them against any congressional encroachments. He, Warren Harding, the country boy from Blooming Grove, was in the succession of Washington and Lincoln and McKinley and Roosevelt. The thought both awed and consoled him. Nor did he fail to resent what he was well aware of, his man-of-straw reputation as a tool of the senior senators. "I think perhaps it has been of some advantage to start into office so poorly appraised," he wrote Jennings in the same letter, "because one does not need to accomplish very much to find himself somewhat marked up in value."

The irreconcilables among the senators were stunned early in May to learn that the President had agreed to let American representatives participate in the London sessions of the Supreme Council of the Peace Conference, the Council of Ambassadors, and the Reparations Commission. When later in the month Senator Borah tacked an amendment onto the annual Naval Appropriations Bill "requesting and authorizing" the President to hold a conference with Japan and Great Britain on the subject of naval disarmament, his Senate colleagues adopted it unanimously. Harding, however, considered the amendment an infringement of his prerogatives and demanded that it be removed. Later he would become so enthusiastic about holding a naval disarmament conference that he would consider the idea his own, but he was not going to accept any directives about foreign affairs from Borah or the Senate. Until an innocuous substitute replaced the Borah amendment, he refused to sign the bill.

Harding's most open challenge to Congress came over a bill to grant the soldiers of the World War a bonus. Demanded by the many unemployed veterans, belligerently backed by the American Legion, the bonus bill— called with virtuous euphony the Soldiers' Adjusted Compensation Bill— was not a measure most election-conscious congressmen would care to oppose. To Harding, pledged to deflation and a balanced budget, such a measure was against his whole conception of normalcy. It would, he told Congress, hinder readjustment and restoration (the alliteration he found unavoidable) and imperil the financial stability of the country. So strongly did he feel about this "treasury raid" that he appeared in person before the Senate and spoke against what otherwise seemed certain of passing both houses. By his independent action Harding deferred the day of the bonus, but he stirred up much bitterness among the veterans and their congressional supporters. Congressman Bourke Cockran of New York was so incensed that he attempted to bring a resolution of censure against Harding accusing him of acting in an unconstitutional manner by thrusting "the personality of the Chief Executive into the grave deliberations of the representatives of the people."

Contrasted with the disintegrating and diminished stature of the Congress, the personality of the Chief Executive had indeed grown during his first months in office. His imperturbable presence in the face of the depression inspired confidence and hope—if not among the unemployed, the farmers, and the ex-soldiers, at least in the middle-class-minded majority. After six months in office Harding was beginning to take on the McKinley image, assuming something of the earlier Ohioan's bronze patina.

One of Harding's early friendly gestures had been to restore the twice-a-week White House meetings with the press that Wilson had given up. Wilson had detested subjecting himself to the overt criticism of such meetings. Harding, the old newspaperman, liked the reporters and they liked him. Press conferences in the Oval Room had the happy atmosphere of reunions. Harding was open with reporters, answering all questions, his only qualification being that they must not quote him directly—although after one embarrassing gaffe on foreign affairs he switched to written questions submitted in advance. They, with rare exceptions, were friendly to him. In July a group of newspapermen presented him with a chair carved from wood taken from the U.S.S. *Revenge,* the "first warship of the American Navy," dating from the Revolution. "It goes without saying that I am delighted to have this token of the esteem of the members of the Fourth Estate," he told them in his speech of thanks. "It touches me rather deeply. . . . I am only the publisher of an interior daily paper, sometimes called a country paper. But if I had my life to live over, with all the experiences that have come to me, I would not change my profession or my occupation."

On July 2 while on a golfing weekend with Frelinghuysen in New Jersey he signed Congress's joint resolution terminating the state of war with the Imperial German government. "Doc" Smithers, a White House aide, had brought the document from Washington and had had to wait an hour and forty-three minutes while the call went out for Harding on the links. Trailed by Frelinghuysen, the President finally arrived, jaunty in a Palm Beach suit, white shirt with removable gold studs, and a red-and-green bow tie. As Harding read through the vellum document, the Frelinghuysens' wire-haired terrier Patsy kept sniffling at his white shoes. When he had finished reading he went into the living room where Frelinghuysen's wife had cleared a small table for him. Writing quickly, he signed his name at the bottom of the page, and a drop of ink fell on the "G." of his signature. "That's all," he said, getting up from the table on his way back to the golf course. The World War had come to an end.

Mark Sullivan by the autumn was pleasantly surprised to find Harding so much better than he had expected in Chicago at the convention, and thought that the President had "undersold himself to the public." If he had not been dominating, neither had he allowed himself to be dominated, and Sullivan credited him with "good housekeeping and business management," adding in his optimism that "no one doubts that the present administration will make a record never equaled before."

September 22 found him writing to George Harvey in London:

> Harding is going very strong. He grows in popularity all the time. But with the Republican majority in the House and Senate it is quite another story. The public makes a clear distinction between the Republican Administration—meaning by that Harding and his Cabinet—and, on the other hand, the Republican Congress. With the former there is general approval; with the latter general disgust.
>
> The chief basis of the disgust with Congress is the failure, at the end of several months, to have written either a tariff bill or a taxation measure. In point of fact, the present session has passed a good many important measures, and under ordinary circumstances would be regarded as having done a good deal of work. But the circumstances are not ordinary. Harding and the Republican party promised tariff legislation and tax legislation. Congress has failed to live up to the promise. Not only that, but the half-hearted, tentative, and rather unintelligent proposals, as respects tariff and taxation, which have come out of Congress so far have satisfied nobody.
>
> The cause of the trouble lies in a total falldown of Republican leadership in the House and Senate. There is no leadership whatsoever. The House is merely a mass meeting. . . . In the Senate, Lodge has all the

official attributes of leadership, but he doesn't seem to know how to put it across. I suspect the real trouble with Lodge is that he is old and tired. . . . Further than this, various personal equations impair the leadership of the other Senators who ought to be leaders. . . . All in all, things in the Senate are very much in a mess. Harding and his Cabinet are deeply concerned about it. Harding is repeatedly urged to assert leadership himself; but both by temperament and principle is disinclined to do so.

Secretary Hoover with his more intimate Cabinet view was equally impressed by Harding's early months. Though years later he was to conclude in his *Memoirs* that the President had neither "the experience nor the intellectual quality that the position needed," he told H. H. Kohlsaat at a dinner in August, 1921: "I want to do my part to make Harding's administration the agency to put the world on its feet. I believe at the end of his term of eight years the world will be normal and Harding will do it."

Hoover was conscious, then and afterward, that Harding "deeply wanted to make a name as President." Fixed in Harding's mind since his boyhood was his awe of the august office of the President. In the country he loved so well he had reached that highest of positions that his mother (like so many mothers) in her pride and love had predicted for him years ago. He was the first man of the United States, and in time to come his name would be affixed to the roster of the Presidents as long as the Republic endured.

Harding, in his cherished image of the Presidency, was capable of a dignity beyond his natural self. It happened that a few weeks after his inaugural a group that included the editor of the *Nation* Oswald Garrison Villard, and the Catholic labor priest Monsignor John Augustine Ryan, had come to the White House to see him about a pardon for the Socialist leader Eugene Debs, then serving ten years in Atlanta Penitentiary for seeking to obstruct the conduct of the war. Wilson had an academic intolerance toward anyone who opposed him. He had put Debs in jail, and he insisted that as long as he was President he would never be pardoned. Harding, with his instinctive good nature, had allowed Debs to come to Washington unguarded for an interview,[9] and planned to release the gentle-minded Socialist—who had already served three years—on July 4. But when the patriotic groups, headed by the American Legion, got wind of this they protested against any lenience for a man they considered a traitor. Daugherty and the Duchess were opposed to freeing Debs. Harding hesitated.

[9] On his arrival in Washington Debs was met at the station by Jess Smith who took him to the Attorney General's office. After the interview Jess drove him back, asking on the way if there was anything he needed. Debs said that he liked quill toothpick and hadn't been able to get any since he went to Atlanta. Smith had the driver stop, dashed into a store, and came out with a huge bundle of toothpicks.

The Debs group, including a number of social workers, had been joined almost in front of the White House by William Allen White. Confronting Harding, Villard, Monsignor Ryan, and White each spoke briefly in favor of Debs's pardon. The President, caught between the Duchess and the deep sea, told them he understood the case and would give it his immediate attention. At this one of the more blatant female social workers interrupted: "Mr. President, that's no way to answer us. We demand a yes-or-no answer now!"

> We were shocked [White wrote]. One of us tried for a second or two to disavow the woman's outburst. But the President straightened himself up. The stoop seemed to come out of his shoulders. A certain gentle dignity enveloped him. He said:
> "My dear woman: you may demand anything you please out of Warren Harding. He will not resent it. But the President of the United States has the right to keep his own counsel, and the office I occupy forbids me to reply to you as I should like to do if I were elsewhere!"

Conscious of the worth of his office, the President of the United States was anxious to be worthy of it. But under the bronze-patinaed presidential image Warren Harding the man grew restive. He longed to be the old W. G., one of the boys, on the golf course, at the poker table, in the bedroom. The White House—half museum and half grand hotel with its long corridors, formal rooms, and clutter of servants—gave him no sheltering privacy. Always he was under the eye of the ushers, the secretaries. Always the Secret Service lurked discreetly in the background. When he was not compulsively playing golf or poker, he busied himself with the trivia of office, pored through the speeches that Welliver and others had written for him. Ike Hoover thought that Harding slept less than any other President he had known. He read no books. The world of art and music was barred to him. His theater visits were confined to the Gayety Burlesque where he watched the girlies from a special box that concealed him from the public. Alone, resourceless, he had not even the consoling relaxation of a hobby like the innocuous if adolescent one of collecting stamps. Sometimes the evening loneliness of the White House—a jail, he called it in his gloomier moments—would overwhelm him and he would flee, to Friendship, to Daugherty's little house, to Mrs. Cromwell's, anywhere to get away. Samuel Hopkins Adams recorded an evening in June, 1921, when Doc Sawyer was holding a little poker party in his suite at the Willard. George Christian, Charlie Forbes, a general, and several high officials were gathered round the chip-strewn table when suddenly the door was thrown open to show the President standing on the threshold. "You fellows can't sneak off and have a party without me," Harding told them in mock aggrieved tones. "I'm here for the evening!"

Later in the year a group of newspapermen who had covered the Front
Porch campaign were holding a reunion dinner in a private dining room
of the National Press Club when an awed Negro attendant appeared to
tell them that the President of the United States was outside and wanted
to join them. Harding spent the rest of the evening there, quietly, free
from the Duchess and among familiar masculine faces.

As long ago he used his railroad passes to still his restlessness, so now as
President he traveled whenever he could evolve a reason. Weekends he
often slipped away from the humid capital aboard the *Mayflower*, usually
taking with him Daugherty, Jess Smith, the McLeans, and kindred boisterous spirits. One weekend he spent with Daugherty at Philander Knox's
farm, Elsmore, near Valley Forge. On July 24 he joined the annual excursion that Edison, Henry Ford, and the Firestones had organized some years
back to get away from "fictitious civilization" in order to experiment in
"Nature's laboratory." Begun as a modest expedition by the naturalist
John Burroughs, the excursion after his death had grown to a safari of
50 automobiles. This year Nature's laboratory—held at Harvey Firestone's
Maryland property, Masons'. Woods, near sluggish Licking Creek—even
had a radio car with a government cipher operator to keep in touch with
the State Department. Edsel Ford and his wife, the younger Firestones,
George Christian, and the reluctant Colonel Starling with his Secret
Service detail were among those fleeing the fictiveness of civilization.
For three days they lived in primitive luxury under canvas, used portable
washstands, slept on canvas cots. Harding took walks with Edison and
Ford, chopped wood, and "bloviated," while Colonel Starling cursed the
flies. A snapshot shows the President in his undershirt shaving under a
tree, gross at the waist, flabby. In his late fifties he was becoming an old
man.

On Sunday Harding attended a pine-grove church service under the
minatory eye of Cincinnati's Methodist Bishop William Anderson, also
one of Nature's laboratory technicians and one who was determined to
have the President sign a total-abstinence pledge. The following weekend
found him aboard the *Mayflower* bound for Plymouth, Massachusetts, to
consecrate the three hundredth anniversary of the landing of the Pilgrims
—held a year late because of technical difficulties in moving Plymouth
Rock. For the occasion and to avoid recurrent embarrassing questions
from tourists, the Rock had finally been shifted from its old high-and-dry
position and placed at the water level where the Pilgrims at least *could*
have landed on it.

Cruising through the Cape Cod Canal, accompanied by the U.S.
Submarine Chaser 408, the *Mayflower* arrived within the long blue arc of
Plymouth Bay outlined by warships and dotted with sailboats. Harding
was piped ashore near the Rock and first greeted by a delegation of

foreign-born school children to whom he presented medals for excellence in English. He seemed "almost buoyantly happy" as he moved among the awe-struck children. For it was in such moments that he felt himself most the President, with the cares of office behind him and only the unencumbered glory left.

After presenting the medals and chatting with the children, the smiling stately President made his way to the temporary wooden stand on Cole's Hill where, flanked by the glum, granite-faced Vice President Coolidge and the vulpine grinning features of the governor of Massachusetts, Channing Cox, he reviewed the Tercentenary Parade. Then in the evening, more restively, he sat through *The Pilgrim Spirit*, the pageant written by Harvard's professor of drama, George Pierce Baker, listened to "the Voice from the Rock," and watched the eight historic scenes culminate in a red-cloaked Priscilla, John Alden, and Miles Standish landing on the Rock and kneeling in prayer—while a battery of searchlights from the warships in the harbor swept illuminating shafts up and down the sky.

Between Harding's election and his inauguration, hundreds and then thousands of letters arrived at the White House addressed to the new President. They were taken to the White House Mail Room where they were opened and sorted by the supervisor, Ira Smith. Not long after Harding took office Smith came across a long envelope addressed in a spidery handwriting and marked "personal." Enclosed was a second envelope on which was written: "This is a confidential and private letter and is to be handed immediately to the President." In it Smith found a letter from Nan Britton with several snapshots of Elizabeth Ann that Nan thought resembled Harding, love messages, and the usual indirect appeal for money. Smith showed the letter to Christian who told him for God's sake to burn it or they would both lose their jobs. Two more letters from Nan arrived, and Smith dutifully destroyed them unopened.

When Nan received no replies, she wrote to Jim Sloan. He carried her message to the President. Harding, his prudence overcome by the sting of desire, told him to make arrangements for Nan to come to Washington. Still complaining of her "general rundown condition" since Elizabeth Ann's birth, Nan had left the child with the Willits—who had formally adopted her on March 15—to go to New York where she planned to take a part-time job and study journalism at Columbia. All this she wrote to her lover, and he from the enforced celibacy of the White House begged her to come to him. Before settling down in New York she paid him her first post-Presidential visit, arriving in Washington on a June afternoon. Sloan met her at the station, a buoyantly girlish figure wearing a floppy picture hat and a black crepe dress trimmed with cerise braid. They drove directly to the White House, entering by the main portico and passing through the hall leading to the Cabinet Room where they had to wait a few minutes. Then a nervous Harding entered alone through a door just behind his official chair at the head of the table. With only a restrained greeting, and telling Sloan to stay in the Cabinet Room, he led Nan through a small adjoining room with a single window—an anteroom, he explained—and then through another door into his private office. Once there he took her in his arms, somewhat circumspectly, for just beyond the long windows sentries were parading back and forth on guard duty. Though they marched with faces rigidly to the front, Harding observed to Nan that some people seemed to have eyes in the sides of their heads.

> Whereupon [Nan wrote], he introduced me to the one place where, he said, he thought we *might* share kisses in safety. This was a small closet in the anteroom, evidently a place for hats and coats, but entirely empty most of the times we used it, for we repaired there many times in the course of my visits to the White House, and in the darkness of a space not more than five feet square the President of the United States and his adoring sweetheart made love.

After they returned to the private office, Nan looking about her noticed a miniature of Harding's mother on his desk and beside it a vase of flowers. Opposite the desk was an open-grate fireplace where, he told her, he burned her letters "after he had committed their message to his heart." Passion spent, they talked. With an older man's jealousy he began to question her about the young men she met and begged her not to go off and marry any of them. Then they discussed how they might best continue writing to each other. Sloan was planning to leave the Secret Service to become Washington manager of the brokerage house of Samuel Ungerleider & Company.[10] Harding told her to seal her future letters in an envelope addressed to his White House valet, Arthur Brooks.

With Brooks as discreet intermediary, no further letters went astray. Whenever she wrote, Nan would always enclose a note in an outer envelope instructing Brooks to hand the inner envelope immediately to the President "in accordance with the President's request." She signed her notes to Brooks "E. Baye," as she had also done to Sloan, E. Baye being derived from Eagle Bay where she had first met Sloan as a courier in the summer of 1920. She agreed to destroy all her lover's letters and, unlike Carrie, she kept her word.

Again in August and on subsequent occasions up until January, 1923, Nan was smuggled in to Harding in the White House. Each time they made makeshift love in the darkness of the coat closet on the floor among

[10] Harding's old liquor-dealer friend of Columbus with the coming of Prohibition had set himself up as a broker instead of a bootlegger and at Harding's request had opened a Washington branch.

the rubbers, and afterward sat and talked on a dilapidated leather sofa in the anteroom. Harding always gave her several hundred dollars, warning her to be careful about spending it, so that people would not talk. If Sloan happened to be away, another Secret Service agent, Walter Ferguson, met her. Growing less cautious as her visits grew more frequent, she asked to see the White House itself, and Harding recklessly allowed Ferguson to show her through the reception rooms, the private dining room, and other rooms usually banned to the public.

Once the Duchess nearly surprised them in their makeshift rendezvous. Ferguson, on Harding's instructions, had gone to the station to meet Nan on her way from Chicago. The train was an hour late. When the two finally arrived at the White House through the back entrance, Harding was waiting for them in his office, boiling over with frustration and anxiety. "Where have you been?" he shouted red-faced at Ferguson. Finally mollified enough to lead Nan to the coat closet, he left Ferguson on guard outside the office door. The Secret Service man had not been there five minutes when the Duchess rushed up, arms akimbo and eyes ablaze. When she demanded that he stand aside, he refused, barring the door and telling her it was a strict Secret Service rule that no one could enter there. Furiously she dashed round to the front entrance through Christian's anteroom office. As soon as she disappeared, Ferguson banged on the closet door to warn Harding, then hustled Nan out the side door, telling her to go to his car and wait for him. Christian, suspecting what was up, took his time about admitting the Duchess, and when she finally burst into Harding's office he was at his desk and there was no sign of Nan. Taking this in at a glance, she rushed out the same side door she had been forbidden to enter, glaring at Ferguson as she brushed past him. Then, spinning round, she returned to the White House by the back, private path. Ferguson decided that it must have been the Duchess's Secret Service man, Barker, who had tipped her off. Later Harding had to face the Duchess alone. "She makes life hell for me!" he once told Nan. Undoubtedly she made it that day.

While Harding as best he could was continuing his fugitive relationship with Nan, Tryon in Marion was developing an autumnal romance with Alice Severns, a buxom local woman five years younger than his own son. In the prospering afterglow of the election Tryon had engaged her as a part-time helper to clean his office, act as an attendant for his few patients, and typewrite his occasional letters. For some weeks after the inaugural he had welcomed reporters to the fusty office. Sitting in his broken-springed "sleepy hollow" chair before the patent gas radiator, he reminisced at great if not wholly accurate length about his President-son and the old days of Blooming Grove and Caledonia. At first the reporters found these great "human interest" stories, but after a time they gave up dropping in to hear the repetitious tales of four-year-old Winnie charging his first pair of red-topped boots at Day's general store, of the enterprising young Warren who painted barns and worked for the Toledo & Central Railroad, of Tryon himself when he had courted Phoebe on a sleighride under the buffalo robe. His day as a reflected celebrity fading, Tryon began to console himself with the unmarried Alice. Like his son, he had always had an eye for the ladies, and even at seventy-seven his sight in that respect was undimmed. On August 12, without telling Daisy or anyone in the family, he and Alice eloped, leaving secretly for Windsor, Ontario, just across the river from Detroit. Finding that they could not get an immediate marriage license in Canada, they drove back to Monroe, Michigan, a quick-marriage town just across the Ohio state line much favored by Ohio elopers. After filling in a license at the Monroe courthouse in which he subtracted ten years from his age and ungallantly added ten to Alice's, Tryon, beaming and uxorious, passed round cigars to officials and even sent a box of them to the office of the local daily paper. Since there was no Baptist church available they were married by the Reverend Doctor Frank T. Knowles in the Monroe Presbyterian Church. Following the quick ceremony, they drove on to Detroit where Tryon had thriftily arranged to spend the night with relatives. Before leaving Monroe he had given the deputy county clerk a dollar to keep the story secret. By the time the couple reached Toledo next day the clerk had tipped off the press, and squads of newspapermen were waiting for him. "I was lonesome, simply unbearably lonesome," he told them while beaming on Alice. That evening the bride and groom arrived in Marion unannounced and were standing on the corner opposite the depot waiting for the streetcar when a carload of reporters discovered them and gave them a ride home. Tryon left his bride at her own house. "Good night, Alice," he told her. "I'll see you in the morning." Then the reporters drove him to the Center Street house five blocks away.

It took several days before Tryon could arrange to bring his bride to the turreted Center Street house. Daisy still lived there, in spite of the plumbing. Unruffled, unchanged by her brother's elevation, she continued to teach her English classes at the newly-named Harding High School. Gradually she found herself being courted by Ralph Lewis, now a widower. It was a slow Sunday-afternoon courtship with the unspoken understanding between the two of them that they were going to get married—someday.

Late in the summer Harding wrote to a friend: "Frankly, being President is rather an unattractive business unless one relishes the exercise of power. That is a thing which has never greatly appealed to me. . . ." It was a somber mood which grew on him as the Republican Congress, so frustrating to his expectations, reconvened on September 21. Thwarted in his personal and private life, thwarted publicly by House and Senate, Harding found an additional and unexpected chagrin in the clash of his Cabinet's "great minds." The anti-conservationist Fall had scarcely settled in the Interior Department before he drew up an executive order, which he sent to Harding for what he considered routine approval, that would have transferred the Forest Service and all the national forests both in the United States and Alaska to the Department of the Interior. The outraged Wallace, aided by such old conservationist friends as Gifford Pinchot, countered by denouncing Fall in the official bulletin of the Department of Agriculture as a conspirator with big business to exploit the public lands. So fierce were the Wallace-backed attacks on Fall that he finally appealed to Harding for protection against such "vicious propaganda."

The question of the transfer of the national forests and of the natural resources of Alaska to Fall's Interior Department finally came up in a Cabinet meeting. "A row ensued that nearly blew the roof off," Wallace told the conservationist Senator Norris. The Secretary of Agriculture let the Cabinet and the President know that if the Forest Service transfer should take place he would resign and denounce Fall in public meetings all through the West. Harding hesitated, tried to compromise, then for the moment agreed not to make the transfer.

There were other setbacks for Fall, in the Cabinet and out, that caused him to write his wife in July that he was ready to quit politics. The governor of New Mexico had appointed Fall's political enemy, Holm O. Bursum, to his vacated Senate seat, and in the ensuing special election Harding swung Federal patronage to Bursum to insure a Republican victory. With Bursum's rise, Fall's political influence in New Mexico declined abruptly. When he and Harding had been senators on the Committee on Foreign Relations he had been Harding's mentor in Mexican affairs. But now in the Cabinet when Fall attempted to "dictate" his chauvinistic Mexican policy, he found himself up against Secretary Hughes, more than ever the bearded iceberg, and the Cabinet member of whom Harding was most in awe. From being in the inner circle, Fall found himself edged to the perimeter. He was further chagrined when Harding appointed Secretary Hoover, "the great engineer," to head the Colorado irrigation project, a position the Secretary of the Interior himself had confidently expected to fill. Fall confided to his wife that he felt he would be freer and more use to Harding outside the Cabinet and added that the President was making "serious mistakes" and "certainly needs good, independent, and STRAIGHT FROM THE SHOULDER advice if ever a man did." When, however, he threatened to resign, Harding placatingly offered him the next vacancy in the Supreme Court.

Rumors of dissension in the Cabinet and of the "farcical" nature of many of the meetings became widespread. When Senator Norris introduced a bill to create a Farmers' Export Financing Corporation, Wallace loudly supported it against the opposition of Hoover and Mellon. There were whispers of an open break between Hughes and Hoover. Wallace began to refer to Hoover as "that man" after the Secretary of Commerce had announced that Wallace's department should limit itself to telling the farmer "what he can best produce based on soil, climatic, and other agricultural conditions." The marketing and disposition of farm products should, Hoover insisted to Harding, be the function and duty of the Department of Commerce. After taking over a moribund department, the aggressively systematic Secretary of Commerce had built it up with great energy and skill, developing a world-wide network of commercial attachés. But his push to expand agricultural exports brought him into increasing conflict with Wallace. And though he had the President's awe, Wallace had his ear. "Hank," Harding called his secretary of Agriculture who—unlike the Secretary of Commerce—could play golf and poker and tell Scotch jokes.

Whatever Harding's private disappointments in his family of great minds, his public stature continued to grow. *The New York Times,* after his nomination, had considered him "the firm and perfect flower of the cowardice and imbecility of the senatorial cabal." Now four months after his inauguration the *Times* had come to feel that "with great domestic and foreign policies before him and with his party divided and without dominant direction in Congress, President Harding is gradually assuming undisputed leadership and without offending his former associates in the Senate." That same month, while avoiding the League of Nations shibboleth, he had informally asked the governments of Great Britain, France, Italy, and Japan to participate in "a conference on the subject of limitation of armaments, in connection with which Pacific and Far Eastern questions will also be discussed." The proposal may have been inspired by Borah's unsuccessfully reiterated resolution. It may have owed more to Secretary Hughes's urgings than to Harding's vaguely formulated hope for world peace. But the final responsibility for calling it nevertheless fell on Harding himself. On August 11 the Secretary of State, on behalf of the President, sent formal invitations to the four powers.

If Harding showed himself the leader of his country in his effort to reach a new understanding with America's wartime allies, he showed himself equally the leader of his party in a surprise speech that he made in Birmingham, Alabama, at the celebration of the city's semi-centennial where he dared to stand in the South and demand civil rights for Negroes. It was the first time since the Civil War that an American President had been bold enough to mention the subject below the Mason-Dixon line. What he intended by this challenging gesture was to establish the

Republicans as a valid minority party on the way to becoming a majority party in the up-until-now Solid South. The last presidential election results had shown it might be possible. True, South Carolina had given only a token 2,244 votes to Harding while giving 64,170 to Cox, and Mississippi Republicans were almost as rare. But in Georgia and Alabama Harding had reached almost half of Cox's total and in North Carolina two-thirds. By carrying the fringe states of Maryland, Tennessee, Missouri, and Oklahoma, Harding had dented the outer edges of the South, and a few thousand Negro votes would even have carried Kentucky. Two Southern voters out of five had voted for him! If he could make the third voter a Negro he could carry the South as he had carried the rest of the country.

Accompanied by the Duchess and Secretary Weeks he first made a flying visit to flag-decked Atlanta, had lunch at Columbus, and crossed the state line early in the afternoon to Alabama. All the way he had a tight schedule. At Birmingham he put on an academic gown to receive a Doctor of Laws degree from the University of Alabama, then within minutes switched into a Masonic apron and hurried across the street under a flashing arch of crossed swords where an honor guard of plume-hatted Masons was drawn up waiting for him to lay the cornerstone of their new temple. Five hundred Masons in Scottish rite regalia stood by as the President smoothed the first batch of mortar with a silver trowel and guided the cornerstone into place. Their swords flashed again as the Master of the Lodge introduced Harding as one of the "trinity of great Masons—Solomon, George Washington, and Warren Gamaliel Harding."

Later in the afternoon Harding spoke to a carefully segregated audience of 20,000 whites and 10,000 blacks at Capitol Park just outside the city. After an affable introduction in which he congratulated the city for its progress and praised the new industrial advances of the South, he told his listeners with disconcerting bluntness that the democracy of the United States was a lie until the Negro was granted political and economic equality. The white majority heard him in shocked silence, but when he mentioned equality, there were yelps of approval from the Negro section. He was not through. Political, economic, and educational equality, he told his divided audience, would benefit not only American democracy but the South as well:

> Just as I do not wish the South to be politically entirely of one party, just as I believe that it is bad for the South, and for the rest of the country as well, so I do not want the colored people to be entirely of one party. I wish that both the tradition of a solidly Democratic South and the tradition of a solidly Republican black race might be broken up. Neither political sectionalism nor any system of rigid groupings of the people will in the long run prosper our country.
>
> I want to see the time come when black men will regard themselves as

full participants in the benefits and duties of American citizenship; when
they will vote for Democratic candidates, if they prefer the Democratic
policy on tariff or taxation, or foreign relations, or what-not; and when
they will vote the Republican ticket only for like reasons. We cannot go
on, as we have gone on for more than half a century, with one great section of our population, numbering as many people as the entire population
of some significant countries of Europe, set off from real contribution to
solving national issues, because of a division on race lines.

The speech was a demonstration in applied political science. "Let the
black man vote when he is fit to vote," he concluded, "prohibit the white
man voting when he is unfit to vote." As a politician he could scarcely
have demonstrated more at the time. Even outside the South the prevailing stereotype of the American Negro remained that of Octavus Roy
Cohen's *Saturday Evening Post* chronicles of the insistently shiftless
Florian Slappey and the Sons and Daughters of I Will Arise. Harding
haunted by his own shadow, spoke for "natural segregation" since "racial
amalgamation there cannot be." It was self-evident to him "that a black
man cannot be a white man, and that he does not need and should not
aspire to be as much like a white man as possible in order to accomplish
the best that is possible for him. He should seek to be, and he should be
encouraged to be, the best possible black man, and not the best possible
imitation of a white man." Harding predicted that Negroes would take
the places until recently filled by the now-excluded immigrants, and told
the stony-faced white section of his audience that unless the South treated
the Negroes well, they would drift to unskilled jobs in Northern factories

To those of a later generation coming across Harding's long-forgotten
Negro rights speech it would seem mild, and even reactionary in its
acceptance of the permanence of social barriers and segregated schools
But at that time it was as challenging a statement as had been made by
political speaker in the South, and the wildly applauding blacks in their
fenced-off section of Capitol Park understood it as such. "The most notable
and courageous expression on the race question made by any President of
the United States since Lincoln," the Negro educator J. Wilson Pettu-
wrote the President.[11]   In contrast to the caste-minded Wilson, Harding
had shown himself, for his day, a race liberal. "Unfortunate," Sen. Pat
Harrison of Mississippi said of the speech, "but to have made it in the
heart of the South where in some states the Negro population predomi-
nates, was unfortunate indeed." Senator Tom Heflin of Alabama, as self-
appointed spokesman for the White South, replied that "God Almighty
has fixt limits and boundary lines between the races, and no Republican
living can improve upon His handiwork."

[11] Only a few radical Negro leaders like W. E. B. DuBois took issue with Harding
"inconceivably dangerous and undemocratic demand" for social inequality.

Jennings gave Harding his always-tempered judgment, writing a few days later: "It was a bully speech—a brave speech, but I can find it in my heart to wish you had not felt it necessary to make it. If it had to be made, it was of course best that it be made in the South." Birmingham, however, absorbed the shock. The speech was soon forgotten in the stir of the twenties. And the Solid South continued as monolithic as Harding had privately predicted that it would.

By September the postwar depression still showed no signs of lifting. More men than ever were jobless. Newspapers ran full-page advertisements urging people to help create jobs in the building trade by starting a new house or at the least by remodeling the one they were living in. When Congress returned, Harding under Hoover's prompting called a Conference on Unemployment, but for all its name the conference produced little that was tangible or hopeful. Depressions, in Harding's view, were part of the inscrutable nature of things, as were indeed a "parasite percentage" of unemployed. "There has been vast unemployment before," Harding told his conferees pontifically, "and there will be again. There will be depression after inflation, just as surely as the tides ebb and flow." Little there was that the Federal government could do about it. Relief measures, the President felt, were a local responsibility and he called upon the mayors of America for action. On that stoic note the conference broke up.

The Sixty-seventh Congress, the do-nothing Congress as it was coming to be called, continued on its dilatory and divided way. Although Senator Knox in April introduced a resolution repealing the 1917 declaration of war against the Imperial German government and the Imperial and Royal —and now non-existent—Austro-Hungarian government, the resolution did not reach Harding for his signature until July. On the reconvening of Congress he sent to the Senate treaties of peace with Germany, Austria, and Hungary, but it was not until late November, three years after the Armistice, that he was able to sign the formal proclamation that the war between the United States and Germany and Austria was terminated. The Secretary of the Treasury's tax-reduction measure took even longer. Mellon had proposed to repeal the wartime excess-profits tax and reduce the tax on large incomes from a maximum of 65 per cent to 33 per cent. But face to face with persisting unemployment and with the resentfully vivid memory of the wartime "profiteers," the Congress was restive. Longworth persuaded Harding that it would be politically preferable to set the maximum at 40 per cent. Even this was too much for the Insurgents who, in the ramshackle bill that evolved, raised the maximum to 50 per cent. It was also too much for William Jennings Bryan. Miami land millionaire though he might be, his populist pulse still quickened at what the papers were calling the administration's tax melon. Bryan liked Harding personally. Before the inauguration the Hardings had visited him in Miami. He had praised the President's inaugural address in a saccharine editorial in his *Commoner*. But now, once more taking up his old cross of gold, he called for a revolt of farmers, laborers, and small businessmen.

The vagaries of the congressional session were soon obscured by the shadow of the Conference on the Limitation of Armaments. As the conception of the conference expanded from naval disarmament to an attempt to resolve great-power rivalry in the Orient, the President through his Secretary of State sent an invitation to China "to participate in the discussion of Far-Eastern questions." And since Belgium, Portugal, and the Netherlands had their own colonial interests in such "pertinent and crucial" problems, they, too, were invited to attend.

Although Japan and the United States had been nominal allies in the war against Germany, there had been bad feeling between the two countries for a generation, a mixture of American apprehensions and Japanese resentments fanned by the cheap journalism of both countries. On the Pacific Coast immigrant Japanese laborers and farmers, frugal, industrious, and acquisitive, prospered and were vindictively feared by the less assiduous native whites. In 1906 the San Francisco school board excluded Japanese children from the public schools. There was continual agitation to keep Orientals from owning land in California or from entering the United States altogether. Over the protests of the Japanese ambassador, the California Assembly in 1913 passed an anti-alien land ownership law aimed chiefly at the Japanese. After the war, a Yellow Peril fever swept the Pacific Coast. Individual Japanese were harassed and in some cases driven from their homes and their holdings. Finally in the 1921 immigration bill Congress, to the great satisfaction of Californians, barred all further Oriental immigrants.

To the Japanese, conscious of themselves as the first modern power in Asia and proud of their new industrial might, this was the ultimate insult. They had just launched the *Mutsu,* the largest and most formidable battleship afloat—paid for with the small coins contributed by Japanese laborers and school children—making the Japanese Navy almost two-thirds the size of the American. As if in answer to the challenge of the Rising Sun, the United States, with a navy almost equal to England's, was rushing construction of six battle cruisers and seven battleships. England, the sun still undimmed above her colonial empire and determined to remain the world's largest naval power, had four super-dreadnoughts of the Hood class on the slips. Though the central theme of the conference was to be the limitations of naval armaments, no such limitation would be possible without Japanese agreement. While lagging behind the other two great naval powers in capital ships, Japan was the most aggressive, and the Anglo-Japanese alliance of 1902—twice renewed and still in effect—made the expanding Japanese Navy seem an open threat to the Philippines and America's position in the Far East.

Of the combatant nations in World War I only the United States and Japan had emerged strengthened. Japan, following the terms of the alliance with England, had declared war in 1914 and within a few months had overrun Germany's Chinese enclave of Kiao-chow and the city of Tsingtad. Prudently refraining from sending urgently requested troops to Europe, the Japanese government had used the war years to consolidate its position in China, monopolize the Chinese trade, seize the former German island possessions, and expand its own industrial plant. By the war's end the world's oldest dynasty had become the world's newest superpower. With the other nations close to exhaustion, the next looming confrontation threatened between the strong but reluctant United States and the dynamic-expansive Japanese Empire. Only if the current naval competition could be brought to a halt might a clash be avoided. To this end Harding's evolving conference seemed a far more tangible hope for mankind than did the League of Nations. The anti-League Borah approved of it as thoroughly as did the pro-League Bryan whose pacifist convictions as Secretary of State had driven him from Wilson's Cabinet in 1915. The Federal Council of Churches endorsed it. So did Samuel Gompers, president of the American Federation of Labor, an otherwise sour critic of Harding and his advocacy of "necessary" wage reductions to revive industry. Al Jolson wrote, offering to "sing Harding's message into men's minds," and enclosed a sample attempt:

> The wives and sweethearts of each nation,
> Have got a longing in their hearts,
> When war turned skies to gray
> They have been the ones to pay,
> So their eyes are turned today
> To Washington—I hear them saying—
> (Refrain)
> Take 'way the gun
> From ev'ry mother's son,
> We're taught by God above
> To forgive, forget and love.
> The weary world is waiting for
> Peace forevermore.
> So take away the gun
> From ev'ry mother's son,
> And put an end to War.

Harding prepared with great care for his conference. He had the campaign-hardy Hays arrange the nationwide publicity. Newspapers, magazines, the moving pictures, all were mobilized. In contrast to the embittered secrecy of the Paris Peace Conference, at least half the meetings of the Washington Conference would be open to the press and public. "To a peculiar degree," a State Department memorandum noted, "this conference is dependent upon atmosphere, open hope, open or warm and friendly disposition, and favorable expectations on the part of the public." It was also to be dependent on the shock of a proposal that Harding's Secretary of State was preparing in secret and that was intended to echo as another shot heard round the world.

Originally the conference had been scheduled for November 11, but on this day, Armistice Day, America's Unknown Soldier was to be buried in Arlington National Cemetery. Harding had already declared the day a legal holiday, and the conference was postponed until the twelfth.

The cult of the Unknown Soldier had begun in England in 1920. No one could determine who had first conceived the idea, but it was quickly taken up with ritualistic fervor by the other Allies, France and Italy, and even by such peripheral participants as Portugal and Jamaica. Through some intricate symbolism each unidentifiable corpse soon came to embody the spirit of the nation. To honor it became in each country an act of national atonement. Although in England the Unknown was buried in Westminster Abbey on Armistice Day, 1920, and the French Unknown lay under the Arc de Triomphe with the grave marked by an eternal flame, the American Unknown Soldier had not yet been chosen. Finally in October, 1921, the bodies of four unidentified soldiers were exhumed in France from the Romagne Military Cemetery and taken to a room in the city hall of Châlons-sur-Marne. There Corp. Edward S. Younger of the Headquarters Company, Second Battalion, 50th Infantry Regiment, had been selected to choose the Unknown. He entered the room, where the four coffins were displayed, carrying a small bunch of white roses, looked at the flag-covered boxes, and then as token of his choice placed the roses on the one farthest to the right. The other three coffins were taken back to the Romagne Cemetery; the coffin of the Unknown was placed in a plain wooden box with a small bronze plaque lettered:

> An Unknown Soldier
> Who Died In
> Defence of His Country

Over the box was placed the flag, and on the flag the bunch of roses.

From Le Havre the Unknown's body was sent across the Atlantic on the *Olympia*, brought by an honor guard to Washington on November 10 and placed in the Capitol's rotunda under the great dome on the catafalque that had borne Lincoln's body. The plain black outer coffin, draped with the American flag to which had been pinned the Grand Cross of the Legion of Honor, was bare except for Corporal Younger's withered roses.

Harding and the Duchess were the first to come to pay their respects. She placed a white ribbon on the coffin that she herself had sewn. At the catafalque's base flowers began to pile up as if it were a flower show—red roses from the President, pink roses and snapdragons from Congress, chrysanthemums and carnations from the Supreme Court, a wreath from the King of England, small anonymous bouquets from those who had lost their sons.

The morning of Armistice Day broke with a wintry chill, the air shimmeringly clear against a cloud-tattered sky whose grayness was broken intermittently by shafts of sunlight. Just after eight o'clock eight soldiers and sailors, acting for the admirals and generals who were the honorary pallbearers, carried the Unknown's coffin from the catafalque to the artillery caisson waiting at the foot of the Capitol steps. At eight-thirty minute guns began to fire and the cortège moved off down the slope toward the White House, led by a brigadier general on horseback and the staff of the Washington garrison. There followed a military display of the armed forces, in precise step to the music of Chopin's "Funeral March" played by the Marine Band: a brown-and-blue composite regiment of infantrymen, sailors, Marines, and national guardsmen; a drum and bugle corps; a battalion of infantry, bayonets flashing; a composite battalion of sailors and Marines; two battalions of engineers; two battalions of artillery with their fieldpieces; two squadrons of cavalry, the horses with muffled hoofs. Then came the caisson with the flag-covered coffin drawn by six black horses.

Harding, in chesterfield and silk hat, walked in the place of honor immediately behind the coffin, with Pershing on his left. The General of the Army, a mourning badge on his sleeve, wore no decoration but the Victory Medal. President and General strode along together, silver-haired, of equal height, in the vigor of their manhood. Harding, preternaturally erect, a shining solemnity to his features, had never looked more a leader of men.

Pursy-faced Vice President Coolidge minced along six steps behind them, accompanied by an admiral. Chief Justice Taft waddled beside him, also with an admiral. Then came the Supreme Court justices, the members of the Cabinet, former commanding generals and admirals, senators eight abreast followed by an awkward squad of congressmen marching in time if not in step to the muffled drums of a following drum-and-bugle corps.

Wearing their white-starred ribbons, a platoon of Congressional Medal of Honor holders marched behind the bugle corps. Then came a solitary victoria, its top down, drawn by a black and a bay horse and driven by a liveried Negro. There was a wave-like murmur as the victoria passed, then scattered applause from the spectators lining the curb as they recognized the ravaged immobile features of the wartime Commander in Chief Woodrow Wilson. He sat with a blanket tucked over his knees, grasping his cane with one hand to hold his sagging figure erect, while with the other he doffed his silk hat and bowed in acknowledgment, his drooped face like a parchment mask. His wife beside him, veiled, with only a single white orchid to break the black of her costume, looked for all her gravity younger than she had on Inauguration Day. Wilson wore a cloth American Legion poppy in his buttonhole, his wife a poppy at her breast. At the sight of their old commander, a group of American Legion men in World War uniforms had sprung forward to form an impromptu guard of honor around the victoria.

A token battalion of World War veterans followed, three from each state, representing the Army, Navy, the Marines, and the Coast Guard. Then came the pathetically ancient survivors of the Grand Army of the Republic in their blue uniforms and wide black hats, and closely behind them, equally ancient but in gray, the Confederate veterans. Then the American Legionnaires, still boys for the most part, some in their new blue Legion dress, most still in their old service uniforms. Then the Gold Star Mothers.

After the Gold Star Mothers a congeries of organizations made up the rest of the parade: Red Cross workers; the Colored Veterans of America; the Salvation Army; the Sons, Daughters, and Children of the American Revolution; the Military Training Camp Association; the Society of the Cincinnati; the American Library Service; and last of all the Georgetown Cadets.

On reaching the White House Harding took his place in a box near the west gate, with the Duchess beside him, to review the civilian contingents that, after passing him, disbanded. As he caught sight of Wilson in his victoria, he bowed. Detached from its civilian appendage, the military cortège continued, making its way the six remaining miles across the Potomac and up the leaf-strewn road to the marble amphitheater of Arlington National Cemetery where at midday the President was to lead the final services for the Unknown Soldier.

So snarled was the traffic across the river that Harding could reach the amphitheater only by having soldiers clear the bridge and then by driving the presidential car off the road and over the grass plots of Potomac Park. Secretary Hughes in his car was so delayed that he never arrived at all. Harding appeared a few minutes before twelve. The coffin had been taken from its caisson and placed on a bier in the center of the amphitheater stage. By the time of the President's arrival the nine sections of the amphitheater were full, three of them with members of Congress and their families. Senators and ambassadors sat in the boxes along the marble colonnade, while the chairs on the stage itself were occupied by the foreign military leaders and heads of state, most of whom had come to Washington for the Arms Limitation Conference.

The bier and the forward part of the stage were banked with flowers; wreaths from the nations of the world, from veterans' organizations, many decorated with American divisional and regimental insignia. One of the most conspicuous wreaths was from the American Legion, a design of white roses with OLD PAL lettered in flowers of a bluish tinge. Behind the marble stage setting and the green leaf-mottled hillside sloping down to the river Washington lay somberly on the horizon, the Capitol dome outlined in miniature against the striated sky. At four minutes before twelve everyone stood as the Marine Band played "The Star-Spangled Banner." Then a chaplain prayed briefly, and exactly at midday a bugler sounded Taps as a signal for two minutes of silence. The band ended the silent minutes with "America." Secretary of War Weeks introduced the President.

As Harding stepped forward beside the coffin the audience rose, and he with a modest gesture motioned them to be seated. He had discarded his chesterfield. From the pocket of his morning coat he took out the small manuscript pages containing his speech. That speech, picked up by the microphones in front of him and carried by telephone wire, would be amplified not only to those gathered on the Arlington grass slopes, but to a vast crowd in Washington, to a packed audience in New York's Madison Square Garden, and even to an early-morning audience gathered in San Francisco's Auditorium. Never before in history had so many thousands simultaneously heard the sound of a single human voice. Harding spoke resonantly and movingly, in the grave generalities that came so easily to him and that carried conviction when he spoke them in his full-throated voice, even if in cold print they defied exacter meanings. Undoubtedly he was deeply moved, and undoubtedly he enjoyed this for-him-alliterative sensation.

If American achievement [he told his audience] is a cherished pride at home, if our unselfishness among nations is all we wish it to be, and ours is a helpful example in the world, then let us give of our influence and strength, yea, of our aspirations and convictions, to put mankind on a little higher plane, exulting and exalting, with war's distressing and depressing tragedies barred from the stage of righteous civilization. . . .

Standing today on hallowed ground, conscious that all America has halted to share in the tribute of the heart, and mind, and soul to this fellow-American, and knowing that the world is noting this expression of the Republic's mindfulness, it is fitting to say that his sacrifice, and that of the millions dead, shall not be in vain. There must be, there shall be the commanding voice of a conscious civilization against armed warfare. . . .

As we return this poor clay to its native soil garlanded by love and

covered with the decorations that only nations can bestow, I can sense the
prayers of our people, of all peoples, that this Armistice Day shall mark
the beginning of a new and lasting era of peace on earth, good will among
men. Let me join in that prayer.

Then, almost as if on impulse, Harding repeated the Lord's Prayer, many
of his audience whispering the words with him. As his silver voice echoed
the Amen, a quartet from the Metropolitan Opera sang "The Supreme
Sacrifice." Silently, the President pinned the Congressional Medal of
Honor and the Distinguished Service Cross beside the Legion of Honor
Medal already on the coffin flag. After the American decorations came
those of the other nations. General Baron Jacques of Belgium, spangled
with medals, stepped forward with his country's Croix de Guerre that he
unpinned from his own breast where it had been placed by the King. He
was followed less colorfully by Lord Beatty, England's Admiral of the
Fleet, who presented the Victoria Cross for the first time to a foreigner.
Foch, in the full-dress uniform of a Marshal of France, laid the Médaille
Militaire and the Croix de Guerre with palms on the coffin. Generalissimo
Diaz, after taking off his high-peaked cap, presented the Italian Medal for
Valor. The generals and ministers of the minor powers followed with
their decorations: the Rumanian Virtutea Militara, the Czechoslovakian
War Cross, the Polish Virtuti Militari.

The generals saluted, the Metropolitan Quartet sang "O God, Our Help
in Ages Past," and at the conclusion of the hymn the Marine Band once
more struck up "Our Honored Dead." Impassively the pallbearers moved
forward to take up the coffin and carry it to its last destination, the opened
crypt in the marble-faced terrace just below the amphitheater. Four
chaplains and the honorary pallbearers followed the pallbearers in the
final procession. Then came Harding and the black-veiled Duchess, Vice
President Coolidge and his wife, and closely after them the marshals and
the generals in their peacock pageantry: Foch in red trousers, black coat
with silver buttons, white plumed hat, and the ribbon of the Grand Cross
of the Legion of Honor across his chest; Generalissimo Diaz, with six
rows of ribbons on his green uniform; the British Admiral of the Fleet
wearing his cocked hat with its gold lace and tassels; Japan's Prince
Iyesato Tokugawa, the last of the Shoguns; the former Prime Minister of
England, Arthur Balfour, in the blue gold-trimmed uniform of the Trinity
Brethren, an honorary society concerned with the licensing of pilots and
the maintenance of lighthouses; and Aristide Briand, Premier of France,
most conspicuous of all in his undecorated civilian black.

At the graveside the band played "Lead, Kindly Light," Harding's
favorite hymn. A chaplain read the brief committal service. As he finished,
Congressman Hamilton Fish, Jr., the author of the resolution providing

for the honoring of the Unknown Soldier, placed a last wreath on the grave. Then, quite unexpectedly, an Indian in a feathered war bonnet, Chief Plenty Coups, stepped forward, took off his bonnet, and laid it with his coup stick beside the wreath.

For all its pageantry the Unknown Soldier's burial on Armistice Day was merely a stage piece, a prelude to the Arms Limitation Conference of the following day. As a planned contrast to the secrecy at Versailles' Hall of Mirrors, and as a reminder of Wilson's violated words about open covenants openly arrived at, the new conference was being held in the open atmosphere of the Continental Memorial Hall belonging to the Daughters of the American Revolution. On that first morning 1,300 spectators had crowded into the galleries and boxes of the white-walled oblong building. Only the floor, marked off by a brass rail, had been kept empty, the usual seats replaced by a central U-shaped table of walnut covered with green baize. Places had been arranged for the delegates— four from each country—each place designated by a blotter, pen, and inkwell. Beyond the table, but inside the brass rail under a shading of potted palms, were seats for the military and naval staff of the various nations.

Shortly before half past ten the delegates filed in to take their places. Harding, defter than his more pedantic predecessor in conciliating the opposition, had picked the irreconcilable Senator Lodge and Alabama's Sen. Oscar Underwood as delegates to accompany Elihu Root and Secretary Hughes. There were whisperings from the galleries and opera glasses were focused at the electric appearance of Briand, the leader of the French delegation, tossing back his shock of blue-black hair and gesturing as he talked with René Viviani, a deputy and former president of the council. Seated next to the French at the baize-covered table were the Japanese: Prince Tokugawa and Admiral Baron Tomosaburo Kato, looking as inscrutable as Orientals are supposed by Occidentals to look. The small earnest Chinese Minister Sao Ke Alfred Sze, with Wellington Koo, president of the League's Council, led his country's delegation; the prim Dutch Minister of Foreign Affairs Jonkheer H. S. van Karnebeek spoke for his country; Viscount d'Alte for Portugal; the blond-bearded, blue-eyed, and most un-Italian appearing H. E. Carlo Schanzer for Italy; and the smoothly turbanned Sirniva Sastri, member of India's Vice-Regal Council —along with Sir John Salmond, K.C., of Australia—for the British Empire. Former Prime Minister Balfour, the color of his Trinity Brethren uniform replaced by a colorless morning coat, led the British delegation, the grim-jawed Admiral Beatty like a bulldog at his heels.

As each delegate took his place he was handed an advance printed copy of the opening prayer and the President's address. Viviani, scanning the prayer, whispered audibly to Underwood that the efficient Americans could get a prayer reproduced on paper before it had even reached the ear of God!

At the near end of the hall, under a large window and above the frieze of potted palms, a wall bracket held flags of the participating powers. Just as Harding entered by a side door, a current of air swirled the flags in a kaleidoscope of color. He looked grave, and in spite of the applause that greeted him his face did not lighten. Mary Roberts Rinehart, sitting in a gallery box, thought that he appeared much changed from the day she had seen him in Marion before the election.

With disarming modesty he waited while the Reverend Doctor Abernathy made his prerecorded prayer, then bowed formally—and rather deeply for an American—and began his speech. He spoke briefly, and on this occasion he was the more impressive because he was so brief. Touched unavoidably to alliteration, he spoke of the Unknown Soldier's burial of the day before, and how "a hundred millions of our people were summarizing the inexcusable causes, the incalculable cost, the unspeakable sacrifices, and the unutterable sorrows; and there was the ever-impelling question: How can humanity justify or God forgive?"

Then with unaccustomed bluntness he told the delegates that "one hundred million, frankly, want less of armament and none of war!" He concluded:

> We are met for a service to mankind. In all simplicity, in all honesty and all honor, there may be written here the avowals of a world conscience refined by the consuming fires of war, and made more sensitive by the anxious aftermath. I hope for that understanding which will emphasize the guaranties of peace and for commitments to less burdens and a better order which will tranquilize the world. In such an accomplishment there will be added glory to your flags and ours, and the rejoicing of mankind will make the transcending music of all succeeding time.

It was Harding oratory, but this time its promise of peace struck home. Clamorously the gallery and the delegates applauded as he walked away, diffident, still bowing slightly and with a shy smile of appreciation. Hughes pushed forward, his face aglow, to seize Harding's hand as he passed. Balfour followed, and then Briand and Viviani and the other delegates reaching out to the smiling, retreating man. Never had Harding seemed more the statesman, never from now on would he seem less so in European eyes for the remainder of his Presidency. Slowly, unruffled, he edged his way past the outstretched hands to the sheltering overhang of the gallery, then with a last wave of his arm stepped rapidly through the door.

When the imperturbable Hughes, as chairman of the conference, rose to address the delegates he realized that he was lighting the fuse of a concealed time bomb that in a few paragraphs would shatter the equanimity of the hall and of the world outside. Eschewing generalizations and rhetorical turns of phrase, he began by announcing that the way to disarm was to disarm. Then he exploded his bomb. Since Japan, England, and the United States were engaged in a naval construction race that was at best a waste of their resources and at worst could lead to armed conflict, he proposed that no more warships of any kind be built for ten years. In addition let the three powers proceed at once to cut down on the fleets they already had. Speaking for the United States he offered to scrap thirty capital ships if England would agree to scrap 19 and Japan 17. His country was ready at once to scrap the 15 ships now being built under the 1916 naval program, as well as 15 older ships. Hughes named off the new ships in his trumpet-clear voice: the unfinished battle cruisers *Lexington, Constellation, Saratoga, Ranger, Constitution,* and *United States;* the battleships *Colorado, Washington, West Virginia, South Dakota, Indiana, Montana, North Carolina, Iowa,* and *Massachusetts*—$330,000,000 worth of warships. In return Hughes demanded that England stop construction of her four new Hood dreadnoughts and scrap all pre-dreadnoughts except those in the George V class. Japan in turn was to abandon construction of seven capital ships still in the blueprint stage and to scrap five that were being built, as well as ten pre-dreadnoughts and second-class battleships in the water.

Beyond Hughes's voice there was a hush in the hall, as if each person present were catching his breath. The members of the diplomatic corps, forgetting their professional aplomb, craned their heads forward, moistening their lips. The Chinese Ambassador lost his bland smile. Balfour, who had been toying with the blotter in front of him, dropped it and in a characteristic nervous gesture caught at his coat lapels with both hands. Admiral Kato held the pen poised with which he had been doodling. At the mention of the name Hood, so sacred to the Royal Navy, Admiral Beatty lurched forward in his chair, his eyes opening wide then narrowing, his bulldog jaw stiff. Then, after the first shocked silence, the galleries rose in maddening applause. William Jennings Bryan, representing the United Press and sitting next to William Allen White in the press section, shed tears of pacifist happiness.

> Into the outburst of the crowd [White himself wrote,] spilled the joy that had tightened its nerves as it listened. Hats waved, handkerchiefs fluttered, men shook one another's hands, hugged one another, slapped one another, exhibited every kind of animal delight of which human beings are capable in their high moments. There was an agenda or program of the conference; but after Hughes had spoken, democracy took charge of the rules and order of business, and as the cheering died, the galleries—after the ancient fashion of American political conventions—began calling out for speakers.

"Briand!" they called out, "Briand!" anglicizing the name of the French Premier beyond his recognition. To the bald pacificist in the press gallery it was the old convention cry for "Bryan," and White had to yank him by the coattail as he tried to stand up in tear-streaked acknowledgment.

The conference adjourned for the weekend with attention focused on it from London to Tokyo. Hughes's proposals would seem the hope of the world, as he well realized when he planned the two-day interlude to let the fact sink in on the delegates. By the time they returned on Monday there was none intrepid enough to challenge the American Secretary of State. For the next twelve weeks the conference deliberated, the delegates cooperating amicably except for the French who with sullen obsessiveness demanded, before any ships were sunk, a guarantee of British and American aid in the event of a future attack by Germany.

In spite of the French minority, the end of the conference in February seemed to justify all its November hopes. Colonel Repington, a British military aide with a mind for statistics, remarked that the American Secretary—in thirty-five minutes—had sunk more ships than all the admirals of the world had sunk in a cycle of centuries. England, the United States, and Japan agreed to keep their naval ratio of five-five-three in capital ships for the next fifteen years with not even replacement construction for the next ten. The French and the Italian navies would each remain about half that of Japan's. In addition, and much to the satisfaction of the United States, the Anglo-Japanese Alliance was to be superseded by a Four Power Treaty between the United States, Great Britain, Japan, and France, in which for the next ten years each power pledged to respect the rights of the others in their Pacific possessions and to consult among themselves if any outside power threatened any of them. The nine powers signed a treaty pledging fairer treatment to China, and Japan agreed to withdraw from the province of Shantung and to give the United States free access to Yap.

Harding did not reappear at the conference until its close. Then, in a final address to the delegates, he told them he believed that the naval holiday would not expire with the treaties:

> Those of us [he concluded hopefully] who live another decade are more likely to witness a growth of public opinion, strengthened by new experience, which will make nations more concerned with living to the fulfillment of God's high intent than with agencies of warfare and destruction. . . . The torches of understanding have been lighted and they ought to glow and encircle the Globe.

In spite of the opposition of the irreconcilables led by Borah, Johnson, and La Follette, the Four Power Treaty was ratified in the Senate 67 to 27.

Lodge and Underwood championed it, and Harding's astuteness in securing their support gave him four more votes than the necessary two-thirds majority required for a treaty. Even the irreconcilables voted for the treaty limiting naval armament, and it was passed with only the dissenting vote of Republican Senator France of Maryland.

Sitting in the White House study before the fireplace where a few sticks were blazing brightly, Harding told H. H. Kohlsaat just before the Senate vote: "The success or failure of this administration depends on the ratification of these treaties. Every administration's name rests on one or two acts. If these treaties are ratified by the Senate, then this administration's name is secure in history. If the treaties are defeated, nothing I can do in the balance of my term will be of more than passing interest."

In contrast to the President's benign public appearance, he continued to fret inwardly more and more at the restraints of the White House, and with the months his restlessness grew. Always he found himself under the observation of servants and secretaries and the Secret Service, to say nothing of the cold eye of the Duchess. Pride of office did not compensate him for his former casual life as senator, nor for the frustrations only furtively and temporarily relieved by Nan's semi-occasional visits. "I'm in jail," he told her at the end of one of their quick encounters, "and I can't get out. I've got to stay." When Senator Brandegee came to the White House to urge the appointment of a friend to the United States Court of Appeals, he asked the President how he liked the job so far. "Frank, it is hell!" Harding exploded. "No other word can describe it."

In addition to his other troubles the American political tradition that saw the justification of a President's first term by his election to a second term was beginning to haunt Harding. Another term would keep him in the White House until March, 1929, when he would be in his sixty-fifth year. More and more he mulled over the idea of freeing himself by restricting the Presidency to a single term. Shortly before the opening of the regular session of the Sixty-seventh Congress on December 5 he sent for Welliver and read aloud to him the galley proofs of his congressional message. Welliver listened without surprise and without comment, until Harding came to a paragraph requesting a constitutional amendment that would limit the President to one term of six years. Noting Welliver's astonishment, Harding stopped and explained that he was tired of buying congressional support with jobs, of always having to take account of his renomination and re-election. It was only when a President was relieved of patronage responsibilities and such things that the civil service could be taken out of politics and put on a real merit basis.

As he continued to discuss the single term with Welliver, the Duchess burst into the room in her unannounced manner and demanded to know what they were talking about. Harding explained that they were talking about including a recommendation for a single six-year presidential term in his new message to Congress. The Duchess's eyes snapped as she snatched up the galley proof. Then she lashed out at Welliver, accusing him of sponsoring an amendment that would be the equivalent of refusing a second term. Welliver tried to tell her that he was against such an amendment, but her flow of angry words overwhelmed him, until finally Harding came to his rescue. Until the renunciatory paragraph was removed the Duchess refused to leave the room. Only after she had gone did Harding nervously tell his secretary that he still planned to make the recommendation before the end of his term.

A heavy snowfall covered Washington just before Christmas, a chill and dreary contrast to the flashing spring inaugural. On December 13 Harding wrote to Richard Washburn Child at the embassy in Rome: "In truth I have decided that it is more fun to be a candidate with all the anxieties of a campaign than it is to be President, with all the annoyances, irritations, and burdens." For several weeks a stream of threatening letters had been pouring into the White House announcing that the President was marked for death. A final anonymous message warned that on Christmas Day "the thing" would happen. The superstitious Duchess, beaten down by presentiments, determined to spend the day somewhere else and telephoned Evalyn Walsh McLean—who at once invited the Hardings for the day to her gold-plated I Street house.

On Christmas morning the Hardings went to church, drove to the McLeans' for lunch, then sat around talking in the enormous drawing room with its three-story Christmas tree until dinnertime. Secret Service men scattered throughout the house while others watched the street outside. Harding took the threats as a joke, but the Duchess remained fearful all day long—jumpy, twitching, and nervous. After dinner Evalyn tucked Harding away upstairs in a sitting room connected with her bedroom as the safest place in the house. There he spent the evening playing poker with Ned, Harry Daugherty, Secretary Weeks, and Charlie Curtis. Downstairs Evalyn and the Duchess watched a private showing of Mary Pickford's Little Lord Fauntleroy. The Duchess kept fingering the diamond sunburst that she wore at her throat. Upstairs they could hear Harding's occasional laugh and his jocose threats of what he was going to do with his friends when he had better cards. "Suddenly," Evalyn recalled in her memoirs, "somewhere in the house there was a loud crashing. Mrs. Harding half-screamed and almost slid from her chair. There was no comedy about her fears; they were too real. A servant came in response to my loud calls and apologized because a door had been slammed."

Harding left about two in the morning. He shook hands with Evalyn and, still amused at the Duchess's fears, said: "I am very grateful to my assassins for a very pleasant Christmas Day." Eight hours later he met with Eugene Debs in his office. Harding, over the personal objections of the Duchess and the political objections of Daugherty, had given Wilson's most hated conscientious objector a Christmas pardon along with 23 other political prisoners, and had asked Debs to call at the White House on his way from Atlanta. "Well," said Harding striding toward him with outstretched hand as Debs introduced himself, "I have heard so damned much about you, Mr. Debs, that now I am very glad to meet you personally." Debs had promised never to reveal what took place at his interview with the President, and he was to keep his word, but he did tell the reporters afterward that "Mr. Harding appears to me to be a kind gentleman. We understand each other perfectly."

For all his efforts at artificial cheer, Harding could not shake off his seasonal gloom. His spiritous adviser, Bishop Anderson, was again after him to sign a total-abstinence pledge that would make him "the moral hero of millions of persons in this country." Harding replied that he would ponder the request very carefully, but admitted that his "personal scruples do not lead me in that direction." During Christmas week his sister Carolyn, despairing of his mood, called that specialist in blithe spirits, Charlie Forbes, to say that Winnie—she still called her brother by their mother's pet name—wanted to see him. Forbes, hurrying to the White House, ran into Doctor Sawyer in the office corridor. "My God! They had a hell of a row this morning," the wispy General told him sadly. He found the President alone at his desk. "Merry Christmas!" said Harding ironically, pulling a plug of Piper Heidsieck tobacco out of the right-hand drawer and taking a chew, then offering Forbes a cigarette. Forbes took the cigarette, lit it as he stood beside the President. "This is a hell of a Christmas!" Harding went on as if he were talking to himself, and when Forbes asked him what the matter was, he replied: "Everything is the matter!"

Years later, when Harding was dead and the man he had appointed head of the Veterans Bureau ruined, Forbes recalled those earlier moments of despairing confidence when Harding had told him how unhappy he was, how empty his life had been. One evening, Forbes wrote, he had gone with the President to the rear lawn of the White House and Harding had cried.

CHAPTER XVIII

Scandal

The Arms Limitation Conference through which Harding thought to secure his administration's name in history is no more than a footnote, one of the futile peace gestures in the interval between World War I and World War II. His administration is recalled, when all else is blurred over, through the name of an eroded sandstone rock shaped somewhat like a teapot and perched over a dome of oil about fifty miles north of Casper, Wyoming. Teapot Dome, its syllables tripping so easily to the tongue, became in the twenties a stone symbol of government corruption. And as Teapot Dome's outline assumed the proportions of a malignant monument, so did Secretary of the Interior Fall assume the shape of the decade's arch villain, the man who sold out his country for cash.

Teapot Dome's history and Fall's involvement are more complex, less definably black and white than the legend. The origins go back to Theodore Roosevelt's administration when the President and Secretary of the Interior Garfield, impelled by such obsessively dedicated Progressives as Gifford Pinchot, first developed conservation as a national policy and a national cause. For Westerners, brought up in the older and more predatory tradition of public lands for the taking, of natural resources open to the enterprising and the shrewd, of progress as represented by the exploitation of the country's minerals and oil fields and water, conservation was seen as an effete and almost effeminate doctrine sponsored by wealthy Easterners uninterested in jobs and opportunities for the people of the West. Taft's Western-minded Secretary of the Interior Ballinger— to the outrage of the conservationists, rallying under the National Conservation Association with Harvard's President Charles W. Eliot as its head—attempted to reverse Garfield's restrictive policies.

Petroleum, from a crude substance refined to bring kerosene lamps to remote households, was becoming the "liquid gold" of power as industries and the navies of the world began to turn from coal to oil. Geologists— erroneously as it turned out—doubted that there would be sufficient oil for the Navy's future use unless it was carefully safeguarded. Until President Taft took office potential oil lands in the public domain still lay open to the prospector and the prospecting company, although Theodore Roosevelt during his administration had already directed his Geological Survey to appraise such lands with the aim of securing them as oil reserves for the future use of the Navy. In 1909 and 1910 President Taft withdrew public lands in California and Wyoming for this purpose. Then in 1912, through his Department of Interior, he set aside two specific oil reserve sites in California: Elk Hills, known as Reserve No. 1; and Buena Vista Hills, Reserve No. 2. Together they contained about a hundred square miles.

In 1914 Wilson's Secretary of the Navy Josephus Daniels speeded up the conversion of the American fleet to oil. When Daniels sought additional oil sources, Teapot Dome was established as a reserve a year later. Although the dome lay next to the Salt Creek field, a rich oil area of withdrawn public lands where many operators had long been active, it was still not a certain oil reservoir.

At the outbreak of World War I the public section had come to occupy an eighth of all the oil lands in the United States. Eyed by the oil companies, guarded jealously by the Navy, this section precipitated a struggle of over a decade between the doctrinaire conservationists and the doctrinaire exploiters, between land reformers and those who for their various reasons resisted land reform. From 1909 on such questions were debated in each session of Congress. Should the public oil lands be disposed of? Should they be leased? Was there danger of the oil being drained away by nearby private wells? How valid were the claims of certain drillers and prospecting companies for compensation for the time and skills and resources spent in developing land—as, for example, in Salt Creek—before the government withdrew it?

The dispute was carried on not only in Congress but within successive administrations. Pinchot had quit his post as head of the Forest Service after his conflict with Taft's anti-conservationist Secretary of the Interior. Wilson's Secretary of the Navy was a strict conservationist but the Secretary of the Interior, Franklin Lane—a corpulent convivial man who liked to extol the pioneer as the "mystic materialist"—sided with the Western developers. When the Honolulu Oil Company claimed occupancy of certain locations in Buena Vista Hills prior to the presidential withdrawal orders of 1909, Lane approved the claims even though it was apparent that many of them were dubious. Secretary Daniels indignantly brought to Wilson's attention what he considered the fraudulent intent of the Honolulu Company, and the President overruled his Secretary of the Interior. Pinchot, still active in conservation and often collaborating with such like-minded legislators as Senator La Follette, accused Lane of being a despoiler of public lands. There were other anti-conservationists in Wilson's Cabinet, such as the new Attorney General, A. Mitchell Palmer, who earned the scorn of the conservationists by refusing to appeal the award by a lower court of a vast acreage in the Buena Vista and Elk Hills reserves to the Southern Pacific Railroad. The railroad had originally claimed the land over the period of 1894–1904, submitting affidavits at the time as to its non-mineral character, affidavits which the government maintained were fraudulent. Daniels, furious at the Southern Pacific's success and at Palmer's complacence, thought the award was the greatest crime he had ever heard of.

"Oil was money, and the struggle for it was earnest and relentless," wrote W. L. Connelly, a Sinclair associate. It affected both parties, with the Republicans by and large more favorable to conservation than the Democrats. On the one hand there were the conservationists like Pinchot, the old Progressives like La Follette, the Easterners, the naval men around Daniels. On the other there were the Westerners, the petroleum lobby, the Department of the Interior. Before 1917 oil claimants asserted their "natural right" to government land, but with the war's coming they demanded access to oil to increase production on the basis of "patriotism and national need." In 1919 the Pitman mineral leasing bill, which would have continued the alienation of public lands and the overgenerous treatment of oil claimants, passed Congress and was defeated in the Senate only by the filibustering La Follette with the back-stairs assistance of Pinchot and the Conservation Association. Finally, in February, 1920, a long and complicated leasing bill more to conservationist taste was approved by Congress and signed by the President. Although no giveaway, the act did provide for prospecting on the lands withdrawn by Taft but not set aside for the Navy, for preferential treatment for claimants whose rights predated the withdrawal orders, for compromises in litigation, and for royalty payments to the states and to the Federal government. It gave the Secretary of the Interior authority in leasing the general public oil lands as well as the naval reserves. The month of its passage Secretary Lane resigned to take a position with the Doheny oil interests at $50,000 a year. Before leaving office, he again asked Wilson to confirm the rejected patents of the Honolulu Oil Company. The President refused.

In his zeal for assuring the Navy an adequate supply of fuel Secretary Daniels had finally come to advocate the nationalizing of the country's entire petroleum resources. In 1920 he learned with alarm of the drainage of the Elk Hills Reserve by private wells on adjoining properties, and at his insistence Congress in June, 1920, passed a special amendment to the naval appropriations bill taking the authority over the management of the Naval Oil Reserves from the Department of the Interior and delegating it to the Secretary of the Navy. However, authority over the portions of

he reserves where there were "pending claims or applications for permits
or leases" remained with the Interior Department.

With the exception of 400 acres in Teapot Dome, the three government
reserves were dotted with lands held outright or claimed by a variety of
individuals and corporations. During the final year of the Wilson administration, after the passage of the leasing bill, leases had been granted
freely. In Buena Vista Hills drainage had gone so far that the whole
Naval Reserve was practically abandoned. Drainage in Elk Hills had
become so serious that Daniels in his last months in office called for bids
to drill 21 offset wells on the western edge of the reserve to tap the
underground oil flow. These bids had not yet come in before the administration changed and he was replaced by Denby.

A month before becoming Secretary of the Interior, Fall wrote his wife
that Harding "thinks the Interior Department is second only to the State
Department in importance and that there is more opportunity for graft
and scandal connected with the disposition of public lands, etc., than
there could be in any other department and he wants a man who is
thoroughly familiar with the business and one he can rely upon as
thoroughly honest." Such was the frame of mind of this sharp-minded and
able man as he took office. The climate of the times was anti-conservationist. His own views on conservation were well known, profanely expressed. As long ago as 1912 he had publicly looked forward to a day
when Congress could abolish the whole Department of the Interior as
redundant. The best place for public land—except in the case of the
national parks—was, in his opinion, in private hands. As for the petroleum
reserves, they should never have existed in the first place.

Fall had long been looking forward to quitting public life. He had been
reluctant to run for a second term in the Senate, and only the importunities of the New Mexican Republican leaders and Theodore Roosevelt's
friendly urging persuaded him. His health was bad. At his New Mexico
ranch he had been gored through the lung by a pet stag before entering
Harding's Cabinet, and this intensified his chronic bronchial troubles,
pleurisy and arthritis. Two of his four children, his thirty-two-year old
son Jack and his daughter Carolyn, had died in the influenza epidemic of
1918. A month before the 1920 Republican convention he told his wife
that he was more and more disgusted with politics and was determined
to get out "as soon as my sense of duty will permit me to do so." He had
never recouped the loss of his Mexican mine holdings in the 1910 revolution, and when he entered the Cabinet he possessed a baronial estate in
New Mexico with very little cash to run it. After a year he planned to
leave Washington for his neglected private affairs and his Three Rivers
ranch in New Mexico's Tularosa Basin.

Lying between the villages of Tularosa and Oscuro, Three Rivers was one of the largest ranches in the state, scattered in tracts of various sizes over a fifty-five mile area twenty-four miles in width and strategically located to contain most of the water holes. Through them Fall controlled three-quarters of a million acres, although some of these acres consisted of leased state lands and range lands of the public domain.

As a poor boy in Kentucky Fall had dreamed of one day owning a blue-grass farm. As a poor and wandering young man he had renewed his dream in New Mexico when he first saw the historic ranch Tres Rios or Three Rivers, belonging to Patrick Coghlan, a friend of Billy the Kid's. Fall never forgot Three Rivers. When, years later, Coghlan failed to keep up his mortgage payments, Fall bought the judgment, took over the ranch, and then continued to buy more land. In 1906 he moved to Coghlan's old adobe ranch house which he now enlarged to a two-story mansion with a classic façade supported by white columns like the Kentucky estates of his childhood. He spent thousands of dollars on irrigation, digging wells and water holes, laying down miles of pipe and concrete ditches, installing tanks and pumping plants to carry water from the San Andreas Mountains. He raised range and thoroughbred cattle, hogs, horses and mules, sheep, hunting dogs, and prize barnyard fowl. He stocked his streams and ponds with fish. He grew alfalfa, corn, wheat, vegetables, apples, peaches, and pecans, and grafted English walnut cuttings on native black walnuts. He organized prospecting on his properties for coal, copper, and iron. His wife ran the small general store, The Three Rivers Trading Company, mostly for his hands and cowboys. His library was renowned in that section of the Southwest. In his settlement dominated by the Ionic-columned mansion, with his wife and four children, in the midst of the rough-rolling acres he loved, Fall became the patriarch of Three Rivers.

After his Mexican financial reverses, Fall tried to put his ranch on a sound footing to insure its continuous development. In 1913 he consolidated most of his holdings with those of Mahlon T. Everhart of the neighboring Hatchet Ranch who had married his daughter Carolyn. Together they formed the Tres Rios Cattle and Land Company, with Fall owning 50 shares, Carolyn 49, and Everhart one. Everhart and Fall then began to round out Three Rivers by buying other pieces of property. They also acquired several hundred registered cattle for breeding with their range herds. All this required outlays of money beyond the profits of the Tres Rios Company. When Fall took his seat in Harding's Cabinet after leaving his son-in-law in control at Three Rivers, he owed the M. D. Thatcher Estates Company of Pueblo $140,500 and was eight years in arrears in his taxes.

As Secretary of the Navy, the inept Denby felt, and indeed was, out of his depth in dealing with Western land problems. For about a month he maintained that the Naval Reserves should be kept intact, then veered round to believing that they should be leased and their management turned back to the Interior Department. Fall later explained that "when Denby, at the door of the Cabinet office, asked me, as Secretary of the Interior, to take over administration of the naval oil reserve lands, and when, afterward, at Denby's request, President Harding directed me to do so, I became officially an agent for the Navy Department. The authority I exerted was executed in cooperation with the Secretary of the Navy and under the direction of the President of the United States." Following his talk with Denby, the Secretary of the Interior drew up a draft for an Executive order to effect the transfer.

Though this transfer of authority over the naval oil lands would later be portrayed as the first step in a sinister conspiracy, it seemed at the time it was announced in the newspapers a routine government transaction. La Follette made a note of it, and some of the senior naval officers raised private objections. Adm. Robert S. Griffin protested to Denby that the Navy had been fighting for ten years to retain its oil reserves and that if the Secretary turned their administration over to the Interior Department "we might just as well say good-bye to our oil."

Fall, once having assumed control of the naval reserves, found himself faced with the same problem of drainage that had plagued his predecessor, the biggest drainer being the Standard Oil Company. The open bids that Daniels had solicited for offset drilling at Elk Hills now arrived on Fall's desk. Since the high bidder was the Pan-American Petroleum and Transport Company, with an offer to the government of 55 per cent of the oil taken from "strip leasing," the lease was given to that company.

The Pan-American Petroleum and Transport Company was the corporate name of Edward Doheny, who so many years before had sweated beside Fall as a penniless hard-rocker in the Grey Eagle Mine. From that joint mining interlude Doheny had wandered on to more adventures if at first with scarcely more success. He had been a book agent, a fruit packer, a mule driver, and a waiter in the Occidental Hotel at Wichita, Kansas. Once he had fought off a mountain lion with nothing but a knife. When on another mining venture he had fallen down a mine shaft and broken both legs he had spent his convalescence studying law. At thirty-five years of age, as he turned to prospecting for oil, he seemed a failure. Yet a dozen years later, after successfully exploring and opening the fabulous Los Angeles district and other rich Californian and Mexican oil fields, the little man with the droopy white mustache and quizzical Celtic face was living on his great estate, Chester Park, outside Los Angeles—when he was not on his yacht *Casiana*—and was reputed to be worth over a hundred million dollars. As president of the Pan-American Company he was considered an enlightened employer and in Washington a reliable expert on petroleum matters. For all his millions he was restless, moving from one new project to another, more concerned with the satisfaction of power than with money. As a Democrat he liked to boast of the former high government officials of both parties whom he employed. Four members of Wilson's Cabinet worked for his Pan-American Company after leaving office—Secretary of the Treasury McAdoo, Sec. of War Lindley M. Garrison, Attorney Gen. Thomas W. Gregory, and Sec. of the Interior Franklin K. Lane. Fall had remained his friend ever since their mining days.

By the act of June, 1920, the royalties from the Doheny lease and others granted earlier by the Wilson administration to private operators on the California reserves went into the general treasury funds, with the Navy being allowed to retain only a half million dollars for its own use. Already $6 million had been paid into the treasury from the Buena Vista Hills Reserve alone. The Navy's General Planning Board, predicting that the United States would exhaust its petroleum resources within fifteen years, had long wanted to construct tanks to store the naval oil that might otherwise be lost through drainage.

From before the Civil War the Secretary of the Navy had held the authority to establish fuel depots for the Navy wherever he felt them necessary. But in 1913 an economy-minded Congress had taken this authority on itself. Since then the Navy had vainly been seeking appropriations to build a string of storage tanks along the Pacific and Atlantic coasts. But in the postwar quest for "normalcy" Congress was much more concerned with cutting down military and naval expenditures than with preparing for battles that might never have to be fought. The probability of a future war with Japan was common wardroom talk in the United States Navy, and the admirals themselves considered a conflict with the ruthlessly Rising Sun as almost inevitable. Harding's conference on the Limitation of Armaments muffled but did not change their opinion. Against this threat from the East naval strategists wanted to construct fueling stations at Pearl Harbor in Hawaii as well as those along America's two coasts. The Navy's "war plans" called for the building of storage tanks at Pearl Harbor to contain a million and a half barrels of fuel oil for the future use of the fleet. Fall felt that with such storage tanks at Pearl Harbor, one-half the battleships then on the Pacific would be worth more than the total number under other conditions.

Another official who thought the tanks a good idea was Griffin's successor as Chief of the Bureau of Engineering, Adm. John Keeler Robison, recently put in charge of the administration of the Naval Petroleum Reserves. Robison, a bluff-faced overly hearty Annapolis graduate of the class of 1891, had commanded the U.S.S. *Huntington* in 1917. One of his junior officers had been Doheny's son, Edward, and when the *Huntington* was in the harbor of Pensacola and Doheny visited his son he also visited the commanding officer. It was in a private talk in Robison's cabin that the oilman was able to instruct the captain in the problem of drainage in the reserves. Robison never forgot the lesson. He was in any case one of those impetuous naval men who felt that war might break out with Japan any day, and he wanted tanks built at Pearl Harbor regardless of how it might be done.

That Congress in its anti-militarist postwar mood would provide funds —estimated by the Navy to run to $200 million—for any such bellicose preparations was out of the question. If the Navy was to construct storage facilities for the oil salvaged from drainage, it could do so only by exchanging a percentage of its oil for tanks and related facilities. Fall determined to establish such a barter system. "My scheme," he wrote in the years after his disgrace, "was going back in a way to the days when men, having no medium of exchange, satisfied their needs by exchanging commodities. Frankly, I thought it was a good idea. I was a little vain about having hit on it."

On April, 1922, as a first step in his scheme, Fall leased the entire Teapot Dome Reserve for twenty years to Harry F. Sinclair, the head of the Sinclair Consolidated Oil Corporation and president of the recently formed Mammoth Oil Company.[1] Sinclair agreed to pay royalties to the government of from 12½ to 50 per cent, depending on the productivity of the wells, not in money—which would have gone into the treasury— but in certificates exchangeable with Mammoth for fuel oil, gasoline, and other petroleum products at 27 seaboard points on the Atlantic and Gulf coasts and in Cuba. Such certificates could also be exchanged for steel tanks to be constructed wherever the Navy needed them. The Mammoth Oil Company also obligated itself to build a pipe line from Teapot Dome to connect with a pipe line running to Chicago.

By the terms of the transfer of naval lands to the Department of the Interior, the Secretary was free to lease the oil reserves without competitive bidding. No other bids were solicited for Teapot Dome, and Fall kept the contract with Sinclair a close secret. Later he explained that it was the only bid he could have considered, because Sinclair's company offered advantages that others could not. He had not asked for outside bids because he knew that without them he could make a better price for the government. His secrecy was justified, since "to call attention to the fact that contracts providing for enormous storages for future use in a crisis of oil were being made off the coast or in certain parts of this country" involved national security.

Fall had known Sinclair for several years. After the inauguration he

Sinclair organized the Mammoth Oil Company specifically for handling the lease and development of Teapot Dome.

had been the oilman's guest on Sinclair's private car *The Sinco*—Sinco being Sinclair's nickname among his associates—at the Kentucky Derby. On the last day of that year *The Sinco* had put into the branch railroad station at Three Rivers for Sinclair and Fall to discuss the prospects and possibilities of the Teapot Dome reserve.

Except for his love of power, his rivalry with Standard Oil, Sinclair did not need Teapot Dome. Starting out in life as a drugstore clerk, he had become one of the richest oilmen in the world, with holdings in Kansas, Oklahoma, Texas, Louisiana, and Wyoming as well as in Mexico, Costa Rica, Panama, and West Africa.[2] Eleven years younger than Harding, he had grown up in Independence, Kansas, first studying pharmacy and working in his father's drugstore. When his father died, he inherited a small amount of money which he used to buy and sell options in the newly discovered Kansas oil fields. In 1905 he bought his first oil well, and within a decade had become one of the largest producers in Kansas as well as the Indian territory of Oklahoma. In his middle years he was a bald, round-faced man with a quiet manner, an enormous grin, and eyes that bulged like a frog's. He owned a racing stable at his Rancocas Farm in New Jersey that would eventually produce a Derby winner, and was part owner of a baseball club, the St. Louis Browns. Theodore Roosevelt had been his friend and just after World War I at the Colonel's request he had given the demobilized Archie Roosevelt a sinecure job with his Mammoth Oil Company. He had long had an envious eye on the government oil reserves.

On April 15, 1922, eight days after signing the Teapot Dome lease, Fall opened proposals for the construction of storage tanks, the building of docks and wharves, the installation of loading mechanisms, and the dredging of a channel into Pearl Harbor. Three companies submitted bids: the Standard Oil Company of California, the Associated Oil Company of California, and Doheny's Pan-American Petroleum and Transport Company. Standard Oil, uncertain that the barter scheme might prove legal, bid on the oil only and not for construction of storage tanks. The Associated Oil Company's bid contained the wary proviso that any contract must first be approved by Congress. Doheny offered two proposals: the first for construction of tanks with a capacity of a million and a half gallons of fuel oil, payment to be made in crude oil from Elk Hills; the second for constructing the tanks for a quarter of a million dollars less (in oil certificates) but with the provision that Doheny's company have a preference on any future lease for the entire Elk Hills reserve. Fall accepted the second proposal. After contracts had been worked out by

[2] At this time Sinclair was trying to get oil property concessions in the Soviet Union. In 1924 Albania would invite him to become its ruler in the hope of settling its troubled economic affairs.

Doheny's subordinates and officials of the Interior and Navy departments, they were signed on April 25, 1922.

The 6 million barrels of crude oil that Doheny had agreed to accept in trade would not have covered the construction costs of the Pearl Harbor tanks. But during the autumn Doheny, in a private talk with Fall and Admiral Robison, proposed that his Pan-American Company should build additional tanks for the Navy, fill them with oil, erect a refinery at San Pedro, California, and build a pipe line from the naval reserves to the refinery. In return for this Doheny asked for a lease on the remaining acres of Elk Hills for fifteen years with unlimited drilling rights. The Secretary and the Admiral agreed, and in December Fall signed the final contract with Doheny, giving Pan-American the exclusive exploitation of about 30 thousand acres of proven oil lands.

While Fall was engaged with the leases to Doheny and Sinclair, he was also faced with the perennial Buena Vista claims of the Honolulu Oil Company as well as the question of the Standard Oil Company's ownership of Section 36 in the heart of the Elk Hills Reserve. The Honolulu Company claimed that it had taken great prospecting risks "in high good faith" but had been mistreated by the government. Fall was sympathetic. He agreed to give the company leases to its claims and would have granted outright patents "but for public opinion." In regard to Section 36, it had long been disputed whether this section, originally granted to the state of California for educational purposes and sold by the state to Standard Oil when oil was discovered there, should not revert to the Federal government. After hearing arguments by both sides, Fall decided in favor of Standard Oil.

In the case of the Honolulu Oil Company and of Section 36 there was no question of collusion or of Fall's having benefited in any way by his decisions. He had decided according to his ingrained anti-conservationist philosophy, just as Pinchot had predicted. In the case of the Doheny and Sinclair leases, however, Fall had privately taken money from both men. Later, and as long as he lived, he would maintain that his personal financial transactions in no way affected his official acts as Secretary of the Interior, but public opinion would not see it that way when such secret transactions came to light.

Fall, in his acquisitive years, had managed to gain control of almost all the land and water sources of the Tularosa Basin. Only one piece in the land pattern was missing, that of the neighboring 3,000-acre Harris Ranch. Called by its owner "the best small ranch in New Mexico," the Harris Ranch controlled the headwaters of Three Rivers Canyon, the source of much of Fall's water. When the ranch came on the market in 1921, Fall felt it was necessary to buy it to protect his own holdings. Still as short of cash as he had been since the 1910 Mexican revolution, in his need he appealed to his old mining pal Doheny. On November 29, the day after Doheny had submitted his formal offer to construct storage tanks at Pearl Harbor in exchange for the Navy's reserve crude oil, Fall telephoned him to say that he was "prepared now to receive that loan." Doheny sent his son Edward, Jr., to the brokerage house of Blair Company with instructions to draw out $100,000 in cash from their accounts. Following his father's instructions, the young Doheny wrapped the bills in paper, put them in a little black bag and took them to Fall in his Wardman Park Hotel suite in Washington. Fall made out a promissory note to Doheny and handed it to the son. The following week Fall arrived in Texas for the Christmas holidays with the bulging bag and on December 5 purchased the Harris Ranch at the office of his son-in-law C. C. Chase, collector of customs at El Paso, for $91,500. Chase's wife, seeing the packages of money on her father's desk, asked about them. Fall told her the money was mortgage money from Doheny that would assure them all of Three Rivers after he himself retired from Harding's Cabinet.

However necessary the purchase of the Harris Ranch may have been to protect Fall's water supply, it did nothing to help the tight financial situation Sinclair found him in on a visit to Three Rivers the last day of 1921. Sinclair arrived on *The Sinco* with his lawyer, Col. J. W. Zevely, and their two wives. Accompanying them in a public coach attached to the same train were Doctor H. Foster Bain, director of the Interior Department's Bureau of Mines, and a former Interior Department official, J. J. Cotter, since become vice president of Doheny's Pan-American Petroleum and Transport Company. Fall was at the branch-line Three Rivers station to meet them.

Bain and Cotter stayed overnight to discuss the Doheny contracts. Sinclair and his party remained three days, exploring the ranch and hunting deer and quail and wild turkeys with the cowpunchers. On New Year's Eve Emma Fall took them to a cowboy dance. During the evenings Fall and Sinclair sat before a log fire in the main ranch house discussing the terms of the Teapot Dome lease. When Fall remarked offhandedly that he would like to have some milch cows on his ranch but could not afford such expensive cattle, Sinclair said he had more than he needed at his Rancocas Farm. After returning to New Jersey he sent Fall six heifers, a yearling bull, two six-month-old boars, four sows, and an English thoroughbred horse for Fall's foreman. For a man of Sinclair's means it was a picayune gift, although in later years much was made of it by Fall's enemies. More was made of the improvements at Three Rivers following *The Sinco's* visit. Neighbors observed a new hydroelectric plant, miles of new wiring, irrigation and power projects, road building and landscaping, new fences, a refurbishing of the ranch house. Fall also bought an additional 6,500 acres to round out his domain.

Six weeks after signing the Teapot Dome lease Fall told his son-in-law, Mahlon Everhart, in Washington, that he was selling Sinclair a third interest in the Tres Rios Company. Following the purchase of the Harris Ranch the company had been reorganized. Sinclair was to be given a third interest in the new company, with Fall and Everhart each having a third and with Everhart acting as Sinclair's trustee. Sinclair's name did not appear on the company books, nor was there any documentary evidence that he owned a third of Fall's ranch.

On May 8, 1922, Everhart met Sinclair on *The Sinco* on a siding in the Washington railroad yards and picked up $198,000 in Liberty Bonds in thousand-dollar denominations. Two weeks later he received an additional $35,000 in bonds from Sinclair in his New York office. Since most of the money so far received was needed to pay the Thatcher Estates and back taxes and to acquire new land, Everhart was instructed by Fall to ask Sinclair for a separate loan of $36,000 to cover operational expenses and improvements. Sinclair paid it, and when he was at Three Rivers in November to get a secondary contract in the Salt Creek fields, he gave Everhart another $10,000. The following January Everhart called on him at the Wardman Park Hotel and received still another payment, this time for $25,000.

Affairs at Three Rivers were such that Fall had real need of the $400,000 he had received from Doheny and Sinclair, small as such a sum might seem to them. Yet as a politician he must have been aware of the implications to be drawn from receiving this money while the lenders were negotiating contracts for government oil lands under his control. He kept the transactions secret, giving Doheny the promissory note but making no written record of any money received from Sinclair. After his retirement, when the oil leases were being investigated by a Senate committee, he would write a letter to the committee denying that he had ever received a cent from either Sinclair or Doheny, and when this was shown to be a lie and the transactions were brought out into the open, he would eventually be convicted of having accepted a bribe from Doheny and sentenced to a year in jail. Fall called that letter his "one greatest blunder," but for the rest of his life he and his loyal wife continued to maintain against all outside disbelief that the money he had received so casually from his friends was not bribe money and had not influenced his official conduct.

If it had not been for the sinister shadow of the Doheny and Sinclair loans, every one of Fall's official actions could have been defended. Was the drainage at Elk Hills and at Teapot Dome sufficient to warrant the construction of storage facilities above ground? Did the Navy receive an adequate return for its oil from the storage tanks and facilities at Pearl Harbor? Was the leasing of the oil reserves justified? Experts differed, and there was no final answer. Fall had never been anything else but a Western anti-conservationist, and for every move he had made there seemed to be a justifiable precedent—except the taking of money.

If Fall had been open about his financial transactions the conservationists would have still done their best to cancel the Interior Department's oil leases and contracts, but his own disgrace and the scandal of Teapot Dome would have been avoided. The questions remain: whether Doheny's loan to his old friend—a bagatelle, Doheny called it—was for friendship or for influence; whether Sinclair's Liberty Bonds were intended to purchase a third interest in the Tres Rios Ranch or the lease of the Teapot Dome Reserve. For multimillionaires like Doheny and Sinclair the sums were insignificant. Fall's secrecy is sign enough of his awareness of the implications of his financial dealings with two prospective lessees of the government's Naval Reserves. Yet, if he had intended to sell the oil leases for personal gain, he knew their value and could easily have demanded outright ten times the amount he received as a loan. As a bribe, $400,000 is simply too small a sum. Even if there had been no question of oil leases, it is most unlikely that Doheny would have turned down his old friend's request for funds or that Sinclair would have hesitated about buying his casual interest in the Three Rivers Ranch. And with Fall's ingrained anti-conservationist attitude he would undoubtedly have turned over the reserves to Doheny and Sinclair, or someone like them, even if he had received no loans or money of any kind.

Fall was to live on almost through World War II, ruined and obscure. Yet never once in those barren years did he show any doubts or regrets about his official acts. Always he hoped for vindication.

> My borrowing the money may have been unethical [he admitted in 1929 just after his bribery conviction] I certainly did not realize it at the time, and my employing a falsehood to prevent a volcano of political abuse pouring upon the administration that had honored me deserves condemnation; but neither one nor the other justifies the charge that I was disloyal or dishonest as Secretary of the Interior and as a member of Harding's Cabinet.

Perhaps Fall's greatest error was his disregard of the continued strength of the conservationist forces in America. From the moment that he became Secretary of the Interior, the conservationists grouped around Pinchot were resolved to drive him from office as they had driven Secretary Ballinger from the Interior Department a dozen years before. Pinchot wrote in 1921 that on the record it would have been possible to pick a worse man than Fall for Secretary of the Interior, "but not altogether easy." Fall's nemesis was a subordinate of Pinchot's, a quiet, obscure Washington lawyer by the name of Harry A. Slattery, who had been clerk-secretary for the Inland Waterways Commission in Theodore

Roosevelt's administration and in the course of his work had come into contact with the pioneers of the conservation movement. So enthusiastically did he welcome the new movement that he resigned from the commission to become Pinchot's secretary. From 1912 to 1917 he served as secretary of the National Conservation Association, then after the war he retired to a small law practice though still corresponding with Pinchot. In the 1920 campaign he had gone to Marion to talk with Harding on the Front Porch and returned convinced that the protean candidate was a friend of conservation.

During Fall's first year in the Department of the Interior Slattery concerned himself primarily with the Secretary's plans for the exploitation of the resources of Alaska, the lifting of all restrictions on trapping and hunting on public lands, and the proposed transfer of the Forest Service from the Department of Agriculture. He kept careful watch on Fall's activities and reported regularly to Pinchot and La Follette. Convinced that Fall was attacking the government's entire conservation program, Pinchot launched a campaign against him in the press. But the major conservationist worries were Alaska and the Forest Service. The oil reserves were an afterthought.

Through his friends scattered in various government departments Slattery managed to learn of Fall's moves and maneuvers almost at their outset. In May he picked up the "unbelievable rumor" that Fall by Executive order had secured the transfer of the Naval Reserves to the Interior Department. Investigating further, he became convinced that the oil transfer was just one of a series of policies "under a veil of secrecy" in a major anti-conservation campaign, and he reported what he had learned and what he believed to Pinchot.

After the transfer of the Reserves to the Interior Department had been made public, Slattery went to Assistant Secretary of the Navy Theodore Roosevelt, Jr., to protest against Fall's actions and attitudes. Roosevelt "hit the ceiling," telling him that Fall had been in the Rough Riders and that he must not "say anything derogatory of this great, good friend." Slattery then went to tell his tale to the more sympathetic La Follette. When Fall heard of Slattery's snooping activities he reacted in the frontier manner. According to Slattery, "Mr. Fall decided he would use some rough tactics. He had a two-gun man named Baracca who had passed several men over the Great Divide. Mr. Fall sent him round to see me, with a threat. I kicked that gentleman out of my office."

Three days after Fall had signed the contract with Sinclair, Slattery learned from a clerk in the Navy Department about the leasing of Teapot Dome. Even before the actual leasing there had been rumors of it. Early in April Walter Teagle of the Standard Oil Company of New Jersey burst into Albert Lasker's office at the Shipping Board to tell him: "I understand the Interior Department is just about to close a contract to lease

Teapot Dome, and all through the industry it smells. I'm not interested in Teapot Dome. It has *no* interest whatsoever for Standard Oil of New Jersey, but I *do* feel that you should tell the President that it *smells*—that he *must* not permit it to go through."

That evening Lasker went to Harding to express his own doubts about the leases. "This isn't the first time that this rumor has come to me," Harding told him, "but if Albert Fall isn't an honest man, I'm not fit to be President of the United States."

Slattery's information leaked to the *Wall Street Journal,* and a week later the *Journal* ran a front-page story reporting that a Teapot Dome lease had been signed and that Department of the Interior officials considered the arrangement "one of the greatest petroleum undertakings of the age and a notable departure on the part of the government in seeking partnership with private capital for the working of government-owned natural resources."

Rumor had preceded the announcement in Wyoming, and Sen. John P. Kendrick of that state had been bombarded with letters and telegrams from his constituents trying to discover what was happening at Teapot Dome. The day following the *Journal's* article Kendrick introduced a mild resolution that the Secretaries of the Navy and Interior Departments "inform the Senate, if not incompatible with the public interest," about "all proposed operating agreements" in the Teapot Dome Reserve. Kendrick's resolution, accepted by the Senate without comment and without a roll-call vote, was supplemented a week later by a much more specific resolution of La Follette's asking that the Secretary of the Interior be directed to send to the Senate all the facts about the leasing of the naval oil reserves to private persons or corporations. Supplied with information from Slattery's private investigations, aided and encouraged by Pinchot, La Follette then made a fiery attack on Fall and Denby to a Senate in which most of the regular Republicans had ostentatiously quit their seats. A great national policy had been reversed, La Follette told the few remaining senators, and the nation was endangered. "Who," he asked, "were the real organizers of the Mammoth Oil Company who were to be favored by the government with a special privilege in value beyond the dreams of Croesus?" Lackadaisically but unanimously La Follette's resolution was adopted, although the Senate would take no further action for another eighteen months.

To lease Teapot Dome it was necessary to make some settlement of the reserve's many entangling claims, even though most of these claims were questionable.[3] Since it would have cost the government much time and

[3] The right of placer mining claims depended on the discovery of oil within lands open to appropriation. Teapot Dome had been withdrawn since 1909, and none of the claims supported oil discovered there before this date.

money to clear the title, Fall required Sinclair to present a quitclaim deed for the encumbering claims before the Teapot Dome contract was signed. The Pioneer Oil and Refining Company, a subsidiary of the Standard Oil Company of Indiana, had managed to buy up most of these claims and now demanded payment for them. To avoid litigation, Sinclair agreed to pay $1 million in settlement, $200,000 in cash, and the rest later in oil.

There were still other lesser claimants whom Sinclair had to pay off. Among the more disgruntled was a Denver politician and oil prospector, John Leo Stack, who had handled various unsubstantial and unsubstantiated claims in the Teapot Dome area including those of the Pioneer Company. When the Pioneer officials offered him what he considered the pittance of $50,000 for his claims, he went to two blackmailing journalist acquaintances in Denver, Frederick G. Bonfils and Albert Tamman, publishers of an ephemeral scandal sheet known as the Denver *Post*. Bonfils— an ex-gambler, and Tamman—a former circus performer, signed an agreement with Stack for a percentage of anything he might collect from the oil company, and the *Post* at once began a lurid campaign against the Teapot Dome lease. Week after week in flaring red-ink headlines Bonfils and Tamman denounced Sinclair, accusing him of consummating "one of the boldest public-land grabs of the century . . . through trickery that verges, if it does not encroach, on the bounds of crime," and mailing copies of their paper to each congressman and senator. They also sent their star reporter, D. F. Stackelback, to Three Rivers, and he soon returned with the sensational news of Fall's unwonted prosperity. The articles nettled but did not alarm Fall. He wrote to Daugherty that he hoped Stack would get his due but added that he objected to any threats of publicity since he felt that there was nothing to be afraid of or to hide in the Teapot Dome dealings.

At first Sinclair stubbornly refused to be blackmailed, and it took some time for Colonel Zevely to persuade him that it would be more sensible to appease Stack and the *Post*. He finally agreed to pay Stack a quarter of a million dollars plus half the profits on 320 acres of Teapot Dome land— although in the end Stack and his associates received no more than the initial payment. As soon as the agreement was signed, the tone of the *Post* changed. No longer was there opprobrious mention of Teapot Dome. Instead, the *Post's* weekly "Great Divide" featured "the gripping story of the sensational rise to fame and fortune of Harry F. Sinclair, one of the most spectacular men of the present day."

A more influential and ostensibly respectable Colorado newspaperman who had to be bought off was John C. Shaffer, publisher of the Denver *Times*, the *Rocky Mountain News*, and the Chicago *Star*. Shaffer, who owned land adjacent to Teapot Dome, had applied unsuccessfully for leases in the reserve in 1917 and 1918, and had had an agreement with the Pioneer Oil Company to receive an eighth interest in any contract the company might negotiate with the government. After selling out its claims to Sinclair, Pioneer paid Shaffer $92,500. Nevertheless, after Fall took office the newspaperman still continued to demand a 640-acre lease.[4] At Fall's suggestion Sinclair tried to muffle Shaffer by offering him a half interest in 420 acres of the Wyoming reserve.

Whatever it cost Sinclair to silence his critics, the sums were a fraction of what he was able to realize almost at once on the Teapot Dome lease. Sinclair Consolidated Oil stock rose to 38¾ in June from a January low of 18¾. Sinclair himself, through a dummy family corporation—Hyva, named after his two children, Harry and Virginia—traded a third of his Mammoth shares for a quarter of a million shares of Sinclair Oil which he was allowed to buy at a unit price of $17 when its public price was $50, making a profit of $17,059,700 before he had even drilled a well at Teapot Dome. With the independent stock trader, Jesse L. Livermore, he then formed a syndicate to buy 400,000 Mammoth shares at $26 which Livermore was able to market to the public at from $40 to $56.50 for an additional $8 million or so profit.

While Sinclair was dealing with Stack and Shaffer, Fall, too, was having his difficulties with dissenters. In New Mexico Carl Magee, to whom Fall had sold an interest he once held in the Albuquerque *Morning Journal,* now began to assail the Teapot Dome leases and, keeping carefully within the laws of libel, to remark on the sudden prosperity of the Three Rivers Ranch. Fall had a sulphurous confrontation with the editor in his office, and in the weeks to come Magee found himself boycotted by advertisers, his bank notes called, and the *Journal* harassed until finally it was forced to close down. In the Teapot Dome reserve itself Fall was faced with the problem of Col. James Darden. Darden, a colonel in the Southern Pickwickian sense, was a friend of Harding and Daugherty who had contributed to Harding's 1920 campaign fund before the convention and served as vice-chairman of the Inauguration Committee. In 1919 he had acquired some land in the Salt Creek area and a worthless claim to a patent in Teapot Dome. After the inauguration, on visiting Daugherty and Jess Smith in their Pickens County shack, he persuaded them to put $2,400 each into his oil business. When the Colonel heard rumors of the impending Teapot Dome lease he arranged with the Mutual Oil Company to begin drilling wells on his fictive patent. Two months after Sinclair had signed his contract with the government, Mutual had set up a large oil-drilling rig on Darden's claim, surrounded it with barbed wire, and begun to pump out oil.

---

[4] Four patents. A patent was for 160 acres.

Fall, who had known and disliked Darden for years, dispatched an order signed by himself and Denby warning the Mutual Oil Company off the premises. On Daugherty's advice Darden went to see Fall who told him he had never filed a proper claim and angrily accused him of being a trespasser. When in spite of warnings the Mutual drillers still persisted, Fall went to Harding to demand that the "squatters" be ejected, explaining that if the government merely brought suit this would "play into Darden's hands and possibly that of fifty other parties with similar worthless claims." The litigation would last for years, Sinclair would relinquish his contract, and no one else would bid for the tract in whole or in part. Fall's suggestion was to use the Marines, the Navy's police force—since the reserve was naval property—and remove Darden's crew by force. Harding was dubious about such peremptory treatment of a loyal Republican and pre-convention contributor. To Fall's objection that Darden was in any case "a low-down son of a bitch," Harding observed that he supposed the Colonel was that when he sent in his campaign check. "By God, Mr. President," Fall told him, "he was!" Some days later Harding wrote Fall that he was arranging an interview with Darden and that "if he does not comply with friendly recommendations we will immediately take steps to eject his company from government property." Darden later gave an account of this interview:

> He [Harding] said, "Jim, how about this property you think you own in Teapot Dome, or in Wyoming," he put it. I said, "I don't know; I couldn't tell you. We feel naturally we own it, because we spent some money to get it." He said, "Fall doesn't think you own it. . . . He is T.N.T." And then we began to discuss it.

Darden was willing to stop the drilling operations if Daugherty so advised him, but Daugherty refused to commit himself, telling Darden that the courts were his only further resource.

Fall sent for Assistant Sec. of the Navy Theodore Roosevelt, Jr., telling him that there were trespassers on the Teapot Dome Reserve and that the President wanted the Marines to put them off the property. It was, he said, a perfectly legal action. Roosevelt, as acting secretary in Denby's weekend absence, dispatched several Interior Department officials and four armed Marines under Capt. George K. Shuler to take over Darden's claim.

The encounter on the oil field was brief and bloodless. Marines advancing in battle order met the foreman at the barbed-wire barrier. Shuler ordered him to stop drilling, and gave him ten minutes to shut down. The superintendent of the Mutual Oil Company then arrived, at first "rather peeved" as he saw the government seal on the rig, but ending up by inviting the battle-ready Marines to lunch.

Colonel Darden, throwing in his hand, did not bother to object further, although the governor of Wyoming protested to Harding against such high-handed means in place of legal action. Harding, defending Fall, replied that the action was "lawful and efficient" and that the removal of the squatters had been managed "sweetly and without conflict."

Whatever the reaction of rival oilmen, financiers, conservationists, and surviving Progressive gadflies like La Follette, the announcement of the Doheny and Sinclair oil leases seemed a technical administrative matter that caused little public interest. Though geologists would continue to debate as to whether there was any real danger of drainage in Teapot Dome by the adjacent Salt Creek wells, the public was reassured by the formal letter of explanation that Harding wrote to the President of the Senate on June 7:

> On April 29th the Senate adopted a resolution directing the Secretary of the Interior to furnish the Senate with certain documents, correspondence, papers, files, executive orders, and all contracts for drilling oil wells on naval oil reserves of the United States, with all detailed information relating thereto. I am today in receipt of a letter from the Secretary of the Interior in which he advises me of his compliance with the Resolution of the Senate and in which he makes to me a full and comprehensive report, probably not contemplated in the resolution, in which he gives to me details of the handling of all naval reserve petroleum matters up to the present date, including all full explanation of the contracts for the disposition of oil and the necessity for such action as has been taken. The report, with the exhibits hereto attached, I am sending to the Senate herewith with the hope that they may be referred to the Senate Committee on Public Lands for such ready reference and information as they will afford the committee in making the investigation contemplated by the Senate.
>
> I am sure I am correct in construing the impelling purpose of the Secretary of the Interior in making to me this report. It is not to be construed as a defense in dealing with the problems incident to the handling of the naval reserves, but is designed to afford that explanation to which the Senate is entitled, and which will prove helpful to the country generally in appraising the administration of these matters of great public concern. I think it is only fair to say in this connection that the policy which has been adopted by the Secretary of the Navy and the Secretary of the Interior in dealing with these matters was submitted to me prior to the adoption thereof, and the policy decided upon and the subsequent acts have at all times had my entire approval.

In January Fall had written a former law partner that he had accomplished as much as he could in the Cabinet without additional legislative acts. Filling a Cabinet post "perfunctorily" had no appeal to him, and he had insisted that the President make known officially that he was resigning and would go out of the Cabinet on March 4. Harding persuaded him to stay on, offering to appoint him later to the Supreme Court, and pointing out that since Hays was resigning on that same date to become the new head of the Motion Pictures Producers and Distributors, if Fall left, too, it would give the impression of dissent in the Cabinet. Fall, still talking of resigning in the summer, wrote to his wife after the Senate resolution that nobody in Washington seemed to be paying any attention to his oil-leasing policies except those opposed to the administration or to him. "Those who know me," he added, "think too little of it even to become indignant."

For four years, through the Harding administration and into the Coolidge succession, Secretary of Commerce Hoover—concealing his distaste—had sat at the same Cabinet table with his colleague, Attorney General Daugherty. Finally, when the winds of scandal had increased to a gale, Hoover had gone with Secretary of State Hughes to warn President Coolidge that for the sake of the new administration the Attorney General must go. "From this man's long-time character," Hoover wrote of Daugherty in his memoirs, "he should never have been in any government."

Challenged from the day he took office, Daugherty was to become second only to Fall in darkening the name of the Harding administration, and Herrick's early warning against having him in the Cabinet would later seem a prophecy. Elihu Root told his biographer that Harding "should have known that Daugherty wasn't fit to be Attorney General of the United States, but he hadn't the nerve to take a course which would appear to be deserting his friends."

Inevitably in his translation to the capital Daugherty brought with him the habits and attitudes of the Ohio political jungle. The vultures and jackals of the Ohio Gang, the politicians of the lower level moving on to Washington in Harding's wake, flocked to him as chief patronage distributor. Although he himself maintained that the term "Ohio Gang" had been concocted by renegade Republicans trying to take over the party in Ohio, rumor and suspicion tagged him in Washington as earlier in Columbus. By the time Coolidge forced him from office he would have been accused of a variety of crimes, from failure to prosecute wartime commercial frauds and profiteering to accepting bribes, selling pardons, and even—it was whispered—to conniving at murder.[5]

Daugherty was sixty-one years old when he entered Harding's Cabinet and in his portly middle years had come to look the politician incarnate, from the agate, dissimilar eyes in a face like flesh-painted steel to the roll of chin fat plumping above his stiff collar and pearl stickpin. Yet behind this impervious mask lurked an uncertain personality haunted by the

[5] Nevertheless, Daugherty's judicial appointments were of strikingly high quality. In naming judges he almost always followed Taft's advice, as in his appointment of the Democrat and Catholic Pierce Butler to the Supreme Court.

accumulation of past disappointments and beyond his depth in the present intricacies of his high office. Of all Harding's Cabinet members he, the gregarious politician, became the least approachable, the least available to the press. From time to time he suffered from spells of physical and psychic collapse in which he would retreat to the Deer Creek shack or to Asheville, North Carolina, or to Florida. Under the burden of his domestic troubles—his wastrel son and invalid wife—his emotional dependence on his "bumper," Jess Smith, increased.

Daugherty became unique among Attorney Generals of the United States in that while he headed the Department of Justice he was subject to two congressional investigations, and after his resignation was twice indicted for malfeasance. His trials were actually for accepting bribes while in office, although because of the statute of limitations he could be charged only with conspiring to defraud the United States of his "honest, impartial, and unprejudiced services and judgment" as Attorney General. "No charge against me was ever proven in any court," he boasted in his ghost-written apologia. But in that book, contrived for his vindication, he neglected to say that in court he had refused to testify on the grounds that he might incriminate himself. Nor did he add that at his first trial the jury failed to agree after sixty-five hours, nine jurors being in favor of convicting him. The jury at his second trial stood eleven to one for conviction, with the lone holdout commonly believed to have been bribed.

Like Fall, Daugherty lived on into World War II, and like Fall he continued to maintain to the end that he was a maligned public servant, innocent of any wrongdoing. His voluminous letters are belligerent in their self-justification. Mark Sullivan, who spent two confidential days at his home in 1935 talking over the Harding period, thought him defiant of any standards outside himself. His conscience, however elastic, was clear. "I felt," Sullivan wrote, "that he lived by a code of his own; if his code did not happen to be identical with the world's conventions, so much the worse for the world's conventions." Daugherty could cover up, with a cold disdain for truth. Although he knew about Nan Britton and must have known about Carrie Phillips, he denied to Sullivan that there had ever been any "woman scrape" in Harding's life. Yet, whatever lies Daugherty may have told, whatever favors he may have done, how many times as head of the Justice Department he may have turned the blind eye, Sullivan felt then, as he had felt earlier, that the Attorney General would never have consciously done anything for his personal benefit to bring discredit on the man he had made President.

So much smoke erupting from the Justice Department in Attorney General Daugherty's term as Attorney General was bound to blacken him permanently. But almost half a century later, when most of the official and unofficial correspondence has been made public, it is still not possible to estimate the proportion of smoke to fire with any exactness. Certain tangible facts remain, nevertheless, obvious and inexplicable. Daugherty had spent his own money so freely in the Harding prenomination maneuverings that by the time he entered the Cabinet he had liabilities of $27,000 and taxable property of only $8,030. His share in the expenses of the Little House on H Street ran to double his official salary of $12,000, yet in the next two or three years he would deposit nearly $75,000 from unrevealed sources in his brother's bank.

During the crusade "to keep the world safe for democracy" 18,000 American industrialists and businessmen had managed to combine patriotism with profit in becoming millionaires, a fact much resented by thirty-dollar-a-month returning soldiers and other losers to the high cost of living. Appealing to those for whom the war and the immediate postwar years had brought more hardship than profit, Republicans in Congress charged that there had been thievery in contracts for ships, planes, munitions, and other war supplies. Wilson's flamboyant Attorney General, A. Mitchell Palmer, had showed himself more interested in deporting Reds and in maneuvering himself as a possible presidential candidate than in uncovering war frauds. Finally, just after Daugherty had taken office, Congress voted the Attorney General's office $3,200,000 for a Bureau of War Transactions to investigate the various wartime contracts. For unexplained reasons, the new Attorney General remained hesitant, dilatory. Finally he put 25 lawyers to work going over some six hundred cases. Eventually, as he was able to boast in his apologia, civil suits that he directed returned $8½ million to the government—a sum that for all his boasting accounted to a mere tenth of 1 per cent of the government's total expenditure for war supplies.

The sudden rearming of a nation unused to large-scale armaments for half a century had brought inevitable mistakes, inefficiencies, bungling, wide-scale waste, and some dishonesty. In the postwar reaction the demand for scapegoats was met neither by Attorney Generals Palmer nor Daugherty. With Daugherty heading the Justice Department, whispers rustled through Washington of indicted or indictable war profiteers with the proper approach being able to come to amicable agreements with the Attorney General's office. An austere and bearded Justice Department investigator, the oddly named Capt. Hazel L. Scaife, uncovered evidence that the Wright-Martin Aircraft Corporation had overcharged the government by $2,267,342 on war contracts while failing to deliver a single fighting plane to France. Scaife, whose impressive beard concealed a naïve and rather gullible reformer, had prepared a dossier on Wright-Martin, only to find that his efforts to bring the corporation to trial were blocked at higher levels both in the Department of Justice and in the War Department. Baffled and disgusted, he resigned. Afterward his report disappeared from the Justice Department files. By ambivalent coincidence—as was later shown—Daugherty on taking office owned 500 shares of Wright-Martin stock, and a year later had acquired 2,000 shares more.

Although the extent could never be determined, other examples of apparent immunity against prosecution kept coming to light. A legal assistant to the Chief of the Army Air Service, Thomas F. Lane, assigned to special duty in the Department of Justice, found evidence of dubious wartime transactions by the Standard Aircraft Company, controlled by the Japanese firm of Mitsui. When a Senate committee began to investigate the case, Lane was forbidden to appear before it. "That is orders," he was told in the Department, and his papers were confiscated. When, in spite of orders, he did testify, he was dropped from the service. Maj. W. O. Watts was another investigator whose career was cut short after he assisted two congressmen to look into war frauds.

Although on becoming Attorney General Daugherty resigned from his firm of Daugherty, Todd and Raney, his partners were not forgotten. Ralph F. Raney, who had married Daugherty's daughter Emily, received an appointment in the New York office of the Alien Property Bureau. The other partner, John E. Todd, found his practice so enhanced by business connected with the Justice Department and the Alien Property Bureau that he felt obliged to open an office in Washington. Though Todd was not invariably successful in resolving his clients' problems with the government, it soon became apparent that he was a useful lawyer to see in tricky cases. Such was the case of Cecil H. Kerns, president of a drug concern who had been sentenced to a term in the Federal prison at Atlanta for bootlegging liquor. Soon after Kerns engaged Todd he found himself paroled. The Miller brothers of Ranch 101 in Oklahoma had equal good luck when they turned to Todd. They had been indicted for swindling the Indians out of oil lands. Long notorious for such chicanery, one of them a convicted counterfeiter, the Millers with their powerful connections in both parties were rarely in difficulties with the law. On being indicted they got in touch with their friend Fall who wrote Daugherty asking for a delay in the trial. Todd then evolved a plan for the Millers to plead guilty, with the understanding that they would be fined and released. Since the special attorney for the Department of Justice, H. M. Peck, was stubborn enough to hold out for prison sentences, arrangements were made to have him removed from the case. When Oklahoma's Sen. John W. Harreld learned of this he warned Daugherty that if Peck were dropped and Todd appeared for the defense there would be an open scandal. The Attorney General expressed surprise that his former partner was connected with the case and advised Todd to withdraw. Peck continued in charge of the prosecution. Shortly afterward Daugherty wired Peck to accept the Millers' plea of guilty, with the fine earlier agreed upon, and when Peck protested he was superseded. Todd kept his retainer, the Millers paid their nominal fine and walked out of court free men, and two investigators from the Indian Bureau who had been overzealous in securing evidence against the Millers were discharged.

Daugherty's trial, in which one stubborn or suborned juryman alone stood between him and jail, was the belated aftermath of a series of financial transactions within the Alien Property Bureau in 1921. As Harding's Alien Property Custodian, Col. Thomas Miller had taken charge of 31,000 active trusts from New England to the Philippines as well as several thousand pieces of real estate. One of the largest of these trusts consisted of the 49 per cent of the shares of the American Metal Company that were owned in 1917 by the German Metallgesellschaft & Metall Bank. On the American declaration of war these shares—then worth about $6 million—were seized as enemy property by the then Alien Property Custodian A. Mitchell Palmer who sold them and invested the proceeds in Liberty Bonds. The bonds, sequestered by the Treasury, had with accumulated interest become worth $7 million four years later when the owners of the Metall Bank, an international banking family by the name of Moses from Frankfurt-on-Main, attempted to regain their property.

A younger member of the Moses family, who had changed his name to Richard Merton, arrived in New York in September, 1921, to lay claim to the confiscated American Metal shares. Merton had served in the German Army as a captain during the war, and although Jewish had absorbed the manner and appearance of a Prussian officer. On behalf of his family he claimed that a Swiss corporation, the Societé Suisse pour Valeurs de Métaux, had bought up the American interests of the Metall Bank in March, 1917, a month before the United States entered the war. The Societé Suisse was also controlled by the Moses family, and Merton admitted that the transfer had been oral.

Once in New York Merton inquired among his Wall Street acquaintances for someone "who could pave the way" to the Alien Property Bureau. They recommended the Republican National Committeeman and former Wood campaign manager John King. King got in touch with Jess Smith, and on September 20 Smith and Miller met with Merton and King for a talk in New York. The next day the Alien Property Bureau agreed formally to Merton's claim, and this was approved two days later by the Attorney General's office.

Within the week Miller drew two checks on the Treasury for a total of $6,453,979.97 and two lots of Liberty Bonds valued at $514,350. These he took to New York for a celebration dinner given by Merton for him, King, and Smith. The grateful Prussian officer presented his guests with two-hundred-dollar cigarette cases as mementos. Afterward he paid King $391,300 in bonds and $50,000 in cash—a fee he did not regard as excessive for such full and rapid service. King turned over $224,000 to Smith "for expediting the claim through his acquaintance in Washington" and $50,000 to Miller, keeping $112,000 for himself, while $55,300 would remain unaccounted for. At Daugherty's trial it was shown that Smith had deposited $50,000 of the Liberty Bonds to a joint account, "Jess Smith Extra No. 3" that he kept in Mally Daugherty's Midland National Bank in Washington Court House. Smith Extra No. 3, as opposed to his two personal accounts, was a political account opened by Daugherty at the beginning of Harding's nomination campaign. According to Daugherty, Smith had deposited the Merton bonds as a part payment for $60,000 he had previously collected for political purposes and failed to turn in. It was impossible to learn more about Extra No. 3 since Daugherty, for reasons he never chose to explain, had burned the bank records before the trial.

Colonel Miller, indicted with Daugherty, was convicted on his second trial and served thirteen months in jail. King, also indicted, suffered a nervous collapse and died before his trial. Smith had killed himself three years earlier. As a result of the trial Daugherty was commonly considered as guilty as Miller. Yet the facts were again ambiguous. George E. Williams, the managing director of the Alien Property Custodian's office, had testified to his approval of the Merton claim, and Daugherty's chief assistant, Guy D. Goff—a lawyer of integrity who would later become senator from West Virginia—assumed full responsibility for certifying the claim and insisted that there had been no attempt to influence him.

"The Department of Easy Virtue," Sen. H. F. Ashurst, a member of the congressional committee investigating the former Attorney General, labeled the Department under Daugherty. Glib though it was, the label was hardly accurate, for most of Daugherty's assistants were men of unquestioned probity, who never lost their belief in the Attorney General's basic honesty. Assistant Attorney Generals Goff and Rush Holland were transparent in their incorruptibility. There was the impeccable Solicitor Gen. James M. Beck, a former assistant Attorney General in the Taft administration. There was Special Assistant Attorney Gen. Hiram C. Todd—no relation to Daugherty's partner—who would later prosecute and convict Daugherty's old associate Thomas Felder. There was Assistant Attorney Gen. John W. H. Crim. In preparing charges of fraud against the Old Hickory Powder Company, a DuPont subsidiary, Crim had found his task obstructed by political road blocks, but he had no doubts about his chief. Testifying before the investigating committee, he told them: "On this question of [Daugherty's] loyalty to an assistant or selling the government in any way for money, why, gentlemen, it is utterly impossible."

Daugherty's narrow escape from jail did not disturb his aplomb. Edgar Mills, a writer for the *Nation*, interviewing him in May, 1926, remarked that the former Attorney General was either the most maligned man in America or the cleverest crook. Daugherty smiled his half-smile, shrugged his shoulders, and told him: "You can take your choice."

To the professionally inquisitive Washington eye no one seemed closer to Harding than Daugherty, the White House semi-resident, the inseparable poker-playing companion, the confidant with the private line to the presidential office. And, obviously, no one was closer to Daugherty than Jess Smith. Subordinates took it for granted that Smith spoke for the Attorney General and possibly for the White House. He wrote letters and gave orders in the Attorney General's name, kept the Attorney General's books, and paid his bills. Official cars were at his disposal; he traveled free by rail on a Justice Department pass. And if Daugherty was not accessible, Jess could always be reached. To those who needed introductions, legitimate or otherwise, to government departments, Smith was their man. He knew all the department heads. In fact, he seemed to know everyone in the government. The Justice Department files were open to him. Easily he moved into the role of what would later be called an influence peddler; a fixer, a go-between, an arranger of pardons and liquor permits, a bagman. His flabby, exuberant face behind the heavy tortoise-shell glasses was ubiquitous. Washington he sensed as a ripe money-tree waiting for him to shake the branches.

One week a month he usually spent in Washington Court House, arriving from the capital with his grips full of whisky which he divided between Mally and Roxy. Once he showed her a money belt stuffed with seventy-five thousand-dollar bills. He boasted to her that he expected to clean up $18,000 by arranging for the nationwide showing of the Dempsey-Carpentier fight films. There was no statute to prevent their being shown; the Federal law merely forbade their transportation across state boundaries. Smith, Daugherty's lobbyist friend Albert Urion, and Jap Muma as entrepreneur had worked out an ingenious scheme to have the films shown in each state by a straw man, preferably representing some veterans' organization. The straw man would be arrested and taken to court where he would pay a small fine, leaving the films then free to be shown throughout the state. All the scheme demanded was a Federal judge complacent enough to fine the straw man rather than jail him. Jess boasted to Roxy that he could fix judges in a dozen states. Eventually the films were shown in twenty states at a profit reputed to be over a million dollars.

When Jess spoke in his loose-lipped drawl, subordinates in the Justice Department and observers heard the voice of Daugherty. Yet for all his freedom of the Department and his coming and going in the White House, he was not nearly as influential and powerful as he—and others—had come to think him. He took the cash, but often let the delivery go—as the

German-born George B. Remus, the "King of the Bootleggers," who was said to have made $40 million in the trade, only discovered on his way to the penitentiary. Remus, a Cincinnati pharmacist and personal teetotaler, had bought up seven distilleries on the cheap after the Volstead Act was passed. To make the distilleries useful to his bootleg ring he needed B permits, issued at the discretion of the state or Federal prohibition commissioner, which allowed bonded liquor to be withdrawn from distilleries or warehouses for medicinal purposes. He also wanted the assurance that he would not be prosecuted by the government.

Remus took his problems to Jess. They met in Washington, in New York, in Columbus, in Indianapolis, and each time Remus paid Jess sums of money that in the end came to over a quarter of a million dollars. The money was not for the permits themselves—those were extra—but for Jess's services in "making connections as far as the withdrawal of permits was concerned."

For a year and a half all went well. Remus paid $19 to $21 a case for withdrawal permits out of which Jess received $1.50 to $2. The cases brought $75 to $90 each on the open bootleg market, and in a little over a year Remus had distributed between 700,000 and 800,000 gallons of liquor. Then suddenly he found himself indicted by the Department of Justice.

Jess reassured him. Although the Department of Justice might put up a "vigorous battle," he would not be convicted. When, in spite of Jess's reassurances, Remus found himself sentenced by the United States District Court to serve several years in the Atlanta Penitentiary, Jess promised him he would never serve a day. On the strength of this promise Remus paid him $30,000 more. Jess told him that the conviction would be reversed in the Court of Appeals, and that in any case through his influence with the Attorney General he would see that Remus got a suspended sentence. But for all Jess's talk and all the money he received, Remus found himself a few months later on the train for Atlanta handcuffed to a Federal marshal.

Jess's reputed influence also failed to prevail in the matter of the distribution of the Dempsey-Carpentier films. Investigators of the Justice Department beyond Smith's reach were readying charges of conspiracy against Jap Muma and his fellow film distributors. Muma panicked when he heard the news. "Fine!" he burst out at Smith. "Jap Muma, general manager of the McLean newspapers. Personal friend of the Attorney General. Old acquaintance of President Harding; called him 'Warren'; calls me 'Jap.' Fine! On my way to Atlanta as a conspirator. The master mind!" Yet the master mind need not have been so alarmed, for Ned McLean with his loftier contacts was soon able to have the conspiracy buried in the Department files; and of the two Department agents who had showed themselves too professionally eager in pursuing the case, one found his work so hampered that he resigned, the other was transferred to Haiti.

After nine months in the Little House on H Street, Daugherty moved to a $7,600 a year suite in the Wardman Park Hotel so that Lucie—now so crippled that she was not able to walk—could stay with him between treatments at the Johns Hopkins Hospital in Baltimore. Jess, who had moved in with Daugherty, acted as nurse when she was in Washington, carrying her round, putting her to bed, taking her over to the window to sit in the sunlight. Daugherty, when he went to sleep, continued to require the comforting assurance of Jess's presence beyond the open door of his bedroom.

In the inclusive world of Washington gossip Jess Smith became the most visible sign of corrupting influence, for he was everywhere to be seen, in and out of the Department of Justice, at the White House, where he aided the Duchess with her correspondence, at Friendship or the McLeans' summer place Briarcliffe at Bar Harbor, in his rocking chair in the Wardman Park lobby, on his favorite corner by the Shoreham Hotel. The Kings and the Remuses and the Jap Mumas and their lesser emulators sought him out, and the green leaves fluttered down from the money-tree.

Yet, for all the pride of a small-town dry-goods merchant in being hailed on the way to the White House by an Albert Lasker, a Coleman DuPont, a John Hays Hammond; for all his natural bonhomie, Jess was from time to time overwhelmed by the shadowy premonition that this good life could not last. His health was bad. He suffered from diabetes, and when in the spring of 1922 he had his appendix removed, the incision never healed and he had to wear a truss. The money that came to him so easily had a way of disappearing almost as easily. After Ungerleider had set up a Washington branch office in the Willard, Jess opened a blind account there—as did Daugherty and Harding himself—and often got stock-market reports during trading hours over the Attorney General's private wire. Yet in spite of his inside tips he lost as often as he tried to play the market. Whenever he was taken by one of his dark moods, he wrote to Roxy for consolation.[6]

If the Justice Department, for all its blemishes under Daugherty, could not be accurately labeled a Department of Easy Virtue, the same could

---

[6] Smith was virtuously indignant when he learned of the sum that Sinclair and his associates had made from the Consolidated Oil stock after the Teapot Dome Lease. He complained to Roxy that "some fellow—five fellows made 35 million the other day in two or three days." When she asked him if he and Harry were in on it, he said no. "That is what we are sore about," he told her. "They were our friends, too."

not be said for its Bureau of Investigation under Daugherty's boyhood friend, William J. Burns. Burns, the founder of the William J. Burns National Detective Agency, was like most detectives more interested in uncovering facts and serving his clients than in ethical and legal abstractions. His father had been police commissioner of Columbus, Ohio, and his experience as a detective had ripened there when at the age of twenty-four he had exposed the notorious election frauds of 1883. As a detective he showed himself skilled, tough, and relentless. He joined the United States Secret Service, and in 1894 uncovered a large-scale counterfeiter who had been forging bills for twenty-five years. Investigating corruption in California, he sent San Francisco's boss Abe Ruef to jail. Later he became Chief of the Secret Service, then retired in 1909 to found the Burns Agency with his son.

The new agency scored some spectacular successes. In 1910 it unearthed such devastating facts against the McNamara brothers, implicated in the bombing of the Los Angeles Times Building, that they confessed. Burns also solved the murder of the New York gambler Herman Rosenthal, with the result that a city police lieutenant and four gunmen were executed. In 1914 he presented such strong evidence of the innocence of the subsequently lynched Leo Frank—sentenced to death in Atlanta, Georgia, for the murder of a girl in his factory—that he himself barely escaped lynching. During World War I, but before the entry of the United States, he undertook various investigations of German activities for the British government and of British activities for the Germans. In 1917 he was found guilty in New York of a misdemeanor, after he had been caught entering a law office and making copies of letters to turn over to a client. He resigned from his company on being appointed head of the Bureau of Investigation which for him was just a larger and more encompassing detective agency. Burns ran the Bureau as he had run his New York office. He had no qualms about search and seizure or about employing criminals and men of dubious reputation. Any inquisitive congressman or senator, any critic of Daugherty or the Department of Justice, would soon find his own affairs investigated by Bureau agents who did not hesitate to break into offices, rifle files, tap wires, and copy private correspondence. Other governmental departments and even congressional offices were not immune to their attentions, as the committees investigating the Attorney General would later discover.

Established in 1908 by Attorney General Bonaparte, the Bureau of Investigation was at first an odd-job detective agency with fuzzy lines of authority and responsibility. In the martial enthusiasm of the war years the Bureau expanded. Aided by civilian volunteers with badges, its agents conducted drives against pro-Germans and draft dodgers, scouring the cities for men without draft cards and locking them up with much fanfare, whatever their excuses. The arrests were often harsh and the results ludicrous—for only one in two hundred of those arrested turned out to be a draft violator. When A. Mitchell Palmer became Attorney General in the first turbulent postwar year, the Bureau turned its efforts to Reds and alien agitators. Palmer, after his Washington house had been bombed and anarchist pamphlets found in the vicinity, became convinced that revolution was just round the corner and sent his Bureau agents out like sheep dogs to round up suspected subversives for deportation. Foreigners were seized in their club halls and homes, without warrant and often at night, marched through the streets handcuffed, crowded into verminous jails, and often mishandled. As in the draft-dodger raids, the proportions of those guilty of any act against the government were ludicrously small. The raids were arbitrary, illegal, savage, and in the case of the two nascent American Communist parties—as the former Communist Ben Gitlow would later admit—effective.

On taking over the Bureau, Burns brought with him a former agent and associate Gaston Bullock Means, a Munchausen in modern dress and the arch-rogue of all the roguish and bizarre figures that infiltrated Washington in the Harding years. Burns and Means had had a profitable collaboration in the early war months, with Burns investigating for the British while Means operated as German Agent E-13. Burns knew Means for what he was, but he also knew his usefulness if there were informers to be bribed or offices to be rifled.

In appearance a wastrel cherub with round face, dimpled smile, sharp chin, and beaming eyes that flickered from time to time with madness, Means was a swindler for the joy of swindling, a liar proud of the credibility of his lies, a confidence man able to make his cheats and deceptions works of art. He bilked, cozened, and blackmailed bootleggers, promoters, and erring millionaires, peddling his assumed influence for hundreds of thousands of dollars. Before his career of larceny and scandal came to an end he had half-persuaded Americans that their President had been murdered. In his middle age he liked to boast that he had been accused of every crime from murder down, and convicted of none.

He was born in 1879 in Concord, North Carolina, of an old plantation family on its uppers. His grandfather, master of slaves and acres, had been a general in the Mexican War; his father, inheriting little more than the General's irascibility, practiced law in Concord and was known locally as the Colonel. Gaston, as a young man with nothing extraordinary about him except his bulk—he was six feet tall and weighed two hundred pounds—attended the University of North Carolina. Good-natured and indolent, he was popular in fraternity row but showed no intellectual interests. In the middle of his junior year he left Chapel Hill.

Back in Concord he taught school briefly, then took a job as traveling salesman for the local Cannon Cotton Mills. As a salesman, with his massively convincing presence and ready dimpled smile, he was a hotshot success. For all his bulk and premature baldness he was a gay blade, involved in a succession of transitory females, sharp for money and able to get it, yet with no signs of being either a thief or a swindler. It was in 1911 at the age of thirty-two that he came to his parting of the ways. While traveling on a sleeper between Detroit and Chicago he landed on his head in the aisle when the chain of his upper berth broke. His injuries were real enough to put him in the hospital. Only afterward was it learned that he had previously taken out accident policies with several companies; and a suspicion grew that he had sawed through a link of the chain. He sued the Pullman Company for $75,000 damages and collected $14,000. From that point on Gaston's legitimate endeavors ceased.[7]

At the age of thirty-four he married a woman eleven years younger than himself who nevertheless remained loyal to him and his vagaries. In 1914 he went to work for Burns. A year later he formed a remunerative acquaintance with Mrs. Maude King, a wealthy scatterbrained widow of alcoholic tendencies who soon trusted him so much that she put all her affairs in his hands. Within two years those hands had disposed of almost half a million dollars, and Gaston was attempting to tap a new ten-million-dollar source by forging the will of her second husband whose first genuine will had left most of his fortune to an old men's home. When Mrs. King's lawyers and relatives began asking awkward questions about the missing half-million, Gaston persuaded her to make a recreational trip to Concord. One evening he took her for a walk down a country road to look for rabbits. He had a pistol with him. Afterward she was found dead with a bullet in her skull. He claimed that she had accidentally shot and killed herself. The District Attorney claimed that Gaston had murdered her. A local jury, outraged by the presence of New York lawyers for the prosecution, easily acquitted him.

In November, 1921, Burns brought Gaston to Washington as a Special Employee of the Department of Justice for ninety days, at seven dollars a day. At his disposal were badge, telephone, official stationery, an office, and the complete files of the Bureau of Information. That was all he needed. At first he was assigned to Captain Scaife who was so impressed by Gaston's swinging presence that he asked to have him as a permanent assistant. Gaston began his operations in a small way by contracting to sell Justice Department reports and papers to those involved, claiming with invincible plausibility that he could offer protection. Through his years of working with Burns he had developed a large underworld acquaintance. As soon as he was installed in his Bureau of Information

[7] Louis Graves, a friend of Gaston's at Chapel Hill and later a New York Times reporter, always felt that Means's head injury had changed his personality.

office he spread the word that he could "fix" Federal prosecutions, obtain favors, and even dispose of incriminating documents. He claimed that he was collection man for Burns and for the Attorney General—whom he met only once—and that he was intimate with the President—whom he never met at all. He did work from time to time with and for Jess Smith and even culled the Justice Department files with him. At first he lived with his family in a suite at the Bellevue Hotel, then in a town house at 903 Sixteenth Street, the lower floor of which he used as a home office. On his salary of seven dollars a day he managed to employ a house staff of three servants and to travel about in his own chauffeur-driven Cadillac.

In February, 1922, Daugherty, refusing to give his reasons, ordered Burns to suspend Means. Captain Scaife, quitting at about the same time and convinced that the Attorney General was not prosecuting war fraud cases as he should, begged Means to go with him and give the facts to some sympathetic congressman. Gaston begged off. While suspended from the Justice Department he undertook to work for Elmer Dover who, as Assistant Secretary of the Treasury, wanted confidential information about the Internal Revenue Director David Blair. Dover hired Gaston as an ostensible customs agent. Meanwhile, Burns kept his ingenious investigator in the Bureau on a temporary basis and finally reinstalled him in May. Assistant Attorney Gen. Rush Holland watched with suspicion as the suspended Gaston failed to vacate his office, and the young Assistant Director J. Edgar Hoover demanded of Burns that Gaston be ordered to stay out of Hoover's office.

By August Gaston, feeling that he had outgrown the Bureau, quit his job. Armed with endless supplies of forged documents supposedly from high government officials, he made a sensation in bootlegging circles with his claims of being able to quash indictments and secure liquor permits. On such promises of protection he collected $50,000 here, $11,500 there, $13,800 somewhere else in quick succession. Unlike Jess Smith, who sometimes delivered on his promises, Gaston never did and never intended to; but it took some time to find him out, and the code of the underworld kept most of his shorn black sheep quiet. With his lawyer, the bloated boozy-faced "Col." Thomas Felder, he shook down his not-so-innocent victims who thought they were bribing the entire Justice Department. After Remus had been sentenced to his prison term, Means offered to fix the case for $125,000. One-quarter of the money, he said, would go to Burns, a quarter to Daugherty, a quarter to Chief Justice Taft, and the rest to himself. But though Remus had been taken in by Smith, he was not gullible enough to believe that Means could bribe the Chief Justice.

Felder had given desk space in his New York office to Draper Daugherty and from time to time paid off the debts of that bibulous young man, no doubt regarding him as a potential hostage in time of trouble. Colonel Miller, with a private line from the Alien Custodian Bureau to Gaston's home office, often dropped in evenings to lay cagey plans and swap confidences over the brown bottles. Gaston also conducted several investigations at Jess Smith's request.

Miller and Felder were frequenters of Daugherty's Little House on H Street as well as the legendary Little Green House on K Street. In the case of both houses legend exceeded fact. The small greenstone-trimmed Victorian town house at 1625 K Street had been rented in May, 1921, by Howard Mannington, the Ohio back-room manipulator who had managed the Front Porch campaign. In Washington Mannington set himself up as a lobbyist. Some of his activities were legal, some were not. Convivial and purposeful, he occupied the house for eight months, until about the time that Daugherty left the H Street house for the Wardman Park Hotel. There were poker parties in the Little Green House, drinks were set up, deals made. Although there is no record but gossip, there may have been women from time to time—call girls have been familiar to Washington before and since. But no major act or scandal took place there in those few months. Admiral Dewey's widow lived close by at 1601 K Street, Mrs. George Vanderbilt at 1612, and Senator Knox lived only a block away—not neighbors who would have tolerated any rowdy revelry. It was the term "Little House," with its overtures of suspicion, bandied about afterward in congressional hearings and in the press, that formed the legend, suggesting rendezvous—sinister, undercover, orgiastic. Although Gaston Means was never in the H Street house and probably not in the Green House on K Street he was as much responsible as anyone for the legend. In a book of fantasy that he afterward dictated to a gullible female novelist he told of a wholly imaginary orgy held in the H Street House one night just before Jess Smith had called him to come over because of "a little trouble." So realistic were Gaston's fantasies, so elaborated with convincing details, that he may even have believed them himself in the telling. He said he had reached the H Street house and walked into a room of the wildest disorder, with half-drunk women and girls sprawled on couches and chairs, "terror on their painted faces." Earlier, in their hilarity, they had been throwing bottles and glasses until one girl had been struck in the head with a carafe. She now lay unconscious on a sofa. Harding, bewildered, was leaning against the mantel, his guards standing near. Gaston, of course, took charge at once, ordering the guards to take the President away and then carrying the girl to his car and driving her to the hospital!

The two Little Houses in the short time that they functioned were in fact clearinghouses, the Little Green House being less important though possibly more convivial. Mannington shared it and its expenses with

M. P. Kraffmiller, a railroad car builder from La Grange, Illinois, whom he had met at the Republican convention. Fred A. Caskey, a Washington lawyer, was the third tenant, too poor at the beginning to contribute to the upkeep although in a few months able to buy a large house on Wisconsin Avenue.

Mannington had charge of Ohio patronage files and made his own private recommendations to Daugherty. He also had files of candidates for Federal judgeships and for Federal criminals for whom pardons might be arranged. Wholesale drug concerns in need of liquor permits came to the Little Green House, as did manufacturers with tax and rebate problems. Jess Smith often conferred with the green triumvirate. Bill Orr, a specialist in the field, kept the house supplied with liquor. His most remunerative specialty was aiding dealers whom Prohibition had left high and dry with warehouses full of legally unsalable liquor. By furnishing them withdrawal permits, he was able to arrange for them to ship their liquor stocks to foreign countries, although somehow most of the liquor had a way of disappearing between the warehouse and the dock.

Among the visitors, casual and otherwise, to the Little Green House were Charlie Forbes, Sinclair, King, Elias A. Mortimer—officially representing the St. Louis contracting firm of Thompson-Black, and unofficially the White House bootlegger—and fellow Ohioans General Sawyer, Secretary Christian, and Prohibition Commissioner Haynes. Thanks to the Commissioner, liquor, guarded by Internal Revenue men with pistols and badges, was delivered at the green K Street door in Wells Fargo Express wagons.

Haynes as Commissioner had early discovered that the fundamentalist pieties of the Ohio hill country could not survive the capital's more secular atmosphere. His patronage-riddled Prohibition Bureau, corrupt from top to bottom with a blatant and obvious corruption, quickly extinguished the dry crusader in him. Only the reach of Haynes's hand under the table is indeterminable, not the fact. In his Bureau, B permits became a form of negotiable security, like Liberty Bonds. Companies headed by known law violators received such permits which Haynes refused to cancel even after the violators had been indicted. A firm of cigar makers in Philadelphia that in the eighteen previous years had not used $480 worth of alcohol received his permission to draw alcohol at the rate of 420,000 gallons a year, or more than enough to treat the entire tobacco crop of the world.

Normal pay for Haynes's prohibition agents was $1,200 to $2,000 a year. Most agents found they could make that much in a month's bribes or less, and they either took the bribes or quit their jobs to work for their ostensible enemies. A "training school for bootleggers," the Bureau was called. Even Harding, though still maintaining that the Eighteenth

Amendment was the will of the people, told Congress in 1922 that "conditions relating to its enforcement . . . savor of nationwide scandal."

The only large-scale administration scandal to break in Harding's lifetime would center round Charlie Forbes, the gay drinking and poker companion of his 1915 Hawaiian trip whom, with the Duchess's approval, he had made head of the much-criticized Bureau of War Risk Insurance. Two years after the war over 300,000 disabled soldiers were being cared for with ranging degrees of efficiency by half-a-dozen disparate government agencies. The wounded for the most part received adequate medical treatment, but the 70,000 veterans disabled by tuberculosis and mental disorders often found themselves shunted from one public institution to another if they were cared for at all. To remedy such anomalies Harding consolidated the War Risk Insurance Bureau, Doctor Sawyer's Federal Hospitalization Bureau, and other overlapping agencies into a central Veterans' Bureau with Colonel Forbes as director. The American Legion enthusiastically approved of the appointment of a legionnaire holder of the Medal of Honor. Only a few insiders—among them Daugherty—were dubious. The new bureau had more money allotted to it than any other government department: almost half a billion dollars a year. Forbes brought with him as general counsel for the bureau a California lawyer, Charles F. Cramer, a small, thin-lipped vulpine man with receding hair, brushed pompadour, and a pince-nez that made his fox face look almost effeminate. On arriving in Washington he bought Harding's old house on Wyoming Avenue for $60,000.

Harding had an intimate and instinctive liking for Forbes, who could always be counted on to jolly the President out of his dreariest moods. The Colonel's brassy manner appealed equally to the Duchess, and the doors of the White House were open to him. Samuel Hopkins Adams described him on his bouncy arrival in Washington at the age of forty-one as

a pursy, rufous, convivial, highly energized individual, full of snappy stories and insinuating gossip, boisterous in mirth and fellowship, a magnetic talker, a ready public speaker, popular with men and alluring to women, with every needful quality of the universal good fellow and high-class confidence man.

Even Daugherty, who disliked him, considered him "handsome, genial, plausible, popular."

Until 1921 a special Army architectural staff had been in charge of the location and construction of veterans' hospitals and had already with reasonable economy and efficiency built 19 such buildings. One of Forbes's first acts as Veterans' Bureau director was to persuade Harding that it would be more efficient to transfer the planning and construction of all future hospitals from the Army to the bureau. To Harding it seemed a logical step in coordinating veterans' services, and he made the transfer by Executive order. Forbes also convinced the President that it would save much time and cut much red tape if he as director had charge of the purchase and disposal of veterans' supplies, then handled by the Quartermaster General's Department. Harding easily agreed, issuing a second Executive order that the disapproving Daugherty had to concede was legal. With the signing of this order the 50 or so huge government storehouses at Perryville, Maryland, crammed with surplus supplies and equipment accumulated during the war, came under Forbes's control.

Forbes rapidly became a gaily conspicuous presence in the relaxed atmosphere of postwar Washington, and it struck no one as extraordinary that he lived so lavishly on a salary of $10,000 a year. He gave elaborate dinner parties in smart restaurants. Sometimes on a weekend he would take over half a floor of an Atlantic City luxury hotel to entertain government officials, Broadway stars, and visiting celebrities. A deft and devoted poker player, he liked to gamble for high stakes. Imperturbably he would win or lose several hundred dollars at the turn of a card or a roll of dice. Separated from his second wife, who had left for Europe taking what securities of his she could lay hands on and threatening him with divorce, he found her threats and her absence no handicap. As director he quickly grew friendly with Carolyn Votaw, moved from her desk in the District of Columbia Police Department to become a personnel director attached to the Veterans' Bureau from the Public Health Service. Carolyn introduced Forbes to Mortimer, then living at the Wardman Park on a ThompsonBlack expense account with his gay and pretty young wife Kathryn. Soon the two couples formed an inseparable foursome—Mort, Charlie, Kate, Carolyn—seen convivially everywhere in Washington at parties, restaurants, and public places.

Obligingly, and with a benevolent eye on Kathryn, Forbes hired her brother Ralph Tullidge, a milkman, at $3,500 a year as one of the bureau's mechanical engineers. Possibly Tullidge was a little short on experience, but qualifications and efficiency did not weigh heavily with the new director. One Francis B. Smith received $4,800 annually from the bureau as a "special expert," for which he admitted he worked about two hours a year. A field agent, R. A. Tripp, wrote a colleague that he earned his pay by keeping "soused to the gills." His motto was: "To hell with central office work!" They set the tone.

Heber Votaw did not approve of the foursome nor of Forbes and his easy, wandering eye. Once the jealous Heber is said to have threatened to throw the director out of his own tenth-story window. The Superintendent of Prisons was having his own problems in the Atlanta Penitentiary where drug peddling had become so open and so common that many prisoners were becoming addicts almost on arrival. A new warden, J. E. Dyche, after investigating on his own, forced two guards to resign, had two others indicted for trafficking in narcotics, and obtained a confession of complicity from the assistant prison physician, himself a prisoner on parole. Dyche then appealed to Votaw and to Director Burns for the help of the Bureau of Investigation in tracking down the outside ring that had been smuggling in the drugs. Burns was willing to put his agents to work, but Votaw, anxious to prevent any unfavorable publicity for his department, balked. He gave orders that there would be no further action on the drug traffic until the two indicted guards were brought to trial. As this might take some time, Dyche protested to Votaw, and as a result of his protest soon found himself without a job. "I was perfectly amazed," he later testified to a Senate investigating committee. "Mr. Votaw was a minister of the gospel; he was a brother-in-law of the President. . . . If there was anybody that ought to want to see that institution cleared up it was Mr. Votaw, and when he took the position he did about stopping the investigation, I was dumfounded."

Rumors of the conditions at the Federal penitentiary somehow reached Harding and he sent his faithful Colonel Forbes to Atlanta to make a private investigation. Whatever Forbes's report contained, it must have reflected on the Department of Justice as well as the Superintendent of Prisons, for Daugherty shortly afterward informed the Colonel that conditions in Atlanta were none of Forbes's damned business.

As soon as Forbes had taken charge of the Perryville warehouses, he pressured the Bureau of the Budget into giving him blanket approval for the sale of a three-page list of supplies he claimed were damaged. To this list he appended two unapproved lists of his own. Then, with an unconcern that amounted to bravado, he proceeded to empty the warehouses of the supplies and equipment accumulated so lavishly during the war years. Some of the goods had indeed deteriorated and might properly have been sold at any price they might bring. But many articles were in good condition, and some like new—including such hospital necessities as sheets, blankets, towels, gauze, bandages, drugs, and soap. Alcohol and drugs Forbes found most profitable to divert directly into illegal channels. In addition to the hospital supplies, of which there was then a country-wide shortage, there were on the warehouse premises thousands of trucks and vast quantities of tools. Without any publicity Forbes arranged for this material, which he represented as surplus and practically useless, to go by private bid to a Boston firm, Thompson & Kelley. Two other firms got wind of the sale and submitted bids, but theirs were disregarded.

Day after day the freight cars moved out of Perryville for Boston with their loads. Thompson & Kelley bought 100,000 pairs of pajamas donated originally to the soldiers by the Red Cross for 30 cents a pair although the actual value was four or five times that amount. Forty-five thousand rolls of gauze that had cost the government $1.33 a roll were marked down to 26 cents; oiled paper "in prime condition," bought at 60 cents a pound, sold for five cents. A million towels that had cost 34 cents each went for 3 cents. Although many government hospitals lacked sufficient bedding, serviceable used sheets sold for six cents each; and 84,000 new sheets in their original packages that had cost $1.27 a pair brought 27 cents at the very time that the Veterans' Bureau was buying sheets on the outside for $1.03. At one point new sheets were being brought in at one end of a Perryville warehouse and loaded out the other end as surplus. All in all Thompson & Kelley bought between $5 and $7 million worth of government goods for which the firm paid $600,000. Forbes was no less lavish in his purchases than in his sales. The Veterans' Bureau bought 70,000 gallons of floor wax and cleaner—enough to last a hundred years— at 98 cents a gallon although its actual value per gallon was 4 cents.

Whatever percentage Forbes received of the Perryville sales, it was trivial compared to the graft he was able to extract from his control of veterans' hospital construction. Congress had appropriated $17 million— and would later double that figure—for needed new hospitals. To replace the Army's well-managed architectural staff, Forbes set up his own architectural sub-department that, although it cost $100,000 a year to run, was so inept that many of its plans had later to be scrapped. The Public Health and the Marine Hospital services had been able to build hospitals at a cost of $2,972 a bed. Forbes's architects raised the cost per bed to $3,957.

In the spring of 1922 Forbes, putting Cramer in charge of the bureau, left with the Mortimers on a continental inspection tour of sites for 12 new hospitals. With Mortimer footing the bills, the journey became a festive one in which business, far from interfering with pleasure, seemed to enhance it. Forbes did not invite Carolyn Votaw since, as he explained to Mortimer, she was engaged in welfare work for the veterans and her presence might interfere with their plans. Their transcontinental drinking parties at chosen spots with chosen companions grew lush enough to surprise the bill-paying Mortimer. There was, in the ribald pleasantries, even a swimming party in full evening dress. At one point Forbes, in the name of the President, awarded a medal to one Alexander, otherwise unknown, who mystified Harding by his letter of thanks. On the way to Chicago Forbes told Mortimer that he was hard up and needed $5,000, which Mortimer agreed to get from Thompson-Black. One Chicago after-noon when Forbes, a bottle of Scotch on the table, was shooting craps with Kate in the living room of their fifty-dollar-a-day suite at the Drake

Hotel, Mortimer arrived, called Forbes into the bathroom and handed him ten five-hundred-dollar bills. The Colonel stuffed them into his trousers pocket, then went back to win $220 from Kate. Later the senior partner of Thompson-Black, J. W. Thompson, held a conference with Forbes and Mortimer in which he agreed to add $150,000 to the nominal cost of each hospital contract awarded his firm. Forbes would receive a third of this, and Thompson also agreed to pay him 35 per cent of all profits that Thompson-Black might make on its work for the Veterans' Bureau. So pleased was Thompson with the arrangements that he threw in a new Packard touring car for Kate.

In San Francisco, two dozen bottles of wine arrived at the suite Mortimer had rented in the Fairmount Hotel, a present from a property owner hoping to unload a lot of land in Livermore as a hospital site. For this land, appraised at $19,257 by the state commander of the American Legion, Cramer arranged for the Veterans' Bureau to pay $105,000, with $25,000 of the money being split between him and the director.

In Spokane, Forbes's old partner in the Hurley-Mason Company, Charles F. Hurley, sat down with Forbes and Mortimer and worked out an agreement that the profits of his firm on veterans' hospital construction —estimated at 10 per cent—should be split three ways: one-third to Forbes, one-third to Hurley-Mason, and one-third to Thompson-Black. Whatever the bids, Forbes awarded contracts only to those firms that "loaned" him money. Somewhere in the Midwest the owners of an enormous brewery tried persuasively to sell the bureau their useless property as a hospital, although architects' plans showed only two windows possible in wards of 90 beds.

At Excelsior Springs, Missouri, Forbes agreed to pay $77,000 for land worth $35,000, then raised the price to $90,000. On the return journey he confided to Mortimer that he expected to become Secretary of the Interior when Fall resigned and that he would then control the huge sums appropriated for reclamation work and be able to give that work to any firm he chose. Yet, by the time they reached Washington, relations between Forbes and Mortimer had begun to cool. Mortimer had already been separated once from his wife and then reconciled, and the Colonel's wandering eye was focusing a little too sharply on Kate. By this time Forbes had collected about $30,000 from Thompson-Black, and the second partner, James W. Black, was coming to the conclusion that the convivial Colonel was a "doublecrosser."

While Fall was disposing of the oil leases, Forbes arranging the Veterans' Bureau to his advantage, and Jess Smith and Gaston Means rustling the money-tree, informed gossip waxed sharp, but to the country at large the new administration seemed worthy of respect. William Allen

White thought that Harding after his first year in office stood well with the people, that although he had made some bad appointments he had made more good ones, and that his Cabinet seemed to be working well. The "crooks and grafters" burrowing beneath the calm surface of the administration were only occasionally visible.

Among the earlier intimations of rougher days ahead were the jarring sounds from Porto Rico [8] after E. Mont Reily had been installed as governor. Though in Washington the sounds were muted by distance, in Porto Rico they became deafening. Governor Reily regarded himself as a pro-consul. At his inaugural, the most splendid ever seen on the island, he congratulated the Porto Ricans on being members of the "Federated Household of the most sublime Government that God has given to man." Independence, then advocated by most younger educated Porto Ricans, he regarded as disloyalty to the United States and traveled around the island denouncing the subversive doctrine in town halls, schools, and village greens. The United States Organic Act had provided that the American President should appoint three members of the Porto Rican cabinet and that the remaining four should be appointed by the governor with the advice and consent of the Senate of Porto Rico. Reily informed the members of the majority Unionist party that he would appoint Unionists to office only if their leader, Antonio R. Barcelo, would publicly renounce the party's independence plank. When Barcelo refused, Reily removed three Unionist cabinet members and replaced them with minority hacks. Political war broke out between the governor and the majority leader, and Reily soon found himself controlling little more than a small alien set of Federal officeholders. He accused Barcelo and the Unionists of treason; they in turn accused him of favoritism, malfeasance, chicanery, and graft. The cables between San Juan, the capital, and Washington sizzled with Reily's voluminous and indignant communications. Eventually affairs on the island grew so embroiled that Daugherty suggested sending a warning destroyer to San Juan. For some time Harding backed his governor's efforts to "Americanize" the Porto Ricans. But, living under a cloud of undetermined scandals and thwarted by hot Latin intransigence, Reily finally resigned "to look after my health." On leaving the island it was his boast that during his administration more American flags had been sold in Porto Rico than in the whole previous period of American control.

A louder, if more ephemeral, uproar occurred overseas when George Harvey two months after his appointment as ambassador to England addressed the annual dinner of the Pilgrim Society of London. To those amateurs of Anglo-American good will he announced professionally, in

[8] Then so spelled.

what one member described as "a spirit of supernationalism and sub-
alcoholism," that the United States had entered the last war because "we
were afraid not to fight. That is the real truth of the matter. So we came
along toward the end and helped you and your allies shorten the war.'
He went on further to undermine the good will of his English listeners
by warning them that the United States could not be "beguiled into the
League of Nations. . . . A majority of 7 million is against it."

After having burned the manuscript of his life of Harding before Post
Office Inspector Zimmerman, Professor Chancellor spent the next year
in Canada, moving from city to city and living cautiously in lodging-
houses and YMCAs. With him he carried a manuscript copy that had not
been burned, revising it and expanding it to cover Harding's first year in
the White House. Early in 1922, and traveling under an assumed name,
he came with his completed manuscript to Dayton where he registered at
the Beckel Hotel and got in touch with two local shysters, Hugh Snepp
and Cedric N. Brown, who formed the law firm of Brown & Snepp.
Working from a corner of their office, Chancellor sent out an "endless
chain" of flyers advertising the forthcoming book and offering shares in
the publishing enterprise at $100 each that he claimed would be worth
$1,800 within six months.

> After a life without one important constructive public achievement [Chan-
> cellor wrote of Harding] and without the advocacy of any public measure
> whatever, he has become the foremost man in America. The singular
> absence of any authentic biography even by his partisan political sup-
> porters has led to the preparation of this work dealing scientifically with
> his ancestry, record, and mental characteristics.

Brown and Snepp felt that in Chancellor's new work they had uncovered a gold mine. They set up a printing press in a vacant loft over
Dayton's Crystal Restaurant and hired a printer. With singular disregard
for the laws of libel and the power of the United States government, they
planned to market four million volumes at five dollars each.

When Zimmerman got wind of the revised book and forwarded a report
to Washington he was ordered to "connect" with Director Burns at the
Department of Justice. Burns asked that all the data on the case now be
sent him, and announced that his bureau would take over the matter from
the Secret Service. In spite of the zeal of government agents, copies of
the book began to appear with the first crocuses, peddled from door to
door throughout Ohio and beyond by fly-by-night salesmen, "tough-
looking fellows" according to Secretary Greer of the Democratic State
Committee whom they approached in his Dayton office saying that the
book was a "quick mover" and asking him to act as state agent for it.

Some copies even reached Washington. But Chancellor had learned discretion from his run-ins with the Post Office and the Secret Service, for the title page now read:

Warren Gamaliel Harding
President of the United States.
A Review of Facts
Collected from
Anthropological, Historical, and
Political Researches
by
William Estabrook Chancellor
formerly
Professor of Economics, Politics, and Social Sciences of
Wooster College, Wooster, Ohio.

Although Chancellor was willing to have himself considered the author, his carefully worded and punctuated title made no such claim. According to its title page the book was "sold and distributed by agents only. The Sentinal Press." Cheaply bound, wretchedly printed, with uncorrected typographical errors strewn across the pages and scattered blurred photographs, the *Review of Facts* nevertheless—in the mass circulation envisaged by Brown and Snepp—held the possibilities of a major scandal that might even unseat Harding in the next election. The President was described as "big, lazy, slouching, confused, ignorant, affable, yellow, and cringing like a Negro butler to the great." Chancellor accused Harding of resorting "to cosmetics to make himself look more white than he really is," of being an Army deserter and of having had several attacks of delirium tremens. The book was a mishmash of obsessive fantasies, lies, occasional shrewd political observations, and a number of facts unrecorded anywhere else. With the author's obvious paranoia and the scurrility of his approach, it is not to be wondered at that no historian has tried to sift the facts from the fantasies. Yet facts are there. While in Marion Chancellor picked up the story of Harding's liaison with Carrie Phillips and made the sole printed mention of her name until the discovery of her long-hidden love letters in 1963:

> The Phillips case illustrates his sex instincts. Mrs. Phillips is the wife of a dry-goods man in Marion, very showy and vain, with a passon [sic] for men. Jim Phillips is a poor little fellow who is part owner of a store that is there.
>
> This woman has made herself useful to men of a kind. She got in with Warren, who as usual, paid no attention to his own wife who is passée through the years.
>
> On frequent occasions, even after the nomination, he and Mrs. Phillips visited together at Upper Sandusky. It is said that Herrick, who knew

about this, went to Jim Phillips and offered to send both himself and the woman to Japan, with an income guaranteed monthly so long as Warren was President. It was reported in every stage of the affair just what was paid. The stake was $25,000 down, and $2,000 a month. The Phillips [sic] went to Japan early in October, but not until Mrs. Phillips, who is a very talkative woman, had told all her friends just what she was to receive.

Chancellor wrote down uncritically all the gossip his quick ear picked up. He recorded that the Washington police records of 1918 showed that Harding had been cut and bruised in a drunken row at the house of "a regular lady friend." But he also recorded the as yet-unpublished fact that Harding suffered from heart trouble. His preoccupation was of course with Harding's alleged Negro blood, yet even in this he confused the issues he was trying to make clear. After calling Harding "our first Negro President" he wrote elsewhere:

> There is no disposition . . . to insist that Warren Harding is by race a negro. It is evident to all that the man is mainly white. What we insist on is that the race consciousness of the Hardings in Blooming Grove caused them to remain negro and that George Tryon Harding, II, never thought of calling themselves [sic] white until after the death of Amos Kling, father-in-law of Warren. Warren, his brother and sisters were reared and treated as colored people.

Chancellor described Harding's grandfather Charles as having "curly, kinky hair, swart complexion, a wide, big body, and great nostrils." He asserted that Senator Foraker once wrote asking for an appointment of a quadroon woman to teach in a colored school, and that this quadroon was Carolyn Harding. The chief claim of his expanded book was that Charles Harding's mother, born in 1799, was a Negress, Mary Ann Dickson or Dixon, although all the Harding genealogies list her as Elizabeth Madison. Chancellor also claimed that Harding's namesake uncle, Warren Gamaliel Bancroft, was a Negro preacher.[9]

[9] Chancellor's gossip is again wrong. Warren Gamaliel Bancroft, Methodist clergyman and chaplain of the Wisconsin State Prison from 1895 to 1897, died in Oshkosh in 1908 at the age of seventy-three and was listed as "white" on his death certificate. Chancellor is equally wrong about Charles Harding who, with his wife Mary Ann Crawford, is listed in the records of the Morrow County Courthouse as white. In 1870 Amos, Elizabeth, and Mordecai Harding were all listed as white. Yet the blood rumor had shadowed the family ever since the Hardings had settled in Blooming Grove. In 1849 David Butler, a Galion blacksmith married to Harding's Great-aunt Jerusha Harding, struck and killed one Amos Smith who had taunted him with "sleeping with a nigger wench." Ninety years after Butler's trial, one of the early *Star* reporters told Samuel Hopkins Adams that "it was generally believed that there was Negro blood in the Harding line, but that W. G. had outgrown it."
There are in Ohio and elsewhere a number of Negro families with the surname Harding, some of whom claim relationship with President Harding. After Harding was

No sooner did Daugherty learn of the book's surreptitious publication than he ordered Jess and Burns to suppress it. Agents of the Bureau of Investigation combed Ohio, buying, borrowing, or seizing every copy they could lay hands on, removing the books from stores, libraries, and institutions. They discovered the loft headquarters of the Sentinal Press and uncovered Snepp's connection with it.

> The officials closed in on poor old Snepp [a Dayton correspondent wrote Adams long afterward]. Snepp, as I understand, was subjected to a severe questioning by certain men who came here for the purpose of finding out all the details and stopping or preventing publication. . . . You may appreciate the amount of sheer terrorism that can be packed into such an investigation, designedly used for intimidation.

On the arrival of the agents in Ohio, Chancellor left secretly for Maine, moving on shortly to Canada where he busied himself as a bond salesman. The plates and the bulk books stored in the Sentinal Press loft were taken away by Burns's agents and destroyed. It is rumored that the plates were dumped into the Ohio River. Gaston Means, who was working on the case with Smith, wrote that the books and plates were brought to Washington in a guarded express car and that he helped burn them, "copyright and all," in the rear grounds of a mansion belonging to a wealthy friend of Harding's, "Douglas Boyd"—which may or may not have been true, since Gaston's stories can never be believed without corroboration. In any case, Chancellor's book became one of the rarest bibliographical items in twentieth-century American history.[10]

In February, 1922, Scott Willits sailed for Europe to study music for a year with Prof. Otakar Sevcik at the Prague Conservatory, with Harding paying his way and his expenses. Stopping off in Washington en route to New York, he and Elizabeth with Elizabeth Ann called on the Votaws. Carolyn took them to lunch with Colonel Forbes in the Senate dining room, still unaware that the prattling child beside her was her niece.

---

nominated for United States senator in 1914 he received a letter of congratulation from F. H. Harding of Marietta who signed himself "your colored namesake."

A curious belief persists in Conecuh County, Alabama, that Harding is a descendant of Hinchie Warren, Jr., son of a plantation owner, and an octaroon slave girl named Lucinda. Hinchie fell in love with Lucinda, took her as his mistress, and some time before the Civil War eloped with her to the free country of Ohio. However, it does not seem chronologically allowable that Lucinda's daughter could have been Harding's grandmother, and no other relationship would be possible.

[10] The New York Public Library possesses a copy, as do the Princeton Library and the library of the Ohio Historical Society. A Marion lawyer is the only private individual I know of who owns the book. On the rare occasion that it finds its way into a bookseller's catalogue it sells for several hundred dollars.

Later they made a tour of the White House although Harding, attending a conference, did not see them.

When Elizabeth returned to Chicago, her sister went with her. Still convinced that she had not recovered from the effects of childbirth, Nan visited a doctor twice a week and spent half her days in bed. Vaguely she nursed the idea of becoming a stage or film star as an outlet for her "suppressed emotions." Although her visits to the White House had fallen away since the narrow escape from the Duchess, she decided in June to go to Harding and talk over her film career and the future of Elizabeth Ann. Sloan brought her to the President's office on a Sunday morning when the Duchess was away. Harding was in his dark cutaway, ready for church, but as soon as he was alone with her he led her to the leather couch.

> And there [she wrote] for a brief space of time—all too brief—we became oblivious to our surroundings, to his identity as President of the United States, and to all the world. "Why don't you tell me you love me, Nan darling?" he coaxed, and I told him over and over again, as I had told him a thousand times, "I love you, darling Warren Harding, I love you."

As he confessed how he dreamed of having her with him all night, she rather tactlessly asked: "How is Mrs. Harding now?" He lifted his eyebrows and shrugged his shoulders and replied in the usual way, "Oh, all right!"

The accustomed vase of flowers stood before the picture of his mother on his desk, this time pink roses. He gave her a rosebud and some money for Elizabeth Ann, then suggested that she let Sloan drive her to church where she could watch the service from the balcony. She said she wished they could go off somewhere alone together instead of separately to church. "Gee, I do, too, dearie!" he told her enthusiastically.

Wearing his rosebud, she sat in the balcony of the Calvary Baptist Church looking down at the Reverend Doctor Abernathy in his Geneva bands and at the fast-whitening head of her lover. After the service she walked back to her hotel, had lunch, and then went to a movie, sitting through two shows in order to see Harding twice in the newsreels before taking the train back to Chicago.

CHAPTER XIX

President II

The winter of 1921–1922 turned into one of the bitterest of the new century. By Christmas the White House grounds were unaccustomedly white. Then at the end of January a blizzard swept across Washington, blanketing the city in 29 inches of snow. The day after the blizzard the roof of the Knickerbocker Theatre—the largest moving-picture house in the city—collapsed under the weight, killing 95 of the 600 or so people in the audience. Harding sent the customary message expected from heads of state when a national disaster occurs.

With the golf courses buried under drifts the President began planning a March trip to Florida with the McLeans. Meanwhile, stimulated by the gift of a horse, "Harbel," from Harvey Firestone, he took up riding again while waiting for the snow to melt on the greens. Firestone had also given the Duchess a mare, "Diamond," but Doctor Sawyer refused to allow her on horseback.

> I may say very truthfully that she rides more than well [Harding wrote to George Harvey]. I wish you might have seen her in the old days when she rode in all her confidence and grace. Sometimes I think she is too busy directing the affairs of government to waste any time on a horse. She was never much of a suffragist, but she is full fledged in expressing her opinion as to how the Executive should perform his duties.

The postwar depression still carried over into 1922, a looming threat to Harding and his party in the autumn mid-term elections. Economists might point out that wages were stabilizing at about 10 per cent above their prewar level, but this was small consolation to a factory worker whose pay had just been cut and who conceived of a dollar as an entity and not a fluctuating value symbol. The four or five million unemployed —at least 11 per cent of the working force—found even less consolation in Harding's Unemployment Conference. Marginal firms and manufacturers had been ruined by the Federal Reserve's grinding deflationary measures. Unions replied to pay cuts and declining membership with a new wave of strikes. The country was restive, ready to react against the party it had so overwhelmingly installed fifteen months before, and Harding with his subtle politician's instinct sensed the gathering reaction. Yet, even as he was confiding to Jennings that the Republicans had possibly lost a quarter of their support, the tide of the business cycle had begun imperceptibly to turn and the waters of the boom ahead were already filtering across the flats of the depression. Unemployment was easing as new expanding industries prepared to surge ahead: the automobile industry, before all others; moving pictures; the radio, still known as "wireless"; advertising; chemicals; the revived building trades. Everyone but the farmers would share in the seven fat years to come.

From the time he had taken over the Department of Agriculture, Secretary Wallace had been urging Harding to call a conference to aid the farmers—40 per cent of the country—whose purchasing power had now fallen to three-quarters of what it had been before the war. Hoover and Mellon opposed such a conference, and Harding hesitated even as Wallace persisted. Finally, on a mild day just before the first snowstorm, as the President and his Secretary of Agriculture were playing golf, Harding glanced up from a putt on the last green, smiled, and said: "Hank, go ahead with your agricultural conference."

The President's National Agricultural Conference met for five days on January 23 and made various legislative recommendations including one "to re-establish a fair exchange value for all farm products with that of other commodities." Beyond that, its members managed to concoct a slogan, "Equality for Agriculture," without, however, specifying how this could be brought about. Harding told the delegates that "legislation can do little more than give the farmer a chance to organize and help himself." His own belief—one that seemed reactionary but would in time come to seem "advanced"—was that the less productive farmers should leave their farms for industry.

Once more, in the new session of Congress, the question of a soldiers' bonus bill came up. Harding warned J. W. Fordney of the House Ways and Means Committee that he would veto any bonus bill that did not carry with it a general sales tax for raising the needed revenue. Even beyond the question of the bonus, he felt that such a tax, where "a man pays according to his expenditure . . . is infinitely preferable to the plan of attempting to penalize success." During the snowy weeks he again revealed his lurking self-doubts in a letter to Judge Gary of the United States Steel Corporation. "It would be a very difficult task," he wrote, "to live very long in the presidential office without exciting or inciting numerous complaints. I am frank to say that I came into a task which has proven vastly more difficult than I had been able to foresee." The doubts did not show on his face. One of his winter visitors, Enrico Caruso, professed himself so struck with the President's likeness to the first President that he took a photograph of Harding and touched it up to resemble Washington, releasing it to the papers as: "Harding Become Father of Country."

As the winter ebbed, the President was faced with the loss of the first member of his Cabinet when Will Hays asked to resign at the end of his office year to become president of the newly formed Motion Picture Producers and Distributors of America. Hays had done as he had promised in "humanizing" the postal service. He had established a welfare department, a merit system, and—as much as the politicians would let him—extended civil service. He had encouraged efficiency and technical improvement, and had built up the air-mail service from its shaky and dangerous beginnings just after the war. But when Lewis J. Selznick and Saul Rogers came to offer him $150,000 a year to supervise and regulate the moving-picture industry Hays—no wealthy man—could not say no. They, in turn, needed Hays to create a more favorable image of the rich-by-night industry summed up in the word Hollywood. For Hollywood's reputation had been tarnished by a series of competitively salacious films and by the less-than-private scandals of the film colony. In 1920 Mary Pickford, America's Sweetheart, had divorced Owen Moore in Nevada to marry Douglas Fairbanks—a divorce many claimed was a fraud. Then a year later a bleached-blonde extra, Virginia Rappe, had died during a wild party given by Fatty Arbuckle in a San Francisco hotel. Afterward Arbuckle had been tried three times for manslaughter. Wallace Reid—a predecessor of Valentino as a film idol—had died mysteriously from drugs; and the death of the director William Desmond Taylor remained even more mysterious. Aroused by such lapses, the rural pieties that had foisted Prohibition on the United States were preparing to challenge the film world. The Southern Baptist Conference, the Christian Endeavor, the General Federation of Women's Clubs all passed resolutions condemning sinfulness in films. Hays, in spite of his ears the image of the churchgoing Hoosier, seemed the answer to outside evangelical criticism and cutthroat competition in the trade, and on March 6 he became the so-called Czar of the film industry. Hubert Work, a former physician less friendly to civil service than Hays, became the new Postmaster General.

On March 8 Harding and the Duchess left for a few weeks of mindless relaxation with the McLeans at Palm Beach. With the presidential party were George Christian, Daugherty, Under Secretary of State Henry Fletcher, Speaker Gillett, and the inevitable Doctor Sawyer. Ned had chartered the houseboat *Nahmeoka* from Bernard Baruch's brother to take the President for a cruise along the coastal canals and rivers. The

Duchess, ailing and on her usual strict diet, spent her days with Evalyn under the awnings of the upper deck. Each morning the men went ashore to play golf, following the *Nahmeoka's* course by car and arriving back in time for dinner. Evenings they played poker. But there was no Scobey with his parlor stories, no Fall to liven up the evenings. Evalyn felt afterward that it had not been a very successful party.

Washington was still wallowing in the muddy aftermath of winter when Harding returned to the White House. He had an old carpet laid on the damp turf behind his office and each morning drove dozens of golf balls all over the South Grounds, some of which Laddie Boy retrieved. The Japanese cherry trees along the Potomac, planted in Taft's administration, burst into bloom to mark the anniversary of his first year in office. Old Progressive William Allen White, who had sweated so despondently through the Coliseum nomination, had now veered round to the opinion that Harding had done some good and wholesome things and that the regime was not in disfavor. Secretary Hughes, still buoyed by the Disarmament Conference, wrote Harding: "Of many happy years, the last has been the happiest—thanks to your constant kindness and to the opportunity you have given to work for worth-while results under your leadership. Such an experience makes one feel younger despite the flight of time."

If in the blossoming spring the autumn elections still seemed a low stratus cloud on the horizon, the threat of impending coal and railroad strikes was like a cumulo-nimbus mass building up in the still-serene sky. Management—no doubt having in mind the pious Bible-literalist Judge Gary's success in breaking the 1919 steel strike—demanded that wages of miners and railroad workers be cut back to the level of the rest of the country, while the unions insisted that wages must stay where they were. Harding, believing that normalcy meant deflation, told John L. Lewis, the new head of the United Mine Workers of America, that miners—like everybody else—would have to take a wage reduction. Lewis, in the President's soft language, had the chance of making himself one of the outstanding labor figures of the nation by persuading his miners to accept such a cut when their contract expired on March 31. Their current wage scale of $7.50 a day, according to the mine owners, was far above competitors in non-union fields and "imposed a burden on the consuming public and the whole industry." What the owners wanted was a return to the 1917 scale of $5.

The pugnacious thatch-browed Lewis, a miner and the son of a Welsh miner, could be as arrogant in his labor way as arch-capitalists like Gary and Frick. He had defied Wilson and won a strike in 1919, and he was equally ready to defy Harding in 1922. Two years before, he had been elected, or rather had elected himself, president of the Mine Workers and had built that loose organization with its autonomous branches into a monolithic union. With his bruiser face and hair that stood up like a picket line, he looked primed for violence, as indeed he was. In June, 1921, he had even attempted to defeat the more conciliatory Gompers for the presidency of the American Federation of Labor.

Lewis, through growing up in the mines, had become tougher and more ruthless than the men he led. He knew what it was to work in the sweat of unventilated tunnels, and he knew disaster. He knew that every time a miner went down into the pits there was one chance in nine of his being injured or killed. To him it was crude, elemental justice, justice that he had the power to enforce, that miners should be among the most highly paid American workers. He refused to listen to Harding's soothing deflationary words any more than he would listen to the coal operators' complaints that they were losing two-thirds of their profits on the present wage scales. "It makes no difference to the organized mineworkers of this country that wage reductions have taken place in other industries," he announced defiantly, "and it makes no difference to the United Mine Workers that men employed in the non-union sections of this country in the coal industry have accepted wage reductions."

The old contract ran until March 31, and on the first of April Lewis called out his men: 446,545 bituminous miners in the United States and Canada, 150,000 anthracite miners in northeast Pennsylvania, and 186,000 non-union miners expected to strike in sympathy.

Behind the coal strike loomed a strike of railroad shopmen and maintenance employees. During the war years their wages had soared, and as late as 1920 they had had another 20 per cent increase. But in 1921 the Railroad Labor Board decreed a 12½ per cent pay cut which the men had accepted. The board had been established during the second Wilson administration and consisted of three members representing the railroads, three representing labor, and three representing the public. In May the Interstate Commerce Commission had ordered the railroad carriers to reduce their rates by 10 per cent. The carriers insisted that such a cut made a further cut in wages necessary, and appealed to the Railroad Labor Board. A week later the Board—its labor members dissenting—ordered a 12½ per cent reduction in the shopmen's wages. Even with the reduction, the board maintained, common laborers would have 44.5 per cent more buying power than in December, 1917, when they averaged 19.3 cents an hour. The higher-paid machinists, with a cut of 7 cents an hour, would still be receiving 70.3 cents, 19 per cent more than five years earlier. Laborers, machinists, and carmen did not see it that way. With the price of food what it was, percentages buttered no bread. They refused to accept the Board's order, and on July 1, 400,000 shopmen across the country left their jobs.

In spite of threatening strikes, economic tensions, and Republican fumblings and dissent in the Congress, Harding in the afterglow of the Arms Limitation Conference remained almost as popular as when he had taken office a year before. If he was not a leader, at least he still looked a leader. Discontent with lesser Republicans enhanced the handsome and affable President. The Boston *Transcript* felt that "Congress is the liability of the Republican party today, the President and his Cabinet its greatest assets." The presidential "honeymoon," that period of stored-up good will based on vague hopes given to most incoming Presidents, still persisted, although *Uncle Henry* of *Collier's* warned that it was "about as personal as the hearty breakfast they give a condemned man." Business was improving in the cities, and although the lot of the farmer did not improve, the folksy Harding image still continued to bemuse the rural areas and the small towns. Whatever Mencken-minded intellectuals might think, such homely gestures as Harding's intervening to save a Russian immigrant's dog, condemned by some outlandish Pennsylvania law forbidding aliens to own dogs, had a mass appeal for latent sentimentalism all over the country.

Harding himself could take pride in such administrative accomplishments as the new Budget Bureau where General Dawes, after a year of establishing a budget on business lines, had reduced government expenses by almost $2 billion. Albert Lasker had been equally successful with the Shipping Board. When he took it over it had been known as "the worst mess in Washington," burdened with a derelict fleet of 2,200 ships that had been built with hasty zeal in the war and were now rotting away at anchor while eating up $200 million a year—a tenth of the Federal budget —in maintenance charges. Lasker salvaged what ships he could from the $3 billion investment while ruthlessly scuttling the rest. With equal ruthlessness he cut down on his office staff, still at its swollen wartime strength of 700 lawyers and 3,000 bookkeepers. Dismissing the drones, hiring experts, he built up a serviceable Shipping Board fleet and managed to cut expenditures to $50 million a year, although he would have preferred to transfer the ships outright to a private merchant marine. Since the Congress balked at passing a ship subsidy bill to make this possible, he operated his fleet commercially. The seized German liner *Vaterland,* the largest ship afloat, he refurbished as the *Leviathan* after first proposing to call her the *Harding*—a proposal that the President found "unseemly." The war seemed further liquidated when his reconstituted ships brought back the last of the American Expeditionary Force from Germany.

Even taciturn Vice President Coolidge was sufficiently carried away by the prevailing optimism to write his chief:

You and your administration give us strength and courage. I am very proud of your accomplishments, and feel certain that no one can examine the record, either now or hereafter, without being thankful for what you have done for the welfare of America.

In mid-spring Harding wrote to Harvey that he personally had no worries and that he was planning a trip to Alaska if Congress would recess in time for him to get away by August 1. As spring gave way to summer, a shower of honorary degrees descended on the President. Topping the list, Harvard offered him its crimson-hooded doctorate, although it was never awarded since he was unable to make the journey to Cambridge, and Harvard—adamant to Presidents and generals—has always refused to award honorary degrees *in absentia*. On June 6 he spoke at the dedication of the Princeton Memorial Monument and received a degree at the hands of President John Grier Hibben, with Wilson's old enemy, Dean Andrew F. West, reading the citation:

WARREN GAMALIEL HARDING

Trained in boyhood to habits of thrift and labor, guided by happy influences at home, schooled in youth, both as student and teacher, in the elemental lessons of our civilization, helping always in the life of his own community, learning and forming public opinion in his editorial career, he further enlarged his views by travel to observe conditions in European states and by continuous service, state and national, and with marked success in the United States Senate. Faithful from the first "over a few things," he has been made "ruler over many things" as the President of our Republic.

Whatever differing party judgments may properly be held as to policies, our people are one in honoring his readiness to seek the best advice, his strict endeavor to find the real truth, his capable handling of complicated difficulties, his immense patience and self-effacing modesty. The sweeping away of extravagant waste and the forming of a budget system show him a master in finance. His vote as Senator for the anti-strike clause in the railroad bill and his attitude as President on the bonus reveal his quiet courage, and the great work of the Conference for limiting armaments, assembled at his call, has won the gratitude of the world.

His charter in things political is the Constitution. His guide in things spiritual is the Bible. First seeking to make American liberty sure, he is well aware that charity begins at home, but does not end there. He stands in the tradition of Lincoln, a man of the people, leading the people, heeding the will of the people and the need of the world.

To match Harding's sheaf of degrees, a peak in Montana was dedicated to him and named Mt. Harding. Edgar Saltus, preparing a limited library edition of his nine books, asked him for a foreword to *Imperial Purple* and Harding supplied one, managing to say nothing with reasonable grace.

One member of the Harding family who failed to share the spring optimism and who wanted no part of the Washington scene was the President's pious doctor-brother. From his thriving sanitorium for the well-to-do insane that he ran in Worthington, near Columbus, Deac could see nothing but apocalyptic visions of doom. At a Seventh-day Adventist World Conference in San Francisco, in May, he predicted that the end of the world was near and that they, the faithful, might expect the second coming of Christ shortly. "We are living in a time predicted by the prophets," he told the delegates. "The end of this phase of our existence is so near at hand that we must work rapidly, for our time is short."

There was no thought of doom in Marion that year, for the little Ohio city, bursting with civic pride at having its own son in the White House as it approached its hundredth birthday, planned a four-day Centennial Celebration beginning on July 2. For its climax the members of the Marion County Federation of Women's Clubs were preparing a pageant, *The Building of Marion*, written by Eleanor M. Freeland, who with her sister Isabel had once lived next door to the Hardings,[1] and had worked at the Harding headquarters in the 1920 campaign. The pageant with its cast of several hundred was to show Marion's history beginning with Holmes's purchase of land from the Delawares and Eber Baker's survey. Intermediate scenes would include the choosing of Marion as the county seat; the escape of "Black Bill," a Negro slave; a patriotic meeting during the Civil War; an old-time singing school. The grand finale would be President Harding addressing the Arms Limitation Conference, and ebullient boosters planned to have him impersonate himself. Harding was greatly distressed when this appeared in the papers and ordered Christian to repudiate it at once.

Although the President might balk at impersonating himself, neither the coal strike—now in its third month—nor the impending railroad strike could keep him from the centennial of the city he loved so well. Always his random thoughts kept drifting back to the Ohio country. Often he imagined retiring to Blooming Grove at the end of his second term. The *Star* and the small affairs of Marion still concerned him. When the crippled Doctor McAfee resigned his pulpit in Trinity Church, Harding was the largest contributor to a fund raised for him; when Fr. Joseph M. Dennig of St. Mary's Catholic Church found himself in undisclosed difficulties, Harding appointed him Agent and Consul General at Tangier. His old friend French Crow he made Marion's postmaster. "You know," he told William Allen White when White dropped in at the White House

---

[1] She later wrote a series of newspaper articles, "The Girl Next Door," about her recollections of the Hardings.

one afternoon to visit him in his private office "every day at three-thirty, here in the midst of affairs of state, I go to press on the Marion *Star*. I wonder what kind of layout the boys have got on the first page. I wonder how much advertising there is; whether they are keeping up with this week last year. I would like to walk out in the composing room and look over the forms before they go to the stereotyper. There never was a day in all the years I ran the paper that I didn't get some thrill out of it." On being presented with a new car in June his first thought was to spend the hot months while Congress dawdled in driving back and forth between Washington and Marion—without the usual accompaniment of the Secret Service, secretaries, and the press, but just on his own, stopping to chat with the people along the way. Christian had to explain to him that for a President this was no longer possible.

A week before Harding left for Marion, violence erupted in southern Illinois, where 60,000 miners were out on strike. At Herrin, a strip-mining center in Bloody Williamson County, a stubborn absentee owner had brought in armed strikebreakers—mostly from Chicago's skid row—and the miners had replied with dynamite, rifles, and even a plane that they hired to drop bombs. Williamson County sheriffs and deputies stayed at home, too fearful to intervene as the miners attacked. Besieged in their mine, outnumbered, unable to save themselves even with machine guns, the strikebreakers raised the white flag. On surrendering they were forced to run a gauntlet of enraged miners, and 21 of them were beaten to death, shot, or lynched. The Herrin Massacre—for which Lewis was held indirectly responsible—although it did not cut short Harding's proposed home trip, alienated sympathy not only for the miners but for the railroadmen and all strikers.

Harding left the White House on July 1, in his official car with the presidential seal emblazoned on the side, for the three-day overland journey to Marion, stopping off the first night at Gettysburg where Gen. Smedley Butler's Fifth and Sixth Regiment of Marines encamped on the old battleground had erected a temporary though elaborate camp of canvas and wood for the presidential party. Traveling with Harding and the Duchess in the motorcade of half-a-dozen cars were General Pershing, former General former Budget Director Dawes and his wife, Doctor Sawyer and George Christian with their wives, the *Star's* red-headed former delivery boy Maj. Ora Baldinger in dress uniform with the glittering gold braid of a presidential aide, Governor Sproul (for the Pennsylvania part of the journey), a carload of Secret Service guards, and another car of reporters.

During the afternoon the President stood on the steps of the observation tower on Cemetery Ridge to watch General Butler's Marines re-enact Confederate General Pickett's last charge that ended in Lee's defeat.

During the night a succession of thunderstorms blew down many tents in the Marine encampment, although Harding's more solid shelter remained intact. In the cleared morning he and his party were awakened by reveille, attended Sunday services, and then left on the winding road over the Cumberland Mountains to Uniontown. Idle miners along the way waved their hats as the President passed. Coming into Ohio, he drove south by way of Cincinnati to visit Grant's birthplace at Point Pleasant. Not until ten of the evening of July 3 did the motorcade reach Marion. Harding stayed with Tryon and his new wife Alice in the frame house on East Center Street, while Pershing stopped more elaborately with the Sawyers at White Oaks Farm.

The centennial celebration had opened decorously on Sunday, July 2, with special morning services in all the churches, while in the afternoon the Shriners' Kadgar Grotto Band and the Marion Choral Society performed at Garfield Park. Monday was given over to welcoming the descendants of Eber Baker. The big day was the Fourth. Early in the morning Harding found himself serenaded by a Civil War Veterans' fife-and-drum corps led by Colonel Christian. After breakfast he dropped in at the *Star* office, shook hands with all the employees and called them by name, then sat at his old desk and wrote an editorial for the centennial edition, concluding with rhetoric undimmed: "The fit counterpart to the city of material success is the city of happy homes, ample education, fortunate and profitable employment, worship of God facilitated, a civic conscience, and a community soul."

Twenty-five thousand spectators filled the grandstand bleachers and half the field within the race track of the fairgrounds, cheering, shouting, and whistling when the sleek black cars of the presidential cortège drove up at two-thirty. Harding in the first car bowed and smiled with easy affability, while the Duchess, stiffly self-conscious beside him, waved her awkward dropsical right arm. With the President rode Pershing in his olive-drab overseas uniform and Reddy Baldinger resplendent in dress blue. Following came Tryon and Alice with Daisy, the crippled Doctor McAfee and his wife, General Dawes, Doctor Sawyer in a general's dress blue, Dick Crissinger with his wife and daughter, and Colonel Christian and Coonie.

The entire grandstand shimmered with American flags. With Pershing sitting at Harding's right and the Duchess on his left, and as the cheering died down, Mrs. Genevra Johnson sang a solo, "I'm Calling You Home." Pershing, the trim martinet in the Sam Browne belt, followed as the first speaker, denouncing—without naming—the Herrin Massacre and invoking "the public spirit and the patriotic enthusiasm of our noble ancestry." While he spoke, a biplane circled in front of the grandstand. When he had concluded, a chorus of 16 soloists under the direction of the chairman of the centennial music committee sang "The Star-Spangled Banner." Harding's speech was the high point of the day.

> If there is anybody in Marion who feels that I have slighted him [he told his fellow townsmen] he must understand it just isn't possible to greet everyone. I would love to have the personal touch with all of you, just as much as anybody in Marion. I wish I could stay a little longer. I will welcome the day when I can come back to stay with you permanently. Some of you may think it is a very fine thing to be President of the United States and it is good to keep thinking it, because when you wake up from your dream you will find it a very different thing.

He did not refer even indirectly to the Herrin Massacre although he did call for the "right to work and live by that work."

Unobserved in the crowd wedged into the space before the grandstand Nan Britton "adored her hero from afar" as he stood bareheaded in the bright sunlight just as she had adored him twelve years before at Marion's Grand Opera House. She had come from Chicago two nights earlier and had driven over to the fairgrounds with her old school chum, Annabel Mouser—now Mrs. John Fairbanks. Harding had no idea that she was there. As she listened, he again recited the four familiar lines of Will Carleton's "First Settler" poem. The silver voice concluded with a rhetorical fanfare too deep for understanding:

> America will go on. The fundamentals of the Republic and all its liberties will be preserved, and government must maintain the supremacy of law and authority. Under these liberty has its fullest fruition and men attain to reveal the glory of liberty's institutions.

After the applause ended, General Dawes spoke. The Duchess was introduced to the crowd. Mrs. Mary Stockwell Durfee sang "Marion, My Marion," written by Isabel Freeland to the tune of "Maryland, My Maryland." At 4:08 the exercises were brought to a close with the members of the Marion Howitzer Company forming a double line from the stands to the official cars. And as the cheering spectators waved their hats and their handkerchiefs, the President and his party passed.

Annabel drove back to her father's house with Nan. When they were together with the family, Grant Mouser, now judge of Marion's Common Pleas Court, suggested that she or his wife Dell drop in at Tryon's "and say how do you do to President and Mrs. Harding." Dell agreed to go, and took her daughter and a hesitant Nan with her.

The President, they found, had gone off to play golf with Dawes and Doctor Sawyer and his doctor son, but the Duchess was holding court on the horsehair sofa in the parlor for Ed Uhler and his wife. Condescendingly cordial, she was to Nan's relief completely unsuspecting as she picked up the thread of her interrupted monologue. "Yes, indeed," she continued, "I keep Wurr'n the best-dressed man in Washington," and the Uhlers nodded in sycophantic agreement.

In the evening a fireworks display illuminated the fairgrounds with the features of Harding, Eber Baker, and Pershing. The following morning was given over to speeches, led off by the president of the Ohio Archaeological and Historical Society, James E. Campbell, Civil War veteran and former governor, and followed by that ancient of days, General Keifer. The event of the afternoon, a historical parade, was reviewed by Harding and his sister Daisy from a bunting-decked temporary stand in front of the Presbyterian Church at the corner of Prospect and Church Streets. Harding was much interested in an old prairie schooner, drawn by 20 mules. One float showing a Colonial mother rocking a cradle made him smile at the inscription: "No Flapper Rocked This." He was equally amused when an AEF veteran in his old uniform edged between the floats in a battered touring car, his wife beside him holding a baby, and a sign on the hood: "First American baby born on the Rhine!"

Nan stood watching on the steps of the house next to the church with the five-year-old twin daughters of her schoolmate Ellen Lucille Mezger Stoll whose brother Roscoe had married Pete DeWolfe's widow, Esther, in 1916. During the whole centenary celebration she was not able to get any closer to her lover than that, and she left for Chicago without his knowing that she had been in Marion. In the afternoon Harding closed the centennial with a speech at the American Legion barbecue held at the fairgrounds, telling the complacent legionnaires that the Legion held the destiny of the country for the next fifty years.

Back in Washington from his Marion interlude, Harding found his accumulating troubles intensified. Fears were growing that after the coal strike there would be another fuel-short winter, that the railroad strike would soon bring most industries to a halt. Congress, still failing to act on tax reduction, was preparing the Fordney-McCumber tariff, the highest tariff act on record; and a soldiers' bonus bill seemed headed for early passage, in spite of the threat of a presidential veto. Between the strikes and the thwarted legislation there would be no chance of a trip to Alaska this year.

Before leaving for Marion Harding had held a futile conference with Lewis and the operators. On July 10 he proposed that the miners go back to work temporarily under the terms of their old contract. During the interval every question in dispute would go to a national commission composed of three representatives of the miners, three of the operators, and five appointed by the President. The commission would not only settle the wage dispute but "inaugurate a searching inquiry into every phase of the coal industry."

The operators agreed to accept the commission and its findings but

Lewis, aware that the majority of the commission would undoubtedly recommend a wage cut, refused the President's "indisputably fair proposal." Angrily Harding appealed to the miners over Lewis's head to go back to the mines—but Lewis's control was absolute and the mines stayed shut. The governors of Minnesota, North Dakota, South Dakota, Wisconsin, and Ohio, telegraphed the President, begging him to take over the mines and the railroads. Briefly Harding considered the idea, but finally decided that "the force of public opinion" had better solve the problem.

Five months after the start of the coal strike the operators capitulated, rescinding all proposed wage cuts and agreeing to Lewis's demands to extend the old contracts for a year and a half. Yet Lewis's was a Pyrrhic victory. Although he could force the mine operators to pay a daily wage of $7.50, he could not force them to give regular daily work to his miners. More and more industries and homes were converting to oil. By the end of the twenties the members of the United Mine Workers would drop from 400,000 to less than 150,000.

The railroad workers in their strike lacked the strategic advantages of the United Mine Workers. Their union, far from being monolithic, was made up of semi-independent branches accustomed to negotiate their own regional controls; and their president, B. M. Jewell, was no John L. Lewis. When the chairman of the Railroad Labor Board, Ben W. Hooper, protested that the shopmen's strike was no longer that of an employee against an employer but a strike against a government tribunal, the railroad directors saw his statement as a green light to move against the unions. Since the workers had not seen fit to obey Hooper's appeal to go back to work, the directors entered lawsuits against the union and began replacing the shopmen by strikebreakers while stationing armed guards around all large stations and freight yards. "The difficulty with the railroad executives' position," Harding complained to Pennsylvania's Sen. George Wharton Pepper, "is that they expect me to enforce to the letter the decisions of the Railroad Labor Board as such decisions relate to the employees, while the railroads have again and again ignored the decisions of the board where fulfillment was encumbent on the railroad managers." He proposed that both sides accept the validity of Railroad Board rulings, that the men go back to work, and that all the strikers be reinstated without loss of seniority or other rights and without any discrimination against them for having struck.

The railroad executives turned down the President's proposal 265 to 2 while refusing any further bargaining. At most they would agree to allow the shopmen to return to work individually at the rate of pay fixed by the Labor Board, but they rejected any nationwide settlement. The shopmen responded to management's obduracy by dynamiting bridges, blocking switches, and destroying railroad property across the country. Non-strikers were assaulted, some died, many had their houses wrecked.

Since the aristocracy of railroad workers—the big four brotherhoods of Railway Trainmen, Locomotive Engineers, Firemen and Enginemen, and Railway Conductors—did not strike, the trains, although the schedules were much curtailed, still ran. Members of the brotherhoods, nevertheless, grew increasingly angry at the belligerence of the armed guards at the stations and at management's intransigence toward the shopmen. Wildcat sympathy strikes broke out, with demands that the armed guards be removed and non-union shopmen discharged. Twenty-five hundred passengers on 12 continental trains found themselves suddenly marooned in the Arizona desert as the crews of the Santa Fé Railroad abandoned their trains out of sympathy with the shopmen. Five hundred more passengers were stranded at Ogden, Utah. At Needles, California, many passengers —some elderly, some small children—collapsed in the 113-degree heat that they were forced to endure for four days. Several babies were born in the aisles of day coaches.

Coming on top of the Herrin Massacre, the casual marooning of innocent passengers in the desert turned public opinion against all strikes and strikers. On August 18 a worn and fatigue-heavy Harding, addressing a joint meeting of the Senate and the House, was much applauded by Democrats as well as Republicans when he condemned the lawlessness growing out of both strikes and promised that "government by law must and will be sustained." He announced that he was resolved to "use the power of the government to maintain transportation and sustain the right of the men to work," but blamed the state authorities for failing to suppress disorders. He condemned the "Herrin butchery" and the cruelty of the train crews in abandoning their passengers, and regretted that the country was at the mercy of the United Mine Workers even though the miners themselves wanted to go back to work. Although asking for no emergency laws he did request a National Coal Agency and legislative action to make the Railroad Labor Board decisions binding on both sides. While he spoke, the Duchess in a plumed hat watched him from the President's box in the gallery, flanked by Welliver, Lasker, and Doctor Sawyer in a white uniform.

To Daugherty, who viewed the world through the vermilion-tinted glasses of his radical-riding predecessor, A. Mitchell Palmer, the 1922 strikers were controlled and manipulated by "Red Agents of the Soviet Government" under the direction of Lenin's associate, Grigori Zinoviev. The Shopmen's Union, he maintained, was being manipulated by "Red borers" determined to force the government to take over the railroads. Fortified by Harding's speech, the Attorney General prepared to move against the shopmen whom he now accused of violating the orders of the Railroad Labor Board, and hence the government itself. "So long and to the extent that I can speak for the government of the United States," he declared, "I will use the power of the government to prevent the labor unions of the country from destroying the open shop." In Chicago he persuaded the sympathetic Federal Judge James A. Wilkerson, whom he had recommended for appointment, to issue an injunction he had already prepared against the Union. On September 1 Judge Wilkerson [2] obliged with one of the most sweeping and drastic injunctions ever issued in the United States. Under it the shopmen could still breathe, but there was little else that they could do. Daugherty did not attempt to conceal his intention of breaking the strike. The strikers could not "loiter" near any railroad station or office, they could not "congregate" near yards, shops, depots, or terminals. They could not picket or attempt to dissuade anyone from taking their jobs. They could not "in letters, circulars, telegrams, telephones, or word of mouth, or through interviews in the papers, encourage or direct anyone to leave or enter the service of the railroad companies."

When Secretary Hoover read the terms of the injunction in next morning's paper he was outraged, feeling that Daugherty and Wilkerson had violated the most rudimentary rights of the shopmen. Walking to the Cabinet meeting, he met Hughes who was equally indignant, and begged Hoover to challenge Daugherty since the matter lay outside the function of the Secretary of State. Hoover acquiesced, and in full Cabinet meeting, with Harding present, denounced the Attorney General's action. Daugherty was "flabbergasted" at Hoover's attack and when the nonplussed Harding asked him for an explanation of this illegal action, could only mumble that it had been approved by the lawyers of his department. Ted Roosevelt, occupying the Secretary of the Navy's chair in Denby's absence, also objected, adding that his father would never have approved such an injunction. According to Fall, in the course of that turbulent meeting he shouted at Daugherty: "You don't know any law and you can't learn any. . . . If the Attorney General is going to be permitted to do such high-handed, damned-fool things, my resignation is in." [3]

Labor's first reaction to the injunction was to declare a general strike, but the cautious Gompers soon thought better of it. The executive council of the American Federation of Labor instructed him to begin impeach-

[2] Judge Wilkerson who in 1931 could have given Al Capone, found guilty of income-tax evasion, a minimum sentence of two and a half years, sent him to Alcatraz for eleven.

[3] Daugherty denied that the Secretary of the Interior had ever shouted any such remarks, although admitted that Fall had opposed the injunction "in a vicious and pronounced way."

ment proceedings against Daugherty. Coached by Gompers's lawyer Jackson Ralston, the Independent Republican congressman from Minnesota, Oscar E. Keller, introduced a resolution in the House impeaching the Attorney General for High Crimes and Misdemeanors in "abridging freedom of speech, freedom of the press, the right of the people peaceably to assemble." Keller also charged that Daugherty had failed to prosecute "malefactors of great wealth"—a phrase he had picked up from Theodore Roosevelt. The House Judiciary Committee, headed by Andrew J. Volstead, agreed to hear his charges in December. By that time Keller had filed fourteen grounds for impeachment, accusing the Attorney General of conducting himself "in a manner arbitrary, oppressive, unjust, and illegal"; of appointing "untrustworthy, dangerous, and corrupt persons"; of "using the funds of his office illegally and without warrant in the prosecution of individuals for certain lawful acts which under law he was specifically forbidden to prosecute"; of "personal, financial, and political favoritism." But Keller, a single-tax fanatic, nervous and unstable, was not the man to tackle the Attorney General. Though enlarging his charges against Daugherty, he declined to present convincing evidence to support them and found himself reduced to telling an unsympathetic committee that he did not want to submit his proofs in advance and that his charges in any case were true until proven untrue. When Volstead snappishly ordered him to produce facts, he lost his temper and stalked from the hearing, refusing to return even when subpoenaed by the sergeant-at-arms. According to a malicious paragraph in Daugherty's apologia, Keller lost his nerve and bolted down the corridor as the sergeant-at-arms approached, soiling himself and the marble tiling as he ran. Finally the Judiciary Committee, with one dissenting vote, reported that all the charges against the Attorney General were unfounded, and the House of Representatives adopted the report by a vote of 204 to 77.

Daugherty remained convinced that the agitation against him was part of a vast Red plot that even included an attempt to poison him. Just before the autumn elections he wrote in his apologia, that when he was addressing an audience of workers in Toledo trying to explain the merits of his injunction, he caught a strange pungent odor coming from an enormous bouquet of flowers that stood beside the speakers' stand.

> The second time I smelled it I caught my breath and thought I was going to faint. It immediately flashed before me that someone had slipped onto the rostrum before I reached it and concealed a deadly gas trap in the flowers.
>
> I moved to the other side of the speakers' stand out of line of the breeze that crossed the flowers, felt no further inconvenience, and closed my speech with a round of applause.

Meanwhile Judge Wilkerson's injunction had broken the back of the railroad strike. Slowly the men drifted back to their old jobs—if they could find them—on the new terms. Some of the railroads signed individual contracts with the Shopmen's Union, some refused to sign. One could not fix a definite date, but by mid-November the strike was over and lost.[4] For the strikers, their only revenge lay in the November elections.

Harding's apprehensive thoughts of the coming elections turned to a much more immediate apprehension when early in September the Duchess, following a severe cold, was struck down with an attack of her old kidney trouble. On September 8 Doctor Sawyer issued the first public bulletin on her condition:

> Mrs. Harding, whose illness is a recurrence of attacks experienced before coming to the White House, developed complications Thursday and Thursday night which make her condition critical. These complications are so serious that recovery is not yet assured. Doctor John Finney of Baltimore was called in consultation tonight and Doctor Charles Mayo is en route from Rochester, Minnesota. Doctor Carl W. Sawyer and Doctor Joel T. Boone have joined in the attendance on Mrs. Harding today.

Harding remained at her bedside all night. It was as if he sensed in such moments how much this ailing, imperious woman whom he could neither accept nor reject had become part of him. Evalyn McLean, whom he had sent for from Bar Harbor, found him slumped at his desk, his arms stretched out before him on the blotter. "I'm afraid Florence is going," he told her. Doctor Finney was even blunter: "Dying now, I think." The Duchess's one kidney being completely stopped, her only chance—an outside one, according to Finney—was for Mayo to operate. This Doctor Sawyer had refused to allow.

Evalyn went upstairs and talked with Sawyer while he paced the floor outside the Duchess's bedroom, a birdlike figure—she thought—hopping along in brown uniform and russet-colored puttees. He squinted at her through his thick glasses and his voice grew shrill as he announced that for all their reputations, Finney and Mayo were not going to operate on the Duchess unless they did it over his dead body! "I know what she can stand, and I know she cannot stand another operation," he told her with tears in his eyes. "I am facing ruin, almost—just because I am convinced that if her heart holds out, the kidney stoppage will open up. I tell you, I'm their *family* doctor." Then he took Evalyn on tiptoe to see the unconscious Duchess. Looking down at her blue-green face, Evalyn thought she must be already dead.

---

[4] Harding wrote privately afterward: "There was no excuse for the railroad strike. The simple truth is that the previous administration allowed railroad labor to fix its own terms at the expense of the Federal Treasury, and the present-day labor leadership is determined to hold that vantage ground regardless of any other considerations."

Nevertheless, the stubborn little homeopath was right, for by the next morning the Duchess showed a trace of improvement, and slowly the bloated kidney began to eliminate the poisons seeping through her body. Harding wrote to Herrick on September 19 that she had turned the critical period and he was confident that she would recover although she would not be able to leave her room for a month or so. During the crisis of the Duchess's illness Wilson and his wife had called and left their cards. Harding, always secretly in awe of his aristocratic predecessor, was touched by Wilson's courtesy, remarking that it was a wonderful thing for a sick man of the opposing party to do. After Harding's death Wilson's card was found carefully tucked in a flap of the blotter on the President's desk.

With the Duchess slowly mending, Harding could concern himself again more directly with Congress. After a dilatory session that had dragged through the languid Washington summer the members were eager to get back to their home districts for their mid-term election campaigning. On September 19 the Senate finally passed the Fordney-McCumber Tariff Act, the so-called "scientific tariff" giving the President the right to raise or lower certain rates up to 50 per cent, a tariff law which Senator Calder considered the best ever enacted. If, indeed, the Senator by "best" meant "highest," he was right; for using the slogan "America First!" the tariff inaugurated the highest rates in the history of the country, with temporary benefits to American industry—including the Mellon aluminum interests—but with permanently disastrous consequences to world trade. With the Fordney-McCumber Tariff Act, that Harding enthusiastically signed, America took the road of economic isolation that would in its turnings wind over the hill to the Depression.

When, at the same time, Congress passed the tariff measure it passed a veterans' bonus bill, Harding—as he had threatened, and in spite of the election year—vetoed it. He refused, he told Congress, to add a $4 billion or one-sixth to the total of the public debt in order to benefit 5 million veterans among 110 million citizens. Although the House of Representatives promptly overrode his veto, the bonus proponents lacked four Senate votes. On that negative vote and on September 22 the regular session of Congress came to an end.

As the November 7 elections neared, more astute Republican leaders privately expected some Democratic gains and were intent merely on holding them to a minimum. The mid-term reaction, the swing of the electorate away from the party in power in the congressional elections held in the middle of each presidential term, is a phenomenon that can be counted on except in periods of profound crisis or economic dislocation. Usually the party in power can expect to lose between 35 and 40 seats in the House of Representatives,[5] although no party officially ever does expect to.

Much of the mid-term reaction is due to men with a grievance who cast their votes against rather than for a party. The overwhelming Republican victory of 1920 was not so much a vote for the Front Porch as against Wilson and the repudiated war that he had come to symbolize. Such protest votes recoil easily, particularly when there is no charismatic leader to head the ticket. But the mid-term reaction of 1922 was far more than the swing of an emotional pendulum. In two years the 7 million Republican majority had melted away. Where there had been 300 Republican and 130 Democratic seats in the old House of Representatives, the mid-term elections brought in only 221 Republicans to 212 Democrats. Members of the Old Guard such as Calder and Frelinghuysen had gone down like ninepins. Even Carmi Thompson, Harding's personal choice to succeed Governor Davis in Ohio, was defeated by A. V. Donahey, the Democratic former state auditor.[6] Only the Republicans-in-name-only of the prairie states, the Farmer-Labor Insurgents, had survived in strength. La Follette—soon to discard the Republican label altogether for the revived Progressive—would with the farm bloc hold the balance of power in both houses in the new Congress.

In the gloomy atmosphere of Republican national headquarters there were even hints that unless conditions changed, the convention would not nominate Harding in 1924. Many Republican leaders blamed the disaster on the new tariff bill. Midwestern farmers, caught in the agricultural depression in which 10 per cent of them had lost their farms by foreclosures, had gone over to the new radical organizations—the Non-Partisan League and the Farmer-Labor party. No longer could they be fobbed off with such palliatives as the regulating of stockyards, the control of grain exchanges by the Secretary of Agriculture. What the farmers wanted, what the farm bloc demanded, was government price support. The wets in the cities were disaffected by Republican endorsement of Prohibition, the rural drys dissatisfied with the enforcement of their pet law. Labor, after the strikes and the Daugherty injunction, was savage against the Republicans, as were the 5 million veterans of the AEF deprived of what they considered their just compensation. And beyond all these tangible reasons for the reaction there were deeper emotional resentments that turned against the regulars of both parties. In 1920 the

[5] The only exception to the mid-term reaction in this century was the 1934 Depression election midway in Franklin Roosevelt's first term when the Democrats raised their total of House seats from 309 to 322 while gaining nine Senate seats.
[6] Two years before, in the Republican sweep, Governor Davis had defeated Donahey by 150,000 votes. This year Donahey defeated Thompson by a 14,000 margin.

country had opted for normalcy, and two years later there was no normalcy.

The mid-term reaction eroded still further Harding's earlier comforting belief that Congress proposes and the President disposes. With his party split between the Insurgents and the Old Guard, leadership devolved on him. "Frankly," he wrote in July to Richard Washburn Child, "being President is rather an unattractive business unless one relishes the exercise of power. That is a thing which has never greatly appealed to me." But after the election setback, those around him noticed a change, a willingness to exercise power that they would not have suspected in the easygoing Senator who had trotted so briskly up the Capitol steps to his inauguration two years before. Finding himself alone, he came to realize how much he wanted to be worthy of his office, to leave a name behind him in the history books, another McKinley from the Buckeye State.

Much as he felt himself imprisoned in the White House, discouraged as he often was by his ignorance of economics and statecraft, distasteful as the office was to his lax habits and manner of life, he still retained his boyhood awe of the Presidency, the homespun path to the White House he had traced in the McGuffey readers. Not since his defeat for governor in 1910 had he suffered such a repudiation as in the 1922 election. Publicly deploring the lack of unity that could so split the Republicans, he privately told the surprised leaders that his views on matters of public concern had "undergone a material and even drastic change." William Allen White hopefully saw the President as finally deciding to "lead the people as their ruler; not as a mere 'subordinate branch of the government.'"

There were indications even before the election that Harding was evolving from the head of his party to the head of his country. As early as April he had written to Judge Gary suggesting that the United States Steel Corporation might set an example to the rest of the industry by reducing its twelve-hour working shift to eight hours and the seven-day week to six. In May he invited 41 leaders of the steel industry to dinner at the White House and afterward gave them his blunt opinion that the twelve-hour day must go. As he wrote to one of the heads of the box board industry, congratulating him for taking the step at which the steel industry still hesitated:

> Nothing will contribute so much to American industrial stability and add so much to American industrial happiness as the abolition of the twelve-hour working day and the seven-day working week. This is far too heavy a draft upon the energies of the workmen employed in any industry and it conforms to our best American ideals to bring about this abolition of excessive hours and excessive days in order that the working forces may have time for leisure, for diversion, for indulgence in the becoming luxuries of life and for a fuller participation in that family life which is essential to the full enjoyment of American freedom and opportunity.

Some of the steel tycoons objected to the President's interference, but they finally agreed to appoint a committee to consider a reduction of the workday "if, and when, practical." The committee after some months concluded that the twelve-hour day of itself had not injured their employees, "physically, mentally, or morally," and that it could not even be said that it denied the worker enough time with his family. To abolish it would dislocate the industry, raise the cost of steel production 15 per cent, and require 60,000 additional and unavailable employees. Harding, still determined to end "such old-time slavish methods," did not flourish a Rooseveltian big stick or denounce as Wilson would have done, but he kept on prodding and urging the reluctant industrialists until finally on August 2, 1923, Judge Gary as president of the American Iron and Steel Institute announced that the elimination of the twelve-hour day would begin at once.

Although Harding recalled Congress two weeks before the regular session of December 4 to consider the Ship Subsidy Bill that he had so long wanted, no vision of the Stars and Stripes waving "in the peace triumphs on the seas of the world" was able to overcome the legislators' deflationary mood. The President told the assembled senators and congressmen that a ship subsidy of $30 million a year would enable the government to convert its fleet into a private merchant marine available for any national emergency, and at a saving of $20 million a year from the $50 million that the fleet now cost the Shipping Board. The only other alternative would be the "supreme humiliation" of selling the ships for scrap. Harding's reasoning fell on deaf Insurgent ears. To them such subsidies were merely a means of enriching Eastern shipowners at the expense of Western farmers. The shipping bill managed to pass the House but in the Senate the shaggy-maned La Follette barred the way.

On December 8 Harding addressed the last, the lame-duck session of the Sixty-seventh Congress. In his evolution he had come so far that he was ready to repudiate the normalcy he had proclaimed. "There will never again be precisely the old order," he told the surprised legislators; "indeed I know of no one who thinks it to be desirable. For out of the old order came the war itself." He now asked for a new law abolishing child labor to replace the one the Supreme Court had struck down. He proposed to investigate the high cost of living, to restrict the issuing of tax-exempt securities, to regulate transport, and provide cheap freight rates for farmers, and—on a less liberal note—to provide for the registration and re-education of aliens. "I have to proceed tactfully," he wrote his friend Jonathan Bourne, "to avoid paralyzing the activities of government. Under the rules of the Senate, as you are well aware, it is very easy to paralyze all activities." Yet for all his political caution, it was an independent Harding emerging from his cracked party shell in the late months of 1922.

Whatever the changes in his political mood, the flat Ohio country still drew him back beyond the boundaries of his presidential term. On October 4 French Crow, acting for him, had bought the old Harding homestead and 266 acres at Blooming Grove. Three weeks later Harding wrote to his aunt Ella Dickerson in Galion:

> My one dream is to restore the old houses of your father and Great-grandfather Harding. I think they can be restored as they were on the exterior and made modern on the interior, and be combined into a very attractive group of farmhouses. . . . The addition of the Finney Farm was made in the hope of acquiring . . . ground along the road for a sufficient distance to provide a nine-hole golf course.

Nostalgic though his feelings might be about the *Star*, he no longer thought of himself as returning to his editor's desk. When a dealer, Jacob B. Shale, suggested buying the paper, Harding replied that the *Star* was not on the market but that if satisfactory arrangements could be made "to protect the minority stockholders (all of whom are officials or employees)" he would be "very glad" to talk about disposing of the property.

"Florence," he wrote to his aunt Ella, "continues to improve. Her recovery, however is exceedingly slow." At Thanksgiving, though still in a wheel chair, she was able to have dinner for the first time in the White House dining room, with Harry Daugherty as their solitary guest. When, a few weeks later, Clemenceau attended a formal White House luncheon she asked to meet him, and received him in her wheel chair in the west hall.

Tryon continued to give his son occasional tremors of discomfort, for after settling down for the third time to married life he had gone off restlessly to become a peripatetic attender of veterans' conventions, as ready to lend his presence to the United Confederate Veterans as to the Grand Army of the Republic. In October, while attending the GAR National convention at Des Moines, he was lent a hotel suite and so royally entertained by the local Democrats that he announced if he lived in Iowa he would vote for the Democratic candidate for United States Sen. Clyde Herring—whom he had met at lunch—in preference to Republican Smith Brookhart.

During that waning autumn the first rumblings of scandal within the administration were becoming audible. Colonel Forbes's prodigal efforts at building veterans' hospitals and the shuttling of goods from the Perryville warehouses could not remain secret long. Doctor Sawyer, from the level of the Federal Hospitalization Board, soon got wind of the happenings and openly and publicly criticized the Veterans' Bureau director, whom he had never liked. Limited as a doctor, comic as a soldier, the wizened homeopath in his pathetic general's uniform was an honest and conscientious public servant. Yet in the less stringent atmosphere of Washington he, for all his hundred pounds and his dentures, had escaped from his wife Mandy's autumnal clutches to the more vernal charms of a lady friend of whom he had become so jealous that he asked the Attorney General to have her shadowed. Daugherty, through Burns, was glad to oblige. Then the Doctor, forgetting his so easily granted request, squired his light o' love about with so little caution that the Bureau of Investigation soon developed a dossier on his amorous activities.[7] But although his heart could still beat passionately behind his thin ribs, although he would often drop into the Little House on H Street for a game of poker and to the Little Green House for a quick one, Doctor Sawyer was professionally and financially incorruptible. His criticism of Forbes even reached the newspapers, and not always to his advantage. At the American Legion convention in New Orleans on October 18, Sawyer was accused of being more interested in economy than in veterans' lives, and the delegates passed a resolution demanding his ouster from the Hospitalization Board while praising Forbes as the veterans' friend.

Forbes continued his deals and his dealings unscathed. Representatives of other firms enviously interested in Thompson & Kelley's monopoly of the profitable Perryville surpluses got short shrift from the Colonel, but they found a more sympathetic listener in the doctor-general at the Hospitalization Board. Sawyer himself had got even shorter shrift when he complained to Forbes that the 20 per cent of the medical supplies supposedly allotted to civilian government hospitals was being shipped elsewhere. Paying an unannounced visit to Perryville, he watched freight cars being loaded by the score. At once he went to Harding and told him that supplies of great value to the Army, Navy, and public health were being disposed of under suspicious circumstances. On November 24 Harding ordered the Perryville shipments stopped, and sent for Forbes.

The glib, plausible Colonel, about whose accomplishments in the Veterans' Bureau Harding had often boasted, had a ready and satisfying explanation. The supplies he sold were deteriorating—he brought several prepared samples to show the President—and he had let them go for what they would bring to cut down on storage expenses which he represented to Harding as being twenty-five times as high as they really were. Whatever minor lapses there might have been in such a large operation, he assured the President that he was on the job and would see that everything was put in order. He even suggested that the War and Navy departments delegate officers to check the Perryville operations, and at his suggestion

[7] On the thread of this story Gaston Means strung one of his imaginative tales of Doctor Sawyer's having had an affair with a Mrs. "Whiteley," an intimate of the Duchess's.

Maj. John Carmody of the Army's Quartermaster Corps and Commander C. R. O'Leary were detailed to investigate. Though there is some doubt that they ever got beyond Forbes's office, they soon reported back that all shipments from Perryville had been legal and proper. Harding, relieved and satisfied, declared that the charges against Forbes were an "abominable libel" and lifted his embargo on shipments, unaware that Forbes had paid no attention to the embargo from the beginning. But Doctor Sawyer's eyes, behind his thick-rimmed glasses, remained watchful.

During the Duchess's slow and tedious convalescence Harding continued to spend much time with her. Their Christmas in the White House that year was a quiet one, with no invited guests. As at Thanksgiving she, dropsical and withered, managed to come downstairs in her wheel chair for dinner and to admire the floral decorations. Harding was becoming aware that he, too, for all his lusty maleness, was growing old, that time was running out on him. Flabby and overweight at 215 pounds, with the "high stomach" that his valet Brooks had noticed, he found now that he could not always finish a round of golf, but after eleven or twelve holes would often be too tired to go on. His face, in spite of its excess flesh, was growing haggard. Often he suffered from attacks of acute indigestion, and his blood pressure remained high. Brooks told Colonel Starling that the President could not sleep nights, that he was listless, that he couldn't lie flat in bed but had to be propped up with pillows because of his difficulty in breathing.

Intimations of mortality may indeed have had something to do with Harding's new seriousness, his resolution to make his mark as President. He had seen nothing of Nan since the late summer, and whenever she suggested visiting Washington he put her off, relieved when she wrote him that she was still living with Elizabeth and working in Evanston as secretary to Walter Dill Scott, the president of Northwestern University. "Gee, Nan," he wrote her in reply, "I think that's just fine." At Christmas he sent her $250 and she bought herself a diamond-and-sapphire link bracelet. Wearying of her job, she decided in January to give it up and enroll as a student at Northwestern. Before the semester began she insisted on making a trip to Washington to see him, first buying herself an "orchid negligee and ostrich-befeathered" mules. In spite of the romantic accessories, the meeting was a brief and gloomy one. Sloan brought her by the usual roundabout way to the President's office where she met Harding, red-eyed and sniffling, having just recovered from influenza. In spite of his jaunty golf knickers he looked ailing, with stooped body and deeply lined face. As they sat on the couch in the corner, Nan, in a belligerent mood, pressed him as to when they could be together for good and he could recognize Elizabeth Ann. He told her he was tied; he would look after her, but he could do no more as long as the Duchess was alive.

His burdens, he said, were more than he could bear, and he was $50,000 in debt. "Nan, darling," he told her, "you must help me; our secret must not come out. Why, I would rather die than disappoint my party."

After their unconsummated meeting he led her down a passage that ran under the pergola and came out near the White House kitchens, and as they stood at the door Laddie Boy came bounding over to meet him. Aware that the kitchen maids were watching them, he shook hands with Nan formally, and she, taking the cue, thanked him for the "conference." Then she watched while he walked slowly toward his private elevator with Laddie Boy gamboling beside him. She was never to see him again.

Evalyn McLean continued to drop in at the White House with casual goodheartedness, jollying the Duchess, bringing her small gifts, making her a lace boudoir cap shaped like a crown. Ned had chartered another houseboat, the *Pioneer,* and was arranging a cruise and golf party for the Hardings in March. This time Harding planned to include Dawes, Gillett, Lasker, Doctor Sawyer, Christian, and Daugherty. The second week in February, with Deac a luncheon guest at the White House, the Duchess stepped outdoors for the first time since her illness, spending several minutes on the south portico.

Before the month was over the smouldering situation at Perryville had burst into flames. Again Doctor Sawyer had visited the warehouses, this time with Surgeon Gen. Hugh S. Cumming of the Public Health Service, and again he found the same bustle of trains and freight cars and goods in transit. He discovered towels that had cost the government 19 cents a piece being shipped to Thompson-Kelley at 3⅜ cents, along with sheets and other items to which the Health Service had a claim and of which it was desperately short. This time Sawyer took the matter to Forbes's enemy, Daugherty, giving him the details not only of Perryville but of the collusion he believed existed in veterans' hospital construction.

The Attorney General carried the matter directly to the White House that afternoon where he found Harding having his portrait painted by Howard Chandler Christy. Waiting until they were alone, he told Harding he had an unpleasant duty to perform. "Shoot!" Harding said—his favorite expression for anyone wanting to tell him something. Daugherty explained what he had heard about Forbes. Harding's face reddened. "That can't be," he insisted, and refused to hear anything more about his merry-andrew favorite. Daugherty suggested that he make his own investigation. Still angry, Harding let his Attorney General leave without inviting him to dinner—the first time he had ever omitted such an invitation. The next day, even more pointedly, Harding failed to call Daugherty on their private telephone line that he usually used from five to twenty times a day. But the day following he sent for Daugherty, put his arm round his shoulder, and asked, "Old man, did I hurt your feelings the last time you were here?" Never since the day they met at Richmond had Harding addressed him so intimately, and Daugherty tried to shrug off his embarrassment by saying that no one could hurt his feelings. Harding admitted that he had had Forbes investigated and had found the charges true. "I am heartsick about it," he said in a shaky voice.

The next afternoon a visitor to the White House with an appointment to see the President was directed by mistake to the second floor. As he approached the Red Room he heard a voice hoarse with anger and on entering saw Harding throttling a man against the wall as he shouted: "You yellow rat! You double-crossing bastard! If you ever . . ." Whirling about at the visitor's approach, Harding loosed his grip and the released man staggered away, his face blotched and distorted. "I am sorry," Harding said curtly to his visitor. "You have an appointment. Come into the next room." On leaving the White House, the visitor asked a doorman who it was who had just gone out after he had come in, and the doorman replied: "Colonel Forbes of the Veterans' Bureau."

To avoid an open scandal Harding let Forbes leave for Europe on the contrived grounds that disabled veterans abroad still needed attention. On January 31 a reorganization of the Veterans' Bureau was announced, and the next day Cramer resigned. Rumors had reached Congress, and on February 12 the Senate passed a resolution directing a committee headed by Senator Sutherland to determine the truth of reports of "waste, extravagance, irregularities, and mismanagement" in the Veterans' Bureau. Congressman Hamilton Fish, Jr. on the following day introduced a resolution providing for an investigation. On February 15 Forbes from Paris cabled his resignation which was at once accepted. It was Harding's first experience of treachery; he never saw Forbes again. The Duchess told Reily afterward that the President "never recovered from Forbes's betrayal of himself and the administration."

At about this time the ubiquitous William Allen White, spending a few days in Washington before going on a Mediterranean cruise, was sent for by Harding who had been pleased with the editorial White had printed in the Emporia *Gazette* on the administration's first anniversary. White arrived a few minutes before his appointment to have a chat with his old friend Judson Welliver.

> Lord, lord, man! [Welliver told him in distress.] You can't know what the President is going through. You see he doesn't understand it; he just doesn't know a thousand things that he ought to know. And he realizes his ignorance, and he is afraid. He has no idea where to turn. Not long ago, when the first big tax bill came up, you remember where there were two theories of taxation for the administration's support, he would listen for an hour to one side, become convinced; and then the other side would get

him and overwhelm him with its contentions. Some good friend would walk into the White House all cocked and primed with facts and figures to support one side, and another man who he thought perhaps ought to know would reach him with a counter-argument which would brush his friend's theory aside. I remember he came in here late one afternoon after a long conference, in which both sides appeared, talked at each other, wrangled over him. He was weary and confused and heartsick, for the man really wants to do the right and honest thing. But I tell you, he doesn't know. That afternoon he stood at my desk and looked at me for a moment and began talking out loud:

"Jud," he cried, "you have a college education, haven't you? I don't know what to do or where to turn in this taxation matter. Somewhere there must be a book that tells all about it, where I could go to straighten it out in my mind. But I don't know where the book is, and maybe I couldn't read it if I found it! There must be a man in the country somewhere who could weigh both sides and know the truth. Probably he is in some college or other. But I don't know where to find him. I don't know who he is, and I don't know how to get him. My God, this is a hell of a place for a man like me to be!"

He put his hand to his head, smiled at his own discomfiture, turned, and walked heavily away. I see something like that going on in him all the time: the combat between folly and wisdom. I never knew a man who was having such a hard time to find the truth. How Roosevelt used to click into truth with the snap of his teeth! How Wilson sensed it with some engine of erudition under the hood of his cranium! But this man paws for it, wrestles for it, cries for it, and has to take the luck of the road to get it. Sometimes he doesn't and sometimes he does, and much he knows about it when it comes.

White found Harding dressed with elegant formality, a flower in his buttonhole, but still haggard after his influenza and with a dark cast to his olive skin. The President offered him a cigar and they sat talking in the morning sunshine that flooded through the long windows. While one of the White House servants came in to put wood on the grate fire, Harding began to reminisce about the *Star*. He told of his stock-distributing plan, and the two editors compared notes about wages for reporters, linotype men, floormen, and the foreman. Harding mentioned county printing and admitted that in Marion they all used to get together before the bid and choose the low bidder who would then add enough "to give us all a little slice of the profits above his low bid." Then with a troubled face he turned to White and cried:

And that's the hell of it. Right now, at the moment, there is a bunch down at the Willard Hotel coming up to see me this afternoon, good friends of mine from Ohio, decent fellows that I have worked with thirty years. Some of them have supported me through thick and thin. Well, there is an energetic young district attorney down East here—maybe New York, or Boston, or Philadelphia, it don't make any difference where—and he has gone and indicted those fellows; is going to put them in jail for violating the antitrust law or some conspiracy law for doing exactly in crockery what I have done in printing for twenty years. *And* (he added) they know all about my method, and they are going to ask me to dismiss the indictment. I can't do that. The law is the law, and it is probably all right, a good law and ought to be enforced. And yet I sit here in the White House and have got to see those fellows this afternoon, and explain why I can't lift a hand to keep them from going to jail. My God, this is a hell of a job! I have no trouble with my enemies, I can take care of my enemies all right. But my damn friends (he wailed with a serio-comic petulance) my God-damn friends, White, they're the ones that keep me walking the floor nights!

Without being able to define it accurately, White, as he left the White House, sensed the inner struggle going on between the limited, complacent Ohio Senator and the President trying uncertainly through his limitations to make himself worthy of his office.

The Arms Limitation had been Harding's personal triumph, and now, urged and encouraged by Hughes and Hoover, he was preparing to lead his country a further step toward peace by bringing the United States into the Permanent Court of International Justice established at The Hague by the League of Nations as a successor to The Hague Tribunal. Elihu Root had been an adviser in forming the court, and another distinguished American jurist, John Bassett Moore, was already a court member. Harding, who in the Senate had called the League a betrayal of America and in his inaugural had praised the wisdom of "non-involvement in old-world controversies," had in two years shaken off his parochial and party limitations enough to admit that there were "rudiments of good in both the League and The Hague Tribunal."

As with the Arms Conference, the unpredictable Borah gave the President his cue by introducing a resolution in the Senate calling for a "judicial substitute for war" modeled on the Supreme Court that would arbitrate compulsorily in international disputes. Ten days later—and in the last week of the congressional session—Harding sent a bombshell message to the Senate, in which he recommended that the United States join the World Court. "Such action," he informed the senators, "would add to our own consciousness of participation in the fortunate advancement of international relationship and remind the world anew that we are ready for our proper part in furthering peace and adding to stability in world affairs." To his message, read to the Senate behind closed doors since it covered foreign affairs, he appended a covering letter from Hughes. In an effort to make the international dose more palatable Hughes explained that adherence to the World Court in no way bound the United

States to the League of Nations; that the United States would have an equal voice in choosing the judges and changing the rules of the court; and that the Congress would decide what part of the expenses should be paid by the United States.

After their first stunned reaction the Republican League-haters, unable to lash out at Harding as they had at Wilson, took the temporizing line that the matter needed much further study. Borah now had his cloudy doubts, calling the court an "international political tribunal." Senator Brandegee, speaking for the Irreconcilables, suggested archly that Harding's proposal be offered as an amendment to the foundering Ship Subsidy Bill.

It was a Democratic senator, William H. King of Utah, who finally introduced the resolution that the Senate sanction adherence to the World Court; whereupon Lodge, the deft parliamentarian, at once buried the resolution in the deep recesses of his Committee on Foreign Affairs. By a vote of 49 to 24 the Senate refused to take up the matter further. Only one Republican voted in favor of consideration. Forty-six Republicans and three Democrats were against it.

So Harding in his role of leader and statesman found himself abandoned by his own party. As a wily politician he had expected no less. In presenting his World Court proposal in the last days of what had been labeled the Do-nothing Congress, he well knew that the lame-duck Senate would never act on it. But in the nine months before the new Sixty-eighth Congress assembled in December he would have the time he needed and wanted to take his case to the people. He was determined, with a determination alien to his easier self, that he would bring his country into the World Court, that he would go down in history as something more than the President who shook the most hands.

> The great hubbub over the World Court [he wrote Jennings] was largely bunk. Most of it emanates from members of the Senate who have very little concern about the favor with which the administration is regarded, and the remainder of it come [sic] from those who are nuts either for or against the League. The League advocates have somewhat embarrassed the situation, but I do not fear the outcome. A good many people have urged me to drop the matter, but I do not find myself ready to accept that sort of a sneaking program.

On March 3, on a gray Sunday morning, the last session of the Do-nothing Congress came to an end. Fall's resignation taking effect at the end of his second year, Postmaster General Work replaced him. Harding had long wanted his friend Harry New in his Cabinet and he now, to the fury of Senators Beveridge and Watson and the Indiana Republican machine, appointed him Postmaster General. New, like Daugherty, disapproved of civil service altogether.

Fall's leaving office occasioned little comment. La Follette's resolution to investigate the oil leases seemed moribund, another political maneuver. Secretary Hoover took the trouble to write his former colleague a week later:

> This note is just by way of expressing appreciation for the many kindnesses I had at your hands during the last two years in the Cabinet. I know that the vast majority of our people feel a deep regret at your leaving the Department of the Interior. In my recollection, that department has never had so constructive and legal a leadership as you gave it.
>
> I trust the time will come when your private affairs will enable you to return to public life, as there are few men who are able to stand its stings and ire, and they have got to stay with it.

As soon as the Congress had adjourned, Harding and the Duchess left for the promised Florida house party with the McLeans. Daugherty had been included in their plans, but shortly after the Keller hearings the steely-faced Attorney General had had a complete breakdown and for six weeks could not leave his bed. Even by the end of February he could sit up for only half an hour at a time. A week after the Hardings, and still in his wheel chair, he left for Miami accompanied by a nurse and a doctor. There were rumors that he might be leaving the Cabinet, and additional rumors that he was writing a book about the administration. Yet, in spite of the flurry over Forbes, Harding still felt as close to his Attorney General as ever. On Daugherty's sixty-second birthday, on January 26, Harding had written him:

> I can make no reference to the birthday anniversary, which is pleasing to my fancy. After one passes fifty they come with such seeming swiftness that I sometimes incline to let them pass unnoticed. I note you are the eldest but one sitting around the Cabinet table, yet I declare you the youngest of all in spirit and if I add "in appearance" I do not know who would dispute.

Cruising with the McLeans, the President took the trouble to stop off at Miami to see the invalid Attorney General. The cruise up the Indian River lasted three weeks, like the other McLean cruises a succession of golf-course visits for the men while the Duchess and Evalyn sat on the upper deck. Harding felt so well at the nine-hole Rio Mar course—that his foursome had to reach by driving through a palmetto jungle—that he played two rounds. But the other three of the foursome—Dawes, Lasker, and Ned McLean—noticed how easily he tired. He broke his days of golf with a two-day fishing trip, then at the cruise's end spent another week in St. Augustine.

While the President relaxed in the warm Florida sun, dark clouds continued to gather in the North. On the very evening of the day Harding had seen the invalid Daugherty, the resigned general counsel for the Veterans' Bureau, Charles Cramer, had killed himself in Harding's old Wyoming Avenue house. After dinner Cramer had driven his wife to the Union Station where she took the train to New York. On returning he sat at his desk upstairs, asked the colored maid for some stamps, and spent most of the night writing letters, including one to the President. When he had finished his writing he took a book of Oscar Wilde's poems and opened it to the "Requiescat," that the young Wilde had written for his dead sister:

> All my life's buried here
> Heap earth upon it.

Marking the place with a newspaper clipping on the Veterans' Bureau investigation, he had closed the book, then he had gone into the bathroom, locked the door, and fired a 45-caliber bullet into his right temple. Mary Roberts Rinehart, living nearby, heard the shot and ran over to the house. She saw Cramer sprawled on the stained tile floor and the letters on his desk. But when she came back later in the morning the letters had disappeared.

The clouds of scandal had not yet begun to gather around Harding's person, yet by the time he left Florida it was obvious to any astute politician that the President's popularity was ebbing. In spite of the now-obvious economic recovery, and at the very time he had determined to prove himself a leader, the country itself was turning against him. Irrational, however solid seeming the reasons, such swings in popularity—although often transitory—are the occupational hazard of political leaders.[8] The chastened Progressive, Beveridge, was convinced that the Democrats would sweep the country in 1924. "The cause," he wrote, "is the public indifference to and disapproval of Harding. The estimate is that he amounts to nothing—is weak and procrastinating. Anyhow, the people are not for him, and their minds are made up." Lasker and Wrigley were even considering supporting Hiram Johnson in 1924. General Dawes, out of office, was trying to organize a counter-trend for the 1924 campaign with his Minute Men of the Constitution. Wearing the black-and-white cockade of the American Revolution, the Minute Men proclaimed respect for the law and the Constitution while condemning class and religious discrimination—which, translated into blunter terms, meant being for the open shop and against the rising power of the Ku Klux Klan. The open-

---

[8] Truman and Johnson are more recent examples. In 1946 Truman's popularity had sunk so low that less than a third of those polled approved of him. Yet two years later he was re-elected. Johnson in 1964 won an even larger majority than Harding's but two years later most of that transitional popularity had ebbed.

shop General felt that the Republican platform of 1924 would, in effect, be Daugherty's railroad injunction and Harding's position on the World Court.

Meanwhile a grass-roots sentiment was springing up for an independent without the gross label of politician, an embodiment of the Alger myth, who was transforming America while remaining himself an unknown quantity. Henry Ford, who with his Model-T automobile had given the country populism on wheels, might, it seemed, make the country an equally popular President.

In 1918 Ford had run for United States senator in Michigan against the Republican Truman H. Newberry at President Wilson's request, and had lost the election by only a few thousand votes. In 1920 he had supported Cox against Harding and argued for the League of Nations. In the spring of 1922 a group of about 140 Dearborn business and professional men without political connections organized a Ford for President Club and printed quantities of cardboard hatbands lettered *We Want Henry*. From a tiny Michigan office they sent letters to friends all over the country trying to set up Ford clubs, and selling the hatbands at a dollar each to defray expenses. By autumn the *Wall Street Journal* was asking "Why Not Ford for President?", and by the spring of 1923 the Washington correspondent of the *New York Herald* could write that "the astonishing growth of popular sentiment for Ford for President is causing deep concern to Democrats and anxiety to Republicans." A poll of a quarter of a million people conducted by *Collier's* gave Ford an 8 to 5 lead over Harding, and *The New York Times* considered him "a powerful and enigmatic figure on the political horizon."

Whatever the waning course of his popularity, Harding's determination to vindicate himself through his re-election grew. No longer was he willing to consider a single-term constitutional limitation. Shortly after his return from Florida he had engaged a Columbus architect to restore the Harding homestead in Blooming Grove by building a Colonial-type house from the remnant of Great-grandfather George's "little old house." But any such dream of a return to his birthplace would have to wait. C. C. Fisher wrote him from Marion that talk of the Democrats nominating Ford was heard everywhere. Harding replied that Ford did not worry him. "It has been my philosophy that if the present administration makes good, there cannot possibly be any doubt about renomination. If it does not make good, there ought to be no renomination."

The announcement that the President would run again came from Daugherty in his Miami wheel chair two days after his meeting with Harding. He told reporters: "The President will be a candidate for renomination. He will ... be renominated and re-elected because the country will demand it."

Whatever Daugherty's motives, whether to counteract rumors of his own resignation or to fortify the President's resolve, Harding was not pleased.

I was a little embarrassed by General Daugherty's announcement of a candidacy [he wrote to Jennings], and have been seeking, in the most consistent way possible, to antidote the impression which that interview may have given that I would travel across the country as a candidate for renomination. I really want to speak as President, and am convinced that I can do so, and I look forward to good results both for me and for the better understanding of the country.

Later speculations as to a breach between the President and his Attorney General are, nevertheless, unfounded. Daugherty had gone from Miami to Asheville, and on April 16 Christian was writing him: "Don't step out too lively, old man, you know from now on we will need you more than ever."

The travel Harding had referred to in his letter to Jennings was his postponed journey to Alaska. But what had originally been planned as an excursion, he now saw in his new earnestness as a "Voyage of Understanding," reaching out and bringing his policies and his great issue of the World Court over the heads of the self-seeking politicians to the people's judgment. He would speak at every city and whistle stop along the way, just as—although the irony escaped him—Wilson had done four years before in defense of his League. Writing to Walter Brown, Harding asked his help in planning the journey from Washington to Seattle to Alaska and back by way of San Francisco and Los Angeles, asking him to visit each scheduled city and to check up on all the local arrangements.

Please make clear [he wrote Brown] that the trip is in no sense a partisan one and that I would like all elements in civic life to be properly represented in public meetings wherever such arrangements are possible.

The trip is unavoidably a very arduous one. People have been so kind in their offering of hospitality and so thoughtful in proposing varied engagements that I have found it necessary to restrict my speaking engagements to one in each city and have also found it necessary to forego the acceptance of the tenders of all private or personal hospitality.

With Harding's determination to overcome his so-often-expressed reluctance to serve came his growing awareness of corruption among his subordinates. What had been the closed gossip of insiders and reporters was becoming more open after Forbes's forced resignation and Cramer's suicide. Stories of Means and his shakedowns were getting into the papers, and Daugherty was receiving so many private complaints that despite Burns he could no longer disregard them. He assigned Assistant Attorney General Crim to investigate Gaston, and then in May appointed

Hiram Todd as special counsel to prosecute that still-blithe confidence man. Todd demanded, and Daugherty gave him, a completely free hand. Gaston countered by retaining Felder as his counsel.

All who saw Harding during this period agree that he was a changing, if not a changed, man. No longer were the highballs passed along the poker table. He had moved his liquor stock to his bedroom, feeling that there at least it was his private concern. But even there he was ferreted out by Wayne Wheeler, as insistent as Bishop Anderson that the President should make an example to the country by signing the abstinence pledge. Harding tried to point out that to give up such a lifelong habit might be harmful to his health. Wheeler was not to be put off. A high moral stand would be an example to the nation. The failure to take such a stand might have unfortunate political consequences. And Wheeler did not need to recall that in last November's election, when Carmi Thompson had been defeated for governor of Ohio, Wheeler had whipped up the Democratic drys behind Republican Simon Fess to defeat the wet Senator Pomerene by 42,000 votes. He made it plain that the President had to choose between his glass and the still-potent Anti-Saloon League support. On the eve of the Voyage of Understanding, Harding let it be announced that he had sworn off alcohol.

Since their brief meeting in January Harding had continued to keep Nan at a distance, although he had once sent for Elizabeth for a private conference. Scott Willits had returned from Europe, and was living not too harmoniously with Elizabeth and Nan in the small Chicago apartment. A friend wrote Nan about an Armstrong summer tour of France that for $525 would include a six weeks' vacation course at the University of Dijon. She wrote to Harding that she thought such a trip would benefit her and he replied by sending her the necessary down payment, adding: "I wish *I* might take you, dearie; I wish we might make the trip together."

As troubled by the undercurrents of scandal as he was uncertain of their extent, Harding found himself bound within the circle of his depression as if it were an iron ring. Early in May he telephoned Nicholas Murray Butler in New York and begged him to come to the White House over the weekend to discuss something he did not want to mention over the telephone. Butler was about to leave for Europe but, putting off his trip, he took the Saturday-night express for Washington, recalling the weekend in his autobiography:

> I had a most extraordinary experience at the White House. The President came to my sitting room before I had finished breakfast and from that time, until I left at half-past eleven to return to the railway station, he hardly ever let me out of his sight for a moment. Evidently, there was something very much on his mind and he was trying to bring himself to tell me what it was. Several times during the morning, afternoon and eve-

ning he seemed to be on the point of unbosoming himself, but he never did so. He came down to the porch of the White House to say farewell, as I took the automobile back to the station, and even then seemed to be trying to tell me something which troubled him. I have never been able to guess what that something was.

Butler felt that Harding had a premonition he would not live out his term. Among the burdens of Harding's mind was the fouled trail of Jess Smith. The President had been informed, in Daugherty's bowdlerized version of events, that Jess was "running with a gay crowd, attending all sorts of parties, and . . . using the Attorney General's car until all hours of the night." When Harding so informed Daugherty, the Attorney General professed to be shocked. He informed Jess that the President would no longer welcome him on the Alaska journey and that he would have to leave Washington.

Jess was shattered by the ban. But even before this ultimate rebuff, in fact ever since his operation, he had the growing sense of fate closing in on him. Shadows followed him, and not only those of his paranoid imaginings. As usual, he sought refuge and consolation with Roxy, but even in familiar Washington Court House he could not shake his fears. A year later she told a Senate committee:

> The last time he came home, I came to Columbus and he grabbed me there in the hotel, in the Deshler, and he threw his arms around me and he said: "I never was so glad to see anyone in my life." He seemed to have forgotten that he was doing something more or less embarrassing—it was not; it was sweet, and he meant it, just in his direct manner. . . . It was like that all the time. He was in fear, he was in mortal fear. He said: "They are going to get me." I said: "No, they won't, Jess." And he said: "They passed it to me." And I knew what he meant. I didn't ask. He was in mortal fear. And I said: "Oh, don't, Jess; you are all right; you are all right." He said: "Let's go home before dark." And I said all right. We took the two o'clock train home. Opposite me was a gentleman apparently asleep, and Jess said: "Don't talk so loud, he will hear you." I said to him I wasn't saying anything of consequence. Jess said: "I don't like the looks of that fellow." I said, "Oh, stop looking at him." He said again: "I don't like the looks of that fellow." And I said: "Yes, but stop looking at him." He walked down the middle of the street at night. He asked different people if they would stay all night with him. I said: "Tell me what the trouble is, Jess, you can trust me; tell me." "No, no, no," he said, "just cheer me up, just brace me up." And I said to him different times: "Now, hold your head up, Jess, straighten up—that is right." And I said to him: "Stand up; straighten up." He said: "Don't you talk cross to me; if you do I'll jump right out of this window." He always used to comfort me if I had troubles, and I tried to do the same thing for him. He had his house absolutely in order. He asked me to destroy his papers. I said: "Tell me all

about it, Jess: I know so much." "No, no, no," he said, "just cheer me up, just cheer me up." It was pitiful. And he would say: "Do you miss me when I am gone?"—and I knew what he was going to do.

Whatever Daugherty's own differences with Jess, they were not enough to keep the two men from traveling back to Ohio on the same train. Just as in sunnier times, they spent several days at the Deer Creek shack. But Daugherty, his nerves still on edge, remained edgy and irritable. It was his habit to take a nap after lunch and Jess's duty to see that his chief remained undisturbed. In spite of orders Jess one afternoon woke Daugherty after an old and importunate friend had arrived insisting that he must see the Attorney General at once. Daugherty, on Jess's waking him, flew into a rage, cursing and abusing his bumper, and ordering him to send for his car at once. So infuriated was Daugherty that he told Jess to find his own way back to Washington Court House, but finally after geting dressed relented enough to give him a lift. They did not speak on the road. Jess got out of the Attorney General's car at the courthouse square and at once headed for Carpenter's hardware store across the street where—in spite of his dread of such things—he bought himself a revolver. "Harry has turned on me," he told Roxy in tears, later that afternoon.

In the evening, his last in Washington Court House, he took her to a dinner dance at the Scioto Country Club. She noticed the change in him from the afternoon as "he came down the street his old self, his head up, and just like as if he were happy and everything, and I saw such a change in him, and I said, 'Are things all right now, Jess?' And he said, 'Yes, they are all right now.' And that is the first time in months he would walk straight and carry his head up. Yet he was making all this preparation."

When Daugherty left for Washington that weekend he agreed to let Jess go along with him and stay at the apartment long enough to see some friends and wind up his business affairs. On the train he noticed that Jess was acting "queer," even though he had not been drinking. They parted company at the Union Station, Jess going to the Wardman Park while Daugherty—by previous arrangement—went to stay a few days at the White House. Concerned about Jess's condition, he sent one of his Justice Department assistants, Warren F. Martin, to stay at the Wardman Park apartment and keep an eye on him.

The day after his return Jess played golf at Friendship with Martin, Harding's naval and medical aide Lieut. Comm. Joel T. Boone, and Maj. Peyton Gordon, the Federal Attorney of the District of Columbia. But he did not join in the drinks after the match, and Boone noticed that he seemed "thoughtful." From Friendship he went to his office in the Justice Department and picked up a brief case full of papers.

Although Friendship with its golf course was open to their friends, Ned McLean and Evalyn had gone to their 2,600-acre Leesburg farm 30 miles away. Early that evening Jess telephoned them to ask if he might come to stay for three or four days. Evalyn, though feeling out of sorts, told him to come along. At about ten he called again to say that a thunderstorm was drenching Washington but that he would be at the farm in the morning. Then at midnight he telephoned for the third time.

Evalyn answered, and he apologized, explaining that he was feeling nervous. When she asked him what was wrong, he replied hesitantly that he was "a little upset." She tried to reassure him, and he promised to be at the farm at seven. "Stay as long as you like," she told him with her usual expansiveness. "I am so glad I can come," he said gratefully in his mincing voice.

Just before his operation Jess had drawn up a complicated will making bequests to 25 people. Daugherty and his brother Mally were to be the executors. Of the estate of $200,000 the Daughertys were each to receive $25,000, with the same amount going to Roxy Stimson to whom Jess also left his Cole sedan. From his prized box of diamonds he willed one each to Harry and Mally Daugherty, Ned McLean, and John King. The residue of his estate he willed to relatives and to charities. Then, on his arrival in Washington, Jess drew up a second will. Brief and unwitnessed, it named Daugherty as sole executor, with the estate to be divided equally among the Daugherty brothers, Roxy, and Jess's cousins Edmund St. John and Louise St. John Thomson. Some time during that stormy evening, after he had called Evalyn, Jess gathered all his accounts, together with his own and Daugherty's private correspondence and the papers he had taken from the Justice Department, and burned them in a metal wastebasket in his bedroom. Then he sat there in the dark, waiting for daylight.

Early in the morning of Decoration Day, Martin, sleeping in the bedroom on the other side of the living room from Jess's, was awakened by a crash as if a door had slammed or a waiter had dropped a tray. Unable to get to sleep again, he went into the living room, and through the open door saw Jess in pajamas and dressing gown sprawled on the floor, his head in the wastebasket among the ashes and a revolver in his hand. He had shot himself in the left temple and the bullet had come out through his forehead to lodge in the doorjamb. Martin sent at once for Burns whose apartment was on the floor below, and Burns took charge so effectively that by the time the police from the Tenallytown sub-precinct arrived they had difficulty finding the revolver. Burns had mislaid it.

Later that morning Mrs. Jaffray on the second floor of the White House heard Daugherty slam the door of his bedroom and hurry down the hall to ask an usher in a loud, angry voice why he could not get a Mr. Smith on his room telephone. "Mr. Smith is dead," the usher told him. "He committed suicide early this morning." Harding had been informed first, and shortly afterward he and Commander Boone came to Daugherty's room intending to break the news. It was a tense, brooding day in the White House. That night Daugherty—still a White House guest—dined with the Hardings. To try to relieve the tenseness, the Duchess had invited a couple to dinner who were close friends of the Hardings'. The two guests remembered that numb, devastating meal afterward like a haunting dream. At table no one spoke more than a fragment of a sentence. After dinner they all adjourned to the upper hall to see a moving picture, sitting mutely before a temporary screen, the silence broken only by the burr of the projector and from time to time by a long-drawn-out "O-o-o-o-o-o-o!" from Daugherty.

Smith's death, following so soon on Forbes's roguery and Cramer's suicide, could not be covered by the blanket of flowers that Harding and the Duchess sent for his coffin. Daugherty wrote a eulogy that was read at the graveside by Judge Charles A. Reid, but he did not go to the funeral. Jess's body was accompanied to Washington Court House by Assistant Attorney General Holland, who, while there, delivered a sealed package to Mally Daugherty at the Midland Bank. After breaking the seal and taking one look at the papers inside, Mally burned them in the bank furnace.

Jess's suicide was front-page news, although no scandal was as yet implied and his act was attributed to ill-health. After his death messages of condolence came to Daugherty from Coleman DuPont, Senator Burton, John Hays Hammond, John Oliver La Gorce of the National Geographic Society, Albert Lasker, and dozens of others. "I mourn with you and your grief is mine," Will Hays wired from Hollywood. Mark Sullivan wrote from London, in words that must later have come to seem strange to him: "I always thought of him [Jess] as a man who enjoyed life fully, and as one who got immense pleasure out of devotion to his friends. I had come to like him with unusual feelings, and to think of myself as a friend of his." Others in Washington were too relieved at Jess's passing, with his thoughtful destruction of records, to bother about letters of condolence. So conveniently timed was his death to avoid a major scandal, that soon there was an undercurrent of talk that he had really been done away with because he knew too much.

Just how much Harding came to know of the termite-like spread of corruption among his subordinates cannot be determined, but it can be surmised. Before his Alaskan trip he told his old friend and campaign biographer, the small-time newspaperman Joe Mitchell Chapple, that "someday the people will understand what some of my erstwhile friends have done for me." Yet however widening his doubts, they did not include Fall or Daugherty.

Fall was planning to leave for Russia in mid-June with Sinclair, hoping to make arrangements for Sinclair's leasing oil lands in the southern part of Sakhalin Island. The Russians were willing to grant such a lease if the United States would recognize the Union of Soviet Socialist Republics within five years, and for this Sinclair felt Fall would be an effective lobbyist. Such recognition had in any case seemed a logical step to Harding, and he had already sent former Gov. James P. Goodrich of Indiana on a special mission to Moscow to explore its possibilities. Before signing his agreement with Sinclair, Fall called on Harding to explain the plan and to ask if his negotiating with the Russians would in any way embarrass the administration. Harding told him: "I know whatever you do in Russia will be done with absolute regard for my policy—I want you to go, and I hope you will make some money." The day before Fall sailed, he and his wife, along with Senator Pomerene, just back from a South American mission for Harding, had lunch at the White House.

The week after Smith's death Harding found a temporary antidote for his low spirits in welcoming the Nobles of the Mystic Shrine who were holding their annual convention in Washington. In the Shriners' honor the capital was decked out in their colors—red, green, and yellow—and for these middle-aged mystics in their red fezzes the White House, by Harding's invitation, became an open house. Twenty thousand Nobles and their families visited it in one day. Harding welcomed the casual, festive chance to be a friendly man among his friendly fellows. In a white linen suit and wearing the fez of Aladdin Temple, he reviewed a four-hour parade of sweaty Shrine patrols in their baggy trousers and bright jackets, and listened to the blaring brass of 110 Temple bands. With him on the reviewing stand in the wilting heat were the Duchess, General Pershing, Secretaries Denby and Weeks, and Imperial Potentate James A. McCandless of Honolulu. At the close of the convention the President—along with George Christian and Theodore Roosevelt, Jr.—was inducted into the Tall Cedars of Lebanon, a new order of Masonry more exclusive than the Shriners, whose ritual was most secret and whose members had the privilege of wearing a three-sided pyramidical skullcap.

By the end of spring Harding's intimates were aware that he intended to run for a second term. Lasker proposed to do all he could to support Harding for re-election in 1924 if Harding would support Hiram Johnson for President in 1928. Since Lasker had gone to Europe in June, the Duchess finally called his wife and said that "we" would agree to it. Charlie Curtis, nursing his own ambitions, tackled Harding about the vice presidency, observing that Coolidge had not been mentioned in Harding's 1924 campaign plans. "We are not worried about that little fellow in Massachusetts," Harding told him, laying his hand on Curtis's shoulder. "Charlie Dawes is the man!"

Facing four more years in the White House, Harding at last gave up the familiar thought of returning to his old editorial desk. A newspaper syndicate had offered him $25,000 a year for editorial contributions after he left office, and he had also been offered $750 for each speech he might deliver. If—as he planned—he should accept the two offers he would have little time left for the *Star*. When two young newspapermen, Louis H. Brush and Roy D. Moore, who owned a chain of small-town papers in Ohio, offered him $550,000 for the *Star*, he felt it was too good an offer to refuse.[9] They completed the purchase and gave Harding their notes shortly before he left for the West. At the same time the new proprietors bought out the Marion *Tribune* and closed it down.

Harding consulted Sam Ungerleider, to whom he was in debt, and arranged for Mellon to discount the Moore-Brush notes. When Ungerleider first set up his Washington office, Harding had opened a small account with him which little by little he kept increasing. Then he opened a second account, using the name of his Secret Service man, Walter Ferguson. Yet for all his hopes, and his need of money, he had lost on both accounts—one proof, at least, that he was not playing the market on inside information. Eager to recoup, and before leaving for Alaska, he bought over half a million dollars' worth of stocks on margin: Mexican Seaboard Railroad warrants, at the suggestion of John Hays Hammond; Bethlehem Steel, on a tip from its president, Charlie Schwab; and Pure Oil. Ungerleider agreed to carry the account until the President's return.

To assert and justify his leadership in a series of speeches, to see and draw attention to his country's neglected Northern territory where no President had yet set foot, to encounter ordinary shirt-sleeved Americans —that was how Harding saw his Voyage of Understanding. In preparing for his Alaskan journey it was as if he wanted to break the threads spun round him in Washington and "bloviate" with his obscure fellow countrymen beyond the city. He sensed his own inner change and confided to his friends that he felt a "conscious spiritual influence" in his actions. Walter Brown's elaborate schedule for the tour now seemed an imposition. He complained to Colonel Starling that Brown was making a circus of the trip and ordered the Colonel to cut every program to the bone. Even so, the President was unavoidably faced with eighteen set speeches, plus innumerable informal talks at rural depots and whistle stops.

The members of his official party formed a more sober group than had traveled with him on his unofficial Florida junkets. He had included three members of his Cabinet most concerned with Alaska: Secretary

[9] After Harding's death the sale was seen as an indirect bribe. Even in 1965 Sinclair in his political biography maintained that the *Star* was sold for twice what it was worth. Actually the *Star* was then making $30,000 a year or 5 per cent on the investment. With Harding's promise of occasional contributions, the paper seems to have been fairly priced.

Work; Secretary Wallace, who planned to join the party at Denver; and Secretary Hoover who would meet them on the West Coast. Speaker Gillett represented Congress, Rear Adm. Hugh Rodman the Army and the Navy.

Daugherty did not plan to go. With Mellon in Paris and Work, Wallace, and Hoover accompanying Harding, "somebody," he wrote, "must keep house for the government." As usual Daugherty, in justifying himself, overestimated his role, for it was Hughes and his assistants in the State Department who, in Hughes's words, were left "sitting on the lid." Yet whatever other reasons Daugherty may have had for staying behind—his health, his brooding over Jess's death, the more immediate problem of his son Draper now confined in a Connecticut sanitarium as an alcoholic—he was in no way estranged from the President. The day before Harding left, Daugherty spent several hours helping him clear his desk. Then, as if some dark premonition were breaking into Harding's plans for the future, he asked Daugherty to help him draw up a new will. In it he left the Mount Vernon Avenue house and all his personal property to the Duchess together with the income from $100,000 and from the money received for the sale of the *Star*. To each of his nieces and nephews he gave $10,000, $4,000 to the DeWolfe children, $2,000 to Trinity Baptist Church, $1,000 to Episcopal St. Paul's, and $25,000 to the Marion Park Commission. The interest only from $50,000 in government bonds was to go to the untrustworthy Tryon. The residue he willed to Deac and his three sisters, with the principal also going to them after the Duchess's death. Nan and Elizabeth Ann he did not mention at all.

Harding's mood as he made the last preparations for his Voyage of Understanding continued morose and restless. He told Welliver before leaving Washington that people he had supposed to be his friends had been "selling him all over this town, and all over the country." But his mind was made up now to run for a second term and at the right time he would go to the country with his story of how his administration had been betrayed. "And the people will believe me," he concluded, "when they hear that story."

[CHAPTER XX]

Last Journey

On June 20, at two o'clock of a humid, heat-heavy afternoon, the presidential train left Washington's Union Station for St. Louis on the first lap of Harding's 1,500-mile two-month Voyage of Understanding. Ten cars made up the train, the last being the *Superb*. As the train pulled out of the station a Navy band struck up a dance tune. Harding and the Duchess waved from the *Superb's* rear platform. The party of 65 persons included, besides Harding's guests and aides, 10 Secret Service men, stenographers, 22 Washington correspondents, 5 photographers, newsreel cameramen, and several technicians from the telephone company who had been sent to install amplifiers and arrange for the long-distance relaying of the President's speeches.

For all his feigned heartiness as he waved good-by, Harding's face was creased with fatigue and his olive complexion sallow. Yet, in spite of his obvious physical and mental weariness, he seemed on the transcontinental journey incapable of resting or relaxing. Confined to the plush and burled-walnut elegance of the *Superb,* he grew restless, never remaining long in his seat but moving from side to side and peering through the windows at the now-browning landscape. Above all he wanted to play bridge, and when not at the bridge table he wanted to talk. Never did he want to be alone.

The *Superb's* first halt was at Martinsburg, West Virginia. From there on, every town and village where the train stopped found the President on the rear platform in his gray Palm Beach suit, always ready with forced affability to pose for photographers or say a few words to any onlookers. From the torpid humidity of Washington the *Superb* moved across Ohio, Indiana, and Illinois into the searing heat of the Midwest. But Harding still insisted on appearing at each whistle stop. His lips grew blistered in the sun, and Doctor Sawyer had to apply ice compresses to them. The amplifier installed by the telephone company could carry his voice easily to the outer edges of even a large crowd, but the crowds were not large and not very responsive between Washington and St. Louis, as Harding was the first to notice.

While he, bareheaded in the sun's glare, was reaching out from the rear platform to shake extended hands, Nan from the deck of the *Roussillon* watched the angular New York skyline recede into the mist. She had sailed on the French Line ship on the first day of spring after being driven to the dock by a Norwegian sea captain, Magnus Cricken, whom she had met while a student at Columbia. "He was at that time very lovely to me," Nan wrote, "and I judged him to be a fine man." She also judged him to be wealthier than he was, and in mid-spring had even invited him to visit her at the Willits's in Chicago. Harding had sent her $400 for incidental expenses, but as she had spent most of this for clothes she was glad to borrow another $50 from Cricken before embarking.

The President had boldly chosen to make his first speech on the World Court in isolationist Missouri at an international convention of Rotary Clubs then being held in St. Louis. Appearing before 10,000 Rotarians at the Coliseum—where Wilson had been nominated in 1916—he was received courteously, but his plea to have the United States join the Court was heard without applause. For the first time a President's address was being broadcast live by radio stations from coast to coast, and Harding was faced with a battery of microphones. He seemed strained, as if he were intimidated by the new instruments. In spite of amplification, his voice sounded subdued, and he had discarded his oratorical gestures. Only when he turned from his text to speak a few extemporaneous sentences did he strike the response that his silver voice usually aroused in an audience. He condemned—without mentioning the understood names of La Follette and Borah—those who wanted the United States to live as a "hermit nation," while reassuring his hearers that he did not intend to enter the League by "back door, side door, or cellar door." Following Hughes's plan to make the World Court more acceptable to the League's enemies, he proposed a court independent of the League, self-perpetuating, with the judges themselves given the authority to fill any vacancies in court personnel. His sincerity shone through the tangle of his rhetoric when he finally told the dubious Rotarians:

> I shall not restrict my appeal to your reason. I shall call upon your patriotism. I shall beseech your humanity. I shall invoke your Christianity. I shall reach to the very depths of your love for your fellow countrymen of whatever race or creed throughout the world. I shall speak, as I now speak, with all the earnestness and power, of the sincerity that is within me and in perfect faith that God will keep clear and perceptive your understanding.
>
> I could not do otherwise. My soul yearns for peace. My heart is

anguished by the sufferings of war. My spirit is eager to serve. My passion is for justice over force. My hope is in the great court. My mind is made up. My resolution is fixed.

The *Superb* left that night for Kansas City. Meeting Harding next morning at the Muehlbach Hotel, William Allen White noticed that "his lips were swollen and blue, his eyes puffed, and his hands seemed stiff when I shook hands with him." In the afternoon the presidential party made a 15-mile motor tour of the city, decked with the usual flags, and with the gawking crowds eager to see a President. Before speaking that night at Convention Hall Harding and the Duchess had dinner in a private suite of the hotel with Senator Capper, Capper's wife, and Emma Fall. Much has been made of Emma Fall's appearance that evening as "an elderly woman, veiled and furtive," a harbinger of disaster bearing a secret message for the President. He, after being closeted with her alone, emerged from the hotel room, according to legend, "scared and shaken." [1] Emma Fall, writing long afterward to a Harding biographer, had a simpler account of the evening. The Hardings

> knew I was to be in Ke several days—and on reaching there had the secretary phone me to dine with them that evening and go to hear the President speak in evening—I expressed a desire that any time or space should be given to someone who had not had the opportunity to know them I had and would have again. The secretary delivered message and called me again to say NO one would dine with them except someone they wanted and invited and would expect me at five-thirty—only six persons at dinner—Senator Capper and wife and myself the only guest—the evening was delightful. I went with them to hear him speak and they left me at my hotel. I never saw the President afterward.

Next day White rode with Harding in the *Superb* from Kansas City in the pitiless heat across Kansas to Hutchinson. Three times during the ride Harding told him that he wanted to have a long talk with him, but the chance never came. Again the President remarked that he could take care of his enemies; it was his friends who were giving him the trouble. At Hutchinson the train made a prearranged stop near a wheat farm in an area of tawny ripening grain extending to a line of low hills in the distance. Under a baking noonday sun Harding, in white flannels and a blue coat, took over the controls of a wheat binder and drove down one side of a 90-acre triangular field while news cameramen scurried across the stubble to take his picture.

Hundreds of farmers from miles around, with their wives, children, and

---

[1] The intimation is that her message had to do with the onrushing Teapot Dome scandal, hardly possible in view of the Falls's friendly relations with the Duchess after Harding's death.

hired men, had driven to the state fairgrounds at Hutchinson to see the President. It was indeed more to see than to hear him, for under those arching Midwestern skies Harding's World Court had little or no meaning. Europe with its broken dynasties and Red mobs was too remote to visualize, and the sunburned farmers could not be concerned about a League or a Court when wheat was threatening to drop below a dollar a bushel on the Chicago exchange. That was not enough to cover the cost of the crops! Harding did his best to reach the farmers, but his efforts to explain how much his administration had done for agriculture, from the high tariff to the Federal Farm Loan Board, could not offset the falling price of wheat.

In Denver, where Harding arrived for the weekend, he told an audience of 12,000 that the Eighteenth Amendment would never be repealed and he demanded rigid enforcement of the Prohibition laws. Then, setting aside his written text, he ended his address with an appeal for the World Court. Sunday, relaxing, he visited the Army General Hospital where, moving still further from his senatorial past, he told the soldiers that, in case of another war, dollars would be drafted as well as men, "if I have anything to do with it." The day of relaxation turned into a day of gloom after he learned that one of his press group, Sumner M. Curtis of the Republican National Committee, had been killed on a Denver Press Club excursion to Buffalo Bill's grave on Lookout Mountain when his car plunged over an embankment at Looking Glass Curve. Two Denver men were killed with Curtis, and the more superstitious in the party were beginning to say that the Voyage of Understanding was an unlucky journey.

Tuesday Harding arrived at Salt Lake City to be met by Senators Smoot and King and taken on the by-now ritual motor tour of the city. He spoke later at the auditorium of the Mormon Tabernacle. Although his subject was taxation, he once more departed from his set text to plead extemporaneously for the World Court.

> I want America to have something of a spiritual ideal. I am seeking American sentiment in favor of an international court of justice. I want America to play her part in helping to abolish war.

His voice was low, with a note of sadness; his tone even; and he made no attempt at gesture or rhetorical emphasis. But when he had finished, he received the most enthusiastic applause since his leaving Washington. He found a respite from formal speechmaking when he moved on next day to Cedar City, on his way to Zion National Park, to dedicate a branch of the Union Pacific Railroad. The 35 miles of track had just been installed, and the presidential special was the first passenger train ever to come to Cedar City. In honor of the event the President was welcomed by 75 Piute Indians in native costume, their faces brightly painted. With the Hardings on their Zion Park excursion were Mormon President Heber J. Grant, Senator Smoot, Utah's Gov. Charles Mabey, and the mayor of Salt Lake City, C. Clarence Neslen. So large was the expanded party that it took over a hundred automobiles to transport everyone from Cedar City.

On arriving at Zion Park Lodge Harding left almost at once on a horse-back excursion to the canyon cleft known as the Narrows. Christian, Doctor Sawyer, Admiral Rodman, and some of the more energetic Utah politicians rode with him, while the Duchess sat in a rocker on the Lodge's front porch and admired the precipitous varicolored scenery. When a party of Boy Scouts passed, she summoned them to the porch and made them a little speech on law observance. Harding did not return until just before lunch. After emerging from the crepuscular canyon he had had to ride for an hour in the glowing noon sunshine, and by the time he reached the Lodge he was hot, sweaty, and sunburned. As soon as the Duchess caught sight of him she clapped her hands and called out in her nasal, peremptory voice: "Wurr'n, you look just like a great big Indian!" Harding flushed, and in the almost tangible silence that followed, the other riders stared at the ground, too embarrassed to raise their eyes.

The next morning, as the *Superb* crossed from Utah into Idaho at Cache Junction, the customary state officials were on hand at the border to greet the President and ride through the state with him on the presidential train. This time the delegation was led by Senator Borah who for the moment was showing a surprising tolerance for the idea of a World Court.

At Pocatello, in an impromptu speech from the rear platform, Harding again spoke of peace and the need for his country to join the Court to make peace secure. In planning his schedule he had intended to mention the Court only twice, but now he found himself introducing it into almost all his speeches. Again in Helena, Montana, he brought up the Court, after setting forth more formally and explicitly what he had promised the soldiers in the Denver hospital—that in the event of another war, money would be conscripted as well as men. Although Montana was a state where the conflict between capital and labor had often been fierce and sometimes desperate, he chose to defend his labor policy there, telling an audience at Helena's Shriners' Hall that "nothing has been further from the purpose of this administration than any thought of destroying the right of either labor or capital to organize." He hoped to lessen the conflict between both, but he was opposed to any "deflation of labor" and to those who held that "organized labor must be crushed." His effort to show himself as labor's friend was sourly received by Gompers who brought up the matter of the Daugherty injunction and remarked that labor would require more than a speech to balance against the acts that had gone on before.

At Butte Harding visited a mine and shook hands with the miners, as did the white-gloved Duchess, brushing aside their awkward objections that their hands were dirty. Then he presented medals to several Boy Scouts for heroic service when their summer camp was struck by lightning. Just as he was boarding the train at the Great Northern Station a miners' brass band outside played "Aloha," and he was so pleased that he walked over and congratulated the leader, asking him if he would play it once more as the *Superb* left the station.

Harding planned to make his weekend a holiday by exploring Yellowstone National Park. The park's Chief Ranger Horace Albright and Colonel Starling had worked out elaborate security arrangements to protect the President, but Harding had made it more difficult for them by insisting that tourists be given a chance to meet him or at least see him. Nevertheless, Albright had about one-hundred-fifty miles of roads patrolled in advance and the adjoining woods combed for strangers. He banned all traffic at night and posted a ranger guard at every place the President was scheduled to stop.

Early on Saturday morning the *Superb* arrived at Gardiner, Montana, near the park's north entrance, where a seven-passenger touring car with the top down headed a line of cars waiting for the presidential party. Harding, on going up to the first car and shaking hands with the driver, was delighted to find a man who looked like Wilson. "It's a wonderful thing," the President said turning to Albright who with Secretary Work was riding with the Hardings, "to be driven around Yellowstone Park by Woodrow Wilson!"

The party had breakfast at the Mammoth Hot Springs Hotel and afterward set out in a snake-like motorcade along the Grand Loop for the Old Faithful Inn 50 miles away. Impressive natural surroundings did not impress Harding much, even when his mood was good. At heart he preferred the even, unspectacular Ohio landscape to this jagged region of bubbling hot springs, foaming waterfalls, and erupting geysers set against the aloof background of the mountains. Besides, he had been to Yellowstone Park on his honeymoon—not the greenest of his recollections.

They passed through Golden Gate with its sheer walls rising above the highway, passed the yellow-green water at the foot of Roaring Mountain, the emerald and blue-green of Twin Lakes, Nymph Lake, and Frying Pan Spring. Harding asked Albright if there would be people along the way. The Head Ranger said they might see moose and deer and possibly elk, but no people. Reassured, the President reached into his pocket, took out a plug of tobacco and bit off a chaw that he had to get rid of quickly when he found a large crowd waiting for him at Norris Geyser Basin.

There he combined looking at the geysers— Constant, Whirligig, Valentine, and one named Congress "because it is in continuous play"—with shaking the hands of some three thousand tourists. On leaving he was flattered to learn that a geyser had just been named after him.

The presidential party had lunch, explored during the afternoon, and spent the night in the huge log cabin that was the Old Faithful Inn. To the delight of ogling visitors, Harding in the early evening sat in front of the gigantic fieldstone fireplace in the lobby popping corn. Next morning the motorcade set out for the Canyon Hotel at the north end of Lake Yellowstone, climbing over eight thousand feet to the Continental Divide where the snow still lay in patches, then down to the turquoise lake in its glacier-gouged basin. Near Tom Thumb Junction a dozen or so waitresses from the hotel, with guitars and carrying bunches of wild flowers, swarmed across the road and brought the President's car to a halt. Alarmed, the Secret Service men tried to push them back, but the girls, their young breasts quivering under their summer blouses, forced the men aside and hopped on the car's running board. There they presented their bouquets to the Duchess and began to sing to Harding. At the sight of their girlish faces and the sound of their voices his gray face lightened and his wrinkles seemed to resolve even as the Duchess's face grew grim. When Albright tried to order them off the car, the President told him, "Let them stay!" Only after much song and chatter were the girls finally persuaded to leave. Harding turned to watch them, then asked Albright if he could not come back the same way that afternoon. Albright said the schedule had been fixed and it was not possible. The Duchess added: "Wurr'n, I watched you while those girls were here! It took you just as long to say good-by to those girls as it did for you to run through 3,000 tourists yesterday at Old Faithful!"

After lunch Harding wanted to climb the steps to the observation tower looking out over Yellowstone Canyon, but Doctor Sawyer insisted that he must not climb stairs since he had not been well the night before. For the Duchess with her thick and swollen ankles the climb was out of the question. Harding had to content himself with feeding gingerbread to a black bear and her cub at the upper end of the lake—to the delight of photographers.

By late afternoon he was once more in the *Superb* and moving west. Even in this brief visit he had been impressed enough by the idea of national parks to advocate adding an additional 400,000 acres to the public domain that would include Jackson Hole Country with part of the Tetons. It was indeed a new Harding who could announce that it was "not desirable that the West should fall into the hands of bonanza corporations seeking to exploit it for the profit of stockholders." On the way to Spokane he amused himself by driving the electric locomotive 12 miles down the steep grade of the Bitter Root Mountains. At Meacham, on the very top stretches of the Blue Mountains of Oregon, the *Superb* halted long enough for him to dedicate a boulder monument marking the new Oregon Trail Highway and to watch a covered-wagon pageant in which —although he did not know it—the Indian participants had had to be paroled from the local jail where they were serving sentences for bootlegging. In Spokane he again defended the World Court, and in Portland at its annual "Rosarian" celebration he received the most enthusiastic welcome since leaving Washington, a welcome scarcely marred by the 22 members of the Joint Amnesty Committee who appeared with placards demanding the release of the remaining IWW prisoners. The British cruiser *Curlew* being in port, a detachment of the Royal Marines paraded July 4 in the President's honor.

Between Portland and Tacoma Harding had his train stop at Centralia, Washington, so that he could put wreaths on the graves of the four former servicemen who had been killed while trying to raid the local IWW headquarters during a patriotic parade on Armistice Day, 1919. At Tacoma the misty air was salt with the smell of the Pacific, and a light rain was falling—the first since the transcontinental journey began. In spite of the rain, Harding spoke at the open-air stadium. Again he brought up the twelve-hour day, obliquely putting further pressure on Judge Gary and the steel industry. "I should be proud, indeed," he told his audience, "if my administration were marked by the final passing of the twelve-hour working day in American life."

Ready at last to embark from Tacoma on his four-day voyage to Alaska, Harding had concluded most of his trip's formal speechmaking although he still planned a major address on the way back at San Francisco on his now dominant and dominating issue of the World Court. Defining himself as he never had before, moving beyond his party in his determination to become leader of his country, he was willing to stake his reputation on the World Court as Wilson had dared to stake his on the League of Nations. Yet, in spite of the fact that his speeches showed him moving toward a new conception of himself and the Presidency, there was an undercurrent of doom to his Voyage of Understanding, a feeling of malignant fate in the offing. Convinced that he had been betrayed, Harding could not shake the feeling.

It was still raining, a soft drizzle, on the afternoon of July 4 when Harding and his party embarked from Tacoma's Municipal Wharf on the refurbished Army transport *Henderson* for the 1,000-mile voyage to Alaska. The *Henderson*, commanded by Captain Allen Buchanan, carried a crew of 21 officers and 460 sailors, a 72-man Marine guard, and a Navy band. In 1917 she had been one of the first transports to carry American troops to Europe. At one time she had caught fire at sea and been abandoned, and it was whispered at the dockside that she was an ill-omened ship. There was nothing ill-omened, however, in the gala departure from Tacoma. As the *Henderson*, her high observation deck banked with flowers, backed into the channel, those on shore sang "God Be with You Till We Meet Again," and batteries from the Army post fired a 21-gun salute. Then, as the *Henderson* glided down Puget Sound with the four-starred presidential flag flying from the masthead and escorted by the destroyers *Hull* and *Curry*, the Navy band blared out with "Yes, We Have No Bananas," followed by "I-o-wa, I-o-wa, That's Where the Tall Corn Grows."

The quick and easy routine of shipboard life followed, as the *Henderson* sailed north along the mountainous primeval coast line: three concerts a day by the Navy band, with group singing of popular songs, led by Malcolm Jennings; moving pictures evenings in the saloon. Harding occupied a cabin reserved for a colonel of the Marines, and the Duchess had an adjoining suite. For Secretary Hoover, who had joined the party at Tacoma, those days at sea were a nightmare voyage that he recalled with pain twenty-eight years later in his memoirs:

> As soon as we were aboard ship he [Harding] insisted on playing bridge, beginning every day immediately after breakfast and continuing except for mealtime often until after midnight. There were only four other bridge players in the party, and we soon set up shifts so that one at a time had some relief. For some reason I developed a distaste for bridge on this journey and never played it again.
>
> One day after lunch, when we were a few days out, Harding asked me to come to his cabin. He plumped at me the question: "If you knew of a great scandal in our administration, would you for the good of the country and the party expose it publicly or would you bury it?" My natural reply was, "Publish it, and at least get credit for integrity on your side." He remarked that this method might be politically dangerous. I asked for more particulars. He said that he had received some rumors of irregularities, centering around Smith, in connection with cases in the Department of Justice. . . . Harding gave me no information about what Smith had been up to. I asked what Daugherty's relations to the affair were. He abruptly dried up and never raised the question again.

Hoover noticed, though, that Harding grew more nervous as the trip continued, and that his gaiety was forced. Alaska lay before them, a territory of forest and lake and mountains as it was before the white man came, a fifth of the land mass of the United States, edged only by the little wooden settlements along the shore. But the renewal that Harding had hoped to find in this land that had been so long in his fantasy he did not find, and the temporary escape that he did find in receptions and parades always left him in the end intolerably alone with himself.

On the late afternoon of the fourth day, with a cloud rack shredding before a fiery sunset, the *Henderson* dropped anchor in Alaskan waters, and as the tide swung the ship's bow west the band serenaded the Duchess with "The End of a Perfect Day" that, with "La Paloma," was her favorite song and one she requested daily. Next morning, Sunday, the President was awakened by the whistle of an approaching tugboat followed by a quick and brassy version of "The Star-Spangled Banner" as played by an Indian band on the deck, the bandsmen barefoot but formal in white trousers, blue coats, and straw hats. After breakfast the presidential party landed by launch at the Indian village of Metlakatla to be greeted by 500 Indians and Alaska's Gov. Scott Bone. They walked under an arch reading *God Bless Our President* along broad sidewalks raised on stilts on either side of which larkspur, fireweed, and daisies grew in brief summer profusion. Harding was presented with a four-foot king salmon, and raised the flag on the new flagpole.

From Metlakatla they sailed past empty forest-covered islands to the salmon-canning town of Ketchikan, a city on a hill built like a great wharf, its wooden streets and sidewalks supported by piles. Then north again, where they were met by blanketed Indians in war canoes and landed at Wrangell, a wooden city like Ketchikan on the side of a mountain, with its buildings and streets planted on tall green stilts above the muddy water of the Stikine River. There the President saw his first totem pole, and in an informal speech said he wanted his administration to go down in history as "a period of understanding."

A heavy rain was falling as Harding arrived at Alaska's capital, Juneau, but, in spite of the rain, long lines of children holding garlands of fireweed formed a guard of honor as he drove with Bone to the governor's residence past a building that looked like a deserted garage and that carried a sign "This Is the Capitol."

On the voyage from Juneau to Skagway Captain Buchanan had the ship's gunners fire several rounds of five-inch shells into the wall of the Taku Glacier so that Harding could watch the flashing ice avalanche. Then came Skagway, a port in a mountain pass, a city of deserted piers, empty streets, and rotting buildings that had once been the outfitting center for thousands of prospectors and adventurers in the Klondike gold rush before their setting out over the Chilkoot Pass for the Yukon and Dawson. Now the ghost city's 484 inhabitants had gathered on the wharf beneath the cliff wall daubed with long-forgotten names to greet the President. Harding, after being met by the mayor, was taken to the one hotel, Pullen House, where he made a brief speech and was presented with a vase of fossilized ivory.

From Skagway the *Henderson* headed west through Joy Strait past Muir Glacier and austere snow peaks named after half-forgotten politicians and into the black waters of the Gulf of Alaska. A chill three days' journey across the gulf brought the presidential party to the winding passage between sheer snow-capped mountains that led to Resurrection Bay, Seward's landlocked harbor. Governor Bone, standing beside the President on the observation deck, suggested naming a glacier or a mountain in his honor. Harding said he would prefer the entrance to the bay, and within an hour Bone had issued a proclamation naming it the Harding Gateway.

Seward was sweltering in an unaccustomed heat wave, with the temperature over ninety degrees. Instead of landing directly, Harding, his face drawn with exhaustion, invited the mayor and welcoming committee aboard, explaining how tired he was, and asking if he might be excused from speeches and public appearances. The Duchess, who had spent her days in the ship's solarium at the stern, did not show herself and sent word that she was indisposed.

The days that followed became a kind of waking dream, a flashing past of transient wooden towns and cities against the unalterable background of sea and sky and glacier, the small party under the enormous sky caught up in the immediacy of the moment that itself slipped away like quicksilver. Yet for Harding there was his underlying sense of doom, sometimes muted, sometimes acute, but always lurking in the shadows of his mind.

From Seward, the sea terminus of the recently completed Alaskan Central Railroad, the travelers found a presidential train made up of all of Alaska's Pullman cars, hastily assembled and with a volunteer amateur staff to carry them to Fairbanks, "farthest north on steel rails." On that long journey toward the Arctic Circle they crossed mountain passes, edged glaciers and waterfalls, looped through tunnels, and coasted down ice-filled canyons. Winding around a great mountain to circle the shores of Turnabout Inlet the train arrived in the evening at Anchorage, the nine-year-old boom town on its tableland above the harbor. Although it was past eleven o'clock, the skies were almost as bright as midday, with a strange yellowish sheen to the air. In spite of the hour, Alaskans had flocked from their bungalow homes to see a real-life President. Harding, met by a committee on arrival and presented with a painting of Mt. McKinley, remarked that he did not know whether to wish them Good Evening or Good Morning. On leaving Anchorage for the two-and-a-half-day journey north the President and his party could even make out Mt. McKinley 60 miles to the north, the highest point in the Western Hemisphere. In the mellow light of Alaska's midnight, the sea below Anchorage looked as if covered with gold leaf. The train puffed along the Susitna River, through the towering Talkeetna Mountains, over high iron bridges, past the abandoned coal mines at Chickaloon, past stations with only numbers instead of names—Milepost 13, Milepost 79. Early in the morning they stopped at Matanuska, and the wife of the deputy United States marshal brought two boxes of strawberries aboard that she had just picked for the President's breakfast. Those up early, or who had not gone to bed at all, could see flocks of reindeer grazing near the Broad Pass of the Alaska Range. At Healy Harding, cap aslant, took over the controls in the engineer's cab for the next 26 miles while the Duchess sat in the fireman's seat opposite. He greeted, but did not pat, the huskies at Kobe, the terminus of the overland dog-team mail trail to the Kuskokwim and Iditarod gold district. In the Yukon District the train stopped at Nenana long enough for him to mark the completion of the Alaskan Railroad by driving a golden spike into a crosstie with a silver sledge hammer—which he succeeded in doing only after two misses.

The moon and the sun were both shining in the night sky as the train reached the rough plain lands of Fairbanks where the presidential party was welcomed with huge bouquets of flowers. In the gold-rush days Fairbanks had had a population of 20,000, a number that had since dwindled to less than fifteen hundred, most of whom lived in log bungalows plastered with moss and mud. Although Fairbanks itself was on frozen ground, there were lush farms on the sunnier slopes, and Harding was proudly taken past them to the new Agricultural and Mining College whose one solitary senior had just graduated that June. After the tour the President was given a midnight banquet at the Model Lunchroom on Main Street where the mayor presented him with a gold-encrusted collar for Laddie Boy. Miners had mushed in from miles around to see their President. He spent the night at the still-uncompleted Hotel Norvale, then spoke next morning at the ball park—the largest place in town—with the temperature at an astonishing 96 degrees. Here at Fairbanks Harding reached his farthest point north, and the fatigue lines had etched still deeper into his face. Doctor Sawyer insisted that he have two days' rest, and canceled the planned drive back over the Richardson Trail in favor of the direct rail route to Seward. As the presidential train pulled out of Fairbanks, a flotilla of cars accompanied it for some distance along the dusty rose-edged road. The *Henderson* had tied up under the shadow of the mountains at the Seward Wharf. When Harding and his party appeared the Navy band blared out "Hail! Hail! The Gang's All Here!" Once aboard Harding, despite Sawyer's orders, worked awhile at his remaining speeches; then, growing restless, he slipped ashore with Joe Chapple, unguarded and unnoticed. They chatted with several children, who failed to recognize the President, and the owner of a fish market who did and who insisted on reciting a poem he had written about Alaska. As they were passing a blacksmith shop, Harding stopped and told Chapple: "The sound of that hammer and anvil is real music to me—reminds me of Harry Cooper's shop at Caledonia."

A twenty-hour sail northeast through Prince William Sound brought the *Henderson* to the mining town of Valdez, the most northern winter port of Alaska. In the ebb tide the ship could not dock, and Harding had to land again by launch. Several hundred prospectors were on hand to greet him. After landing he drove out for some miles on the Richardson Trail, crossing the 27 bridges that spanned the gray glacial stream to the Keystone Canyon. Then when he had re-embarked, the *Henderson* turned south through island-dotted channels, docking at Cordova, the copper capital, a vertical city clinging to its mountainside and ablaze with flags for the great occasion even though the President and the Duchess had to ride through the waving streets in the only available transportation—an Army truck.

From Cordova there was another three-day voyage back across the Gulf of Alaska to Sitka, the former capital, where Russian warships once anchored. During those days Harding, when he was not playing bridge, was playing shuffleboard, but it was obvious that he was abstracted, troubled, hag-ridden by obsessive thoughts he could not shake off.

Already misunderstandings to the south were intruding on the Voyage of Understanding as wireless messages arrived daily. Wheat had dropped to below a dollar on the Chicago market. The talk of Ford for President in 1926 was growing stronger. At Anchorage, while Harding was having breakfast in the Curry Hotel, he learned by telegraph that Magnus Johnson, the Swedish-born candidate of the Farmer-Labor party, had beaten the regular Republican in the special Minnesota senatorial election by 60,000 votes. Johnson, a gallus-snapping farmer in the old Populist tradition, who still pronounced his J's like Y's, announced that he was for the common people, was common himself, and didn't "give a damn for books." He stood for a redistribution of income, public ownership of railroads, the soldiers' bonus, a curb on the Supreme Court, and a government guarantee to the farmers of a "reasonable profit." And he was against all foreign entanglements, from Wilson's League of Nations to Harding's World Court. His election in a state that Harding had carried by 376,000 votes three years earlier showed the Western farm revolt spreading like a brush fire and promised little support for any World Court proposal. Borah made this even more specific a few days later in New York after his return from Europe. "What we condemned under a Democratic administration we will not accept under a Republican administration," he told the 1,200 guests attending a testimonial dinner at the Waldorf-Astoria. La Follette saw Johnson's election as the harbinger of Farmer-Labor Social Democracy in the United States; and that most staid of Republican morning papers, the Boston *Herald,* concluded in editorial gloom that the President's 7 million majority of 1920 had been wiped out and that he would be defeated for re-election.

While the *Henderson* was poking her way south along the glacier and mountain-edged coast, a naval seaplane caught up with her bringing a long, coded message to the President from Washington. After reading it Harding suffered something like a collapse. For the rest of the day he seemed half-stunned, muttering to himself and breaking off to ask whoever was with him what a President should do when his friends were false. What the message contained not even Welliver was able to find out although both he and Hoover noticed the President's distress.

The long northern light was fading when the *Henderson* on July 21 slipped through the narrow channel of Sitka's island-dotted harbor. Harding and his party landed by launch while the bells in the green onion-shaped dome of the old Russian cathedral rang out in welcome. Children, descendants of Russians and of formerly hostile Indians, strewed flowers in Harding's path as he made his way to the village green near the old prison and customhouse. Little girls were on hand to serve plates of cookies and salmonberries, and afterward they sang "Alaska, My Alaska" for the Duchess.

On the next day, Sunday, Harding and the Duchess attended a brown wooden mission church, sitting in the fourth row, with bobbed-haired Indian girls in white blouses occupying the pews ahead of them. After church they inspected the Alaskan relics in the Sheldon Jackson Museum, and Harding was particularly struck by the effigy of an Indian with an ivory tusk piercing his upper lip. On leaving the museum they were driven on a tour down Lovers' Lane, a path through a hemlock and spruce forest edged with totem poles. Chapple noticed the face of a man on one pole wearing a tall hat and thought it might represent a missionary. The line of totem poles led them to the old blockhouse, the site of the last battle between Russians and Indians. On the way back Harding stopped at the Russian Cathedral of St. Michael, a small church built of logs and clapboards, with a green roof, a green carrot-shaped belfry containing six bells, and a lower onion-shaped steeple. The priest, Father Pontelarf, showed him old ikons, tapestries, crucifixes, and paintings donated by the Romanovs from the time of Peter the Great. Then as Harding was leaving the priest, as the highest honor he could bestow, opened the doors of the sanctuary for the President to see the treasures inside. Late Sunday afternoon the *Henderson* slipped down the harbor. Harding, now leaving Alaska behind him, stood in the opalescent sunset on the upper deck for his last glimpse of Sitka with its verdigrised cathedral spires and red-tiled roofs and windows beginning to light up.

At some brief stop along the coast Reddy Baldinger had bought a mess of giant crabs that he had the cook boil for him. Late one evening as he was sitting in the empty dining room, with a plate of crab claws and a dish of butter in front of him, the President in one of his troubled fits of night restlessness wandered in and found him. Reddy asked him to share the feast, and Harding sat down. For over an hour the old editor and his delivery boy squatted there in their shirt sleeves, elbows on the table, cracking the shells and picking out the meat as they talked of old times in Marion, their relaxed faces smeared with butter.

By the time the *Henderson* reached Vancouver another heat wave had settled in, but the undeterred Canadians outdid themselves in welcoming the man they considered the peace President, the first American President to make a speech on their soil. Soldiers in pith helmets, arms swinging shoulder high, marched past Harding in review to the slow rhythm of kilted pipe bands, with all the imperial display that Canada had inherited from England. Yet the welcome that would usually have aroused him left him this time listless. He did his best, making five impromptu speeches and then speaking bareheaded to 40,000 people at Stanley Park, but he appeared worn and in spite of his bulk almost frail. His uneasiness was spreading to the other members of the party. Nevertheless, at a banquet in his honor he managed to summon up enough of his homely self to call the Canadians his neighbors and fellow Americans and to conclude in the terms of his boyhood: "I like that word—neighbors. I like the sort of neighbors who borrow eggs óver the back fence."

A heavy fog had blanketed Vancouver Harbor when the *Henderson* next evening moved out to sea, the bell buoys ringing and the foghorns wailing in the darkness. Some time in the black early-morning hours near Port Townsend, as she edged into Puget Sound, she struck the destroyer *Zeilen* amidships. After the first grinding crash, there was the cry of "All hands on deck!" Brooks, hurrying to Harding's cabin, found him lying on his bed, his face hidden in his hands. Without uncovering his face, the President asked what had happened, and Brooks told him there had been a slight collision. Even though everyone had been ordered on deck, it was not serious. Harding lay there, motionless. "I hope the boat sinks," he said softly, his face still hidden.

The fog had lifted in the morning light by the time the *Henderson* reached Seattle harbor to find the United States fleet lined up in review. "Ruffles and Honors" kept echoing all the forenoon under the blazing sun as admiral after admiral came aboard to pay his respects to his Commander in Chief. Since daybreak thousands of people had lined the streets and hills of the hilly city waiting to see the President.

Hoover had written the speech on Alaska that the President was to deliver at Seattle Stadium that afternoon, although Harding had gone over the text and introduced what Hoover called "his usual three-dollar words and sonorous phrases." For all its sonorities it was a surprising speech, a rebuke to Fall and his kind. Harding came out for a policy of thoroughgoing conservation. He would not, he said, see the territory turned over to exploiters to loot "as the possibility of profit arises." Undoubtedly, in his own words, he declared that Americans must "regard life in lovely, wonderful Alaska as an end and not a means."

On landing, the President rode in an auto parade, attended a boys' picnic, then stood bareheaded for two hours at an open-air reception under a torrid sun. When he appeared to make his Hoover-prepared speech he found 60,000 waiting in the quivering heat of the stadium. Those near him could see the exhaustion written into his slack face, the slightly green tinge to his cheeks, the way his jaws set in pain. Several times while speaking he hesitated, slurred his words, called Alaska "Nebraska." Then, halfway through he faltered, dropped the manuscript, and clutched the lectern in front of him with both hands. An alarmed and solicitous Hoover, sitting directly behind him, managed to pick up the scattered pages from the floor, handed him the next few, and sorted out the rest while the President caught his breath and continued speaking.

That evening Harding felt he had recovered enough to address the Press Club at its postponed luncheon, but he sat down afterward in a state of collapse. Hoover, Work, Gillett, and Doctor Sawyer then hustled him to the train and put him to bed where he complained of violent cramps and indigestion. Sawyer blamed the midnight snack of crabmeat, and released a bulletin that the President was suffering from some bad sea food and would take two days to recover.

Harding had planned to make major speeches in Portland, San Francisco, and Los Angeles, and preliminary texts of the speeches, prepared by his White House staff, reached him in Vancouver. Now, under the threat of his collapse, the engagement in Portland was canceled and the train ordered to run straight through to San Francisco. As the *Superb* moved through southern Oregon without stopping—to the vocal disappointment of the crowds gathered at way stations—Boone took Hoover aside to tell him he felt the President was suffering from far more than indigestion. Boone with the former physician Doctor Work had examined Harding and found his heart alarmingly enlarged. On learning this Hoover telegraphed ahead to have Doctor Ray Lyman Wilbur, the president of Stanford University and of the American Medical Association, meet the train in San Francisco.[2]

Doctor Sawyer still maintained that the attack was nothing more than "a slight attack of ptomaine" with "no serious aspects," and Harding

[2] Doctor Samuel A. Levine of Boston's Peter Bent Brigham Hospital, the first doctor to have made a diagnosis of acute coronary thrombosis, on reading the successive Sawyer bulletins, was convinced that Harding had had a heart attack. "I felt so firmly about this," he wrote, "that I suggested to Doctor Harvey Cushing, the celebrated brain surgeon, who was surgical chief at my hospital, that we should telephone Doctor Sawyer. . . . After thinking this over, Doctor Cushing replied that it was not our business and we should not interfere."

himself thought he was feeling better when his train pulled into the San Francisco ferry station on Sunday morning, July 29, where Doctor Wilbur and the noted heart specialist, Doctor Charles Minor Cooper, were uneasily waiting. Over their protests he insisted on dressing himself. Rejecting the wheel chair brought for him, he walked from the *Superb* to the limousine at the curb outside the station. Mayor Rolf and a small crowd were there to greet him. There were no cheers. Reporters noted that the President looked "old and worn." A chance news photograph—that would turn out to be his last—snapped in the early-morning light shows an aging, flabby-faced man with slack chin and puffy eyes, forcing himself into a half-smile as he squints into the sunshine.

At the Palace Hotel he went to bed at once in his suite, Room 8064 on the eighth floor overlooking Market Street, but sent out word that after resting he would surely deliver his scheduled speech on Wednesday. He insisted that Hoover and Work have rooms near him. The Duchess had her own suite across the corridor. On Monday he turned worse, with a temperature of 102 and a pulse rate of 120. "His acute illness came to a peak on Monday night," Doctor Wilbur wrote, "with the rapid development of a bronchial pneumonia. The quick, irregular, and labored breathing distressed him and when, by stimulation, he had been relieved after a sharp attack of breathlessness, he said, 'I feel much relieved, but, oh, so very tired.'" The whole remaining California schedule was canceled.

On Tuesday the President seemed better, more cheerful, and already convinced that he would soon be well. Doctor Sawyer, observing the lung area clearing up, announced that he would shortly take a vacation himself. Since Harding could no longer consider delivering his World Court speech in San Francisco, he authorized Hoover to release it to the press—to the fury of Hiram Johnson, who attacked Hoover as the real author. On Wednesday the President was so much improved that he was able to sit up in bed, take solid food, and read the papers. His temperature was normal, his pulse under 100. Doctor Sawyer announced proudly that the crisis was past, although Wilbur and Cooper privately left orders that his future appearances must be canceled and that he would have to take a two months' rest.

On Thursday even the more pessimistic Boone felt encouraged. The President looked well and had "had a most splendid afternoon." Harding himself thought that he might go home on Sunday. He sent George Christian to Los Angeles to deliver the address he had prepared for the Knights Templar of the Hollywood Commandery assembled in the Hollywood Bowl to receive the Beauseant, the traveling banner symbolic of the order. Supposedly the Beauseant was the successor of the banner borne by the Templars in the Crusades, although this particular Beauseant had originated in Buffalo, New York, and was being carried to Hollywood by members of Harding's Marion Commandery. Harding took such rituals quite seriously, and his address was full of references to the Grail and the Holy Land and the idealism of fraternal orders.

Daugherty, having kept in touch with the presidential party daily from Washington, arrived in San Francisco on Wednesday and went directly to the Duchess who scolded him for not staying at the Palace where Christian had made reservations for him. He said he did not feel he should see the President and burden him with unnecessary talk, although the Duchess said Harding had been asking for him, but he talked with her every few hours and arranged to have dinner with her on Thursday. Malcolm Jennings managed to slip into the sickroom late Thursday afternoon and found the President weak but cheery, saying that he felt "out of the woods" but "so tired, so tired."

Early in the evening Colonel Starling found him propped up in bed, affable as of old, regretting that he had not caught a single fish in Alaska but promising himself and Starling some good deep-sea fishing at "Bill Wrigley's place" on Catalina Island. The Duchess, after her dinner with Daugherty, came back to read him a *Saturday Evening Post* article about himself by Samuel Blythe, "A Calm View of a Calm Man." Blythe's calm view was of a President following a steady, competent course, quietly pursuing his task with a deaf ear to the howls of critics and factions. Harding was pleased with the image. "That's good," he said to the Duchess. "Go on; read some more." After finishing the article she went to her room across the corridor. Harding remained as she had left him, in a half-sitting position, his eyes shut, his back and head resting on a couple of pillows. His day nurse, Ruth Powderly, had gone for a glass of water to give him with his night medicine. As she came out of the bathroom, diagonally across from his bed, she saw his face twitch sharply and his mouth drop open. Then his body slumped and his head lolled to the right, and in that moment she knew that he had died. Rushing from the room, she called the Duchess who hobbled into the corridor shrieking, "Get Doctor Boone! Get Doctor Boone!" Work and Hoover reached the bedroom a few seconds later, followed by Doctor Sawyer. They found the nurse standing by the door and the Duchess sitting by the bed sobbing, "Wurr'n, Wurr'n, Wurr'n!" The pillows had already been removed and the body, wrapped in a white dressing gown, lay flat on the bed. Harding's mouth had been closed; his face was relaxed and his expression peaceful. It was 7:32.

Sawyer diagnosed the cause of death as a cerebral hemorrhage, but the other doctors after they arrived disagreed. The Duchess refused to allow an autopsy or even to have a death mask made. In the anteroom adjoining the President's bedroom the five doctors—Sawyer, Wilbur, Cooper, Work, and Boone—after some debate finally signed an official bulletin that

death was apparently due to some brain evolvement, probably an apo-
plexy. During the day he [Harding] had been free from discomfort and
there was every justification for anticipating a prompt recovery.

As Pershing and other members of the official party were still struggling
down the jammed and milling corridor to the death room, newsboys on
the street below began hawking extra editions announcing Harding's
death. Hearing their cries, the Duchess sent for copies. Colonel Starling
ordered the Secret Service men to clear the hotel and assigned city police-
men to guard all elevators and stairs. On the main floor the lights dimmed
as the announcement was made that "Your President is dead." Those
having dinner at the Palace's Palm Court stopped eating and left
immediately.

When the Secret Service men had cleared the corridors sufficiently,
two undertakers and an embalmer from N. Gray & Company arrived with
a brown metal coffin. Shutting themselves in the death room, they began
to prepare Harding's body for burial. While they worked, the Duchess
sat in her suite across the corridor, her lips trembling, talking ceaselessly
of her Wurr'n to the women who kept watch with her—Mrs. Work, Mrs.
Sawyer, Mrs. Hoover, Mrs. Jennings, and Harding's sister Chat who had
arrived from Santa Ana with her two daughters the day before. By early
morning the undertakers had finished their work, and the body—dressed
in a cutaway with black trousers—was placed in the coffin and moved to
the adjoining drawing room.

During that long, fog-streaked night while the Palace stirred and
hummed like a beehive that has been disturbed, far on the other side of
the country in the quiet of a Vermont hill village, Calvin Coolidge—the
prim, tight-lipped Yankee whom the Duchess despised—was being sworn
in by lamplight as the thirtieth President of the United States.

By midmorning the large drawing room of the presidential suite bulged
with flowers and people. The open coffin had been placed against the wall
between two windows. Harding's face, primped and painted, looked more
that of a waxwork figure against the white silk of the coffin lining. Mark
Sullivan thought that under his heavy layer of make-up he had a placid
and unworried look. Sullivan found the room almost cheerful, with its
high ceilings and the many tall windows through which the sunshine was
streaming. Workmen were draping the front of the Palace with crape,
and the President's flag hanging over the entrance had been replaced by
an American flag at half-mast.

All day the flowers poured in, filling the suite and the corridors with
the cloying, overpowering scent that has come to seem the odor of death.
The Duchess remained in seclusion in her room while aides and secretaries busied themselves making schedules for the funeral train across the

continent. At five in the afternoon the Reverend Doctor James S. West of the First Baptist Church offered a simple prayer over the body; the coffin was closed, and covered by a flag. Only the immediate members of the presidential party were present, including the newsmen who made the Alaska trip and one reporter from each of the San Francisco papers. Escorted by General Pershing, the coffin was carried down the red-carpeted corridor to the freight elevator by two soldiers, two sailors, two Marines, and two California national guardsmen. On reaching the ground floor, they passed through the Palm Court to New Montgomery Street where Gray's Pierce-Arrow hearse and a fleet of limousines were waiting.

The impromptu funeral procession moved slowly the half mile from the Palace to Third and Townsend streets where the train had been temporarily halted. The Duchess and Chat rode in the first car. After them came the honorary pallbearers—Hoover, Daugherty, Work, Wallace, Pershing, Gillett, the mayor and the governor, and the commanders of the San Francisco military and naval districts—followed by detachments of cavalry and infantry. The crowds along the sidewalks were silent, with the only sounds those of the hobnail boots of the marching men and the more irregular click of horses' hoofs until their thin clatter was resolved by the insistent strains of Chopin's "Funeral March" played by a Marine Corps Band. The coffin was placed on a bier in the rear of the *Superb* just above window level so that the public could watch its passing. A second private car, the *Elmonte,* had been attached to the train for the Duchess, but she insisted on remaining in her old compartment. Doctor Sawyer and Malcolm Jennings and their wives stayed with her in the *Superb*.

At seven-fifteen, in the cool but still-bright evening, the funeral train moved out of the Southern Pacific Station, its eight-wheeled mogul locomotive twined with strips of black and white bunting. The awning and the rail of the *Superb's* platform had been hung with crape. Through the open rear door the blue field and the stars of the flag covering the coffin were visible, and—less distinctly—two soldiers, a sailor, and a Marine standing at parade rest at each corner of the bier with their rifles. At the clanging of the brass engine bell, those clustered in the station sang Harding's favorite hymn, "Lead, Kindly Light."

For Americans, lacking the continuity of a dynasty, the death of a President is a profoundly disturbing experience, as if the mortal man should have been shielded by the immortality of his office. There is no "the President is dead, long live the President," but a void in which political and party differences dissolve. In the grief for the lost leader—who now looms so much larger than life—there is an ephemeral sense of national unity combined with an anxiety for the leaderless future that easily turns to feelings of guilt. The President, the political *salvator mundi*, has died for us—and we are unworthy of his sacrifice. So it was with Lincoln, slandered and uncertain of re-election a few months before his death yet after his assassination almost immediately apotheosized in a country-wide sweep of emotion as Father Abraham.

It was even, if briefly, true of Garfield, the four-month President who took two months to die after he had been shot by a disgruntled office seeker. Flowers were strewn across the tracks and Civil War veterans knelt along the way as a funeral train carried his body from Washington to Ohio. McKinley's death day, marked by tolling bells and newspapers edged in black, was one of general fear as well as of grief. People sensed uneasily that an era had come to an end—as indeed it had, for the Victorian era in the United States ended with McKinley's death in September, 1901, just as it had ended eight months earlier in England with the death of the old queen.

Lincoln, Garfield, and McKinley were murdered, and public grief and anger could find an outlet in vengeance on their assassins—Booth and his companions, Guiteau and Czolgosz. But Harding, the life-loving, had been struck down by fate; and America itself was guilty. Assistant Secretary of the Navy Theodore Roosevelt, Jr., summed up the feeling when he said that Harding "gave his life for the service of our country as truly as anyone in our history." "I have lost the best friend I ever had," George Christian told reporters, "and so has every American."

As the first dismay at the news of Harding's death became absorbed by grief, as the black-streamered train moved east across the continent, ordinary Americans became suddenly aware—although they would soon forget—how much they loved their white-haired President with the face of a Roman senator. Never since Lincoln's death had there been such a quick, spontaneous outpouring of public sorrow. Newspapers that had attacked Harding now appeared edged in black to praise the virtues of "the beloved President." Editorial pages were filled with spontaneous poetry and with solemnized drawings: Columbia with bent head offering up her wreath; an etherealized Harding, in a stiff collar, surrounded by trumpeting angels; Laddie Boy in the (for a dog) anatomically impossible act of shedding tears. "A great calamity," said Taft and Wood in the same words; "an irreparable loss," said Hiram Johnson. Pomerene called his rival colleague "a great American," and, from Hollywood, Hays claimed that the President "gave his life to his country." Nicholas Murray Butler felt that Harding had sacrificed himself "in trying his best to fullfil the duties of his great office." Only with Senator Lodge did the formal mask of grief momentarily slip. When a reporter called him at his Nahant summer home to break the news, the old man was nearly asleep. "My God!" he shouted in the first overwhelming realization, "that means Coolidge is President!"

There had been nothing like the four-day return journey of the *Superb* across the continent since the twelve-day passage of Lincoln's funeral train—interrupted by ten separate funerals along the way—from Washington to Springfield, Illinois, fifty-eight years before. To avoid the San Francisco Bay ferry crossing, Harding's train had been routed down the peninsula by way of San Jose to the Overland Limited Line. No stops were planned on the funeral journey except to change engines, but whenever the train made an unscheduled halt, bystanders rushed to bring flowers to the *Superb* until the ceiling was hidden by great festoons of China asters. In the darkness a soft light flooded the coffin.

Millions watched the *Superb* pass, packing the city railroad stations, standing all night along the tracks in remote country districts to honor their dead President, their lost friend and leader. Masons in helmets and plumes waited at small-town depots as did World War veterans in their high-collared AEF uniforms, and self-conscious Boy Scouts in their new low-collared tunics, and the ancients of the Grand Army of the Republic, waiting for Harding as they had waited for Lincoln and Garfield and McKinley. School children strewed wild flowers on the tracks, and as the clanging bell of the locomotive invaded the dark silence there was a flicker of white garments and the watchers began "Lead, Kindly Light" or sometimes the hymn that Harding had also loved and that was McKinley's favorite, "Nearer, My God, to Thee."

At Stockton, California, all theaters and restaurants were closed, and the train passed to a tolling of bells; at one in the morning, in the little town of Auburn, 300 persons—a quarter of the population—bowed their heads in silence; at Reno, where the locomotive was changed, all the bells tolled. Hundreds were gathered at Sparks, Nevada, just as the sun broke over the horizon. Night and day the train rolled on, slowed by the thousands gathered beside or on the tracks in the cities, picking up speed as it crossed Nevada and Utah and Colorado and Nebraska, the deserts and the mountains and the sagebrush country and the plains. Farmers stood bareheaded, motionless in the fields. Workers in factories downed their tools. Boys perched on telegraph poles and trees and the roofs of barns. Others put pennies on the rails and scrambled for the flattened pieces of copper as good-luck charms after the train had passed. At Cheyenne, Wyoming, regular Army units and a mounted cavalry band joined watch with Civil War, Spanish-American War, and World War I veterans. On the plains of the Platte, farmers who had driven in for miles in their Model-T Fords waited in the rain. At Omaha 40,000, drenched and patient, stood through a thunderstorm at two in the morning.

Those not within traveling distance of the railroad line held memorial services—church and civic groups, veterans' organizations, in the Midwest the burgeoning Ku Klux Klan. Throughout Ohio the Klan held midnight services in every county, the robed and hooded members of each Konklave holding torches of red fire to form a living cross. Church and courthouse bells throughout the country tolled.

By the time the train reached Chicago 300,000 inhabitants of that polyglot city had clustered along the tracks or were swarming in and through the railroad station. Many of the women burst into tears at the sight of the flag-draped coffin. A delegation of aldermen carrying a large wreath of white roses and lilies met the *Superb*. To the clangor of the Chicago bells was added the sound of steamboat sirens from the lake. The 122nd and 124th Field Artillery of the Illinois National Guard fired 21-gun salutes. Far overhead planes flew back and forth trailing long black streamers.

As the train passed through Ohio early on the morning of August 7 it was hours behind schedule, but the Duchess insisted nevertheless on cutting down speed. Ohioans by the thousands had been waiting all night, sleeping on benches or railroad trucks in the stations or on the grass outside or in wagons and cars. Whenever she saw such a group she had the train stop for them.

Not until ten twenty-two that evening did the train finally arrive at Washington's Union Station, backing in so that the *Superb* could be close to the exit. The concourse milled with the devout and the curious, and the gathering crowd swelled against the iron grating behind the platform. At the gate the new President and his Cabinet were waiting. The Duchess was the first to get off, leaning on George Christian's arm, with Doctor Sawyer at her other side. Under the arched roof the throbbing of the engine's air pump echoed above the restless shuffle of the crowd. Then a band in the concourse began "Nearer, My God, to Thee."

A detachment of soldiers, sailors, and Marines carried the coffin—on which the Duchess had placed a single wreath—through the station and to a waiting artillery caisson drawn by three pairs of horses. Outside a squadron of cavalry and a battery of field artillery were drawn up. As soon as the coffin was set in place and strapped down, an officer gave a low-voiced command in the darkness, the troopers saluted with their sabers, and the cavalcade moved off in slow columns to the White House.

Harding's body was placed on a bier in the East Room under the massive central chandelier where Lincoln had lain in state for the first of his many funerals. Floral pieces, elaborate in all their intricate ingenuity, were banked against the walls and at the foot of the coffin, but only the Duchess's wreath rested on the flag. Evalyn McLean, speeding down from Bar Harbor, was at the White House when the coffin arrived. Dry-eyed, sleepless, the Duchess sat with her through the night hours in the upstairs sitting room of the house that was no longer her home. At half past one she suddenly stood up and told Evalyn that she must keep her husband company. The two women, with George Christian following, walked slowly down the curving marble stairway, Evalyn grasping the old woman's puffy arm. Once in the East Room, the Duchess told Christian: "Put back the casket lid," and he obeyed at once, silently. To Evalyn, Harding at first glimpse looked quite alive. The softer artificial light, muting the touches of rouge and lipstick, made him seem almost himself. In the heavy air Evalyn found the cloying scent of the flowers, that masked but did not conceal the pervasive odor of formaldehyde, overpowering. They stood there for what seemed to her to be almost endless minutes until finally the Duchess began to talk. Christian brought her a chair and she sat at the head of the coffin, her face near her husband's. "Wurr'n," she told him, "the trip has not hurt you a bit." And she continued to talk to him for over an hour, on and on, her grating voice almost a singsong. "No one can hurt you now, Wurr'n," she concluded. Then looking about the room, examining the massed flowers, the roses and lilies and giant chrysanthemums and the rest in their oversized stands, she suddenly stooped down, as if she were in a garden, and picked up a home-made bouquet of country flowers, daisies and nasturtiums. Then, ordering Christian to close the lid, she placed the little bouquet on the coffin.

The morning broke with a thin fog layer, quickly shredded by the rising sun. It was to be another day of overwhelming heat. At ten o'clock a bell in a tower near the White House struck the hour and the massive entrance doors under the North Portico swung open. After a brief and private service in the East Room, Harding's body was carried by a detachment of soldiers, sailors, and Marines to the black caisson with its six brown horses drawn up under the portico. A tall sailor watched to see that the flag was not disarranged as the others lifted the coffin into place. Then a bugler gave the signal, and the caisson moved slowly down the drive, followed by the other cars of the funeral cortège, each of which stopped under the portico to pick up passengers.

Justices of the Supreme Court and members of Congress and the Diplomatic Corps had been waiting in the Blue Room until the procession was ready to start, giving rise to the thorny if familiar question of precedence. Who came first, the justices or the foreign ambassadors? This was finally and quickly settled by making the justices honorary pallbearers and sending them ahead with the Cabinet.

The Duchess, swathed in layers of black, her face hidden under a mourning veil, and leaning on Christian's arm, stepped forward into the front limousine with its drawn blinds. The honorary pallbearers followed in the sequence of cars behind her: Senators Lodge, Curtis, Watson, Kendrick, Overman, and Fletcher of Florida; Speaker Gillett and Congressman former Senator Burton, Congressmen Butler of Pennsylvania, Cooper of Wisconsin, Garrett of Tennessee, Garner of Texas. Then came the new President Coolidge and the old President Taft, and behind them, in an obsolete Pierce-Arrow that had once been his official car, Woodrow Wilson. Wilson had driven up with his wife at half past nine—he wearing a black tie, she in mourning—and the chauffeur had parked by the west side of the portico where the ravaged former President waited, too feeble to alight. Harding's death had shocked the dying man, perhaps as a portent of his own mortality.[3]

The funeral cortège moved down the curving drive and out to Pennsylvania Avenue to join the military units already drawn up there in the blazing sunshine under the command of General Pershing, on horseback—his first command since he had left Europe. So great was the heat that the dust rose, and spectators along the way tried to shield themselves with umbrellas. Several Marines waiting in formation fainted. Soldiers, sailors, and Marines made up the long escort, with a squadron of the Third Cavalry. The sunlight glanced along the lines of bayonets like flashing rain as the ranks passed, moving to a march-step version of "Onward, Christian Soldiers" played by a Marine band. Halfway down Pennsylvania Avenue the caisson halted, and a group of children sang "Nearer, My God, to Thee," while those nearest the street scattered flowers under the caisson's wheels. Then the cortège moved up the slope to the Capitol, three Presidents following a dead president, over the same route that Harding had taken to his inauguration twenty-nine months before.

Minute guns of the artillery firing in the distance announced the arrival of the caisson at the Capitol. While the uniformed men carried the coffin to the Rotunda, the Marine band played "Lead, Kindly Light," and the crape-draped President's flag dipped in salute. Harding's body was placed on a black catafalque directly under the core of the central dome that looked down from its height like a celestial eye. That same catafalque had originally been built for Lincoln, after the model of the Masonic Lodges of Sorrow, and had borne the bodies of Garfield, McKinley, and the Unknown Soldier. Folding chairs occupied every inch of the Rotunda's tiled floor. Ten truckloads of flowers had been brought from the White House, and with these bouquets ranged against the walls or at the base of the catafalque, the odor was overwhelming in the humid heat. The Duchess, still veiled, took her place in an armchair next to the coffin.

Everyone in the packed room rose when President Coolidge entered. Thin-lipped and silent, he placed a large wreath on the catafalque. Following him, Taft presented a wreath in behalf of the judiciary; and Gillett and the president pro tempore of the Senate, Albert Cummins, a third wreath from Congress. Then a male quartet standing near the great sculptured head of Lincoln sang "Lead, Kindly Light." The Reverend Doctor J. Freeman Anderson of the Calvary Baptist Church conducted

---

[3] Wilson died six months later, on Harding's death day.

the brief service, assisted by the chaplain of the House of Representatives, James Shera Montgomery. A reading of the eighth verse of the sixth chapter of Micah, the same passage on which Harding's fingers had rested at his inaugural, was followed by the now almost inevitable sequel of "Nearer, My God, to Thee." At the Amen the congregation recited the brief Twenty-Third Psalm, the words echoing and reverberating from the giant dome. A benediction concluded the service, which ended at three minutes before twelve.

At noon, and simultaneously all over the country, there was a moment of silence. A bugler sounded Taps on the Capitol steps and at the same time the slow notes of another bugle echoed in the canyons of New York's financial district. Within the Rotunda the folding chairs had been moved away, the wreaths placed to one side, and the coffin again opened, though at this time it had been covered by a sheet of plate glass. For the next five hours Harding's body lay in view, and thousands passed four abreast to catch their last glimpse of him. At four forty-five the military escort drew up in formation in the plaza facing the steps to the Rotunda. At five o'clock Coolidge and his Cabinet, the honorary pallbearers, and the honor guard of generals and admirals came to bid official farewell to their dead chief. Newsmen noticed Daugherty in particular, bent with grief, "a pathetic figure." Then the coffin was closed and taken to the Union Station for the overnight journey and final funeral in Marion.

Again the funeral train moved across the country, and newspapermen exhausted their adjectives in trying to describe the journey. There were seven Pullman cars in addition to the *Superb*, a dining car, a combination car, and two express cars filled with flowers. The locomotive draped in purple and black crape carried a black-edged photograph of Harding just below the headlight. In the late afternoon the train passed through Baltimore and in the early evening through York, Pennsylvania, and Harrisburg. Among those aboard were the members of Harding's Cabinet, Gillett and Cummins, the Duchess, Doctor Sawyer, George Christian and his wife Stella, Judson Welliver, Daisy, Carolyn, Chat and her children, Deac and his two boys, Heber Votaw, the Jennings, Ned McLean (Evalyn did not feel up to the journey), newspapermen, and photographers. Over and over the two theme hymns rang out in the darkness. Cars waiting beside the road turned on their headlights as the *Superb* passed. At 4:35 A.M. of August 9, just as the sky was beginning to lighten, the train crossed the Ohio line. For those who had waited all night to catch a glimpse of the flag-covered coffin the Duchess had the train stop frequently. At Mansfield a locomotive of the Erie Line, draped in black and white, was waiting to act as pilot engine into Marion. Church bells began to toll at thirty-second intervals as soon as the train crossed into Marion County. The last stop—for two minutes—was at Caledonia.

Scheduled to arrive at ten in the morning, the *Superb* did not pull into the Union Station until twelve thirty-five. The penny craze had spread to Marion, and hundreds had placed coins on the tracks, scrambling madly for the flattened metal as soon as the train had passed. National guardsmen had already cleared the station. A soldier and a sailor were the first to alight from the funeral car. The Duchess walked behind them in her heavy veil, then the Harding relatives. Other members of the funeral party followed behind the coffin, carried by the guard of honor through an archway a short distance to a gray hearse that would take it to the bay-windowed house on East Center Street.

Since daybreak the roads around Marion were choked with cars. The population had quadrupled for the day, and thousands lined both sides of Center Street in the scorching noon sun. Every store and public building was draped in black, and Harding's black-edged picture stood in almost every window. Reddy Baldinger and Captain Adolphus Andrews, commander of the *Mayflower,* mourning bands on the sleeves of their uniforms, walked ahead of the hearse on its slow passage from West to East Center Street. Soldiers, sailors, and Marines moved solemnly beside the coffin while behind it came the long line of funeral cars. Soldiers were stationed along the curb at intervals of 40 feet, with uniformed Boy Scouts and Girl Scouts self-consciously filling the spaces between. A mounted trooper guarded each intersection. The bells continued to toll as the coffin passed the unfinished Harding Hotel, Uhler-Phillips'—this time draped like the other stores—the now-seedy Hotel Marion that Amos Kling had sponsored so long ago and its barbershop where W. G. used to go for his shave, the Corinthian courthouse, the brick jail with its key-shaped weather vane, the *Star* building. In the editor's office a black-and-white ribbon had been stretched across Harding's old desk and his office chair stood draped in black.

Carpenters had had to remove the railings of the Center Street house to allow the coffin to pass through the doorway. Tryon was waiting just inside the threshold in his GAR uniform, mute in his sorrow. The bearers carried the coffin to the little parlor, its shades drawn, cleared of its miscellaneous furniture and whatnots. Only a sepia reproduction of Watt's "Hope" and a crayon drawing of Tryon still hung on the wall. Tryon remained at the head of the coffin, flanked by its guard of four soldiers and sailors, until the flag was drawn back and the half-lid opened. Two tall electric candelabra cast a softening glow on Harding's features under glass, the yellow light absorbing the garish cosmetic tints. One old acquaintance on seeing him thought that he looked healthier than he had at the Marion centenary. Flowers banked the walls almost to the ceiling, spilled over to the front yard where the undertakers had spread green matting over the browned and scraggly turf as far as the curb. Under the front-yard maple trees the ground was covered with wreaths of all sizes and shapes, the flowers worked into designs of lodge emblems or the initials of service clubs—Kiwanis, Lions, Rotary.

Early in the afternoon the public was allowed to file past the coffin. People had driven or taken the train from all over Ohio, whole families with small children, many bringing lunch baskets with them, coming to Marion out of awe for the dead, respect for the Presidency, morbid curiosity. They waited quietly four abreast on the sidewalk in the hot sun in a line that stretched down East Center Street to the courthouse and beyond; old folk, children, parents carrying infants. At the rate of 35 a minute they filed past, all the afternoon, and the line seemed no smaller at sunset. Some of the hundred or so newspapermen, paralyzed by writing variations of the same story for over a week, took refuge in contrived sentimentalism, packing their copy with accounts of grieving children; the little girl of eight who after passing the bier laid her small offering of wild flowers beside a "more pretentious" floral display, then "a tiny hand wiped tears from her eyes as she descended the steps in silence."

The Secret Service men had been ordered to close the parlor at ten in the evening, but when the line in the darkness still stretched as far as ever the Duchess ordered them to "keep open as long as they come, even if it takes until daylight." From her darkened bedroom window upstairs she watched the shadowy line moved forward. Not until two in the morning did the last stragglers file past.

By sunrise a new line had formed that was even longer than the one of the night before. At nine the front door was again opened. Many of those waiting had brought campstools with them. For five hours the sweaty files shuffled forward. Over a dozen persons collapsed from the heat. When at last the guards closed the coffin there were still 20,000 waiting outside.

At two o'clock a gun boomed, and the gray hearse, preceded by a naval chief petty officer bearing the blue eagle-crested presidential flag, drew up near the hitching post where Tryon usually left his horse and buggy. Ohio national guardsmen in wrinkled slept-in uniforms were ranged along both sides of the wide brick-paved street as far as one could see. Then the flag-covered coffin appeared in the doorway as the six servicemen eased it through the entrance. Major Baldinger and Commander Andrews walked ahead to the hearse. The narrow-shouldered President Coolidge, who had arrived on his own special train that morning, followed with the wide-shouldered Chief Justice Taft, both holding their glossy silk hats close to their chests. Then came the members of the Cabinet, Speaker Gillett and Senate President Cummins, governors, and old friends such as Crissinger. Grace Coolidge, her graciousness not to be concealed by the mourning she was wearing, was accompanied by a military aide in white. Finally the Duchess walked down the steps, heavily veiled, escorted by Christian and by Doctor Sawyer who looked as shriveled and forlorn in a cutaway as he did in his general's uniform.

Harding had come back to Marion at last for the leading part in his own pageant. The hearse pulled away from the curb, the final procession—without bands or music—began its slow mile-and-a-half journey to the Marion Cemetery, down East Center Street and again past the Star building, left to State Street just before the courthouse, across Church Street and up the rise of Delaware Avenue almost within sight of the Phillips house on Gospel Hill.

From Tryon's house to the cemetery the route was again lined with silent thousands. In the distance cannon boomed at regular intervals. At the cemetery entrance the cortège was joined by a squadron of cavalry mounted on black horses. Small boys clustered perilously along the branches of the great elms that arched overhead.

Harding's body was to be left temporarily in the cemetery's receiving vault, an arched Victorian-Gothic stone building set into the hillside with a forward covered porch overgrown with ivy. Its grilled iron gates, opening in, had been folded back, and a low brown-velvet catafalque placed just in front of the entrance. The hearse halted by the vault, and the guards transferred the coffin to the catafalque where it was received by the new pastor of Trinity Baptist Church, the Reverend Doctor George Landis, the Reverend Doctor Jesse Swank of the Duchess's Epworth Methodist Church, and Bishop Anderson. Vault and hillside with its overhanging birches were decked with truckloads of flowers that kept arriving until the very moment that the three clergymen walked slowly down the tree-lined avenue bordered by graves to the foot of the coffin. Two of the eagle-topped columns that had marked the Victory Way in the 1920 campaign stood on either side of the vault entrance, but this time trimmed with black. To the left under a lacework of birches five admirals and a Marine general in white flanked the coffin, to the right beside the presidential flag six major generals in khaki. President Coolidge and Chief Justice Taft with the members of the Cabinet stood before the coffin bareheaded and balding, looking in their black mourning clothes like a flock of bedraggled blackbirds. The Duchess and Tryon, their relatives and friends, including Thomas Edison, Henry Ford, and Harvey Firestone, gathered in an enclosed space just beside the vault.

As the three clergymen took their places, the Trinity Baptist girls' choir, dressed in white and partially concealed by the shrubbery, sang "Lead, Kindly Light." Beyond the diapered pattern of the vault's varicolored slate roof, in the middle distance, tents of the encamped national guard glittered in brown contrast to the verdant turf. So hot was the afternoon sun that a number of the floral pieces were already beginning to wilt.

The fourth and final funeral service was mercifully brief. Pastor Landis read from Scripture. A prayer was offered by Pastor Swank. The choir sang "Nearer, My God to Thee," and at the Amen, Bishop Anderson, at last having the last word, pronounced the benediction.

No one else moved while the soldiers, sailors, and Marines of the honor guard carried the coffin through the ivy-grown gateway into the penumbral interior. They came out into the light to stand at stiff attention before the porch in a double line. A bugler with a silver cornet stepped forward to sound Taps, and, as the last notes faded, a rifle detachment fired a 21-volley salute.

The powder smoke looped in strands through the heavy air. There was the slight simultaneous click of metal as the riflemen ordered arms. The Duchess whispered through her veil to George Christian, then walked forward alone past the double line of servicemen and into the shadow of the vault. For several minutes she stayed there, invisible. The President of the United States, the Chief Justice, the others waited. Then she reappeared, the indomitable matriarch, walking firmly, her veil thrown back, her chin high, and her eyes without tears.

CHAPTER XXI

History

A reporter, Boyden Sparkes, saw the Duchess's eyes "shining" as she walked resolutely from the vault. If so, it was a more terrestrial glitter than Sparkes had supposed. With the funeral rites over, she left almost at once with Doctor Sawyer—again in uniform—George and Stella Christian and Reddy Baldinger aboard the *Superb* for Washington. Arriving early the following morning, August 11, still dressed in her widow's weeds, she drove in the official limousine to the White House through the silent, long-shadowed streets.

As the car drew up under the North Portico, Harry Barker stepped forward to open the door. President Coolidge and his wife were waiting on the steps. After the two women had embraced, the Duchess, her ankles more swollen than usual, walked haltingly into the entrance hall where her personal secretary, Laura Harlan, and the rest of the White House staff stood waiting to offer their condolences. Slowly, in full control of herself, the Duchess moved from one to the other until each had shaken her hand. Then, turning to Baldinger who was several paces behind her, she told him sharply: "Reddy, come along. Bring Laura and Harry and let's get to work. Everything has to be sorted and packed. The furniture, Wurr'n's clothes, his papers." Under her direction they worked until noon. Reddy sent some clothes to the Smithsonian Institution. Others he had packed to be shipped to relatives or to Paddock's Storage Warehouse in Marion. The Duchess snipped buttons from several of her husband's coats which she mailed with sentimental notes to young relatives and admirers.

Just after midday she broke off to drive with Evalyn McLean to Friendship for lunch. Fall, back from Russia, was there with Emma to meet her, as were several senators. But by midafternoon the Duchess was back at the White House at her self-imposed task. With Baldinger at her side, she went through Harding's desk and the wall safe in the second-floor study. Some of the papers she let Baldinger burn at once in the fireplace. Some she insisted on burning herself, standing by the hearth as they went up in flames and stirring the ashes with a poker. For the next five evenings until after midnight, aided by Barker and Miss Harlan, she continued to sort, pack, or destroy. Baldinger prepared a shipment of personal effects for the Marion warehouse that included many of Harding's personal and confidential papers. Laddie Boy the Duchess gave to Barker, at the very time that children all over the country were collecting pennies to be melted down for a Laddie Boy statue. Meanwhile in the Executive Wing George Christian, under her orders, was busy packing and sorting the papers and documents in Harding's office.

On the evening of August 17 the Duchess, accompanied by George Christian and Harding's nurse Ruth Powderly, left the White House for good, driving with the Coolidges through the rain-filled dusk to Friendship where she planned to stay with Evalyn for the next three weeks. The rain had faded and cicadas were shrilling in the darkness as Evalyn and her guest walked across the lawn under the shade trees after dinner.

"Now that it is all over," the Duchess said, "I am beginning to feel it is for the best." In the privacy of Friendship she continued sorting through the mass of papers she had taken with her, burning whatever she felt should be destroyed. Each morning Baldinger reported to her. One morning they removed the contents of a safe-deposit box from a Washington bank. On another day they made a fire of several boxes of Professor Chancellor's book in the back garden. On that same day she ordered Reddy to toss a locked suitcase onto the bonfire. As it broke open under the enveloping flames, he could see masses of papers and letters but he said nothing. "Reddy," she warned him, "we must be loyal to Wurr'n and preserve his memory."

On September 5 the Duchess left Friendship for Marion to probate Harding's will which—after several weeks' search—had been located in a Marion safe-deposit box. Her home from now on would be Doctor Sawyear's White Oaks Farm. Reddy Baldinger was given extended leave from the Army to serve her. The five large boxes of documents and papers that had been forwarded to Paddock's Warehouse she now had brought to Harding's old office at the *Star*. There for the next six weeks, as her strength allowed, she spent her mornings with Baldinger searching through Harding's papers and handing to Reddy those she had selected to be burned in the potbellied stove. At first she gave him single pages, but as she grew more fatigued she handed him whole files.

Each day during those September weeks that were still as sultry as summer she returned at noon to White Oaks Farm, exhausted and grimy to the elbows. Under the strain of such concentrated sorting she became almost panicky, ripping off headings and endings from letters she did not choose to burn, tearing portions of the text from outgoing carbons only to leave the original incoming letter intact. Between six and eight boxes of letters had been shipped from the White House office, each box about ten feet long, a foot wide, and a foot deep. All were tightly packed. By the time the Duchess had finished her culling, two boxes remained.

When Harding, gray and broken, arrived in San Francisco, Nan had been several weeks in Dijon and was already becoming bored with the desultory summer course for foreigners. Aboard the *Roussillon* she had looked over the young men who might be "fitted for the role of foster father," but the young man she picked as wealthy enough to meet her standards paid her no attention. At Dijon, where she lived in a pension, she became friendly with a young Italian lawyer, so well to do and so much a gentleman that she considered marrying *him* as "the convenience father" of Elizabeth Ann. On August 1 she was shaken by the news of Harding's pneumonia, but when next day's paper announced that he was much better she felt sufficiently encouraged to go to dinner and to the theater with her Italian who on their walk back to the pension proposed to her "for the severalth time." That night Harding died, she had—or claimed she had—a premonitory dream that same hour of

> a coffin draped with, and trailing about it, American flags, and heaped with red, red roses! A coffin, ascending on my left, rising so slowly that it seemed suspended in mid-air, yet ever moving upward and away from me . . . the whole, mounting majestically, lifted by an invisible force, upward, onward, protectingly shrouded by white, white clouds!
>
> So he had come to me! He had come in this way that I might be the first to know he was leaving this earth! . . . Perhaps he had been too tired, too tired to bend over me, too tired even to murmur before he went away, "I love you, dearie!" But I knew. I understood. He meant to waft me sweet kisses in his sleep.

This portentous vision did not, however, prevent her from buying a cerise dress next day for a foreign students' dance to be held in the evening. She also cabled Captain Cricken for more money, he having already sent her $200 in reply to a previous cable. Then, that afternoon, one of the Armstrong group mentioned to her casually that Harding was dead. "The world seemed without bottom," she wrote. "Things suddenly lost their meaning. The world, people, life itself, were like a horrible nightmare. I felt, like the coffin, as though I were balanced in mid-air."

Borrowing $90 from her Italian lawyer, she left Dijon to catch the next ship for America, sailing on the *France* on August 11. When she arrived in New York she found $200 at the American Express office that Cricken had left her before going to sea. This, she felt, would be enough to tide her over until she received the large settlement which she was convinced that Harding had arranged for her and Elizabeth Ann. In September she visited Marion to call on Daisy, still living at Tryon's Center Street house but now engaged to Ralph Lewis. Daisy knew nothing of any liaison or legacy, nor was Nan yet ready to reveal her secret. The Duchess was not so uninformed, for when Nan wrote her a note asking if she could "be of service" to the newly established Harding Memorial Fund, she received a curt reply from the Duchess's secretary informing her that there was nothing she could do.

On returning to New York, Nan took a job in the appointment office of Columbia University. For a while Elizabeth Ann stayed with her, but soon she felt compelled to send the child back to the Willitses in Chicago. Cricken kept proposing to her every time he was in port. She told him finally that before she could marry anyone, she required a check for $25,000 or $30,000 in advance. He managed to persuade her that, although his money was too tied up to give her so much cash, he was worth over $125,000 and would be quite willing to have Elizabeth Ann as his foster daughter. So, in spite of his somewhat slovenly dress, she decided that she would accept this "diamond in the rough." They were married on January 5, 1924, even though—as she wrote—"it seemed almost sacrilegious to me to yield to my husband the body which had belonged so completely to Warren Harding." She soon discovered that the Captain's tales of Norwegian inheritances were sailors' yarns, and that Cricken had nothing more in the world than his pay as a ship's master. Nor was the husband so generous as the suitor had been. Money was again her problem. For all her inquiries she could find no hint that Harding had made any provision for her. Her funds ran so low while Cricken was at sea that she pawned her wedding ring and his watch. When he returned, they arranged to have their marriage annulled, he agreeing to pay her so much a month until the annulment.

Another financial victim of Harding's unexpected death was his undercover broker, Sam Ungerleider. Following Harding's hasty margin purchases, the stock market had gone into a decline. Pure Oil that he had bought at 23½ in June was 17⅛ in August. Bethlehem Steel had dropped from 55¼ to 46¼, and Mexican Seaboard Certificates from 20 to 11¾. The value of the amount that he carried in his own name had shrunk by about $170,000, and the smaller account in Ferguson's name was $30,000 below the purchase price of the stocks. Ungerleider, left without adequate margin in violation of Stock Exchange rules, had no one to turn to either for more collateral or for permission to sell out the account. Each day saw his losses grow. His lawyer, Newton Baker, felt he had a right to file a claim against the Harding estate, but Ungerleider refused, knowing that such a claim would become a public document and a possible public scandal. As the stocks continued to go down, he took his problem to

Daugherty who arranged for a conference with Hoke Donithen, the lawyer for Harding's estate. Deac and the three Harding sisters joined Donithen when he met with Ungerleider and Baker in Columbus. Ungerleider told them that all he wanted was for someone in authority to give him permission to sell out the stocks he was still secretly carrying. Baker felt that at the very least the estate should pay the loss on the Ferguson account. After some talk the Hardings agreed to pay that off, since a third party was involved. The next day Donithen called Ungerleider to say that Deac authorized him to sell the stocks, but that the Hardings did not feel it their obligation to make good on the $170,000. Ungerleider, persuaded of his (tax-deductible) patriotism, made no attempt to collect the debt.

A few days after the funeral Hoke Donithen persuaded a number of Harding's friends to form an association to erect a suitable memorial to Marion's President and maintain the Mount Vernon Avenue house as a shrine. In October the Harding Memorial Association was incorporated, with President Coolidge as its honorary president, George Christian as secretary, and a board of trustees that included Hoover, Mellon, Wallace, Weeks, Denby, Daugherty, Dawes, Ned McLean, and Hoke Donithen. Hoke was the driving force behind a nationwide campaign to raise money for a monument that would also serve as a permanent resting place for the dead President. In his will Harding had requested nothing more than "a simple marker at my grave," but Hoke envisioned a mausoleum that would be the glory of Marion.

For a time it seemed that Harding could not be memorialized enough.

> Martyr of fate, child of a Nation's sorrow
> Deathless in death that near divinity brings.

So wrote an apotheosizing poet, one of the many inspired to verse by the President's sudden end. Even the icily aloof Charles Evans Hughes extolled the dead man as "a martyr in fidelity to the interests of the people." Dozens of towns and cities began their own memorials. Peaks and bays were renamed Harding. A sequoia in Giant Forest, California, the second largest tree in the world—five thousand years old, 32 feet in diameter, and 280 feet high—was named the Warren Harding Tree (the largest tree in the world had already been named after General Sherman). The Mint began striking off silver Harding medallions with his likeness on one side and the date of his birth, inauguration, and death on the other. Money poured into Hoke Donithen's monument fund from every state.

In October the Marion vault was opened and Harding's coffin placed in a 2,600-pound asphalt sarcophagus. A detachment of 30 soldiers from Fort Hayes, Columbus, had been detailed to guard the vault for six months following the interment. But even in his temporary resting place, Harding was not to sleep quietly. Before the six months' guard duty was up, the image of the martyr President had begun to disintegrate.

On October 22, six weeks before the opening session of the new Sixty-eighth Congress, the Senate Committee on Public Lands investigating the naval reserve oil leases held its first hearing in the marble decorum of the Senate's large caucus room. Two geologists occupied the first day in testifying that Teapot Dome contained 30 per cent less oil than had been estimated and that the existing reserve was draining steadily into adjacent areas. At the end of that unsensational session the chairman, Senator Smoot, observed that, if the geologists' reports were accepted, Fall had been entirely justified in making his leases.

Fall appeared as the first witness on the following day. Although Harding's friend Smoot was the designated chairman, Democratic Sen. Thomas J. Walsh of Montana, urged and encouraged by La Follette, had taken over as chairman in all but name. Ever since La Follette's resolution of eighteen months before, Walsh had been working his way through the masses of documents supplied by the Department of the Interior, assisted by Pinchot's associate Harry Slattery whose distrustful eyes had been for so long fixed on Fall. Unlike Pinchot and Slattery, Walsh as a Westerner was not a conservationist, and he had undertaken the investigation reluctantly. But during his months of delving into records he had come by degrees to feel that there was much in the oil leases detrimental to the public service and to the government and that possibly fraud and bribery were involved.

"Austere" was the word usually applied to Walsh. Like Fall, he was a self-taught lawyer, a Westerner by choice, but there the resemblance ceased. A second-generation Irishman, Walsh had been born in Wisconsin where he had managed at least to spend one year at the university. On passing his bar examinations he first practiced law in the Dakota Territory, then moved still farther west to Montana. Between the Texas land baron and the ascetic Montana Senator with his conviction that honorable public service was the highest good, there could be little in common but mutual mistrust. As they faced each other under the crystal chandeliers, separated by the green length of a baize-covered table, Fall stared at Walsh with amused arrogance. Walsh's dark, emotional eyes meeting Fall's cold blue ones were like positive and negative electrical poles that sent out sparks on contact. Sitting bolt upright in the witness chair, Fall belligerently defended his leasing policies and his secret contracts. He told the committee that he was very proud of what he had done to construct oil storage tanks at Pearl Harbor. Secrecy, he insisted, had been necessary in the interests of national security. What he had done he would readily do over again, since his actions had more than doubled the strength of the Pacific fleet.

To Walsh's question as to whether he had ever been given any compensation by Doheny or Sinclair, Fall replied that he had never suggested any compensation and had received none.

More geologists with contrary opinions to those of the first two followed Fall in the witness chair. Then the committee recessed for a month. The hearings had aroused little public interest and Walsh, at a dead end, was even considering abandoning them. But during the recess, information kept coming to him surreptitiously from various disgruntled individuals in New Mexico about Fall's unwonted prosperity in a period when other ranchers found conditions so bad that they had been turning their cattle out on the open range and letting them wander into Mexico in search of food. The twin questions kept growing larger in his mind. Where had Fall's windfall come from? Had the money any connection with the oil leases? Beyond these questions, Walsh's combative nature was aroused by clumsy attempts to silence him. His office was ransacked, and he soon became aware that his telephone was tapped, his mail was being opened. Government agents probed into his past. Once his daughter was accosted on the street while wheeling her three-year-old daughter and warned that her father had better drop his investigations.

When the hearings resumed, several witnesses from New Mexico were on hand to testify to the "beautiful" improvement on the Three Rivers ranch as well as Fall's purchases of additional land and payments of back taxes for ten years; a total expenditure of $175,000, by Walsh's calculations. A subpoenaed Doheny followed them. He and Walsh had long been friends. Walsh, on the verge of a breakdown after the death of his wife, had even stayed for a time in Doheny's Los Angeles house. But the Jansenistic rectitude of the Montana Senator could not be swayed by friendship. Doheny, mild and friendly in manner, told the senators that the contracts he had made through Secretary Fall were saving the people about a million dollars and were of great advantage to the Navy. Walsh forced him to admit that the Navy could have stopped drainage without leasing the whole Elk Hills reserve. Then the Senator questioned him sharply about his relations with Fall. Doheny explained that he had known Fall since 1866 when they "mined in the same camp," and told the senators he felt very bad about the reflections made on his friend's integrity. When Senator Lenroot asked whether Fall had profited in any way, directly or indirectly, through making the Elk Hills contract, Doheny replied: "Not yet. I want to say right here, though, that I would be very glad to take Mr. Fall in my employ if he ever wanted to come to us."

At the end of December Sinclair, appearing before the committee for the second time, told of visiting Three Rivers. He admitted that he had sold Fall some livestock—seven cows and a bull—but denied that he had ever made a gift of any kind in return for the Teapot Dome lease. With his

denial, following that of Doheny and Fall, it looked as if Walsh's investigation had reached its inconclusive conclusion.

Yet, as the Montana Senator continued to delve into the financial intricacies of Three Rivers, as Fall's New Mexican neighbors enlarged on
his sudden affluence, the former Secretary of the Interior began to lose his
nerve. He sent his son-in-law C. C. Chase to ask Price McKinney, a rich
mining and steel man of Cleveland with whom Fall had traveled West in
1921, if he would state that he had lent Fall money to rehabilitate Three
Rivers. McKinney refused. The money mystery grew deeper. Instead of
explaining it or fighting back, Fall ran away. He took to drinking heavily.
His blue eyes grew clouded. Leaving Three Rivers, he traveled to Chicago
and from there to New York (where he conferred with Doheny, Sinclair,
and Zevely), to Washington, and finally to Atlantic City where he entered
a hospital. When the committee again sent for him, his doctor telegraphed
that he was "too rundown" to appear. From Chicago he had called Ned
McLean at Friendship to ask if he could spend a few days there. Ned told
him to come along, but heard nothing more until a week later when Emma
Fall telephoned Evalyn from Atlantic City begging her to send Ned to
see her husband at once on "a matter of life or death."

Postponing a trip to Palm Beach, Ned left for Atlantic City on *The Enquirer* that same day. He found Fall in his hotel room wrapped in a dark-
red dressing gown, trembling, and "in terrible condition." Fall said he was
in trouble and asked Ned if he would tell Walsh's committee that he had
lent him $100,000. "It has nothing to do with Harry Sinclair or Teapot
Dome," Fall reassured the gullible Ned. "They [the committee] are bark-
ing up the wrong tree." Without further thought Ned agreed to say that
he had lent the money, and made out a dummy check to that effect. The
day after Christmas Fall wrote the committee a long, rambling letter in
which he explained that in order to enlarge his ranch holdings he had, in
November, 1921, borrowed $100,000 from Edward B. McLean, "a gentle-
man" with whom he had had a "pleasant and close personal relationship"
and from whom he had borrowed money before. Although "some evil-
minded persons" were insinuating that Sinco had put up the money for
the Harris ranch, Fall thought it needless to say that he had never received from Sinclair or Doheny "one cent on account of any oil lease or
upon any other account." He did not wish to discuss the matter further.
In fact, he found "the entire subject . . . more or less humiliating ever to
refer to." Ned sent a corroborating wire to the committee from Palm
Beach that he had lent Fall the money. To most people, the investigation
had now come to seem a tempest in a teapot. Walsh, feeling that the tea
was not even warm, agreed with Smoot to end the hearings within the
week, except for possible later testimony from Ned McLean.

Fall later admitted that the greatest blunder of his life was in writing the letter to the committee. If he had told Walsh the truth about Doheny's loan, his reputation would certainly have suffered to some extent, and the oil reserve leases and contracts might even have been canceled, but he would never have been brought to trial for bribery and conspiracy. When his lies about his financial affairs were at last revealed, they cast a sinister light on every aspect of the naval oil transactions. According to Emma Fall, her husband had intended to tell the truth at the hearing, but Doheny had persuaded him that it would be too damaging to Doheny's business interests. At this time Doheny was trying to raise $20 million for the Pan American Western Corporation, a new subsidiary of his company, and he feared such unfavorable publicity would make it impossible to float the stocks and bonds. And it was Doheny who suggested that Fall say the loan came from McLean.

Ned, aware that he, too, might be subpoenaed, had added A. Mitchell Palmer to his stable of lawyers. From Palm Beach, Palmer wired the committee that his client's health required him to stay in Florida, and Ned's doctor certified that he was suffering from such an acute sinus infection that it was out of the question for him to return North. Fall had meanwhile gone to Palm Beach as a guest of the McLeans, arriving on the last day of the year at the Breakers Hotel where he spent most of each day sitting on the porch and looking out to sea. "For the first time in my life," Evalyn wrote, "I saw a man crumble right before my eyes. . . . Drinking had changed him from a virile, sharp-witted man into a trembling wreck." Fond of him in her open-hearted, empty-headed way, she begged him again and again to tell what he knew. "I can't tell without bringing ruin to some others," he would answer, "but I tell you I have done nothing wrong."

For the first time in his casual life Ned now found himself faced with a threat that neither his lawyers nor his money could avert. He had done Fall the favor of committing perjury, and if this were discovered even the McLean millions might not keep him from jail. Thoroughly alarmed at the prospect of being called on to swear to the truth of a lie, he set up a task force to prevent his appearance before the committee. His Republican lawyers called on Republican senators, A. Mitchell Palmer called on the Democratic senators. Republicans and Democrats together tried to persuade Walsh that Ned was not only ailing but had never met Sinclair, Doheny, "or any of the so-called oil crowd." Two informants in the Department of Justice—one of them the wife of Ned's confidential secretary—kept him in touch with developments there. So many hundreds of telegrams passed between the McLean cottage and Washington that Ned finally had a private line set up to his office at the *Post*. When it became apparent that Walsh was going to come to Florida, Ned panicked. Besides his Department of Justice badge he had a copy of its secret code, and he made up codes of his own as well. The wires to the *Post* hummed with such enigmatical messages as:

JAGUAR BAPTISTICAL STOWAGE BEADLE
HUFF PULSATOR COMMENAL FITFUL.
LAMBERT CONATION FECUND HYBRIDIZE.

Decoded, that particular message read: "Walsh leaves Coast Line twelve-thirty-five tonight instead of Seaboard. Lambert on same train." In the bizarreries of code, Walsh was "Jaguar," Fall "Apple," Ned "The Big Bear," Daugherty "Sonatone," Evalyn "Wyhol."

Before Walsh arrived at Palm Beach he had already come to doubt Ned's story and to suspect that Fall's loan had in some way come from Sinclair. He was "dumbfounded" when the harried Ned now informed him that he had never really given Fall any money, merely a couple of checks in November, 1921, that Fall had returned uncashed a few days later, saying that he had made other arrangements. Ned produced the checks but could produce no corresponding stubs in his checkbook, nor indeed had he had enough money in the bank at the time to cover such a sum.

Fall from his suite at the Breakers refused to see Walsh or even to receive a letter from him outlining what McLean had said. Finally Walsh threatened to send a sheriff with the letter, but relented enough to let Ned take it to Fall's room. Ned found Fall at his desk composing a telegram to Doheny informing him that he was going to tell the committee where he had got the $100,000. For the first time the astonished Ned now learned that the money had come from Doheny, although Fall was not ready to tell Walsh this. In his reply to Walsh's letter he admitted that he had not taken McLean's money, maintaining he had found other sources, none of which were in any way connected with Sinclair or Teapot Dome or any oil concession. He still refused to see Walsh, ending his letter by saying that because of his physical condition he did not care to go into the matter further.

That day at Palm Beach was the turning point in the investigation, the day that would eventually make Teapot Dome a household phrase and begin the erosion of Harding's reputation even before the guard had been relieved at his temporary tomb. Conflicting opinions on oil reserve drainage and offset drilling or the construction of storage tanks in relation to the strength of the Pacific fleet had been too abstruse to sway public opinion one way or the other. But a rich playboy who had lied to a Senate committee, a mysteriously missing $100,000, a former Cabinet member who had arranged the oil leases and now refused to talk—these were concrete elements of scandal comprehensible to any tabloid reader.

Walsh on his return to Washington told newsmen that Fall had deceived the committee. After Ned's story of the $100,000 had appeared in the papers, Sen. T. H. Caraway of Arkansas denounced the former Secretary on the floor of the Senate as a liar and a Benedict Arnold. One of the side results of the McLean revelations was that Harry Sinclair left on the next boat for Europe. Archie Roosevelt from his sinecure security in the Sinclair organization grew disquieted by Sinclair's abrupt voyage. When he asked Sinclair's secretary, Gustav D. Wahlberg, what was the reason for such a sudden departure, Wahlberg told him it was probably "on account of the turn in the investigation occasioned by McLean's testimony in Florida." Archie then asked Wahlberg point-blank whether he thought Sinclair had bribed Fall. The Swedish-born secretary replied that bribery was a nasty word but he thought "somebody might have lent Mr. Fall money." He added that he was worried about a payment of $68,000 to a foreman of Fall's ranch for which he still held the canceled checks. Archie began to feel he ought to resign, and he telephoned his brother Ted for advice.

Three days later, on January 21, in a caucus room for the first time jammed with spectators, Walsh reported on his visit to Palm Beach. Then the doors opened and a detachment of Roosevelts marched down the aisle of the hushed room, Ted leading Archie like a delinquent schoolboy, followed by their wives and Princess Alice with her husband. With the clan there to give him courage, the confused and apprehensive Archie told his rambling story, not forgetting the $68,000 payment to the foreman. Wahlberg, on his turn in the witness chair, denied that he had said any such thing. He had been talking about cattle shipped to Fall and had said "six or eight cows" not "sixty-eight thous" that Archie had thought he heard! Between Archie's confusion and Wahlberg's reticence it was impossible to settle on just what had happened, but Wahlberg did admit that "some money might have been lent to Mr. Fall." Democratic senators pricked up their ears at his incidental mention of Sinclair's loan of Liberty Bonds to Chairman Hays of the Republican National Committee during the Harding campaign.

On January 24 Doheny again appeared before the committee, this time at his own request. After apologizing for not having related the full facts before, he now admitted that he had loaned Fall $100,000 after Fall had telephoned to ask him for help in fulfilling his ambition, "amounting to an obsession," of acquiring the Harris ranch. He told how his son had brought the money in a black satchel, a method of delivery that Doheny found no more extraordinary than he did the loan, which to him was "no more than $25 or $50 perhaps to the ordinary individual." The loan had had nothing to do with the oil contracts, Doheny insisted, for in these Secretary Fall had not profited directly or indirectly. He sturdily defended his Elk Hills lease as a patriotic move on his part to help his country set up storage tanks at Pearl Harbor in preparation for any future Pacific war. Some of the officials of his own company had considered the contract unfavorable, but Doheny did admit under Walsh's questioning that by investing $100 million in Elk Hills he expected to make an additional hundred million in thirty years' time—an amount that Sinclair had said he expected to make from Teapot Dome. In spite of Doheny's stubborn insistence that there had been no collusion, black headlines all over the country made his Elk Hills lease appear a corrupt transaction.

A few hours after Doheny had finished testifying, a haggard and faltering Fall arrived in Washington with Colonel Zevely. "I am a sick man," he told reporters. Although he had been subpoenaed to appear on Tuesday, January 29, his lawyer submitted a statement from four doctors that it would be detrimental to his health for him to leave his bed. Since he was unavailable, the committee turned again to Doheny who this time was able to produce the note Fall had given him, although with the signature torn off. Doheny had himself torn this off, he explained, so that if he and his wife happened to die his friend would not be embarrassed by his executors. After Senator Lenroot, who had taken over from Smoot as chairman, suggested that the committee had been misled, Doheny turned belligerent, and when questioned further announced defiantly that four former members of Wilson's Cabinet worked or had worked for him: Gregory, Lane, Garrison, and McAdoo, as well as the former chairman of Wilson's wartime Committee on Public Information, George Creel. Mark Sullivan, attending the hearings, wrote that Doheny "called the roll of these like an ostentatious king giving an inventory of his possessions, like a parvenu art collector calling the roll of his Rembrandts and Van Dykes." To further questions, Doheny snapped back, "I hired them for their influence." McAdoo he had engaged to assist him in his Mexican interests, in no way connected with the oil leases. But the name of Wilson's son-in-law injected into the ballooning scandal smeared his reputation and destroyed any chance he might have had of fulfilling his old ambition to succeed his father-in-law in the White House. Though his employment by Doheny was legitimate, the connection was enough to account for the small margin by which he missed the Democratic presidential nomination of 1924.

The following day Zevely added another dubious postscript by admitting that Sinclair had given Fall twenty-five to thirty thousand dollars' worth of Liberty Bonds before they left for Russia. Not until Saturday morning did Fall at last appear to face the committee. He entered the caucus room with difficulty as the Senate attendants elbowed a path for him through the spectators massed in the entrance. Gone was the pugnaciously erect Westerner with the fierce mustache and the arrogant blue eyes, the set jaw concealing a tongue ready for instant vitriolic debate. Instead, an old man in a wrinkled and baggy blue-serge suit shambled down the aisle leaning on the cane that he had once carried so jauntily. His cheeks were sunken, his mouth seemed to have drooped with his mustache, and his blue eyes were muted by gold-rimmed spectacles. Guided to his seat by his lawyer who seemed more a nurse, he did not look at his former colleagues. Slowly, in a flat but still clear voice, he read a prepared statement. After denying that the committee had any authority to conduct its investigations, he concluded with the ritual phrase: "I decline . . . to answer any questions, on the grounds that it may tend to incriminate me." Then, his eyes still fixed on the ground, he took his lawyer's arm and moved slowly toward the door, the silence of the room broken only by his shuffling feet and the tapping of his cane.

Whatever his degree of guilt, Fall, tapping his way down the marble corridor, would wear a thief's brand for the rest of his life. Sinclair, called again before the committee, also declined to answer, not on Fall's grounds of self-incrimination but because he considered that the committee lacked jurisdiction and he was reserving his evidence for the courts. Ten times he refused point-blank to answer Walsh's questions. After the hearings he was indicted in criminal court for contempt of the Senate.

Doheny and Sinclair loomed as the villains of the melodrama. And to round it out there was the clown's relief of Ned McLean with his BONKA SULTRY TKVOUEP PROZOICS telegrams and his disarming "I'll be goldarned if I know, Senator!" Elk Hills became absorbed under the name Teapot Dome which in itself developed into a metonym for the whole oil scandal.[1] Teapot Dome was a spout that would spatter oil as far as Harding's vault in Marion; it was a name that would be linked to his and that of his administration after all other links had become eroded by time.

On the same day that Fall was making his abject appearance in the capital, Congress passed a joint resolution calling on President Coolidge to appoint special counsel independent of the Justice Department to begin suit to cancel the oil leases. Coolidge had once observed to Hoover that "if you see ten troubles coming down the road, you can be sure that nine will run into the ditch before they reach you and you have to battle with only one of them." His temperament preferred inaction, but he was astute enough to know when he had to act. Teapot Dome was the one trouble that refused to run into the ditch. Methodically he made his own inquiries, even sending for Harry Slattery to enlighten him with his opposing views about Elk Hills and Teapot Dome. He would, he announced, name one well-known Republican and one well-known Democrat with unlimited authority to investigate and prosecute any oil lease frauds. At the end of February he appointed two prosecutors: the

---

[1] Bruce Bliven wrote that "nobody cared about Teapot Dome when it was a question of conservation, only when it became a scandal of personality and corruption did the public wake up and lick its lips."

Republican Owen J. Roberts, a former professor at the University of Pennsylvania Law School; and Ohio's Democratic former Senator Pomerene. When, however, the Senate requested that the President remove Denby from office, Coolidge balked. Matters concerning his Cabinet, he let the senators know, were not the prerogative of the Senate. Denby, too stupid to realize his own stupidity, attempted to bluster through, but Coolidge—after making his point against the senators—saw to it that his Secretary of the Navy resigned before the month's end.

Coolidge's appointment of Roberts and Pomerene over the head of the Justice Department was a tacit admission that the department under its present Attorney General was not to be trusted. Daugherty tried to minimize the affront by publicly placing the facilities of his department at the disposal of Roberts and Pomerene and by offering them his own services. With cold politeness they declined his offers.

On January 29 Montana's freshman Sen. Burton K. Wheeler had introduced a resolution in the Senate calling on the President to ask for Daugherty's resignation on the grounds of his failure to prosecute corruption in high places. Walsh meanwhile announced that the Justice Department had failed to produce "one scintilla of evidence" for his committee. The heat was on Daugherty, and after Denby's departure he was left alone in his vulnerable isolation. Coolidge, his Yankee caution reinforced by his wish not to discredit his predecessor or his party, hesitated. He would have preferred to have Daugherty resign of his own accord and even sent Chief Justice Taft to sound him out. But Daugherty, from his Ohio days, had never been noted for taking hints.

Wheeler followed up his first resolution with a second to create a select committee to investigate the Attorney General. He accused Daugherty of failing to prosecute large corporations for illegal monopolies as recommended by the Federal Trade Commission, for illegal sales of liquor permits to bootleggers, for conniving in the distribution of the Dempsey-Carpentier films, for participation in stock-market pools. Everybody knew, Wheeler told the Senate, that Daugherty was a friend of McLean, Sinclair, Doheny and such "grafters." Other Democratic senators took their turn, amid Republican silence, in denouncing Daugherty without restraint and without mercy. On March 1 the Senate finally authorized an investigation of the Attorney General by a vote of 66 to 1.

Daugherty, under attack, counterattacked with the same indiscriminate ruthlessness he had learned long ago in Columbus. Wheeler, like Walsh before him, found his office ransacked and himself shadowed, as did La Follette and other Justice Department critics. When Wheeler, picking up the gossip about Roxy Stinson, went to Ohio to persuade her to testify in the coming hearings, unknown persons made a crude attempt to frame him in a hotel room with a woman. A similar crude attempt had been made to intimidate Roxy. She and the Daughertys had been at outs ever since Mally, as Jess Smith's executor, had refused to pay over to her Jess's blind account with Ungerleider that she claimed he had opened for her. It amounted to $11,000 and she needed the money to build a house. Mally held that the money had to go into the general estate. She sued him, and when he retaliated by having her telephone tapped and by trying to compromise her, she warned him that things might come out that he and his brother would not like to have made public.

Wheeler's committee investigating the Attorney General met under the chairmanship of Smith W. Brookhart in the Senate Office Building on March 12. Roxy, still simmering with anger at the Daughertys and more devoted to Jess's memory than she had been to the living man, was the first witness. At forty she had kept much of her earlier charm, and Wheeler could not have contrived a more dramatic opening than this slim, still-handsome woman set against the fleshy background of senators. With her testimony, Washington's back-stairs gossip became black headlines across the country: the Little House on H Street; the Little Green House on K Street; Jess's shadow relationship with Daugherty. She told of deals and payoffs, suitcases of liquor, stock certificates, and thousand-dollar bills—everything she could remember that Jess in his boastfulness or his anxiety had told her, even to the "they" who were out to get him.

Gaston Means was the next and most sensational witness. Wheeler had been steered to Means early in 1924, and Gaston, glib and plausible, had spent every night for several weeks with him before the hearings elaborating on the affairs of Daugherty's Justice Department. Gaston's trial for larceny and conspiracy was on the June docket. Before that date he aimed to create such turmoil in the Justice Department that his own prosecution would be forgotten. On the eve of the Wheeler hearings he sent word to Daugherty that he was going to blow the lid off, but that there was still time for him to refuse to testify if Daugherty would stop his prosecution. The Attorney General told Gaston to go to the devil. Faced with that prospect, Gaston intended to take Daugherty with him.

On the morning of March 14 Gaston appeared in the committee room bringing with him two large accordion cases which he said contained his diaries of the government years. Dimpled and beaming, he almost seemed to blow kisses to the spectators as he made his way to the witness chair. Grandly he waived immunity, saying that he asked for no quarter and would give none.

Roxy Stinson's unembroidered recollections of what Jess had told her were soon dwarfed by Gaston's super-fabrications. Yes, he admitted to the committee, he had worked for and with Jess Smith, collecting a quarter of a million dollars in graft and payoffs. He had collected $100,000 alone from an agent of Mitsui & Company to settle the Standard Aircraft case; he had been paid about half that in distributing the Dempsey-

Carpentier fight films. All this money had been turned over to Jess. Once he had seen Jess with $100,000 in his hand. While testifying in his easy, convincing voice, he kept smoking one cigarette after the other, mugging for the crowd, shooting the smoke through his nostrils or jetting it high in the air with a thrust of his mobile lower lip. Occasionally he would dig into one of his accordion cases and pick out a paper to read from. Masterfully at ease, he knew all the members of the committee by name, and answered and sometimes asked questions as if he and the senators were old friends. He told of Mannington and Smith working with Daugherty in the sale of liquor permits in New York, of Daugherty's efforts to have Prohibition enforcement taken from the Treasury and placed under the Department of Justice, of high meetings in the two Little Houses.

Gaston had a particular grudge against Secretary Mellon who had thwarted his various ingenious efforts to infiltrate the Treasury Department. So Mellon, according to Gaston, had been engaged in issuing illegal liquor permits, and Harding had employed Gaston as a confidential agent to investigate him. Gaston's aplomb, his easy marshaling of uneasy facts deftly corroborated by the accordion case grabbags, impressed the committee. One of the senators, Henry F. Ashurst of Arizona, after complimenting Gaston on the valiant service he had rendered the cause of truth and justice, concluded punningly that for the first time he had "seen the end justify the means."

Following Roxy and Gaston, a parade of lesser figures carried the hearings through until the end of May. Wheeler did not have Walsh's cold instinct for facts and although he marshaled witnesses to give a lurid gossip picture of the Harding era and insinuated much more, he proved little. As an investigator Wheeler showed himself more a prosecutor, but he did attain his primary objective of making the Attorney General's position untenable. Whatever the truth—if any—of Gaston's charges, the fact remained that he had been the highly valued collaborator of the head of the Bureau of Investigation, and Burns had been Daugherty's friend. Jess—whose death seemed more and more mysterious—had been Daugherty's shadow. Their affluence, although obvious, remained unexplained. Daugherty himself refused to appear before the committee, claiming that it was not investigating but putting the Attorney General on trial.[2] He also refused on the same grounds to turn over departmental records requested by Walsh.

[2] An accountant for the committee looking through the books of Mally's Midland National Bank had found records of deposits of $78,000 by the Attorney General, as well as certificates of $63,000 and $50,000 in Liberty Bonds for Jess Smith and Daugherty. Mally then barred the accountant from the bank and abstracted the records. Cited for contempt of the Senate, he appealed to the local Federal Court and it was there that an obliging judge sustained him and condemned the committee.

On the way back from Marion after Harding's funeral, Coolidge told Hoover that he planned no Cabinet changes. "Had he known," Hoover later wrote, "what bugs crawled about under the paving stones of the Harding regime, he would not have been so inclusive." From the beginning Coolidge's prim rectitude had been dismayed by the Harding entourage. On entering the White House for the first time as President, he had told Ike Hoover that he wanted things "as they were," and the head usher understood at once that he meant the decorum of Wilson's day. Alice Roosevelt Longworth found the atmosphere of the White House under the Coolidges "as different as a New England front parlor is from the back room in a speakeasy." Yet Coolidge's Yankee caution was reinforced by his thoughts of the November election in which he would certainly be the Republican candidate. When Borah came to him demanding Daugherty's resignation, the President told him: "Daugherty was Harding's friend. He stands high with the Republican organization. I do not see how I can do it." Senators Lodge and Pepper arrived at the White House to reinforce Borah's demand, and Borah himself faced Daugherty in Coolidge's presence. "I don't know why you want me to resign," the Attorney General told him. "I have never had to turn you down." Hughes suggested another way out. "If it will ... aid ... you in displacing Daugherty, I'll arrange to have the entire Cabinet resign," he told the President after a Cabinet meeting. Coolidge, on the way to the door, turned back. "No, don't do that!" he replied with the wry Vermont wit he concealed beneath his taciturnity. "It might leave me alone with Daugherty!" Finally, on March 28, after Daugherty had refused to open the Department of Justice files to Brookhart's Investigating Committee, Coolidge sent him a blunt note requesting his immediate resignation. On resigning Daugherty wrote a long and angry personal letter to Coolidge. As he walked down the steps of the Justice Department for the last time, tough and truculent, he again saw the red hand of Moscow in his difficulties. Wheeler and Brookhart were, he explained in his apologia, Communists at heart, "received in the inner Soviet circles as comrades," and he had withheld his files from them in the interests of national security.

While the Wheeler and Walsh hearings were building up to their egregious climaxes, still another congressional committee began probing into the affairs of the Veterans' Bureau under Colonel Forbes, more briefly but with equally lurid results. Star witness for this committee was the aggrieved Elias Mortimer, still seething with jealousy at Forbes's seduction of his wife. "I'm going to get that bastard if I go up for life," he told the feature writer Will Irwin, and to the current stories of Teapot Dome and Fall and Jess Smith and the Little Houses, he contributed his own recollections of graft and revelry and booze parties at government expense.

The Veterans' Bureau hearings ended in February with Forbes's indictment assured. The investigations of the oil leases and of the Attorney General extended into May, but long before then they had lost their headline-capturing explosiveness, petering out in a dry debate of geologists. By the end of Wheeler's hearings the senators of the committee as well as the press of the country were having disturbing second thoughts about Gaston's veracity. His entire story depended for verification on the documents that he claimed he possessed, but at each request of the committee to see his documents he stalled. Finally he arrived one morning in apparent distress claiming that his files of five years, contained in three large suitcases and a trunk, had been purloined the night before by two men claiming to be assistant sergeant-at-arms of the Senate. Gaston had used such dodges too often to have anyone believe him, particularly after special investigators returned to the committee from Atlanta with the news that knowledgeable convicts considered Means the swindler of the century.

Gaston's testimony had failed in its aim of quashing his conspiracy indictment, and on June 17 he went on trial. Colonel Felder acted as his counsel until forced to drop out because of an advanced case of syphilis. Again Gaston made headlines by implicating Harding, Mellon, and Daugherty in his swindles, but for all his plausibility he failed to convince the jury of his own innocence. He was found guilty and sentenced to two years in Federal prison. During his appeal he turned again to Daugherty, signing a statement repudiating his charges before the Wheeler committee and confessing that, prompted by Wheeler, he had perjured himself all along.

Walsh, taking a hint from Wahlberg's testimony, had gone so far as to examine the Republican national convention of 1920 for traces of oil. A former train robber from Oklahoma, Al Jennings, had his brief self-glorying moment in the limelight when he told the committee that Jake Hamon had told him that Harding's nomination had cost him a million dollars and that Daugherty and Will Hays had promised to make Hamon Secretary of the Interior.[3] Although no more than the flimsiest gossip, it made even Harding's nomination suspect to a public increasingly willing to believe the worst.

In the early months of 1924, with the three-ring hearings in session at the capital unfolding headline-shrieking scandals almost daily, there seemed little hope for the Republicans in the November presidential elections. Seizing Teapot Dome as a slogan to embrace all the scandals, the Democrats banked on public indignation sweeping them into the

[3] The most likely explanation was that of another witness who said that "when Jake had a few drinks he talked pretty big."

White House. Ickes told Pinchot in February that Coolidge had been slipping for some time and that his descent would be accelerated. Borah thought that the question was not so much whether the Republican party would be defeated as whether it would survive. Oil had become the chief subject of conversation in Washington, and Coolidge's position seemed in peril, his future in doubt.

Whatever his inner feelings about the oil and Justice Department scandals and the men involved, Coolidge preserved his Yankee mask of inscrutability. Only once did his anger flare up in private when he snapped at Hoover: "There are three purgatories to which people can be assigned: to be damned by one's fellows; to be damned by the courts; to be damned in the next world. I want these men to get all three without probation." Making no public statement, he moved with a determination so quiet that it seemed inaction—until he acted. Denby he replaced by an Annapolis graduate, Chief Justice Curtis D. Wilbur of the California Supreme Court. For his new Attorney General he picked the irreproachable Harlan F. Stone, former dean of the Columbia Law School. Within weeks Stone had shaken up the Bureau of Investigation, replacing Director Burns—who had described Gaston to the Wheeler committee as one of the "ablest investigators" he had ever known—by the assistant director, J. Edgar Hoover, whose views of Gaston were unprintable.

Although Coolidge might look, in Alice Longworth's supercilious phrase, as if he had been weaned on a pickle, he was steadily surrounding himself with an atmosphere of probity from the inner circle of his Cabinet outward. Americans tend to respond to any new President, however narrow his election margin or fate-chanced his succession; and although they may later make a scapegoat of him, at the beginning of his term they bring him a large measure of critical good will. The man from Vermont, sober of mien, a symbol of ancestral thrift and virtues, with his dry reserve and quacking voice appealed to the folksiness of the country however much a mannikin he would remain to intellectuals. Incongruously this rufous contracted man would give his name to the era—the seven fat gaudy years of expansion that would come to seem autumnal in the lean decade ahead.

Though Doheny was a Democrat, and Democratic bystanders of varying degrees of innocence had been spattered with the oil from Teapot Dome that had so smeared the Republicans, Coolidge emerged from the debris untainted and untouched. Ford's presidential balloon had long since been deflated. Democratic hopes of capitalizing on Republican sins, already diminished by Doheny's scornful exposures, were further lessened by the bitter struggle in the June Democratic national convention at New York's Madison Square Garden. There for two weeks McAdoo, with the support of the drys and the covert unsolicited support of the Ku Klux

Klan, fought the wet Catholic governor of New York, Al Smith, to an unforgiving standstill. For the first time a convention's proceedings were broadcast, and over a million Americans clamped on their earphones to listen in on what became a howling, raging mob. Only on the 103rd ballot did the exhausted delegates finally pick as their candidate the conservative lawyer and former ambassador to England, John W. Davis. By contrast the Republican convention was routine and foreordained, nominating Coolidge on the first ballot with Hell 'n Maria Dawes as his running mate, but it was clear by the short shrift given to Lodge and the elders of four years before that the President was slowly remaking the party by taking it away from the Old Guard.

La Follette, misreading the country's mood, thought the time had come to unite farm and labor discontent with dissenters from both parties by reviving the Progressive name in a third party that even if it did not win might throw the election to the House of Representatives where the Insurgents held the balance of power. A Conference for Progressive Political Action nominated him as the Progressive presidential candidate, with Wheeler—who had now bolted the Democratic party—as the candidate for vice president.

Though Democrats and Progressives alike flaunted the issue of Teapot Dome, they could draw no response from the canny Coolidge. During the campaign he spoke briefly of such accomplishments of the Harding administration as the budget and the Arms Limitation Conference, while saying nothing at all about the scandals. His New England-granite calm, exasperating to his opponents, was convincing to the electorate. Harding's cronies, it became clear, had been guilty of unconscionable swindling, but the country did not hold the Republican party or such stalwart stand-bys as Nicholas Murray Butler, Henry Cabot Lodge, William Howard Taft responsible. Republican leaders took to execrating Fall and saying as little as possible about the Marion martyr in his temporary tomb. "Keep Cool with Coolidge" was the slogan.

In spite of the brief recession of 1924, the growing prosperity dimmed any widespread demand for change. Even farm income was rising at last, while farm costs declined. Jokes about Coolidge's silence or his thrift were making him into a folk figure, and the public looked with affection on the unpretentious, unrhetorical man who spoke in aphorisms and who even as President still paid $32 a month rent for his half of a two-family house in Northampton, Massachusetts. Coolidge, with his unassailable personal probity, became by autumn the savior of his party. The campaign itself was a lackluster one, foreordained, with none of the fervor that voting *against* can arouse. Only 51 per cent of those eligible bothered to vote at all. Of the 29,085,000 votes cast, Coolidge received 15,725,000, carrying 38 states with 7,334,000 more votes than Davis. La Follette, with 4,826,000 country-wide votes, managed to carry only Wisconsin. Although the Republicans in Congress did not keep pace with Coolidge, they still managed to offset much of the previous mid-term reaction, gaining 19 seats in the House and 2 in the Senate. In Minnesota the regular Republican Congressman Thomas D. Schall overwhelmed the Farmer-Labor Sen. Magnus Johnson. Supreme Court Justice Oliver Wendell Holmes summed up the country's mood when he wrote to Harold Laski: "While I don't expect anything very astonishing from [Coolidge] I don't want anything very astonishing."

For the first few months after Harding's death, money for the proposed memorial poured into the offices of the Harding Memorial Association. Schoolchildren sent their pennies and nickels; from all parts of the United States came quarters and halves and dollars. Seven hundred thousand dollars arrived before the stream began to trickle off, with the spreading doubts and rumors about the martyr President. A special committee appointed by the Memorial Association had been considering a design by John Russell Pope when a dismayed member pointed out that all the monument needed was a handle to look like a teapot. Pope was never mentioned again. The committee finally settled on a design by the dapper École des Beaux Arts graduate and architect of New York's Hell Gate Bridge, Henry F. Hornbostel. Hornbostel's plan, derived from Roman tombs along the Appian Way, was of a vast hollow drum of Georgia white marble consisting of an exterior colonnade of Tuscan columns surrounding an Ionic peristyle that edged on an open inner court. The Tuscan and Ionic together would add up to 48 columns, symbolic of the 48 states of the Union.

While the committee members were pondering on tombs and the shape of teapots, the Duchess continued to live at White Oaks Farm. On a brief visit to Washington in January she had had an interview with Doctor Charles Moore of the Library of Congress who had written her earlier suggesting that she turn over her husband's papers to the Library. She now told Moore that she had burned them all. To the publisher Frank N. Doubleday she gave the same answer, explaining that she had destroyed such correspondence because she "feared some of it would be misconstrued and would harm his [Harding's] memory."

On September 23 Doctor Sawyer's frail amorous heart gave way and he died in his sanitorium office almost in the Duchess's presence. Shocked by his death, she herself had a premonition of her own. Evalyn McLean, passing through Ohio in her private railroad car in October, stopped over at Marion and persuaded the Duchess to have dinner with her aboard *The Enquirer*. When the older woman left that evening, she told Evalyn somberly that she would never see her again. Evalyn tried to jolly her out of the mood, promising her that she would soon be visiting at Friendship. The Duchess knew better. "This is the end," she said as they parted. A month later she was dead.

The Duchess died on November 21, after an attack of her old kidney ailment and a week's gradual decline. Doctor Carl W. Sawyer, who had inherited the sanitorium from his more martial father, was with her during the last days. Again Marion went into official mourning, but only for half a day. The Reverend Doctor Jesse Swank conducted the service in the Duchess's own Methodist Church, assisted by the Baptist Pastor Landis. Then on a raw and windy afternoon the hearse with the Duchess's coffin moved slowly down the leaf-littered drive of Marion Cemetery to the receiving vault where the iron gates had already been swung open. An honor guard from the 10th United States Infantry, Fort Thomas, Kentucky, presented arms as the coffin was taken from the hearse, Pastor Swank prayed briefly, and a bugler sounded Taps. As the last notes faded, the Columbus Glee Club, standing almost knee-deep in drifted leaves, sang "The End of a Perfect Day." The Duchess was thrust home.

In her will she left the Mount Vernon Avenue house and all its fittings to the Memorial Association. More important for the future status of Harding documents was the will's final clause in which she declared:

> I also give to said the Harding Memorial Association all books, writings, and manuscripts of every description, belonging to me, or which came to me by or under the terms of the will of my late husband, including all his public letters all of which are now in my possession and all other articles, writings and manuscripts and letters of historical interest, . . . it being my intention in making the gifts, herein specified, that all of the same, of every description, shall be forever preserved to the public, for the benefit of posterity.

Not long after the Duchess's death, Hoke Donithen as secretary of the association resumed negotiations with Doubleday, Page for the publication of Harding's remaining papers, and selected Judson Welliver to write an official biography. A young Doubleday editor, John Van Bibber, came to Marion and prepared 5,000 typewritten pages from the letters the Duchess had not destroyed. George Christian objected to the whole project. No one had stood closer to Harding or thought more of his own ability than Christian. He felt that he should be the official biographer, and when he found he could not persuade Donithen he wrote to Daugherty. The harried former Attorney General undoubtedly had reasons of his own for not wanting the administration's papers published. Together with Christian he forced Frelinghuysen to call a meeting of the association in the autumn of 1925. At that meeting Hoover, Donithen, and Frelinghuysen favored the proposed publication, but in the end let

Daugherty and Christian override them. The project was abandoned, and the papers in the association's control ordered sealed until 1975.

Not so easily sealed was Nan Britton. While Harding was alive he had paid her $500 a month through the Willitses for Elizabeth Ann, a sum she and they had lived on and had come to feel their right. She was convinced that Harding must have provided for her, and when she lost that conviction remained equally convinced that he should have. After her annulment there was no more money from Cricken. The pattern of her life kept repeating itself. She would get a job as some sort of assistant secretary, rent an apartment too expensive for her salary and live there with Elizabeth Ann, and sometimes her mother, until ejected by the landlord for falling behind on the rent. Then she would send the child back to Chicago and move to some cheap single room. But within a few months she would have borrowed enough money to be back for Elizabeth Ann. At one point she wrote to Jim Sloan from New York. The next time he was in the city he called on her and she confessed to him then that her daughter was Harding's child. She told him she thought that she was entitled to $50,000 from the Harding estate to provide for Elizabeth Ann. He felt it would be difficult to persuade any of the Hardings to part with their money but promised to take up the matter with some of Harding's friends.

Sloan first talked with Crissinger and Hoke Donithen. When they refused to have anything to do with the affair, he went to see Lasker, Curtis, Weeks, Dawes, and other of Harding's old political cronies. Ten of these, apparently not surprised, agreed to contribute $5,000 each to pay the woman the sum she demanded. Unfortunately they left Hell 'n Maria Dawes to deal with the temperamental Nan. When at his invitation she came to his office, he lived up to his nickname by pacing up and down and calling her a blackmailer, trollop, and whatever else came to his easily indignant mind. In the midst of his tirade she walked out.

Nan's next stop was at Marion where she decided to let Daisy know about Elizabeth Ann and ask her what the Hardings were prepared to do. Daisy had at last married Ralph Lewis and they were living in a new house in Vernon Heights, the area of empty land beyond the cemetery that Lewis with premature optimism was trying to develop. Sitting on the couch in Daisy's living room, with a picture of Harding and Laddie Boy on the table facing her, Nan told her story. Daisy seemed neither surprised, shocked, nor unfriendly. At most she felt concerned about her brother's reputation, and asked Nan to say nothing as yet to the Votaws or anyone else. At the mention of $50,000, she told Nan that she and her husband had invested so heavily in real estate that they were afraid they had nothing more.

Back in New York, where she was now working as assistant to the executive secretary of the Town Hall Club, Nan kept writing to Daisy that she "simply must" have money. Daisy replied with postal orders for $65, $110, and once as much as $400. Over the year she sent $840. The Votaws were neither as understanding nor as generous. When they heard the news from Daisy they preferred not to believe it, and met it with silence. Finally Nan wrote them in exasperation:

> I was quite sincere when I wrote you that I should exhaust every effort to make you people—and that means all the brothers and sisters of Mr. Harding—see your responsibility to Elizabeth Ann, and I mean to do so.

Heber, forced from the ease of his Federal prison post and now secretary of the Seventh-day Adventists' Religious Liberty Association, forwarded the letter to Deac.

In March, 1926, five months after Nan had first told her secret to the Hardings, Daisy sent for her. Nan quit her Town Hall Club job and took the next train for Marion, arriving at the Lewis's house the morning of April 1. She found Daisy still friendly, still apparently understanding, and after lunch the two women washed the dishes together. Then early in the afternoon Deac arrived by car from Columbus in a snow flurry. He shook hands with Nan, but without a smile. Sitting on the edge of the rocker in the living room, a notebook poised on his knee, he spent the next two hours tersely questioning her. When did the alleged "first intimacy" take place? Where and when were the other meetings and trysts? Deac was not interested in sentiments. He wanted exact dates and names, and each answer he wrote in his notebook. Finally he asked her coldly what her idea of a settlement was—that is, if they could ascertain she was telling the truth. She said she wanted what Elizabeth Ann was entitled to as Harding's daughter. "You mean, you mean *all* the Harding estate?" he stammered, almost jumping out of the chair. She told him that all she wanted was a $50,000 trust fund for Elizabeth Ann plus $2,500 for herself to settle her debts. He gave her no set reply.

After their confrontation they had dinner with the Lewises, and Deac hurried away. When Nan left, Daisy kissed her good-by. "If this should get out, Nan," she told her sadly, "they would take the Harding name away from the high school!" In New York, without a job, she as usual found her funds running low. As she had done before, she turned to Jim Sloan who at various times had lent her small sums amounting in all to $327. This time he failed to answer her letter. Desperately she wired Daisy and received in reply another postal order with a note saying that she could spare no more after this "for I, too, have obligations." Deac's eventual answer, as Sloan had predicted, was that the other Hardings felt no obligation to help her.

Through an employment agency Nan at last found a job with the Bible

Corporation of America as secretary to Richard Wightman whom she described as a fatherly, gray-haired man of "ministerial mien" and who was then writing advertising copy for a picture edition of the Bible. Nan soon confided in him about Harding, Elizabeth Ann, and her own difficulties with the Harding family. For all his mien, Wightman had a sharp nose for money and he took her to his lawyer, William F. Ashley, who also happened to be the lawyer for Samuel Gompers. Ashley listened to her story and asked her how long it would take her to write up an outline with approximate dates of her relations with Harding. She said she could do it in two or three hours. That evening on a rented typewriter she began. But, under the spell of her own words, the hours turned to days, and the outline to a tome. Again she quit her job, working uninterruptedly through the long summer days. After typing eight hours a day for three weeks she handed the completed manuscript to Wightman who brought it to Ashley. "Wonderful, wonderful, wonderful!" was the lawyer's comment as he skimmed the many pages. She instructed him to take legal steps at once against Harding's brother and sisters to claim a portion of the estate for Elizabeth Ann.

Before any such legal action got under way, Nan decided to expand her outline to a book. She had long dreamed of becoming a writer yet without knowing what to write about, and now at last she had found her theme— the story of her love affair with Warren Harding, the defense of all the illegitimate children in the world. "Would not Warren Harding approve of my attempting to do something for humanity, for all mothers who longed, as I did, to have their children with them?" she later wrote. "Certainly he would!"

She talked over her prospective book with Wightman, and he grasped the financial possibilities of the project at once. In his eagerness his voice lost its ecclesiastical unction, and he spoke so sharply that she was momentarily shocked. First he gave her a contract to sign. He would advise her and be her sole representative, and they would share all profits on a fifty-fifty basis. Nan borrowed more money and went to Oscawanna-on-the-Hudson where she lived for two months at the Valeria Home and worked on her great project. Then she moved to Saybrooke, Connecticut, to stay with Wightman and his wife Patricia under the name of Lea Benson at the cottage they called their "hunting lodge." Patricia, younger than her husband, was a Greenwich Village artist without art who ran an antique shop and did at least possess a draughty studio. There through the increasingly chill days Nan sat writing at an old kitchen table, warmed by a pair of cylindrical Simplex oil heaters. Evenings she would read over what she had written to the Wightmans and they would comment on it. As she developed her life story she found an emotional release in her writing that spilled over into the four stanzas of a poem she wrote about Harding's eyes. Under the name Ninon Britton and with the title "Her Eyes," she sent it to *The New York Times*. The poem was accepted and appeared in the August 30 edition. As a poem it was the equal of most of the fugitive pieces that appeared each day in the *Times*, and better than many:

> Sometimes her eyes are blue as deep sea-blue,
> And calm as waters stilled at evenfall.
> I see not quite my child in those blue eyes,
> But him whose soul shines wondrously through her.
> Serene and unafraid he was, and knew
> How to dispel the fears in other hearts,
> Meeting an anxious gaze all tranquilly:
> These are her father's eyes.

While the days grew shorter Nan remained at the hunting lodge, her typewriter clicking as she worked away at the kitchen table on her 175,000-word time-bomb. Wightman, sensing the gold beneath her tinsel prose, encouraged her in every way, provided for her, whenever she got restive took her to Saybrooke in his old Essex coach to a moving picture.

Most Presidents have been lucky enough to carry the worst scandals in their life and works to their graves, to be examined later with a measure of historical detachment. But Harding, in his asphalt cocoon, had no such luck. Each year following his death brought its own new sensations, new reminders, new exposures of himself and his administration. In the winter of 1924–1925 Forbes and his friend John W. Thompson of the Thompson-Black Company went on trial in Chicago on charges of bribery and conspiracy. Mortimer in his bitterness at Forbes's seduction of his wife— whatever Kathryn's degree of cooperation—had turned state's evidence. Although Assistant Attorney General Crim had agreed with the defense to protect the reputations of Harding and his family, it was not possible to cover up Carolyn Votaw's merry junketings nor the implications of the trail that led to the White House. On January 30, 1925, a jury found Forbes and Thompson guilty, and three days later they were sentenced to two years' imprisonment and a fine of $10,000, although with various appeals Forbes was able to postpone entering Leavenworth for over a year.

Such cold winds withering Harding's reputation only increased the determination of the Memorial Association's committee members to build a memorial mausoleum that by its very size and grandeur would still criticism. Three-quarters of a million dollars had been raised, and ground was finally broken on April 26. Vice President Dawes came from Washington to lay the cornerstone on Memorial Day. Nan in her anger at the

Hardings was considering coming to Marion with her daughter to interrupt the ceremony, but fortunately for the peace of mind of Christian,
Crissinger, Hoke Donithen, and other local members present she did not.

The marble memorial was not half finished before Daugherty, together
with Harding's Alien Property Custodian, Colonel Miller, was indicted
for conspiracy by a New York grand jury and placed on trial. Daugherty
was charged specifically with having failed to prosecute the fraudulent
transactions in the American Metal Company case. He maintained that he
had nothing to do with the American Metal Company or with the transfer
of its assets to Merton's German firm, that he had done nothing except
sign his name to decisions already made by others. His burning of the
Jess Smith Account No. 3 records, however, and other circumstantial
evidence so told against him that everyone felt he would have to take the
stand on his own behalf. When the time came for him to do so, he sat
stolidly in his chair, his politician's face inscrutable as he scribbled in
pencil on a scrap of paper:

> Having been personal attorney for Warren G. Harding before he was
> Senator from Ohio and while he was Senator, and thereafter until his
> death . . .
>   And having been Attorney General of the United States during the time
> that President Harding served as President . . .
>   I refuse to testify and answer questions put to me, because: The answer
> I might give or make and the testimony I might give might tend to
> incriminate me.

The effect of the former Attorney General's evasion was even more
devastating than Fall's, for it implicated the dead President directly in the
corruption of his associates. Daugherty's counsel, the noted trial lawyer
Max D. Steuer, made matters even worse by stating that if the jurors
knew the real reason why Daugherty had burned the Jess Smith account
records in the Washington Court House bank "they would commend
rather than condemn him." It was syllogistic that if Daugherty had had to
go to such lengths to protect Harding, there was obviously much detrimental to Harding remaining hidden. Although the jury could not agree
on a verdict, its sixty-five-hour deliberation was no vindication for
Daugherty—or for Harding. Daugherty's out-of-court explanation for refusing to testify was that "not a line of testimony had been introduced
against me." [4]

---

[4] Mark Sullivan, writing his sixth volume of *Our Times* nine years later, found
Daugherty's motives as inexplicable then as he had at the time. Sullivan asked him
if a woman could have been involved, and Daugherty, looking him straight in the eye,
replied that if there had been a "woman scrape" in Harding's life he would have
known of it—and he knew of none. "Of one thing I am sure," Sullivan wrote, none
of the money Jess Smith got to facilitate the American Metal case went into
Daugherty's pocket. Chief Justice Taft, too, remained convinced that Daugherty was
personally honest.

Scarcely had the echoes of Daugherty's defiant silence faded when they were succeeded by the reverberations from Samuel Hopkins Adams's novel *Revelry*. Adams as a newspaperman in Washington knew the facts and had picked up most of the gossip about Harding and his associates, material which he wove into the plot of his book in a thin fictional guise. As a novel *Revelry* was jejune, with a slang dialogue never spoken in America before or since, but as an exposé it was overwhelming. Published by Boni & Liveright in November, it sold out three editions in three weeks.

Revelry's characters were easily recognized, even to their transparent names. Willis Markham, President of the United States, a good-natured sloven with a talent for high-flown meaningless oratory, was of course Warren Harding. The Crow's Nest on Blue Street that "slept by day and woke at night," where the opening chapter found Markham and his cronies playing poker, was the House on H Street. Dan Lurcock was Harry Daugherty, even to the cast in his eye. Jeff Sims was Jess Smith; the gay Cholly Madrigal, Charlie Forbes; Duke Forrest, Elias Mortimer; Secretary Andy Gandy, Albert Fall; Sig McBride, Ned McLean; Clairborne, Sinclair; Zoa Farley, Roxy Stinson. The Cabinet members, Sheldon, Covert, and Maxson, were obviously Hughes, Hoover, and Mellon, while Markham's crude niece had much of Carrie Votaw in her. Edith Westervelt, the heroine, was Adams's compliment to Alice Roosevelt Longworth, although Edith's attempts to regenerate Markham would have been fastidiously eschewed by Princess Alice. Adams even included a fictionalized account of Harding in the Red Room shaking Forbes like a rat. At the conclusion Adams had Willis Markham, realizing his betrayal by his friends, commit suicide. It was a shocking conclusion, but rumors had long been circulating in Washington that Harding had not died a natural death. With *Revelry*, that story at last burst into print. The book was made into a play and a moving picture. And worse was to follow.

By January, 1927, Nan in the draughty seclusion of Saybrooke had finished the story of her love life. She had told all, from her schoolgirl infatuation, her first meeting with Harding in New York, to their hotel nights, their love-making in the litter of the White House coat closet, Elizabeth Ann's birth, Harding's death, and Nan's financial impasse with his family. Far from sparing the details, she enlarged on them, with an innocent eroticism unhampered by taste or style. Wightman, who had fastened on the compelling title of *The President's Daughter*, tried the manuscript out on a succession of New York publishers, beginning with Boni & Liveright. That house, still recovering from the heat engendered by *Revelry*, did not fancy being burned again. "Take back your ball of fire," its reader, T. H. Smith, told Wightman. "We're passing up a hundred thousand dollars and we know it!" The editor of *Cosmopolitan* read 20,000 words without lifting his eyes from the pages and said it was the most astounding document he had ever read—but he refused to print it in his family magazine. Alfred Knopf's wife read it and said No for him. Simon & Schuster declined it, as did William Morrow and Albert & Charles Boni.

Since no publisher or editor would risk sponsoring the book, Wightman and Nan decided to follow Smith's advice and publish it privately. Incorporating themselves in April as the Elizabeth Ann League "to sponsor the cause of all so-called illegitimate children," they acquired a backer, Stephen U. Hopkins—who had been a delegate to the 1920 Republican convention—and a commercial printer, the Polygraph Company of America, willing to undertake the job. As Hopkins had advanced over $10,000 for printing expenses, he was made treasurer of the Guild, and under the Guild's name publication was set for June 25. Fifteen days before that date six policemen, accompanied by John S. Sumner of the New York Society for the Suppression of Vice, raided the Polygraph Company's plant and seized the plates and printed sheets as "obscene, lewd, lascivious, and indecent, and in violation of the Penal Law of the State of New York." Next day the news was out, as the *Graphic* announced: *STATESMAN NAMED IN CHARGES BY GIRL.* Through a writ of replevin the Elizabeth Ann Guild was able to overturn a lower magistrate's ruling and regain the plates and sheets, and on June 29 the case was dismissed. *The President's Daughter,* "dedicated with understanding and love to all unwed mothers, and to their innocent children whose fathers are usually not known to the world," made its unheralded appearance a few days later. Ignored by the reviewers, declined by bookstores, it advanced by whispers. Yet it did advance. The silence was finally broken by Mencken with a two-column article in the Baltimore *Sun*. Then the rush began. Brentano's reversed itself and ordered 10 copies, then 50, then 100, then 1,000. By September *The President's Daughter* was on all the best-seller lists. Belatedly the other reviewers took it up. Harry Hansen in his *New York World* column "The First Reader" called it "a highly romantic and thrilling story of a love affair with . . . the ring of truth in it." Heywood Broun considered it "often absorbingly interesting." The October sales kept climbing. Even the aged and deaf Thomas Edison managed to hear of it. Its artless authenticity seemed accentuated by badly reproduced photographs of Elizabeth Ann, Nan herself, and Harding and his sisters. Copies circulated so hectically in official Washington that finally the Democratic Senator from Arkansas, John N. Tillman, felt called on to denounce the book on the floor of the Senate as "obscene, filthy, and lewd, . . . a blast from hell," and added that he did not believe Nan wrote it but "some fellow of the baser sort for money." She replied by offering a $5,000 reward if he could prove she did not.

After the suicides of Jess Smith and Cramer, the conviction of Forbes and Miller, the disgrace of three Cabinet members, the Teapot Dome inquiries, Roxy Stinson's vengeful testimony and the lurid revelations of Gaston Means, after Mortimer and Votaw and Burns and the parade of other dubious figures, and now after Nan Britton's confessions, Harding's memory—as Mark Sullivan wrote—became almost a rag in the gutter. In the prideful days of 1921 the law school of Ohio Northern University—numbering among its graduates Senators Fess and Willis—had become the Warren G. Harding College of Law, the name cut in a large stone slab over the library entrance. Gradually the name was removed from the official stationery and from the university catalogue until finally it was excised from the stone.[5] It was a name that Republicans from Coolidge down would have liked to excise from the party. What seemed peripheral corroboration of the scandals continued to crop up: the news that the Duchess had burned her husband's private papers; the airing of long-current rumors by a retired New York banker, Frank A. Vanderlip, that the Marion *Star* had been sold for twice its value to two men of no financial standing. In a Lincoln Day speech to a Rotary Club, Vanderlip said that every Washington correspondent knew this but "no one wants to look under the edge of a shroud." Though he was later forced to admit he had no factual basis for his statement, although he was later sued for damages by Brush and Moore, the impression persisted that the sale had been a means of transferring dubious undercover money to Harding.

In the summer of 1927 the vast marble cylinder of the Harding Memorial was completed,[6] and four days before Christmas at a private service the bodies of Harding and the Duchess were interred in the central grass plot, each under a two-ton slab of Labrador granite. Yet no dedication followed. According to the etiquette of such things no one less than a living President could fittingly dedicate the tomb of a President, but at any mention of it Coolidge—according to Herbert Hoover—"expressed a furious distaste." The seasons passed. Tourists came and went and bought souvenir postcards. The tomb remained undedicated.

While *The President's Daughter* held its place on the best-seller lists, Teapot Dome continued to spout its own scandal. In the government's civil suit against Doheny, Pomerene and Roberts had succeeded in voiding the Elk Hills contract because of the fraud implied in the $100,000 given to Fall. Their first suit against the Teapot Dome lease ended in failure, and although they were able to show that Fall had received $233,500 in Liberty Bonds from the Continental Trading Company of Canada they were not as yet able to trace them through the company to Sinclair. The decision of the lower court was at last reversed by the

[5] A trustee of the university offered $50,000 to the Law School "if that name comes off."

[6] Because of the falling off in donations, the Memorial Association committee reduced the number of columns to 46.

United States Circuit Court of Appeals which held that the Teapot Dome
lease was invalid, having been made with collusion and fraud. Both
decisions were upheld by the United States Supreme Court, Fall being
branded by Justice Butler as a faithless public servant "willing to conspire
against the public interest."

As early as June, 1924, Fall, Sinclair, Doheny, and Doheny's son had
been indicted in the District of Columbia Supreme Court, Fall and
Doheny charged with conspiracy, Fall and Sinclair charged with conspiracy, and Fall and the two Dohenys charged with bribery. After the
first indictments were dismissed on a technicality, new indictments were
returned a year later. In November, 1926, Fall and Doheny faced a jury
for the first time: Fall frail, trembling, and silent; Doheny pallid and with
his arm in a sling because of an infection, but cocky. That it would be a
flamboyant trial was insured by the dapper presence of Doheny's defense
lawyer, Frank J. Hogan, a rhetorical dandy who found himself at times so
carried away by his own rhetoric that he broke down. To him the crucifixion of his client could only be compared to the Crucifixion of nineteen
hundred years ago, and he summoned Harding as a silent character
witness from "his sacred tomb in Marion." Properly impressed, the jury
after an all-night debate found the two men not guilty. Fall, suffering
from tuberculosis, went back to the isolation of New Mexico. The more
robust Doheny, on returning to California, was given a hero's welcome at
a huge testimonial dinner attended by the mayors of Los Angeles and
San Francisco.

In March, 1927, Sinclair was tried for contempt of the Senate for his
refusal to answer Walsh's questions. He was quickly found guilty and
sentenced to three months in jail—the first sentence to be imposed on any
of the oil lease defendants. Seven months later he and Fall went on trial
in Washington for criminal conspiracy. Sinclair, though nervous, appeared
jaunty, "a fashion plate in blue"—if anyone who so much resembled a
bullfrog could be so described. Fall, still wearing his black string tie and
broad-brimmed black Western hat, looked old and ill and sad. For all the
skills of his lawyers, Sinclair believed in leaving nothing to chance. As
soon as he learned that the jury would not be locked up, he had the
William J. Burns Agency send him 12 operatives plus a captain and
lieutenant to shadow the jurors and probe their weaknesses.

A garrulous juror of shady background, Edward J. Kidwell, boasted in
a speakeasy that he expected to get $150,000 to $200,000 for deadlocking
the case, and his boasting was passed on to the editor of the Washington
Herald. Then one of Burns's agents rebelled at being ordered to frame
another juror and took his story to Roberts who had already come to learn
of some of the Burns Agency's activities. When Sinclair's jury-tampering
efforts were then brought to the attention of the judge, he declared a

mistrial, and, as the news exploded, new overtones were added to the sensationalism of Teapot Dome. Sinclair and Burns now found themselves on trial for criminal contempt. Burns, who had been replaced as head of his agency by his son, maintained he knew nothing about any jury shadowing. He was sentenced to a nominal fifteen days. Sinclair, in spite of his 15 voluble lawyers, was found guilty and received a sentence of six months in the Washington Asylum and Jail.

Yet, even after four years of investigations and civil and criminal trials, there were still gaps in the story of the oil leases. To complete these, to get to the murky bottom of Teapot Dome, Walsh was authorized to re-convene his committee in January, 1928. As his first witness he summoned Fall's son-in-law, Mahlon Everhart. Since the three-year statute of limita-tions had expired, Everhart for all his reluctance to testify could no longer plead self-incrimination. Either he must now speak or find himself prosecuted for contempt of the Senate. Faced with this dilemma, he told the story of his conveying the Liberty Bonds from Sinclair to Fall, although he still maintained that Sinclair had not been bribing Fall but had actually bought a third interest in the ranch, intending to turn it into a club. He could produce no documents of any kind to prove Sinclair's ownership.

Walsh was now able to establish the links between the Canadian-incorporated Continental Trading Company, Sinclair, and Fall. That defunct company had remained for a long time a mystery within a mystery. Although its president was a Toronto lawyer, H. S. Oster, the company had been organized in New York by Col. A. E. Humphreys of Humphreys Mexico and Humphreys Texas Oil Company; Harry M. Blackmer, chairman of the board of Midwest Refining Company; James E. O'Neil, president of the Prairie Oil and Gas Company; Col. Robert W. Stewart, president of Standard Oil of Indiana; and Sinclair. Once orga-nized, the Continental Company contracted for 33,333,333 barrels of crude oil at $1.50 a barrel from Humphreys's companies and on the same day sold the oil to Sinclair and to Prairie Oil and Gas for $1.75 a barrel. Stripped of its mystery, the trading company was an ingeniously simple device by the heads of companies to rob their stockholders. In a year the Continental Company had accumulated over $2 million which was then invested in Liberty Bonds and distributed to the five principals. When the company dissolved in 1924, all records and papers were destroyed. Only the serial numbers of the Liberty Bonds remained on file beyond the reach of destruction, and it was finally through them that Walsh's investi-gators were able to determine that the bonds given by Sinclair to Everhart were part of the $757,000 in bonds that he had received as his share of the Continental Trading Company.

After Walsh had traced an additional $26,000 worth of Sinclair bonds to the Republican National Committee, he subpoenaed former National Chairman Will Hays for an explanation. Once the Czar of the Moving Pictures had laid aside his Hollywood absolution to appear before the committee, he showed himself a bumbling commoner. Squirming and wriggling like an outraged rabbit, sometimes so rattled that he jumped out of his seat, he was forced to admit that even as the Teapot Dome scandal was beginning to break he had appealed to his good friend Harry Sinclair to help make up the $1,200,000 Republican campaign deficit. Sinclair had "loaned" him $260,000 in Liberty Bonds, of which $100,000 had been paid back. Following the old political adage of not looking a campaign contribution in the mouth, Hays had peddled these "hot" bonds to various prominent Republicans. He had sent $50,000 worth to Mellon who had returned them saying that he preferred to contribute an equal sum from his own funds. The ascetic financier, too, was summoned to the hearings and left not wholly unscathed after admitting that although he knew the bonds were from Sinclair he had never felt called on to say anything to the committee about it. "A fence," Sen. T. H. Caraway of Arkansas afterward summed up Hays, who "knew that certain goods were stolen goods and was trying to help the thief find a market for them; the Secretary of the Treasury, although he declined to aid in the marketing of the goods . . . handed them back so that the fence could find somebody else who would act for him."

Sinclair went on trial in April for conspiracy to defraud the government. Since Fall's doctors reported him a dying man, his trial was severed from Sinclair's. The defense was now ready to admit that Sinclair had given Fall Liberty Bonds and cash, but maintained this was for the third interest in the Three Rivers ranch. Washington juries had long shown a notorious hostility to government cases, and Sinclair's jury was no exception. After debating an hour and fifty-six minutes the jurors found him innocent, to the dumbfounded amazement of Roberts and Pomerene.

Walsh's renewed hearings ended in May without arousing any of the fevered interest and indignation of four years earlier. The country was not in a crusading mood. As far as Teapot Dome went, the oil leases had been canceled; the residue had become somewhat boring, out of date now like the narrow golf knickers Harding had worn and that had long been replaced by plus-fours. With the disgruntled exception of the farmers, Americans found 1928 their most profitable year, the peak year in industry, with no visible unemployment, a booming stock market, and few signs of gloom, domestic or foreign. Of more concern than old scandals was the long waiting list for the Model-A Ford. The incandescent sunset of the Coolidge prosperity seemed a new dawn. Reflecting its brightness, the 1928 presidential election resulted in another Republican landslide, Hoover defeating Al Smith by 6½ million votes. With prosperity plus

Smith's wetness, his Catholicism and the dowdiness of his wife as the chief issues, Hoover won by 444 electoral votes to Smith's 87, taking Florida, Texas, North Carolina, and even Virginia from the less-than-solid South.

So deliberate was the course of justice, that Coolidge had left the White House by the time Sinclair arrived in his limousine on May 9, 1929, to begin his concurrent sentences in the gloomy seventy-year-old Washington Asylum and Jail. Assigned to the jail's pharmacy, he served his full term, being released after seven-and-a-half months with the usual time off for good behavior. On the same day that he had gone to jail, Fall's Three Rivers ranch was bid in at a sheriff's sale by Doheny for $168,250. In October Fall went on trial in the District of Columbia Supreme Court for accepting a bribe from Doheny. Confident of saving his friend as he had himself, Doheny dispatched the flamboyant Hogan to be Fall's lawyer. Hogan staged the scene with his customary pathos. Haggard and ashen pale, Fall appeared in the courtroom in a wheel chair, attended by a nurse and a doctor. As he was being helped into the witness chair he gasped for breath, and the nurse wrapped him in a blue automobile robe. His ill-health, though staged, was no contrivance, for at the first day of the trial he collapsed suddenly with a hemorrhage. Three court-appointed physicians reported that he was in no condition to continue, and the prosecution lawyers—not wishing to appear persecutors—asked for a postponement. Fall insisted that the trial go on. Hogan informed the court that his client was entitled to "vindication before he passes into the Great Beyond."

In addition to sending Hogan to Washington, Doheny came in person to testify for his old friend. Eight months before, his son Edward—who had carried the little black bag from his father to Fall—had been shot and killed by his insane secretary. When the boy's name was mentioned, the old man broke down. Hogan did his best to wring the jurors' hearts, even providing the prop of Fall's small granddaughter as he begged them to send a broken old rancher back to the sunshine of New Mexico. But for once Hogan's well-rehearsed appeal to the heart failed. After debating overnight the jury found Fall guilty, though recommending mercy. At the verdict Fall slumped in his chair. His wife and daughter burst into tears, as did Doheny who was heard to mutter "that damned court." Although the maximum penalty was three years, in consideration of Fall's health and the jury's recommendation, the judge sentenced him to a year in jail and a $100,000 fine.

In March, 1930, in the same courtroom and before the same judge, Doheny went on trial for giving Fall the same bribe. Hogan again laid on the pathos, presenting a bent, white-haired man who had done nothing more than help the friend of his young manhood. Step by step he led Doheny through the stages of his life, Doheny again shedding tears when his son was mentioned. Enlarging on Doheny's patriotic willingness to build the storage tanks at Pearl Harbor, Hogan appealed to the jurors in conclusion: "Ned Doheny says to you from the grave, that ... can you believe that a man who a few years before had offered his only son to his country had fallen so low that he took him, the expected solace of his old age, and made him an instrument of bribery? It isn't human to believe it."

The jury was human. Though Fall had been found guilty of taking the bribe, the jurors found Doheny not guilty of giving it. Cheers and applause greeted the verdict. Taking his wife's arm, Doheny walked to the jury box and thanked each juror personally.

For over a year after Fall's sentencing his lawyers did their ingenious best to keep him out of jail. But after the Court of Appeals had upheld the conviction and the Supreme Court refused to hear the case, the only further recourse was an appeal to the President to remit the sentence because of Fall's health. Hoover, as he grimly watched the blast of the Depression rip his Coolidge-inherited prosperity to tatters, was in no mood to be lenient to his old Cabinet associate even when petitioned by all the members of the New Mexico Legislature. Although doctors claimed that Fall was suffering from arteriosclerosis, myocarditis, arthritis, tuberculosis, and pleurisy, nevertheless on July 18, 1931, he was taken in an ambulance from his Three Rivers ranch to serve his sentence at the State Penitentiary in Santa Fé.

During the same year that Fall's lawyers were making their various appeals, a book appeared, *The Strange Death of President Harding*—purportedly compiled from the diaries of Gaston Means—that, in the lurid light it cast on the dead President, put all other such books in the shade. Without benefit of publisher it rapidly reached the top of the best-seller list. Those who had thought that Harding's reputation could sink no lower, that the scandals of his life had played themselves out, had not reckoned on Gaston's ingenuity. His chief and most shocking assertion, told with all the plausible piling up of detail of his fertile mind, was that the Duchess had poisoned her husband in San Francisco to prevent his being impeached and to save his honor through death. Gaston also claimed that Cramer and Smith had been murdered, and that there was a sinister mystery in the deaths of King, Doctor Sawyer, and even Colonel Felder who had died suddenly in Savannah after his conviction.

Gaston, according to his own story, had been an intimate of the White House, the Duchess's trusted private investigator. On her orders he had trailed Nan Britton and had even broken into the Willits's apartment in Chicago to filch her private diaries and the letters written to her by

Harding. The diaries, he related, were tied with pink silk corset ribbon. By such descriptive touches did Gaston convince. He told of terrible scenes at the White House with Harding shaking his fist in the Duchess's face and shouting at her: "I never loved *you*. You want the truth. You ran me down!" Furthermore, he claimed that he, Jess, Daugherty, Miller, and Felder had been responsible for all the "stern undercover work" of the administration, and he boasted that he had collected over half a million dollars for Jess with whom he had worked intimately. Actually Means had not known Daugherty and had never been inside the White House, but what he said sounded all too true to willing ears.

While Gaston was serving time in Atlanta he had come in contact with May Dixon Thacker, the wife of a Southern evangelist and sister of the Reverend Doctor Thomas Dixon whose bombastic novel *The Klansman* had been made into the moving picture's first epic, *The Birth of a Nation*. Mrs. Thacker herself contributed to *True Confessions*. On Gaston's release in 1928 she wrote him that when he was ready to tell his story to the world she would help him. Gaston, short of money, was indeed ready. Day after day he spent dictating to her, letting his imagination range at will, using Nan's book and what he remembered of Roxy Stinson's testimony and his own Bureau of Investigation experiences as his starting point. Evenings he and his wife would laugh about the tall stories he had invented during the day.

Gaston's first thought was to have the Elizabeth Ann Guild publish his book, but Nan refused to have anything to do with him or it. He did manage to entice Nan's advertising manager, Maurice Fryefield away, and the two of them formed the Guild Publishing Company and published the book on their own. The results exceeded even Gaston's over-buoyant expectations. Americans had acquired a will to believe anything derogatory about Harding.[7] Their will to believe brought him in a small fortune. Since for all his tall talk he was never able to produce his diaries or any other documentation for Mrs. Thacker's doubtful eyes, she, the following year, repudiated the book she had written "in the spirit of righteous exaltation." Her repudiation merely spurred its sales.

As *The Strange Death of President Harding* continued to pass from hand to hand, the tomb in Marion was becoming another national scandal following an article in *Plain Talk* by Robert S. Harper, a young editor on the staff of the *Ohio State Journal*. Harper pointed out angrily that the

[7] Gaston's book is chiefly responsible for the vague but durable conviction that Harding did not die a natural death. Frederick Lewis Allen in his *Only Yesterday* felt that both the suicide theory and the Means story were plausible. Oswald Garrison Villard thought that there was foul play and suspected more in Doctor Sawyer's death. James Truslow Adams wrote in *The March of Democracy* that the mystery of Harding's death had never been cleared up.

dedication had originally been announced for July 4, 1927. Yet three more Glorious Fourths had passed, a presidential election had come and gone, and still the great marble drum remained undedicated. He let it be known that Hoover had even suggested to the members of the Harding Memorial Association's executive committee—now narrowed to residents of Marion —that they arrange a dedication without the presence of the President. Secretary Mellon went even further. He urged Frelinghuysen as the association's president to drop all plans for a dedication and instead hold a simple annual memorial service. "A bunch of cowards," Committee Chairman Hoke Donithen retorted from Marion.

The *Plain Talk* article caused so much stir, the members of the association's executive committee brought so much pressure to bear, that Hoover in the dismal spring of 1931 finally agreed to dedicate the "haunted tomb" on June 16. As the Depression spread, he, too, seemed a fading leader, his own repute almost as diminished as Harding's, his name a term of opprobrium applied by the unemployed to their shanty towns. Whether he was aware of the irony or not, he found himself, a discredited President, extolling an even more discredited President.

It was an embattled group of Marionites and Republicans who gathered at the stately circle of marble columns on that summer afternoon. Former Senator Frelinghuysen, presiding feebly over the exercises, presented the monument to the Harding Memorial Association. Former President Coolidge, forced by Hoover's example to swallow his own distaste, accepted the monument for the association as its honorary president. Coolidge said what he had to say, cannily, neither more nor less. Hoover in his dedicatory address could have confined himself to Harding's sunny ways, his love of country and faith in democracy. But his Quaker conscience could not let the day pass in platitudes. Directly behind him, among the trustees of the association, sat Harding's beady-eyed Attorney General, neither bloody nor bowed. When Hoover spoke of Harding, it seemed to many present as if he were addressing Daugherty:

> Here was a man [he said] whose soul was seared by a great disillusionment. We saw him gradually weaken not only from physical exhaustion but also from mental anxiety. Warren Harding had a dim realization that he had been betrayed by a few of the men whom he had trusted, by men whom he had believed were his devoted friends. It was later proved in the courts of the land that these men had betrayed not only the friendship and trust of their staunch and loyal friend but they had betrayed their country. That was the tragedy of the life of Warren Harding.

Daugherty's own soul was so seared by Hoover's words that he was unaware of "The End of a Perfect Day," sung by the Columbus Glee Club, or of the Reverend Doctor Jesse Swank's benediction. Stirred at last to fulfill his old promise (or threat) of writing his memoirs, assisted in his prose niceties by Mrs. Thacker's brother, the Reverend Doctor Thomas Dixon, he now set out to compose his own answer to detractors, a book that would show him in the white light of Ohio truth as the savior of his country as well as the victim of the Red menace, the friend, guide, confidant, and protector of that President whom future generations would come to see as "a modern Lincoln." [8]

Fall survived his sentence in spite of his health and was released from the penitentiary in May, 1932, just six months before the stiff-collared Hoover was overwhelmed in his bid for re-election. Fall's release marked the end of the active scandals of the Harding era. With Hoover's retirement the twenties were no longer part of a past that intruded into the living present. To the New Deal-dominated thirties they soon seemed as remote as the 1914 world had seemed to the Harding-Coolidge era. New problems, new threats, new economics, new theories of government had replaced the hectic glow of Coolidge's sunset with the gray sunrise of the early Roosevelt years.

There was an echo of the Harding past when Gaston Means's name again flashed across the country in connection with the kidnaping of the Lindbergh baby in March, 1932. Knowing no more of the case than any other newspaper reader, but perennially short of money, Gaston went to Evalyn McLean, persuading her that he had made contact with the kidnapers and that for $100,000 ransom plus a few thousand dollars for his own expenses he was the one person who could produce the missing child. She in her gullible good will believed his involved story and gave him the money.[9] Only gradually did she realize that Gaston had no underworld contacts except in his imagination nor any knowledge of the baby's whereabouts, and that she had been swindled. Gaston went on trial for larceny, all injured innocence but refusing to testify because his "life could be snuffed out." He was found guilty and sent to the penitentiary at Leavenworth, Kansas, for fifteen years where—still conniving—he died of a heart attack six years later. The $100,000 was never recovered.

The other characters in the Harding melodrama, even Nan Britton, were fading into their anonymous backgrounds. While the money flowed in

[8] Daugherty's ghost-written book, *The Inside Story of the Harding Tragedy*, was published in 1932.
[9] Since Ned's humiliating appearance before the Teapot Dome Committee, the McLeans had been living in—for them—quiet retirement. By the time of the Lindbergh kidnaping Ned was confined permanently in the Sheppard-Pratt Hospital, a private mental institution in Towson, Maryland. Hostile to all outsiders, he insisted that he was not Ned McLean, and went into a rage whenever he was addressed by his right name.

from *The President's Daughter*, Nan had had a staff of 18 at her Elizabeth Ann League which she envisioned as a clearinghouse for girls "in trouble." She put most of her royalties into the league, Wightman put his into his pocket. But when, as eventually with all best sellers, sales from the book began to taper off, Nan and Wightman parted company. Wightman's wife Patricia had already sued for separation, claiming that Nan had disrupted her home and that her husband was the real author of the book. As her funds diminished, Nan, for all her sense of mission, was forced to cut down on her staff and finally to dissolve the league. Spurred by the hope of another literary success, she started a novel, but could not go on with it. She attempted to turn *The President's Daughter* into a play and, when she could not manage this, began negotiations with a Hollywood agent for a "picturization" of her book. Czar Hays squelched any idea of a moving picture.[10]

While *The President's Daughter* still sustained its unsponsored place on the best-seller list, Joseph deBarthe, a former editor of the Buffalo *Times* with a self-conferred doctor's degree, arrived in Marion with the announced purpose of writing a confutation of Nan's book. Staying at the dilapidated Hotel Marion, he ran up an extended bill and then ran out of money. Charles A. Klunk, the owner and manager of the hotel, a sporting type willing to gamble that such a book would be another best seller, offered to keep on boarding deBarthe in return for a half share in the profits.

Shortly after completing his manuscript deBarthe died from a fall down the hotel's main staircase—presumably while drunk. When Klunk was unable to find a publisher for the manuscript, he had it printed at his own expense, convinced that he had inherited a small gold mine. It was published anonymously as *The Answer*, printed on only one side of each page to pad it out. Nowhere did it get reviewed, and except for the few copies retailed in the hotel lobby it did not sell. DeBarthe's thesis, his answer acquired from the Harding family, was that Harding had been sterile since an early attack of mumps and hence incapable of siring a child. As for Nan Britton, she was described as a blackmailer, a "common woman" of loose morals. On reading *The Answer* Nan sued Klunk for $100,000 damages.

Klunk's lawyer, Judge Mouser, did his best to discredit Nan, but all his investigations merely seemed to confirm her story. Two of his lawyer friends on going to New York found Harding's recognizable handwriting in the register of the Hotel Imperial where he had first signed in with Nan as Hardwick. By bribing the clerk they managed to steal that page from the register. Nowhere could they find that she had lied. Nan's case against

[10] "I had no notion that the trunk of the elephant swept so far," a Hollywood lawyer wrote her.

Klunk was tried in the Toledo Federal Court in October, 1931. As a lawyer Judge Mouser was well aware that *The Answer* was libelous, but he also knew his Ohio juries, and he instructed his fellow defense lawyers accordingly:

> We won't waste much time on cross-examination of Nan Britton, and we won't put on much of a defense—just enough to prevent a directed verdict against us. When we go to the jury, we will divide the time, with one of you talking just a little about the case. Then I'll come on.
>
> I'm going to walk up and down in front of that jury box, and tell them how I met Harding when I first came to Marion to practice law. I'll tell them how we both lived on East Church Street, and how I used to meet him every morning as we walked down to work, and how he was always full of ideas about things that would be good for Marion, and how he would ask me for advice as to what he could say in his paper to put over those ideas.
>
> Then I'll wind up by mentioning the scandals of his administration, and tell them I never heard anybody even hint that Warren G. Harding personally profited from any wrongdoing. I'll sort of bear down on repeating that he was a fine and good man, betrayed by his associates in all walks of life. I probably won't even mention this Britton girl's name, but the jury will get the point, and do their duty, unless I have lost my touch. Remind me to wear a wrinkled suit, and to have some cigar ashes spilled on my vest.

The jury, after being out an hour and casting three ballots, brought in a verdict in favor of Klunk.

A few months later Nan produced her second and final book, *Honesty or Politics,* an account of her money struggles with the Harding family, her writing of *The President's Daughter,* and her difficulties in getting it published. Lacking either novelty or any coat-closet titillations, the new book was not a success. Discouraged by these twin failures, Nan moved with Elizabeth Ann to Evanston, Illinois, where she found a job with an employment agency, the Davis Personnel Service. Later she and the proprietor, Gertrude Davis, became partners and shared an Evanston apartment at 618½ Sheridan Road. In 1938 Elizabeth Ann graduated from Sullivan High School as Elizabeth Ann Harding, and in her application for Lake Forest College gave her father's name as Warren G. Harding and his birthplace as Blooming Grove. Instead of entering Lake Forest in September, however, she married Henry Blaesing, an office building manager.

After her daughter's marriage Nan started another novel, but her literary impulse had run dry and she was unable to finish it. Over the years she paid occasional fleeting visits to Marion. To the indignation of aging Harding partisans she openly attended her fortieth high-school class reunion, even visiting the Mount Vernon Avenue house, open daily as a museum.

The decades brought their attrition to the Hardings as well as to the town. Tryon, warming his old bones in California, died there in November, 1928, and his widow returned to Marion. Deac, still anticipating the Seventh-day Adventist resurrection, fell into his last sleep on January 18, 1934. Daisy died in March, 1935. Three years after her death Ralph Lewis married the widowed Hazel Kling Longshore, Amos Kling's granddaughter and the Duchess's niece.

On the Phillips's leisurely return from their Republican-sponsored trip abroad Jim had sold out his interest in the store to the Uhlers. Carrie persuaded him to turn over his property and the Gospel Hill house to her. They continued to live in his retirement with the extravagance to which she was accustomed. Then in the Depression, when he had lost most of his money, she turned him out of the house to which he had once brought her. He died of tuberculosis in 1939. During those Depression years, a pathetic wandering figure along Main Street, he lived in a back room of the Hotel Marion. Shortly before he died he asked the editor of the *Star* to give him credit in his obituary for his civic work and booster efforts of so long ago when he was a rising young merchant.

Carrie, still a striking-looking woman, became increasingly eccentric after his death. She moved from Gospel Hill to a house on Mount Vernon Avenue about a mile from Harding's old home. Alienated from Marion, estranged from her daughter, she lived the life of a recluse, trying to supplement her thin income by raising German shepherd dogs and getting into difficulties with the Board of Health because of the stench of her back-yard kennel.

As World War II approached, interest in Harding had so faded that historians passed him by. Toward the end of Franklin Roosevelt's second term, Samuel Hopkins Adams—who since *Revelry* had kept up a quixotic interest in Harding—published his *Incredible Era,* a lively journalistic account of Harding, his administration scandals, and the personalities involved. Now that the receding era could be viewed in perspective, few contemporary feelings remained to be ruffled. Adams might stir Daugherty in his Columbus retirement to momentary indignation, but such indignation scarcely extended beyond the boundaries of Ohio. There was more durable indignation over Adams's book in Marion, among the small dominant group centered in the Marion Club and the now-inbred Harding Memorial Association. Adams, in addition to his chapters on the later scandals, gave the first extended account of Harding's shadowed ancestry while making a wider public familiar with the relatively unfamiliar Chancellor book. His open-minded conclusion that "if Negro blood there were in his [Harding's] line, he honorably and courageously lived down the handicap" was something the Memorial Association and the Harding relatives wished emphatically not to have mentioned. Even after the Post

Office Department had tactlessly issued 1½ cent stamps with Harding's portrait in black, and later in brown, the Hardings said nothing. On this subject they preferred silence.

Another who regretted any renewed mention of the Chancellor book was Chancellor himself. In 1927 he had quietly come back to Ohio from Canada and resumed teaching at the University of Cincinnati. Intent on a peaceful old age, he now denied to Mark Sullivan and others that he had ever had anything to do with the book ascribed to him.

> I did not write this book [he wrote to Adams in 1939]. I did not authorize its publication. . . . I denied then and I now deny all connection with the affair. I do not know who issued the book. I have no copy of it. Nor do I even know or even try to guess who got up these schemes to involve me. As a matter of fact, I despise all race hatreds and all such political trickeries.

Two decades of silence followed the publication of *The Incredible Era*, decades in which the Harding administration was recalled chiefly by back-page obituaries. Ned McLean, still confined to the closed ward of his mental hospital, died in July, 1941, at the age of fifty-five. Daugherty followed him three months later. The former Attorney General had divided his last years between Columbus and Palm Beach, a serene elder statesman and political philosopher, writing voluminous letters defending his official past, his serenity undisturbed even by the failure of his brother's bank and Mally's subsequent sentencing to ten years in the Ohio State Penitentiary for embezzlement, false entries, concealing loans, and the deception of bank examiners.[11] Fortunately for the serenity of Mally's old age, the conviction was reversed by an understanding Ohio judge of the Court of Appeals.

At the end of 1944, as the American and British forces were preparing for their D-Day assault on Nazi-held Europe, Fall died obscurely in a Santa Fé hospital. Three years after his release from prison the Doheny interests had foreclosed the mortgage on Three Rivers and evicted him from his ranch.[12] He and his wife moved to a shabby house they still owned in El Paso where Emma supported the two of them by running a lunchroom and by canning fruits and vegetables at home. She died the year before he did.

Evalyn Walsh McLean survived World War II, a fabulous aging hostess,

---

[11] Mally had become president of the Ohio State Bank, a consolidation of his Midland National Bank with the Commercial Bank and the Fayette County Bank. The new bank closed after a run on it in May, 1930, and never opened again.

[12] Doheny, bedridden, half insane, and with only a few months to live when the foreclosure took place, undoubtedly had no idea what his subordinates were doing to his old friend.

still wearing the Hope Diamond, entertaining soldiers during the war in a smaller edition of Friendship. Her twenty-year-old daughter, named after her, married Sen. Robert Reynolds of North Carolina, a parody of a Southern statesman, fifty-seven years old and already married four times. Five years later, in 1946, the daughter committed suicide. Evalyn herself died the following year.

Carrie Phillips lived on until 1960, but by 1956 she was penniless and had deteriorated so far that Probate Court Judge Edward J. Ruzzo appointed a Marion lawyer, Don Williamson, as her guardian. The house, decayed and filthy from a dozen unhousebroken dogs, Williamson took over and sold. He placed Carrie in the Willetts Home for the Elderly. Her possessions he catalogued and auctioned off. There had been old rumors that she had used much of her Harding money to buy diamonds and jewelry. Williamson searched all over the house without discovering any, but in his searches he did find a locked closet and inside the locked closet a locked box. It was this box that contained the letters from Harding to his "beloved and adored" Carrie.

Williamson wrote several times to Carrie's daughter Isabelle, who ran a small antique shop in Genoa City, Wisconsin, but he never received a reply. After the money from the auction and the house was exhausted, Carrie lived on state old-age assistance from the Department of Public Welfare.

A generation is said to encompass thirty years, and as the United States moved through the post-World-War-II expanding fifties, interest quickened in that thirty-year-earlier postwar generation. Just as the twenties had looked back nostalgically to what it called the Gay Nineties, so the fifties looked back to the Harding-Coolidge era, labeled with some glibness the Roaring Twenties. Dance tunes and dances like the Charleston, flapper fashions, and F. Scott Fitzgerald were rediscovered. But beyond the musical-comedy aspect of this revival lay a very real problem of scholarship. No adequate biography of Harding had ever been written, as historians were beginning to observe. Even the studies of his times were basically exposures. What was Harding actually like as a man? What were his accomplishments, if any? What was it like to live in the twenties?

The difficulty in finding the answers to such questions lay in the documentation. Outside Marion it was scanty and scattered. Since 1934 the Harding papers in Marion were controlled by the bald, deaf, and increasingly crotchety Doctor Sawyer who refused to make them available to anyone.

In 1929 workmen making repairs in the basement of the White House had found 39 letter-file cases of Harding correspondence. Doctor J. Franklin Jameson, head of the manuscript division of the Library of Congress, was most anxious to acquire this vast store for the Library's meager Harding collection.[13] After examining the cases hurriedly, he wrote to Charles Schaffner, the administrator of Harding's and the Duchess's estates. On Sawyer's advice, Schaffner by return mail ordered the papers sent at once to Marion. When Jameson, mindful of earlier holocausts, tried to delay, Schaffner wrote directly to President Hoover demanding their return under the terms of the Duchess's will. Two months after the file cases were discovered, to Jameson's chagrin they ended up in Marion in the closed custody of the Memorial Association.

Harding's former Cabinet members, President Hoover, New, and Work, agreed with Jameson, as did the retired Frelinghuysen, that the Library of Congress was the logical depository for all the Harding papers. Jameson visited Hoke Donithen in whose office the papers were being stored. Donithen, although sympathetic, pointed out the difficulty in bringing the trustees to any formal action. He also revealed that there was "a trunk or box of other papers" being held in the Duchess's bank.

In 1934, on a second visit to Marion, Jameson found that all the Harding papers had been removed to the basement of the Mount Vernon Avenue house, but this time Donithen showed himself willing to return them to Washington. The two men drew up an agreement according to which the papers, while remaining the property of the association, would go to the Library of Congress where they could be seen only with permission of the association's executive committee until twenty years after Harding's death. Before the transfer could take place, Donithen died. Then later that year George Christian, who had come to know Jameson, turned over to the Library seven large and three small wooden boxes of Harding papers that he had been keeping—eight boxes containing presidential campaign and official correspondence; the other two personal and private papers. Christian followed these up with 18 letter-file cases relating to Harding's career as senator, as well as other cases dealing with his election as President. All these, to Jameson's repeated chagrin, were claimed and had to be shipped to the Memorial Association.

Until he resigned as president of the Memorial Association, Frelinghuysen had regarded the Harding papers as a possible hornet's nest that he had no intention of disturbing. Doctor Carl Sawyer on assuming the presidency showed himself more actively inactive. For over a quarter of a century he kept the papers sealed. Then in 1961, when Daniel Reed, Jameson's successor in the Library of Congress, came to spend a day at White Oaks Farm, Sawyer hinted that he was engaged in arranging and numbering the Harding correspondence and might eventually turn all the files over to the Library. A year later the doctor told a reporter that

[13] It seems most likely that this collection was packed by George Christian in 1923 from the papers in the Executive wing.

Harding's papers would not be released until 1973, fifty years after his death, and possibly not even then. "There's something America doesn't know," he concluded enigmatically, "and may not for a hundred years."

For several years the Ohio Historical Society had been making a self-conscious effort to collect the papers of Harding's contemporaries. With the backing of the trustees, the curator of documents, Kenneth Duckett, now tried to persuade Sawyer that the association's Harding papers be given to the society to form the core of a Harding collection that would be the most important in the country. The Doctor, as stubborn as his martial father, needed considerable persuading, but finally, on October 4, 1963, he formally donated the Memorial Association's collection to the society.

Six days later, on a bright clear morning, an Atlas Moving Company van with a five-man crew pulled up in front of 380 Mount Vernon Avenue ready to load the filing cases from the basement. The society staff, in rehearsals with the moving company, had set up a split-second timetable. To reassure Doctor Sawyer, who feared a possible hijack by "those Teapot Dome people"—and not unmindful of the publicity—the society's public-relations officer had enlisted the support of an armed state highway patrol to escort the van, containing some three hundred thousand documents, to Columbus.

Early in the afternoon the van arrived at the society's headquarters on the campus of Ohio State University, to be met by TV cameras, newsreel photographers, wire-service men, and reporters. The news was now officially released that the society had acquired *all* the Harding papers and that they would be opened to researchers within six months.

The release was not wholly accurate, for the feared hijacking had already taken place the day before when Doctor Sawyer had removed two files from Mount Vernon Avenue to his White Oaks Farm. Those files, comprising Harding's political and personal as well as business correspondence from 1895 to 1914, were potentially the richest source in the surviving papers. But not until the following March could Sawyer be persuaded to turn over these approximately ten thousand withheld pieces to the society. The manuscript department, forced to mark time while waiting for Doctor Sawyer, began a frantic rush to get all the files arranged and catalogued for the official opening of the Warren G. Harding Papers at the society's annual meeting on April 26. Still sequestered at White Oaks were two boxes containing Harding's personal correspondence from 1915 to 1920 that the Doctor had earlier found stored away among his father's papers.

The 1964 annual meeting of the Historical Society was more than usually festive. An all-day reception, with a buffet lunch, was held at the society's cavernous gray building. The three living former Presidents of the United States sent letters of felicitation. Reporters flocked in like starlings. To the members of the society the day seemed the bright beginning of a re-evaluation of Harding, the opportunity at last with adequate documentation to put the old scandals in perspective and give the man from Marion a presidential stature worthy of Ohio.

Yet even as they nursed these improving thoughts over their chicken-salad lunch, another scandal from the blue as sensational as any of the earlier ones was poised to strike. At the opening of the meeting the society's president, Fred J. Milligan, a Columbus lawyer, told the 15 trustees —his hoarse voice edged with anger—that the Harding papers being released to view that day were not quite all. There were still other letters, some extraordinary private correspondence to consider. The board then sent the stenographer from the room and went into executive session. What went on at that session can only be learned piecemeal. But Milligan informed the trustees that a large collection of Harding's love letters to another man's wife had come into the possession of the society.

CHAPTER XXII

Centenary

Since it was through me that the 105 letters written by Harding to Carrie Phillips were uncovered and later delivered to the Ohio Historical Society, and since my discovery has become part of Harding history, this concluding chapter is necessarily more personal. I first came to Marion at the end of a belatedly warm Indian summer afternoon in October, 1963. Like most tourists I stopped first on the outskirts of the city at the columned marble drum of Alexandrian immensity in whose core Harding and his Duchess are buried. Leaving my car at a parking inlet in the road, I walked up the long concrete walk to the Memorial. Curious an architectural amalgam as it was, it managed somehow to be harmonious and even impressive. Through the locked iron gate within the outer circle of columns I could see the two rectangular slabs of what the guidebook called "emerald pearl Labrador granite" marking the graves. In spite of the official description, the granite looked black to me. Harding's grave was marked by a bronze palm wreath, the Duchess's by a bronze wreath of roses. Peace and love, perhaps.

The Harding Hotel—another memorial of sorts a mile beyond on West Center Street—seemed almost empty on that languid afternoon. In the vague, paneled lobby I found only two people: a drowsy, middle-aged bellhop tilted back on a chair near the deserted reception desk, and a traveling man sprawled under a simpering oleographic portrait of Harding. A bent, silent woman, apparently an elderly pensioner, ran the one elevator still in operation.

When the hotel had been started with a glow of civic zeal, practically every businessman and merchant and lawyer in town had bought a few shares in the enterprise. Each towel and blanket had Harding's Roman profile woven into it. Murals in the dining room displayed a lushly vegetative landscape with a swan-filled river in the foreground and, beyond an umbrageous line of trees, a distant glimpse of the Washington Monument and the White House and the Capitol embowered like dream castles. The Harding Hotel was to be more than a hotel, it was to be a shining center for the presidential Marion.

Somehow things never worked out that way. After Harding died, the hotel's name endured and the Rotary and other service clubs held their weekly luncheons there, and occasionally over a football weekend there might be a flutter of guests, but the stock certificates in Marion bank vaults paid no dividends and the brick building itself remained almost as much a mausoleum as the marble drum beyond the cemetery.

Except for my single room, the whole eighth floor was empty. Forty years had bleached the wallpaper roses, the carpet was threadbare, and the pre-chromium plumbing flecked with verdigris. Any Roman profile had long since vanished from the towels of the not-too-clean bathroom. From my window I could see an indeterminate flatness beyond the boulevard lined with small factories and punctuated by traffic lights, and the waning perspective of roofs and chimneys. The afterglow of the sunset was a bilious mauve and saffron above the brown unbroken horizon curve. Not one person did I know as yet among the 40,000 inhabitants of that blurred city. Somehow I found myself thinking of the passage in Goethe's autobiography where, arriving in Strasburg for the first time, he climbed the great cathedral tower to look down at the Alsatian plain. There it lay below him, still unknown, containing the pattern of the future—the people he would meet, the course his life would take. Marion was no Strasburg and I no Goethe. Even so, that flat Ohio landscape with its pattern of die-straight streets—north and south, east and west—platted so long ago by Eber Baker contained my own immediate future.

After I had changed my clothes I wandered up Center Street, like an alien ghost in the gathering twilight. Across from the hotel the marquee of the Palace Theatre announced *Beach Party* and *Where the Boys Are*. Uhler's department store—the name Phillips forgotten—was having its fall clothing sale. The streetcar tracks had long since been removed. Yet, in spite of the chrome-and-glass glitter of modernized façades, neither the street nor the city had altered basically since Harding's day. The brick Gothic jail with its key-shaped weather vane was the same, as was the Corinthian courthouse, although the statue of Justice that topped its aluminum-painted dome had been replaced by the sheriff's short-wave radio antenna. What was once the Star Building had been masked by a veneer of artificial stone, becoming the central office of the Marion Water Company. The new *Star* offices were round the corner near the jail. Harding, if he could have strolled along with me, while admiring the improvements, would have felt as much at home as ever going back from the office and under the maple-shaded side streets to the green house with its wart-like porch. Marion's population had increased by a quarter since his day, but I found the same intimate folksiness of houses close together, their yards running into each other unseparated by hedge or fence. In the mild evening the yellow lights of the front windows shone out warmly, interspersed here and there with the cooler bluish reflection of a television screen. There were, of course, gaps. Amos Kling's brick mansion had been replaced by a filling station, Tryon's turreted white box by a real estate and insurance office. But Carrie's house still stood on Gospel Hill, and on the street directly behind it Doctor Britton's old bungalow still showed a light in the gabled upstairs room where Nan so long ago had pasted up newspaper photos of her darling Warren.

Several new industries had come into Marion after World War II—one, requiring much female clerical help, brought there by a computer oracle that revealed the city as having a greater supply of high-school girl graduates than any other small city in Ohio. But the Marion Steam Shovel Company still remained the biggest plant and largest employer. Residential growth had been mostly in the peripheral ranch houses, now reduced to the size of the log cabins of Eber Baker's day. The new managers and the next generation of wealth had moved out to Vernon Heights where Ralph Lewis's quixotic stubbornness had at last come to seem extraordinary foresight as his decades-empty lots blossomed with super-ranch houses and glittering imitations of New England colonials. Lewis was still alive, a millionaire at last, charitable if tottering, a leading citizen and zealous golfer who in the older Marion tradition fled to Florida each year from the ferocious Ohio winter.[1]

I was to talk with Lewis, and I had also hoped to talk with Doctor Chancellor in Wooster. But Chancellor, I learned, had died eight months before my coming to Ohio. After retiring from teaching in 1940, he had gone to Kent, where during the fifties he lived in the Golden Glow Home for the Aged. A few years later, nearly blind, he returned quietly to Wooster. There were few others I wanted to see, although I knew there were a number of Harding and Kling relatives scattered throughout Marion, and I had heard that the several-times-married daughter of Pete DeWolfe still lived in the city. What I did not know was that the Willets Home for the Aged contained Harding's stepmother and Tryon's third wife, Alice Severns.[2]

Noon, I discovered next day, was the one period when the dining room of the Harding Hotel filled up. Through wars and depressions, expansion and change, Marion had remained a tight little community, with its ruling clique of bankers, lawyers, lawyer-politicians, businessmen, the larger property owners, the wearers of the Rotary pin with the diamond center, the trustees of the Harding Memorial Association. Each day a number of

[1] Lewis died in Florida, March 27, 1967.
[2] She died at the age of ninety-five on November 27, 1964, three weeks after her President stepson's ninety-ninth birthday.

them took their lunch at the hotel. With the years the faces changed, as did some of the names, but the structure remained. What had happened, what was happening, what would happen within the city and the county, they, "the set," knew. And, as in most small towns, the lawyers knew it first. Marion's lawyers gathered daily and informally at a round central table that held a scant dozen places and that had become known over the years as the Lawyers' Table. There one might meet anyone from John Bartram, whose position as a fourth-generation Marion lawyer was almost feudal, to Judge Ruzzo whose arrival from the other side of the tracks to that staid Anglo-Saxon environment was so recent that he still felt sensitive about his Latin and barbershop origins.

Because I had the necessary introductions I was able to break the blank wall that the set usually presents to inquisitive outsiders. Several of the younger businessmen took me to lunch with some of the younger members of the Lawyers' Table in the more intimate atmosphere of the Country Club. One of the questions I had long had in mind was the identity of a woman, mentioned but not named, in William Allen White's *Masks in a Pageant.* White had been in Marion for the opening of the 1920 Front Porch campaign and had observed the stark brick front of the undecorated Uhler-Phillips building among the other decorations. On asking the reason, he "heard one of those stories about a primrose detour from Main Street which Florence Kling, the Duchess, had chosen to ignore." When I asked at the luncheon table who the woman might be, the answer came almost in a chorus, "Why, Carrie Phillips, of course." Everyone in Marion, they told me, knew that; everyone being two or three hundred persons out of a population of 40,000, but including the association trustees and the Lawyers' Table. A young chief of Rotary offered to take me to see another Marion lawyer who was said to have some of Harding's letters to Mrs. Phillips still in his possession. That was how I met Don Williamson.

Ever since Williamson had discovered the letters seven years earlier, he had been uneasy about them. Although no scholar, he had a sense of history, and he believed that anything written by a President of the United States ought to be preserved. He also knew that if he turned over the letters to anyone in the Harding Memorial Association they would go up in smoke. So, not knowing what else to do, he kept them in his basement.

I first talked with Williamson, a plump, pleasant man in his middle forties, in his old-fashioned office near the courthouse in an old-fashioned building camouflaged by a modernistic grille. He told me of his problem with the letters, his fear that they might be destroyed, his vain efforts to get in touch with Carrie's daughter Isabelle. "If you want to look at them," he told me finally, "come to my house some night on Bellefontaine Avenue and I'll show them to you." Taking no chances that he might change his mind, I went that very evening. He brought the letters to me in a cardboard box which he set on the kitchen table, and I spent till midnight in the kitchen with him and his wife going through them. Tossed helter-skelter in the box, some were in their envelopes, some out of them, others with the envelopes lost. Often the pages were disarranged or parts of individual letters separated. Some letters were fragments. Many, written in pencil on scratch-pad paper, ran to 30 or 40 pages. A few were on United States Senate stationery. I recognized at once the angular Harding handwriting.

Even before I read them I could see that they confirmed Nan Britton, for in her book she had told of receiving letters 40 pages long, written in pencil and enclosed in blue envelopes. I had thought such length preposterous and doubted her story because of it, but here were penciled letters equally long, and enclosed in similar blue envelopes. Here the same expressions that he had used to Nan popped out of the scrawled pages: [- -]

The next morning I managed to continue reading the letters alone in Williamson's office while he attended to some matter at the courthouse. But the more I followed Harding's blubbery passion from page to page, the more I began to worry about the difficulties Williamson might find himself in if the news got out. When he returned at lunchtime, I told him that he ought to seal the letters and present them to the Ohio Historical Society. He said he had just been talking with Judge Ruzzo, and Ruzzo had told him the same thing.

Before he could think twice about it, I picked up the telephone and called the Ohio Historical Society's curator of documents, Kenneth Duckett, in Columbus. Duckett I had met briefly on my way to Marion and I had confidence in him. He struck me as a quiet professional type, younger than most curators. But he would know how to handle the letters, and I hoped he would get the credit for discovering them.

I had thought of the Ohio Historical Society as a staid and respectable organization, much like the Massachusetts Historical Society. Only later did I come to realize that it was predominantly political, heavily subsidized, and supervised by the state legislature, and that its trustees were appointed for reasons of politics rather than scholarship. So far as I could determine, the qualifications of its president, Fred Milligan, consisted of his being a Rhodes Republican and a former traveling secretary for his Ohio State fraternity, Phi Delta Theta. My first impression—when I met him in his Columbus office—was of a lawyer-politician, a man of aggressive naïveté. Mementoes of old college pursuits hung about his office walls like testimonials—fraternity scrolls, diplomas, group pictures, an inspirational note about Lincoln's having been a failure at fifty. I found his talk crude and his voice harsh. Although he had read little and written nothing, he was apparently very proud of seeing his name printed as the president of the society.[3] Erwin C. Zepp, the society's director, was scarcely more than his shadow.

But of the true state and status of Ohio's Historical Society I knew nothing as I met that afternoon with Duckett in Williamson's office. We packed the letters in two shoeboxes, tied them with string, and sealed them with Scotch tape. Then I dictated a letter to Williamson's secretary —which she typed on Ohio Historical Society stationery that Duckett had brought with him—to the effect that Williamson was making a free gift to the society of two sealed boxes of Harding letters and that no financial considerations were involved. The secretary made three copies: one for Williamson, one for the society, and one which went to Judge Ruzzo.

Duckett and I drove back to Columbus in the long-shadowed afternoon with the two shoeboxes in the back seat. The memorial drum sparkled like a wedding cake as we passed it, yet somehow it didn't seem as substantial as when I had first seen it earlier in the week. By the time we reached Columbus the Historical Society building was closed, but Duckett rang for the night watchman, and after signing the register, we retreated to the double-doored privacy of the directors' room where we opened the shoeboxes and spread the letters across the long table. Then we spent the evening trying to classify and arrange them. Many were undated or fragmented. We discovered several postcard photographs of Carrie, taken aboard ship and afterward sent from Germany. She seemed a large, full-bosomed woman, handsome in the Gibson-girl manner of the period.

The following morning I went through the letters again. Duckett was fearful that if the news got out while he was still negotiating with Doctor Sawyer for the remaining two boxes of Harding's personal correspondence, the testy doctor would never release them. He told Zepp of a separate Harding acquisition that he wanted to keep secret for the time being. But Zepp asked no questions, and Duckett volunteered no more information.[4] Duckett knew the society, and I did not. During the winter, after I had returned to New England, he made microfilms of the Phillips letters against the possibility that the originals might later be destroyed. He also informed the historian J. H. Rodabaugh with whom he had worked when Rodabaugh was head of the Society's History and Science Division until political maneuverings forced him out.

Shortly before the festive annual meeting of 1964, Duckett let Zepp know what the secret acquisition contained. Zepp, aghast and goggle-eyed,

[3] In one of those political transformation scenes, familiar to Ohio since the days of Boss Cox, Milligan in October, 1965, was named by Gov. James A. Rhodes as "expeditor" for the state's Historical Society program of capital improvements and chief planner for the new $10 million Ohio Historical Center.
[4] Zepp's lack of inquisitiveness would eventually cost him his job.

at once relayed the news to Milligan. After the angry Milligan in turn had told the trustees at the annual meeting in his leathery voice, the brightness went out of the spring afternoon. Some of the more irascible trustees exploded. Judge Lehr Fess became quite violent and demanded that the letters be destroyed at once. The lawyers present pointed out that this was no longer possible since an outsider had already read them. Their existence was known beyond the society; who owned them legally was still an open question.

The problem, as it developed in Milligan's mind, was how the society could rid itself of its unwelcome legacy. After the annual meeting he sent for Duckett and drove with him to Marion where together with Williamson they met in Judge Ruzzo's chambers. Ruzzo, anxious to please the establishment as represented by the head of the Ohio Historical Society and conscious that he was primarily responsible for the letters having left Marion, at first took the indignant view that anything damaging to the image of an American President should be suppressed to protect the younger generation. There were, he announced, too many juvenile delinquents as it was. But when his Latin temper had settled he told them, according to a 1964 deposition of Duckett's: "You want a solution to your problem, send the things back up here and we will get rid of them." . . . And Milligan said, "Fine," twice.

Milligan later gave Duckett an hour to hand over the letters or face suspension. This Duckett refused to do until he received assurance that they were not going to be destroyed. Finally Milligan agreed that the shoeboxes would be deposited in a safety-deposit box of the Ohio National Bank. One key would go to Duckett, the other to Milligan, and the letters would remain there until it could be decided what to do with them.[5]

When I talked with Milligan shortly afterward, he admitted that the letters were in the bank vault and that Judge Ruzzo was going to issue an order impounding them. The letters would remain there in the official custody of the Ohio Historical Society, he told me, "probably for years and years, like the judge sees it."

True to his promise, Judge Ruzzo provided a way out for the society's embarrassing acquisition, and his solution was ingenious. After creating a Carrie Phillips estate, he appointed a Marion lawyer, Paul Michel—the nephew of Hoke Donithen and secretary of the Harding Memorial Association—as its administrator. Ruzzo then issued an order that the letters be surrendered into Michel's custody. Faced with a court order, Duckett felt he had no choice but to go with Milligan to the bank and hand over the sealed packets. Before evening the letters were once more

[5] There was another angry confrontation at the bank when Milligan, accompanied by Zepp and another trustee, declined to give the second key to Duckett. Duckett, the letters still in his possession, refused to hand them over until he received the key.

in Marion. It was all very deftly arranged, with Deac's son, Doctor George Tryon Harding III, in the background.

Doctor George, a chubby affable man with no resemblance at all to his "Roman" uncle except for the over-fleshy nose, carried on the family tradition of Seventh-day Adventist piety. After Deac's death, he had taken over the Worthington sanitorium. Although he had known vaguely of his uncle's affair with Carrie Phillips, the letters were a shock to him. Defense of the family seemed more important than any claims of history as he hurried to his lawyer, Byron E. Ford, of Congressman Vorys's old firm. If Doctor George had anything to say about it, the letters would never again see the light of anyone's day. Ford admitted casually to a reporter that "my clients would like to destroy the letters, but I don't think that will happen. They want to suppress them."

Disturbed by the undercurrents of gossip, Milligan sometime in July called a meeting of the staff and employees of the Historical Society. To them he explained that from the beginning Williamson had not technically had the legal right to give the Phillips letters to the society, and that the society had not had the right to accept them, and that on order of the probate court they had been returned to Marion. As far as the society was concerned, the affair was over. "Our hands are clean," he concluded, and the meeting ended abruptly without the usual question period.[6] Shortly before this Zepp had "resigned" as director.

For myself, I had no intention of making public any news about the letters unless there seemed a clear danger of their being destroyed. But by the summer of 1964 too many people knew about them for the secret to last. The 17 trustees of the Historical Society had probably told their wives. Most of the lawyers in Marion were in on it, as were a number in Columbus. I was surprised that the story kept as long as it did. Just before the Republican national convention in July I learned that someone had leaked a garbled account to the Toledo *Blade*.[7] Wishing to set forth the fact as accurately as possible, I confirmed certain data which appeared in a story in *The New York Times* about the Harding letters.

[6] I heard the end of Milligan's talk which sounded more like a harangue. In spite of the legal correctness of his explanation, it is a fact that nearly every historical society holds letters and documents to which its rights are unclear. If a Washington letter turned up, the far-distant heirs of the addressee might claim physical ownership, and Washington's equally remote heirs the common-law copyright. The same would apply to a letter from, for example, Theodore Roosevelt or Calvin Coolidge. One can scarcely imagine, in such cases, a recourse to the probate courts. Nor can one imagine a historical society seeking to rid itself of the papers of any other President or historical figure. All the Ohio Historical Society needed to do for the preservation of its documents was to keep the letters safely in the archives while trying to persuade any Phillips heirs either to donate or sell them to the society. No such attempt was made.
[7] Rodabaugh, at odds with the society, had written Prof. Randolph Downes of Toledo about the letters, Downes, preparing a Harding biography, told his assistants. One of the assistants talked too much in a Toledo bar, and the news was out.

The coast-to-coast, and even European, reaction was more than I had bargained for. Once more, forty-one years after Harding's death, a Harding scandal occupied the front pages of the country's newspapers. Some of the more sensational California papers had headlines about HARDING's PARAMOUR that dwarfed the convention news. The news weeklies ran feature articles. Reporters, reviving the older scandals, discovered Nan Britton living obscurely in Evanston, and one enterprising reporter managed to interview Elizabeth Ann who as the forty-four-year-old Mrs. Henry Blaesing was living in Glendale, California, with her husband and her three unsuspecting children.

As a result of this new scandal just after the Harding papers had at last been opened and preparations were beginning in Ohio for the Harding Centenary Year, Doctor George filed a suit asking for the impounding of the letters and for a million dollars in damages, claiming that he and the other heirs had been "irreparably damaged" by publication of extracts. Defendants named were myself, Duckett, the McGraw-Hill Publishing Company, and the magazine *American Heritage*.[8] Judge Henry L. Holden of the Court of Common Pleas in Columbus issued an order forbidding the defendants from "publishing, producing, copying, exhibiting, or making any use whatsoever" of the letters pending a final hearing and a decision on the suit.

With the letters safely bottled up, the Hardings turned their attention to Duckett who, they now learned to their dismay, had made microfilm copies. On Milligan's instructions, Duckett was ordered to produce the microfilms or face suspension from his job at the Historical Society. The films, Duckett was told, would either be burned or given to the Phillips estate or to the Harding heirs. Instead of complying, Duckett sent the film roll to *American Heritage* Magazine in New York for safekeeping.[9] With Nevins's formidable backing the society hesitated to suspend Duckett although in October he was given an official reprimand signed by Milligan, with the matter to be "continued for further action hereafter." Before any such action was taken, Duckett quit his position as curator of documents in the spring of 1965 to become archivist at Southern Illinois University.

With Doctor George's lawsuit still in its preliminary stage, Michel in

---

[8] The latter two were named because McGraw-Hill was my publisher and *American Heritage* planned to publish my article on the Phillips letters. The Hardings later added *The New York Times* to their list.
[9] Professor Allan Nevins, Chairman of the Advisory Board of *American Heritage* and former president of the American Historical Society, told the press: "[Duckett] had a duty to American history and the whole body of American historians. It was in execution of that duty that he made reproductions of the Harding-Phillips letters solely for the purpose of insuring their historic safety. In this he followed precisely the right course. . . ."

Marion arranged to have the letters appraised. Ralph Newman of Chicago's Lincoln Bookstore and two other appraisers, after examining the letters, set their value at $15,000. Carrie's daughter could of course only claim the letters after she had paid the outstanding debts of her mother's estate. On being told of the letters, she had engaged John Bartram to look after her interests. The debts came to $7,807.68, a sum that included $3,854.11 owing the Ohio Department of Public Welfare, $3,000 for lawyers' fees, and $936.40 for the appraisal.

In September, 1964, I made an offer of $15,000 for the letters and was informed by the estate lawyers that there might be no public sale if Mrs. Matheé chose to pay the debts and costs of administration. The Hardings instructed their lawyers that whatever I might bid, they would bid $500 more. However, they were not forced to this but were able to come to an amicable and less expensive private agreement with Isabelle. On February 20, 1965, Ford, acting on behalf of Doctor George Harding, paid all the debts of the Phillips estate, and the originals of the letters at last came under the control of the Harding family.

Like the prolonged shadow of Blooming Grove, the Phillips letters cast their own shadow over the Harding Centennial. In early preparation for the anniversary, Ralph Lewis had provided the Ohio Historical Society with money for an elaborate bronze marker trimmed with buckeyes to designate the Blooming Grove site of Harding's birthplace. There, on a chill snow-streaked December day in 1963, in the presence of Doctor George and 75 other Harding descendants, a rubicund and beaming Milligan dedicated the marker as the opening ceremony of the centennial celebration.

Much of the association's efforts and $75,000 of its funds were spent during the following year in restoring the interior of the Mount Vernon Avenue house to its domestic state when the Hardings lived in it. Since Harding's death it had become a museum-junkshop, displaying on the first floor all the detritus of the presidential years, the gewgaws and elaborately useless bric-a-brac that fall to all Presidents—vases, glass bowls and goblets, carved stone ash trays, inkwells, ship models, canes, scrolls, trinkets in gold and silver. Harding's senatorial desk and chair were on display, as well as the desk embossed with the American eagle at which he had been sworn in. And there were the Duchess's fans and ostrich plumes and evening slippers in glass cabinets and the stuffed remains of the canary Pete, to say nothing of such early objects as family photographs, and the statuary, china, and beer steins bought abroad. A television mast sprouted anachronistically from the caretaker's quarters upstairs. The caretaker himself sold admission tickets, postcards, felt souvenir banners and buckeyes at a counter near the front door.

By 1965 all that had been changed. Gewgaws and bric-a-brac had been banished to the old 1920 press bungalow that, refurbished, painted white, and flying the Stars and Stripes and the Ohio state flag, had been transformed into the Harding Museum. The house itself had been so carefully restored that, according to Doctor Warren C. Sawyer, the vice president of the Memorial Association and grandson of the medical general, "should Harding enter the house today he would find it as it was when he last saw it." From the upright piano and the tasseled piano lamp downstairs to the brass double bed in the master bedroom upstairs, everything was indeed as it used to be. Combination gas and electric lighting fixtures had been recalled from banishment. The kitchen had its gas stove on stilts, its bronze hot-water boiler, its sink with the brass faucets, even its wooden coffee mill and enamel coffeepot. In the library, Harding's rocking chair stood by his table with its tobacco jar and a rack of unread books. The oak dining-room table was set for dinner. A potted fern with a brass stand stood by the stairway. Wallpaper of a revived Victorian pattern extended the prevailing brown tone. To the unwary visitor the effect was of a giant dolls' house from the McKinley era.

In May, 1965, the house was officially reopened as the Harding Home. Then on June 4, with the two Harding nephews present, the association held an open house followed by a dinner at the Country Club. One hundred and seventy Harding friends and relatives were present as well as all the teachers of American History in Marion County. During the long presidency of the crusty Doctor Carl Sawyer, he had seen to it that none of the Hardings was among the trustees or even a member of the Harding Memorial Association.[10] But now in his senility, his doctor-son had arranged to have Doctor George Harding elected a member of the association and then appointed to its board of trustees.

As Harding's hundredth birthday neared, the historical markers proliferated. In September a buckeye-trimmed bronze was dedicated to mark the site of Ohio Central College and inform the tourist that here Harding and a friend had founded the *Iberia Spectator*. Another historical marker was placed in front of the Home, now considered a national shrine and inscribed as a National Historical Landmark on a bronze tablet set beside the steps leading to the Front Porch. Still another bronze plaque had been contributed by the Brush-Moore newspaper syndicate to memorialize the old press headquarters.

Harding's birthday celebration began with a Rotary Club luncheon in the ballroom of the Harding Hotel, the principal speaker being Edwin K. Gross of Buffalo, New York, a former reporter and press agent. Gross, a self-appointed rehabilitator of Warren Harding, had for the past eighteen

---

[10] Doctor Sawyer, who had come to regard the association as his personal possession, remarked privately that he did not want any Hardings interfering in his affairs. He died February 22, 1966.

years been studying, collecting documents about and defending the twenty-ninth President. In his quest he had founded the American Society for the Faithful Recording of History—that awarded annual booby prizes as well as prizes—and had written and published a 100th Birthday Memorial, *Vindication for Mr. Normalcy*. Described as "a good book which crowds the dirty books off the shelves," Gross had prefaced it with a poem, which he read to the Rotarians and several rather stunned academic historians, concluding:

> Now, opening of documents
> so diligently saved by wife
> conveys new image—and the true!
> they sing the greatness of his life,
> and writing craft must disinter
> the good, revise his history;
> Americans will cheer, as ends
> the Harding saga happily;
> Ohioans will proudly fete
> his century; belatedly
> in justice sweet, a wrong's made right,
> reward for Mr. Normalcy!

At one o'clock a memorial service was held at the drum sepulcher, the usual wreaths were laid, and a Harding High School sophomore in a striped sweater sounded Taps. The High School Band, in red and blue uniforms, was on hand at 380 Mount Vernon Avenue at two-thirty to play "The Star-Spangled Banner" when the Home was formally dedicated as a National Historic Landmark and a certificate presented to the Memorial Association by Doctor S. Sydney Bradford, Jr., of the National Park Service. Standing on the Front Porch with the two Harding nephews and the third Doctor Sawyer, the zealous David Porter, who had replaced the unzealous Zepp as director of the Historical Society, made a few laudatory remarks about the association. Then, led by the younger Doctor Sawyer, and as the band struck up "The End of a Perfect Day," the official party made a tour of the Home and the Museum.

At four-thirty a panel discussion took place in the cafeteria of the Harding High School under the chairmanship of Congressman Jackson E. Betts of Ohio's 8th District. The frail and elderly Prof. Randolph Downes, of the University of Toledo's Department of History, spoke first on Harding's early life. Downes, distinguished for his three-volume definitive history of Lake Shore, Ohio, had been twelve years preparing his equally definitive but still uncompleted three-volume Harding biography. His version was of a young Harding "always hard working, always proud, always driving." He was followed by Prof. Dale E. Cottrill, a former Marion boy who had risen to become chairman of the Department of

Rhetoric, Fine Arts and Humanities of McComb County College, Mount Clemens, Michigan. Mesmerized by Harding's oratory, Professor Cottrill had devoted his scholarship to tracking down the unpublished speeches of Warren G. Harding, of which he had already turned up a thousand and hoped to uncover several thousand more. A younger Harding scholar, Prof. Dean Albertson, the biographer of Franklin Roosevelt's Secretary of Agriculture, Claude R. Wickard, concluded the symposium. From the remoteness of New York's Brooklyn College Albertson had become engrossed in a Harding biography because, as he explained in the idiom of Everest, "he was there." Maintaining a discreet friendship with Nan Britton, he at the same time became so intimate with the Harding family that Doctor George trusted him to produce the authorized version of his uncle's life. So great was the Doctor's confidence in the young historian that, under the guise of appraisal, he even allowed him to read (but not take notes on) the Phillips letters. Albertson concluded the day by telling the Marionites that "in spite of what has been written, in spite of what has been said, in spite of what has been inferred, none of you need have the slightest hesitation to say, with pride, to anyone who asks: 'Warren G. Harding was born here.' "[11]

As an ironic prelude to the Harding Centennial Year, oil was suddenly discovered in Morrow County, and by the time of Harding's hundredth birthday his old city had taken on the aspect of a boom town.[12] No longer were there vacant floors in the Harding Hotel. An oilman had bought the building, and for the first time in its history the hotel was making money. The lobby filled up daily with wide-hatted prospectors, fast-buck boys, and hangers-on. White Continental convertibles clogged the parking lots, the courthouse was jammed with strangers looking up titles, every lawyer's office hummed, and cowboy boots were beginning to appear in the windows of Center Street shoestores.

When I returned to Marion a year after my first quiet visit I found every

[11] A year later, at a Harding Memorial Association banquet in the ballroom of the Harding Hotel to honor Harding's one-hundred-and-first birthday, Downes was again one of the speakers. With Doctor George Harding sitting only a few feet from him, he put aside his usual mild manner to denounce the Hardings's secrecy in regard to the Phillips letters, their allowing their house historian Albertson to read them while denying them to him as the definitive biographer. Doctor Harding was so disturbed by Downes's remarks that he published an apology. Gross, following Downes as speaker, attempted to defend Harding and his habits. His original reaction to the Phillips letters was that they were forgeries, but when the Hardings themselves accepted them as genuine, he concluded that "in Adam's fall we sinnéd all." After his vigorous defense of Harding, Gross dropped dead of a heart attack while leaving the ballroom.
[12] Although west of Morrow County, Marion was the nearest city with any hotel accommodations.

room in the Harding Hotel taken. The dining room overflowed at each meal, even breakfast. In the lobby a battery of telephones flanked the wall across from the reception desk, a brokerage firm had installed offices next to the barbershop, and the basement had been made over into the Harding Petroleum Key Club.

I did not stay long in the oil-fevered town, nor did I return for the centennial celebration. Marion may have been Gertrude Stein's favorite American small city, but it was not mine. Yet, in spite of the cowboy boots and the white convertibles, it looked calm enough on the rainy October afternoon when I drove away for the last time. The leaves were again clogging the gutters and it was just beginning to grow dark as I drove by the Mount Vernon Avenue house, its green woodwork and white trim dazzling under layers of fresh paint. Without stopping, I continued out the avenue to the right-angle curve of Vernon Heights Boulevard that ends next to the Harding Memorial at the junction with Route 23. Once more I paused in the indented parking space while the rain came down harder, but this time I did not get out. The wet massive columns glistened under a diffused lemon-yellow glow from concealed spotlights that had just been turned on. Like a monument to an emperor, the Memorial loomed up along Ohio's Appian Way to Columbus. Peering at it through my drizzled windshield, I sensed that I should never again pass through this flat, melancholy landscape, along these die-straight parallel roads that seemed to meet in some unimagined infinity. Such as it was, I had made my own centenary pilgrimage to Ohio's Roman whose image had been so eroded by the years. There in the rain, under two tons of black granite, he lay at last and at least beside his Duchess. Death, I could not help but think as I drove away, makes strange bedfellows.

Acknowledgments

This book has been written to the accompaniment of a million-dollar lawsuit brought by the Harding heirs against me following my discovery of the Phillips letters. I am at least grateful to them for the ensuing publicity. I am more lastingly grateful to Don Williamson of Marion and Kenneth Duckett, former curator of documents of the Ohio Historical Society, for their sense of historical obligation in preserving the letters—at much personal cost to themselves—against those who would have destroyed them. Equally am I grateful to Oliver Jensen and *American Heritage* for their moral and legal support in the controversy. Beyond the Phillips letters, I should like to acknowledge the assistance of the Ohio Historical Society and its library staff, the Marion Public Library, Widener Library, the Boston Athenaeum, the Yale and Princeton libraries, the New York Public Library, the Library of Congress, and the National Archives. David Stratton has been kind enough to allow me the use of his unpublished thesis on Albert Fall while furnishing me with much additional information. Through the courtesy of Syracuse University I was able to read H. F. Alderfer's unpublished doctoral thesis, *The Personality and Politics of Warren G. Harding*, from which Samuel Hopkins Adams drew so much of his material. I am above all grateful to Gordon Ray and the John Simon Guggenheim Memorial Foundation for the two fellowships that have made the writing of this book possible.

Since my intention has been to write for the general reader rather than the specialist, I have not included a detailed bibliography, contenting myself with mentioning my chief sources incidentally in my notes. My primary source has of course been the vast amount of material now in the custody of the Ohio Historical Society. This includes the recently acquired mass of the Harding Papers themselves, the material on Harding's early life collected by Ray Baker Harris and Cyril Clemens, the Walter Brown

Papers, the Charles E. Hard Papers, the Malcolm Jennings Papers, the Frank E. Scobey Collection, the voluminous correspondence of Harry Daugherty with Harris, and others. At present the Phillips letters—essential as they are to a knowledge of Harding—are sequestered under the control of Doctor George Harding.

Notes

[CHAPTER I]

Many of the details of the inauguration are from the *New York Times*. Both Mrs. Wilson and Admiral Grayson in their memoirs describe the early-morning hours in the White House. Senator Lodge's encounter with Wilson in the President's Room is dealt with in Garraty's *Life of Lodge*. Harry Daugherty, to be trusted only when he is not apologizing for himself, gives the account of Fall's confirmation by the Senate. The elephant story has many versions but the original occurs in a letter to Harding from his sister Carolyn while she was still in Burma. Almost all the incidents of the inaugural day that concern Wilson have been assiduously collected by Gene Smith in *When the Cheering Stopped*.

[CHAPTER II]

Most of the information about the Harding family comes from "The Ancestry of President Harding" in Volume XXI of the *Proceedings of the Wyoming Historical and Geological Society*, and in Wilbur Harding's *The Hardings in North America*. A description of the early days in Ohio and in Blooming Grove is given in the *History of Morrow County* and other county histories. A chapter by Helen Harding Meredith in *The Hardings in North America* contains the most extended explanation of the mixed-blood legend.

[CHAPTER III]

The Ray Harris Papers are the primary source on Harding's background and early life. Harris was well acquainted with the surviving members of the Harding family, corresponded with them over several decades, and was granted access to their private letters. Tryon Harding gave several press interviews in his old age. The account of his death in the *Star* adds details about his military service.

[CHAPTER IV]

A surviving copy of the *Iberia Spectator* in the Ohio Historical Society archives furnishes much incidental knowledge of Harding's old school. The *Star* printed the text of his speech at the Marion centenary. Harris has solid information about the Iberia years. Jack Warwick, Harding's old partner, recorded some of the Caledonia incidents.

[CHAPTER V]

The evolution of Harding's editorial career and its conflicts are to be traced in the files of the *Star*, the *Mirror*, and *the Independent*. I am indebted to Mrs. Ada Denman, a double cousin of Harding's, for the version of Florence Kling's first marriage, a more accurate and less sensational account than that found in Samuel Hopkins Adams's *The Incredible Era*. The *Northwest Ohio Quarterly* has reprinted Jack Warwick's ephemeral reminiscences, *Growing Up with Warren Harding*. But the most consistent information on these not-too-well documented years is in the private correspondence of the *Star* now in the Harding Collection of the Ohio Historical Society.

[CHAPTER VI]

Samuel Hopkins Adams in a 1939 visit to Marion picked up much information about Florence Kling's early life, some of it erroneous. Unfortunately most of what he wrote came from verbal sources and can be checked only through elderly witnesses such as Mrs. Denman. The record of Florence's divorce proceedings is on file in the Marion courthouse while Pete's decline and fall are traceable in the *Star's* random social notes. The *Star*, the *Independent*, the *Mirror*, and the *Transcript* have furnished the substance of this chapter along with Harding's personal correspondence in the Ohio Historical Society. Daugherty told Mark Sullivan of his Richmond meeting with Harding—which Sullivan overembroidered—and then wrote another version in *The Inside Story of the Harding Tragedy*. Robert S. Harper gave a good brief account of Daugherty's early career in *Plain Talk* of July, 1928, to which James Cox in his autobiography added a few unflattering additional episodes.

[CHAPTER VII]

By far the most comprehensive book on Ohio politics during the period of Harding's political life up to his years in the United States Senate is Hoyt Landon Warner's *Progressivism in Ohio, 1897–1917*. Though written with Progressive sympathies the book is accurate, unbiased, and encyclopedic. Foraker's autobiography is a tedious book; the facts are there, if trickily embalmed. Everett Walters's *Joseph Benson Foraker: An Uncompromising Republican*, is as indispensable as it is dull. Herbert D. Croly's biography of Mark Hanna is still standard although a new assessment is overdue. Frederick C. Howe's *The Confessions of a Reformer* has much about Boss Cox and the seamy side of Ohio politics. Lincoln Steffens both interviewed and investigated Cox, recording his impressions in *Ohio, The Tale of Two Cities*. In this chapter and subsequent ones I have traced Harding's political career through his personal correspondence, the files of the *Star*, the Cincinnati *Enquirer*, the Columbus *Dispatch*, and the *Ohio State Journal*.

[CHAPTER VIII]

The general background for this chapter, like that of much of Chapter VII, and of the Ohio political chapters to follow, is to be found in *Progressivism in Ohio*, with details from the files of the *Enquirer*, the *Dispatch*, the *Ohio State Journal*, the *Star*, and Harding's private correspondence. Alderfer's study is also useful. Harding's career in Masonry I learned from a history of the Marion Lodge of Masons and from talks with the present lodge secretary. The library of the Mount Vernon Avenue house, before its books had been purged and prettified for the centennial year, provided a key of sorts to Harding's cultural attainments. Details of his family come from the so-called *Star* correspondence, Harding's political and personal files from 1895 to 1914 that Doctor Sawyer had held back when he handed over the bulk of the Harding Papers to the Historical Society and that Duckett was able to persuade him to release the following spring.

[CHAPTER IX]

Among the additional sources for this chapter are Pringle's *Life and Times of William Howard Taft*, his *Theodore Roosevelt*, and Isabel Ross's Taft history, *An American Family*.

[CHAPTER X]

Harding's letter from Madeira was acquired by the Historical Society some time before the Harding Papers.

[CHAPTER XI]

If Nan Britton had not written *The President's Daughter* nothing would have been known of her relationship with Harding except among intimate circles in Marion. Although the more stalwart defenders of Harding have tried to make her out a blackmailer, the external evidence that can be assembled shows her story to be true. Harding's *nom d'amour* in the New York hotel register is as she claimed. His true signature and hers as Elizabeth Christian are in the register of Plattsburg's Hotel Witherill, where she described the 1918 lovers' meeting. The story of a letter that she sent to the White House and that went astray was corroborated long after by a White House mail clerk. Comparisons of photographs of Harding and of Elizabeth Ann show that they had the same ear structure. Above all Harding's letters to Carrie Phillips confirm Nan's story, for Nan had described just such letters—long, scrawled in pencil on scratch paper, enclosed in blue envelopes, and with the same hackneyed endearing terms. Nan has hinted that she has letters of Harding's that could prove her case still further. Pete DeWolfe's decline has to be unraveled from scattered notes in the *Star* and brief letters in Harding's personal correspondence. For the Washington picture, Archie Butt as military aide preserved a wealth of intimate White House information in his *Taft and Roosevelt*. George E. Mowry's *Theodore Roosevelt and the Progressive Movement* is one of the most useful books in tracing Roosevelt's evolution into the Bull Moose leader, as is Joseph

B. Bishop's *Theodore Roosevelt and His Time* for the latter stages of Roosevelt's career. Laylin's reply to Harding's surprising request to be appointed ambassador to Japan is to be found in the Ohio Historical Society's Harding Papers.

[CHAPTERS XII AND XIII]

Besides the previously mentioned sources on Ohio politics I have used Forrest Cressey's *Theodore E. Burton, American Statesman*. Harding reserved his most confidential thoughts for his cronies Scobey and Jennings, and I have found their letters invaluable. Some of the most intimate information about the Hardings in Washington comes from Evalyn Walsh McLean's ghost-written *Father Struck It Rich*. I am indebted to Professor Stratton for the use of his unpublished *Albert B. Fall and the Teapot Dome Affair*. Harding's warning letter to Carrie Phillips, now in the possession of *American Heritage*, I bought from a dealer in Ohio. Other letters to James Phillips appeared in booksellers' catalogues in the thirties, and several were reprinted in Ohio papers at the time.

[CHAPTER XIV]

Hermann Hagedorn's admiring life of Leonard Wood is encyclopedic. The best single book on the convention, campaign, and election of 1920 is Wesley M. Bagby's *The Road to Normalcy*. Robert Harper's "Before Revelry" gave an unflatteringly detailed picture of Jess Smith. Daugherty's lengthy correspondence in his meditative years with Ray Baker Harris is an adequate and on the whole truthful account of how he shaped the nomination for Harding. For information about Jake Hamon I am indebted to Mrs. Marion B. Atkins of the Oklahoma Historical Society. Madam Marcia's fanciful recollections appeared in *Liberty*.

[CHAPTER XV]

To establish what happened at the Republican national convention of 1920 is like fitting together an extremely complicated jigsaw puzzle. Bagby's *The Road to Normalcy* sets the general pattern and is a conclusive demolishing of the myth of the Smoke-filled Room. But the individual pieces come from the press accounts of the time; from William Allen White's autobiography and his *A Puritan in Babylon;* from Mark Sullivan who, like White, was there; from Hagedorn's life of Wood with its many quotations from Wood's diary; from Nan Britton; from Daugherty, both in his letters and his time-serving apologia, *The Inside Story of the Harding Tragedy;* from Samuel Hopkins Adams; from William T. Hutchinson's *Lowden of Illinois;* from Nicholas Murray Butler; from Joseph W. Martin; from Willis F. Johnson's *George Harvey;* from Alice Roosevelt Longworth's *Crowded Hours,* and a dozen other lesser biographies and memoirs; and of course from the Harding Papers in the Ohio Historical Society.

[CHAPTER XVI]

I have taken the day-by-day account of the campaign from the *New York Times* and other papers, Mark Sullivan, William Allen White, Samuel Hopkins Adams, and the correspondence of Harding Papers. Chancellor in his surreptitious Harding biography later mentions the Phillips pay-off and Carrie Phillips by name. Adams's *Incredible Era* goes at length into the question of Harding's Negro strain but draws no conclusions. Edith Bolling Wilson in *My Memoir* tells of Tumulty's excited arrival at the White House with the Chancellor-derived rumor. Olive Ewing Clapper, who spent the campaign months in Marion with her husband, is responsible for the toothbrush story. The fullest account of the presentation of the gold make-up rule is in Sherman A. Cuneo's ephemeral *From Printer to President*. Harding's small-town friend Joe Mitchell Chapple was among the newsmen on the Panama trip, as he was later to be on Harding's last voyage to Alaska; he wrote the most extended account of both voyages. Edith Wilson caustically recorded her first meeting with the Duchess. Taft wrote about his visit to Marion in a long letter to his wife.

[CHAPTER XVII]

The Harding Papers are the chief source for the official activities of Harding's presidential years. Taft's appointment as Chief Justice is covered in Ishbel Ross's *An American Family* and in Alpheus T Mason's *William Howard Taft: Chief Justice*. Hoover in his memoirs describes his inadvertent appearance at a White House poker party. Ike Hoover, Colonel Starling, Mrs. Jaffray, and the mail clerk Ira Smith have supplied gossipy recollections of the White House under the Hardings. Louise Cromwell Brooks, after she had become Louise Cromwell Brooks MacArthur Atwill, told the Washington columnist Betty Beale in 1943 about her White House china acquisition. Olive Clapper observed Harding closely on the foggy morning at Hoboken Pier and afterward wrote down her impressions. Tryon's third marriage made brief headlines in Ohio. William Allen White, Nelson Trusler Johnson, and a score of others wrote their recollections and reminiscences of the Arms Conference, Joe Chapple took in more of the conference with his admiring eye than did most reporters present.

[CHAPTER XVIII]

For the background to the oil scandals the most informative book is J. Leonard Bates's *The Origins of Teapot Dome,* a prelude to Burl Noggle's *Teapot Dome: Oil and Politics in the 1920's. The Teapot Dome Scandal* by M. R. Werner and John Starr is interesting for its details but less accurate. I found Burton K. Wheeler's memoirs, *Yankee from the West,* a helpful accompaniment to two indispensable government publications: *Investigation of the U.S. Veterans' Bureau, 1923,* and *Hearings before the Senate Committee on Investigation of the Attorney General, 1924.* Gaston Means can be given credence neither in his testimony before the Senate Committee nor in his ghost-written *The Strange Death of President Harding* nor anywhere else. Edwin P. Hoty in *Spectacular Rogue* has winnowed truth from fiction in his biography of this Munchausen figure. *Incredible Era* is still the best book on the Harding scandals and includes much inside information that would otherwise have been lost.

[CHAPTER XIX]

Russell Lord in *The Wallaces of Iowa* gives the background of the disputes between Wallace and Hoover in the Cabinet. The *Ohio Archeological and His-*

torical Publications of 1920 relates the course of the Marion Centennial Celebration. Hoover wrote of his outrage over Daugherty's rail-strike injunction in his memoirs. Daugherty of course defended himself with flamboyant rhetoric in his apologia. Adams records the story of the Red Room encounter.

[CHAPTER XX]

I am deeply indebted to A. A. Hoehling for the voluminous material on Harding's last journey and death that he placed at my disposal. Joe Mitchell Chapple wrote an indiscriminatingly encyclopedic account of the Alaska trip. Malcolm Jennings also wrote an account, and Hoover recorded his impressions in his memoirs. Horace Albright, Yellowstone Park's Chief Ranger at the time of Harding's visit, made a tape recording of what he remembered. Emma Hall's letter on her meeting with Harding is in the possession of the Ohio Historical Society. The society possesses a voluminous scrapbook on the progression of the funeral train and Harding's burial.

[CHAPTER XXI]

Kenneth Duckett, former curator of documents of the Ohio Historical Society, collected the information about Florence Harding's destruction of her husband's papers for an *American Heritage* article of February, 1965. In that same article Duckett explained his role in the releasing of the Harding Papers by the Harding Memorial Association to the Ohio Historical Society. Nan Britton's continued story is from her book. Her legal difficulties with the Hardings she set down in a second book, *Honesty or Politics*. Samuel Ungerleider was kind enough to furnish me with an account of Harding's gambols in the stock market. I have taken the account of Daugherty's dismissal from Donald R. McCoy's *Calvin Coolidge: The Quiet President*. "Harding's Haunted Tomb" by Robert S. Harper in *Plain Talk* of September, 1930, is the article that finally forced Hoover to dedicate the Harding Memorial. Evalyn McLean tells in her autobiography of her last meeting with the Duchess. Friends in Marion have brought me up to date on the later years of the Lewises and the Phillipses. Chancellor's last years are recorded in an otherwise worthless article about Harding's Negro blood that appeared in the now-defunct *Fact*.

[CHAPTER XXII]

Most of this chapter is current history. Historians owe a debt of gratitude to Don Williamson of Marion for his self-sacrificing insistence in preserving Harding's letters to Carrie Phillips. The full story of the letters is contained in *American Heritage*, February, 1965. For much of the information in this chapter, including the events of the centenary celebration and after, I am indebted to friends in Marion as well as to current issues of the *Star*.

Index

About the Author

Francis Russell has contributed historical and critical articles to such distinguished publications as *American Heritage, Horizon, The Yale Review,* and the London *Observer.* He is the author of one of the more intimate books on America's "Roaring '20's," *The Great Interlude,* as well as an investigation of the facts behind the Sacco and Vanzetti Trial, *Tragedy in Dedham.* In addition, he has written a volume of critical essays on Joyce, Kafka, and Gertrude Stein, a study of Albrecht Dürer, and is the author of *The American Heritage History of the Making of the Nation, 1783-1860.*

Mr. Russell was born in Boston in 1910. He attended the Roxbury Latin School there and went on to do most of his undergraduate work at German universities. When he returned to America he completed his A.B. at Bowdoin College and his A.M. at Harvard. After serving as a captain in the Canadian Army in World War II, he traveled extensively and lived for various periods in France, England, Holland, Ireland, and Germany. He held Guggenheim Fellowships in 1964 and 1965. With his wife he lives in a seventeenth-century house, "The Lindens," in Sandwich on Cape Cod.